Organization Theory
Cases & Applications

Fourth Edition

Richard L. Daft
Vanderbilt University

Mark P. Sharfman
University of Oklahoma

West Publishing Company
Minneapolis/St. Paul New York Los Angeles San Francisco

WEST'S COMMITMENT TO THE ENVIRONMENT

In 1906, West Publishing Company began recycling materials left over from the production of books. This began a tradition of efficient and responsible use of resources. Today, up to 95% of our legal books and 70% of our college texts and school texts are printed on recycled, acid-free stock. West also recycles nearly 22 million pounds of scrap paper annually—the equivalent of 181,717 trees. Since the 1960s, West has devised ways to capture and recycle waste inks, solvents, oils, and vapors created in the printing process. We also recycle plastics of all kinds, wood, glass, corrugated cardboard, and batteries, and have eliminated the use of Styrofoam book packaging. We at West are proud of the longevity and the scope of our commitment to the environment.

Production, Prepress, Printing and Binding by West Publishing Company.

Contents

Preface

In this fourth edition of *Organization Theory: Cases and Applications,* we again bring the student and instructor a collection of organization theory cases and exercises that we believe are meaningful in terms of both practice and theory. We have designed this edition with the belief that the purpose of an Organization Theory course is to provide the student both with a conceptual framework within which to understand organization level phenomena and some practical experience in addressing the problems that managers face. The cases and exercises vary in both difficulty and complexity because we believe that an effective Organization Theory course challenges the student with the same range of issues she or he will face in the business world.

In this edition we have made several major and minor changes which we believe will be beneficial to our readers. The following is a discussion of the key changes:

1. The most critical change from the third edition is the overall organization of the book. For each new edition, we solicit feedback from instructors who are familiar with the current edition. The feedback that we heard most often from these faculty for this revision was that it would be helpful if the fourth edition was organized in a way that was more consis-

tent with Professor Daft's text *Organization Theory and Design*. Because we value the feedback from our reviewers and because the suggestion was so often mentioned, we decided to change the organization of this edition. The book now carries a structure that is essentially identical to Professor Daft's text. To those instructors who use another textbook as a companion to this casebook, we wish to reiterate that first and foremost *Organization Theory: Cases and Applications* is appropriate for use with any high quality Organization Theory textbook — not just Professor Daft's book.

2. As part of our continuing efforts to keep this casebook up-to-date, we have added about 40 percent new material. Because the world of organizations changes very rapidly we believe that it is necessary to regularly refresh our stock of cases.

3. In selecting the new material for this edition, we again added material to reflect the changing world of organizations. Several topics are represented in the book for the first time. We have added cases that address diverse new areas such as self-managed teams, downsizing, total quality management, workplace diversity, stakeholder management, electronic data interchange, global integration, manage-

ment in newly emerging or developing countries, and drug testing. In selecting these new areas, we again relied heavily on the advice of our reviewers. In their feedback they provided us with several topic areas that they wished to have added to the book. We have been able to find quality cases to address many of the suggested areas.

4. We are especially pleased with the number of interesting new international cases that we have included in this edition. We have added new cases set in the Czech Republic, India, Japan, Spain, and Sweden. As the globalization of the business world continues, it becomes critical that students have as broad an understanding of international issues as possible.

5. In this edition we have continued a practice that we started in the earlier versions of this book. In making the decision to add a case or an exercise to this edition, we have concentrated on materials that require the student to apply ideas, concepts and skills from other courses in their business school curriculum. The core in each new case or exercise is still an organizational level phenomenon. However, another trend we see in the business world is the use of cross-functional teams to solve cross-functional problems. The best way a student can prepare for working in cross-functional teams is to have worked on projects and cases that require her or him to integrate material across the curriculum. We have included several new cases that give students an opportunity to use the breadth of their training and experience.

6. As a final note to the instructor, we have again included a topic matrix in the instructors' manual to aid you in determining the uses of the materials in the book. Our decision to leave the topic matrix out of the instructors' manual for the third edition was greeted uniformly with negative comments. Bowing to popular demand, we have reintroduced this element to the instructors' manual.

Acknowledgements

As is always the case, this books reflects the work and influence of several people in addition to the authors. First, we must thank the case authors. They studied the companies, developed the cases and granted us permission to use their work.

We also have to thank all of the publishers who granted us permission to use already published works. We also wish to extend our appreciation to administrators and colleagues at Vanderbilt University and the University of Oklahoma who were helpful and supportive during the development of this fourth edition. Martin Geisel, Dean of the Owen Graduate School of Management at Vanderbilt; plus Nim Razook, Chair, Division of Business Strategy and Legal Studies; and Richard Cosier, Dean of the College of Business Administration, both at the University of Oklahoma, have created excellent climates for research of all types and have provided some of the resources for this project. We also must thank Lisa Tullius of the College of Business at the University of Oklahoma for her assistance in the development of the manuscript and the instructors' manual plus with securing permissions. Our thanks also go to Betty Robbins for her assistance on the final draft.

We feel a great debt to the colleagues who took the time to give us such detailed reviews of the third edition. Their assistance made the development of the fourth edition much easier. Our thanks go to Sonny Ariss, University of Toledo; Janet Barnard, Rochester Institute of Technology; Ronald Klocke, Mankato State University; Meryl Reis Louis, Boston University; James Swenson, Moorhead State University; Larry Wall, Western Illinois University; Jack Wimer, Baylor University; and Frank Winfrey, Kent State University.

We also wish to thank several people at West. As usual, without Esther Craig's assistance, support and patience, this edition would not have happened. Rick Leyh has been an important source of support and resources throughout the process, and we thank him for his help.

We also wish to thank Marilyn DeBrase at Esther Craig's office, Kathy Morton in Permissions and Carol Yanisch in Marketing for all of their assistance. Finally, we wish to thank Jim Somers and crew at Sonora Marketing and Graphics for their high quality production services.

As befits it, we save our most important acknowledgement until last. We believe that we owe our greatest debt to the students and instructors who have used the previous editions of this book. This new edition is for you. We have as our on-going goal making the examination of organization level phenomena an interesting, challenging and exciting part of the curriculum. As noted above, we have added several things to this edition while retaining the best parts of our previous efforts in order to achieve our goal. It is our hope that the materials included in this book will help the students develop both a conceptual understanding of the phenomena we have addressed as well as gain some of the practical skills they will need to be successful in today's fast-paced, changing business world.

R.L.D.
M.P.S.

A General Diagnostic Model for Organizational Behavior: Applying a Congruence Perspective

Most of the job of management is the struggle to make organizations function effectively. The work of society gets done through organizations, and the function of management is to get those organizations to perform that work.

The task of getting organizations to function electively is a difficult one, however. Understanding one individual's behavior is a challenging problem in and of itself. A group, made up of different individuals and multiple relationships among those individuals, is even more complex. Imagine, then, the mind boggling complexity inherent in a large organization made up of thousands of individuals, hundreds of groups, and relationships among individuals and groups too numerous to count.

In the face of this overwhelming complexity, organizational behavior must be managed. Ultimately the work of organizations gets done through the behavior of people, individually or collectively, on their own or in collaboration with technology. Thus, central to the management task is the management of organizational behavior. To do this, there must be the capacity to *understand* the patterns of behavior at individual, group and organizational levels, to *predict* what behavioral responses will be elicited by different managerial actions, and finally to use understanding and prediction to achieve *control*.

How can one achieve understanding, prediction, and control of organizational behavior? Given its inherent complexity and enigmatic nature, one needs tools to help unravel the mysteries, paradoxes, and apparent contradictions that present themselves in the everyday life of organizations. One kind of tool is the conceptual framework or model. A model is a theory which indicates which factors (in an organization, for example) are most critical or important. It also indicates how these factors are related, or which factors or combination of factors cause other factors to change. In a sense, then, a model is a road map that can be used to make sense of the terrain of organizational behavior.

The models we use are critical because they guide our analysis and action. In any organizational situation, problem solving involves the collection of information about the problem, the interpretation of that information to determinespecific problem types and causes, and the development of action plans. The models that individuals utilize influence what data they col-

Written by David A. Nadler and Michael L. Tushman. Published by permission of the authors, who retain all rights. A version of this paper was originally published in J. R. Hackman, E. E. Lawler, and L. W. Porter (eds.), *Perspectives on Behavior in Organizations* (New York: McGraw-Hill, 1977).

lect and what data they ignore; models guide how people attempt to analyze or interpret the data they have; finally, models aid people in choosing action plans.

Indeed, anyone who has been exposed to an organization already has some sort of implicit model. People develop these road maps over time, building on their own experiences. These implicit models (they usually are not explicitly written down or stated) guide behavior (Argyris & Schon, 1974). These models also vary in quality, validity, and sophistication depending on the nature and extent of the experiences of the model builder, his or her perceptiveness, his or her ability to conceptualize and generalize from experiences, etc.

We are not solely dependent, however, on the implicit and experience based models that individuals develop. The last four decades have witnessed intense work including research and theory development related to organization behavior (see, for example, Dunnette, 1976). It is therefore possible to think about scientifically developed explicit models for the analysis of organizational behavior and for use in organizational problem solving.

This paper will present one particular research-and theory-based model. It is a general model of organizations. Rather than describing a specific phenomenon or aspect of organizational life (such as a model of motivation or a model of organizational design), it attempts to provide a framework for thinking about the organization as a total system. The major thrust of the model is that for organizations to be effective, their subparts or components must be consistently structured and managed—they must approach a state of congruence.

The paper will be organized into several sections. In the first section, we will discuss the basic view of organizations which underlies the model—systems theory. In the second section, we will present and discuss the model itself. In the third section, we will present an approach to using the model for organizational problem analysis. Finally, we will discuss some of the implications of this model for thinking about organizations.

A Basic View of Organizations

There are many different ways of thinking about organizations. Typically, when a manager is asked to "draw a picture of an organization," he/she responds with some version of a pyramidal organizational chart. The model this rendition reflects is one which views the most critical factors as the stable formal relationships among the jobs and formal work units that make up the organization. While this clearly is one way to think about organizations, it is a very limited view. It excludes factors such as leader behavior, the impact of the environment, informal relations, power distribution, etc. Such a model can only capture a small part of what goes on in an organization. It is narrow and static in perspective.

Over the past twenty years, there has been a growing consensus that a viable alternative to the static classical models of organizations is to think about organizations as social systems. This approach stems from the observation that social phenomena display many of the characteristics of natural or mechanical systems (Von Bertalanffy, 1968, Buckley, 1967). In particular, it is argued that organizations can be better understood if they are considered as dynamic and open social systems (Katz & Kahn, 1966; 1978).

What is a system? In the simplest of terms, a system is a set of interrelated elements. These elements are related; thus, change in one element may lead to changes in other elements. An *open system* is one that interacts with its environment. Thus, it is more than just a set of interrelated elements. Rather, these elements make up a mechanism that takes input from the environment, subjects it to some form of transformation process, and produces output (Exhibit 1). At the most general level, it should be easy to visualize organizations as systems. Let's consider a manufacturing plant, for example. It is made up of different related components (different departments, jobs, technologies, etc.). It receives input from the environment, including labor, raw material, production orders, etc., and

EXHIBIT 1 The Basic Systems Model

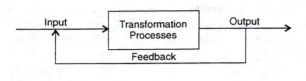

subjects those inputs to a transformation process to produce products.

Organizations as systems display a number of basic systems characteristics. Katz and Kahn (1966; 1978) discuss these in detail, but a few of the most critical characteristics will be mentioned here. First, organizations display degrees of internal *interdependence* (Thompson, 1967). Changes in one component or subpart of an organization frequently have repercussions for other parts—the pieces are interconnected. Returning to our manufacturing plant example, if changes are made in one element (for example, the skill levels of the people hired to do jobs), other elements will be affected (the productiveness of equipment used, the speed or quality of production activities, the nature of supervision needed, etc.). Second, organizations have the capacity for *feedback* (see Exhibit 1). Feedback is information about the output of a system that can be used to control the system (Weiner, 1950). Organizations can correct errors and indeed change themselves because of this characteristic (Bauer, 1966). If, in our plant example, the plant management receives information about the declining quality of its product, it can use this information to identify factors in the system itself that contribute to this problem. It is important to note that, unlike mechanized systems, feedback information does not always lead to correction. Organizations have the potential to use feedback and be self-correcing systems, but they do not always realize this potential.

A third characteristic of organizations as systems is *equilibrium*. Organizations develop energy to move towards states of balance. When an event occurs that puts the system out of balance, it reacts and moves towards a balanced state. If one work group in our plant example

were suddenly to increase its performance dramatically, it would throw the system out of balance. This group would be making increasing demands on the groups that supply it with information or materials to give it what it needs. Similarly, groups that work with the output of the high performing group would feel the pressure of work in process inventory piling up in front of them. Depending on the pay system used, other groups might feel inequity as this one group begins to earn more. We would predict that some actions would be taken to put the system back into balance. Either the rest of the plant would be changed to increase production and thus be back in balance with the single group, or (more likely) actions would be taken to get this group to modify its behavior to be consistent with the levels of performance of the rest of the system (by removing workers, limiting supplies, etc.). The point is that somehow the system would develop energy to move back towards a state of equilibrium or balance.

Fourth, open systems display *equifinality*. In other words, different system configurations can lead to the same end or lead to the same type of input-output conversion. This means there is not a universal or "one best way" to organize. Finally, open systems need to display *adaptation*. For a system to survive, it must maintain a favorable balance of input or output transactions with the environment, or it will run down. If our plant produces a product for which there are decreasing applications, it must adapt to the environmental changes and develop new products or ultimately the plant will simply have to close its doors. Any system therefore must adapt by changing as environmental conditions change. The consequences of not adapting to the environment can be seen in the demise of many once prosperous organizations (such as the eastern railroads) which did not alter in response to environmental changes.

Thus, systems theory provides a different way of thinking about the organization, in more complex and dynamic terms. While systems theory is a valuable basic perspective on organizations, it is limited as a problem-solving tool. The reason is that as a model systems theory is too abstract to be used for day-to-day organizational behavior problem analysis. Because of the level of abstraction of systems theory, we need to develop a more specific and pragmatic model based on the concepts of the open systems paradigm.

A Congruence Model of Organizational Behavior

Given the level of abstraction of open systems theory, our job is to develop a model which reflects the basic systems concepts and characteristics, but which will also be more specific and thus more usable as an analytic tool. In this section, we will describe a model which attempts to specify in more detail what are the critical inputs, what are the major outputs, and what are the transformation processes that characterize organizational functioning.

The model puts its greatest emphasis on the transformation process and in particular reflects the critical system property of interdependence. It views organizations as made up of components or parts which interact with each other. These components exist in states of relative balance, consistency, or "fit" with each other. The different parts of an organization can fit well together and thus function effectively or fit poorly, thus leading to problems, dysfunctions, or performance below potential. Given the central nature of these "fits" among components in the model, we will talk about it as a *congruence model of organizational behavior*, since effectiveness is a function of the congruence among the various components.

The concept of congruence is not a new one. Homans (1952), in his pioneering work on social processes in organizations, emphasized the interaction and consistency among key elements of organizational behavior. Leavitt (1965), for example, identified four major components of organization as being people, tasks, technology and structure. The model we will present here builds on these views and also draws from fit models developed and used by Seiler (1967),

Lawrence and Lorsch (1969), and Lorsch and Sheldon (1972).

It is important to remember that we are concerned about modeling the *behavioral* system of the organization—the system of elements that ultimately produce patterns of behavior and thus performance of the organization. In its simplest form, we need to deal with the questions of what inputs does the system have to work with, what outputs does it need to and actually produce, and what are the major components of the transformation process, and how do these components interact with each other?

Inputs

Inputs are those factors that are, at any one point in time, the "givens" that face the organization. They are the material that the organization has to work with. There are several different types of inputs, each of which presents a different set of "givens" to the organization. (See Exhibit 2 for an overview of inputs.)

The first input is the *environment*, or all of those factors outside of the boundaries of the organization being examined. Every organization exists within the context of a larger environment which includes individuals, groups, other organizations and even larger social forces, all of which have a potentially powerful impact on how the organization performs (Pfeffer & Salancik, 1978). Specifically, the environment includes markets (clients or customers), suppliers, governmental and regulatory bodies, labor unions, competitors, financial institutions, special interest groups, etc. The environment is critical to organizational functioning (Aldrich & Pfeffer, 1976). In particular, for purposes of organizational analysis, the environment has three critical features. First, the environment makes demands on the organization. For example, it may require the provision of certain products or services, at certain levels of quality or quantity. Market pressures are particularly important here. Second, the environment may place constraints on organizational action. It may limit the types of kinds of activities in which an organization can engage. These constraints

EXHIBIT 2 Key Organizational Inputs

Input	Environment	Resources	History	Strategy
Definition	All factors, including institutions, groups, individuals, events, etc., outside of the boundries of the organization being analyzed, but having potential impact on that organization.	Various assets that organization has access to, including human resources, technology, capital, information, etc., as well as less tangible resources (recognition in the market, etc.).	The patterns of past behavior, activity, and effectiveness of the organization which may have an effect on current organizational functioning.	The stream of decisions made about how organizational resources will be configured against the demands, constraints, and oprotunities, within the context of history.
Critical Features of the Input for Analysis	■ What demands does the environment make on the organization? ■ Does the environment put constraints on organizational action?	■ What is the relative quality of the different resources that the organization has access to? ■ To what extent are resources fixed, as opposed to flexible, in their configuration?	■ What have been the major stages or phases of development of the organization? ■ What is the current impact of historical factors such as strategic decisions, acts of key leaders, crises, core values, and norms?	■ How has the organization defined its core mission, including: ■ What markets it serves? ■ What products/services it provides to these markets? ■ On what basis does it compete? ■ What supporting strategies has the organization employed to achieve the core mission?

could range from limitations imposed by scarce capital, all the way to governmental regulatory prohibitions. Third, the environment provides opportunities which the organization can explore. In total, then, the analysis of an organization needs to consider what factors are present in the environment of the organization and how those factors individually or in relation to each other create demands, constraints, or opportunities.

The second input is the resources of the organization. Any organization faces its environment with a range of different assets to which it has access and which it can employ. These include human beings, technology, capital, infor-

mation, etc. Resources can also include certain less tangible assets such as the perception of the organization in the marketplace, or a positive organizational climate. A set of resources can be shaped, deployed, or configured in diferent ways by an organization. For analysis purposes, there are two features that are of primary interest. One aspect of resources concerns the relative quality of those resources, or what value they have in light of the nature of the environment. The second factor concerns the extent to which resources can be reconfigured, or how fixed or flexible different resources are.

The third input is the *history* of the organization. There is growing evidence that the contemporary functioning of many organizations is greatly influenced by events in the past (see Levinson, 1972; 1976). In particular, it is important to understand what have been the major stages or phases of development of the organization over time (Galbraith & Nathanson, 1978) as well as understand the current impact of events that occurred in the past, such as key strategic decisions that were made, the acts or behavior of key leaders in the past, the nature of past crises and the organizational responses to them, and the evolution of core values and norms of the organization.

The final input is somewhat different from the others in that it in some ways reflects some of the factors in the environment, resources, and history of the organization. The fourth input is strategy. We will use this term in its most global and broad context (Hofer & Schendel, 1978) to describe the whole set of decisions that are made about how the organization will configure its resources against the demands, constraints and opportunities of the environment within the context of its history. Strategy refers to the issue of matching the organization's resources to its environment, or making the fundamental decision of "what business are we in?" For analysis purposes, several aspects of strategy are important to identify (Katz, 1970). First is what is the core mission of the organization, or what has the organization defined as its basic purpose or function within the larger system or environment? The core mission includes decisions about what markets the organization will serve, what products or services it will provide to those markets, or what basis it will use to compete in those markets. Second, strategy includes the specific supporting strategies (or tactics) that the organization will employ, or is employing, to achieve its core mission. Third is the specific performance or output objectives that have been established.

Strategy is perhaps the most important single input for the organization (see discussion in Nadler, Hackman & Lawler, 1979). On one hand, strategic decisions implicitly determine what is the nature of the work that the organization should be doing, or the tasks that it should

perform. On the other hand, strategic decisions, and particularly decisions about objectives, serve as the basis for determining what the outputs of the system should be. Based on strategy, one can determine what is the desired or intended output of the system.

In summary, there are three basic inputs: environment; resources; and history; and a fourth input, strategy, which reflects how the organization chooses to respond to or deal with those other inputs. Strategy is critical because it determines the work that the organization should be performing and it defines the nature of desired organizational outputs.

Outputs

Outputs describe what the organization produces, how it performs, or globally, how effective it is. There has been a lot of discussion about what makes for an effective organization (see Steers, 1978; Goodman & Pennings, 1978; Van de Ven & Ferry, 1980). For our purposes, however, it is possible to identify a number of key indicators of organizational output. First, we need to think about system output at different levels (see Exhibit 3). Obviously we can think about the output that the system itself produces, but we also need to think about the various other types of output that contribute to organizational performance, such as the functioning of groups or units within the organization as well as the functioning of individual organization members.

At the organizational level, three factors are important to keep in mind in evaluating organizational performance. The first factor is goal attainment, or how well the organization meets its objectives (usually determined by strategy). A second factor is resource utilization, or how well the organization makes use of resources that it has available to it. The question here is not just whether the organization meets its goals, but whether it realizes all of the potential performance that is there and whether it achieves its goals by continuing to build resources or by "burning them up" in the process. A final factor is adaptability, or whether the organization continues to position itself in a favorable position

EXHIBIT 3 Key Organizational Outputs

ORGANIZATIONAL FUNCTIONING
- Goal Attainment
- Resource Utilization
- Adaptability

GROUP/UNIT FUNCTIONING

INDIVIDUAL FUNCTIONING
- Behavior
- Affective Reactions

---

vis-a-vis its environment—whether it is capable of changing and adapting to environmental changes.

Obviously, these organizational level outputs are contributed to by the functioning of groups or units (departments, divisions, or other subunits within the organization). Organizational output also is influenced by individual behavior, and certain individual level outputs (affective reactions such as satisfaction, stress, or experienced quality of working life) may be desired outputs in and of themselves.

The Organization as a Transformation Process

So far, we have defined the nature of inputs and outputs for the organizational system. This approach leads us towards thinking about the transformation process. The question that any manager faces, given an environment, a set of resources, and history, is "How do I take a strategy and implement it to produce effective organizational, group/unit, and individual performance?"

In our framework, the means for implementing strategies, or the transformation mechanism in the system is the organization. We therefore think about the *organization* and its major component parts as the fundamental means for transforming energy and information from inputs into outputs (see Exhibit 4). The question then is what are the key components of the organization, and what is the critical dynamic which describes how those components interact with each other to perform the transformation function?

Organizational Components

There are many diferent ways of thinking about what makes up an organization. At this point in the development of a science of organizations, we probably do not know what is the one right or best way to describe the different components of an organization. The question then is to find approaches for describing organizations that are useful, help to simplify complex phenomena, and help to identify patterns in what may at first blush seem to be random sets of activity. The particular approach here views organizations as composed of four major components: (1) the task, (2) the individuals, (3) the formal organizational arrangements, and (4) the informal organization. We will discuss each one of these individually. (See Exhibit 5 for overviews of these components.)

The first component is the *task* of the organization. The task is defined as the basic or inherent work to be done by the organization and its subunits. The task (or tasks) is the activity the organization is engaged in, particularly in light of its strategy. The emphasis is on the specific work activities or functions that need to be done, and their inherent characteristics (as opposed to characteristics of the work created by how the work is organized or structured in this particular organization at this particular time). Analysis of the task would include a description of the basic work flows and functions, with attention to the characteristics of those work flows, such as the knowledge or skill demands made by the work, the kinds of rewards the work inherently provides to those who do it, the degree of uncertainty associated with the work, and the specific constraints inherent in the work (such as critical time demands, cost constraints, etc.) The task is the starting point for the analysis, since the assumption is that a primary (although not the only) reason for the organization's existence is to perform the task consistent with strategy. As we will see, the assessment of the adequacy of other components will be dependent to a large degree on an understanding of the nature of the tasks to be performed.

A second component of organizations con-

EXHIBIT 4 The Organization as a Transformation Process

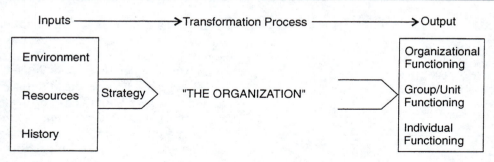

Inputs ──────────────► Transformation Process ──────────────► Output

Environment			
Resources	Strategy	"THE ORGANIZATION"	Organizational Functioning
History			Group/Unit Functioning
			Individual Functioning

cerns the *individuals* who perform organizational tasks. The issue here is identifying the nature and characteristics of the individuals that the organization currently has as members. The most critical aspects to consider include the nature of individual knowledge and skills, the different needs or preferences that individuals have, the perceptions or expectancies that they develop, and other background factors (such as demographics) that may be potential influences on individual behavior.

The third component is the *formal organizational arrangements*. These include the range of structures, processes, methods, procedures, etc., that are explicitly and formally developed to get individuals to perform tasks consistent with organizational strategy. "Organizational arrangements" is a very broad term which includes a number of different specific factors. One factor of organizational arrangements is organization design (how jobs are grouped together into units), the internal structure of those units, and the various coordination and control mechanisms used to link those units together (see Galbraith, 1977; Nadler, Hackman & Lawler, 1979). A second factor in organizational arrangements is how jobs are designed (Hackman & Oldham, 1980) within the context of organizational designs. A third factor is the work environment, which includes a number of factors which characterize the immediate environment in which work is done, such as the physical working environment, the work resources made available to performers, etc. A final factor includes the various formal systems for attracting, placing, de-

veloping, and evaluating human resources in the organization.

Together, these factors combine to create the set of organizational arrangements. It is important to remember that these are the formal arrangements, formal in that they are explicitly designed and specified, usually in writing.

The final component is the *informal organization*. In any organization, while there is a set of formal organizational arrangements, over time another set of arrangements tends to develop or emerge. These arrangements are usually implicit and not written down anywhere, but they influence a good deal of behavior. For lack of a better term, these arrangements are frequently referred to as the informal organization and they include the different structures, processes, arrangements, etc., that emerge over time. These arrangements sometimes arise to complement the formal organizational arrangements by providing structures to aid work where none exists. In other situations they may arise in reaction to the formal structure, to protect individuals from it. It may, therefore, either aid or hinder organizational performance.

A number of aspects of the informal organization have a particularly critical effect on behavior and thus need to be considered. The behavior of leaders (as opposed to the formal creation of leader positions) is an important feature of the informal organization, as are the patterns of relationships that develop both within and between groups. In addition, there are different types of informal working arrangements (including rules, procedures, methods, etc.) that develop.

EXHIBIT 5 Key Organizational Components

Component	Task	Individual	Formal Organizational Arrangements	Informal Organization
Definition	The basic and inherent work to be done by the organization and its parts.	The characteristics of individuals in the organization.	The various structures, processes, methods, etc., that are formally created to get individuals to perform tasks.	The emerging arrangements, including structures, processes, relationships, etc.
Critical Features of Each Component	▪ The types of skill and knowledge demands the work poses. ▪ The types of rewards the work inherently can provide. ▪ The degree of uncertainty associated with the work, including such factors as interdependence, routineness, etc. ▪ The constraints on performance demands inherent in the work (given a strategy).	▪ Knowledge and skills individuals have. ▪ Individual needs and preferences. ▪ Perceptions and expectancies. ▪ Background factors.	▪ Organization design, including grouping of functions, structure of subunits, and coordination and control mechanisms. ▪ Job design. ▪ Work environment. ▪ Human resource management systems.	▪ Leader behavior. ▪ Intragroup relations. ▪ Intergroup relations. ▪ Informal working arrangements. ▪ Communication and influence patterns.

Finally, there are the various communication and influence patterns that combine to create the informal organization design (Tushman, 1977).

Organizations can therefore be thought of as a set of components, the task, the individuals, the organizational arrangements, and the informal organization. In any system, however, the critical question is not what the components are, but rather the nature of their interaction. The question in this model is, then, what is the dynamic of the relationship among the components? To deal with this issue, we need to return to the concept of congruence or fit.

The Concept of Congruence

Between each pair of inputs, there exists in any organization a relative degree of congruence, consistency, or "fit." Specifically, the congruence between two components is defined as follows:

the degree to which the needs, demands, goals, objectives and/or structures of one component are consistent with the needs, demands, goals, objectives and/or structures of another component.

Congruence, therefore, is a measure of the

goodness of fit between pairs of components. For example, consider two components: the task and the individual. At the simplest level, the task can be thought of as inherently presenting some demands to individuals who would perform it (i.e., skill/knowledge demands). At the same time, the set of individuals available to do the tasks have certain characteristics (i.e., levels of skill and knowledge).

Obviously, when the individual's knowledge and skill match the knowledge and skill demanded by the task, performance will be more effective. Obviously, even the individual-task congruence relationship encompasses more factors than just knowledge and skill. Similarly, each congruence relationship in the model has its own specific characteristics. At the same time, in each relationship, there also is research and theory which can guide the assessment of fit. An overview of the critical elements of each congruence relationship is provided in Exhibit 6.

The Congruence Hypothesis

Just as each pair of components has a degree of high or low congruence, so does the aggregate model, or whole organization, display a relatively high or low level of system congruence. The basic hypothesis of the model builds on this total state of congruence and is as follows:

other things being equal, the greater the total degree of congruence or fit between the various components, the more effective will be the organization, effectiveness being defined as the degree to which actual organization outputs at individual, group, and organizational levels are similar to expected outputs as specified by strategy.

The basic dynamic of congruence thus views the organization as being more effective when its pieces fit together. If we also consider questions of strategy, the argument expands to include the fit between the organization and its larger environment. An organization will be most effective when its strategy is consistent with the larger environment (in light of organ-izational resources and history) and when theorganizational components are congruent with the tasks to be done to implement that strategy.

One important implication of the congruence hypotheses is that organizational problem analysis (or diagnosis) involves description of the system, identification of problems, and analysis of fits to determine the causes of problems. The model also implies that different configurations of the key components can be used to gain outputs (consistent with the systems characteristic of equi-finality). Therefore, the question is not finding the "one best way" of managing, but of determining effective combinations of components that will lead to congruent fits among them.

The process of diagnosing fits and identifying combinations of components to produce congruence is not necessarily intuitive. A number of situations which lead to congruence have been defined in the research literature. Thus, in many cases, fit is something that can be defined, measured, and even quantified. There is, therefore, an empirical and theoretical basis for making assessment of fit. In most cases, the theory provides considerable guidance about what leads to congruent relationships (although in some areas the research is more definitive and helpful than others). The implication is that the manager who is attempting to diagnose behavior needs to become familiar with critical aspects of relevant organizational behavior models or theories so that he or she can evaluate the nature of fits in a particular system.

The congruence model is thus a general organizing framework. The organizational analyst will need other, more specific "sub models" to define high and low congruence. Examples of such submodels that might be used in the context of this general diagnostic model would be (1) Job Characteristics model (Hackman & Oldham, 1980) to assess and explain the fit between individuals and tasks as well as the fit between individuals and organizational arrangements (job design); (2) Expectancy Theory models of motivation (Vroom, 1964; Lawler, 1973) to explain the fit between individuals and the other three components; (3) the Information Process-

EXHIBIT 6 Definitions of Fits

Fit	The Issues
Individual-organization	To what extent individual needs are met by the organizational arrangements. To what extent individuals hold clear or distorted perceptions of organizational structures, the convergence of individual and organizational goals.
Individual-task	To what extent the needs of individuals are met by the tasks. To what extent individuals have skills and abilities to meet task demands.
Individual-informal organization	To what extent individual needs are met by the informal organization. To what extent the informal organization makes use of individual resources, consistent with informal goals.
Task-organization	Whether the organizational arrangements are adequate to meet the demands of the task, whether organizational arrangements tend to motivate behavior consistent with task demands.
Task-informal organization	Whether the informal organization structure facilitates task performance, whether it hinders or promotes meeting the demands of the task.
Organization-informal organization	Whether the goals, rewards, and structures of the informal organization are consistent with those of the formal organization.

ing model of organizational design (Galbraith, 1973; Tushman & Nadler, 1978) to explain the task-formal organization and task-informal organization fits; or (4) an Organizational Climate model (Litwin & Stringer, 1968) to explain the fit between the informal organization and the other components. These models and theories are listed as illustrations of how more specific models can be used in the context of the general model. Obviously, those mentioned above are just a sampling of possible tools that could be used.

In summary, then, we have described a general model for the analysis of organizations (see Exhibit 7). The organization is seen as a system which takes inputs and transforms them into outputs. At the core of the model, the transformation process is the organization, seen as composed of four basic components. The critical dynamic is the fit or congruence among the components. We now turn our attention to the pragmatic question of how to use this model for analyzing organizational problems.

A Process for Organizational Problem Analysis

The conditions that face organizations are frequently changing, and as a consequence, managers are required to continually engage in problem identification and problem solving activities (Schein, 1970). To do this, managers must be involved in gathering data on the performance of their organizations, comparing these data to desired performance levels, identifying the causes of problems, developing and choosing action plans, and finally implementing and evaluating these action plans. These phases can be viewed as a generic problem solving process. For long-term organizational viability, some sort of problem-solving process needs to continually be in operation (Schein, 1970; Weick, 1969).

Experience with using the congruence model for organizations to do problem analysis in actual organizational settings has led to the development of an approach to using the model, based on the generic problem solving processes described above (see Exhibit 8). In this section, we will walk through this process, describing the different steps in the process and discussing how the model can be used at each stage. There are eight specific steps in the problem analysis process, and each one will be described separately.

1. *Identify symptoms:* In any situation there is

EXHIBIT 7 A Congruence Model for Organizational Analysis

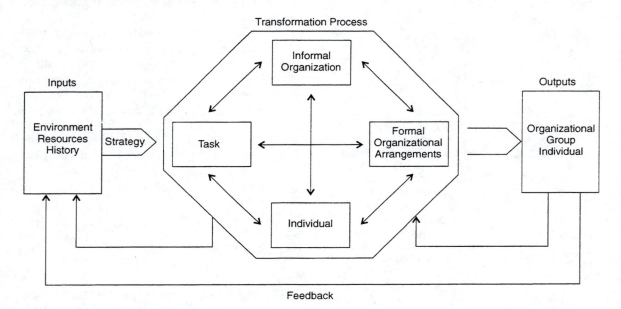

initial information that presents itself as indications that problems may exist. We can think of this information as symptomatic data. These data tell us that a problem might exist, but they do not usually indicate what the problem is or what the causes are. Symptomatic data are important to note, however, since the symptoms or problems that present themselves may be important indicators of where to look for more complete data.

2. *Specify inputs:* Having noted the symptoms, the starting point for analysis is to identify the system and the environment in which it functions. This means collecting data about the nature of environment, the type of resources the organization has, and the critical aspects of its history. Input analysis also involves identifying what the strategy of the organization is, including its core mission, supporting strategies, and objectives.

3. *Identify outputs:* The third step is an analysis of the outputs of the organization at the individual, group, and organizational level. Output analysis actually involves two elements. The first is to define what is the desired, or planned output. This usually can be obtained from an analysis of strategy which should explicitly or implicitly define what the organization is attempting to achieve in terms of output or performance indicators. The second is to collect data that would indicate what type of output the organization is actually achieving.

4. *Identify problems:* Symptoms indicate the possibility of problems. For our purposes, we will define problems as the differences between expected output and actual output. A problem exists when a significant and meaningful difference is observed between output (at any level) that is desired or planned and the output that is actually being obtained. Thus problems would be discrepancies (actual vs. expected) of organizational performance, group functioning, and individual behavior or affective reactions. These data thus tell us that problems exist, but they do not specify what the causes are.

Gap Analysis

EXHIBIT 8   BASIC PROBLEM ANALYSIS STEPS USING THE CONGRUENCE MODEL

Step	Explanation
1. Identify symptoms	List data indicating possible existence of problems.
2. Specify inputs	Identify the system. Determine nature of environment, resources, and history. Identify critical aspects of strategy.
3. Identify outputs	Identify data that defines the nature of outputs at various levels (individual, group/unit, organization). Should include: Desired outputs (from strategy). Actual outputs being obtained.
4. Identify problems	Identify areas where there are significant and meaningful differences between desired and actual outputs. To the extent possible, identify penalties, i.e., specific costs (actual and opportunity costs) associated with each problem.
5. Describe components of the organization	Describe basic nature of each of the four components with emphasis on their critical features.
6. Assessment of congruence (fits)	Do analysis to determine relative congruence among components (draw on sub-models as needed).
7. Generate hypotheses to identify causes	Analyze to associate fit with specific problems.
8. Identify action steps	Indicate what possible actions might deal with causes of problems.

Where data are available, it is frequently useful to also identify what are the costs associated with the problems, or the penalties that the organization incurs by not fixing the problem. Penalties might be actual costs (increased expenses, etc.) or opportunity costs, such as revenue that could be realized if the problem were not there.

5. *Describe organizational components:* The next step begins analysis to determine the causes of problems. Data are collected about the nature of each of the four major organizational components, including information about the component and its critical features in this organization.

6. *Assess congruence (fits):* Using the data collected in step 5 as well as applicable sub-models or theories, an assessment is made of the positive or negative fit between each of the pairs of components.

7. *Generate hypotheses about problem causes:* Having described the components and assessed congruence, the next step is to link together the congruence analysis with the problem identification (step 4). Given the analysis, which poor fits seem to be associated with or account for the output problems that have been identified? The patterns of congruence and incongruence which appear to cause the patterns of problems are determined.

8. *Identify action steps:* The final step in problem analysis is to identify possible action steps. These steps might range from specific changes to deal with relatively obvious problem causes on one hand, to additional data collection to test the hypotheses developed concerning relatively more complex problems and causes.

In addition to these eight steps identified, some further steps need to be kept in mind. Having identified possible actions, problem solving involves making predictions about the consequence of those actions, choosing particular action steps, implementing those action steps, and evaluating the impact of those actions. In each case, it is, of course, important to have a general diagnostic framework to monitor what the effects of actions are.

The congruence model and this problem analysis process outline are tools for structuring and dealing with the complex reality of organizations. Given the indeterminate nature of social systems, there is no one best way of handling a particular situation. The model and the process do, however, facilitate one in collecting data, analyzing the meaning of that data, and making decisions about possible action. If these tools have merit, then it is up to the manager to use them along with his or her intuitive sense (based on experience) to make the appropriate set of diagnostic, evaluative, and action decisions over time.

Future Directions

The model that we have presented here reflects a particular way of thinking about organizations. If that perspective has merit, then it may make sense to think about the possible extensions of that model as a tool to think about more complex problems or to structure more complex situations. A number of directions for further thought, research, and theory development are as follows:

1. *Organizational change:* The issue of organizational change has received a good deal of attention from managers and academics alike. The question is how to implement organizational changes effectively. Much talk has centered on the lack of a general model of organizational change. In one sense, however, it is hard to think about a general model of organizational change in the absence of a general model of organizations. The congruence perspective outlined here may provide some guidance and direction towards the development of a more integrated perspective on the processes of

organizational change. Initial work in that area (Nadler, 1981) is encouraging in terms of the applicability of the congruence model to the change issue.

2. *Organizational development over time:* There has been a growing realization that organizations grow and develop over time, that they face different types of crises, evolve through different stages, and develop along some predictable line (see, for example, Greiner, 1972; Galbraith and Nathanson, 1978). A model of organizations such as the one presented here might be a tool for developing a typology of growth patterns by indicating what are the different configurations of task, individual, organizational arrangements and informal organizations that might be most appropriate for organizations in diferent environments and at different stages of development.

3. *Organizational pathology:* Organizational problem solving ultimately requires some sense of what types of problems may be encountered and kinds of patterns of causes one might expect. It is reasonable to assume that most problems that organizations encounter are not wholly unique, but rather predictable problems that one might expect. The view, often heard, that "our problems are unique" reflects in part the fact that there is no framework of organizational pathology. The question is, are there certain basic "illnesses" which organizations suffer? Can a framework of organizational pathology, similar to the physician's framework of medical pathology be developed? The lack of a pathology framework in turn reflects that lack of a basic functional model of organizations. Again, development of a congruence perspective might be able to provide a common language to use for the identification of general pathological patterns of organizational functioning.

4. *Organizational solution types:* Closely linked to the problem of pathology is the problem

of treatment, intervention, or solutions to organizational problems. Again, there is a lack of a general framework to consider the nature of organizational interventions. In this case, too, the congruence model could have value as a means for conceptualizing and ultimately describing the diferent intervention options available in response to problems (see one attempt at this in Nadler & Tichy, 1980).

Summary

This paper has presented a general approach for thinking about organizational functioning and a process for using a model to analyze organizational problems. This particular model is one way of thinking about organizations. It clearly is not the only model, nor can we claim that it definitively is the best model. It is one tool, however, that appears to be useful for structuring the complexity of organizational life, and helping managers in creating, maintaining, and developing effective organizations.

References

Aldrich, H. E., & Pfeffer, J. Environments of organizations. *Annual Review of Sociology*, 1976, 2, 79-105.

Argyris, C., & Schon, D. A. *Theory in practice.* San Francisco: Jossey-Bass, 1974.

Bauer. R. A. Detection and anticipation of impact: The nature of the task. In R. A. Bauer (Ed.), *Social indicators*, pp. 1-67. Boston: M.I.T. Press, 1966.

Buckley, W. *Sociology and modern systems theory.* Englewood Cliffs, N.J.: Prentice-Hall, 1967.

Dunnette, M. D. *Handbook of industrial and organizational psychology.* Chicago: Rand-McNally, 1976.

Galbraith, J. R. *Designing complex organizations.* Reading, Mass.: Addison-Wesley, 1973.

_____, *Organization design.* Reading, Mass.: Addison-Wesley, 1977.

_____, & Nathanson, D. A. *Strategy implementation: The role of structure and process.* St Paul, Minn.: West, 1978.

Goodman, P. S., & Pennings, J. M. *New perspectives on organizational effectiveness.* San Francisco: Jossey-Bass, 1977.

Greiner, L E. Evolution and revolution as organizations grow. *Harvard Business Review*, 1972.

Hackman, J. R., & Oldham, G. A. *Work redesign.* Reading, Mass.: Addison-Wesley, 1979.

Hofer, C. W., & Schendel, D. *Strategy formulation: Analytical concepts.* St. Paul, Minn.: West, 1978.

Homans, G. C. *The human group.* New York: Harcourt Brace Jovanovich, 1950.

Katz, D., & Kahn, R. L. *The social psychology of organizations.* New York: Wiley, 1966, 2d ed., 1978.

Katz, R. L. *Cases and concepts in corporate strategy.* Englewood Cliffs, N.J.: Prentice-Hall, 1970.

Lawler, E. E. *Motivation in work organizations.* Belmont, Calif.: Wadsworth, 1973.

Lawrence, P. R., & Lorsch, J. W. *Developing organizations: Diagnosis and action.* Reading, Mass.: Addison-Wesley, 1969.

Leavitt, H.J. Applied organization change in industry. In J. G. March (Ed.), *Handbook of organizations*, pp. 1144-1170. Chicago: Rand-McNally, 1965.

Levinson, H. *Organizational diagnosis.* Cambridge, Mass.: Harvard, 1972.

_____, *Psychological man.* Cambridge, Mass.: Levinson Institute, 1976.

Litwin, G. H., & Stringer, R. A. *Motivation and organizational climate.* Boston: Harvard University Graduate School of Business Administration, 1968.

Lorsch, J. W., & Sheldon, A. The individual in the organization: A systems view. In J. W. Lorsch and P. R. Lawrence (Eds.), *Managing group and intergroup relations.* Homewood, Ill.: Irwin-Dorsey, 1972.

Nadler, D. A. An integrative theory of organizational change. *Journal of Applied Behavioral Science*, 1981.

_____, & Tichy, N. M. The limitations of traditional intervention technology in health care organizations. In N. Margulies & J. A. Adams, *Organization development in health care organizations.* Reading, Mass.: Addison-Wesley, 1980.

_____, Hackman, J. R., & bawler, E. E. *Managing organizational behavior.* Boston: Little, Brown, 1979.

Salancik, G. R., & Pfeffer, J. *The external control of organizations.* New York: Wiley, 1978.

Schein, E. H. *Organizational psychology.* Englewood Cliffs, N.J.: Prentice-Hall, 1970.

Seiler, J. A. *Systems analysis in organizational behavior.* Homewood, Ill.: Irwin-Dorsey, 1967.

Steers, R. M. *Organizational effectiveness: A behavioral view.* Pacific Palisades, Calif.: Goodyear, 1977.

Thompson, J. D. *Organizations in action.* New York:

McGraw-Hill, 1967.

Tushman, M. L. A political approach to organizations: A review and rationale. *Academy of Management Review*, 1977, 2, 206-216.

Van de Ven, A., & Ferry, D. *Organizational assessment.* New York: Wiley Interscience, 1980.

Von Bertalanffy, L. *General systems theory: Foundations, development applications* (Rev. ed.). New York: Braziller, 1968.

Vroom, V. H. *Work and motivation.* New York: Wiley, 1964.

Weick, K. E. *The social psychology of organizing.* Reading, Mass.: Addison-Wesley, 1969.

Wiener, N. *The human use of human beings: Cybernetics and society.* Boston: Houghton Mifflin, 1950.

I

Organizations
as Systems

1
Kao Corporation

Dr. Yoshio Maruta introduced himself as a Buddhist scholar first, and as President of the Kao Corporation second. The order was significant, for it revealed the philosophy behind Kao and its success in Japan. Kao was a company that not only learned, but "learned how to learn." It was, in Dr. Maruta's words, "an educational institution in which everyone is a potential teacher."

Under Dr. Maruta's direction, the scholar's dedication to learning had metamorphosed into a competitive weapon which, in 1990, had led to Kao being ranked ninth by Nikkei Business in its list of excellent companies in Japan, and third in terms of corporate originality (Exhibit 1). As described by Fumio Kuroyanagi, Director of Kao's overseas planning department, the company's success was due not merely to its mastery of technologies nor its efficient marketing and information systems, but to its ability to integrate and enhance these capabilities through learning. As a result, Kao had come up with a stream of new products ahead of its Japanese and foreign competitors and, by 1990, had emerged as the largest branded and packaged goods company in Japan and the country's second largest cosmetics company.

Since the mid 1960s, Kao had also successfully used its formidable array of technological, manufacturing and marketing assets to expand into the neighbouring markets of SE Asia. Pitting herself against long established multinationals like Procter & Gamble and Unilever, Kao had made inroads into the detergent, soap and shampoo markets in the region. However, success in these small markets would not make Kao a global player, and since the mid-1980s, Kao had been giving its attention to the problem of how to break into the international markets beyond the region. There, Kao's innovations were being copied and sold by her competitors, not by Kao itself, a situation the company was keen to remedy. But would Kao be able to repeat its domestic success in the US and Europe? As Dr. Maruta knew, the company's ability to compete on a world-wide basis would be measured by its progress in these markets. This, then, was the new challenge to which Kao was dedicated: how to transfer its learning capability, so all-conquering in Japan, to the rest of the world.

This case was written by Charlotte Butler, Research Assistant, under the supervision of Sumantra Ghoshal, Associate Professor at INSEAD. It is intended to he used as a basis for class discussion rather than to illustrate either effective or ineffective handling of an administrative situation.
Copyright ©1992 INSEAD-EAC, Fontainbleau, France. Used with permission.

Exhibit 1-1 The Ranking of Japanese Excellent Companies (1990)

I. Honda Motors	79.8
2. IBM-Japan	79.4
3. SONY	78.4
4. Matsushita Electrics	74.5
5. Toshiba	69.9
6. NEC	69.8
7. Nissan Motors	69.8
8. Asahi Beer	67.4
9. KAO	66.6
10. Yamato Transportation	66.4
11. Fuji-Xerox	66.3
12. Seibu Department Store	66.2
13. Suntory	65.8
14. Nomura Security	65.4
15. NTT (Nippon Telegraph & Telephone)	65.3
16. Omron	65.1
17. Ajinomoto	64.3
18. Canon	64.3
19. Toyota Motors	63.9
20. Ohtsuka Medicines	63.8

Note: Points are calculated on the basis of the following criteria:

1. the assessment by Nikkei Business Committee's member corporate originality, corporate vision, flexibility, goodness;

2. the result of the researches among consumers;

Source: Nikkei Business 9.4.1990

Exhibit 1-2 The Trend of Kao's Performance

	Billions of Yen						Millions of US$
Years ended March 31	1985	1986	1987	1988	1989	1990	1990
Net Sales (Increase)	398.1	433.7 +8.9%	464.1 +7.0%	514.4 +10.9%	572.2 +11.2%	620.4 +8.4%	3,926.8
Operating Income (Increase)	16.5*	19.853*	31.7	36.5 +15.2%	41.1 +13.5%	43.5 +5.1%	275.5
Net Income (Increase)	9.4	10.5 +12.3%	12.9 +22.5%	13.4 +4.2%	17.5 +30.4%	17.8 +1.7%	112.7
Total assets	328.3	374.4	381.0	450.4	532.3	572.8	3,625.5
Total shareholders' equity	114.4	150.9	180.2	210.7	233.8	256.6	1,624.1

* non-consolidated

Note: The U.S. dollar amounts are translated, for convienience only, at the rate of ¥156 = $1, the approximate exchange rate prevailing on March 30, 1990.

Source: KAO Corporation

The Learning Organization

Kao was founded in 1890 as Kao Soap Company with the prescient motto, "Cleanliness is the foundation of a prosperous society." Its objective then was to produce a high quality soap that was as good as any imported brand, but at a more affordable price for the Japanese consumer, and this principle had guided the development of all Kao's products ever since. In the 1940s Kao had launched the first Japanese laundry detergent, followed in the 1950s by the launch of dishwashing and household detergents. The 1960s had seen an expansion into industrial products to which Kao could apply its technologies in fat and oil science, surface and polymer science.

The 70s and 80s, coinciding with the presidency of Dr. Maruta, had seen the company grow more rapidly than ever in terms of size, sales and profit, with the launching of innovative products and the start of new businesses. Between 1982 and 1985, it had successfully diversified into cosmetics, hygiene and floppy disks.

A vertically integrated company, Kao owned many of its raw material sources and had, since the 1960s, built its own sales organization of wholesalers who had exclusive distribution of its products throughout Japan. The 1980s had seen a consistent rise in profits, with sales increasing at roughly 10 percent a year throughout the decade, even in its mature markets (Exhibit 2). In 1990, sales of Kao products had reached 620.4 billion ($3,926.8 million), an 8.4 percent increase on 1989. This total consisted of laundry

Exhibit 1-3　Review of Operations

OPERATIONAL REVIEW (NONCONSOLIDATED BASIS)

HOUSEHOLD PRODUCTS

Personal Care

Cosmetics

toilet soap, body cleansers, shampoo, hair rinse, hair care products, cosmetics and skin care products, toothpaste and toothbrushes

34%

Net Sales *(Yen in billions)*

Year	Value
90	183.7
89	176.7
88	158.9
87	133.3
86	115.0

0　50　100　150　200　250

Laundry and Cleansing

laundry, kitchen and other household detergents, laundry finishing agents

40%

Net Sales *(Yen in billions)*

Year	Value
90	220.2
89	211.1
88	196.1
87	177.2
86	164.7

0　50　100　150　200　250

Hygiene

sanitary products, disposable diapers, bath agents

13%

Net Sales *(Yen in billions)*

Year	Value
90	69.5
89	64.7
88	69.5
87	68.8
86	59.5

0　30　60　90　120　150

CHEMICAL PRODUCTS

Fatty Chemicals

edible fats and oils, fatty acids, fatty alcohols, glycerine, fatty amines

4%

Net Sales *(Yen in billions)*

Year	Value
90	22.9
89	22.6
88	22.1
87	21.2
86	26.2

0　30　60　90　120　150

Specialty Chemicals and Floppy Disks

surface active agents, polyurethane systems and additives, plasticizers for synthetic resins, polyester resins, floppy disks

9%

Net Sales *(Yen in billions)*

Year	Value
90	49.0
89	46.3
88	43.4
87	40.6
86	40.3

0　30　60　90　120　150

Source: Kao Corporation annual report 1990, p.5.

and cleansing products (40 percent), personal care products (34 percent), hygiene products (13 percent), specialty chemicals and floppy disks (9 percent) and fatty chemicals (4 percent) (Exhibit 3). Net income had increased by 1.7 percent, from 17.5 billion ($110 million) in 1989 to 17.8 billion ($112.7 million) in 1990.

Kao dominated most of its markets in Japan. It was the market leader in detergents and shampoo, and was vying for first place in disposable diapers and cosmetics. It had decisively beaten off both foreign and domestic competitors, most famously in two particular instances: the 1983 launch of its disposable diaper brand *Merries* which, within twelve months, had overtaken the leading brand, Procter & Gamble's *Pampers* and the 1987 launch of its innovative condensed laundry detergent, the aptly named *Attack*; as a result, of which the market share of Kao's rival, Lion, had declined from 30.9 percent (1986) to 22.8 percent (1988), while in the same period Kao's share had gone from 33.4 percent to 47.5 percent.

The remarkable success of these two products had been largely responsible for Kao's reputation as a creative company. However, while the ability to introduce a continuous stream of innovative, high quality products clearly rested on Kao's repertoire of core competences, the wellspring behind these was less obvious: Kao's integrated learning capability.

This learning motif had been evident from the beginning. The Nagase family, founders of Kao, had modelled some of Kao's operations, management and production facilities on those of US corporations; and in the 1940s, following his inspection of US and European soap and chemical plants, Tomiro Nagase II had reorganised Kao's production facilities, advertising and planning departments on the basis of what he had learned. As the company built up its capabilities, this process of imitation and adaptation had evolved into one of innovation until, under Dr. Maruta, a research chemist who joined Kao in the 1930s and became President in 1971, "Distinct creativity became a policy objective in all our areas of research, production and sales, supporting our determination to explore and de-velop our own fields of activity."

The Paperweight Organization

The organizational structure within which Kao managers and personnel worked embodied the philosophy of Dr. Maruta's mentor, the 7th century statesman Prince Shotoku, whose Constitution was designed to foster the spirit of harmony, based on the principle of absolute equality: "Human beings can live only by the Universal Truth, and in their dignity of living, all are absolutely equal." Article 1 of his Constitution stated that "If everyone discusses on an equal footing, there is nothing that cannot be resolved."

Accordingly, Kao was committed to the principles of equality, individual initiative and the rejection of authoritarianism. Work was viewed as "something fluid and flexible, like the functions of the human body;" therefore, the organization was designed to "run as a flowing system" which would stimulate interaction and the spread of ideas in every direction and at every level (Exhibit 4). To allow creativity and initiative full rein, and to demonstrate that hierarchy was merely an expedient that should not become a constraint, organizational boundaries and titles were abolished.

Dr. Maruta likened this flat structure to an old fashioned brass paperweight, in contrast to the pyramid structure of Western organizations: "In the pyramid, only the person at the top has all the information. Only he can see the full picture, others cannot... The Kao organization is like the paperweight on my desk. It is flat. There is a small handle in the middle, just as we have a few senior people. But all information is shared horizontally, not filtered vertically. Only then can you have equality. And equality is the basis for trust and commitment."

This organization practised what Kao referred to as "biological self control." As the body reacts to pain by sending help from all quarters, "If anything goes wrong in one department, the other departments should know automatically and help without having to be asked." Small group activities were encouraged in order to link

Exhibit 1-4 Organizational Structure

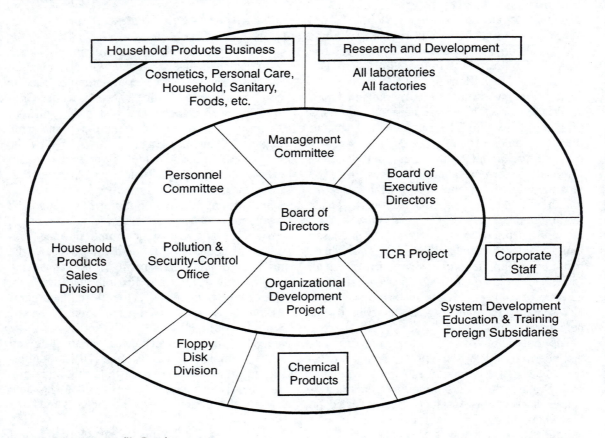

Source: Company Profile Brochure

ideas or discuss issues of immediate concern. In 1987, for example, to resolve the problem of why Kao's Toyohashi factory could achieve only 50 percent of the projected production of Nivea cream, workers there voluntarily formed a small team consisting of the people in charge of production, quality, electricity, process and machinery. By the following year, production had been raised to 95 percent of the target.

In pursuit of greater efficiency and creativity, Kao's organization has continued to evolve. A 1987 program introduced a system of working from home for sales people, while another will eventually reduce everyone's working time to 1800 hours a year from the traditional level of 2100 hours. Other programs have aimed at either introducing information technology or re-vitalising certain areas. 1971 saw the "CCR movement," aimed at reducing the workforce through computerization. "Total Quality Control" came in 1974, followed in 1981 by Office Automation. The 1986 "Total Cost Reduction" program to restructure management resources evolved into the "Total Creative Revolution," designed to encourage a more innovative approach. For example, five people who were made redundant following the installation of new equipment, formed, on their own initiative, a special task force team and visited a US factory which had imported machinery from Japan. They stayed there for three months until local engineers felt confident enough to take charge. Over time, this group became a flying squad of specialists, available to help foreign production plants get over their teething troubles.

Managing Information

Just as Dr. Maruta's Buddha was the enlightened teacher, so Kao employees were the "Priests" who learned and practised the truth. Learning was "a frame of mind, a daily matter," and truth was sought through discussions, by testing and investigating concrete business ideas until something was learned, often without the manager realizing it. This was "the quintessence of information... something we actually see with our own eyes and feel with our bodies." This internalised intuition, which coincides with the Zen Buddhist phrase *kangyo ichijo*, was the goal Dr. Maruta set for all Kao managers. In reaching it, every individual was expected to be a coach, both to himself and to everyone else, whether above or below him in the organization.

Their training material was information. Information was regarded not as something lifeless to be stored, but as knowledge to be shared and exploited to the utmost. Every manager repeated Dr. Maruta's fundamental assumption: "in today's business world, information is the only source of competitive advantage. The company that develops a monopoly on information, and has the ability to learn from it continuously, is the company that will win, irrespective of its business." Every piece of information from the environment was treated as a potential key to a new positioning, a new product. What can we learn from it? How can we use it? These were the questions all managers were expected to ask themselves at all times.

Access to information was another facet of Kao's commitment to egalitarianism: as described by Kuroyanagi, "In Kao, the 'classified' stamp does not exist." Through the development of computer communication technologies, the same level of information was available to all: "In order to make it effective to discuss subjects freely, it is necessary to share all information. If someone has special and crucial information that the others don't have, that is against human

equality, and will deprive us and the organization of real creativity."

Every Director and most salesmen had a fax in their homes to receive results and news, and a bi-weekly Kao newspaper kept the entire company informed about competitors' moves, new product launches, overseas development or key meetings. Terminals installed throughout the company ensured that any employee could, if they wished, retrieve data on sales records of any product for any of Kao's numerous outlets, or product development at their own or other branches. The latest findings from each of Kao's research laboratories were available for all to see, as were the details of the previous day's production and inventory at every Kao plant. "They can even," said Dr. Maruta, "check up on the president's expense account." He believed that the increase in creativity resulting from this pooling of data outweighed the risk of leaks. In any case, the prevailing environment of *omnes flux* meant that things moved so quickly "leaked information instantly becomes obsolete."

The task of Kao managers, therefore, was to take information directly from the competitive environment, process it and, by adding value, transform it into knowledge or wisdom. Digesting information from the market place in this way enabled the organization to maintain empathy with this fast moving environment. The emphasis was always on learning and on the future, not on following an advance plan based on previous experience. "Past wisdom must not be a constraint, but something to be challenged," Dr. Maruta constantly urged. Kao managers were discouraged from making any historical comparisons. "We cannot talk about history," said Mr. Takayama, Overseas Planning Director. "If we talk about the past, they (the top management) immediately become unpleasant." The emphasis was rather, what had they learned today that would be useful tomorrow? "Yesterday's success formula is often today's obsolete dogma. We must continuously challenge the past so that we can renew ourselves each day," said Dr. Maruta.

"Learning through cooperation" was the slogan of Kao's R&D; the emphasis was on information exchange, both within and outside the department, and sharing "to motivate and activate." Glycerine Ether, for example, an emulsifier important for the production of Sofina's screening cream, was the product of joint work among three Kao laboratories. Research results were communicated to everyone in the company through the IT system, in order to build a close networking organization. Top management and researchers met at regular R&D conferences, where presentations were made by the researchers themselves, not their section managers. 'Open Space' meetings were offered every week by the R&D division, and people from any part of the organization could participate in discussions on current research projects.

A number of formal and informal systems were created to promote communication among the research scientists working in different laboratories. For example, results from Paris were fed daily into the computer in Tokyo. The most important of these communication mechanisms, however, were the monthly R&D working conferences for junior researchers which took place at each laboratory in turn. When it was their own laboratory's turn to act as host, researchers could nominate anyone they wished to meet, from any laboratory in the company, to attend that meeting. In addition, any researcher could nominate him or herself to attend meetings if they felt that the discussions could help their own work, or if they wanted to talk separately with someone from the host laboratory. At the meetings, which Dr. Maruta often attended to argue and discuss issues in detail, researchers reported on studies in progress, and those present offered advice from commercial and academic perspectives.

The Decision Process

"In Kao, we try collectively to direct the accumulation of individual wisdom at serving the customer." This was how Dr. Maruta explained the company's approach to the decision process. At Kao, no one owned an idea. Ideas were to be shared in order to enhance their value and achieve enlightenment in order to make the right decision. The prevailing principle was *tataki-dai*; present your ideas to others at 80 percent completion so that they could criticise or contribute before the idea became a proposal. Takayama likened this approach to heating an iron and testing it on one's arm to see if it was hot enough. "By inviting all the relevant actors to join in with forging the task," he said, "we achieve *zoawase*; a common perspective or view." The individual was thus a strategic factor, to be linked with others in a union of individual wisdom and group strategy.

Fumio Kuroyanagi provided an illustration. Here is the process by which a problem involving a joint venture partner, in which he was the key person, was resolved: "I put up a preliminary note summarizing the key issues, but not making any proposals. I wanted to share the data and obtain other views before developing a proposal fully... This note was distributed to legal, international controllers to read... then in the meeting we talked about the facts and came up with some ideas on how to proceed. Then members of this meeting requested some top management time. All the key people attended this meeting, together with one member of the top management. No written document was circulated in advance. Instead, we described the situation, our analysis and action plans. He gave us his comments. We came to a revised plan. I then wrote up this revised plan and circulated it to all the people, and we had a second meeting at which everyone agreed with the plan. Then the two of us attended the actual meeting with the partner. After the meeting, I debriefed other members, discussed and circulated a draft of the letter to the partner which, after everyone else had seen it and given their comments, was signed by my boss."

The cross fertilization of ideas to aid the decision process was encouraged by the physical lay out of the Kao building. On the 10th floor, known as the top management floor, sat the Chairman, the President, four Executive Vice Presidents and a pool of secretaries (Exhibit 5). A large part of the floor was open space, with one large conference table and two smaller ones, and chairs, blackboards and overhead projectors strewn around: this was known as the Decision Space, where all discussions with and among the

Exhibit 1-5 Layout of KAO Offices

Top Management Floor

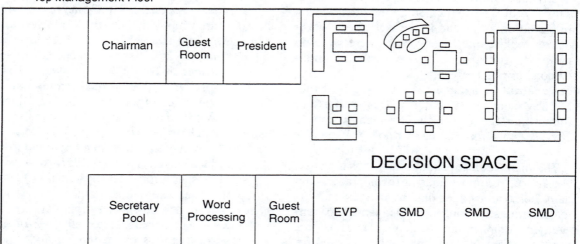

Other Floors

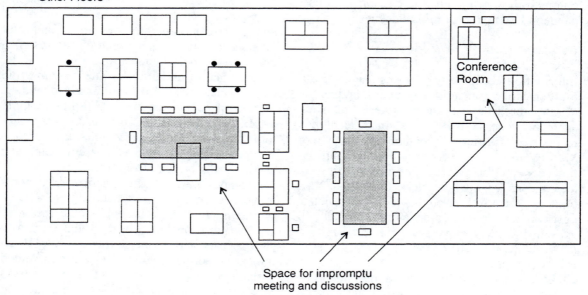

Space for impromptu
meeting and discussions

top management took place. Anyone passing, including the President, could sit down and join in any discussion on any topic, however briefly. This layout was duplicated on the other floors, in the laboratories and in the workshop. Workplaces looked like large rooms; there were no partitions, but again tables and chairs for spontaneous or planned discussions at which everyone contributed as equals. Access was free to all, and any manager could thus find himself sitting round the table next to the President, who was often seen waiting in line in Kao's Tokyo cafeteria.

The management process, thus, was transparent and open, and leadership was practised in daily behaviour rather than by memos and formal meetings. According to Takayama, top management "emphasizes that 80 percent of its time must be spent on communication, and the remaining 20 percent on decision making." While top management regularly visited other floors to join in discussions, anyone attending a meeting on the 10th floor then had to pass on what had happened to the rest of his colleagues.

Information Technology

Information Technology (IT) was one of Kao's most effective competitive weapons, and an integral part of its organizational systems and management process. In 1982, Kao made an agreement to use Japan Information Service Co.'s VAN (Value Added Networks) for communication between Kao's head office, its sales companies and its large wholesalers. Over time, Kao built its own VAN, through which it connected upstream and downstream via information linkages. In 1986 the company added DRESS, a new network linking Kao and the retail stores receiving its support.

The objective of this networking capability was to achieve the complete fusion and interaction of Kao's marketing, production and R&D departments. Fully integrated information systems controlled the flow of materials and products, from the production planning of raw materials to the distribution of the final products to local stores; no small task in a company dealing with

over 1,500 types of raw materials from 500 different suppliers, and producing over 550 types of final products for up to 300,000 retail stores.

Kao's networks enabled it to maintain a symbiotic relationship with its distributors, the *hansha*. Developed since 1966, the Kao *hansha* (numbering 30 by 1990) were independent wholesalers who handled only Kao products. They dealt directly with 100,000 retail stores out of 300,000, and about 60 percent of Kao's products passed through them. The data terminals installed in the *hansha* offices provided Kao with up-to-date product movement and market information, which was easily accessible for analysis.

Kao's Logistics Information System (LIS) consisted of a sales planning system, an inventory control system and an on-line supply system. It linked Kao headquarters, factories, the *hansha* and Logistics centres by networks, and dealt with ordering, inventory, production and sales data (Exhibit 6). Using the LIS, each *hansha* sales person projected sales plans on the basis of a head office campaign plan, an advertising plan and past market trends. These were corrected and adjusted at corporate level, and a final sales plan was produced each month. From this plan, daily production schedules were then drawn up for each factory and product. The system would also calculate the optimal machine load, and the number of people required. An on-line supply system calculated the appropriate amount of factory stocks and checked the *hansha* inventory. The next day's supply was then computed and automatically ordered from the factory.

A computerized ordering system enabled stores to receive and deliver products within 24 hours of placing an order. Through a POS (point of sale) terminal, installed in the retail store as a cash register and connected to the Kao VAN, information on sales and orders was transmitted to the *hansha's* computer. Via this, orders from local stores, adjusted according to the amount of their inventory, were transmitted to Kao's Logistics centre, which then supplied the product.

Two other major support systems, KAP and RSS, respectively helped the wholesale houses in ordering, stocking and accounting, and worked with Kao's nine distribution information service

Exhibit 1-6 Kao's Information Network

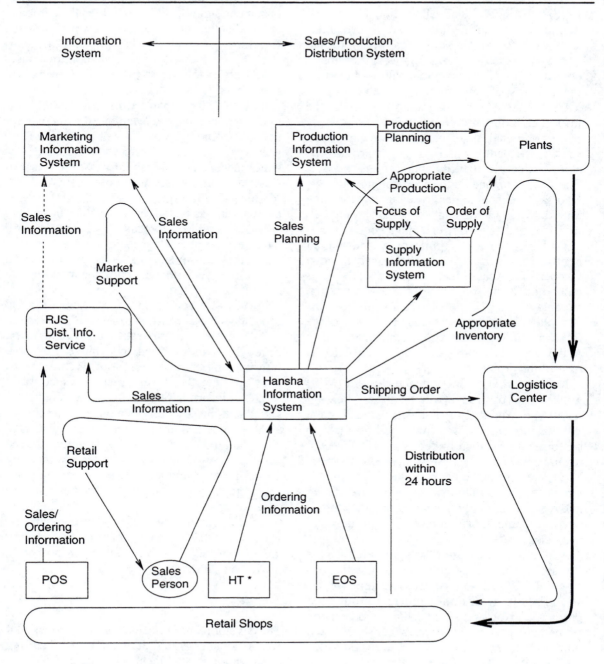

Source: Nikkei Computer Oct. 9, 1989 (Nippon Keizai shinbunsha)

companies: the Ryutsu Joho Service Companies (RJSs). Each RJS had about 500 customers, mainly small and medium sized supermarkets who were too small to access real-time information by themselves. The RJSs were essentially consulting outfits, whose mandate was to bring the benefits of information available in Kao VAN to those stores that could not access the information directly. They guided store owners by offering analysis of customer buying trends, shelf space planning and ways of improving the store's sales, profitability and customer service. The owner of one such store commented: "A Kao sales person comes to see us two or three times a week, and we chat about many topics. To me, he is both a good friend and a good consultant... I can see Kao's philosophy, the market trend and the progress of R&D holistically through this person." According to Dr. Maruta, the RJSs embodied Kao's principle of the information advantage: their purpose was to provide this advantage to store owners, and the success of the RJSs in building up the volume and profitability of the stores was ample evidence of the correctness of the principle.

Kao's Marketing Intelligence System (MIS) tracked sales by product, region and market segment, and provided raw market research data. All this information was first sifted for clues to customer needs, then linked with R&D 'seeds' to create new products. New approaches to marketing were sought by applying artificial intelligence to various topics, including advertising and media planning, sales promotion, new product development, market research and statistical analysis.

Additional information was provided by the Consumer Life Research Laboratory which operated ECHO, a sophisticated system for responding to telephone queries about Kao products. In order to understand and respond immediately to a customer's question, each phone operator could instantly access a video display of each of Kao's 500 plus products. Enquiries were also coded and entered into the computer system on-line, and the resulting data base provided one of the richest sources for product development or enhancement ideas. By providing Kao with "a direct window on the consumer's mind," ECHO enabled the company to "predict the performance of new products and fine tune formulations, labelling and packaging." Kao also used a panel of monitor households to track how products fitted into consumers' lives.

In 1989, Kao separated its information systems organization and established a distinct entity called Kao Software Development. The aim was to penetrate the information service industry which, according to Japan Information, was projected to reach a business volume of ¥12,000 billion($80 billion) by the year 2000. In 1989, the market was ¥3,000 billion($20 billion). One IBM sales engineer forecast, "by 2000, Kao will have become one of our major competitors, because they know how to develop information technology, and how to combine it with real organization systems."

In 1989 Kao's competitors, including Lion and Procter & Gamble, united to set up Planet Logistics, a system comparable to Kao's VAN. Through it, they aimed to achieve the same information richness as Kao. But Dr. Maruta was not worried by this development. Irrespective of whatever information they had collected, he believed that the competitors would not be able to add the value and use it in the same way as Kao did: "As a company we do not spend our time chasing after what our rivals do. Rather, by mustering our knowledge, wisdom and ingenuity to study how to supply the consumer with superior products, we free ourselves of the need to care about the moves of our competitors. Imitation is the sincerest form of flattery, but unless they can add value to all that information, it will be of little use."

Sofina

The development of Sofina was a microcosm of Kao's modus operandi. It illustrated the learning organization in action since it sought to create a product that satisfied the five principles guiding the development of any new offering: "Each product must be useful to society. It must use innovative technology. It must offer consumers value. We must be confident we really understand the market and the consumers. And, finally, each new product must be compatible with the trade." Until a new product satisfied all these criteria, it would not be launched on the market. At every stage during Sofina's creation, ideas were developed, criticised, discussed and refined or altered in the light of new information and learning by everyone involved, from Dr. Maruta down.

The Sofina story began in 1965 with a "vision." The high quality, innovative product that finally emerged in 1982 allowed Kao to enter a new market and overtake well-established competitors. By 1990, Sofina had become the highest selling brand of cometics in Japan for most items except lipsiicks.

The Vision

The vision, according to Mr. Daimaru (the first Director of Sofina marketing), was simple: to help customers avoid the appearance of wrinkles on their skin for as long as possible. From this vision an equally simple question arose: "What makes wrinkles appear?" Finding the answer was the spring that set the Kao organization into motion.

Kao's competence until then had been in household and toiletry personal care products. However, Kao had long supplied raw materials for the leading cosmetics manufacturers in Japan, and had a technological competence in fats and soap that could, by cross pollination, be adapted to research on the human skin. Accordingly, the efforts of Kao's R&D laboratories were directed towards skin research, and the results used in the company's existing businesses such as Nivea or Azea, then sold in joint venture with Beiersdorf. From these successes came the idea for growth that steered the development of Sofina.

The Growth Idea

The idea was to produce a new, high quality cosmetic that gave real value at a reasonable price. During the 1960s, there was a strong perception in the Japanese cosmetics industry that the more expensive the product, the better it was. This view was challenged by Dr. Maruta, whose travels had taught him that good skin care products sold in the US or Europe were not as outrageously expensive. Yet in Japan, even with companies like Kao supplying high quality raw materials at a low price, the end product was still beyond the reach of ordinary women at ¥10,000-20,000.

As a supplier of raw materials, Dr. Maruta was aware of how well these products performed. He also knew that though cosmetics' prices were rising sharply, little was being spent on improving the products themselves, and that customers were paying for an expensive image. Was this fair, or good for the customer? Kao, he knew, had the capacity to supply high quality raw materials at low cost, and a basic research capability. Intensive research to develop new toiletry goods had led to the discovery of a technology for modifying the surface of powders, which could be applied to the development of cosmetics. Why not use these assets to develop a new, high quality, reasonably priced product, in keeping with Kao's principles?

To enter the new market would mean a heavy investment in research and marketing, with no guarantee that their product would be accepted. However, it was decided to go ahead; the product would be innovative and, against the emotional appeal of the existing competition in terms of packaging and image, its positioning would embody Kao's scientific approach.

This concept guided the learning process as Sofina was developed. It was found that the integration of Kao's unique liquid crystal emulsification technology and other newly developed materials proved effective in maintaining a "healthy and beautiful skin." This led Kao to emphasize skin care, as opposed to the industry's previous focus on make-up only. All the research results from Kao's skin diagnosis and dermatological testing were poured into the new producuct and, as Dr. Tsutsumi of the Tokyo Research Laboratory recalled, in pursuing problems connected with the product, new solutions emerged. For example, skin irritation caused by the new chemical was solved by developing MAP, a low irritant, and PSL, a moisturiser. By 1980, most of the basic research work had been done. Six cosmetics suitable for the six basic skin types had been developed, though all under the Sofina name.

During this stage, Kao's intelligence collectors were sent out to explore and map the new market environment. Information on products—pricing, positioning, the competition and above all, the customers—was analysed and digested by the Sofina marketing and R&D teams, and by Kao's top management. Again and again Dr. Maruta asked the same two questions: How would the new product be received? Was it what customers wanted?

The Growth Process

Test marketing began in September 1980, in the Shizuoka prefecture, and was scheduled to last for a year. Shizuoka was chosen because it represented 3.0 percent of the national market and an average social mix; neither too rich or too poor, too rural or too urban. Its media isolation meant that television advertisements could be targeted to the local population, and no one outside would question why the product was not available elsewhere. The local paper also gave good coverage. In keeping with Kao's rule that "the concept of a new product is that of its advertising," the Sofina advertisements were reasoned and scientific, selling a function rather than an image.

Sofina was distributed directly to the retail stores through the Sofina Cosmetics Company, established to distinguish Sofina from Kao's conventional detergent business and avoid image blurring. No mention was made of Kao. Sofina's managers found, however, that retailers did not accept Sofina immediately, but put it on the waiting list for display along with other new cosmetics. The result was that by October 1980, Kao had only succeeded in finding 200 points of sale, against an objective of 600. Then, as the real parentage of Sofina leaked out, the attitude among retailers changed, and the Sofina stand was given the best position in the store. This

evidence of Kao's credibility, together with the company's growing confidence in the quality and price of the product, led to a change of strategy. The 30-strong sales force was instructed to put the Kao name first and, by November, 600 outlets had been found.

Sofina's subsequent development was guided by feedback from the market. Direct distribution enabled Kao to retain control of the business and catch customer responses to the product at first hand. To Mr. Masashi Kuga, Director of Kao's Marketing Research Department, such information "has clear added value, and helps in critical decision making." During the repeated test marketing of Sofina, Kao's own market research service, formed in 1973 to ensure a high quality response from the market with the least possible distortion, measured the efficacy of sampling and helped decide on the final marketing mix. This activity was usually supported by "concept testing, focus group discussions, plus product acceptance research." Mr. Daimaru visited the test market two or three times each month and talked to consumers directly. Dr. Maruta did the same.

Every piece of information and all results were shared by the Sofina team, R&D, Kao's top management, corporate marketing and sales managers. Discussions on Sofina's progress were attended by all of these managers, everyone contributing ideas about headline copy or other issues on an equal basis. Wives and friends were given samples, and their reactions were fed back to the team.

From the reactions of customers and stores, Kao learnt that carrying real information in the advertisements about the quality of the product had been well received, despite differing from the normal emphasis on fancy packaging. This they could never have known from their detergent business. Another finding was the importance of giving a full explanation of the product with samples, and of a skin analysis before recommending the most suitable product rather than trying to push the brand indiscriminately. They also learned the value of listening to the opinion of the store manager's wife who, they discovered, often had the real managing power, particularly for cosmetics products.

Decisions were implemented immediately. For example, the decision to improve the design for the sample package was taken at 3.30 p.m., and by 6.30 p.m. the same day the engineer in the factory had begun re-designing the shape of the bottle.

The results of this test marketing, available to the whole company, confirmed the decision to go ahead with Sofina. Kao was satisfied that the product would be accepted nationally, though it might take some time. A national launch was planned for the next year. Even at this stage, however, Dr. Maruta was still asking whether consumers and retail store owners really liked Sofina.

The Learning Extended

Sofina finally went on nationwide sale in October 1982. However, the flow of learning and intelligence gathering continued via the *hansha* and MIS. Kao, the *hansha*, the retailers and Sofina's customers formed a chain, along which there was a free, two-way flow of information. The learning was then extended to develop other products, resulting in production of the complete Sofina range of beauty care. In 1990, the range covered the whole market, from basic skin care to make-up cosmetics and perfumes.

In fact, the product did not achieve real success until after 1983. Dr. Tsutsumi dated it from the introduction of the foundation cream which, he recalled, also faced teething problems. The test result from the panel was not good; it was too different from existing products and was sticky on application. Kao, however, knowing it was a superior product that lasted longer, persevered and used their previous experience to convert the stickiness into a strength: the product was repositioned as "the longest lasting foundation that does not disapper with sweat."

In the early 1980s, while market growth was only 2-3 percent, sales of Sofina products increased at the rate of 30 percent every year. In 1990, sales amounted to ¥55 billion, and Kao held 15.6 percent of the cosmetics market behind Shiseido and Kanebo. Though taken individu-

ally, Sofina brands topped every product category except lipsticks.

Within Japan, Sofina was sold through 12,700 outlets. According to Mr. Nakanishi, Director of the Cosmetics Division, the marketing emphasis was by that time being redirected from heavy advertising of the product to counselling at the point of sale. Kao was building up a force of beauty counsellors to educate the public on the benefits of Sofina products. A Sofina store in Tokyo was also helping to develop hair care and cosmetics products. A Sofina newspaper had been created which salesmen received by fax, along with the previous month's sales and inventory figures.

Knowledge gathered by the beauty advisers working in the Sofina shops was exploited for the development of the next set of products. Thus, Sofina "ultra-violet" care, which incorporated skin lotion, uv care and foundation in one, was positioned to appeal to busy women and advertised as 'one step less.' The Sofina cosmetics beauty care consultation system offered advice by phone, at retail shops or by other means to consumers who made enquiries. From their questions, clues were sought to guide new product development.

A staff of Field Companions visited the retail stores to get direct feedback on sales. Every outlet was visited once a month, when the monitors discussed Kao products with store staff, advised on design displays and even helped clean up. Dr. Maruta himself maintained an active interest. Mr. Kuroyanagi described how Dr. Maruta recently "came down to our floor" to report that while visiting a certain town, he had "found a store selling Sofina products, and a certain shade sample was missing from the stand." He asked that the store be checked and the missing samples supplied as soon as possible.

Despite Sofina's success, Kao was still not satisfied. "To be really successful, developing the right image is important. We've lagged behind on this, and we must improve."

As the Sofina example showed, in its domestic base Kao was an effective and confident company, renowned for its ability to produce high quality, technologically advanced products at relatively low cost. Not surprising then, that since the 1960s it had turned its thoughts to becoming an important player on the larger world stage. But could the learning organization operate effectively outside Japan? Could Kao transfer its learning capability into a very different environment such as the US or Europe, where it would lack the twin foundations of infrastructure and human resources? Or would internationalization demand major adjustments to its way of operating?

Kao International

When the first cake of soap was produced in 1890, the name 'Kao' was stamped in both Chinese characters and Roman letters in preparation for the international market. A century later, the company was active in 50 countries but, except for the small neighbouring markets of SE Asia, had not achieved a real breakthrough. Despite all its investments, commitment and efforts over 25 years, Kao remained only "potentially" a significant global competitor. In 1988, only 10 percent of its total sales was derived from overseas business, and 70 percent of this international volume was earned in SE Asia. As a result, internationalization was viewed by the company as its next key strategic challenge. Dr. Maruta made his ambitions clear; "Procter and Gamble, Unilever and L'Oréal are our competitors. We cannot avoid fighting in the 1990s." The challenge was to make those words a reality.

The Strategic Infrastructure

Kao's globalization was based not on a company-wide strategy, but on the product division system. Each product division developed its own strategy for international expansion and remained responsible for its worldwide results. Consequently, the company's business portfolio and strategic infrastructure varied widely from market to market.

South East Asia

As Exhibit 7 illustrates, Kao had been building a platform for production and marketing throughout SE Asia since 1964, when it created its first overseas subsidiary in Thailand. By 1990, this small initial base had been expanded, mainly through joint ventures, and the company had made steady progress in these markets. The joint ventures in Hong Kong and Singapore sold only Kao's consumer products, while the others both manufactured and marketed them.

One of Kao's biggest international battles was for control of the Asian detergent, soap and shampoo markets, against rivals like P&G and Unilever. In the Taiwanese detergent market, where Unilever was the long established leader with 50 percent market share, Kao's vanguard product was the biological detergent, *Attack*. Launched in 1988, *Attack* increased Kao's market share from 17 percent to 22 percent. Subsequently, Kao decided on local production, both to continue serving the local market and for export to Hong Kong and Singapore. Its domestic rival, Lion (stationary at 17 percent), shortly followed suit. In Hong Kong, Kao was the market leader with 30 percent share and in Singapore, where Colgate-Palmolive led with 30 percent, had increased its share from 5 percent to 10 percent. Unilever, P&G and Colgate-Palmolive had responded to Kao's moves by putting in more human resources, and consolidating their local bases.

In Indonesia, where Unilever's historic links again made it strong, Kao, Colgate-Palmolive and P&G competed for the second position. In the Philippines, Kao had started local production of shampoo and liquid soap in 1989, while in Thailand it had doubled its local facilities in order to meet increasing demand. To demonstrate its commitment to the Asian market where it was becoming a major player, Kao had established its Asian headquarters in Singapore. In that market, Kao's disposable diaper *Merrys* had a 20 percent share, while its *Merit* shampoo was the market leader.

Exhibit 1-7 The History of Kao's Internationalization

Area	Company	Year	Capital	Main Products
ASIA				
Taiwan	Taiwan Kao Co. Ltd	1964	90	detergent, soap
Thailand	Kao Industrila Co. Ltd Kao	1964	70	hair care products
Singapore	Private Ltd	1965	100	sales of soap, shampoo, detergents
Hong Kong	Kao Ltd	1970	100	sales of soap, shampoo, detergents
Malaysia	Kao Ptc. Ltd	1973	45	hair care products
Philippines	Pilippinas Kao Inc.	1977	70	fats and oils
Indonesia	P. T. PolcKao	1977	74	surfactants
Philippines	Kao Inc.	1979	70	hair care products
Indonesia	P. T. Dino Indonesia Industrial Ltd	1985	50	hair care products
Malaysia	Fatty Chemical Sdn. Bdn.	1988	70	alcohol
Singapore	Kao South-East Asia Headquarters	1988		
Philippines	Kao Co. Philippines Laboratory			
NORTH AMERICA				
Mexico	Qvmi-Kao S. A. de C. V.	1975	20	fatty amines
	Bitumex	1979	49	asphal
Canada	Kao-Didak .Ltd	1983	89	floppy disk
U. S. A.	Kao Corporation of American (KCOA)	1986	100	sales of household goods
	High Point Chemical	1987	100 (KCOA)	ingredients
	Kao Infosystems Company	1988	100 (KCOA)	duplication of software
	The Andrew Jergens		100 (KCOA)	hair care products
U. S. A	KCOA Los Angeles Laboratories	1988		

Source: KAO Corporation

Exhibit 7 (con't) The History of Kao's Internationalization

Area	Company	Year	Capital	Main Products
EUROPE				
W Germany	Kao Corporation GmbH	1986	100 (KCG)	sales of household goods
	Kao Perfekta GmbH	1986	SO (KCG)	toners for copier
	Guhl Ikcbana GmbH	1986	50 (KCG)	hair care products
	Kao Corporation S. A.	1987	100	surfactants
Spain	Goldwcll AG	1989	100	cosmetics
W. Germany France	Kao Co. S. A. Paris Laboratories			
Spain	Kao Co. S. A. Barcelona Laboratories			
W. Germany	Kao Co. GmbH Berlin Laboratories			

Source: KAO Corporation

North America

Step 1 — Joint venture

In 1976, Kao had embarked on two joint ventures with Colgate-Palmolive Company, first to market hair care products in the US, and later to develop new oral hygiene products for Japan. The potential for synergy seemed enormous: Colgate-Palmolive was to provide the marketing expertise and distribution infrastructure, Kao would contribute the technical expertise to produce a high quality product for the top end of the US market.

1977 saw a considerable exchange of personnel and technology, and a new shampoo was specially developed by Kao for the US consumer. Despite the fact that tests in three major US cities, using Colgate-Palmolive's state of the art market research methods, showed poor market share potential, the product launch went ahead. The forecasts turned out to be correct, and the product was dropped after 10 months due to Colgate-Palmolive's reluctance to continue. A Kao manager explained the failure thus; "First, the product was not targeted to the proper consumer group. High price, high end products were not appropriate for a novice and as yet unsophisticated producer like us. Second, the US side believed in the result of the market research too seriously and did not attempt a second try... Third, it is essentially very difficult to penetrate a market like the shampoo market. Our partner expected too much short term success. Fourth, the way the two firms decided on strategy was totally different. We constantly adjust our strategy flexibility. They never start without a concrete and fixed strategy. We could not wait for them."

The alliance was dissolved in 1985. However, Kao had learned some valuable lessons about US marketing methods, about Western lifestyles, and, most of all, about the limitations of using joint ventures as a means of breaking into the US market.

Step 2 — Acquisition

In 1988, Kao had made three acquisitions. In May, it bought the Andrew Jergens Company, a Cincinnati soap, body lotion and shampoo maker, for $350 million. To acquire Jergens' extensive marketing know-how and established distribution channels, Kao beat off 70 other bidders, including Beiersdorf and Colgate-Palmolive, and paid 40 percent more than the expected price. Since then, Kao has invested heavily in the company, building a new multi-million dollar research center and doubling Jergen's research team to over 50. Cincinnati was the home town of P&G, who has since seen Jergens market Kao's bath preparations in the US.

High Point Chemical Corporation of America, an industrial goods producer, was also acquired in 1988. As Kao's US chemical manufacturing arm, it had since begun "an aggressive expansion of its manufacturing facilities and increased its market position." The third acquisition, Info Systems (Sentinel) produced application products in the field of information technology.

In Canada, Kao owned 87 percent of Kao-Didak, a floppy disk manufacturer it bought out in 1986. A new plant, built in 1987, started producing 3.5 inch and 5.25 inch diskettes, resulting in record sales of $10 million that same year. Kao viewed Floppy Disks as the spearhead of its thrust into the US market. As Mr. Kyroyanagi explained, "This product penetrates the US market easily. Our superior technology makes it possible to meet strict requirements for both quantity and quality. Our experience in producing specific chemicals for the floppy disk gives us a great competitive edge." In what represented a dramatic move for a Japanese company, Kao relocated its worldwide head office for the floppy disk business to the US, partly because of Kao's comparatively strong position there (second behind Sony), but also because it was by far the biggest market in the world. The US headquarters was given complete strategic freedom to develop the business globally. Under the direction of this office, a plant was built in Spain.

Europe

Within Europe, Kao had built a limited presence

in Germany, Spain and France. In Germany, it had established a research laboratory, and through its 1979 joint venture with Beiersdorf to develop and market hair care products, gained a good knowledge of the German market. The strategic position of this business was strengthened in 1989 by the acquisition of a controlling interest in Goldwell AG, one of Germany's leading suppliers of hair and skin care products to beauty salons. From studying Goldwell's network of beauty salons across Europe, Kao expected to expand its knowledge in order to be able to develop and market new products in Europe.

Kao's French subsidiary, created in January 1990, marketed floppy disks, skin toner and the Sofina range of cosmetics. The research laboratory established in Paris that same year was given the leading role in developing perfumes to meet Kao's worldwide requirements.

Kao's vanguard product in Europe was Sofina, which was positioned as a high quality, medium priced product. Any Japanese connection had been removed to avoid giving the brand a cheap image. While Sofina was produced and packaged in Japan, extreme care was taken to ensure that it shared a uniform global positioning and image in all the national markets in Europe. It was only advertised in magazines like *Vogue*, and sales points were carefully selected; for example in France, Sofina was sold only in the prestigious Paris department store Galeries Lafayette.

Organizational Capability

Organizationally, Kao's international operations were driven primarily along the product division axis. Each subsidiary had a staff in charge of each product who reported to the product's head office, either directly or through a regional product manager. For example, the manager in charge of Sofina in Spain reported to the French office where the regional manager responsible for Sofina was located, and he in turn reported to the Director of the Divisional HQ in Japan. Each subsidiary was managed by Japanese expatriate managers, since Kao's only foreign re-

source was provided by its acquired companies. Thus, the German companies remained under the management of its original directors. However, some progress was made towards localisation; in Kao Spain (250 employees) there were "only six to ten Japanese, not necessarily in management." Kao's nine overseas R&D laboratories were each strongly connected to both the product headquarters and laboratories in Japan through frequent meetings and information exchange.

Mr. Takayama saw several areas that needed to be strengthened before Kao could become an effective global competitor. Kao, he believed "was a medium sized company grown large." It lacked international experience, had fewer human resource assets, especially in top management and, compared with competitors like P&G and Unilever, had far less accumulated international knowledge and experience of Western markets and consumers. "These two companies know how to run a business in the West and have well established market research techniques, whereas the Westernization of the Japanese lifestyle has only occurred in the last 20 years," he explained. "There are wide differences between East and West in, for example, bathing habits, that the company has been slow to comprehend."

Kao attempted to redress these problems through stronger involvement by headquarters' managers in supporting the company's foreign operations. Mr. Kuroyanagi provided an insight into Kao's approach to managing its overseas units. He described how, after visiting a foreign subsidiary where he felt change was necessary, he asked a senior colleague in Japan to carry out a specific review. The two summarized their findings, and then met with other top management members for further consultation. As a result, his colleague was temporarily located in the foreign company to lead certain projects. A team was formed in Japan to harmonize with locals, and sent to work in the subsidiary. Similarly, when investigating the reason for the company's slow penetration of the shampoo market in Thailand, despite offering a technologically superior product, headquarters' managers found that the product positioning, pricing and packaging policies developed for the Japanese market were unsuitable for Thailand. Since the subsidiary could not adapt these policies to meet local requirements, a headquarters' marketing specialist was brought in, together with a representative from Dentsu — Kao's advertising agent in Japan — to identify the source of the problem and make the necessary changes in the marketing mix.

Part of Mr. Kuroyanagi's role was to act as a "liaison officer" between Kao and its subsidiaries. Kao appointed such managers at headquarters to liaise with all the newly acquired companies in Europe and Asia; their task was to interpret corporate strategies to other companies outside Japan and ensure that "We never make the same mistake twice." He described himself as "the eyes and ears of top management, looking round overseas moves, competitors' activities and behaviours and summarizing them." He was also there to "help the local management abroad understand correctly Kao as a corporation, and give hints about how to overcome the cultural gap and linguistic difficulties, how to become open, aggressive and innovative."

Kao's 1990 global strategy was to develop "local operations sensitive to each region's characteristics and needs." As Mr. Takayama explained, these would be able "to provide each country with goods tailored to its local climate and customs, products which perfectly meet the needs of its consumers." To this end, the goals of the company's research centres in Los Angeles, Berlin, Paris and Santiago de Compostela in Spain, had been redefined as "to analyze local market needs and characteristics and integrate them into the product development process," and a small market research unit had been created in Thailand to support local marketing of Sofina. Over time, Kao hoped, headquarters' functions would be dispersed to SE Asia, the US and Europe, leaving to the Tokyo headquarters the role of supporting regionally based, locally managed operations by giving "strategic assistance." There were no plans to turn Jergens or other acquired companies into duplicate Kaos; as described by Dr. Maruta "We will work alongside them rather than tell them which way to go."

The lack of overseas experience among Kao's managers was tackled via a new ¥9 billion training facility built at Kasumigaura. The 16 hectare campus, offering golf, tennis and other entertainment opportunities, was expected to enjoy a constant population of 200, with 10 days training becoming the norm for all managers. To help Kao managers develop a broader and more international outlook, training sessions devoted considerable attention to the cultural and historical heritages of different countries. A number of younger managers were sent to Europe and the United States, spending the first year learning languages and the second either at a business school, or at Kao's local company offices.

"If you look at our recent international activity," said Mr. Kuroyanagi, "we have prepared our stage. We have made our acquisitions... The basis for globalization in Europe, North America and SE Asia has been facilitated... We now need some play on that stage." Kao's top management was confident that the company's R&D power, "vitality and open, innovative and aggressive culture" would ultimately prevail. The key constraints, inevitably, were people. "We do not have enough talented people to direct these plays on the stage." Kao could not and did not wish to staff its overseas operations with Japanese nationals, but finding, training and keeping suitable local personnel was a major challenge.

Kao expected the industry to develop like many others until "there were only three or four companies operating on a global scale. We would like to be one of these." Getting there looked like it would take some time, but Kao was in no rush. The perspective, Dr. Maruta continually stressed, was very long term, and the company would move at its own pace. "We should not," he said, "think about the quick and easy way, for that can lead to bad handling of our products. We must take the long term view... and spiral our activity towards the goal... We will not, and need not hurry our penetration of foreign markets. We need to avoid having unbalanced growth. The harmony among people, products and world wide operations is the most important philosophy to keep in mind... Only in 15 years will it be clear how we have succeeded."

2
Artisan Industries

Artisan Industries was a $9-million-a-year, family-run manufacturer of wooden decorative products. It was approaching its first fall sales season since last year's successful turnaround under the direction of the new 29-year-old President, Bill Meister. Last fall had begun with a year-to-date loss of $125,000 and, through Meister's actions, had ended with a $390,000 profit. This had been the first profit in several years and capped a challenging eight months for the new president.

Meister had hired his first man while his father was still president, bringing in 27-year-old Bob Atwood from the local office of a "Big Eight" firm to begin modernizing the accounting system. On June 10, 1977, Bob was in Bill's office for further and, he hoped, final discussion of plans for this fall season. Artisan's sales were quite seasonal, and on June 10, there were about two more months during which production would exceed sales. Atwood, concerned with the company's limited capital, proposed a production plan to hold the inventory build-up to $1.6 million, or about twice the level shown on the last full computer listing.

The president, based on his feel for conditions after the successful 1976 season and viewing sales in the first weeks of 1977, believed total sales for this year would really beat Bob's estimate of the same as last year's and reach $9 million. But he would like to have stronger support for his opinions; a lot rested on this estimate. If sales were much beyond their plans, he could expect to lose most of them and create difficulties with his customers. New customers might even be lost to the competition. Bill was also concerned with developing contingency plans for dealing effectively with the potential oversold condition. Besides getting more production from the plants at the last minute, there might be good ideas that involved the customers and salespeople. For example, if all orders couldn't be filled, should some be fully shipped and others dropped, or should all be shipped 75-95 percent complete? Overall, in 1976 orders had been shipped 75 percent complete, and during the peak months this had fallen to 50 percent. Partial shipments might be a way to keep everyone happy. If orders are canceled, should they be the ones from the small "mom and pop" stores or the large department stores? The small stores are more dependable customers, but on the other hand large department stores systematically evaluate suppliers on their order completion history. Also the department store buyers must commit funds when they place an order; thus,

Reprinted by permission of Frank C. Barnes, Associate Professor, University of North Carolina at Charlotte.

their resources are idle until the order is filled. There are potential benefits from good communications, for if you inform the buyer of any delay quickly, he can cancel that order and order something he can get. Such sensitivity to the customer's needs could win the company many friends and aid Meister in building a desirable reputation. On the other hand, poor communication could cause the opposite. Meister wondered if there was some way to usefully involve the salespeople, many of whom had left a sales representative organization six months earlier to work solely for Artisan.

After about mid-August, total annual sales were limited to what had been built up in inventory beforehand and production through mid-November. Thus, holding back now put a lid on total sales for the season.

If, on the other hand, the sales plan was not reached, there could also be serious consequences. Last year after the fall sales period, the inventory loan had been paid off for the first time since the 1960s. This had made a very favorable impression on the lending institutions and brought a reduction in the high interest rates (from 12 percent to 10 percent). They considered Bill a "super-star," with his youth, professional appearance, and modern ideas, and their fears for the Artisan loan were diminishing. Trouble at this time might erase all this and suggest last year was just a fluke.

If sales didn't materialize, inventories could be held down by cutting back on production. But Bill believed the plants operate inefficiently during any cutbacks, and such moves very likely saved nothing. He held a similar opinion of temporary second shifts. In many past years, over-production early in the year had resulted in a big layoff in December and January and in the financial drain of carrying over large inventories. Meister was highly interested in building an effective work environment for people at Artisan, where attitudes were historically poor. The employees — workers and supervisors — had little exposure to "professional" managers and had much to learn. The long process had been begun, but a layoff now could undermine all his efforts and, he felt, lose him what little

confidence and support he had been able to encourage.

The strategy for this fall was of critical importance to Bill and his hopes for Artisan and his future.

Artisan's History

Artisan Industries is the product of a classical entrepreneur — W. A. (Buddy) Meister. After a variety of attempts at self-employment, such as running a dry-cleaning shop, a food shop, and an appliance store, he began to have some success making wooden toys. One try in 1950 with his father and brothers failed, leaving Buddy with an old tin building and some worn-out equipment.

During the next few years, Buddy put his efforts into making a collection of 10 to 15 toys, sold via direct mail, house-to-house, on television, and on the roadside, all without a sales representative. One day a visiting gummed-tape salesman offered to take on the line, and a pattern of using outside sales reps was established.

The first attempt at a trade show was a last-minute entry into the regional gift show 40 miles away. Out of sympathy for Buddy, Artisan was allowed to pay the $25-a-week rent after the show. Buddy brought home $3,000 in sales but lacked the money to produce them until a friend offered a loan. The orders were produced in a dirt-floor barn. In the following months, Buddy and his wife drove off to other markets, showing the goods in their motel room.

In 1953, sales reached $15,000, then climbed to $30,000 in 1954, $60,000 in 1955, and $120,000 in 1956. Then in April, the plant, or barn, burned down destroying everything. With hardly a delay, Buddy jumped into rebuilding, and sales continued to. double. In 1958, success allowed Artisan to move into a 30,000-square-foot building and continue using its two old buildings for finishing and shipping. Then in March of 1960, these two burned down. Again Buddy fought back and sales doubled into 1961. The rate of growth slowed to 50 percent in 1962.

The third and most disastrous fire occurred in February 1963. The entire main plant was burned to the ground with the exception of the new office, which stood under one foot of water and was damaged by smoke and water. The company was in the middle of manufacturing its show orders and the only thing saved was the inventory in the paint shop. All the jigs were burned, and before work could begin, new jigs and patterns had to be made. "Only the plant in Spencer, built only a year before, saved us. The entire operation, with the exception of the office, was moved to Spencer; and working three shifts, we were able to keep most of the 200 employees. Many employees worked night and day for approximately six months to help us get on our feet again." Before Christmas of 1963, the company was back in full operation in the main plant.

Sales reached $4 million in 1967 and $8 million in 1972. During that six-year span, Buddy's five children reached ages to begin full-time jobs in the company. The youngest, Bill, was last to join. Typical of the youngest, he had it it best, having all the "toys" his father could provide. He attended Vanderbilt, where he majored in business administration and the "good life." But his good time was at last interrupted by graduation and retirement to Artisan.

Bill wanted no major role in the company, but over the next three years found himself getting more involved. Buddy had developed no modern management systems: accounting was ineffective, sales was in the control of outside reps, manufacturing was outdated and unprofessional. The lack of order fit Buddy's style — close personal control and manipulation. As the company problems increased, family conflict intensified. Bill's older brother lost the support of his father and the support of the other side and left. Bill moved up to the role of spokesman, for a change.

In early 1975, though sales were booming, the financial situation at Artisan was "tight." A second shift was in operation, though production was generally inefficient. By October, sales had slackened; and in November, to hold inventories down, layoffs began. Accounts receivable were worsening and the worried bankers were forcing the company to pay off some of its $2.5 million loan. The inventory was reduced some and accounts payable were allowed to increase. In December, the plant was closed for three weeks and $100,000 in cash was raised through a warehouse sale. But in the end, 1975 closed with a loss of over a million dollars.

As 1976 began, the sales picture looked bad. Even with the large inventory, there was difficulty shipping because it contained the wrong things. Since it tied up capital, production of salable items was limited. There were more layoffs and shut-downs in January. Some old suppliers cut off the company's credit. In February, under the threat of the local bank calling the loan, Bill and Bob negotiated a new loan with a New York firm. This was composed of an inventory loan with a ceiling of $500,000, an accounts receivable loan of up to $1 million, and a long-term loan on the warehouse and real estate of approximately $350,000. "The package was finalized and the funds transferred about one week prior to payment deadline with the Bank. Had we not completed the deal with the other group, there was no way we could have made the $25,000 payment," according to Bill.

As the troubles deepened in the spring, Buddy had few solutions and, worse, blocked Bill's actions. The atmosphere in the company became grim. As Bill put it, "It became a fight between who was going to make decisions about what. Through the spring, the conflict between us continued at a heightened pace. The effect was that most people became very nervous because no one understood who was really in control. With the company in the financial condition it was in, the last thing it needed was a power struggle over who should be in charge. So in April I went to Buddy and explained the situation that the company needed one person who was clearly in authority and in control, that one person would be better than two, and that I felt that he should leave or I should leave. He suggested that since he had gotten there first, I should leave." Bill went to the mountains for good.

But two weeks later, under pressure from the lenders, Buddy stepped aside and Bill became the chief executive.

In May 1976 when Bill Meister became president, Artisan was in critical condition. Sales had fallen off dramatically, there had been little profit for three years, the number of employees had fallen from 600 to 370, modern management systems existed in no area of the company, and there were few qualified managers. "When I took over, sales were running 50 percent off and we could not get a line of credit through our suppliers, we were on a cash basis only, inventory was still relatively high, accounts receivable were running over 120 days, manufacturing was without anyone in charge, and the company was sustaining a loss of approximately $10,000 a week. The general situation looked pretty hopeless."

Bill Meister's First Year as President

When Bill became president in May, changes began. Although Bill controlled many of the changes, others were the result of actions by his managers or outside forces. By mid-summer of 1976, he had reestablished contact with a business professor he particularly respected at his alma mater and was in regular contact with a management professor at a local school. The small number of trained managers, their lack of experience, and the absence of cooperation among them were serious handicaps to his rebuilding effort. He hoped interaction with the professors would make up for the lack of inside managers to interact with.

Exhibit 2-1 shows the organization chart in June 1977. Buddy moved up to chairman, but remained around the office. Bill's sister Edith and uncle Sam helped in the sales area. Another sister, Sally, worked for Bob Atwood in accounting. A new man, Will Shire, was over production, mainly Plant One. Two long-term men, Charles Scott and Jack Lander, headed the plants. Two other long-term employees were in management: Cal Robb over the computer and Richard Bare over purchasing. A young man, Richard Barnes, had been hired recently for plant engineering. Paul Morgan had been with Artisan about two years in design.

Marketing

The company was one of four making up the wooden decorative products industry. Sales were seasonal, peaking with the Christmas period. Artisan's customers were some 13,000 retail shops that were serviced by outside sales representatives. Regional market shows were an important part of the marketing activity. The product line consisted of over 1,400 items and included almost anything for the customer. The largest item was a tea-cart, and the smallest a clothespin-type desk paper clip. New products were continually coming up; about 100 a year were added to the line. Practically no items were ever dropped. The top 100 products averaged 5,000 units a year. The first 25 items had double the sales units of the next group. Two hundred and fifty sold over 1,000 units. The average wholesale price was $3.75. The top item sold 31,000 units last year for about $75,000 in sales. The 200th had sales of over $10,000.

Marketing was the function where Bill wanted to spend most of his time. His father had left this mainly with outsiders, but Bill was determined to put the company in charge of its own marketing. He attended all shows and found out firsthand what was going on. He felt the outside sales reps had let Artisan slide into making anything they could sell easily, regardless of costs and profits.

Bill hired a local young man with good design talent, but little experience, to set up a design department. They soon came up with a new "theme" line of items that became the talk of the industry, and Bill planned to try others. He engaged a New York advertising agency for a professional program of advertising in the trade journals and publicity in the newspapers. He produced an artistic catalog with color photographs rather than the dull listing used before.

There had been no price increases in quite a while, and with the recent inflation Atwood estimated the current prices would not yield a profit. In mid-October, an immediate price in-

Exhibit 2-1   Organization Chart — Artisan Industries — June 1977

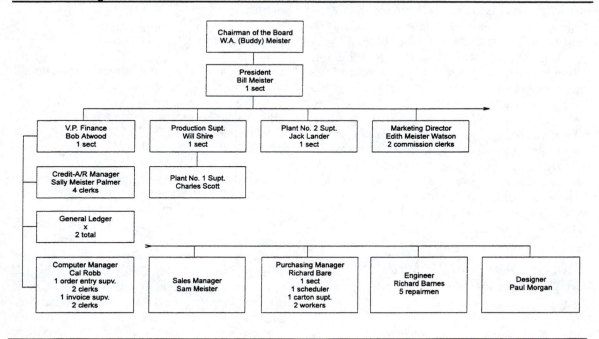

crease appeared imperative if 1976 was to end with a profit. But there was great concern about the advisability of such action in the middle of the major sales season. Also, waiting on new price lists to institute the increase in an ordinary manner would not accomplish a 1976 profit; orders already acknowledged or in-house but not yet acknowledged exceeded what could be shipped. In fact, as Bill, his sister Edith from sales, Bob Atwood, the computer manager, Cal Robb, and the university professor met to decide what to do, a 30-page order from one store chain for $221,000 at the old prices sat in front of them. Bob and Cal took the position that no further orders should be acknowledged until the customer had been written that prices were increased and asked to mail a reconfirmation if they still wanted the goods. Edith felt the price increase was very risky and would be very difficult to implement at this time, if even possible. But she had difficulty explaining her views and Bob, with Cal, out-talked her. Bill listened to their arguments as little was accomplished. Only when the consultant added his weight to Edith's

views and pointed out the manipulation and lack of good problem solving did any practical ideas develop.

A 16 percent price increase was instituted immediately. The orders awaiting acknowledgment were examined that afternoon, and on a priority basis the salespeople were called and informed of the necessity of the increase and asked to contact their customers for immediate approval. When possible, and with moderation, orders at the new prices were given priority over those at the old prices. Within a few days, the new prices were contributing to profits.

Bill's most aggressive move was to cancel, in November 1976, the company's long agreement with E. Fudd Associates, a sales representative firm. Accounting for 60 percent of their sales, Fudd, with 50 salespeople, had handled Artisan's business in about 20 states for many years and had even lent the company money during the previous December. But Fudd was an old-style "character" much like Buddy—and Bill had been unable to systematically discuss market strategies or improvement ideas with him. Bill felt the 15 percent commission Fudd was setting could be better used as 10 percent directly to the salespeople and 5 percent in a company-controlled advertising budget.

Bill had planned to deal with E. Fudd Associates after the first of the year. It would take careful action to break with Fudd and assist any reps wishing to go independent on Artisan's line. But an accidental leak forced Bill's hand in the middle of the critical sales season. Bill did not back off but broke with Fudd immediately. Fudd countered with suits against Artisan, threats of displacing Artisan's goods with others, claims of tossing Artisan out of major regional market shows, and even withholding unpaid commissions on salespeople going with Artisan. Fudd spread rumors of Artisan's impending bankruptcy and sued any sales reps leaving him. Though there were bad moments, Bill held firm, and in a few weeks it was over. Bill had gotten all the sales personnel he wanted, he was lined up for his own space in the critical shows, and the rumors were going against Fudd.

Accounting

With the hiring of Bob Atwood in the fall of 1975, improvement in the accounting systems began, though slowly. By the spring of 1977, the outside service bureau had been replaced by a small in-house computer to handle order entry and invoicing, including an inventory listing.

The small computer system was delivered in January 1977. Prior to that, $85,000 to $100,000 a year had been spent for assistance from the service bureau. This assistance had been primarily invoicing. After orders were manually checked for accuracy and credit, they went to the service bureau where a warehouse picking ticket was prepared. Then after shipment, a form went back to initiate the invoice. Besides invoicing, they produced a monthly statement of bookings and shippings that summarized activity by item, customer, and state. The bureau was not involved with accounts receivable; aging was a manual process that took 30 days and was possibly only accurate to within $25,000. In 1975, checks had been posted, taking about three hours

per day, and then forwarded directly to the lender. This had added three to four days of work for Atwood.

The computer had caused a small management crisis for Bill. Cal Robb and Bob Atwood, neither of whom had any special knowledge or experience with computers, had selected the system they wanted with no help beyond that of computer salespeople. With only verbal agreements and several contract notebooks from the supplier, they pressured Bill for his approval. When he failed to act, they saw him as dragging his feet and lacking respect for their opinions. With the counsel of the university consultant, Bill took the unpopular step of sending them back to prepare a proper proposal and timetable. In working with the vendor, several serious omissions were found and corrected, and all agreed the further documentation had been worthwhile. Bill approved the project.

The new system consisted of a 48K "small" computer with a 450-line-per-minute printer, two disc drives with two million bytes each, and seven CRTs. Monthly rental amounted to about $4,000. The software was developed in-house by Robb, using basic systems supplied by the vendor at no charge. Robb was the only staff for the computer. He was 36, with a business administration degree with some concentration in accounting from a good state university. Prior to Atwood's hiring, he had been controller.

By May, inventory accounting was on the computer. The inventory listings computing EOQs were available but inaccurate. Atwood believed a couple of months of debugging was necessary before computer inventory control would be possible. The data needed for the EOQ model were all old and inaccurate; lead times, prepared by a consultant years ago, were considered by all to be way off. They and the standards hadn't been studied in five to six years. For now, Atwood felt these listings would be of some help in operating the existing production scheduling system. (EOQ stands for the Economic Order Quantity inventory model.)

By June, invoicing was fully on the computer and the lender had stopped requiring the direct mailing of the checks. About 3,000 invoices were prepared each month. The A/R systems, including statements and weekly aging of delinquent accounts, were operational, and about 2,500 statements were being prepared monthly. The controller felt both systems were running well and providing for good control. The computer supplier felt they had been lucky to get the system operational as quickly as they did. (A/R means accounts receivable, A/P means accounts payable.)

Cal expects inventory control will be on the computer by February. In another month, he will add A/P payroll and general ledger. Production control must wait on others' work and input.

Monthly preparation of financial statements had begun in January. Production costing for the statements had been based on historical indices, but Bob reported little resulting error. The statements were out, in typed form, 30 days after the close of the period.

Production

There were two plants, roughly identical and five miles apart, each with about 60,000 square feet. Kiln dry lumber, mainly high-quality Ponderosa pine, was inventoried in truck trailers and covered sheds at the rear of the plant. The lumber width, totally random, depended on the tree, and the length was from 8 to 16 feet, in multipies of two. The thickness started at the lumber mill at four, five, or six "quarter" ("quarter" meaning one-quarter inch; therefore, four quarters is one inch). By the time it reached the plant, it was about an eighth of an inch less.

The rough mill foreman reviewed the batch of production orders he was given about every week and decided on the "panels" the plant would need. A panel is a sheet of wood milled to a desired thickness and with length and width at the desired dimension or some multiple. Clear panels, ones with no knots, can be made from lower grade lumber by cutting out the defects and then gluing these smaller pieces into standard panels. Artisan did no such gluing but cut high-quality, clear lumber directly to the desired length and width. The necessary panels would be made up in the rough mill from lumber or

from purchased glued panels. Artisan spent about as much on purchased panels as it did on raw lumber, paying about twice as much for a square foot of panel as for a square foot of lumber. Surfacers brought the wood to the desired thickness, the finished dimension plus some excess for later sanding. Rip saws cut the lumber to needed width and cut-off saws took care of the length. About 30 people worked in this area, which had about 12 percent of the labor cost.

The plant superintendent worked with the machine room foreman to decide on the sequence in which orders would be processed. Scheduled due-dates for each department were placed on the orders in production control, but they followed up on the actual flow of orders only if a crisis developed. In the machine room 22 workers (17 percent of the labor cost) shaped panels to the final form. The tools included shapers, molders, routers, and borers. Patterns and jigs lowered the skill requirements, still the highest in the plant. This part of the plant was the noisiest and dustiest.

In the third department, sanding, the parts were sanded by women working mainly at individual stations. There were 24 people here. The sanded components were moved to a nearby temporary storage area on the carts, which originated at machining. It was estimated there were six to eight wooden parts in an average item. In addition, there were purchased parts, such as turnings and glass or metal parts. Sanding added about 19 percent of the direct labor to the products.

The assembly foreman kept an eye on the arrival of all parts for an order. Assembly began when all parts were available. Eighteen people assembled the items using glue, screws, nail guns, or hammer and nails. Jigs assisted the work where possible, and usually only one person worked on an order. Fourteen percent of direct labor derived from this step. Little skill was needed and dust and noise weren't a problem.

The assembled items were moved promptly to the separate finishing area. Here they were dipped by hand into stains and sprayed with several clear coats. After oven-drying, they proceeded to packing. Most were packed individually into cartons made in the company's small plant. Finishing and packing employed about 50 people and accounted for 34 percent of direct labor costs. The new 60,000-square-foot finished goods warehouse was two miles away.

The labor rates ranged from $2.65 to $5.60 per hour. The average was probably $3.00, with about a dozen people making over $4.00. Factory overhead was about 60 percent of direct labor. Labor costs as a percent of the wholesale selling price ran about 20 percent; direct material, 35 percent. Variable costs totaled about 75 percent, with about another $1.8 million in total company fixed costs. There was a three-percentage-point difference between the plants in labor costs. The capacity of the plant with 150 people working was estimated to be less than $110,000 a week. Indirect labor amounted to about 12 percent of plant overhead.

Most jobs did not require high skill levels. The average jobs in the rough mill and machine room, where the skilled jobs were, required no more than five weeks to master because the person would usually already have advanced skills. Elsewhere, a week was adequate. Everyone but the supervisors and workers considered the work pace quite slow.

Production Scheduling

The production control department began the scheduling process. Exhibit 2-2 outlines the production scheduling system. About every week, sometimes longer, the clerk prepared a batch of production orders for each plant. Several factors determined when a batch of orders was prepared: whether the plants said they needed more work, how sales were doing, what the situation was in the warehouse, etc. The clerk examined the "Weekly Inventory Listing" for items that appeared low and the file of "Progress Control Charts" to see if the items were already on a production order. He converted the information to an available supply in weeks and selected any with less than eight weeks. If the total of orders gotten this way did not add up to an aggregate amount he had in mind, such as $60,000 to

$100,000, he went back through the lists for more things to run.

"Production Sheets," or shop orders, were prepared for each item. These contained a drawing and a list of materials and process steps. The data were already prepared and came from consultant studies several years old. The order contained a date the part was due through each department based on standard lead times, for example, one week in the rough mill, three days in machining, etc. The actual work in the plant at the time did not alter lead-times. At the same time, a "Progress Control Chart" was prepared for each order. These remained in production control to trace the flow of orders.

The batch of orders was then handed to the plant superintendent who decided exactly how the items would be run. Daily, each department gave production control a "Parts Completion Report," listing production from that department — order number, part number, and number produced. The production control clerk posted this information to the "Progress Control Charts." This reporting cycle used to be every two hours. The clerk reported these charts were not actually used to control production progress; they aided in locating an order if a question arose, but one still had to go out on the floor to be sure.

A brief look at the inventory listing for December showed the first 20 items were 23 percent of the inventory value. The tenth group of 20 items was 2 percent of inventory; the cumulative value to this point was 82 percent. The fortieth item had $1,800 in inventory and the two-hundredth, $625.

Turning through the notebook for Plant One "Process Control Charts" on one day showed almost 300 open orders, perhaps 30 percent to 50 percent of them past the due date. Several items had two or even three different production orders two weeks or so apart. The order size appeared to average 200 at most. One in 10 was for more than 250 pieces. Only a couple were for 500 or more; the maximum was 1,000 pieces. The typical items appeared to contain about six parts, and each took three to five processing steps.

The engineer was trying to estimate stan-

Exhibit 2-2 Production Scheduling System

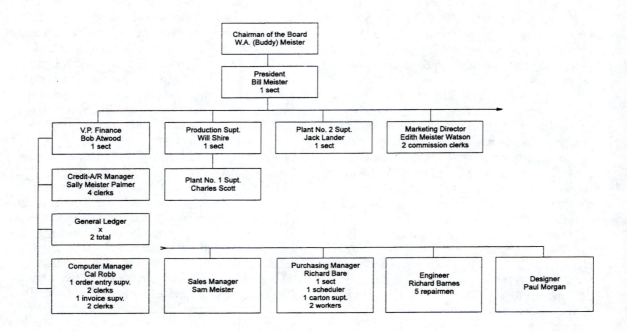

dards for new items as they were priced. A quick look at eight of them showed a total of 1,800 minutes of set-up time for the eight and a total of 6,400 minutes per 100 units of runtime. The set-up times ranged from 100 to 250 minutes for the products, but several of the parts required no set-up in some departments and where there was set-up it amounted to 25 percent to 50 percent of the run time for 100. Many parts required less than 30 minutes of processing in a department. The lot size on these ranged from 100 to 200 units; seven were priced around $4 and one at $25.

Production Problems

Bill feels production efficiency is a major problem. In talks with machinery salespeople and other visitors to the plant over recent years, Bill has come to feel the machinery is generally appropriate. But based on guesses about his competitors, he feels his labor costs must be reduced. Earlier attempts to work with the plant superintendents and the various supervisors to systematically improve output met with no success. The supervisors had been unable to identify the needs for change in the plant or to develop the programs for bringing about improvement. To help the supervisors begin to improve their operations, a weekly production meeting was begun in June 1976. At the meeting, the supervisors were to examine the total dollar output and total labor cost for each plant for the past week, compare it to the labor percent goal of 16 percent, set by Bill, and think about what could be done to improve operations for the coming week. Data on department performance was not available. During the first several meetings, the visiting consultant had to provide direction and ideas; the plant superintendent and his supervisors volunteered no ideas about what specifically limited last week's output. Bill reported that some discussion of problems began three or four months later. It was Bill's opinion that this kind of thinking and planning was not required under his father's management. The supervisors in general felt nothing was wrong in the plant and really seemed puzzled at the thought of doing anything except continuing what they had always done.

In March 1977, after a good deal of thought and search, Bill hired two young men for the production system. One man, Will Shire, aged 28, was hired to be general superintendent over everyone in production, and the other, Richard Barnes, aged 27, was to be manufacturing engineer. It appeared the plant simply needed good management rather than any single big change that could be brought from the outside. Both of these men were young, college trained, and experienced in a wood industry.

Significant resistance from the old superintendent and most of the supervisors seemed probable. Consequently, the new men were briefed on this problem. As expected, things did not advance smoothly. Even as the new men gained familiarity with the operation, no significant changes were observed. The expected complaints and rumors were heavy, and Bill ignored them as best he could. However, after three months on the job, the complaints still persisted and, more importantly, the new superintendent did not appear to have command of the situation. He had not developed his appraisal of what needed to be done and had no comprehensive plan for improvement. Bill recently received very good evidence that Will had some

major difficulties in supervising people. One of the supervisors who did not appear to be a part of the rumor campaign and was conscientiously concerned about the company gave Bill examples of the new man's mistakes. Bill felt he may have made a mistake in hiring Will.

Richard's responsibilities have also been narrowed to more technical tasks. He is supervising the five-person repair crew, engineering some of the new products, examining the procedures for producing samples of new products, and beginning to examine a major redesign of the rough-mill area.

Major Competitor's Production

The major competitor is Sand Crafters, Inc. A managerial person familiar with both operations provided these comments. Demand for Sand Crafters' products exceeded their capacity, and this, in the person's opinion, was the main reason Artisan existed. Its sales were somewhat less than Artisan's, they had no debt, and its equipment was described as new. It was located in a small community where the workers were relatively skilled for this kind of business. The work force was primarily white male. The manager characterized the Artisan worker as about two-thirds as good as Sand Crafters. The workers in the third company in the industry were rated as one-half as good. The quality of manufacture of Sand Crafters was considered first, Artisan second, and the third company a close third. Sand Crafters' weakness was in poor engineering of the products and an outdated approach to marketing. Sand Crafters schedules long runs in manufacturing with the objective of having three months' stock of top priority items. It does not use the EOQ Model because it is limited in its work-in-process space.

In describing the Artisan manufacturing system, the person noted that two-thirds of the equipment is idle at any time and that neither capacity nor optimum production mix have yet been determined. The largest run size he claimed to have seen had been 250. Setup costs he estimated to average $30. He commented that this was the least directed operation he had ever seen, with the slowest pace and the lowest level of knowledge of this type of work He felt its employees knew only the simple way of doing the job. Only one man in the company, for example, was able to count the board feet of lumber, and there was no lumber rule in the plant. He stated that this was a skill that the smallest cabinet shop would have and that it was essential for any kind of usage control.

The Workforce

Bill was greatly interested in the newest concept of management, frequently pointing to the latest book or sending a copy of an article to his managers or anyone with whom he was interacting. The behavioral writings made a lot of sense to him, and he was very perceptive of behavioral processes in meetings or situations. The participative management systems and cooperative team environments were ones Bill wanted for Artisan. However, he recognized his managers and the work force were not ready for this yet. His managers manipulated more than cooperated, and the workers were neither skilled nor very productive. When he discussed the workers' desires with the supervisors, he was told they wanted a retirement program and higher pay, nothing else. Bill felt this was really what the supervisors themselves wanted.

As a basis for beginning change in this area, an outside consultant conducted an employee attitude survey in May 1977. All employees in the company were assisted in small groups in completing the written questionnaire. The questionnaire was designed (1) to find out what they wanted, for example, more pay, retirement plans, more or less direction, etc.; (2) to gain insight into the probable impact of participative management moves; (3) to establish benchmarks of employee satisfaction so that changes over time could be monitored; (4) to develop an objective profile of the workers; and (5) to look for significant differences in attitudes between the various stratifications possible.

The survey included questions developed specifically for this situation as well as a highly regarded attitude instrument, the Job Descrip-

tive Index (JDI). Although the wording is considered simple, many of the workers did not understand such words as "stimulating," "ambitious," or "fascinating," and it became necessary to read the entire questionnaire to them.

The study showed minorities accounted for 80 percent of the 300 employees; white females were the largest group at 40 percent. The work force was 58 percent female, 57 percent white, and 39 percent over 45 years old. As many people have been with the company under two years as over 10 years — 24 percent. The pay was only a little above the legal minimum, but many workers felt fortunate to have their jobs. There did not appear to be a "morale" crisis; the five JDI measures located the company in about the middle of the norms. The supervisory group was highest in "morale," while management was lowest.

Exhibit 2-3 summarizes the Job Descriptive Index scores. The numbers in parentheses show the norms.

Employees were also questioned about a number of aspects of their work climate that could be improved. Exhibit 2-4 shows these questions.

Their expressed view of the organizational climate was relatively good. They claimed to enjoy their work, looked for ways to improve it, and felt they were expected to do a good job. They especially felt that their co-workers were good to work with and felt part of a team. They appeared to like their supervision.

Their views did not suggest need for a different manner of supervision. And they did not respond positively to the suggestions of being more in charge of themselves, did not feel strongly about having more of a say in how things are done, and did not feel there were too many rules.

The survey revealed no critical problems, differences between groups were not extreme, and the resulting view of the worker was moderate. However, the workers were relatively unsophisticated, and there was concern they might not have expressed themselves on the instrument.

Exhibit 2-3 Summary of JDI Scores by Level (Percentile)

Group	Number	Overall	Co-worker	Work	Supervision	Promotion	Pay
					Attitude toward:		
(Maximum score)		25	54	54	54	27	27
Total company	318	17.4	41.2	32.3	40.4	11.1	7.1
Management	7	15.9	38.0	39.4	48.0	18.7	15.9
(%)			(35)	(60)	(70)	(80)	(55)
Office	18	16.6	45.8	36.6	47.4	6.9	7.7
(%)			(60)	(50)	(65)	(50)	(25)
Supervision	13	19.7	46.8	39.2	46.1	16.1	12.2
Plant No. 1 hourly	141	17.1	40.4	31.6	38.4	11.7	6.6
Plant No. 2 hourly	101	18.1	39.8	31.3	42.6	11.0	5.9

The Meeting with Bob on June 10

The last months of 1976 had been very good in spite of fears caused by the price increase and the changes in the sales organization and had resulted in a $390,000 profit. Bob Atwood reported that the original plan for 1977 had been for no major changes — a regrouping, doing as in late 1976, just better. However, there was no formal written plan. As actual sales in January and February ran well ahead of the prior year, production was allowed to stay higher than the plan. Bill believed Bob's estimate of sales at $6.5 million was very low. A quite conservative estimate, he felt, was $9 million. This level became accepted as the premise for production planning in the first part of the year. But March and April were disappointing and May was only fair. Bill still felt the $9 million was reasonable, as the normal retail sales patterns had been upset by inflation and the fuel crisis. But he recognized the risks and was concerned. He hoped the gift shows in July would settle what 1977 would hold.

On June 10, 1977, Bob Atwood had returned to Bill's office to press for some decision on the inventory level. He wanted Bill to pull back on plans for 1977. As sales had been slower coming in and inventories had increased more than expected, Bob had become increasingly wor-

ried. The level on the last full inventory listing prepared about six weeks before stood at $800,000 in wooden goods. The current level was nearer $1.1 million. From a financial perspective, Bob was willing to accept a level as high as $1.6 million. But this called for limiting production now. His report dated May 13 presented several alternative production levels for the fall, comparing particularly $600,000 and $720,000 per month. The advantages and disadvantages of $600,000 versus $720,000 production levels are as follows:

Advantages and Disadvantages

Advantages of $600,000 production level:
1. Reduces scope of operation to afford high degree of control.
2. Maintains positive cash flow position for remainder of year.
3. Maintains more liquid corporate position.

Disadvantages of $600,000 production level:
1. More customer dissatisfaction from possible low service level.
2. Probable lost sales if orders increase.

Advantages of $720,000 production level:
1. High service level to accounts.
2. Low probability of decrease in service if orders increase.

Exhibit 2-4 Results of Attitude Survey: May 1977

What is Your Opinion on the Following Statements? Do You Agree or Disagree?	Average Employee Response
I enjoy taking the test.	3.97
My pay is fair for this kind of job.	2.26
My co-workers are good to work with.	4.14
My complaints or concerns are heard by management.	3.22
Things are getting better here.	3.45
The supervisors do a poor job.	2.35
I am fortunate to have this job.	3.95
Working conditions are bad here.	2.55
I benefit when the company succeeds.	3.11
I have all the chance I wish to improve myself.	3.19
The company is well run.	3.29
Communications are poor.	2.91
I don't get enough direction from my supervisor.	2.56
I enjoy my work.	4.13
I look for ways to improve the work I do.	4.21
I need more of a chance to manage myself.	3.11
I don't expect to be with the company long.	2.35
Morale is good here.	3.55
We all do only what it takes to get by.	2.19
I am concerned about layoffs and losing my job.	3.51
I like the way my supervisor treats me.	4.02
We need a suggestion system.	3.75
I want more opportunity for advancement.	3.86
My supervisor knows me and what I want.	3.56
We are not expected to do a very good job here.	2.01
There are too many rules.	2.58
I feel like part of a team at work.	3.82
The company and my supervisor seek my ideas.	3.06
I can influence department goals, methods, and activities.	3.01
There is too much "family" here.	2.77
This company is good for the	

5 = Strongly Agree
1 = Strongly Disagree

Disadvantages of $720,000 production level:

1. Risk of inventory buildup.
2. Risk of being in a layoff situation if orders do not increase.

He advocated a $60,000 per month level.

Bob recommended they immediately cut production and make Richard Bare, the purchasing agent, production control manager with the responsibility for guiding the controlled inventory buildup. Since the desired total inventory level of $1.6 million was twice the level shown on the last computer listing that included recommended run sizes (EOQs), he felt they could use this part of the computer system as a guide in selectively increasing the inventory. They could double either the Re- Order Points (ROPs) or the lead times in the computer, return the report, and use the new EOQs to double the inventory in a balanced form. Bob felt there had been unnecessary delay in making a decision and was impatient for Bill to put this to rest without further delay.

3
Organizational Diagnosis Questionnaire

Instructions for Use of the ODQ

Goals

I. To assist participants in understanding the process of organizational diagnosis.

II. To show participants how the various formal and informal aspects of an organization work together.

III. To provide participants with a method for understanding the functioning of the internal environment of an organization.

Group Size

May be administered individually or in small groups of six to eight. May be used with students as a training tool or as part of an organizational analysis.

Time Required

Approximately two hours.

Materials

I. A copy of the Organizational Diagnosis Questionnaire (ODQ) and score sheet for each participant.

II. A newsprint flip chart or chalk board for the instructor.

Physical Setting

A room large enough so that individuals/ groups can work undisturbed. Movable chairs should be provided.

Process

Step I.   Introduction (10 min.)
The instructor announces the goals of the activity, distributing copies of the ODQ, its score sheet and the associated handout. The participants are instructed to read the handout.

Step II.   Overview (15 min.)
The instructor presents an overview of the Weisbord Six-Box Organizational Model, provides examples, and elicits questions.

The ODQ and its introduction were prepared by Robert C. Preziosi. Reprinted from: J. William Pfeiffer & John E. Jones, (Eds.), *The 1980 Annual Handbook for Group Facilitators*, San Diego, CA: University Associates, Inc., 1980. Used with permission.

Step III.   Complete the ODQ (30 min.)
Participants are told to think of an organization with which they have some knowledge. This can be a firm where they have worked, a club to which they belonged, etc. They are told to think of that organization as they respond to the items on the ODQ.

Step IV.   Score the ODQ (10 min.)
After completing the ODQ, the instructor explains the scoring system, and participants score their own questionnaire.

Step V.   Small Group Discussion (I5 min.)
Participants are then asked to form small groups and discuss why the organizations they analyzed came out the way they did.

Step VI.   Change Strategies (10 min.)
(Optional)
Participants are asked to think of activities they might instigate in their organizations to change some of the negative issues that surfaced in their analysis.

Step VII. Large Group Discussion (20 min.)
(Optional)
Instructor brings the entire group together and solicits volunteers to discuss the specifics of their particular organization.

Introduction to the Questionnaire

Both internal and external organization development (OD) consultants at some point in the consulting process must address the question of diagnosis. Recently the need for two levels of diagnosis, preliminary and intensive, was addressed (Lippitt & Lippitt, 1978). The purpose of the Organizational Diagnosis Questionnaire (ODQ) is to provide survey feedback data for intensive diagnostic efforts. Use of the questionnaire either by itself or in conjunction with other information-collecting techniques (such as direct observation or interviewing) will provide

the data needed for identifying strengths and weaknesses in the functioning of an organization and/or its subparts. The questionnaire produces data relative to informal activity.

A meaningful diagnostic effort must be based on a theory or model of organizational functioning. This makes action research possible as it facilitates problem identification, which is essential to organization development. One of the more significant models in existence is Weisbord's (1976) Six-Box Organizational Model (Exhibit 3-1). Weisbord's model establishes a systematic approach for analyzing relationships among variables that influence how an organization is managed. It provides for assessment in six areas of formal and informal activity: purposes, structure, relationships, rewards, leadership, and helpful mechanisms. The outer circle in Exhibit 3-1 determines an organizational boundary for diagnosis. This boundary clarifies the functioning of the internal environment, which is to be analyzed to the exclusion of the external environment.

The Instrument

The Organizational Diagnosis Questionnaire is based on Weisbord's practitioner-oriented theory. The ODQ generates data in each of Weisbord's suggested six areas as well as in a seventh, attitude toward change. This item was added as a helpful mechanism for the person involved in organizational diagnosis. In attempting any planned-change effort in an organization, it is wise to know how changeable an organization is. Such knowledge helps the change agent understand how to direct his efforts.

Thirty-five items compose the ODQ, five in each of the seven variables. Respondents are asked to indicate their current views of their organization on a scale of 1 to 7, with a score of 4 representing a neutral point.

Uses of the ODQ

The ODQ can be administered to a work unit, an entire organization, or a random sample of each. It might also be used to analyze staff or line

EXHIBIT 3-1 ■   The Six-Box Organizational Model[1]

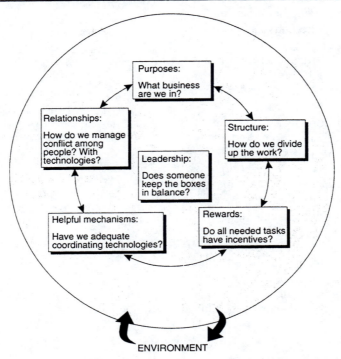

[1]Reproduced from M. R Weisbord, "Organizational diagnosis: Six places to look for trouble with or without a theory."
Group & Organization Studies,1976. 1(4), 430-447, by permission of the publisher and the author.

functioning as well as to assess the thinking of different levels of management or supervision. It should be administered by the consultant or process facilitator in order to insure that an adequate explanation of the questionnaire and its use will be given. The consultant could also train others to administer the questionnaire.

■ *Administration and Scoring* The administrator of the questionnaire must emphasize to the respondents that they be open and honest. If they are not, data that yield an inaccurate assessment of the organization on any or all of the seven variables may be produced. All ODQ statements are positive and can easily be discerned as such, which may influence the manner in which the respondents react to the questionnaire.

Scoring the questionnaire may be done in more than one way. Aggregate data will be most useful; an individual's set of responses is not significant. A self-scoring sheet is provided for each individual. Individual scoring sheets could then be tabulated by the consultant, an assistant, or, for large-scale studies, a computer.

■ *Processing the Data* Once aggregate data have been collected, they must be processed. The first task is to prepare a bar or line graph (or any similar technique) to present the data so that they can be readily understood. The consultant/facilitator should present the data first to the organization's president or the work unit's supervisor (whichever is applicable) to establish understanding, commitment, and support.

Next, a meeting with the work group is essential. During this meeting, the consultant/facilitator must weave a delicate balance between task and maintenance issues in order to be productive. During this meeting, a number of things take place: information is presented (feedback);

information is objectively discussed; group problem solving is encouraged; brainstorming for solutions is facilitated; alternative solutions are evaluated against criteria; a solution is chosen; an action plan is developed; and a plan for future evaluation is determined.This process is presented in detail in Hausser, Pecorella, and Wissler (1977).

The ODQ produces information about the informal system. As Weisbord suggested, the formal system must be considered also. A consultan/facilitator may review an organization's charter, operations manual, personnel policies, etc. Gaps between the two systems lead to a diagnosis of what is not happening that should be happening, or vice versa.

In sum, the ODQ is useful for diagnostic efforts insofar as it provides data about people's perceptions of their organization. It is an instrument that may be used separate from or in addition to other information-collecting techniques.

References

Hausser, D. L, Pecorella, P. A. & Wissler, A. L. *Survey-guided development: A manual for consultants.* San Diego, CA: University Associates, 1977.

Lippitt, G., & Lippitt, R. *The consulting process in action.* San Diego, CA: University Associates, 1978.

Weisbord, M. R. "Organizational diagnosis: Six places to look for trouble with or without a theory." *Group & Organization Studies,* 1976, 1(4), 430-447.

Organizational Diagnosis Questionnaire

From time to time organizations consider it important to analyze themselves. It is necessary to find out from the people who work in the organization what they think if the analysis is going to be of value. This questionnaire will help the organization that you work for analyze itself.

Directions: Do not put your name anywhere on this questionnaire. Please answer all thirty-five questions. Be open and honest. For each of the thirty-five statements, circle only one (1) number to indicate your thinking.

1 - Agree Strongly
2 - Agree
3 - Agree Slightly
4 - Neutral
5 - Disagree Slightly
6 - Disagree
7 - Disagree Strongly

1. The goals of this organization are clearly stated.

   1   2   3   4   5   6   7

2. The division of labor of this organization is flexible.

   1   2   3   4   5   6   7

3. My immediate supervisor is supportive of my efforts.

   1   2   3   4   5   6   7

4. My relationship with my supervisor is a harmonious one.

   1   2   3   4   5   6   7

5. My job offers me the opportunity to grow as a person.

   1   2   3   4   5   6   7

6. My immediate supervisor has ideas that are helpful to me and my work group.

   1   2   3   4   5   6   7

7. This organization is not resistant to change.

   1   2   3   4   5   6   7

8. I am personally in agreement with the stated goals of my work unit.

   1   2   3   4   5   6   7

9. The division of labor of this organization is conducive to reaching its goals.

   1   2   3   4   5   6   7

10. The leadership norms of this organization help its progress.

    1   2   3   4   5   6   7

11. I can always talk with someone at work if I have a work-related problem.

    1   2   3   4   5   6   7

12. The pay scale and benefits of this organization treat each employee equitably.

    1   2   3   4   5   6   7

13. I have the information that I need to do a good job.

    1   2   3   4   5   6   7

14. This organization is not introducing enough new policies and procedures.

    1   2   3   4   5   6   7

15. I understand the purpose of this organization.

    1   2   3   4   5   6   7

16. The manner in which work tasks are divided is a logical one.

    1   2   3   4   5   6   7

17. This organization's leadership efforts result in the organization's fulfillment of its purposes.

    1   2   3   4   5   6   7

18. My relationship with members of my workgroup are fiiendly as well as professional.

    1   2   3   4   5   6   7

19. The opportunity for promotion exists in this organization.

    1   2   3   4   5   6   7

20. This organization has adequate mechanisms for binding itself together.

    1 2 3 4 5 6 7

21. This organization favors change.

    1 2 3 4 5 6 7

22. The priorities of this organization are understood by its employees.

    1 2 3 4 5 6 7

23. The structure of my work unit is well designed.

    1 2 3 4 5 6 7

24. It is clear to me whenever my boss is attempting to guide my work efforts.

    1 2 3 4 5 6 7

25. I have established the relationships that I need to do my job properly.

    1 2 3 4 5 6 7

26. The salary that I receive is commensurate with the job that I perform.

    1 2 3 4 5 6 7

27. Other work units are helpful to my work unit whenever assistance is requested.

    1 2 3 4 5 6 7

28. Occasionally I like to change things about my job.

    1 2 3 4 5 6 7

29. I desire less input in deciding my work-unit goals.

    1 2 3 4 5 6 7

30. The division of labor of this organization helps its efforts to reach its goals.

    1 2 3 4 5 6 7

31. I understand my boss's efforts to influence me and the other members of the work unit.

    1 2 3 4 5 6 7

32. There is no evidence of unresolved conflict in this organization.

    1 2 3 4 5 6 7

33. All tasks to be accomplished are associated with incentives.

    1 2 3 4 5 6 7

34. This organization's planning and control efforts are helpful to its growth and development.

    1 2 3 4 5 6 7

35. This organization has the ability to change.

    1 2 3 4 5 6 7

ODQ Scoring Sheet

Instructions: Transfer the numbers you circled on the questionnaire to the blanks below, add each column, and divide each sum by five. This will give you comparable scores for each of the seven areas.

■ *Purposes*

1	_____
8	_____
15	_____
22	_____
29	_____
Total	_____
Average	_____

■ *Structure*

2	_____
9	_____
16	_____
23	_____
30	_____
Total	_____
Average	_____

■ *Leadership*

3	_____
10	_____
17	_____
24	_____
31	_____
Total	_____
Average	_____

■ *Relationships*

4	_____
11	_____
18	_____
25	_____
32	_____
Total	_____
Average	_____

■ *Rewards*

5	_____
12	_____
19	_____
26	_____
33	_____
Total	_____
Average	_____

■ *Helpful Mechanisms*

6	_____
13	_____
20	_____
27	_____
34	_____
Total	_____
Average	_____

■ *Attitude Toward Change*

7	_____
14	_____
21	_____
28	_____
35	_____
Total	_____
Average	_____

ODQ Profile and Interpretation Sheet

Instructions: Transfer your average scores from the ODQ Scoring Sheet to the appropriate boxes in the figure below. Then study the background information and interpretation suggestions that follow.

Background

The ODQ is a survey-feedback instrument designed to collect data on organizational functioning. It measures the perceptions of persons in an organization or work unit to determine areas of activity that would benefit from an organization development effort. It can be used as the sole data-collection technique or in conjunction with other techniques (interview, observation, etc.).

Weisbord's Six-Box Organizational Model (1976) is the basis for the questionnaire, which measures seven variables: purposes, structure, relationships, rewards, leadership, helpful mechanisms, and attitude toward change. The first six areas are from Weisbord's model, while the last one was added to provide the consultant/facilitator with input on readiness for change.

The instrument and the model reflect a systematic approach for analyzing relationships among variables that influence how an organization is managed. The ODQ measures the informal aspects of the system. It may be necessary for the consultant/facilitator also to gather information on the formal aspects and to examine the gaps between the two.

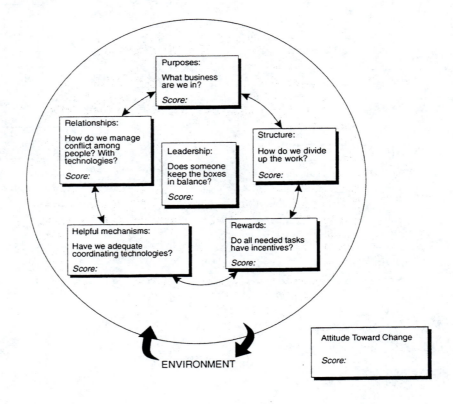

Using the ODQ is the first step in determining appropriate interventions for organizational change efforts. Its use as a diagnostic tool can be the first step in improving an organization's or work unit's capability to serve its clientele.

Interpretation and Diagnosis

A crucial consideration is the diagnosis based upon data interpretation. The simplest diagnosis would be to assess the amount of variance for each of the seven variables in relation to a score of 4, which is the neutral point. Scores above 4 would indicate a problem with organizational functioning. The closer the score is to 7 the more severe the problem would be. Scores below 4 indicate the lack of a problem, with a score of 1 indicating optimum functioning.

Another diagnostic approach follows the same guidelines of assessment in relation to the neutral point (score) of 4. The score of each of the thirty-five items on the questionnaire can be reviewed to produce more exacting information on problematic areas. Thus, diagnosis would be more precise. For example, let us suppose that the average score on item number 8 is 6.4. This would indicate not only a problem in organizational purpose, but also a more specific problem in that there is a gap between organizational and individual goals. This more precise diagnostic effort is likely to lead to a more appropriate intervention in the organization than the generalized diagnostic approach described in the preceding paragraph.

Appropriate diagnosis must address the relationships between the boxes to determine the interconnectedness of problems. For example, if there is a problem with relationships, could it be that the reward system does not reward relationship behavior? This might be the case if the average score on item 33 was well above 4 (5.5 or higher) and all the items on relationships (4, 11, 18, 25, 32) averaged above 5.5.

4
The University Art Museum

Visitors to the campus were always shown the University Art Museum, of which the large and distinguished university was very proud. A photograph of the handsome neoclassical building that housed the Museum had long been used by the university for the cover of its brochures and catalogues.

The building, together with a substantial endowment, was given to the university around 1912 by an alumnus, the son of the university's first president, who had become very wealthy as an investment banker. He also gave the university his own small, but high quality, collections — one of Etruscan figurines, and one, unique in America, of English pre-Raphaelite paintings. He then served as the Museum's unpaid director until his death. During his tenure he brought a few additional collections to the museum, largely from other alumni of the university. Only rarely did the museum purchase anything. As a result, the museum housed several small collections of uneven quality. As long as the founder ran the museum, none of the collections was ever shown to anybody except a few members of the university's art history faculty, who were admitted as the founder's private guests.

After the founder's death, in the late 1920s, the university intended to bring in a professional museum director. Indeed, this had been part of the agreement under which the founder had given the museum. A search committee was to be appointed; but in the meantime a graduate student in art history, who had shown interest in the museum and who had spent a good many hours in it, took over temporarily. At first, she did not even have a title, let alone a salary. But she stayed on acting as the museum's director and over the next 30 years was promoted in stages to that title. But from the first day, whatever her title, she was in charge. She immediately set about changing the museum altogether. She catalogued the collections. She pursued new gifts, again primarily small collections from alumni and other friends of the university. She organized fund raising for the museum. But, above all, she began to integrate the museum into the work of the university. When a space problem arose in the years immediately following World War II, Miss Kirkhoff offered the third floor of the museum to the art history faculty, which moved its offices there. She remodeled the building to include classrooms and a modern and well-appointed auditorium. She raised funds to build one of the best research and reference libraries in art history in the country. She also began to organize a series of special exhibitions

Case #3, "The University Art Museum: Defining Purpose and Mission" (pp. 28-35), from *Management Cases* by Peter F. Drucker. Copyright © 1977 by Peter F. Drucker. Reprinted by permission of Harper & Row, Publishers, Inc.

built around one of the museum's own collections, complemented by loans from outside collections. For each of these exhibitions she had a distinguished member of the university's art faculty write a catalogue. These catalogues speedily became the leading scholarly texts in the fields.

Miss Kirkhoff ran the University Art Museum for almost half a century. But old age ultimately defeated her. At the age of 68 after suffering a severe stroke, she had to retire. In her letter of resignation she proudly pointed to the museum's growth and accomplishment under her stewardship. "Our endowment," she wrote, "now compares favorably with museums several times our size. We never have had to ask the university for any money other than for our share of the university's insurance policies. Our collections in the areas of our strength, while small, are of first-rate quality and importance. Above all, we are being used by more people than any museum of our size. Our lecture series, in which members of the university's art history faculty present a major subject to a university audience of students and faculty, attracts regularly three hundred to five hundred people; and if we had the seating capacity, we could easily have a larger audience. Our exhibitions are seen and studied by more visitors, most of them members of the university community, than all but the most highly publicized exhibitions in the very big museums ever draw. Above all, the courses and seminars offered in the museum have become one of the most popular and most rapidly growing educational features of the university. No other museum in this country or anywhere else," concluded Miss Kirkhoff, "has so successfully integrated art into the life of a major university and a major university into the work of a museum."

Miss Kirkhoff strongly recommended that the university bring in a professional museum director as her successor. "The museum is much too big and much too important to be entrusted to another amateur such as I was 45 years ago," she wrote. "And it needs careful thinking regarding its direction, its basis of support, and its future relationship with the university."

The university took Miss Kirkhoff's advice. A search committee was duly appointed and, after one year's work, it produced a candidate whom everybody approved. The candidate was himself a graduate of the university who had then obtained his Ph.D. in art history and in museum work from the university. Both his teaching and administrative record were sound, leading to his present museum directorship in a medium-sized city. There he converted an old, well- known, but rather sleepy museum to a lively, community-oriented museum whose exhibitions were well publicized and attracted large crowds.

The new museum director took over with great fanfare in September 1971. Less than three years later he left — with less fanfare, but still with considerable noise. Whether he resigned or was fired was not quite clear. But that there was bitterness on both sides was only too obvious.

The new director, upon his arrival, had announced that he looked upon the museum as a "major community resource" and intended to "make the tremendous artistic and scholarly resources of the Museum fully available to the academic community as well as to the public." When he said these things in an interview with the college newspaper, everybody nodded in approval. It soon became clear that what he meant by "community resource" and what the faculty and students understood by these words were not the same. The museum had always been "open to the public" but, in practice, it was members of the college community who used the museum and attended its lectures, its exhibitions, and its frequent seminars.

The first thing the new director did, however, was to promote visits from the public schools in the area. He soon began to change the exhibition policy. Instead of organizing small shows, focused on a major collection of the museum and built around a scholarly catalogue, he began to organize "popular exhibitions" around "topics of general interest" such as "Women Artists through the Ages." He promoted these exhibitions vigorously in the newspapers, in radio and television interviews, and, above all, in the local schools. As a result, what had been a busy but quiet place was soon knee-deep in school children, taken to the museum in special buses that cluttered the access roads around the museum and throughout the campus. The faculty, which was not particularly happy with the resulting noise and confusion, became thoroughly upset when the scholarly old chairman of the art history department was mobbed by fourth-graders who sprayed him with their water pistols as he tried to push his way through the main hall to his office.

Increasingly, the new director did not design his own shows, but brought in traveling exhibitions from major museums, importing their catalogue as well rather than have his own faculty produce one.

The students too were apparently unenthusiastic after the first six or eight months, during which the new director had been somewhat of a campus hero. Attendance at the classes and seminars held in the art museum fell off sharply, as did attendance at the evening lectures. When the editor of the campus newspaper interviewed students for a story on the museum, he was told again and again that the museum had become too noisy and too "sensational" for students to enjoy the classes and to have a chance to learn.

What brought all this to a head was an Islamic art exhibit in late 1973. Since the museum had little Islamic art, nobody criticized the showing of a traveling exhibit, offered on very advantageous terms with generous financial assistance from some of the Arab governments. But then, instead of inviting one of the University's own faculty members to deliver the customary talk at the opening of the exhibit, the director brought in a cultural attache of one of the Arab embassies in Washington. The speaker, it was reported, used the occasion to deliver a violent attack on Israel and on the American policy of supporting Israel against the Arabs. A week later, the university senate decided to appoint an advisory committee, drawn mostly from members of the art history faculty, which, in the future, would have to approve all plans for exhibits and lectures. The director thereupon, in an interview with the campus newspaper, sharply attacked the faculty as "elitist" and "snobbish" and as believing that "art belongs to the rich." Six months later, in June 1974, his resignation was announced.

Under the bylaws of the university, the academic senate appoints a search committee. Normally, this is pure formality. The chairperson of the appropriate department submits the department's nominees for the committee who are approved and appointed, usually without debate. But when the academic senate early the following semester was asked to appoint the search committee, things were far from "normal." The dean who presided, sensing the tempers in the room, tried to smooth over things by saying, "Clearly, we picked the wrong person the last time. We will have to try very hard to find the right one this time."

He was immediately interrupted by an economist, known for his populism, who broke in and said, "I admit that the late director was probably not the right personality. But I strongly believe that his personality was not at the root of the problem. He tried to do what needs doing, and this got him in trouble with the faculty. He tried to make our museum a community resource, to bring in the community and to make art accessible to broad masses of people, to the blacks and the Puerto Ricans, to the kids from the ghetto schools and to a lay public. And this is what we really resented. Maybe his methods were not the most tactful ones — I admit I could have done without those interviews he gave. But what he tried to do was right. We had better commit ourselves to the policy he wanted to put into effect, or else we will have deserved his attacks on us as 'elitist' and 'snobbish.' "

"This is nonsense," cut in the usually silent and polite senate member from the art history faculty. "It makes absolutely no sense for our museum to try to become the kind of community resource our late director and my distinguished colleague want it to be. First, there is no need. The city has one of the world's finest and biggest museums, and it does exactly that and does it very well. Secondly, we have neither the artistic resources nor the financial resources to serve the community at large. We can do something different but equally important and indeed unique. Ours is the only museum in the country, and perhaps in the world, that is fully integrated with an academic community and truly a teaching institution. We are using it, or at least we used to until the last few unfortunate years, as a major educational resource for all our students. No other museum in the country, and as far as I know in the world, is bringing undergraduates into art the way we do. All of us, in addition to our scholarly and graduate work, teach undergraduate courses for people who are not going to be art majors or art historians. We work with the engineering students and show them what we do in our conservation and restoration work. We work with architecture students and show them the development of architecture through the ages. Above all, we work with liberal arts students, who often have had no exposure to art before they came here and who enjoy our courses all the more because they are scholarly and not just 'art appreciation.' This is unique and this is what our museum can do and should do."

"I doubt that this is really what we should be doing," commented the chairman of the mathematics department. "The museum, as far as I know, is part of the graduate faculty. It should concentrate on training art historians in its Ph.D. program, on its scholarly work, and on its research. I would strongly urge that the museum be considered an adjunct to graduate and especially to Ph.D. education, confine itself to this work, and stay out of all attempts to be 'popular,' on both campus and outside of it. The glory of the museum is the scholarly catalogues produced by our faculty, and our Ph.D. graduates who are sought after by art history faculties throughout the country. This is the museum's mission, which can only be impaired by the attempt to be 'popular,' whether with students or with the public."

"These are very interesting and important comments," said the dean, still trying to pacify. "But I think this can wait until we know who the new director is going to be. Then we should raise these questions with him."

"I beg to differ, Mr. Dean," said one of the elder statesmen of the faculty. "During the summer months, I discussed this question with an old friend and neighbor of mine in the country, the director of one of the nation's great museums. He said to me: 'You do not have a personality problem, you have a management problem. You have not, as a university, taken responsibility for the mission, the direction, and the objectives of your museum. Until you do this, no director can succeed. And this is your decision. In fact, you cannot hope to get a good man until you can tell him what your basic objectives are. If your late director is to blame—I know him and I know that he is abrasive—it is for being willing to take on a job when you, the university, had not faced up to the basic management decisions. There is no point talking about who should manage until it is clear what it is that has to be managed and for what.' "

At this point the dean realized that he had to adjourn the discussion unless he wanted the meeting to degenerate into a brawl. But he also realized that he had to identify the issues and possible decisions before the next faculty meeting a month later. Here is the list of questions he put down on paper later that evening:

1. What are the possible purposes of the University Museum?
- to serve as a laboratory for the graduate art-history faculty and the doctoral students in the field?
- to serve as major "enrichment" for the undergraduate who is not an art-history student but wants both a "liberal education" and a counter-weight to the highly bookish diet fed to him in most of our courses?
- to serve the metropolitan community—and especially its schools—outside the campus gates?

2. Who are or should be its customers?
- the graduate students in professional training to be teachers of art history?
- the undergraduate community—or rather, the entire college community?
- the metropolitan community and especially the teachers and youngsters in the public schools? any others?

3. Which of these purposes are compatible and could be served simultaneously? Which are mutually exclusive or at the very least are likely to get in each other's way?

4. What implications for the structure of the museum, the qualifications of its director, and its relationship to the university follow from each of the above purposes?

5. Do we need to find out more about the needs and wants of our various potential customers to make an intelligent policy decision? How could we go about it?

The dean distributed these questions to the members of the faculty with the request that they think them through and discuss them before the next meeting of the academic senate.

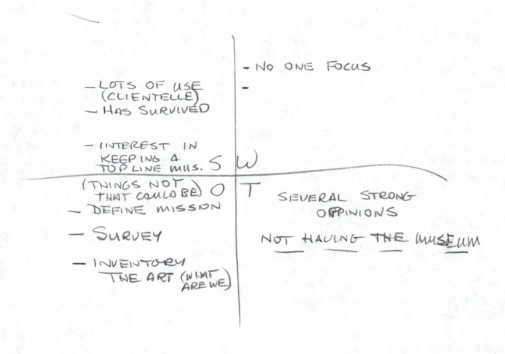

— NO ONE FOCUS
—

— LOTS OF USE (CLIENTELLE)
— HAS SURVIVED

— INTEREST IN KEEPING A TOP LINE MUS. S | W

(THINGS NOT THAT COULD BE) O | T
— DEFINE MISSION

— SURVEY

— INVENTORY THE ART (WHAT ARE WE)

SEVERAL STRONG OPPINIONS

NOT HAVING THE MUSEUM

DEFINE MISSION, DIRECTION, OBJECTIVES

5
Gillette Metal Fabrication

Jon Ball

Jon Ball had worked for Gillette Metal Fabrication for 8 years. He was 34, had a wife, three kids, a mortgage, a car payment, and had feared losing his job for 8 years. The company seemed constantly about to go under. Many of Gillette's competitors had already failed, developments all Gillette's employees followed closely. Everybody in the plant knew that if they lost their job at Gillette, it was very unlikely that they would ever find similar high-paying production work.

All things considered, Jon liked working at Gillette. The work was often challenging, he had the freedom to develop and use his own procedures for getting the job done, and he liked his co-workers. The downside was the insecurity of the job and the constant pressure of the Methods Department looking over his shoulder.

Machine Shop

Gillette's machine shop worked on the piece rate system. You got paid for what you produced, which was sometimes fair, sometimes not. If a job was timed wrong, you had to work for the guaranteed day rate of $12 an hour, hardly enough to make ends meet. When a job was timed right, you could earn a bonus of up to $8 an hour without alerting Methods that you were actually making some money for a change. But if you went over $20 per hour, Methods would be on you like flies on a cow pile. And you would end up working for day rate.

All the workers in the shop were well trained and experienced hands. Jon was no exception. He had trained as a machinist in a vocational program at Community College before joining Lockheed as a machinist. He had worked at Lockheed for 4 years, then made the move to Gillette. He was attracted to the job at Gillette because of the work variety, the opportunity to expand his skills, and the possibility of making more money working for a piece rate. He was a better machinist now than he ever could have become at Lockheed, and he was making better money. Not a lot better, but better.

There was a strict pecking order in the machine shop. Vern and Bud were the two most respected workers in the place. Both were in their late 50s and had been working at Gillette since the dawn of time, at least as far as Jon could tell. They had worked every machine and job in the place. They knew more about machining than any humans alive. And as a result, the machine shop was their domain.

Pappy Mitchell was the shop foreman. Pappy had been around a long time, was a good friend with the Gillettes, and was in charge of job assignments. If you crossed Pappy, you would be working day rate for the rest of your life. So everyone gave Pappy a lot of room. He as a grouch, but lovable in his own way. If you did not make problems for Pappy, Pappy would not make trouble for you.

Gravy and "Shit" Jobs

The jobs in the machine shop fell into two categories: gravy and "shit". A gravy job was any job where you could make a significant bonus above the $12 an hour guaranteed rate, which the workers called the "day rate." Most of the guys would not "bust ass" unless they could make at least $16 an hour on a job. Jon felt this was a good rule of thumb. Given the choice between cruising through the day at $12 an hour and being stressed out for $14 an hour, Jon preferred the $12 an hour. And by not killing himself for a measly $2 an hour, he had the energy he needed to crank when he hit a real gravy job.

Jon was to the point on some jobs that he could work at rates that approached $30 an hour. Of course, because of the quota maintained by the workers to avoid retiming by Methods, he could only turn in $20 an hour for the day. On days when he was finished early, Jon either worked on projects for the shop he had at home or left early. It seemed ridiculous to him that he was forced not to work a good portion of the time, but it was the way the shop ran.

The day rate was paid on jobs that were not timed, rework, jobs that were one-time work and would not be timed, and on jobs that were in the process of being timed by Methods. The "timing" process was a joke. Some young, green industrial engineer from Methods would come down and watch one of the guys run the job, then divine a piece rate. It was all hocus-pocus gues-

stimation as far as Jon could tell. The guys doing the timing could not run the machines if their lives depended on it, and the guys being timed were dogging it to try to get a good time. If Methods wanted to know the right time, all they had to do was ask Vern. When Vern said a rate should be X, it should be X. You could count on it. And if a rate was below X, it was a "shit" job.

Anything that did not pay a bonus was a "shit" job. And there was more "shit" in this place than anybody liked. When you worked "shit", you settled for the day rate. By working to the rules, you could run the job at an easy pace and take time to have some coffee, talk to the other guys, and maybe even catch an afternoon nap out in the warehouse. The warehouse stayed cool in the summer, and it was sometimes hard to find a spot to curl up on hot summer afternoons.

David Wade's Project

Jon had been good friends with David Wade, who had worked in the shop for a year some time back. It turned out that David had been doing a study of the behavior in the shop for a Ph.D. in anthropology at Midwestern University. Jon had thought David was quick, but he did not come across as a real brainy type. He was — all things considered — a pretty mediocre machinist. It was a good thing he had something else to fall back on.

David had finally told Jon about the project he was doing after he left. He apologized for the secrecy, but said he had to be "one of the guys" to get honest observations. Jon was a little miffed at first, but David was his friend and had been straight with him otherwise. They still got together for beers on occasion and were going on a fishing trip over the summer. And now that David was no longer undercover — at least not to Jon — Jon was getting some interesting information from David.

David had mapped the pattern of productivity in the machine shop. Jon found this pretty interesting. Judging from this data, there was a lot of wasted time in the shop. "How in the hell does this relate to the company's problems?" Jon wondered. If the company did not come down so hard on productivity, it seemed like output levels could go up, and Jon sure would like to know that he was going to have a job in a year.

Appendix 1: Excerpts from David Wade's Field Notes

Day 1

I started the day with an orientation session with Nick Whitman, Director of Personnel. As per the agreement between Dennis, Walt Gillette, and myself, no one is supposed to know I am studying the machine shop. Whitman did not seem to give me any special treatment. In fact, he was abrupt and hurried. I think my status as "employee" is secure.

Whitman indicated that I was hired because I had excellent experience. I asked him about pay. I know the shop is on a piece rate, but with no experience, it is difficult to know how I will do. Whitman told me I should average about $20 per hour working under the piece rate. Sounds pretty good, especially given my job last summer only paid $14 an hour.

After going over the company's health and benefits package, Whitman walked me down to the shop and introduced me to Pappy Mitchell, the shop foreman. Pappy is a piece of work. His office is an unbelievable mess of papers, tooling, bits, and scrapped parts. Whitman scurried back to his office after Pappy growled at him, "What the hell you hangin' around for?"

Pappy talked to me for about an hour after Whitman left, asking me questions about my previous experience, what jobs I had run at my last job, and all the training I had from high school on. Although he did not come out and say it, his line of questioning let me know that I was neither as experienced nor as trained as he would have liked. Our conversation ended with "You've got some things to learn" and my assignment as a drill press operator, the lowest rung on the machine shop ladder.

Today was slow. I did not have any work assigned. I spent most of the day wandering around and getting acquainted; figuring out the procedures for checking tools out of the tool crib and for requisitioning materials; filling out job slips; and meeting the guys in the shop. Things must have been slow for everyone, because I spent two hours in the afternoon with Vern and Bud sitting in the warehouse, talking about the Skyhawks and drinking coffee.

Day 2

I was assigned a housing with four holes at four different angles when I arrived this morning. Pappy told me to pick up the jig from the tool crib and get to work. The job looked simple enough and had a piece rate of $1.50 an hour. I was figuring I should be able to do a hole a minute, which would translate into $22.50 an hour. I was expecting a good day.

An hour into the job, I realized I was in Fantasyland when I started calculating my earning. I had only finished 4 pieces, was cursing the malevolent sinner that had designed the jig I was using, and had attracted the attention of several of my co-workers. Bud, who appears to be one of the "personalities" in the shop, decided to give a play-by-play of my work to those gathered around. I glared at him initially and made a remark about work piling up over on his bench, but my reaction only encouraged him. And not a lot of encouragement was needed, judging from the laughter that followed my repeated efforts to loosen the jig and remount it to drill the next hole. The group broke up when Pappy walked up and yelled at everyone to "Get the hell back to work!" Then he turned to me and offered the closest thing to encouragement I had heard yet: "Just don't turn all those parts into scrap. That's all I ask."

I got a lot of ribbing over lunch. Bud was still on me about my inability to handle "the sweetest of all gravy jobs." As best I can figure, the job I have has been performed at a rate generating tremendous bonuses by every man in the shop at some point in time. And they were all greatly amused by my inability to even make the guaranteed pay rate. I could feel myself getting angry, but I had to admit that I was not a wizard of productivity. Even though I had experience, I had never had to crank out volume work with tight tolerances, and that was the name of the game in this shop.

After I got going again after lunch, Vern came over to take a look at what I was doing. After watching me run through a mounting cycle, he stepped up and said "Watch me run this." He drilled the first hole according to procedure, but then he took a small clamp out of his pocket and remounted the piece without adjusting the jig. He did the same thing after each of the next two holes, finishing the piece in 3 minutes maximum. He then handed me the clamp he had and said "Hang onto this. Be good to this job and it will be good to you."

I asked Vern why he did not use the jig as it was designed, and he gave the obvious answer: "I'll start using the jigs when the jigs are designed by someone who knows something about running these damn machines." It turns out that Vern had designed the clamp himself and used it for several years while he was still being given an occasional drill press job.

I was not a whiz, even with Vern's help. But I did do better this afternoon, producing close to $15 per hour by the end of the day. I finished the job with an hour to work, but Pappy did not offer me anything else. "Just be thankful for day rate while you are learning the ropes," was all he said. I took this comment, plus his admonishment to "Get the hell out of my office," as an indicator that I was done for the day.

Day 7

Half way through my second week and I have finally figured out what is "gravy" and what is "shit". Gravy jobs are what I thought they were: jobs where it is easy to make a premium above "day rate," which is shop lingo for the $12 per hour guarantee. "Shit" jobs — as in "I cannot believe I am stuck working on this piece of shit" — are jobs where no one can make a premium, even the very experienced guys like Vern.

Everybody dogs it on the "shit" jobs. At first I thought it might be a good idea to try to get the "shit" jobs over with so I could move onto something else, but Bud laid it out for me. "Why bust your hump for day rate? If you try to work through a "shit" job, you are playing right into management's hands. Why do you think the rates on some of these jobs are so lousy? It is because management expects us to scurry around for the few crumbs they throw our way. Well I am not willing to play their game, and neither are the rest of the guys. If management wants us to work a job, they are going to have to raise the rate to make it worth our while."

The basic logic everybody follows on the "shit" jobs is to punish management into changing the rate. Bud, for instance, went out to the warehouse for some material in the middle of his "shit" job, returning two hours later looking like he had just gotten up. He assured me my perception was accurate. Bud only got his job half run by mid afternoon, then he split at 2:00 PM to go to softball practice for his city league team. He said Ronny would punch him out.

Pappy came around looking for Bud about 3:30, but Vern covered for him. Pappy ranted and raved for about 20 seconds, then walked off cursing. It scared the hell out of me, but Vern was unconcerned. "It is okay to go home early if you finish up a gravy job early, but only Bud has the balls to leave with a "shit" job in the queue. But that is because Pappy knows that he can count on Bud when there is rush work to be done. The secret to getting along with Pappy is to make sure you always make him look good. Never, and I mean never, make Pappy look bad to a customer or management. If you do, you will find out just how many "shit" jobs actually exist in this shop."

Day 18

There was an argument this morning between Vern and Bud over whether a valve body grinding job was "shit" or gravy. Bud said it was "shit" and Vern said he thought it might be gravy. Vern was not as adamant as Bud and decided to put the part to a test. I asked Ronny about the argument, and he indicated that "if Vern says it's shit, it's shit. If Bud says it's shit, it probably is shit, unless Vern proves that it is not. But then sometimes Vern is the only guy that can make gravy on it." It was clear to him.

The word came down on coffee break. The job was "shit". Vern had tried it and could do no better than $14 per hour. I expressed the opinion that $14 sounded pretty good to me, but Vern sat me straight. "Do you mean to tell me that you are willing to bust your hump for an extra $16 a day?" Actually, at this point, I was, but I could tell 'yes' was not the right answer. "Kid, life is too short to kill yourself for $2 an hour when you can use the energy the next day to do a job that will get you $8 an hour gravy. You got a lot of years working in front of you. Put your effort into something with some returns. You cannot bust hump every day in here and stay human."

Day 43

Jon Ball and I went out last night after work and killed a few million gray cells, and I am feeling it today. I guess he and I are becoming pretty good friends. He is a kind of stand back guy, but he has been a big help the past two months. I have picked up a lot of pointers from him. If I make gravy anytime soon, it will be because of his help.

An interesting thing happened today. The timing men were down riding Vern on the valve body that he and Bud had the argument over awhile back. They were trying to persuade him that the milling operation could be done faster than he said it could be done. He told us about it later. "Those method guys got their heads up their ass. They do not know what they are talking about. They want a rate of $15 to mill those valve bodies. They are out of their mind. It is going to take 2 hours minimum to run that job right. Every step on that thing is "shit". Somebody bid the price on that thing too low a year ago, and now methods wants to take it out of my ass. Well, I can tell you right now that they are not getting any more than a piece every three hours out of me."

When Vern was doing the method study, there was little doubt that he was "doing it right." The job has very precise tolerances, and Vern was playing them for all they are worth, adjusting his machine after ever step and double checking every procedure. The methods guys knew he was dogging it, but what are they going to do? Vern is the only guy in the shop who can do this job with any kind of productivity at all.

Day 45

We got the rate on the valve body today, and we were floored: $18 a piece! Bud lit up the lunch room, "What do those methods assholes think we are, a charity shop? They might as well ask us to work for free! Did you see Vern working on that job?

Three hours per piece! If they are going to keep setting rates like this, we may as well pack it in. My kids are going to go hungry if this is what I am getting paid. What the hell do I care if the company folds if my family is going hungry because I am working here?"

I asked Jon about it later. "If Vern says it's shit, it's shit." I pointed out that Vern was really dogging it when they timed him, something the industrial engineers couldn't help but notice. "Yeah," Jon said, "but they should have listened to Vern in the first place. If it is a 2 hour job, then the rate should be $30. It is the most complex piece in the shop. It has very precise tolerances and a lot of steps. They are lucky Vern can do it at all."

All the guys in the shop were bent out of shape over the valve body, even though most of us would never work the job. It was an interesting kind of anger, not really directed at anybody. One of the things that I have noticed here is that relations with the industrial engineers from the methods department are pretty good. They are generally an okay bunch of guys, willing to joke around, and helpful most of the time. But "Methods" is the enemy around the shop. The guys in the shop do not blame the individual engineers when they get screwed on a rate, but there is a lot of anger with the system here.

Day 68

I made out big for the first time today! I was cranking out pieces all morning, when Vern came over to see how I was doing. When I showed him how I was doing, he became concerned. "Hey, you are doing great. But be careful. You are going to have to quit at noon at this rate. You might want to stretch it out a little. If you do this all day, we are going to have Methods down here tomorrow resetting the rate on this. Milk it a little, because you do not want to lose it. If you stretch it out until after lunch, Pappy will be too busy to notice you finished up with it. Then you can take your time cleaning your machine and get out of here. I will punch you out."

I would like to have cranked the parts all afternoon to build a kitty, but they are too big to store in my locker. Jon has a job he does all the time, and he can usually store up enough of a kitty that he does not have to work the job every third or fourth time. He uses the extra time to work on the bench he is building for his garage at home. It is a thing of beauty. He should have it finished in another month; then he can come in on Saturday when no ties are around and pick it up from the warehouse.

The quota really impacts what people do around here. But you have to respect it. If you don't, Methods will cut all the rates, and we'll all end up working for day rate. It sure would be nice to bring home $24 an hour for a change, however. But the company won't let it happen. Bud told me how Ronny and Vern got into a competition a couple of years back "to see who was champ on the milling machine. They had a big job that they worked on for a week, cranking out the pieces at $30 an hour by the end. Methods was down here the next week retiming that job so that we could not make more than $10 an hour on it. Now nobody will work it. We make Ronny and Vern deal with that shit. It's their fault that we lost a gravy job. You got to respect the quota, because otherwise we will all be working day rate."

Day 74

I screwed up big time today. I was not watching my piece count very closely and ended up turning in $22 an hour for the day. Pappy seemed surprised but did not say anything. If the job gets retimed, the guys will be pissed. When Jon has the job, he can run it at $32 an hour. If it comes back with the rate halved, he is going to be pissed. And the job will be mine for life.

Day 92

Methods was back today, working on Vern and the valve body again. Vern and Ronny have been

running the job at 2-3 hours per piece and are none too happy about it. Apparently methods is not either. Three engineers were down working with Vern, trying to get him to try some new procedures and discussing tolerances. They spent the whole day on the part, and Vern was pissed. "A whole day on day rate because those methods bastards got a problem. I will be running that piece of "shit" all day tomorrow because they screwed up the price to the customer. The only way they are getting any output on that job is if they set the rate at $30 a piece. It is a 2 hour job, and there is no getting around it."

Day 93

The job I busted quota on came back around again today. Thank god Methods did not retime it. I got lucky this time. I am going to be more careful. I cannot afford to screw things up for the rest of the guys.

Day 145

The saga of the valve body continues. They have retimed the job 5 times in the last six months. Vern finally got a $24 a piece rate out of them two weeks ago. Then he got 30 pieces to do this week. "I am going to spend the rest of my life working this piece of shit" was his comment on Monday. Well, he finished the job today. After a day of dogging it, he got fed up and started working the job. By Thursday, he was doing a piece an hour.

I asked him about it when we were having afternoon coffee. "I guess this is some real gravy after all. I am glad Methods finally set a reasonable rate. If they had set a decent rate in the first place, I would not have been working day rate a third of the time for the past three months."

Walt Gillette

Walt Gillette took over Gillette Metal Fabrication from his father, William, in 1984. The company was founded in 1947 to do subcontracting work for firms supplying parts to the automobile industry. Durable goods sales boomed in the post-WWII period, as consumers made up for the shortages of the war years, and Gillette Metal Fabrication grew significantly during this period. The company continued to prosper over the next two decades as automobile sales soared in direct proportion to the wealth of the American consumer. The company never grew beyond approximately 200 employees, but the margins in the business were good. As a result, the Gillettes amassed enough of a fortune to be comfortable, but not ostentatious.

The company began to encounter difficulties with the first oil shock. As the automobile industry's fortunes waned under the combined effects of model downsizing and foreign auto3mobile imports, Gillette Metal Fabrication fell on hard times. The company managed to survive largely because William Gillette was willing to operate the company without drawing a salary. And he had long established relationships in the industry that kept sufficient work flowing his way to keep the company alive, although just barely.

By 1989, Walt had 5 hard years behind him and was beginning to wonder if there was any point keeping the company going. Japanese suppliers and subcontractors had become a significant presence in the industry, and it did not look like Gillette could compete with them. For reasons that were not apparent to Walt, Gillette's Japanese competitors were selling at prices well below Gillette's production costs. Walt did not see how they could make any money at the prices they were charging. They had the same basic labor costs that Gillette had, the same materials costs, and they bought their equipment from the same manufacturers. But they were beating Gillette's prices by a significant amount on every contract that came up for bid. Walt figured he could keep the company open for another year the way things were going. But if profits did not improve, he was going to close down. There were no other options.

"The Project"

Walt had gone to high school and college with Dennis Gordon. Dennis had continued his edu-

cation right through to a Ph.D. in anthropology. He now worked as a professor at Midwestern University in Chicago. He and Walt were lifelong friends, so no favor seemed too big. When Dennis asked if he could send one of his Ph.D. students — a young man named David Wade — down to do a year-long field study inside Gillette's machine shop, Walt was not thrilled. But it was Dennis. After meeting the kid and finding out that he had prior experience as a machine operator, Walt okayed the project, figuring at worse he was getting a motivated employee for a year and was helping the university.

The kid had finished up his work late last year, but Walt had never heard anything about the dissertation. Walt and Dennis were talking one day on the phone, and Walt was bemoaning the fragile state of Gillette's finances. Dennis paused, then said "Walt, you need to take a look at Wade's dissertation. Things are not working the way you think they are in that plant of yours." Walt was shocked to hear Dennis express any opinion on a business matter. Dennis refused to discuss the matter over the phone, so the next day Walt was on his way to Chicago.

"Walt, you are not going to like what I am about to show you, but you need to see it. Wade's dissertation research shows your workforce is not working half the time." Dennis was serious.

Walt was stunned by what he saw in David Wade's field notes. He knew that the people that worked for him goofed off every now and then, but what Wade reported was systematic cheating. Workers were having their friends clock them out and going home for the afternoon. Workers were finishing their work for the day by noon and spending their afternoon in the warehouse talking and hatching practical jokes. And a long coffee break was not 5 extra minutes, it was three extra hours. If Wade's estimates were right, the shop employees at Gillette Metal Fabrication spent much of their time not working.

The Compensation System

The employees in the machine shop where Wade had worked were paid a piece rate, a common practice in the industry. Every job had a per piece compensation rate (e.g., machining a transmission shaft paid $8 per shaft, so a machine operator that could finish two an hour was paid $16 per hour for the job). The rates were set by the firm's two industrial engineers. They based the rate on a timing study conducted the first time a job was run for a customer. Times were updated whenever material changes were requested, the part was modified by the customer, or industrial engineering came up with improved processing techniques. The engineers set the rate by watching a trained employee perform the job, then estimated the percent effort the employee was putting out during the timing period to come up with the final "realistic" rate for the job based on the company's compensation philosophy.

The piece rate system was designed to provide an incentive for Gillette's employees to work harder. The system design called for a mean rate slightly higher than the average hourly rate for machine shop workers locally. In addition, Gillette had a guaranteed base rate of $12 per hour to protect workers from timing errors. This base rate was also the hourly rate used when workers were doing rework, conducting timing studies, and working on jobs that had not yet been timed or were one-time, special order work. The basic design of the compensation system is shown in Exhibit 5-1. Workers always were paid a minimum of $12 per hour, even when working on jobs where their actual production was less than $12 per hour on the piece rate.

The firm's cost accounting data indicated that the system worked as designed. Exhibit 5-2 shows the most recent numbers that Walt had on the distribution of hourly pay for the employees in the machine shop. As expected, the employees were working at the guaranteed rate less than half the time. The rest of the time, they were receiving a bonus based on superior output. The firm's average hourly cost of labor was $15.43, which was consistent with historical performance net inflation adjustments.

Bimodal Output Pattern

Although the accounting data were consistent with management's expectations, David Wade's study indicated the employees' actual output was distributed in a bimodal pattern, not the bell-shaped pattern of the expected normal distribution. The pattern observed by Wade is shown in Exhibit 5-3. Based on Wade's data, the employees were only producing at an average rate of $8.18 per hour, considerably below what was expected. Since labor costs were 50% of Gillette's cost of goods sold, this explained a great deal of the firm's cost disadvantage in recent years.

Wade's research indicated that the bimodal pattern of output reflected two distinct responses to the piece rate system. First, the machine shop workers engaged in goldbricking (i.e., they took it easy) when the piece rate was close to or below the guaranteed rate. Even if the worker could do the job for $11.50 per hour on the piece rate, the typical response was to work slowly and take the guaranteed $12 per hour. Based on Wade's data, the employees were only working at $5.22 per hour on jobs where they were earning $12 per hour. In addition, Wade's data indicated the machine shop employees even gold bricked on jobs where they could earn as much as $15 per hour. The logic for this completely escaped Walt.

The second response to the piece rate system was a "quota restriction" developed by and policed by the employees. According to Wade's observations, the employees enforced a maximum work rate of $20 per hour on the piece rate. The cost accounting information that Walt had indicated that workers were turning in work in excess of the $20 quota, but only 3% of the jobs turned in were above quota, well below the 18% of the jobs completed at a rate above $20 per hour. According to Wade's description of the shop, more often than not, once the employees produced enough pieces to achieve $20 per hour for the day, they quit working for the rest of the day.

Given Wade's observations as graphed in Exhibit 5-3, the workers were sacrificing an average of $21.65 a day in earnings on quota jobs.

Exhibit 5-1 Piece Rate System

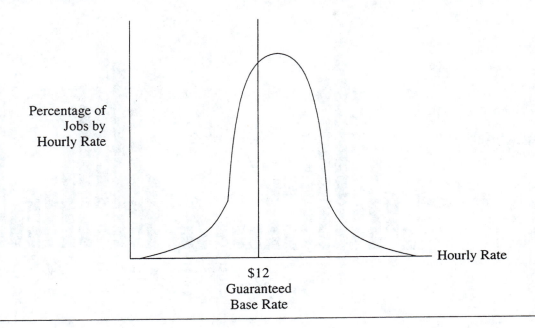

Exhibit 5-2 Cost Accounting Data on Earnings Rate Frequency for Machine Shop Employees

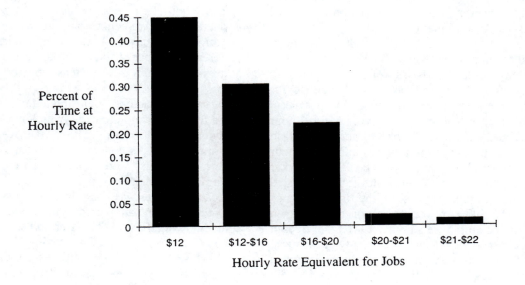

EXHIBIT 5-3 David Wade's Data on Output Frequency by Hourly Rate

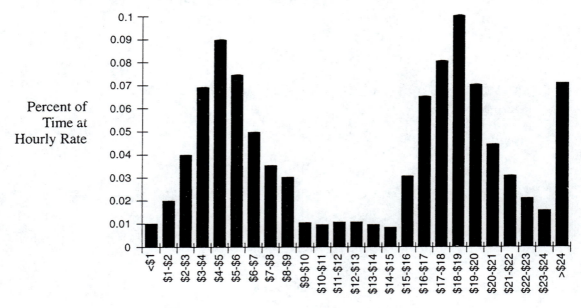

Percent of Time at Hourly Rate

Hourly Rate Equivalent for Jobs

Walt found this especially baffling, because in some cases the workers were giving up more than $32 a day — representing 20% additional earnings per day — in order to do nothing. Why? Walt had no explanation.

The costs to the firm of lost productivity due to goldbricking were obvious. But the quota- restriction was costing the firm as well. The firm bid jobs on a per piece price, not on an hourly rate. So, for instance, a job with a piece rate of $16 per piece, a materials cost of $10 per piece and $6 per hour fixed cost, might be bid at $40 per piece. If an employee produced eight pieces in an eight-hour shift, the firm's earnings would be $64 per worker day on the job. If the em- ployee produced 10 pieces in an eight-hour shift, the firm's earnings would be $92 per worker day on the job, even though the employee's hourly earnings increased to $20 per hour. This was the beauty of the piece rate for the firm and its employees; both gained from increased productivity. The employee's gain was increased earnings per hour based on acquired skills. And the firm's earnings increased with

workforce productivity because fixed costs per piece went down as productivity increased. So if the workers were producing at $24 per hour on a $16 job (12 pieces per day) — a rate of production they were not claiming because of the quota restriction — the firm's earnings would be $120 per worker day, almost double the earnings from a 50% increase in productivity.

The same productivity logic applied to the jobs where the workers goldbricked, which made this behavior doubly distressing. The workers were not only drawing $12 per hour and working at a much lower rate, they also were eating up any earnings the firm might make by being unproductive.

Because Gillette was being hammered by foreign competition, an increase in productivity would allow the firm to bid lower and still make money. The firm was barely breaking even and steadily losing work. A 50% increase in productivity could make the firm competitive and profitable, the two conditions that Walt needed to meet to keep the firm in business. And Wade's data indicated a 50% productivity increase could be achieved if the employees just worked an 8 hour day.

Machine Shop Workforce

The pattern of work behavior uncovered by Wade was not apparent in the cost accounting data for two reasons. First, the accounting information only indicated what the workers were paid, so the lower hump was summed as work at the guaranteed rate. Second, Wade's analysis indicated the workers managed their "turn-in" rate to conform to the quota restriction, which resulted in a pattern of payment that appeared more in compliance with the expected pattern than was in fact the case. There was no way the cost accounting system could identify the bimodal pattern Wade had discovered, because the accounting system could only capture work turned in, not actual work behavior. Walt Gillette depended on his shop foremen to motivate and control his employees' work behavior.

The machine shop was the domain of Fred "Pappy" Mitchell. Pappy had worked for Gillette Metal Fabrication for over 30 years and had been machine shop foreman for 18 years. Pappy assigned all the jobs, deciding who would work on what job based on job difficulty, the employee's skills, and customer service considerations. Walt had always believed Pappy was a good man and could be trusted to run the shop in the best interests of the company. Sure, he was a little coarse, sloppy in following company reporting rules, and not always completely cooperative with industrial engineering, but the men in the machine shop seemed to love him and would do anything he asked to get an emergency order out to a customer.

The employees in the machine shop were all graduates of trade schools and had all completed some kind of apprenticeship period before Gillette hired them. Times were too tough for Gillette to train anyone on the job. All the employees were highly qualified and had significant experience. They had the skills to be productive. The question that Walt had to wrestle with was "Why aren't they producing as expected?" The incentives were in place, but the workers were working contrary to the rewards of the compensation system. It just did not make sense.

What Next?

Walt was deeply disturbed by what he had seen in David Wade's field notes. If the information was correct, most of the firm's productivity disadvantages were due to goldbricking and quota restriction by the employees. Walt tossed and turned that night in bed, wondering what he was going to do next.

6
Reviewing Objectives and Strategies: A Planning Task for Managers

Goals

I. To review and evaluate an organization's accomplishments of the past year.

II. To clarify the organization's mission.

III. To prepare objectives and action steps for major organizational efforts in the next year.

Group Size

Eight to twelve persons who can assume the roles of the top management of an organization or organizational unit, including the chief executive officer.

Time Required

Approximately one to two hours.

Materials

I. At least six copies of the Reviewing Objectives and Strategies Sheet for each participant.

II. Newsprint and felt-tipped markers.

III. Masking tape.

Physical Setting

One large room furnished with a work table, chairs, and easel for the newsprint. Smaller rooms, furnished similarly, for individual or small-group work are helpful but not necessary.

Process

Step I. Overview (five min.)
The facilitator reviews the goals of the activity and indicates that these goals will serve as the agenda for the session and that the majority of the time will be spent on Goal III.

Step II. Review of Accomplishments (20 min.)
Explaining that planning must be based on some data, the facilitator invites the participants to review an organization's accomplishments for the past year. This organization can be one at which a participant works; one with which participants are familiar; or one from a case. The facilitator leads the group in brainstorming answers to the question "What have they accomplished during the past year?" The facilitator may ask prodding questions during this step and/or may post a list to encourage the partic-

Prepared by Cyril Mill. Reprinted from J. William Pfeiffer and John E. Jones (eds.), *The Annual for Facilitators, Trainers and Consultants*. 1982 University Associates, Inc., San Diego, CA pp. 65-68.

ipants to think in terms of such things as size, growth, profit, new organizational structures, new policies, new personnel, new technical resources, new linkages to outside groups, impact on the market or community, events (e.g., conferences), awards, and new learnings. All answers are listed on newsprint, and the list then is reviewed to eliminate redundancies and non-pertinent items. This could be done as an out-of-class assignment and reported in class.

Step III. Review of Shortcomings (20 min.)
The brainstorming procedure is repeated for the question "What have been the organization's failures or shortcomings during the past year?" This could be done as an out-of-class assignment. The list of organizational weaknesses is reviewed and narrowed down by the participants.

Step IV. Organizational Mission (30 min.)
The facilitator introduces the goal of clarifying and reaffirming the organizational mission by commenting on the following points:

1. A management team should be clear about and in agreement on the organization's mission.

2. All activities of an organization should help to achieve its mission.

3. A mission statement may be a phrase, a few sentences, or a lengthy document.

The facilitator announces that the group's task at this point is to state the organization's mission in a few sentences with which all agree. The facilitator serves as process and catalytic consultant during the group's discussion, which concludes with the writing of a mission statement on newsprint. Guidelines for the discussion may include:

1. State a *goal* rather than *operations*. A mission is more related to purpose than it is to activities.

2. A statement can be too broad or too narrow, thus limiting its usefulness. Avoid high-sounding generalities as well as specifics.

3. The statement should distinguish this organization from others.

4. Throughout the discussion, be alert to problems of interpretation or emphasis and work to clarify and rationalize these differences.

Step V. Preparing Objectives (30 min.)
The facilitator explains that the third goal, to prepare objectives and action steps for the next year, will be accomplished in two phases. In the first phase, which will take about thirty minutes, the participants will work individually on familiar material; in the second phase, the group members will work together in planning new organizational efforts.

The facilitator gives each participant six copies of the Reviewing Objectives and Strategies Sheet and instructs the participants that they may either work individually or consult freely with one another and that their task is to prepare as many objectives and strategies as they can, limiting themselves to *present operations and ongoing tasks*. The facilitator states that the emphasis of the activity is on quantity of ideas rather than on technicalities and reminds the group members that an objective is simply a statement of intention, whereas strategies are statements of steps that one will take to reach the objective. After thirty minutes, the participants are directed to tape their Reviewing Objectives and Strategies Sheets to newsprint sheets and to post them around the room so that everyone can walk around and read them.

Step VI. Summarization (20 min.)
The group reviews the statements, summarizing and categorizing wherever possible, and prepares an initial statement of goals and objectives.

Variations

I. If the group has difficulty in working through an issue during Step VI, the facilitator can direct the participants to form three groups and announce that the task for each group is to prepare three charts as follows:

1. Chart I. State the issue or the problem.
   a. What do they do well?
   b. What do they do poorly?

2. Chart II.
   a. Write a pessimistic statement that describes their approach to _____.
   b. Write an optimistic statement that describes their approach to _____.

3. Chart III.
   a. What objectives must be established to move from the pessimistic statement to the optimistic one? List three to five objectives that are clear and measurable.
   b. What strategies must be followed to accomplish each objective? List as many as are needed and indicate the resources that are needed.

II. If a block of time devoted to "thinking about the future" would be more productive than steps 5 or 6, the following procedure can be used:

1. The facilitator comments that even though the future is unpredictable, it can be useful to ask "What might happen?" and "How would they cope?"

2. The facilitator divides the participants into three groups, distributes four sheets of newsprint and felt-tipped markers to each group, and gives the following instructions: "Your group's task for the next ten minutes is to identify four significant trends, internal or external to the organization, that could have an impact within five years on the organization. Consider the four trends as future problems with which your group will have to grapple. Write a trend or problem at the top of each of the sheets of newsprint."

3. Each group is directed to give two of its newsprint sheets to each of the other groups. Each group now has four new problems with which to work. The facilitator then gives the following instructions: "Identify strategies to cope with each of the problems you have received. Be as imaginative as you wish, but do not assume that you will have unlimited resources of money or personnel. Write your solutions for each problem on the sheet of newsprint." (Forty minutes.)

4. The facilitator suggests that, as each solution is presented, the members feel free to cheer and clap to show approval of a solution as well as to boo and hiss to show their disapproval.

Reviewing Objectives
and Strategies Sheet

1. Objective: (What is your intention; what do you plan to achieve? What end result do you want?)

2. Mission relationship: (What is the relationship of this objective to the organizational mission?)

3. Strategies: (What action steps will be necessary to reach the objective? If you are not the person to take these steps, identify the person who is.)

   a.

   b.

   c.

   d.

4. Who will be responsible?

5. Resources needed: (If money or people or other resources are needed for this item, indicate them here.)

7
All The President's Men

John Henry is usually an optimist, but on the afternoon of March 4, 1986, his mood was as bleak as the late-winter Washington weather. He had just left a boisterous hearing on Capitol Hill, and the realization was sinking in that his company, then only five years old, might die long before it could ever bring a product to market.

Henry had known from the start that biotechnology was a tough business. The science was exotic. Technological dead ends would appear frequently. The burn rate of his venture capital would be be high. At best, profits were a decade away. Still, by 1986 Crop Genetics International was looking at a promising future. Henry's "gene jockeys" were developing a plant vaccine that could, if it worked as planned, eventually replace many chemical pesticides.

Henry was pursuing the same kind of radical change in farming as had his distant ancestor Cyrus McCormick, who invented the reaping machine in 1831 and commercialized it by founding International Harvester Corp. McCormick had carried the industrial revolution to the farm; now, Henry was helping to usher in the next great wave of change through biotechnology.

The newer technology, though, was charged with the kind of danger and controversy that had never touched McCormick's invention. The reaper was a mechanical device that greatly increased the productivity of human labor; Henry's product is a biological agent that carries the seeds of both growth and destruction. And it is that very real threat of destruction—what unintended perils might arise from the release of new biological agents into the environment?—that has raised public concern to such a pitch that it could bring down Henry's company.

It didn't help that the biotech industry was shooting itself in the foot. The hearing that day had been called by the oversight subcommittee of the House Science, Space and Technology Committee to investigate a company named Advanced Genetic Sciences Inc. (AGS). In November 1985 AGS had been granted the first permit from the Environmental Protection Agency for a test "release" of a genetically engineered organism contained in a product called Frostban, which gave strawberries greater resistance to frost damage.

But the *Washington Post* had reported that

Written by Jay Finegan. Reprinted with permission, *Inc.* magazine, February, 1989. Copyright © 1989 by Goldhirsh Group, Inc., 38 Commercial Wharf, Boston, MA 02110.

long before acquiring its EPA approval, AGS had injected the test bacterium into more than 45 fruit trees on the rooftop of its Oakland, Calif., headquarters. When the news broke, the EPA suspended AGS's license and levied a $20,000 fine. (The Frostban tests were later conducted by scientists in protective suits and masks.) The incident crystallized public suspicion that biotech companies were dangerously out of control, ethically dubious, and poorly regulated. Could they, as some critics warned, unleash some deadly new organism, an Adromeda strain?

John Henry was hardly an innocent in the Byzantine drama of Washington politics. He had spent three years on the staff of the Senate Foreign Relations Committee after graduating from Harvard College in 1971. But he wasn't prepared for the spectacle that unfolded before him in the hearing room that March day. The place was jammed with environmental activists, EPA officials, and journalists, and the atmosphere was chaotic.

Medical biotech is regulated by the Food and Drug Administration. But the EPA was trying to cope with the agricultural side of the industry with regulations aimed at chemicals; it had not devised any long-term policy for the release of new life forms into the environment.

By the time the hearing ended, some members of Congress were talking about creating a brand-new regulatory system for agricultural biotech. Crop Genetics might not survive several years in regulatory limbo. With a dwindling supply of venture capital and a business plan that allowed no time to spare, Henry reckoned he could be bankrupt before his technology ever got out of the gate. "My overwhelming feeling as I left that hearing was fear," he recalls. "Everything we had worked for since 1981 could go down the tubes."

It was then that Henry decided on an unusual strategy. By and large, U.S. industry and the regulatory system regard each other with mutual hostility. But Henry decided to consider the EPA not an adversary but a partner; environmental activists were to be regarded as "a fourth branch of government." Government relations

would become just another business discipline, like marketing or research. And the dominant discipline at that: for the foreseeable future, government relations would be the business of Crop Genetics.

Three weeks after the hearing, Henry walked into the Washington office of a Seattle-based law firm called Perkins Coie to see William D. Ruckelshaus.

Ruckelshaus is a veteran on the Washington scene. He has been EPA administrator twice, first in 1970, when the agency was new, and again in 1983, when it was struggling to regain credibility in the wake of the Rita Lavelle perjury trials. In between, he was deputy U.S. attorney general. In March 1986 he was back in private life. Henry figured if anyone understood the regulatory zeitgeist, had stature and credibility, and knew how to deal with the government, that person was Bill Ruckelshaus.

Philip Angell, who had served as Ruckelshaus's chief of staff at the EPA, was a consultant to Perkins Coie. As a confidant of his old boss, he attended that first meeting. "Henry believed very deeply in what he was doing, and he asked us how to deal with a regulatory situation that was fraught with emotionalism," says Angell.

Ruckelshaus and Angell concluded that what Henry needed was good advice on sidestepping the political perils befalling other biotech outfits. They decided to put together a brain trust of Washington wise men.

In the annals of entrepreneurship, this may have been the most high-powered advisory panel ever assembled. Henry recruited Douglas M. Costle, who had headed the EPA in the Carter Administration. Ruckelshaus brought in Robert M. Teeter, a prominent Republican pollster who in 1988 would become co-chairman of the George Bush Presidential transition team. And he enlisted his old Justice Department boss, former attorney general Elliot L. Richardson, who has held a record number of Cabinet posts—Defense, Commerce, and Health, Education and Welfare.

It might seem odd that a small company with no profits could attract such heavy-gauge talent, but there was a certain logic to it. Ruckelshaus, for instance, had been a director of Monsanto Co., a chemical industry giant. Richardson, for his part, was intrigued by the idea that the plant vaccine could trim the use of chemical pesticides, a leading cause of groundwater pollution, food contamination, and bird kills. (Some 1.4 billion pounds of chemicals are dumped on U.S. farms every year, twice the amount applied just 25 years ago.) Crop Genetics paid the members $1,000 for each of the formal brainstorming sessions the committee held and gave them stock options in the company.

Henry required their advice to achieve one clear strategic objective. Because his plant vaccine is designed to kill insects, it is classified as an insecticide. And he could not conduct the first, all-important field trial without an experimental-use permit from the EPA. It was absolutely critical that the company get that permit and do its test on time.

The test was scheduled for summer 1988. The company planned to conduct it on just an acre of corn at its farm on Maryland's Chesapeake Bay. A second round of tests the following summer, to be held in the Midwest, would be far more extensive. Both field trials would have to succeed before the EPA would register the product and sales could begin. Henry aimed to introduce his product in the fall of 1991 in the United States and France, Europe's largest corn producer, envisioning a market of about $100 million. He planned to market it for use on the world's three major crops: first corn, then rice and wheat.

The EPA requires pesticide tests that prove safety. In this case, the safety question centered on the difficult issue of "spread." Could the organism move from target plants to other plants?

Henry was reasonably sure they could not. After all, his biopesticidal vaccine grew inside the plant. An organism that operated inside plants was containable, at least in theory. And anyway, lab tests showed that the microbe could survive only in the sap of living plants. Outside, in soil or water, it died.

Furthermore, the biopesticide in question is a benign, naturally occurring organism called Bt that has been used for decades with no ill effects on mammals, fish, birds, or nontargeted insects. What made the new product unique — and patentable—was its delivery system. The company had found an obscure type of bacterium called an endophyte. Lab work showed that it could be made to multiply through cell division inside more than 80 kinds of plants, from pansies to pumpkins. By splicing a single Bt gene into this endophyte, Crop Genetics scientists could "grow" pesticides inside plants — something nobody had ever attempted before.

Henry believed that farmers would clamor for the product. After all, chemical pesticides affect farmers more than anyone else. They contaminate the water they drink and the air they breathe. This new product promised to be safer and less expensive. And consumers would approve because it would solve the problem of pesticide residue on fruits and vegetables.

"The beauty of the system is that it requires virtually no manufacturing," says Peter Carlson, Crop Genetics' cofounder and chief scientist. "We enjoy a huge material advantage over chemical insecticides. Once our product is inside a plant, it acts like a tiny microbial factory, manufacturing pesticides around the clock. Only 20 pounds will stop the European corn borer— our first target pest—from damaging Iowa's 10-million-acre corn crop."

The corn borer, the nation's greatest uncontrolled corn pest, infests more than half of America's 70 million acres of corn, inflicting some $400 million in damage every year. Acting like a biological Roto-Rooter, it eats its way up and down the stalk until the plant grows so weak it simply blows over in the wind. For Crop Genetics, a vaccine for corn was to be just the beginning. But in the spring of 1986, the company's fate hinged on one thing: obtaining the EPA permit to conduct that field test. "Without that," Henry says, "we were dead meat."

There was, however, an interesting political wrinkle at work. Given the electrified atmosphere surrounding biotech, the EPA was unlikely to issue the permit without the approval of the country's main environmental groups. For Henry, the uncertainty was nerve-racking. Political risks were piling up on top of scientific risks. It was a hell of a way to have to run a business.

The essence of our strategy was 'no surprises to anybody,' Angell recalls. "We wanted to involve all the pertinent people as early as possible, to touch every base in sight. We wanted to contact anyone who could conceivably be interested in this experiment—to tell them who we were and what the company was doing."

And always there was an eye to the inevitability that, sooner or later, Jeremy Rifkin and his Foundation on Economic Trends would take a lively interest in the company's plans. Rien was not to be taken lightly. Through sheer force of personality and a charismatic stage presence, he had made himself a force to be reckoned with in biotech.

Working through the courts, Rifkin had stalled the Frostban tests for several years. Later, by threatening to sue the EPA, he had caused the agency to reject a permit application from Monsanto. Rifkin was waging biotech battles nationwide, with an opposition to the new science that amounted to a crusade. He almost certainly could be counted on to fight Crop Genetics.

Richardson, though, was not intimidated. "The most effective way to deal with the Rifkins of this world is to be in a situation in which you're hiding nothing, to be prepared to answer any fair questions," he says. "And if people then attack you in some way that seems to call your good faith into question, they weaken their own position, not yours." He advised a policy of maximum disclosure of the company's work.

In the summer of 1986, the federal government decided that it wouldn't need a new law for biotech — the threat that had lingered after that congressional hearing in March. Instead, it devised the so-called "combined coordinated framework for biotechnology." The idea was to ensure that existing regulatory standards meshed to present a unified federal approach.

This was a welcome development. Instead of operating on uncertain regulatory terrain, Henry knew the rules. But as it turned out, the new system placed yet another hurdle in his path. He was no longer dealing with just the EPA. He now

had to obtain a separate test permit from the U.S. Department of Agriculture's Animal and Plant Health Inspection Service (APHIS).

Henry accepted this burden with equanimity. "You can't have a wild reaction to regulation," he says. "You have to take the world as you find it, and make it work for you. That is the tremendous insight that Bill Ruckelshaus and Elliot Richardson helped me with."

For openers, he sent his top scientists down to EPA headquarters to meet with the agency's pesticide specialists, the people who actually made the decisions. This was in mid-1986, more than a year before the company applied for its first permit.

"We explained our technology and asked them to tell us what the safety issues were," he says. "We did the lab tests, and then went back to them. Each time, we narrowed the areas of concern about our biopesticide. Does it spread? Is it harmful? Is it in the food? We entered a process of first getting a consensus on the issues, and then going out to get the data they wanted."

Next Henry turned his attention to politicians and environmental activists in Maryland, where the test would be held. It was critical to have local opinion makers on his side to offset the not-in-my-backyard syndrome. To orchestrate this delicate operation he brought in yet another high-powered advisor, Russell "Tim" Baker Jr.

Baker, a product of Harvard Law School, had been a partner in the Baltimore firm of Piper & Marbury. In 1986 he had narrowly lost a bid to become attorney general of Maryland. A Democrat, he had enjoyed unanimous support from the state's environmental groups, for whom he'd done a great deal of pro bono legal work. He also had strong connections in state politics, stemming from eight years as a federal prosecutor, including four as U.S. Attorney for Maryland.

After the election, Baker had worked with two of the venture capital firms backing Crop Genetics. Once he understood that the new technology could help eliminate chemical pesticides, he applied himself fervently to the company's cause.

"John asked me to take him around and introduce him to a series of groups," he says. "We wanted everybody to know about us before they read about us in the *Washington Post*. We were afraid the reporters would quote Rifkin saying how horrible this project was. So we talked to community associations and PTAs. We held a town meeting. We talked to local politicians, people in the governor's office, the state's U.S. senators and representatives—some 40 politicians in all. We explained that the technology was safe, that they shouldn't be worried. Their eyes just glazed over.

"But in talking to friends, I happened to point out that if this technology works, it's going to replace pesticides, which is one of the largest unsolved problems in the pollution of the Chesapeake Bay. John had been hesitant about bringing this up for fear of arousing the competitive juices of the chemical giants. But when you talk about eliminating chemical pesticides, you're hitting apple pie and motherhood. So we quickly started including that in our presentation."

On a Saturday morning in early December 1987, Baker made his major strategic move. He appeared at a meeting at the Baltimore home of Ajax Eastman, a prominent environmentalist and member of the Maryland Conservation Council. Among the more than 50 guests were leaders of the local chapters of the Sierra Club, the Nature Conservancy, and others.

"I knew this was the group that would be Rifkin's natural allies," Baker says. "Our strategy all along had been to isolate Rifkin. I knew that if this group analyzed this technology objectively, they would not ally with him on this one."

For this presentation, Baker brought in Peter Carlson, the mastermind behind the new product. Carlson, a former college professor, is as much a salesman as a scientist when he speaks, taking off his jacket, pacing around, gesturing emphatically. At first the audience was skeptical. For 90 minutes, Carlson explained the plant-vaccine technology. Even as he spoke, Baker could sense attitudes changing. He knew things were looking up when Malcolm E. King, founder of a national conservation outfit called Save Our Streams, asked the first question. He wanted to know how he could buy some Crop Genetics stock.

When it came to the national environmental groups, the company employed a similar strategy. Three of the most prominent organizations concerned with biotechnology—the National Wildlife Federation, the Environmental Defense Fund, and the National Audubon Society—had been heavily funded by the Joyce Foundation of Chicago to analyze the implications of biotech for the Farm Belt. National Wildlife, which received $210,000 over three years, had gone further, establishing the National Biotechnology Policy Center to study the new industry.

Center director Margaret Mellon, an attorney and molecular biologist Ph.D., sums up the concerns. "Society must identify the environmental problems raised by biotechnology before they occur, not after," she says. "Otherwise, we could confront in 50 years the biotech equivalents of hazardous-waste dumps, greenhouse gases, and pesticides that persist in the environment and devastate wildlife."

In keeping with Richardson's advice of "maximum disclosure," Henry dispatched Carlson to these three groups and had him bring a 500-page document that described the company's work in mind-boggling detail. It paid off. The Audubon Society praised the company, telling the EPA that "such openness and cooperation are rare, and reflect well upon the company's sensitivity to environmental and public concerns."

All this was taking an enormous amount of Henry's time and energy. On the one hand, he had the normal challenges of managing a growing company—he was up to almost 100 employees. On the other, several tough scientific problems still had to be solved, a big technological gamble. As he puts it, "I had to move a lot of pieces down the chessboard at the same time." And if the EPA refused to grant the permit, it was checkmate.

He had, however, anticipated these demands and had styled his management structure accordingly. "I have things pretty well staffed, so I'm not needed day to day," he says. "I can go where the problems are. I have really talented people, and I delegate."

But there was no denying that lobbying was complicating progress on one vital front. For the field trial, the company planned to inject each corn plant with the recombinant microbe. For commercial use, however, the organism will have to be inoculated into seed corn, a process that requires new technology.

Crop Genetics would need seed-company partners to help invent and install seed-inoculation machines; no such machines existed. But, as Henry says, "It would have been absurd to ask seed companies to team up with us for that kind of work if we couldn't successfully launch even this small-scale test." So this fundamental component of the business—marketing and distribution—had to be put on hold.

Money, at least, wasn't a pressing problem. True, Henry had spent almost $14 million in venture capital. But early in 1987 the company had gone public. Ruckelshaus had spoken on the company's behalf to investors in New York City. Richardson appeared when the road show played in Switzerland. With their help, the offering brought in $23 million, enough to fuel the firm for two more years.

But Henry, who had spent two years as a Wall Street securities lawyer, was already planning a second offering for 1988. And he knew that if his permit application failed, he could forget that.

Honing yet another prong in his offensive, Henry emphasized the public interest. On Richardson's counsel, he approached the Agricultural Research Service (ARS), a prestigious test facility of the Department of Agriculture. Scientists at the ARS-operated experimental farm in Beltsville, Md., agreed to collaborate with the company in testing the vaccine by planting an acre of test corn.

The collaboration benefited Crop Genetics. ARS had special labs and expertise that the company lacked. The government scientists would publish their studies, which Henry hoped would augment the company's own test analysis. Teaming up with ARS would also give him the imprimatur of government sanction and help expedite the APHIS permit. It was a brilliant move.

In December 1987 Crop Genetics formally filed its permit application with the EPA, a massive document three inches thick and crammed with scientific data.

Waiting for the permit was not uneventful. In March, all hell broke loose because of a mistake of the company's making.

The company's PR firm, Fenton Communications, Inc., issued a press release inviting Washington reporters to a breakfast briefing at the Hay-Adams Hotel featuring Henry, Carlson, and Elliot Richardson, by now a director. The idea was to explain the company's work so that when the permit was issued, the press would have the background. It seemed harmless.

But David Fenton, seeking a sexy angle, couldn't resist inserting this little nugget: "The principal chemical pesticide now used against the European corn borer is Furadan, which a recent EPA study said could be responsible for as many as 2.4 million deaths of birds nationwide [including] as many as 13 bald eagle deaths since 1985 in the Chesapeake Bay area, where the national bird has been making a comeback."

Now as it happened, Furadan was manufactured by FMC Corp., which was represented in Washington by Harold Himmelman, one of the country's top pesticide lawyers. In fact, he was the very same attorney Henry had hired a year earlier to represent Crop Genetics before the EPA. FMC was not amused by Fenton's "chemical bashing," and in the dustup that ensued, Himmelman dropped Crop Genetics in favor of his much larger client.

"Here it was March, less than two months before what we viewed as the climactic lawsuit with Rifkin that we'd have to win fast, and there we were without a law firm," says Tim Baker. "It was like the eighth inning and the team quits. John told me, 'Go out and find a new team, we're up next.'"

Baker frantically began interviewing law firms. Oddly enough, he was on good terms with Himmerman. They had been classmates and lacrosse teammates at Williams College in the 1960s. And Himmelman recommended that Baker try the law firm of Weil, Gotshal, & Manges, where he met Jim Davis, a young partner.

Davis turned out to be yet another Washington insider who could make water flow uphill.

Not only did he have a scientific background — a Ph.D. in chemistry from California Institute of Technology — but he also had spent two years as special assistant to John Moore, then the EPA's assistant administrator for pesticides and toxic substances. Davis knew the EPA, biotech, and regulatory nuances like nobody's business. Baker signed him up immediately. (Henry later hired him as general in-house counsel.)

In April the three major environmental groups submitted to the EPA their comments concerning the permit application. Not one of them would fight it. Only Rifkin weighed in with an opposing view, arguing that the delivery microbe is known to cause a stunting disease that could spread to other plants.

"Spread" was something that had also troubled Rebecca Goldburg of the Environmental Defense Fund. "I'm concerned that it might infect wild plants," she says. "I don't want to make wild plants resistant to the insects that feed on them. I mean, wild plants are the basis of the food chain." Still, given the containment procedures the company planned for its field test, she felt confident that spread would, if anything, be minimal.

As the action moved into May, Davis went into crash mode to prepare for a Rifkin legal challenge. If Rifkin sued the EPA for issuing a permit, the Justice Department would represent the agency. But Baker was skeptical. "Having been a deputy assistant attorney general there, I knew the department could get itself fouled up," he says. "I didn't want to count on them to carry the load. I thought we should get ready ourselves."

By mid-May the Crop Genetics team was set for combat. "If Rifkin sued, he'd run into a buzz saw," Baker says. "We were prepared to fight in state court or federal court. We tried to figure out every angle Rifkin might use to come after us, then have a strategy ready for it. If he filed, we'd file our papers the next day.

"We couldn't afford to lose any time. Rifkin couldn't beat us on the merits, but he wouldn't have to. All he'd have to do was get some judge confused long enough and it would end up being mid-July—it would be too late to plant the test crop."

In late May, the EPA and APHIS issued the two experimental-use permits. It was an event of such moment that it made the "CBS Evening News." Crop Genetics was the only biotech firm in the country to have made it through the first round of regulatory hoops without being delayed or stalled.

Rifkin didn't sue. He and his staff attorney, Andrew Kimbrell, concluded that they didn't have much of a case after all—not this time, anyway. But that didn't soften the blow when John Henry opened the legal bills: Baker's came to $50,000.

"The cost of this thing was just incredible," Baker says. "And how do you price all the time that John Henry and Peter Carlson put in, and their scientists? It turned out that we could afford it, and we did everything right. We had played error-free ball, and we were lucky. But what happens to a company that isn't lucky, or doesn't play it so well?"

At this writing, in December, Crop Genetics has harvested its test corn and is compiling the results. Mind you, all this had nothing to do with proving that the product will work. It was only to show that the microbes didn't spread into surrounding plants. So far, says Henry, "things look good."

Already, he is preparing another application to conduct large-scale held tests next summer in the Midwest with his four new seed-company partners. They include DeKalb-Pfizer Genetics, the second-largest producer and marketer of field-corn seed in the world, and Rogers Brothers, the largest sweet corn-seed company. Those tests, Henry hopes, will demonstrate that the product's delivery system works.

The only thing he knows for sure is that this time around the action will be more bruising. "We'll be there for this one," says Andrew Kimbrell, Rifkin's attorney. Rifkin himself pledges that the first company that tries to test recombinant microbes on a large scale will face "years of battle in the courts and in Congress."

The big environmental groups also will be much more aggressive next time. "We thought there was very little risk associated with a small-scale test of this organism," says Margaret Mellon. "We based that largely on the containment features. But we are not as sanguine about the large-scale use of the product."

John Henry waxes whimsical about all this. "Sometimes I wonder why I ever got into such a complicated business," he muses. But he knows why—a huge new market beckons, just as it did for his ancestor, Cyrus McCormick. Still, he says, "It's a long, long march."

8

Beer Brouhaha

Trend Worries Little Guys

Pleasantville, N.J. - One day, five stops, Robert Beale, merchandising manager for Coors beer distributor Kramer Beverage Co., chats with customers as he replaces banners, straightens pallets of beer cases on discount-store floors and puts up table tents and posters at bars.

Across the country, at LaCosta's Liquor Store in Sea Isle City, Kramer sales representative Betsy Ludman cheerfully fulfills a request for a Coors Extra Gold keg sign, taking down a competing Anheuser-Busch Co.'s sign in the process. And Jerry Sanford, one of Kramer's draft technicians, stops at the Good Guy's Pub at a quiet rural-highway intersection here to banter behind the bar, clean draft-beer lines and shine levers on the Coors taps.

It's another day of details on the front lines of the nation's beer wars. While new brands and glitzy advertising campaigns grab attention, it is the wholesale distributors like Kramer that mobilize over placements of tap handles and inches of prime shelf space, local promotions and special services to customers. And as operatives in the field, they gather crucial market intelligence to filter back to the big breweries' marketing gurus.

Darwinian Struggle

This detail patrol is critical to small bars and retailers, but it no longer can be taken for granted. The nation's beer distributors now are not just jostling one another for shelf space, they are also pitted against their own brewers and retailers for survival.

Today's deep-discount warehouse clubs and big grocery chains exert considerable marketplace leverage. As they pressure brewers to cut their costs, the middlemen—the wholesale distributors—are obvious targets. The U.S. beer distribution system now is under attack legally, politically and economically. Distributors' only hope is that legislators in Florida and a court in San Francisco believe the current system is integral to maintaining a variety of retail outlets for consumers, according to industry observers.

"The alternative is that we all go the Sam's direction," says Charles Kramer, owner of Kramer Beverage, referring to Wal-Mart Stores Inc.'s discount club stores. "It would mean lower prices, sure, but fewer and fewer retail outlets."

Creating a Middleman

The three-tier system of beer making and marketing—brewer, distributor and retailer—was created by Congress in 1933 to keep brewers from gaining control over the sale of beer to the public, as they did before Prohibition. The mandated middleman role led to the establishment of today's 3,000 distributors, mostly small businessmen with fewer than 30 employees, which manage the $24 billion business of delivering beer. A brewer may legally own a distributor—and some do—but distributors cannot own retailers.

Today, battles to change that system are being fought in California and Florida, trendsetting states in the beer business where brewers seeking to cut costs in a stagnant market are bypassing their regular distributors, which serve small as well as big customers, and begin to provide beer exclusively to big retailers through special distributors. The next step, if the courts allow, could be direct deliveries from brewers to retailers. "It's an antiquated system," argues Donald Beaver, president of the California Grocers Association. "Eventually it must be changed."

For Mr. Kramer, 51, who runs Kramer Beverage with his wife Lynn, 50, these developments hint like faraway thunder of an approaching storm. While his big customers have yet to bypass him, he knows they would, if given the chance. "The big retailer could live without the wholesalers," he warns, "but no one else could. If the big accounts disappeared, I don't know how I could survive."

Worried Small Retailers

If he doesn't, then neither will his smallest customers—bars, taverns and restaurants, venues whose deliveries look more like trunkloads than truckloads. With their volume of business, big retailers have the economic power to command direct deliveries from brewers at heavily discounted prices if that becomes clearly legal. Linda Scanlon, manager of the bayside Deauville Inn near Atlantic City, N.J., doesn't. "Who would deliver to me if I only need two kegs a week?" she asks.

Further, if direct deliveries from brewers to retailers help cut the big package stores' costs, and those savings are passed on to customers, Mr. Kramer and industry experts wonder whether enough smaller stores would survive to keep the distribution business alive. "The neighborhood package store has as great a future as the family farmer," says Mark Rodman, a Boston attorney and industry consultant.

The current three-tier system has its obvious failings. The practice of loading beer onto brewery trucks, unloading it at distributor warehouses, putting it back on distributor trucks and then sending it out to retailers may be too costly in today's penny-pinching retail environment. For customers who can buy entire truckloads, direct deliveries from the brewery make more sense. Computers, able to transmit retail inventory data to brewers, make the sales and inventory-tracking functions of the distributor superfluous we well—at least for the big retailers. More and more retailers are ordering private-label beers—and don't need any marketing and inventory help from wholesalers to sell them.

The brewers each have hundreds of distributors granted exclusive territories as small as a single town or as big as several counties (except in Indiana, the only state where exclusive territories are prohibited). For distributors with popular brands like Coors, exclusivity long made life easy. With no place else to go for beers that were in demand, retailers were forced to pay the wholesalers' price and take whatever service was offered. For years, for example, New York distributors piled beer on the sidewalks outside customers' stores, refusing to haul it inside, retailers say.

But, with as much as 90% of beer being sold at discount in some markets, beer has become more like a commodity, and brands have become less important. Distributors have been forced to make more and more concessions on price and service. As a result, profits as a percentage of sales declined to 1.6% in 1990, the most recent figures available, from 2.5% in 1982, according to Barsby & Associates, a beer- industry market-research firm in Molalla, Ore.

A crazy quilt of state laws hinders distributors from banding together into more cost-efficient national networks. Some states won't allow distributors to offer customers volume discounts; the rules governing contests, promotions, advertising and bottle deposits differ from state to state, making multistate distributorships a logistical nightmare.

Forced to compete with the huge marketing budgets of industry leaders Anheuser-Busch, Adolph Coors Co. and Miller Brewing Co., smaller brewers seek out ways to cut costs in order to keep product prices down. Thus, struggling G. Heileman Brewing Co., which produces a host of largely regional beers, and S&P Co., brewer of declining old-line brands Pabst and Falstaff, decided to bypass their regular distributors in California and ship to their biggest customers—chains such as Safeway, Von's and Liquor Barn—through special distiributors that sell beer only to large retailers and at a sharp discount.

Lutz Issleib, executive vice president of S&P, said that the change in Pabst and Falstaff distribution in California wasn't his idea but was the brainchild of a distributor. But he isn't arguing with the results. Sales of Pabst in California have gone from 6,000 barrels in 1986 to 256,000 barrels in 1993, largely because of the distributor's sales to chain stores, he says.

Mike Sadler, merchandising manager for Liquor Barn Inc., San Francisco, says that because of Heileman's program, he was able this summer to reduce the price of the Henry Weinhard brand to $5.99 a 12-pack from $7.50 or $8.

"It's pretty simple," explains Mr. Sadler, "You're looking for a competitive edge, a way to grow your piece of a shrinking pie, and the brewers saw an opportunity to provide us with a better price." But the brewers' regular distributors say these "special distributors" are a sham, a way to get around the letter of the law mandating separate distributors. Twenty-two Heileman distributors have filed suit against the brewer in a federal court in San Francisco, alleging that the brewer abrogated their exclusive contracts to deliver beer. Heileman won't comment on the suit.

Similarly, some large retail chains in Florida have contracted with brewers for beer packaged under private labels to be delivered through special discount distributors, knocking the brewers' regular distributors out of the loop. The distributors' state trade group, in response, unsuccessfully sought legislation barring such deliveries from brewers to retail chains. "We got stepped on," says Buddy Griddley, president of the Florida Bar Industry Association. "I'm not sure where we're headed now."

Where they're headed could be for radical change. In speeches and newsletters, all the major brewers have warned their distributors that they are under pressure to deliver beer directly to big retailers. Those retailers have a great deal of power—in California, for example, six chains control 40% of retail beer sales, the trade publication Beer Marketer's Insights reports. Industry experts say that if the court in California upholds Heileman's new delivery system, the practice surely will spread. "The major brewers know they've got to change," says Mr. Beaver, of the California grocers group. "It's happening today in all other products."

Coors' 24 distribution centers around the country are perfectly suited to deliver directly to retailers, says Mr. Rodman, the industry consultant. All it would take to start the trend, adds Ed Peterson, general manager of Coors' Denver distributor, is for one of the big brewers to lose significant market share in the pivotal California or Florida territories to a smaller competitor's discount-distribution system.

For Mr. Kramer, the possibility of losing the business founded by his grandfather in 1924 brings back unpleasant memories. The distributor, which employs 86 people full time at a big metal warehouse in this town just west of Atlantic City, saw his business nearly die once before over price wars. Regional beers such as Piers, Ballantine and Heileman products went into sharp decline in the 1980s, leaving Anheuser-Busch and Miller, a division of Phillip Morris Cos., as the industry leaders. Distributors were affected accordingly, and Kramer handled regionals.

So seven years ago, Mr. Kramer waged a year-long lobbying campaign to win an exclusive franchise from Coors, which was expanding sales into New Jersey. His application to the Golden, Colo., brewer included photos of 12 of his best trucks—he hid the clunkers—and of his 16-year-old son, Mark, whom he touted as the fourth generation of distributors in the Kramer family. Kramer Beverage got the franchise.

Without Coors, Mr. Kramer says, "we wouldn't have lasted five years." Now, he has doubled the size of his warehouse and sells more than three million cases of beer a year, well above distributors' national average of less than a million cases.

While Kramer customers were glad to get Coors products, they haven't all been pleased with the distributor. "It would be nice if you could buy from another wholesaler," grouses Russell Waddell, the unhappy owner of Cherry Hill Liquors in Cherry Hill, N.J. Over the busy Fourth of July weekend, Mr. Waddell notes, Kramer didn't make its usual Thursday delivery deadline. In fact, the beer didn't arrive until the following Wednesday, and Mr. Waddell ran out of beer during one of the biggest beer-drinking weekends of the year. "Doesn't he understand I'm a customer of his, he's not a customer of mine?" Mr. Waddell fumes.

William Critchfield, Kramer's general manager, says all distributors had trouble keeping up with the holiday demand, although he concedes that most retailers got better service than Mr. Waddell did. Mr. Waddell's complaints notwithstanding, a large part of Kramer Beverage employee hours goes to keeping small customers like him happy, attending to minutiae that occupy a distributor's life. Mr. Critchfield also points out that small retailers looking to buy directly from breweries would find that brewers don't offer the credit terms distributors do, and brewers don't find it economical to deliver partial truckloads.

But Kramer's biggest customers don't need that kind of attention, and it will be much harder to hang onto them if they can choose direct deliveries. Mr. Critchfield cites Canal's Discount Liquors in Williamstown, part of a large local chain, as an example. The store sells strictly on price, eschewing the promotional displays distributors like Kramer provide. And because of Canal's size, Kramer frequently puts up with minor indignities.

One day, the Kramer driver sat behind a Canal's store for four hours waiting for store employees to unload the truck. The customer earns a "forklift discount" for doing the unloading, but Mr. Critchfield says the discount agreement calls for customer unloading to be timely. "To us, that's 45 minutes," Mr. Critchfield says.

How eager are brewers to dump their distributors? Executives at most breweries decline to be interviewed on the subject, saying they don't want to take sides. But W. Leo Kiely, president of Coors, says his company isn't planning any direct deliveries. Still, he calls the California experiment by Heileman and S&P "a wake-up call to the industry that we'd better innovate. Wholesalers do a good job of serving bars and restaurants. But we really haven't addressed the issue of how to service the large retailers."

Indeed, at meetings with their distributors, brewers are sounding like they are the ones under attack, caught between loyalty to their distributors and the need to please the big retailers. Jack MacDonough, chairman of Miller, recently pledged his support for the three-tier system at a meeting with Miller wholesalers in Florida. He warned, however, that retailers were pressuring beer makers to change.

"We need the three-tier system," he said, according to a report in Beer Marketer's Insights. "I only wish we could come up with a way of supporting it more strongly without getting our retailers almost boycotting us if we do."

The Wall Street Journal
Monday, November 22, 1993

9

The Audubon Park Zoo: An Urban Eden

The Audubon Park Zoo was the focus of national concern in the early 1970s, with well-documented stories of animals kept in conditions that were variously termed an "animal ghetto,"[1] "the New Orleans antiquarium," and even "an animal concentration camp."[2] In 1971, the Bureau of Governmental Research recommended a $5.6 million zoo improvement plan to the Audubon Park Commission and the City Council of New Orleans. The local Times Picayune commented on the new zoo: "It's not going to be quite like the Planet of the Apes situation in which the apes caged and studied human beings but something along those broad general lines."[3] The new zoo confined people to bridges and walkways while the animals roamed amidst grass, shrubs, trees, pools, and fake rocks. The gracefully curving pathways, generously lined with luxuriant plants, gave the visitor a sense of being alone in a wilderness, although crowds of visitors might be only a few yards away.

The Decision

The Audubon Park Commission launched the $5.6-million development program, based on the Bureau of Governmental Research plan for the zoo, in March 1972. A bond issue and a property tax dedicated to the zoo were put before the voters, with renovations to begin the day following passage. The New Orleans City Planning Commission finally approved the master plan for the Audubon Park Zoo in September 1973. But the institution of the master plan was far from smooth.

The Zoo Question Goes Public

A revenue-generating proposal was put to the voters by Mayor Moon Landrieu on November 7, 1972. When it passed by an overwhelming majority, serious discussions began about what

©1987, Claire J. Anderson, Old Dominion University, and Caroline Fisher, Loyola University, New Orleans. Used by permission. The authors wish to acknowledge the contributions of graduate students Martha McGraw Hamilton and Debbie Longo, who aided in research and contributed many helpful suggestions in developing the case. The case was designed for classroom discussion only. It was not meant to depict effective or ineffective administration.

EXHIBIT 9-1 The Audubon Park Zoo

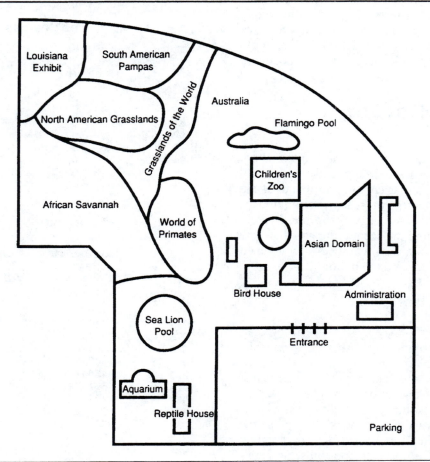

should be done. Over two dozen special interests were ultimately involved in choosing whether to renovate and expand the existing facilities or move to another site. Expansion became a major community controversy. Some residents opposed the zoo expansion, fearing that a "loss of green space" would affect the secluded character of the neighborhood. Others opposed the loss of what they saw as an attractive and educational facility.

Most of the opposition came from the zoo's affluent neighbors. Zoo Director John Moore ascribed the criticism to "a select few people who have the money and power to make a lot of noise." He went on to say that "[T]he real basis behind the problem is that the neighbors who

live around the edge of the park have a selfish concern because they want the park as their private backyard."[4] Legal battles over the expansion plans continued until early 1976. At that time, the Fourth Circuit Court of Appeals ruled that the expansion was legal.[5] An out-of-court agreement with the zoo's neighbors (The Upper Audubon Association) followed shortly.

Physical Facilities

The expansion of the Audubon Park Zoo took it from 14 to 58 acres (see Exhibit 9-1). Under the master plan developed by the Bureau of Governmental Research, the zoo was laid out in geographic sections: the Asian Domain, the World

of Primates, the World's Grasslands, the Savan-
nah, the North American Prairie, the South
American Pampas, and the Louisiana Swamp.
Additional exhibits included the Wisner Discov-
ery Zoo, the Sea Lion exhibit, and the Flight
Cage.

Purpose of the Zoo

The main outward purpose of the Audubon Park
Zoo was entertainment. Many of its promotional
efforts were aimed at creating an image of the
zoo as an entertaining place to visit. Obviously,
such a campaign was necessary to attract visitors
to the zoo. Behind the scenes, the zoo also preserved and bred many animal species, conducted
research, and educated the public.

New Directions

One of the first significant changes made was the
institution of an admission charge in 1972. Admission to the zoo had been free before the
adoption of the renovation plan. The initial purpose behind instituting the admission charge
ostensibly was to prevent vandalism,[6] but the
need for additional income was also apparent.
Despite the institution of and subsequent increases in admission charges, admissions increased dramatically (see Exhibit 9-2).

Operations

Friends of the Zoo

The Friends of the Zoo was formed in 1974 and
incorporated in 1975 with 400 original members. The stated purpose of the Friends was to
increase support and awareness of the Audubon
Park Zoo. Initially, the Friends of the Zoo tried
to increase interest and commitment to the zoo,
but its activities grew dramatically over the years
until it was involved in funding, operating, and
governing the zoo.

EXHIBIT 9-2 Admissions

Admission Charges

Year	Adult	Child
1972	$0.75	$0.25
1978	1.00	0.50
1979	1.50	0.75
1980	2.00	1.00
1981	2.50	1.25
1982	3.00	1.50
1983	3.50	1.75
1984	4.00	2.00
1985	4.50	2.00
1986	5.00	2.50

Admissions

Year	Number of Paid Admissions	Number of Member Admissions
1972	163,000	
1973	310,000	
1974	345,000	
1975	324,000	
1976	381,000	
1977	502,000	
1978	456,000	
1979	561,000	
1980	707,000	
1981	741,000	
1982	740,339	78,950
1983	835,044	118,665
1984	813,025	128,538
1985	854,996	144,060
1986	915,492	187,119
1987	439,264*	93,327 *

*Through the end of the second quarter.
Source: The Audubon Park Zoo

The Friends of the Zoo had a 24-member
governing board. Elections were held every year
for six of the board members, who served staggered four-year terms. The board oversaw zoo
policies and set guidelines for memberships,
concessions, fund-raising, and marketing. Actual policy making and operations were controlled by the Audubon Park Commission, however,
which set zoo hours, admission prices, etc.

Through its volunteer, the Friends of the Zoo
staffed many of the zoo's programs. Members of

the Friends of the Zoo volunteered as "edZOO-cators," who were specially trained to conduct interpretive education programs, and "Zoo Area Patrollers," who provided general information about the geographic area of the zoo and helped with crowd control. Other volunteers assisted in the Commissary, Animal Health Care Center, and Wild Bird Rehabilitation Center, or helped with functions related to membership, public relations, graphics, clerical work, research, or horticulture.

Fund-Raising

The Audubon Park Zoo and the Friends of the Zoo raised funds through four major activities: Friends of the Zoo memberships, "Adopt an Animal," "Zoo-To-Do," and capital fund drives. Zoo managers from around the country came to the Audubon Park Zoo for tips on fundraising.

■ *Membership* Membership in the Friends of the Zoo was open to anyone. Even though membership fees increased over the years, as summarized in Exhibit 9-3, the number of members grew steadily, from the original 400 in 1974 to 33,000 in 1987. Membership allowed free entry to the Audubon Park Zoo and many other zoos around the United States. Participation in "Zoobilation" (an annual members-only evening celebration at the zoo) and the many volunteer programs described earlier were other benefits of membership.

Increasing membership required a special approach to marketing the zoo. Chip Weigand, director of marketing for the zoo, stated,

... [I]n marketing memberships, we try to encourage repeat visitations, the feeling that one can visit as often as one wants, the idea that the zoo changes from visit to visit and that there are good reasons to make one large payment or donation for a membership card, rather than paying for each visit.... [T]he overwhelming factor is a good zoo that people want to visit often, so that a membership makes good economical sense.

In 1985, the zoo announced a new member-

EXHIBIT 9-3 Membership Fees and Membership

Year	Family	Individual	Number Memberships
1979	$20	$10	1,000
1981	20	10	7,000
1982	20	10	11,000
1983	25	15	18,000
1984	30	15	22,000
1985	35	20	26,000
1986	40	20	30,000
1987	45	25	32,000
	45	25	33,000

Source: The Audubon Park Zoo

ship designed for businesses, the Audubon Zoo Curator Club, with four categories of membership: Bronze, $250; Silver, $500; Gold, $1,000; and Platinum, $2,500 and more.

■ *Concessions* The Friends of the Zoo took over the Audubon Park Zoo concessions for refreshments and gifts in 1976 through a public bidding process. The concessions were run by volunteer members of the Friends of the Zoo, and all profits went directly to the zoo. Prior to 1976, concession rentals brought in $15,000 in a good year. Profits from the operation of the concessions by the Friends of the Zoo were $400,000 a year by 1980 and were expected to be over $900,000 in 1987.

■ *Adopt an Animal* Zoo Parents paid a fee to "adopt" an animal, the fee varying with the animal chosen. The names of Zoo Parents were listed on a large sign inside the zoo. They also had their own annual celebration at the zoo: Zoo Parents Day.

■ *Zoo-To-Do* Zoo-To-Do was an annual black-tie fund-raiser with live music, food and drink, and original, high-class souvenirs, such as posters or ceramic necklaces. Admission tickets, limited to 3,000 annually, were priced starting at $100 per person. A raffle conducted in conjunction with Zoo-To-Do offered items ranging from an opportunity to be zoo curator for a day to the use of a Mercedes Benz for a year. Despite the rather stiff price, Zoo-To-Do was a sellout every

year. Local restaurants and other businesses donated most of the necessary supplies, which cut
the cost of the affair. In 1985, Zoo-to-Do raised
almost $500,000 in one night, more money than
any other nonmedical fund-raiser in the country.[7]

Advertising

The Audubon Park Zoo launched impressive
marketing campaigns in the 1980s. The zoo received ADDY awards from the New Orleans
Advertising Club year after year.[8] In 1986, the
film *Urban Eden*, produced by Alford Advertising and Buckholtz Productions Inc. in New Orleans, finished first among 40 entries in the
"documentary films, public relations" category
of the 8th Annual Houston International Film
Festival. The first-place Gold Award recognized
the film for vividly portraying the Audubon Park
Zoo as a conserving, rather than a confining,
environment.

During the same year, local television affiliates of ABC, CBS, and NBC produced independent news spots on the theme: "One of the
World's Greatest Zoos Is in Your Own Back Yard
... Audubon Zoo!" Along with some innovative
views of the Audubon Park Zoo being in someone's "backyard," local news anchor personalities enjoyed "monkeying around" with the
animals and the zoo enjoyed some welcome free
exposure.[9]

In 1986 and 1987, the zoo's advertising budgets were just over $150,000, its total public rela-
tions budgets were over $300,000, and the total
marketing budgets were over $1,000,000 each
year, including salaries. The marketing budgets
included development or fund-raising and membership as well as public relations and advertising. Percentage breakdowns of the public
relations budget for 1987 can be found in Exhibit
9-4.

The American Association of Zoological
Parks and Aquariums reported that most zoos
find that the majority of their visitors live within
a single population center in close proximity to
the park.[10] Thus, in order to sustain attendance
over the years, zoos must attract the same visitors repeatedly. A large number of the Audubon

EXHIBIT 9-4 Public Relations and Media Budgets

Public Relations Budgets

Category	1987 Percent
Salaries and overtime	24.3%
Education, travel and subscriptions	1.1
Printing and duplicating	2.4
Professional services	1.5
Tourist brochures for hotel rooms	3.6
Special events	24.1
News releases	0.4
Entertainment	0.7
Photography	0.9
Miscellaneous supplies	0.6
Advertising	40.3

Media Budgets

Category	1986 Percent	1987 Percent
TV and radio	28.0%	46.3%
Special promotion contingency	32.3	13.2
Tourist publications	10.5	9.2
Streetcar and bus	6.9	7.3
Magazines	4.2	5.0
Newspaper		1.1
Production	18.1	17.8

Source: The Audubon Park Zoo

Park Zoo's promotional programs and special
events were aimed at just that.

Promotional progress was slow among people
outside of New Orleans. For example, Simon &
Schuster, a reputable publishing firm, in its 218-
page Frommer's 1983-84 Guide to New Orleans
managed only a three-word reference to a "very
nice zoo." A 1984 study found that only 36
percent of the zoo's visitors were tourists, and
even this number probably included to some
extent an overflow from the World's Fair.

Promotional Programs

The Audubon Park Zoo and the Friends of the
Zoo conducted a multitude of very successful
promotional programs. The effect was to have
parties and celebrations going on continuously,

EXHIBIT 9-5 Audubon Park Zoo Promotional Programs

Title (Activity)	Month(s)
Photography contest	January
Fit for Life (aerobics)	March
Zoo-To-Do for Kids	April
Easter Family Days	April
Zoo-To-Do	May
Musical Zoo Revue (symphony concert)	May
Summer Concert Series	April to August
Breakfast with the Beasts	June
Ice Cream Sunday	June
Zoobilation (members party)	June
Play-Doh Invitational (architects compete with Play-Doh designs)	June
Teddy Bear Affair (teddy bear contests)	August
Press Party	September
Symphony Run	September
Louisiana Swamp Festival	October
Halloween	October
Beast Ballet (ballet performance)	November
Annual Essay Contest	November
Holiday Celebration	December
Annual Members' Christmas Sale	December

Source: The Audubon Park Zoo

attracting a variety of people to the zoo (and raising additional revenue). Exhibit 9-5 lists the major annual promotional programs conducted by the zoo.

In addition to these annual promotions, the zoo scheduled concerts of well-known musicians, such as Irma Thomas, Pete Fountain, The Monkeys, and Manhattan Transfer, and other special events throughout the year. As a result, a variety of events occurred each month.

Many educational activities were conducted all year long. These included (1) a "Junior Zoo Keeper" program for seventh and eighth graders, (2) a student-intern program for high school and college students, and (3) a Zoomobile, which took live animals to special education classes, hospitals, and homes for the elderly, among other sites.

Admission Policy

The Audubon Park Commission recommended the institution of an admission charge. Those who argued against such a charge held that it would result in an overall decline in attendance and a reduction of nongate revenues. Proponents held that gate charges would control vandalism, produce greater revenues, and result in increased public awareness and appreciation of the facility. In the early 1970s, all major international zoos charged admission, as did 73 percent of the 125 U.S. zoos.

The commission argued that there is no such thing as a free zoo; someone must pay. If the zoo is tax supported, then locals carry a disproportionate share of the cost. At the time, neighboring Jefferson Parish was growing by leaps and bounds and, it was argued, surely would bring a large, nonpaying constituency to the new zoo. Further, most zoos are tourist attractions, so tourists should pay since they contribute little to the local tax revenues.

The average yearly attendance for a zoo may be estimated by multiplying projected population figures by a "visitor generating factor." The average visitor generating factor of 14 zoos similar in size and climate to the Audubon Park Zoo was 1.34, with a rather wide range from a low of .58 in Phoenix and Miami to a high of 2.80 in Jackson, Mississippi.

Attracting More Tourists and Other Visitors

The romantic paddle wheeler Cotton Blossom took visitors up the Mississippi River from downtown to the zoo. The Zoo Cruise originally began at a dock in the French Quarter, but was later moved to a dock immediately adjacent to New Orleans' newest attraction, the Riverwalk, on the site of the 1984 Louisiana World Exposition. Not only was the riverboat ride great fun, it also lured tourists and conventioneers from the downtown attractions of the French Quarter and the new Riverwalk to the zoo, some six miles upstream. A further attraction of the riverboat ride was a return trip on the New Orleans Streetcar, one of the few

EXHIBIT 9-6 Seven Reasons Given for Not Altending the Audubon Park Zoo

Relative Importance of Reasons Respondent Does Not Visit (in percentages)

Reason (Close Ended) Characterstic	Very Imp. w/ Emphasis	Very Imp. w/o Emphasis	Somewhat Important	Unimportant
The distance of the zoo's location from where you live	7	11	21	60
The cost of a zoo visit	4	8	22	66
Not being all that interested in zoo animals	2	12	18	67
The parking problem on weekends	7	11	19	62
The idea that you get tired of seeing the same exhibits over and over	5	18	28	49
It's too hot during the summer months	25	23	22	30
Just not having the idea occur to you	8	19	26	48

remaining trolley cars in the United States. The Zoo Cruise drew more visitors to the zoo, generated additional revenue through landing fees paid by the New Orleans Steamboat Company, and kept traffic out of uptown New Orleans.[11]

Financial

The zoo's ability to generate operating funds has been credited to the dedication of the Friends of the Zoo, continuing increases in attendance, and creative special events and programs. A history of adequate operating funds allowed the zoo to guarantee capital donors that their gifts would be used to build and maintain top-notch exhibits. See Exhibit 9-7 for sources of operating budgets over the years. The 1986 combined balance sheet and the statement of revenue and expense for the Audubon Park Commission are in Exhibits 9-8 and 9-9.

Capital Fund Drives

The Audubon Zoo Development Fund was established in 1973. Corporate/industrial support of the zoo has been very strong—many corporations have underwritten construction of zoo displays and facilities. A partial list of major corporate sponsors is in Exhibit 9-10. A sponsorship

was to be for the life of the exhibit. The zoo's development department operated on a 12-percent overhead rate, which meant that 88 cents of every dollar raised went toward the projects. By 1987, the master plan for development had been 75-percent completed. The fund-raising goal for 1987 was $1.6 million.

Management

The Zoo Director

Ron Forman, Audubon Park Zoo director, was called a "zoomaster extraordinaire" and was described by the press as a "cross between Doctor Doolittle and the Wizard of Oz," as a "practical visionary," and as "serious, but with a sense of humor."[12] A native New Orleanian, Forman quit an MBA program to join the city government as an administrative assistant and found himself doing a business analysis project on the Audubon Park. Once the city was committed to a new zoo, Forman was named an assistant to the zoo director, John Moore. In early 1977, Moore gave up the battle between the "animal people" and the "people-people,"[13] and Forman took over as park and zoo director.

Forman was said to bring an MBA-meets-menagerie style to the zoo, which was responsible for transforming it from a public burden into an almost completely self-sustaining operation. The result not only benefited the citizens of the city, but also added a major tourist attraction to the economically troubled New Orleans of the 1980s.

Staffing

The zoo had two classes of employees: civil service through the Audubon Park Commission and noncivil service. The civil service employees, who included the curators and zoo keepers, were under the jurisdiction of the city civil service system. Employees who worked in public relations, advertising, concessions, fundraising, and other such activities were hired through the Friends of the Zoo and were not part of the civil service system. See Exhibit 9-11 for further data on staffing patterns.

Moving Into the Future

A visitor to the new Audubon Park Zoo could quickly see why New Orleanians were so proud of their zoo. In a city that was labeled as one of the dirtiest in the nation, the zoo was virtually spotless. This environment was the result of adequate staffing and the clear pride of those who worked at the zoo and those who visited it. One of the first points made by volunteers guiding school groups was that anyone seeing a piece of trash on the ground must pick it up.[14] A 1986 city poll showed that 93 percent of the citizens surveyed approved highly of the zoo — an extremely high rating for any public facility.

Kudos came from groups outside the local area as well. Delegates from the American Association of Zoological Parks and Aquariums ranked the Audubon Park Zoo as one of the three top zoos of its size in America. In 1982, the American Association of Nurserymen gave the zoo a Special Judges Award for its use of plant materials. In 1985, the Audubon Park Zoo received the Phoenix Award from the Society of American Travel Writers for its achievements in

EXHIBIT 9-7 Operating Budget

Year	Operating Budget	Gov't Support	Self-Generated
1978	$1,700,000	$700,000	$1,000,000
1980	2,800,000	840,000	1,960,000
1986	4,469,000	460,000	4,009,000

Source: The Audubon Park Zoo

conservation, preservation, and beautification.

By 1987, the zoo was virtually self-sufficient. Money received from government grants amounted to less than 10 percent of the budget. The master plan for the development of the zoo was 75-percent complete and the reptile exhibit was scheduled to open in the fall of 1987. The organization had expanded with a full complement of professionals and managers. (See Exhibit 9-12 for the organizational structure of the zoo.)

While the zoo made great progress in 15 years, all was not quiet on the political front. In a court battle, the city won over the state on the issue of who wielded ultimate authority over Audubon Park and Zoo. Indeed, the zoo had benefited from three friendly mayors in a row, starting with Moon Landrieu, who championed the new zoo, then Ernest "Dutch" Morial and Sidney Barthelemy, who in 1987 threw his support to both the zoo and a proposed aquarium being championed by Ron Forman.

New Directions for the Zoo

Zoo Director Ron Forman demonstrated that zoos have almost unlimited potential. A 1980 New Orleans magazine article cited some of Forman's ideas, ranging from a safari train to a breeding center for rare animals. The latter had the added appeal of being a potential money-maker since an Asiatic lion cub, for example, sells for around $10,000. This wealth of ideas was important because expanded facilities and programs are required to maintain attendance at any public attraction. The most ambitious of Forman's ideas was for an aquarium and river-

EXHIBIT 9-8 Audubon Park Commission Combined Balance Sheet, December 31, 1986

Assets	Operating Fund	Enterprise Fund	Designated Funds	Total
Current assets				
Cash - Noninterest bearing	$ 12,108	$ 0	$ 131,411	$ 143,519
- Interest-bearing	306,483	0	0	306,483
Time certificates of deposit	301,493	0	107,402	408,895
Investments	100	0	0	100
Accounts receivable:				
Friends of the Zoo, Inc.	321,774	0	1,177	322,951
Other	13,240	7,842	75,698	96,780
Due from operating fund	0	309,208	320,463	629,671
Due from enterprise fund	0	0	300,000	300,000
Due from other designated funds	0	0	66,690	66,690
Prepaid expenses	166,862	3,371	0	170,233
Total current assets	1,122,060	320,421	1,002,841	2,445,322
Fixed assets				
Equipment	0	159,455	0	159,455
Less: Accumulated depreciation	0	75,764	0	75,764
Total fixed assets	0	83,691	0	83,691
Total assets	$1,122,060	$404,112	$1,002,841	$2,529,013
Liabilities				
Cash overdraft	$39,700	$ 0	$ 0	$39,700
Accounts payable:				267,185
City of New Orleans	267,185	0	0	72,658
Friends of the Zoo, Inc.	0	72,658	0	75,904
Other	68,805	7,099	0	14,337
Payroll taxes payable	14,337	0	0	9,552
Accrued salaries	7,973	1,579	0	46,899
Due to operating fund	0	0	46,899	309,208
Due to enterprise fund	309,208	0	0	573,564
Due to designated funds	273,564	300,000	0	66,690
Due to other designated funds	0	0	66,690	1,475,697
Total liabilities	980,772	381,336	113,589	
Fund equities				
Fund balances	141,288	0	889,252	1,030,540
Retained earnings	0	22,776	0	22,776
Total fund equities	141,288	22,776	889,252	1,053,316
Total liabilities and fund equities	$1,122,060	$404,112	$1,002,841	$2,529,013

front park to be located at the foot of Canal Street.

Although the zoo enjoyed political support in 1987, New Orleans was suffering from a high unemployment rate and a generally depressed economy resulting from the depression in the oil industry. Some economists were predicting the beginning of a gradual turnaround in 1988, but any significant improvement in the economy was forecasted to be years away. In addition, the zoo operated in a city where many attractions competed for the leisure dollar of citizens and visitors. The Audubon Park Zoo had to vie with the French Quarter, Dixieland jazz, the Superdome, and the greatest of all attractions in the city — Mardi Gras.

The New Orleans Aquarium

In 1986, Forman and a group of supporters proposed the development of an aquarium and

EXHIBIT 9-9 Audubon Park Commission Statement of Revenue, Expenditures and Changes in Operating Fund Balance — Actual and Budgeted Year Ended December 31, 1986

	Annual Budget	Actual	% of Budget
REVENUE			
Intergovernmental			
City of New Orleans	$ 600,000	$ 450,000	75.0%
State of Louisiana	25,000	10,913	43.7
Other governmental	25,000	0	0.0
Total intergovernmental	650,000	460,913	70.9
Charges for services			
Animal rides	115,000	127,671	111.0
Binocular receipts	4,000	2,604	65.1
Education programs	10,000	930	9.3
Events	10,000	4,701	47.0
Food and drink	458,000	569,259	124.3
Gift shops	140,000	136,369	97.4
Mombasa Railroad	40,000	40,030	100.1
Race fees	30,000	30,844	102.8
Swimming Pool	17,000	15,992	94.1
Tennis	0	10,167	0.0
Train	10,000	0	0.0
Travel program	14,000	5,508	39.3
Zoo admissions	2,420,000	2,718,254	112.3
Total charges for services	3,268,000	3,662,329	112.1
Interest income	10,000	34,867	348.7
Miscellaneous			
Animal sales	10,000	38,446	384.5
Aquarium campaign	0	124	0.0
Friends of the Zoo	525,000	640,869	122.1
Miscellaneous	12,000	8,569	71.4
Riverboat	35,000	36,278	103.7
Stables	8,400	7,887	93.9
Total miscellaneous	590,400	732,173	124.0
Total revenue	4,518,400	4,890,282	108.2%
EXPENDITURES			
Personal services			
Life insurance	$2,000	$23,106	1,155.3%
Medical insurance	100,000	103,321	103.3
Pension	150,000	160,543	107.0
Payroll taxes	198,000	155,961	78.8
Salaries - regular	1,883,652	1,959,205	104.0
Salaries - overtime	59,570	61,937	104.0
Terminal leave	10,000	1,169	11.7
Uniform allowance	19,900	17,287	86.9
Workmen's compensation	50,000	38,779	77.6
Total personal services	2,473,122	2,521,308	101.9
Contractual services			
Advertising	131,200	111,863	85.3
Aquarium	90,000	248,082	275.6

	Annual Budget	Actual	% of Budget
Building repairs	5,400	18,790	348.0
Communications	100	166	166.0
Convention and travel	29,950	32,445	108.3
Delivery and parking	10,850	12,639	116.5
Dues and subscriptions	7,910	7,636	96.5
Duplicating services	14,500	5,021	34.6
Entertainment	5,800	12,350	212.9
Equipment rental	22,750	12,215	53.7
Insurance	260,000	254,079	97.7
Laboratory services	8,100	9,762	120.5
License fees	550	1,108	201.5
Minor repairs	10,300	12,265	119.1
News releases	6,000	1,551	25.9
Penguins	0	10,957	0.0
Personal contracts	46,200	0	0.0
Postage and freight	40,350	33,322	82.6
Printing	18,700	9,207	49.2
Professional services	342,890	362,050	105.6
Swimming pool	48,000	42,835	89.2
Telephone	40,000	50,634	126.6
Utilities	40,000	41,902	104.8
Vehicle repairs	10,000	12,307	103.1
Waste removal	18,800	18,011	95.3
Total contractual services	1,208,350	1,321,197	109.3
Supplies and materials			
Amphitheater	$ 3,400	$ 2,264	66.6%
Art and essay	900	518	57.6
Artifacts	1,000	0	0.0
Building supplies	57,750	63,151	109.4
Display supplies	32,100	17,172	53.5
Educational supplies	10,050	49,626	493.8
Electrical supplies	10,300	25,283	245.5
Events	50,200	45,989	91.6
Feed and forage	187,780	172,398	91.8
Fuel	38,000	23,874	62.8
Graphics supplies	4,500	8,152	131.2
Hand tools	4,000	3,120	78.0
Horticultural supplies	20,000	17,788	88.9
Hospital and laboratory supplies	15,300	13,711	89.6
Janitorial and cleaning	51,500	50,018	97.1
Junior keeper	500	817	163.4
Medical supplies	1,750	1,300	74.3
Minor equipment	28,950	30,384	105.0
Motor vehicle supplies	30,000	10,285	34.3
Office supplies	34,150	29,768	87.2
Photographic supplies	5,150	6,138	119.2
Plants, shrubs, and trees	18,300	16,574	90.6
Police supplies	1,500	3,128	208.5
Public information	0	638	0.0

	Annual Budget	Actual	% of Budget
Read the Zoo	7,000	7,675	109.6
Safari carts	3,000	1,136	37.9
Special education	10,000	12,731	127.3
Teacher in-service	6,000	2,562	42.7
Uniforms	5,060	4,329	35.6
Zoomobile	3,000	1,138	37.9
Total supplies and materials	641,140	621,667	97.0
Equipment			
Animals	$22,400	$14,359	64.1%
Automotive	40,000	56,722	141.8
Communications	1,150	847	73.7
Construction projects	50,000	32,418	64.8
Educational and recreational	0	96	0.0
General plant	7,000	5,621	80.3
Hospital and medical	4,200	2,947	70.2
Office furniture and equipment	8,500	35,897	422.3
Total equipment	133,250	148,907	111.8
Other expenditures			
Claims	12,000	10,385	86.5
Miscellaneous	1,000	19,461	1,946.1
Total other expenditures	13,000	29,846	229.6
Total expenditures	4,468,862	4,642,925	103.9
Excess of revenue over expenditures	49,538	247,357	499.3
OTHER FINANCING USES			
Operating transfers out	49,538	150,000	302.8
Excess of revenue and other financing sources over expenditures and other uses	$ 0	97,357	
OPERATING FUND BALANCE AT BEGINNING OF YEAR		43,931	
OPERATING FUND BALANCE AT END OF YEAR		$ 141,288	

riverfront park to the New Orleans City Council. In November 1986, the electorate voted to fund an aquarium and a riverfront park by a 70-percent margin — one of the largest margins the city has ever given to any tax proposal. Forman hailed this as a vote of confidence from the citizens as well as a mandate to build a world-class aquarium that would produce new jobs, stimulate the local economy, and create and educational resource.[15]

Once the voters had appproved the bond proposal, the New Orleans City Council had many decisions to make. Should the management structure of the aquarium be placed within the same organization as the Audubon Park Zoo or under a separate structure? Where should the aquarium be located and how large should it be?

A feasibility study prepared by Harrison Price Company projected a probable 863,000 visitors to the aquarium by the year 1990, with 75 percent of them coming from outside the metropolitan area.[16] The location of the new aquarium was to be adjacent to the Riverwalk, providing a logical pedestrian link between New Orlean's major attractions of the Riverwalk and the Jax Brewery, a shopping center in the French Quarter.

The aquarium would face major opposition

EXHIBIT 9-10 Major Corporate Sponsors

Amoco Corporation
American Express
J. Aron and Company
Breaux Mart
Chevron USA, Inc.
Conoco, Inc.
Consolidated Natural Gas Corporation
D. H. Holmes, Ltd.
Dr. G. H. Tichenor Antiseptic Company
Exxon Corporation
First National Bank of Commerce
Freeport-McMoRan, Inc.
Frischhertz Electric Company
Goudchaux/Maison Blanche
Hibernia National Bank
Kentwood Spring Water
Louisiana Coca-Cola Bottling Company, Ltd.
Louisiana Land and Exploration Company
McDonald's Operations of New Orleans
William B. Reily and Company
Texaco USA
Trammell Crow Company
Wendy's of New Orleans
Whitney National Bank
Frank B. Williams and Company

Source: The Audubon Park Zoo

EXHIBIT 9-11 Employee Structure

Year	# of Paid Employees	Number of Volunteers
1972	36	
1973	49	
1974	69	
1975	90	
1976	143	
1977	193	
1978	184	
1979	189	
1980	198	
1981	245	
1982	305	
1983	302	56
1984	419	120
1985	454	126
1986	426	250
1987	358*	287 *

*Through the end of the second quarter.
Source: The Audubon Park Zoo

from several groups: riverfront developers, the Vieux Carre Commision (preservationists of the old French Quarter), the Dock Board (responsible for riverfront property usage), the U.S. Park Service, and businesses from downtown and other parts of the city. Serveral of these groups argued that the proposed site was not safe from river accidents. One counter plan was for the aquarium to be located on the west bank of the Mississippi River. The West bank was accessible from downtown only by two major bridges and ferry boats. The east bank contained the major tourist and visitor attractions of the French Quarter, the Convention Center, the Lakefront (Lake Pontchartrain restaurants and facilities), the historic Garden District, and major shopping areas. A diferent downtown site was pushed by an opposing political group.

Meanwhile, the Audubon Park Zoo had its own future to plan. The new physical facilities and professional care had paid off handsomely in increased attendance and new animal births. But the zoo could not expand at its existing location because of a lack of land within the city. Ron Forman and the zoo staff considered several alternatives. One was incorporating the new aquarium. Another was little "neighborhood" zoos to be located all over the city. A third was a separate breeding area to be located outside the city boundaries, where land was available. With the zoo running smoothly, the staff seemed to need new challenges to tackle and the zoo needed new facilities or programs to continue to increase attendance.

EXHIBIT 9-12 Audubon Park Zoo Organizational Structure

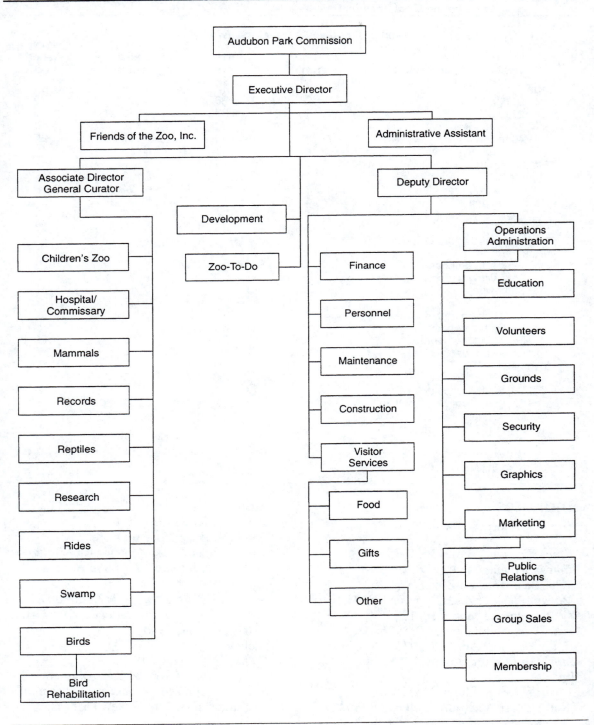

EXHIBIT 9-13 Respondent Characteristics of Zoo Visitors According to Visitation Frequency (in Percentages)

	Number of Zoo Visits Over Past Two Years			
Respondent characterstic	Four or more	Two or three	One or none	Never visited zoo
Age				
Under 27	26	35	31	9
27 to 35	55	27	15	3
36 to 45	48	32	11	9
46 to 55	18	20	37	25
Over 55	27	29	30	14
Marital status				
Married	41	28	20	11
Not married	30	34	24	13
Children at home				
Yes	46	30	15	9
No	34	28	27	12
Interest in visiting the Orleans Aquarium				
Very, with emphasis	47	26	18	9
Very, without emphasis	45	24	23	12
Somewhat	28	37	14	11
Not too	19	32	27	22
Vote intention on aquarium				
For, with emphasis	46	33	16	5
For, without emphasis	39	31	16	14
Against or don't know	11	40	32	17
Member of FOTZ				
Yes	67	24	5	4
No, but heard of it	35	30	24	12
No, and never heard of it	25	28	35	13
Would you be interested in joining FOTZ (nonmembers only)				
Very/somewhat	50	28	14	8
No/don't know	33	29	26	12

Endnotes

[1] *Times Picayune* March 30, 1975.

[2] *Times Picayune* January 20, 1976.

[3] Millie Ball, *"The New Zoo of '82," Dixie Magazine Sunday Times Picayune* June 24, 1979.

[4] *Times Picayune* March 30, 1975.

[5] *Times Picayune* January 20, 1976.

[6] *Times Picayune* April 29, 1972.

[7] *Jefferson Business* August 1985.

[8] Ibid.

[9] *Advertising Age* March 17, 1986.

[10] Karen Sausmann (ed.). *Zoological Park and Aquarium Fundamentals*, (Wheeling, W.V.: American Association of Zoological Parks and Aquariums, 1982) 111.

[11] *Times Picayune* November 30, 1981.

[12] Steve Brooks, *"Don't Say 'No Can Do' to Audubon Zoo Chief,"* Jefferson Business May 5, 1986.

[13] Ross Yuchey, *"No Longer Is Heard a Discouraging Word at the Audubon Zoo"* New Orleans August 1980, 53.

[14] Yuchey, 49.

[15] *"At the Zoo",* Winter 1987.

[16] *Feasibility Analysis and Conceptual Planning for a Major Aquarium Attraction,* prepared for the City of New Orleans, March 1985.

EXHIBIT 9-14 Chronology of Events for the New Zoo

1972   The Audubon Zoological Society asked the Audubon Park Commission to institute an admission charge "in an amount sufficient to reduce the possibility of vandalism but not so great as to inhibit visits by family groups and less affluent members of the community" (*Times Picayune*, April 29, 1972).

1973   The City Planning Commission approved a master plan for the Audubon Park Zoo calling for $3.4 million for upgrading. Later phases called for an additional $2.1 million and were to be completed by 1978.

1974   Friends of the Zoo formed with 400 members to increase support and awareness of the zoo.

1975   Phase I renovations began: $25 million in public and private funds to expand from 14 acres to 58 acres.

1977   John Moore went to Albuquerque; Ron Forman took over as park and zoo director.

1978   Phase II began.

1980   Phase III began.

1980   First full-time education staff on duty at the zoo.

1980   Last animal removed from antiquated cage — a turning point in zoo history.

1981   Contract signed allowing New Orleans Steamboat Company to bring passengers from downtown to the zoo.

1981   Delegates from the American Association of Zoological Parks and Aquariums ranked the Audubon Park Zoo as one of the top three zoos of its size in the United States.

1981   Zoo accredited.

1982   The Audubon Park Commission reorganized under Act 352, which required the commission to contract with a nonprofit organization for the daily management of the park.

References

Beaulieu, Lovell. "It's All Happening at the Zoo." *The Times Picayune*, Sunday, January 28, 1978.

Ball, Millie. "The New Zoo of '82." *Dixie Magazine, Sunday Times Picayune*, June 24, 1979.

Brooks, Steve. "Don't Say 'No Can Do' to Audubon Zoo Chief." *Jefferson Business*, May 5, 1986.

Bureau of Governmental Research, City of New Orleans. Audubon Park Zoo Study, Part I, Zoo Improvement Plan, August 1971. New Orleans: Bureau of Governmental Research.

Bureau of Governmental Research, City of New Orleans. *Audubon Park Zoo Study, Part II, An Operational Analysis*, August 1971. New Orleans: Bureau of Governmental Research.

Donovan, S. "*The Audubon Zoo: A Dream Come True.*" *New Orleans*, May 1986, 52-66.

Feasibility Analysis and Conceptual Planning for a Major Aquarium Attraction, prepared for the City of New Orleans, March 1985.

Forman, R., J. Logsdon, and J. Wilds. *Audubon Park An Urban Eden. New Orleans*: The Friends of the Zoo, 1985.

Poole, Susan. *Frommer's 1983-84 Guide to New Orleans*. New York: Simon & Schuster, 1983.

Sausmann, K., ed. *Zoological Park and Aquarium Fundamentals* Wheeling, W.V.: American Association of Zoological Parks and Aquariums, 1982.

Yuchey, R. "*No Longer Is Heard a Discouraging Word at the Audubon Zoo.*" *New Orleans*, August 1980, 49-60.

Zuckerman, S., ed., *Great Zoos of the World*. Boulder, Colorado: Westview Press, 1980.

10

"Pardner, this town ain't big enough for the both of us"

[People] think that this four thousand acres will save the creek...[but] if there is land out there to be bought, people are going to buy it. You can't shut the world down.[1]

There may be frowns at City Hall, but Barton Springs Eternal; Smoggy air and urban sprawl, but Barton Springs Eternal; There may be traffic jams downtown, drunk and loony convention clowns, confusion spreading all around, but Barton Springs Eternal.[2]

Introduction

The case study you are about to read is merely a microcosm of a battle that is being waged daily in the United States. On one side are development interests and investment firms who view the environment as a resource to be used and exploited for the betterment of mankind. On the other side are environmental interests, who believe that there are some natural areas which are so precious that they should be protected from development, despite the economic costs. The conflict becomes especially attenuated when the two groups are acutely interested in developing or preserving the same natural area. This is precisely the situation which arose in the Hill Country of Central Texas, an area designated by the Nature Conservatory as one of the twelve "last great places" on earth.[3] It is here that our story begins.

Background of the Conflict

Just west of the City of Austin, Texas, lays the rolling dark-green hills known as the Hill Country. The area and topography are truly unique, consisting of a series of creeks, rivers, lakes and caves which serve as home to many different species, five of which are considered endangered. The rugged beauty is also a developer's dream. Minutes from Austin, the capital of

---

[1] Jim Bob Moffett, Chief Executive Officer of Freeport-McMoRan, Inc., a prime developer of property, in environmentally sensitive West Austin, commenting on the citizen effort to protect Barton Creek Watershed. Quoted in "A Showdown in Austin", *The Greater Baton rough Bus. Rep.*, Apr. 7, 1992, at 26.

[2] Bill Oliver, "Barton Springs Eternal", on *Environmental Songs for the World*.

[3] Scott Pendleton, "Austin Texas", *Christian Sci. Monitor*, Jan. 2, 1992, at 10.

By Everett H. Eissenstat. The author retains all rights. Used with permission.

Texas, it is perfectly situated for residential and commercial development.

However the area sits on top of much of the "recharge zone"[4] of the Edwards Aquifer.[5] The Edwards Aquifer is made up of a series of limestone caves and tiny pockets which hold and help move water underground. About 300,000 acre-feet of water is stored in these underground chambers.[6] A series of watersheds[7] feed six creeks which in turn feed the Aquifer.[8] As the creeks flow towards Town Lake and the Colorado River, water percolates through cracks in the creek beds down to the Aquifer itself.[9] Eventually the creeks run dry until the water is flowing totally underground. The water in Barton Creek usually remains completely underground (depending on the amount of rainfall) for several miles until it erupts suddenly at Barton Springs, minutes from the center of downtown Austin.[10] A similar process takes place in the five other creeks.[11]

The water of Barton Springs has been described as "clean, clear [and] mystical."[12] It remains a constant 68 degrees year-round, providing the citizens of Austin with a welcome respite from the searing summer heat.[13] The Spring itself is 997 feet long and is "considered one of the 10 best swimming holes in the country."[14]

Unfortunately, the watersheds, creeks and Barton Springs are extremely sensitive to water pollution. This is because "run off," or non-point source, pollutants enter the watersheds when it rains. Run-off pollution is caused by things such as spilled motor oil, antifreeze, gasoline, pesticides and herbicides. Because of the thin topography of the watersheds, any run off pollutants which enter the Edwards Aquifer through the recharge zone travel unfiltered through the underground limestone and creek beds.[15] These pollutants travel directly to the creek beds, through the Edwards Aquifer and eventually emerge at Barton Springs. Because of this unique combination of natural factors, the Texas Water Commission declared the 150-square-mile Barton Springs portion of the Edwards Aquifer to be the "most susceptible watershed" to pollution in the State of Texas.[16]

Urban development directly impacts upon the amount of run-off pollutants in an area. As more residential and commercial construction is undertaken, the amount of ground cover which is available to filter the pollutants before they enter the Aquifer is reduced. This is because the ground cover is being replaced with smooth surfaces such as asphalt and concrete.[17] In addi-

[4] The "recharge zone of an aquifer is that portion of the land surface which, because it is composed of permeable soils, is the principal source of ground water inflow." James T. B. Tripp and Adam B. Jaffe, "Preventing Groundwater Pollution: Towards a Coordinated Strategy to Protect Critical Recharge Zones", 3 Harv. Envtl. L. Rev. 1, 3 (1979) The replenishment of groundwater is known as recharge.

[5] An aquifer is "a rock layer that will yield enough water to serve as a water supply for some use." Texas Water Commission, "The Underground Subject: An Introduction to Ground Water Issues in Texas" (1989). The Edwards Aquifer consists of a massive area of land extending from Bell County in the North to Kinney County in the Southwest. It is divided into three sections: the Southern Edwards, in the south central portion of the Texas near San Antonio; the Northern Edwards, extending from Austin through Georgetown and Salado; and the Barton Springs section, which encompasses 155 square miles of Travis and Hays counties. 1' Barton Springs section is the section of the aquifer which provides water to Barton Springs. Austin Parks and Recreation Department, et al., Hill Country Oasis: Barton Springs. Barton Creek. Edwards Aquifer 14 (1992). It is this third portion of the Edwards Aquifer which we will focus upon in this paper.

[6] Austin Parks and Recreation Department, et al., Hill Country Oasis: Barton Springs, Barton Creek. Edwards Aquifer 14 (1992).

[7] A watershed is basically a drainage basin. Rain falling into a watershed is carried by a network of tributaries to the parent creek. Austin Parks and Recreation Department, et al., Hill Country Oasis. Barton Springs. Barton Creek. Edwards Aquifer 14 (1992).

[8] Id. These six creeks are the Barton, Williamson, Slaughter, Bear, Little Bear and Onion.

[9] Austin Parks and Recreation Department et. al. op. cit.

[10] "Barton Springs: Link to the Past. Hope of the Future", Austin American-Statesman, July 1, 1990, at A8.

[11] The Hill Country Foundation, "What You Should Know About Barton Springs" (1991).

[12] Id. Native Americans believed that the Springs were created by the Great Spirit, who hurled a rainbow against the limestone of the Edwards Aquifer, splitting the rock so that the cool, clear water could flow forth. Bill Collier, "SOS Initiative Springs to Landslide Win", Austin American-Statesman, Aug. 9, 1992, at Al, A19.

[13] Austin Parks and Recreation Department, et al., Hill Country Oasis: Barton Springs. Barton Creek. Edwards Aquifer 7 (1992).

[14] Scott Pendleton, "Austin Texas", Christian Sci. Monitor, Jan 29, 1992, at 20.

[15] Kaye Northcott. "Soul vs. Salvation: Referendum Focuses on Development of Barton Springs", The Houston Chron., May 31, 1992, at 3.

[16] Robert Sullivan, "Should Barton Springs Be Out of Bounds?", Sports Illustrated, Aug. 19, 1991, at 8.

[17] These smooth surfaces are known collectively as impervious cover.

tion, the construction of more houses and businesses naturally leads to the increased use of such things as bug spray, motor oil, herbicides and gasoline—precisely the type of pollutants which detrimentally impact the water quality of the Aquifer.

Early Efforts to Protect the Watersheds

Initially protection of the watersheds was not of great concern for the City of Austin. Austin had only 290,000 inhabitants in 1973, and new developments had not yet begun to encroach heavily upon the environmentally sensitive areas of West Austin.[18] The 1970s and 80s were somewhat of a "boom" time for the city however, and by 1980 the population had risen at a faster rate than San Antonio, El Paso, Dallas or Houston.[19] By 1989 the population had reached 749,000.[20] With the population increase came a demand for more housing, more recreational facilities and more commercial development.

Public pressure to protect the environmentally sensitive Hill Country Watersheds from overdevelopment mounted. In response to this pressure, the City Council for the first time undertook measures to protect the watersheds with the adoption of a series of watershed ordinances in 1980 [the 1980 Ordinances].[21] The 1980 Ordinances approached the problem in a piecemeal fashion, incorporating four regulatory strategies: water quality zones, density controls, impervious cover limits, and structural controls.[22] The pollution problems in the watersheds continued however, and in 1985 the City was forced to impose a moratorium on the Bear and Onion Creek watersheds in the extreme southern portion of Austin's extraterritorial jurisdiction.[23] The purpose of the moratorium was "to preclude undesired development until water quality controls could be devised and applied in those areas."[24] In 1986 the City Council adopted the Comprehensive Watersheds Ordinance [Comprehensive Ordinance]. This ordinance consolidated the previous series of watershed ordinances into a single document. The Comprehensive Ordinance was strict and considered by many environmentalists to be in "the vanguard of efforts to protect urban watersheds."[25] Despite the potential strength of the Comprehensive Ordinance to prevent watershed pollution, development and pollution in the area continued. This was in large part attributed to the fact that the Comprehensive Ordinance contained a number of exemptions. These exemptions were included by the City Council as part of a "compromise" with business and development interests which city officials asserted was necessary to enable the Comprehensive Ordinance to be passed at all.[26] The end result was continued development. Between 1986 and 1990, 86% of all development projects proposed for construction in the Barton Creek watershed were exempt from the Comprehensive Ordinance.[27] New malls, country clubs and housing additions were built to the south and west of Austin. New roads were constructed to connect the additions to the city, spurring even greater growth in the area. With each new proposed project, came cries of environmental degradation from the environmental community.[28] Conflicts between development

[18] Dan Balz. "Austin May be First City in Sun Belt to Question if Growth is Too Rapid", The Washington Post, July 12, 1981, at A4.

[19] Mary Lenz, "Austin's Caves, Flyways Become Development Targets", Christian Sci. Monitor, Aug. 17, 1989, at 8.

[20] Id.

[21] "Barton Springs: Link to the Past Hope of the Future", Austin American-Statesman, July 1, 1990, A1, at A8.

[22] James B. Duncan and Terry D. Morgan, "Growth Management at the Local Level-The Austin. Texas. Experience", in Proceedings of the Institute on Planning. Zoning, and Eminent Domain, 7-1, at 7-18 (1986).

[23] Id.

[24] Id.

[25] Scott Pendleton, "Austin, Texas", Christian Sci. Monitor, Jan 29, 1992, at 10.

[26] Bill Collier, "Comparing SOS and City Ordinances", Austin American-Statesman, July 19, 1992, CI, at C5.

[27] Id.

[28] For example, the construction of Barton Creek Mall in 1980 led to heavy opposition by environmental activists through the "Save Barton Creek" movement. Mary Lenz, Austin's Caves. "Flyways Become Development Targets", Christian Sci. Monitor, Aug. 17, 1989, at 8. In 1989, members of Earth First! and other environmental groups, including the Texas Nature Conservancy, protested Ross Perot's development of 330 acres in western Travis County. Id. A few months later, contemplated construction of a plant for the microchip manufacturer,

interests and environmentalists became more commonplace, and more visible. As it turned out, however, these conflicts were just preliminary skirmishes in a war over the development of West Austin that was to last over three years.

The "Spark' that Started a Revolution

The first shot was fired, unknowingly, by the developers in February of 1990 when construction of a $100 million planned unit development (PUD) over the environmentally sensitive Barton Creek Watershed was submitted for approval to the Austin City Council[29] for approval. The proposed PUD as originally planned would develop 4,000 acres into 4,200 single-family and multi-family residences and 3.2 million square feet of commercial and light industrial space.[30] The PUD was designed to accommodate "upper crust" home buyers, with the community centered around three golf courses and two clubhouses.[31] These facilities would complement two golf courses which had already been constructed in the area.[32]

The project was proposed by Freeport-McMoRan, a New Orleans- based energy firm. According to one reporter, the "project would be the culmination of land deals involving a who's who

of University of Texas alumni."[33] The Chief Executive officer of Freeport-McMoRan is James "Jim Bob" Moffett, a former University of Texas[34] football star. Also involved in the proposed project are Darrell Royal, former University of Texas football coach; and professional golfer Ben Crenshaw, who is a former member of the University of Texas golf team.[35] The three alumni formed a corporation called Barton Creek Properties for the sole purpose of developing the PUD. Barton Creek Properties is also working with Club Corp. International, whose chairman, Robert Dedman is another University of Texas alumnus.[36]

Both companies were aware of the environmentally sensitive nature of the 4,000 acres upon which they planned to build. To accommodate the sensitive aquifer recharge zone, Freeport-McMoRan planned to set aside 700 acres to serve as a water quality buffer zone.[37] Construction plans also called for inclusion of 53 acres of public and private parkland with hike and bike trails.[38] The plans included construction of "state-of-the-art innovations such as 'wet ponds' to treat water run off and a sophisticated water quality monitoring system"[39] to control pollution.

The group was also aware of the public opposition to such development projects in the past. Before the City Council vote on the project, Freeport-McMoRan began an advertising campaign to persuade Council Members and the public that the project would "be both beautiful

28 cont. U.S. Memories to be built over the Edwards Aquifer in Travis County was abandoned after conservation groups, led by the Sierra Club, vowed to fight the project." Austin Aquifer Site Scrapped for U.S. Memories", *UPI Press Release*, Nov. 2, 1989. In March of 1990 environmental groups filed suit in federal district court to force the Texas Department of Highways to conduct an environmental impact study of two major highway projects that crossed the Edwards Aquifer. "Road Projects Over Texas Aquifer Halted Pending Environmental Impact Study", 20 *Envt. Rep.* 1866 (BNA) (1990).

29 The City of Austin is a "Home Rule" city with a "council-manager government." Austin, Tex. *Charter of the City of Austin* art. I, 2 (1953). 'The City Council consists of seven council members, one of whom is the mayor of the City of Austin. Austin, Tex., *Charter of the City of Austin* art. II, 1 (1953). The council is elected every three years for staggered terms, and is required to appoint a city manager "who shall serve as the chief administrative and executive officer of the city." Austin, Tex., *Charter of the City of Austin* art. V, 1 (1953).

30 "Austin Council Nixes Barton Creek Development", *UPI Press Release*, June 8, 1990.

31 "John MacDougal, $100 Million Development Planned Near Barton Creek", *Austin Bus. J.*, Feb. 19, 1990, 1, at 1.

32 "Austin Council Nixes Barton Creek Development", *UPI Press Release*, June 8, 1990.

33 "John MacDougal, $100 Million Development Planned Near Barton Creek", *Austin Bus. J.*, 51, at l.

34 The University of Texas is located in Austin, Texas. It is the largest publicly financed university in the state.

35 Royal and Crenshaw own ten percent of the corporation, with Moffett holding the other ninety percent. "John MacDougal, $100 Million Development Planned Near Barton Creek", *Austin Bus. J.*, 1, at l.

36 Id.

37 These seven hundred acres, along with an additional one-hundred, would also serve as habitat for the golden-checked warbler, a bird placed on the endangered species list. "John MacDougal, $100 Million Development Planned Near Barton Creek", *Austin Bus. J.*, 1, at l.

38 Id.

39 "Austin Council Nixes Barton Creek Development", *UPI Press Release*, June 8, 1990.

and environmentally sound."[40] A full-page newspaper advertisement was placed in the *Austin American-Statesman*, with both Darrell Royal and Ben Crenshaw supporting the project in an open letter to then Mayor Lee Cooke.[41] Other groups in Austin, however, opposed the project. The Sierra Club, the National Audubon Society, the Save Barton Creek Association, Earth First! and Save Austin's Neighborhoods and Environment began to pressure city hall to reject the development project and to work towards tightening the city's water quality ordinances.[42] One day prior to the council vote, the score was four council members for the project, and three opposed.[43]

The People Fight Back

Apparently the environmentalists had won the preliminary battle over public sentiment. On the day of the vote, over 800 people swarmed the Council Chambers to protest construction of the PUD and to speak out against the project.[44] A 13-hour marathon public meeting ensued, lasting through the night until 6:00 a.m. the following morning. "Outside the packed council chambers...hundreds of...demonstrators chanted so loudly that at times they drowned out the speakers inside."[45] By the end of the night, the council rejected the proposal 7-0.

It was clearly the public opposition to the proposed PUD that swayed council members to reject the project.[46] Prior to public protest, it is likely that the project would have been approved by the City Council 4-3. Ironically, the developer's attempts to garner public sentiment through the news media may have actually damaged their objectives in the short-run. It is possible that the increased publicity only served to make more Austin citizens aware of the proposed development and that it would have some impact, whether it was actually serious or not, upon the Barton Creek Watershed.

There is one thing that is clear from the vote, however. The people of Austin, through a spontaneous political movement, were able to address the City Council and effectuate the direction of public policy in the city. It is a clear example of democracy at work in perhaps its purest form. The council members were elected to serve their constituents, and their constituents adamantly opposed construction in the area. That night the council responded. Unfortunately, the vote was only one battle in what proved to be a long and divisive war, the remainder of which was not nearly so clean.

As a result of public pressure, the City Council passed a resolution in 1990 which called for "non-degradation" of the existing water quality in the watersheds.[47] This was by far the strictest standard ever proposed for the Edwards Aquifer watersheds, a measure strongly supported by environmental interests. The City Council also imposed a moratorium on new development in the Barton Creek Watershed to enable the environmental department to draft and implement new regulations (Revised Comprehensive Ordinance).

Development interests were incensed. The non-degradation standard sharply limited the amount of development permitted over the watersheds and they believed that the revised "rules could put a halt to development in the watershed[s]."[48] They also felt that compliance with the new regulations would be prohibitively costly.

---

[40] "Royal, Creenshaw Back Barton Creek Area Development", *UPI Release*, June 6, 1990.

[41] Id.

[42] Id.

[43] Id. The three council members opposed were: Robert Barnstone, George Humphrey and Max Nofziger. g.

[44] "A Showdown in Austin", *The Greater Baton Rouge Bus. Rep.*, Apr. 7, 1992, 1, at 26. The Austin City Charter requires that "all council meetings shall be open to the public except as may be authorized by the laws of the State of Texas." Austin, Tex., *Charter of the City of Austin*, art.II, 9 (1953).

[45] "Austin Council Nixes Barton Creek Development", *UPI Press Release*, June 8, 1990.

[46] In fact one council member, Smoot Carl-Mithchell, was quoted as saying that "he voted against the project because of the overwhelming outpouring of opposition from Austin residents." "Austin Council Nixes Barton Creek Development", *UPI Press Release*, June 8, 1990.

[47] "Scott Pendleton, Austin Texas", *Christian Sci. Monitor*, Jan. 29, 1992, at 10.

[48] "Bill McCann, Watershed Regs Halted for Study", *Austin Bus. J.*, Feb. 11, 1991, 1, at l.

The Conflict Intensifies

Both sides began to see the need for broad public support. Thus, while continuing their pressure upon the council, both groups also began to turn increasingly towards other means of achieving their goals. Freeport- McMoRan went before the Texas Water Commission in an attempt to override the City Council's rejection of the PUD development.[49] The development firm also threatened to sue in district court or incorporate the area as a separate city if their project was rejected.[50]

The developers also began to undertake "an extraordinary number of measures to try to win support from a decidedly hostile public."[51] These measures included establishing the Barton Creek Foundation as a trust fund to provide financial support for research and testing of Barton Springs, as well as a permanent board of directors to oversee long-term development and preservation in the area; providing seed money to endow the trust; establishing a community information program; and revising planned water-quality control facilities for the area.[52]

Engineers for the Barton Creek PUD asserted that they needed the variances from the Comprehensive Watershed Ordinance to enable them to implement water quality measures such as wet ponds, structures designed to trap and filter run off. A spokesman for the PUD contended that they could "do the development and have less pollutants go into the creek than if the land is left in its natural state, and certainly less than if we followed the Comprehensive Watershed Ordinance."[53]

Despite the developer's efforts and promises to protect Barton Springs, opponents were not satisfied. They contended that, "Not even compliance with the city's ordinances would maintain Barton Creek's pristine condition."[54] Environmentalists began a boycott of Franklin Federal Bancorp, a thrift 80% owned by ClubCorp. International and Robert Dedman, two prime developers of the Barton Creek Watershed. In addition to the boycott, activists asked residents to write letters protesting the banks poor minority lending practices to the Federal Deposit Insurance Corp., the Texas Water Commission and the state congress.[55] This was the first time either group sought to identify themselves with minority issues in their campaign over development of the watershed. Obviously, the environmentalists saw this as an opportunity to increase their support among minorities by identifying themselves with a minority issue, accusing the bank of redlining,[56] as well as supporting the Barton Creek development project.

Pro-development interests also began to organize and place pressure upon City Council to reject the Revised Comprehensive Ordinance. The Austin Chamber of Commerce began to write letters to the City Council on behalf of development interests,[57] and PUD related Political Action Committee (PAC) funds began to filter in to various council members.[58]

Apparently, some of the pressure worked. One month before the building moratorium imposed in 1990 was to expire, the City Manager called for separate economic assessments of the Revised Comprehensive Ordinances. The studies were ordered under "provisions of an ordinance

[49] Ken Martin, "Barton creek Case Goes to Water Board", *Austin Bus. J.*, Aug. 6, 1990, 1, at l.

[50] Texas state law gives developers the option of incorporating the area and proceeding with the project under their own regulations and those of the state and Lower Colorado River Authority. "Austin Council Nixes Barton Creek Development", *UPI Press Release*, June 8, 1990. Of course, this would result in a loss of tax revenue to the City of Austin.

[51] Ken Martin, "Barton Creek Case Goes to Water Board", *Austin Bus. J.*, Aug. 6, 1990, 1, at l.

[52] Id.

[53] Id.

[55] Bob Lowry, "Environmentalists Target Thrift for Protest", *UPI Press Release*, July 26, 1990.

[56] The accusations of redlining, which is the illegal practice of denying loans for reasons other than poor credit risk, followed a report released by the Southern Bank Finance Project, which accused Franklin Federal and five other lenders of not making sufficient loans in minority communities. Ken Martin, "Barton Creek Case Goes to Water Board", *Austin Bus. J.*, 1, at l.

[57] Bill McCann, "Watershed Regs Halted for Study", *Austin Bus. J.*, Feb. 11, 1991, 1, at l.

[58] The following council members received the following amounts of PUD related PAC money: Mayor Bruce Todd, $12,000; Louis Epstein, $6,250; Ronney Reynolds, $4600; Charles Urdy, $2250; Gus Garcia, $1500; and Bob Larson, $200. *Austin Chron.*, Oct. 18, 1991 at 13.

that gives the city manager authority to take such action if a proposed law could have a major impact on the Austin economy."[59] The move was significant in several ways.

First, the economic impact assessments could take up to six months to complete. This would enable the City Council to implement less stringent watershed regulations during the interim between the expiration of the moratorium and the termination of the economic studies. Second, the six months would also enable the City Council to avoid voting on the controversial Revised Comprehensive Watershed Ordinances until after the May 4 City Council elections.[60] As was pointed out by one council member who was not seeking re-election, "If there was to be an economic assessment, that decision should have been made months ago—not when the moratorium is about to expire."[61] The council member added that he believed "political considerations were behind the decision."[62]

Fortunately for environmentalists, the Revised Comprehensive Watershed Ordinances were adopted on an interim basis, pending the results of the economic impact assessments.[63] Nevertheless, despite the interim ordinance, the effects of development on Barton Springs Watershed were becoming more and more pronounced. During 1991, Barton Springs was closed for 23 days because of fecal coliform bacteria or sediment pollution.[64] During hearings before the Texas Water Commission in May of 1991, it was disclosed that the Springs should have been closed for an additional three-day period when more than 1,000 people used the pool.[65]

At the same time, pro-development interests were becoming more-and more organized.

When the City Council held a hearing on the content of the Revised Comprehensive Watershed Ordinances in September, the business community had an unprecedented showing of support before the City Council. More than fifty individuals from engineering, building, and real estate groups, in addition to several Chambers of Commerce, signed up to speak in opposition to the ordinances.[66]

An additional hearing in October on the Revised Ordinances brought in support from all sides. They remembered how important the "crowd tactic" was to the environmentalists' initial victory over the PUD in 1990, and over 300 people from both sides of the issue were brought in to speak for or against adoption of the Revised Ordinances.[67]

But the environmentalists were prepared to wage the battle on another front if their efforts failed to get the interim Revised Comprehensive Watershed Ordinances approved by council vote in October. During the skirmishes, the environmentalist formed the Save Our Springs Coalition (SOS), an umbrella organization representing more than a dozen environmental groups. The initial focus of the group was to get "hordes of people" to pack Council Chambers for the October vote. If SOS failed at the City Council level, the group vowed to take the issue to the people in the form of a citizen initiative.[68]

Showdown at City Hall

The Council Chamber was packed the night that the Revised Ordinance was put to a vote. Environmentalists filled one side of the room and developers the other. Apparently, the developers also sought to incorporate minority issues into

[59] Bill McCann, "Watershed Regs Halted for Study", *Austin Bus. J.*, Feb. 11, 191, 1, at I.

[60] Id.

[61] Id. (quoting council member Smoot Carl-Mitchell).

[62] Id.

[63] Id.

[64] Robert Sullivan, "Should Barton Springs Be Out-of-Bounds", *Sports Illustrated*, at 8.

[65] Id.

[66] Bill McCann, "Watershed Rules Stir Growth Fight", *Austin Bus. J.*, Sept. 30, 1991, 1, at 1. The organizers acknowledge that they "took a cue from environmentalists, who often pack the chambers when they are trying to get the council's attention on an issue." Id. In fact, one group even chartered a bus to bring opposition in from the outlying areas of Austin. Id.

[67] Bill McCann, "Watershed Rules Stir Growth Fight", *Austin Bus. J.*, Sept. 30, 1991, 1, at I.

[68] Id. (quoting Brigid Shea: "We are concerned that the council does not represent a majority of the voters. If the council doesn't do it, we want to give the voters the chance to say they want the springs protected").

their struggle. As council member Charles Urdy, a supporter of the PUD project, stood up before the council and explained "to the predominantly white crowd of environmentalists why there were no blacks in their midst. 'They are not here, because in all of this discussion you have not spoken to their primary issue, which is their kids.'"[69] This "drew a huge hand from the even more predominantly white developer crowd, who stood and applauded reverently."[70] This was countered by Council Member Gus Garcia, who proclaimed in Spanish that "La contaminacion del medio ambiente no tiene fronteras (the contamination of the environment has no borders)."[71] Reportedly, "The environmental side went wild, giving Garcia a long, rousing standing ovation."[72] After significant debate, a new composite ordinance replaced the Revised Ordinance, which had been initiated on an interim basis by a vote of 6-1. The environmentalists were "outraged that the interim ordinance was weakened."[73] Part of their dismay was caused by the fact that the ordinance actually adopted by the City Council carried over all but one of the exemptions which had created such a problem in the 1986 Comprehensive Watershed Ordinance. As they did in 1986, council members again asserted that the exemptions were necessary as part of a compromise to get the ordinance passed before the council.[74]

The Battle Begins on a New Front

Perhaps anticipating that they would lose at the Council level, SOS had organized early and secured two environmental canvassing groups[75] to begin gathering voter signatures for the initia-

tive.[76] The SOS coalition quickly gathered the 24,000 signatures needed to get the initiative petition before the City Council[77] (SOS Ordinance). Once the City Council had the initiative ordinance, the Charter of the City of Austin provided them with three alternatives: (1) pass the initiated ordinance within sixty days of receipt; (2) submit the ordinance without amendment to the voters within ninety days of receipt; or, (3) submit the ordinance without amendment to the voters along with "an alternative ordinance on the same subject proposed by the council."[78]

The council chose the third alternative and proposed an alternative ordinance in May of 1992 [Council Ordinance] to be placed on the ballot.[79] If they had to put the strict SOS Ordinance to a vote of the people, they at least wanted the opportunity to provide them with a less stringent alternative. The Council initially sought to pit the two ordinances against one another on the ballot, presenting voters with an "either/or" alternative. However, the Texas Election Code prohibits this practice, requiring that voters have the opportunity to vote yes or no on b o t h proposed ordinances. Thus, the Council was required to amend the Council Ordinance to provide that, if both proposed ordinances were approved by the voters, the Council Ordinance would be suspended indefinitely.[80]

The Council Ordinance calls for a Regional Quality Action Plan to protect the sensitive wa-

[69] Daryl Slusher, "Council Watch. Hunting Season Opens", *Austin Chron.*, Oct. 18, 1991, 12, at 13.

[70] Id.

[71] Id.

[72] Id.

[73] Scott Pendleton, "Austin Texas", *Christian Sci. Monitor*, Jan. 29, 1992, at 10.

[74] Bill Collier, "Comparing SOS and City Ordinances", *Austin American-Statesman*, July 19, 1992, Cl, at C4.

[75] Clean Water Action and Texas Citizen Action.

[76] Bill McCann, "Watershed Rules Stir Growth Fight", *Austin Bus. J.*, Sept. 30, 1991, 1, at 1. The Charter of the City of Austin "reserve[s] the power of direct legislation by initiative" to the citizens of Austin. Austin, Tex., *Charter of the City of Austin* art. IV, 1 (1953).

[77] Kaye Northcott, "Soul vs. Salvation: Referendum Focuses on Development of Barton Springs", *Houston Chron.*, May 31, 1992, at 3. The Charter of the City of Austin enables the people to propose an ordinance to City Council via a petition signed by ten percent of the qualified voters of the city. "Austin, Tex.", *Charter of the City of Austin* art. IV, 1 (1953). "Austin, Tex.", *Charter of the City of Austin* art. IV, 5 (1953).

[78] "Austin, Tex.", *Charter of the City of Austin* art. IV, § 5 (1953).

[79] The Council Ordinance was proposed by council member Ronney Reynolds and approved by council members Reynolds, Louise Epstein, Bob Larson, and Charles Urdy. Three council members, Mayor Bruce Todd, Gus Garcia and Max Nofziger, voted against the Council Ordinance. "SOS Controversy Continues: Dueling Ordinances", *Austin Bus. J.*, July 13, 1992, 1, at l.

[80] "SOS Question and Answer", *Austin American-Statesman*, July 6, 1992, at B4.

tersheds to be developed in coordination with the Texas Water Commission, the City of Austin and the Lower Colorado River Authority. It also provides for the purchase of sensitive land in order to prevent its development and "retrofitting," or repairing, existing damage to the creeks and watershed.[81] Finally, the Ordinance requires run off to meet measured standards for four pollutants.

The unique aspect of the Council Ordinance is that it would apply to the entire Barton Springs Watershed and not just the 30% that is within the Austin's city limits and extraterritorial jurisdiction (ETJ).[82] However, no funding source for the retrofitting or purchase of land was designated by the Council Ordinance.[83] The Council Ordinance also contains a number of exemptions and permits impervious cover[84] of up to 70%.

The SOS Ordinance strictly limits impervious cover to 15 to 25%. It contains practically no exemptions and requires run off to meet measured standards for 13 pollutants.[85] However, the SOS Ordinance only applies to the 150 square miles of the watershed which are within the city limits and its extraterritorial jurisdiction. This leaves roughly 200 square miles unprotected.[86] The legal effect of the SOS Ordinance would be to supplement and replace certain provisions of the Comprehensive Watershed Ordinance but not to replace it. This is because the ordinance was written "to be cumulative of other city ordinances."[87] Thus a developer faced with conflicting provisions of the SOS Ordinance and prior city ordinances would have to comply with the most stringent of the two.

Once these two ordinances were proposed and placed on the ballot there was little political maneuvering which could be done on the City Council level. The controversy had been thrown into the political arena to the people of Austin. From this point forward the two sides effectively were limited to political campaigning. The only question left to be resolved at the City Council level was <u>when</u> the elections would be held.

Proponents of the SOS ordinance sought to have an early election on the ordinance, hoping to have it on the ballot by May 2, 1992. However a majority of the City Council voted against it.[88] Instead, the vote was placed on the ballot for August 8, 1992. In addition, the City Council opted to place over 22 bond propositions on the August 8 ballot in June of 1992.[89]

Development interests finally reacted to the creation of the SOS coalition on May 11, 1992 when they formed Citizens for Responsible Planning (CRP). CRP is a coalition of business, civic and Chamber of Commerce leaders formed specifically to oppose the SOS Ordinance.[90] Both CRP and SOS realized that the key to achieving their goals on August 8 was to persuade the voters that their proposal was not only the best way to prevent environmental degradation in the Barton Creek Watershed, but also the best way to ensure the economic development and business growth of the City of Austin. How-

---

[81] "SOS Controversy Continues: Dueling Ordinances", *Austin Bus. J.*, July 13, 1992, 1, at l.

[82] Id.

[83] Bill Collier, "Comparing SOS and City Ordinances", *Austin American-Statesman*, July 19, 1992, Cl, at C5.

[84] Impervious cover is the amount of land covered by buildings, streets and parking lots.

[85] "SOS Controversy Continues: Dueling Ordinances", *Austin Bus. J.*, July 13, 1992, 1, at l.

[86] Scott Pendleton, "Austin's War of the Watershed", *Christian Sci. Monitor*, Aug. 7, 1992, at 2.

[87] "SOS Question and Answer", *Austin American-Statesman*, July 7, 1992, at B2.

[88] Bob Burns, "99 Development proposals Filed Since October for Springs Zone", *Austin American-Statesman*, July 22, 1992, at B3.

[89] Mike Todd, "How Deep Does Austin's Debt Go?", *Austin American-Statesman*, July 19, 1992, Cl, at C4. The bond package calls for issuance of $170.6 million in general revenue bonds to fund projects such as improvement in police and medical services, cultural museums, libraries, parks, street construction d electric and water utilities. For a complete list of all proposed bonds, see appendix VII. The most interesting and unique proposals provide for the borrowing of $20 million to expand the Barton Creek Greenbelt (See map Appendix VIII) and $22 million to enable the city to purchase over 11,725 acres as a part of the Balcones Cayonlands Protection Plan to protect endangered species west of Austin. (See map appendix IX). This in itself provides for a very interesting study in the inter-workings of local government and interrelationship of federal agencies to city government. Unfortunately, the subject is beyond the scope of this paper. For an interesting analysis of some of the issues involved, see J. B. Ruhl, "Regional Habitat Conservation Planning Under the Endangered Species Act: Pushing the Legal and Practical Limits of Species Protection", 44 *Sw. L.J.* 1393, 1413- 23 (1991).

[90] Bob Burns, "$460.000 Flows to Campaigns in Water Debate", *Austin American-Statesman*, July 11, 199, Al, at A20.

ever, the nature of the issues was extremely complex and highly technical. Thus both sides began to appeal directly to the voters' sentiments through print and media advertisements and began to seek endorsements from various civic leaders and groups. As one campaign manager explained "endorsements tell you who your friends are."[91] Endorsements can also provide campaign workers with much needed credibility among certain groups which they would otherwise not have.[92]

Almost immediately after its formation, CRP spent $34,000 to mail a tri-fold brochure to around 72,000 voters, asking them to vote against the SOS Ordinance.[93] This supplemented a several hundred-thousand dollar television blitz begun by Freeport-McMoRan in January of 1992. The ads were geared towards demonstrating to the Austin community that Freeport-McMoRan was an environmentally sensitive company.[94] Unfortunately, some of these ads were pulled by Austin TV stations when the National Wildlife Federation complained that the ads were misleading.[95]

In response, SOS also began to run a series of television commercials "aimed at convincing the voters that the proposed water quality ordinance would be good for the local economy."[96] The ad featured three prominent area business persons who spoke out in praise of the business aspects of the SOS Ordinance.[97] CRP countered these commercials with a new television advertisement designed to repeat "many of the same themes the anti-SOS forces had been trying to drive home over the past several weeks as the election campaign heated up."[98] Another tactic employed by anti-SOS forces was the release of a study in late July (just weeks before the polls opened) conducted by a professor of environmental engineering at the University of Texas at Austin. The report stated that passage of the SOS Ordinance "would make collective water and wastewater systems unprofitable and would force proliferation of septic tanks that leak into the aquifer," thus actually increasing the amount of pollution in the water.[99] SOS responded to the study, calling it "junk science" and asserting that the study was based upon faulty data and non-supported assumptions.[100]

CRP also argued that the SOS Ordinance would only serve to "hurt or destroy the life savings of many small-property owners caught in the cross-fire."[101] SOS countered this argument through an economic study conducted by a University of Texas at San Antonio economics professor which stated that the SOS Ordinance would actually increase the value of existing homes in the watershed due to increased demand and limited supply of housing in the area.[102]

Both groups also portrayed the economic well-being of the City of Austin as being intimately intertwined with passage of their proposed ordinance. CRP asserted that the SOS Ordinance would erode the city's tax base with the ultimate effect of depriving Austin's schools, and hence the children of Austin, with enough money for education.[103] They also asserted that the SOS Ordinance would expose the city to limitless financial exposure because of litigating inevitable takings-claims which would be filed by disgruntled landowners.

---

[91] Bob Burns, "Endorsements Weighty Amid SOS Confusion", *Austin American-Statesman*, July 18, 1992, at B5. The SOS coalition claimed more than 300 endorsements, to which the CRP stated that it had endorsements from more than 700 businesses and individuals.

[92] Bob Burns, "Endorsements Weighty, Amid SOS Confusion", *Austin American-Statesman*, July 18, 1992, at B5.

[93] "SOS Controversy Continues: Dueling Ordinances", *Austin Bus. J.*, July 13, 1992, 1, at l.

[94] "A Showdown in Austin", *The Greater Baton Rouge Business Rep.*, Apr. 7, 1992, 1, at 26.

[95] Id.

[96] Bob Burns, "SOS. Business Group Unveil Television Ads", *Austin American-Statesman*, July 14, 1992, at B2.

[97] Id.

[98] Bob Burns, "TV Campaign Begun by Anti-SOS Group", *Austin American-Statesman*, July 28th, 1992 at B2. For text of the advertisement, see appendix XII.

[99] Bob Burns, "Study: SOS Plan Would Backfire", *Austin American-Statesman*, July 22, 1992, at B1.

[100] Id.

[101] John Lewis, "Myth: Only Developers Hurt by SOS", *Austin American-Statesman*, July 9, 1992, at A17.

[102] Mary Ann Neely, "Investment in Austin", *Austin American-Statesman*, July 9, 1992, at A17.

[103] John Lewis, "Myth: Only Developers Hurt by SOS", *Austin American-Statesman*, July 9, 1992, at A17.

At the same time, environmentalists argued that the SOS Ordinance would enhance, rather than harm, the city's economic future, stating that "Barton Creek and Barton Springs are key elements of Austin's outstanding quality of life, protecting them enables [the city] to compete more effectively for the highly sought after high-tech business, as well as a vibrant tourist industry."[104] The argument continued that investing in the protection of the watersheds now would actually save the City of Austin money in the long-term, as prevention of pollution is much less costly than repairing environmental damage in the future.

Endorsements continued to be crucial to the campaign on both sides. Freeport-McMoRan began to funnel funds into public interest projects around the city, particularly those supported by minority groups. The firm donated money to Austin's ballet company, the symphony and gave "large sums" of money to a program for Austin's poor youth.[105] Meanwhile SOS had gained the endorsement of several prominent minority organizations, including the United League of Latin American Citizens, the South Austin Mexican American Democrats and the East Austin Strategy Teams.[106] SOS also won the support of the National Association for the Advancement of Colored People who felt that "promoting growth in [the Barton Creek] watershed is counterproductive to the long-neglected needs of East Austin."[107]

SOS also sought to increase support among business groups in Austin, sending more than 3,300 letters to Greater Austin Chamber of Commerce members.[108] The mailing contained a list of over 99 business and professionals that supported SOS. In addition, business leaders formed the coalition Austin Business Leaders for the Environment (ABLE) to show support for the SOS Ordinance. The group, "comprised of more than 330 local businesses ranging from high-tech firms to local clubs and restaurants," began a series of print ads expressing their support for the SOS Ordinance.[109]

Meanwhile, the Greater Austin Chamber of Commerce threw its full support behind the Council Ordinance. The Chamber mailed two separate flyers to more than 5,000 individuals and companies asking them to vote against the SOS Ordinance and for the Council Ordinance.[110] The civic organization also used its monthly publication, *Skyliner*, as a forum to express opposition to the SOS Ordinance.[111]

As can be seen, both SOS and CRP employed similar campaign strategies, seeking to broaden their coalitions while at the same time portraying the other group as overreactive and unconcerned with either the economic (for SOS) or environmental (for CRP) impacts of their proposed ordinances. CRP sought to dampen concerns that the Council Ordinance would be inadequate to protect the Barton Creek Watershed through the print media. They also sought to show that the SOS Ordinance would not only harm the economic interests of the City of Austin (including the public schools) but would also be inadequate to protect the sensitive watershed. SOS on the other hand sought to assure the people of Austin that environmental protection and economic growth were not incompatible, but rather an intricate part of Austin's future. Both groups were trying to be all things to all people.

---

[104] Mary Ann Neely, "Investment in Austin", *Austin American-Statesman*, July 9, 1992, at A17.

[105] "A Showdown in Austin", *The Greater Baton Rouge Business Rep.*, Apr. 7, 1992, 5 1, at 26.

[106] Bob Burns, "Endorsements Weighty, Amid SOS Confusion", *Austin American-Statesman*, July 18, 1992, at BS.

[107] "NAACP Endorses Save Our Springs", *Austin American-Statesman*, July 30, 1992, at B2. East Austin is primarily inhabited by minority and lower income groups.   Apparently civic groups in the area were taking lessons from the political mobilization of the SOS coalition. A few months prior to the August 8 vote on the bond propositions, over 29 minority and other civic groups banded together to form the Neighbors for Inner-City Environments (NICE). The coalition was formed to persuade voters to support inner-city bond projects. See Mike Todd, "29 Civic Groups call for Passage of Bonds for Inner-City

Projects", *Austin American-Statesman*, July 9, 1992, at B3.

[108] Sarah Barnes, "Businesses Spring to Fund SOS Fight", *Austin American-Statesman*, July 25, 1992, at El.

[109] Bob Burns, "SOS. Business Group Unveil Television Ads", *Austin American-Statesman*, July 14, 1992, at B2.

[110] Sarah Barnes, "Businesses Spring to Fund SOS Fight", *Austin American-Statesman*, July 25, 1992, El, at E2.

[111] Glenn E. West, August 8th...and Beyond!, *Skyliner*, Aug., 1992, at 3.

The Vote and the Fallout

When the polls finally opened, the voting was intense. The election, although not record setting, brought 27.6% of the registered voters to the polls, a turnout "considered high for an election devoid of City Council Candidates."[112] In the end, the SOS Ordinance won by a ration of almost 2 to 1, 64% in favor and 36% opposed. The Council Ordinance lost by almost the same margin, with 35% in favor and 65% opposed.[113] As one SOS supporter noted, the victory was "a loud and clear message to the City Council."[114]

Voters also approved all but three of the proposed revenue bonds. Every environmentally related proposition passed by strong margins. In addition, propositions for increased police, medical and cultural facilities passed. The only propositions which failed to carry the voters' support were a proposition for purchase of a performing arts center; a bond proposition for the expansion of the George Washington Carver Museum in East Austin; and a bond proposition for construction of a Mexican American Cultural Center in downtown Austin.[115]

The minority community "blamed the defeat [of the cultural bonds] on ballot placement and inadequate support from people backing the [SOS] water quality initiative."[116] Some minority leaders were more vocal, stating that "SOS supporters who had sought the backing of East Austin failed to return the favor by getting out the vote for the cultural centers."[117] Some went even further, attributing the loss to "cultural indifference and racial insensitivity."[118]

Supporters of the Council Ordinance were also bitter about the loss. The campaign by CRP was called "amateurish and ineffective," which "succeeded only in underscoring the absence in Austin of a business community that is both united and coherent."[119] The campaign itself was led largely by real estate interests who had no real central organization to turn to for support.

The Greater Austin Chamber of Commerce clearly came out a loser, as business leaders did not believe that the organization was effective in coordinating business interests, in large part because of its broad membership. In fact, after the election, Chamber members bluntly asserted that they had "made a mistake in opposing SOS and misread[ing] its membership."[120] According to an article in the *Austin Business Journal*, the Chamber is making a conscious effort to move from a "white boys' club" to include more Hispanics, blacks, environmentalists and women. Kerry Tate, a member of the Chamber's executive committee, summed up the Chamber's new direction: "Our goal is to move from the image of the Chamber of Concrete to the Chamber of Conscience."[121] Apparently this move was too little too late. In January of 1993 more than one hundred small businesses banded together to form the Independent Chamber of Commerce (ICC). The ICC acknowledged that the SOS debate served as a catalyst for forming the group and that their organization was committed to both economic growth and a healthy environment.[122]

While some groups, such as the Chamber of Commerce, sought to heal the wounds over SOS, others vowed to continue the fight. The battle now shifted from the City Council level to the state legislature and the courts.[123] Since passage of the SOS Ordinance, five area landowners have filed a consolidated suit in the

---

[112] Bill Collier. "SOS Initiative Springs to Landslide Win", *Austin American-Statesman*, Aug. 9, 1992, Al, at A19.

[113] Id.

[114] Id.

[115] Mike Todd, "Voters Reject Cultural Center Bonds. Embrace Capital Improvements", *Austin American-Statesman*, Aug. 9, 1992, at A18.

[116] Id.

[117] Id. (quoting Cathy Vasquez, Planning Commission member).

[118] Id.(quoting Dennis Garza, president of the League of United Latin American Citizens).

[119] Michele Kay, "SOS Shows Split Business Community", *Austin American-Statesman*, Aug. 16, 1992, at G3

[120] Rickie Windle, "Economic Growth Expected: Predictions are Good for Austin", *Austin Bus. J.*, Jan 25, 1993, 1, at 1 (quoting Angelos Anelou of the Greater Austin Chamber of Commerce).

[121] Amy Smith, "The Other Chamber", *Austin Bus. J.*, Feb. 1, 1993, 1, at 1.

[122] Id.

[123] Bill Collier, SOS Initiative Springs to Landslide Win, Austin American-Statesman, Aug. 9, 1992, Al, at A19.

District Court in Travis County.[124] In addition, two bills have been introduced in the state legislature which have a serious impact upon the continued validity of the SOS ordinance.

Texas House Bill 1307 was introduced in March of 1993. This bill amends Section 26.177 of the Texas Water Code to require that any city ordinance designed to abate or control pollution within the city's boundaries or extraterritorial jurisdiction be enforced "within the city...to provide equal protection for all residents of the city and its extraterritorial jurisdiction."[125] The bill also requires that an ordinance in effect in one part of the city be automatically extended to every part of the city.

The clear impact of this bill would be to make the SOS Ordinance prohibitively expensive and impractical. As noted in this paper, the SOS Ordinance was designed to deal with an extremely sensitive part of the City's terrain. This area makes up only a small portion of the City's total area. Unlike the majority of the creeks and watersheds within the City's jurisdiction, it is not highly developed. Therefore, the City is able to demand a higher standard from future construction than that which would be required in areas which are already damaged by development. In these highly developed areas it would be virtually impossible to achieve the same level of water quality as can be maintained in the watersheds west of the City.

The rationale behind the bill is that the residents of Austin should all be entitled to the same amount of environmental protection, not just those affluent white residents who generally inhabit West Austin.[126] While the goals of the bill might be laudable, it would effectively "gut" the

SOS Ordinance.

The second bill was introduced in April of 1993. It amends Section 481.142(a)(3) of the Local Government Code to clarify that any proposal submitted to a city regulatory agency must be evaluated solely upon the basis of the regulations in effect at the time the proposal was submitted.[127] It also provides that any project which is "interrupted for any reason...as a result of an action taken by a regulatory agency or governmental entity" be regarded as "in a continuous process of completion," thus enabling the project to take advantage of the new legislation.[128]

This bill seems to have been tailor-made for the Barton Creek PUD project. In April of 1992 Freeport-McMoRan filed preliminary subdivision and site plans for the PUD with the City of Austin. Interestingly, these plans were filed during the interim period after the weaker 1991 Ordinance was approved by the City Council but prior to the August 1992 vote on the SOS initiative. In fact, more than 99 development proposals for the Barton Creek area took advantage of this "window of opportunity" and filed preliminary plans.[129] If House Bill 2135 is enacted, all of these projects, including the Barton Creek PUD, would be exempt from the SOS Ordinance. Both bills are currently pending before the Texas State Legislature.

On another front, Jim Bob Moffett is now seeking to sharpen his image before the Austin public, launching a massive ad campaign that portrays him and his project in a favorable light.[130] To aid in this effort, his company, Free-

[124] Quick, et al. v. City of Austin, No. 92-12387 (147th Judicial District, Travis County, Tex.). The suit alleges that the limit on impervious cover violates the Texas Local Government Code, which prohibits the city from regulating in its extraterritorial jurisdiction (ETJ) the size of buildings or the ratio of building floor space to and square footage. "Texas Landowners File Lawsuit Against Ground Water Ordinance", Ground Water Monitor, Sept. 8, 1992. The suit is pending as of the date of this paper. For Contra authority, see City of Austin v. Jamail, 662 S.W. 779 (Tex. Civ. App.-Austin 1983, writ dism'd) (upholding the City of Austin's authority to enforce watershed ordinance in its extraterritorial jurisdiction).

[125] 1993 Tex. H.B. 1307, 73rd Legis. Sess. (1993); 1993 Tex. S.B. 1305, 73rd Legis. Sess. (1993) (duplicative bills).

[126] The rational behind this bill becomes even more justified when one considers the City of Austin's poor environmental record in predominantly black and Hispanic East Austin. For insight into this problem, see "Scott W. Wright Oil Company Lawyer: Stricter Controls Not Needed at Tank Farm", Austin American-Statesman, July 30, 1992, at B3; "Enrique J. Gonzales, Tank Farm Neighbors Accept Offer of Medical Assistance", Austin American- Statesman, July 17, 1992, at B5 ("The tank from has been the center of a health controversy since earlier this year when it was reported that ground water under the tanks was contaminated with gasoline-related chemicals [in East Austin].)

[127] 1993 Tex. H.B. 2135, 73rd Legis. Sess., (1993); 1993 Tex. S.B. 1029, 73rd Legis. Sess., (1993) (duplicative bills).

[128] 1993 Tex. H.B. 2135, 73rd Legis. Sess., (1993); 1993 Tex. S.B. 1029, 73rd Legis. Sess., (1993) (duplicative bills).

[129] Bob Burns, "99 Development Proposals Filed Since October for Springs Zone", Austin American-Statesman, July 22, 1992, at B3.

[130] "Can Reporter Rewrite Developer's Image?", Austin Bus. J., Nov. 2, 1992, 1, at l.

port-McMoRan, hired *Austin American-Statesman* journalist Bill Collier to serve as the company's newly-created public relations director. The hiring of Mr. Collier is significant as he is a long- time resident of the Austin community and widely respected by the environmental community.

The Last Chapter?

Moffett seems to be seeking conciliation on other fronts as well. A few months after the SOS Ordinance passed, Moffett met privately with Austin Mayor Bruce Todd to see if a mutual agreement could be reached that would enable him to develop the Barton Creek PUD while maintaining the high water quality mandated by the SOS Ordinance. Apparently, the City of Austin was looking for a means to resolve the controversy as well. On January 21, 1993, the City Council unanimously enacted a City Ordinance calling for the creation of a Citizens' Task Force with the "general goal of protect[ing] the City's economic future while protecting its environmental interests in the context of development planning for the Barton Creek Watershed."[131] The Citizens' Task Force is made up of environmentalists, governmental leaders and business leaders. The Ordinance also called for the creation of an Advisory Committee to make interim reports to the City Council on the Task Force's recommendations.[132]

The Task Force's work has been exemplary. After receiving proposals from Freeport-McMoRan, the Save Our Springs Coalition and other interested parties, the group presented the "Oles-Scanlan proposal" within three months of its formation. The response of all sides was promising. Both Freeport-McMoRan and the SOS coalition agreed in principle with the ma-

jority of the proposal's provisions.[133] One month later, on April 5, 1993, the Task Force submitted revised recommendations to the City Council. After extensive public debate and discussion among the City of Austin, Freeport-McMoRan and the SOS Coalition, the Citizens Task Force submitted its final recommendations to the City Council on April 14, 1993.

The proposal, which has been approved in principal by both environmentalists and developers, is a model of compromise. Under the proposal, Freeport-McMoRan would set aside a 1,000 foot park corridor along Barton Greek and reduce the size of its proposed PUD.[134] The development firm would also move many of its proposed development sites south of the Barton Creek Watershed onto the Latana tract, which is better equipped to support extensive development. Impervious cover would be reduced below the 20% required by SOS on the Barton Creek tract, but expanded to 45% on the Latana tract. Freeport-McMoRan would also adopt water pollution control and halt all legislative and court challenges to the SOS Ordinance. In an interesting twist, Freeport would undertake efforts to relieve the financially troubled Southwest Travis County Road District No. 1 of some of its debt obligations. This would enable the City of Austin to purchase two tracts of land needed to complete the Balcones Cayonland Conservation Project.

In exchange, the Barton Creek PUD would be annexed into the city limits and served by city sewage system. This would also work to the City of Austin's advantage as it would place the PUD within the city's tax base. The company would also receive development offsets from the City of Austin which could be charged against development fees in the future. The City of Austin would also purchase some of Freeport's property to be used as part of the Balcones Cayonland Protection Project. The proposal would enable Barton Greek Properties to continue construction on its PUD while protecting the environ-

[131] Austin, Tex. Ordinance No. 930121, part 2(1) (Jan. 21, 1993).

[132] The Ordinance required the committee to be a broad-based group, mandating that it consist of one representative from each of the following organizations: Travis County Commissioner's Court; Lower Colorado River Authority; Barton Springs/Edwards Aquifer District; Texas Parks and Wildlife Commission; Resolution Trust Corporation; U.S. Fish and Wildlife; Sierra Club; Audubon society; Texas Water Commission; National Parks Service; Trust for Public Land; and the Texas Department of Transportation. Austin, Tex. Ordinance No. 930121, part 1(B) (Jan. 21, 1993).

[133] Mike Todd, "Vote on Barton Creek Compromise Could Be Near", *Austin American-Statesman*, Apr. 3, 1993, at A1.

[134] Mike Todd, "Panel OKs Barton Plan: 6 Issues Left", *Austin American-Statesman*, Apr. 15, 1993, Al, at A12.

ment at the same time.

The plan is complex and still not final. Six significant issues remain unresolved which could prove to be the plan's undoing.[135] The bills pending before the state legislature could also cause the agreement to fall apart.[136] Another problem is the inclusion of SOS as a signatory to the agreement, a proposition which Freeport-McMoRan rejects. Nevertheless, if these issues are resolved, the parties would enter into a long-term binding contract which would govern the development of the PUD and the Barton Creek Watershed for decades to come. It would be a landmark compromise in the continuing battle between development and the environment.

---

[135] Id.

[136] The agreement provides that both parties may withdraw if the either legislation passes the Texas State Legislature. Id.

II

Organization Structure and Design

11

RASCO:
The EDI Initiative

In 1988, the Reynolds Aluminum Supply Company (RASCO) initiated development of Electronic Data Interchange (EDI) technology — the electronic exchange of transaction-processing information between two firms. RASCO believed that EDI could benefit the company in two ways. First, EDI would make internal systems more economical and efficient than previously by eliminating the clerical requirements of paper-based systems. Second, EDI capability would improve RASCO customer service (See Appendix 1 for a technical discussion of EDI. Exhibit 11-2 of the appendix shows how a basic EDI system works). It could also serve as an additional marketing tool for improving sales. For these reasons, former RASCO General Manager Richard N. Peters believed that EDI technology had to be developed. He was concerned, however, about resolving important issues surrounding the technical aspects and the marketing efforts of RASCO's EDI initiative.

Reynolds Aluminum Supply Company

RASCO was one of 12 divisions within Reynolds Metals Company of Richmond, Virginia, the second largest aluminum producer in the United States. RASCO began in 1950 when Reynolds acquired the building products supplier, Southern States Roofing Company of Savannah, Georgia. In 1951, Reynolds purchased Clingan & Fortier, a Los Angeles, California, metals distributor. Southern States and Clingan & Fortier were then consolidated in 1963 to form a new Reynolds division called RASCO. Six years later, RASCO gained its Midwest foothold through the acquisition of Industrial Metals of Kansas City, Missouri. In 1988, RASCO operated 24 branches serving approximately 40 states. These branches were located throughout the country, except in the highly industrial and unionized areas of the upper Midwest.

RASCO was the nation's largest distributor of aluminum mill products and the second largest for stainless-steel mill products. The products were used in the manufacture of such items as highway signs, automobile hoods, commercial kitchen equipment, hospital equipment, aircraft skins, aluminum siding, and wine tanks. RASCO was part of the highly fragmented metal service-center industry, which was composed of about 450 companies operating 1,300 facilities nationwide.

RASCO's strategic objective was to establish the largest service-center network in the United States for aluminum, stainless steel, and nickel-alloy products. Management had set specific market-share objectives for each strategic business unit (SBU), and RASCO's 1988 strategy had five areas of emphasis:

1. A marketing orientation centered around customer, quality, and service
2. Geographical expansion
3. Complementary product-line extension
4. Extension of capability to offer higher value-added processing services
5. Technology-based services such as customer computer order entry and inventory control.
6.

Since 1981, when its first business plan was developed, RASCO had become, in its own words, "a lean, but potent" organization. Shipments per employee in 1988 were 80 percent higher than in 1978. Total shipments were up 60 percent, while head count was down 12 percent. Ten years previously, a turnover problem existed to such an extent that the average employee had only five years of service. In 1988, the average RASCO employee had been with the company twelve years. Top management had been in place since 1980. Incentive programs existed for corporate staff, field managers, and the sales force; and promotion almost always occurred from within, supported by an in-house training program.

RASCO placed heavy emphasis on inventory turnover. The company's goal was to achieve 5 turns a year by 1993. Currently, inventory turned 4.2 times annually, which was better than the industry average. Various buying and selling mechanisms were in place to help achieve this objective.

Benjamin C. McLean, manager of Administrative Systems, believed EDI could serve as a tool to increase inventory turnover and could also help vendors reduce their lead times. Other internal benefits of EDI included reductions in clerical help, in data-entry errors, and in paper and mailing costs.

Industry Characteristics

The large, regional suppliers in this industry were pursuing national distribution. Producing mills (RASCO's suppliers) had shortened their manufacturing cycles and were producing more product in a semi-processed state. This move had given service centers the opportunity to provide value by carrying out the finishing process historically completed at the producing mill. As a result, service centers were rapidly expanding their processing capabilities.

On the demand side, large-volume metal users (RASCO's customers) had changed their buying strategies and expectations. In an effort to become low-cost producers, metal users were streamlining the purchasing process by reducing their number of suppliers. They also expected suppliers to provide just-in-time inventory. The service centers were using computer technology to improve productivity and customer service by offering just-in-time inventory availability, material requirements planning, quality assurance, and EDI. Metal users were also looking at ways to improve the way they could manage their own operations by asking suppliers to provide vital information on the quality and types of metals in advance of physical delivery. This would enhance the ability of metal users to pre-set their own operations to work with the different metals as they arrived from the suppliers.

RASCO Supplier Strategies and Relationships

RASCO had centralized much of its purchasing function at its Richmond headquarters in order to minimize costs. It evaluated each vendor, including parent-company Reynolds, on an annual basis. Each supplier was given an actual report card that rated the vendor's timeliness of delivery, product quality, and general service level. RASCO's policy was not to award firm supply contracts but rather to establish long-term relationships characterized as gentlemen's agreements. Mr. Peters noted,

"We forge lasting and mutually supportive relationships with our suppliers. As a result,

RASCO is a difficult company to sell to. But once you are a RASCO supplier, it is difficult to lose that status."

RASCO believed it would not have any problem finding a vendor willing to commit to establishing an EDI link with it. In fact, Mr. McLean already had a vendor in mind: Allegheny Ludlum Steel.

Allegheny, with 1987 sales of approximately $870 million and net income of approximately $47 million, was the US leader in the specialty-steel industry. In 1986, the company had considered EDI technology, because General Motors Corporation, an Allegheny customer, required its suppliers to have EDI capability in order to remain a GM vendor. Allegheny had begun exploring EDI technology and alternatives when suddenly GM retracted its ultimatum.

RASCO was one of Allegheny's biggest accounts, and the relationship was characterized by as many as 25 daily transactions. Accordingly, Allegheny had to manage tremendous amounts of paper flow to provide RASCO with the service it needed for all of its locations. Allegheny had a sophisticated computer system that indicated the cost of an item anywhere along the milling and processing cycle. The costing system was considered the best in the industry, and Allegheny was the industry low-cost producer.

RASCO Customer Strategies and Relationships

Most of RASCO's customers were industrial manufacturers who purchased metals for fabrication into a variety of finished products. Customer requirements were diverse: some might purchase just one piece of metal per order, while others ordered by the truckload. Some customers might purchase as often as several times a week; others would buy only once a year. RASCO had approximately 3,000 open accounts, although only 17 customers purchased more than $1 million annually (increased from eight million-dollar accounts during the previous year). Most of the million-dollar accounts were large-volume, multifacility operations that preferred to purchase metal under a single buying arrangement or contract.

Marketing the EDI concept to customers was a different challenge from marketing it to suppliers. To help him, Mr. McLean consulted RASCO's National Marketing Director William A. Fagan. Mr. Fagan was optimistic about the sales potential for RASCO and the metal service-center industry in general. The service-center segment was expected to grow faster than the metal-producing industry, and market-share growth for the service centers was forecasted to grow from 31.9 percent to 34.5 percent by 1992. In reality, growth was occurring more rapidly than anticipated.

RASCO had geographic coverage in 80 percent of the national market; however, 48 percent of the revenue in the metal service-center industry was generated in the upper Midwest and Northeast. Although active penetration into these regions was a future possibility, Mr. Fagan's current concern was to strengthen RASCO's leadership in its existing markets. Several aggressive competitors, including O'Neal Steel, Rio Algom, and J. T. Ryerson, had recently entered RASCO's existing market areas. Industry market shares are shown in Exhibit 11-1.

RASCO has undertaken several measures to strengthen customer relations. First, it developed a controlled inventory release program that could be used by customers for large orders. A customer placed an order, but instead of taking immediate delivery of the entire order, the customer had the option of receiving the material in incremental releases. RASCO was essentially providing customers with a warehousing service that lowered inventory-holding costs and reduced warehouse space. This service had enabled many customers to implement just-in-time inventory procedures.

RASCO had also improved its ability to provide value-added products. Because customers were expecting more preprocessing capabilities from their suppliers, RASCO had established processing locations in Altanta, St. Louis, and Los Angeles. Furthermore, RASCO had intro-

Exhibit 11-1 Estimated Industry Market Shares

COMPANY	LOCATIONS	ALUM	S/S	NICKEL
A. M. Castle & Co.	16	2.6%	3.8%	21.2%
Central Steel & Wire	4	3.1%	2.0%	0.0%
Copper & Brass Sales Inc.	8	1.7%	0.0%	0.0%
Edgcomb Corporation	22	2.6%	5.5%	0.0%
Inland Steel Corp.				
J. T. Ryerson & Son	26	4.3%	9.9%	2.6%
J. M. Tull Metals	10	2.0%	2.0%	2.6%
Earle M. Jorgensen Co.	24	1.4%	1.2%	0.0%
Metal Goods, a Div. of Alcan				
Alum. Corp.	20	4.0%	6.9%	17.6%
Prime Metals	6	2.3%		
Production Supply Co.	5	1.6%		
Reliance Steel & Alum.	14	2.8%	2.0%	
Thypin Steel Co. Inc.	4	0.0%	4.1%	
Rio Algom Ltd.				
Vincent Metals	10	2.6%	2.7%	
Williams & Co.	8	3.1%	4.1%	8.8%
Total share estimated (other than RASCO)		34.1%	40.1%	52.8%
RASCO	23	8.7%	8.4%	15.0%

duced such new processing technology as slitting and blanking equipment, which it planned to install at various locations. RASCO was also trying to find ways to help customers streamline operations by providing information on the quality and other properties of metals in advance of actual delivery.

Offering technology-based services was another element of RASCO's strategy to strengthen customer service. Mr. Fagan believed that electronic order entry would be a significant factor in RASCO's attempt to solidify its position in current markets. In addition, he thought that by streamlining the customer's purchasing function through electronic order entry, RASCO could cultivate stable and long-term supply relationships. To Mr. Fagan, a stronger relationship resulted in customers who were more tolerant and less likely to switch suppliers.

Developing an EDI relationship would contribute to this strategy because it was a bilateral arrangement requiring a commitment from both partners in order to be successful. This commitment not only required a financial and human resources investment but also compelled the par-

ticipants to make mutually satisfying agreements regarding the data, communications standards, and operational details of EDI. This cooperation, Mr. Fagan believed, further encouraged customers who undertook these investments and efforts to buy from RASCO. EDI would make doing business with RASCO simpler and easier, while at the same time strengthening the supplier-customer relationship.

Technological Considerations

RASCO was grappling with a host of technical issues in considering the design of an appropriate EDI architecture. Should separate and different EDI architectures be developed for suppliers (vendors) and customers? Should RASCO establish computer-to-computer links with each vendor and supplier? Should personal computers be installed in customer locations? Should RASCO develop proprietary standards or adopt ANSI X.12? If ANSI X.12 were adopted, should translation software be purchased or developed in-house? Should a value-added-network (VAN) be used? Because of so many different types of customers and vendors, these decisions were difficult and important.

Mr. McLean decided to determine and quantify some of the alternatives. On the supplier side, he believed the only option from a hardware standpoint was a computer-to-computer link via either direct connection or a VAN. RASCO would certainly not benefit from accessing the different suppliers' order-entry systems via a personal computer (PC). From a software standpoint, Mr. McLean could develop proprietary document and communications standards. It would probably cost RASCO only six months of an in-house programmer analyst's time to develop an EDI link with a vendor using proprietary data standards. If, instead, Mr. McLean opted to use the ANSI X.12 data standards, he would have to purchase the documentation from ANSI for a minimal cost of $200 or so. Again, it would probably take six months for a programmer analyst to develop the interface between ANSI X.12 standards and RASCO's internal document standards, or RASCO could purchase commercially available translation software for about $15,000. One advantage of purchasing the software was that the software vendor would provide RASCO with updates as the data standards changed. RASCO still needed to work out mutually agreeable communications protocols with its vendors or employ the services of a VAN. The VAN would charge a $700 monthly flat fee plus $.35 per document sent.

On the customer side, handling transactions using ANSI X.12 was the most desirable approach, but many customers were not mature with respect to using information systems and did not have ANSI X.12 capability. Mr. Mclean was faced with having customers of different technological capabilities all wanting the benefits of EDI capabilities. One option was to connect customers to RASCO's order-entry system. Mr. McLean reasoned that most customers probably had a PC, and possibly a modem. The only cost to RASCO would be a phone line, for which the customer might be willing to pay, and the human-resource time required to teach the customer how to access and use the RASCO system. For customers who didn't have a PC, RASCO could provide them one for a few thousand dollars. If RASCO decided to establish computer-to-computer links, and/or used the VAN, the costs and human-resource commitment would be equivalent to those for the vendor alternatives.

Marketing the EDI Concept

Our marketing philosophy is to try to keep one eye on real, day-to-day activity and the other on where RASCO wants to be four or five years down the road. If we become too marketing oriented and disassociate ourselves from the market's daily activity, we lose sight of what is the essence of our business—serving our customers' business needs now.

Bill Fagan
National Marketing Director

Mr. Fagan was eager to get the EDI initiative underway. For most customers, he believed that any competitive advantage brought about by being an industry pioneer would only last a decade or so. He thought that in ten years EDI would no longer be a differentiating factor; doing business via EDI would be as commonplace as the telephone. Therefore, it was necessary to establish EDI as soon as possible with these accounts.

For its large, national customers, however, RASCO's advantage could be sustainable indefinitely. The national accounts would have the same motivations as RASCO did to move toward a paperless operating environment: fewer clerical needs and data-entry errors, reduced costs for forms and mailing, and reduced vendor lead times. In addition, national accounts were very interested in lowering inventory-holding costs by implementing just-in-time and material requirements planning procedures. National accounts were also setting the precedent toward supplier consolidation. Furthermore, the investments and efforts necessary to make EDI work would be much greater for the larger accounts than the smaller ones. The selected vendors, therefore, would most likely benefit from the lion's share of the national accounts' metal needs.

EDI was becoming a hot item in the metals industry. Customers of all sizes were very eager to implement EDI under their strategic plans. Because of the diversity among his customer base, however, Mr. Fagan was unsure how to identify those customers with whom it would be best to pursue a relationship. Demand would probably be so great that RASCO would not be able to accommodate every customer who wanted to implement EDI. Mr. Fagan thought that some metals users simply wanted to jump on the EDI bandwagon and hadn't given much thought to how EDI could specifically improve the efficiency of their systems. Some, such as PMI Food Equipment Group (formerly Hobart Corporation), a maker of commercial food equipment, had integrated computer technology into every facet of their businesses, but most of the small metal-fabricating shops probably did not even use a PC. Some customers had well-designed internal systems, while others had completely uncoordinated operations.

Mr. Fagan thus had to develop an efficient and equitable way to determine who among the enthusiastic customers were truly ready for, and could benefit from, an EDI partnership with RASCO. The EDI initiative was bilateral in nature and, therefore, had to provide a win-win situation for both participants to be successful.

Mr. Fagan also realized that his decisions would have to be made in consideration of the alternatives facing Mr. McLean. The two of them would need to assess the long-term strategic importance of this initiative and determine the implications of the various options.

Above all, Mr. Fagan wanted to maintain control of the EDI relationship, even though customers typically held power over suppliers. How could this be done? What types of service should RASCO offer? Should it provide any and all customers with direct access to the order-entry system? Should RASCO develop a partnership only with those customers who could afford and justify maintaining direct computer-to-computer or computer-to-VAN-to-computer links?

Once these questions had been answered, Mr. Fagan had to decide whether or not it should be the responsibility of the RASCO sales staff to determine which customers were best suited for EDI. Furthermore, what would happen if RASCO identified a customer who could benefit from EDI but wasn't ready to make the commitment necessary for its successful implementation? Because of the strategic aspects of these decisions and the fact that RASCO had 3,000 customers, the undertaking was a challenge. These decisions had to be well thought out.

Appendix 1 Technical Information on Electronic Data Interchange"

At its simplest, EDI automates existing paper flows between organizations in much the same way as paper flows within organizations have been automated. EDI can also represent the opportunity to rethink and restructure the relationships between organizations. While the benefits are significant, so too are the pitfalls that can derail EDI initiatives, or their business impacts.

Extending Internal Transaction Processing Systems

Transaction processing systems of the organization can be extended beyond the organization's boundaries and linked electronically with the business and information systems of other organizations. Instead of paper documents linking the organizations, electronic equivalents of the documents would be transmitted. This substitution requires efforts in three broad areas. First, each organization must replace the manual interpretation of incoming documents with computer software. Second, the two organizations must replace the functions of the postal service with an agreement on a telecommunications link. Finally, the two organizations must establish the terms and conditions governing electronically placed orders and agree on the operational details of an electronic link.

Exhibit 11-2 Basic Components of an EDI Linkage

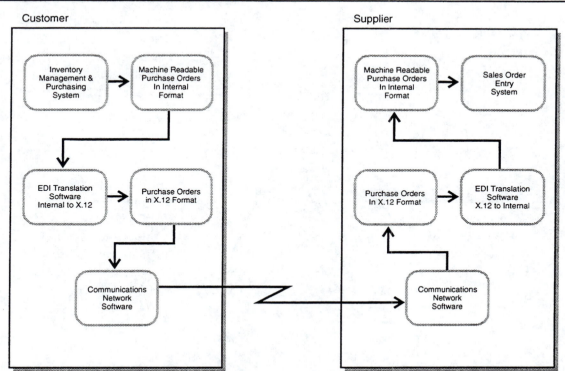

Components of an EDI Linkage

Most organizations have developed unique formats for their business forms. Although the information content of a purchase order is similar from organization to organization, there is still substantial interpretation and clerical effort to transcribe information from the range of incoming formats into an organization's internal format. A first step, therefore, in replacing a paper document (e.g., a purchase order) with its electronic equivalent is for the two organizations to agree on the data items to be exchanged, together with agreements on their format and sequence. These agreements must cover such details as where the customer's name and address will appear in the electronic transmission, how they will be formatted, how part numbers will be entered so that customer and vendor number systems will correlate, how units of measure (cases versus tons, for example) will be speci-

fied, and how the end of the document will be recognized (so that both organizations are assured that line items have not been lost in transmission). Since one of the goals of an EDI link is to minimize human intervention, precise agreements need to be reached to cover all of the idiosyncrasies of paper-based documents which are normally managed by human insight and judgment.

Once message formats have been worked out, the organizations must then agree on the technical details of a communications link. This linkage might be either direct computer-to-computer or via a value-added network service (VAN). A direct communications link between two organizations requires agreement on questions such as whether the link will be a permanent or dial-up link, and what communication protocols for sending and receiving data will be used. With the variety of possible technical protocols, finding a workable match may require

Exhibit 11-3 Adding EDI Trading Partners

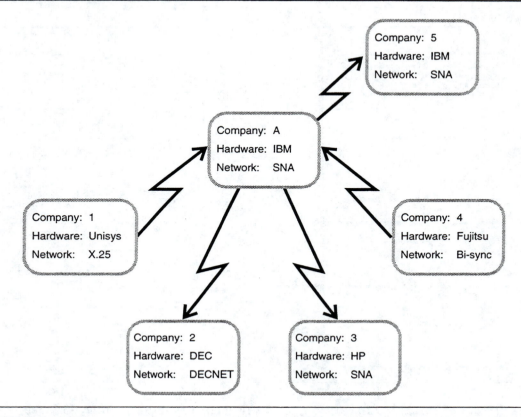

one partner or the other to invest in new equipment or software. Linking by way of a VAN implies establishing two linkages instead of one. On the other hand, a VAN linkage can provide store and forward capability in the form of "electronic mailboxes" that eliminate the requirement for coordinating schedules between organizations.

Finally, operational and procedural details must be established. If the link is to be a dial-up link, which organization will place the phone call and which will answer? What times of day can orders be sent or received? If an order is sent in error, what procedures must be followed to stop shipment? How will changes in pricing or the introduction of new products be announced? All of the mechanisms which have evolved to carry out business in a paper-based environment must be examined in an electronic context. The procedural details ensure that operations in each

organization can be coordinated with minimal disruption and that orders sent by one organization can be interpreted and honored by the other. Once the initial procedural details have been worked out, organizations must worry about how to manage organizational relationships which are mediated by electronic links. Exhibit 11-2 identifies the basic components of a link between two trading partners who are starting from existing automated systems for purchasing and order entry.

The ANSI X.12 Standards for EDI

In 1979, TDCC and the Credit Research Foundation[1] began work on developing a generic standard for EDI under the auspices of the

---

[1] The CRF was part of the National Association of Credit Management, a not-for-profit trade organization. CRF was concerned with interchange issues from the perspective of electronic funds transfer.

Exhibit 11-4 EDI Via Third Party Services

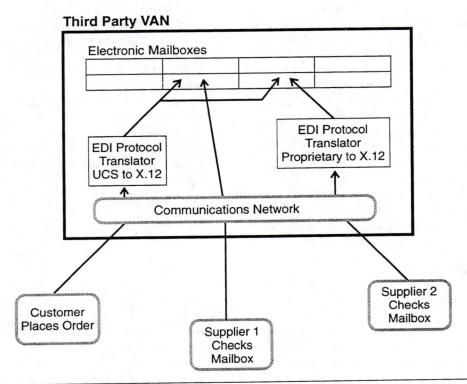

American National Standards Institute. These standards are know as the ANSI X.12 EDI standards after the designation of the ANSI subcommittee which developed the standards. The X.12 standards specify the overall structure for EDI transactions and the details for individual transactions.

The X.12 standards closely followed the logic of the existing TDCC standards. Essentially, the X.12 standards specify a series of codes and rules for interpretation that permit a generic paper document to be converted into an interpretable machine-readable format. To achieve a standard applicable across a range of industries, the X.12 committee created standards with room for flexibility and interpretation. Industries committing to EDI can take the X.12 . standards as a starting point and specify the interpretations necessary to adapt to industry practices. Interpretations required to make X.12 usable might include, for example, rules for identifying specific organizations or shipping locations. The X.12 standard specifies that a DUNS[2] number will be used as an organization's unique identifier. Not all organizations have a DUNS number, however. Further, a DUNS number only identifies the parent organization; it does not identify specific shipping locations or branch offices. Because of the flexibility inherent in X.12's generic approach, standards within an industry frequently display some measure of conflict with standards in other industries.

Third Party Service Providers of EDI

Establishing a link between any two companies is straightforward, with or without standards. With standards, it is conceptually simple to add new trading partners. Message standards specify

[2] Assigned by Dun & Bradstreet for their credit reporting services.

data formats, and communication standards specify how to physically link the two companies' computer centers. However, the operational details of establishing computer-to- computer communication links with multiple trading partners can severely limit the ability of a company to set up EDI links with more than a handful of its major trading partners. Exhibit 11-3 suggests the complexities of adding trading partners. Two companies, for example, may use incompatible communications hardware or software. Establishing an EDI link entails one company or the other investing in new equipment.

The second response to these operational problems has come from commercial time- sharing companies and computer service bureaus such as McDonnell Douglas Automation, IBM's Information Network, General Electric Information Services Company, and AT&T offering Value-Added Network (VAN). These are companies which traditionally sold computer time to companies who could not afford their own computer systems or needed access to highly specialized software. The larger vendors had made substantial investments in computer hardware and in extensive data communications networks.

Exhibit 11-4 depicts the basic structure of services which these independent (as opposed to industry captive) vendors offered to support EDI. Each of these VAN services operates in a similar fashion. The service establishes an "electronic mailbox" for a company where that company can accept electronic orders. The service bureau takes responsibility for accepting input from other companies in a variety of formats and standards and translating these input orders into the correct standard. Many service bureaus have developed translation programs between the common standards and support a wide variety of communications standards and protocols. Serv-

ice bureau costs include fixed costs to maintain a mailbox and charges for characters transmitted. At normal transaction volumes, service bureau charges for processing a purchase order and its acknowledgement were approximately $1.50 per purchase order in the mid-1980s.

Although the third party EDI VAN concept was initially introduced to alleviate the operational problems of multiple EDI links, it presents operational problems in its own right. With one more organization involved in the business transaction, there is one more layer to manage and one more layer to deal with in resolving problems.

Conclusion

EDI is moving out of a long start-up phase and moving into the knee of the growth curve. Some consultants have predicted that more than 10,000 companies will be using EDI in the United States by the early 1990s. The 1988 market for various software and third party services is on the order of $60 million. EDI holds out the promise of great improvements in productivity and substantial changes in business practices. EDI promises to become a central characteristic of routine business practice in the 1990s.

This technical note provides a rich and thorough treatment of EDI concepts. It was based on a technical note by James McGee and Professor Benn Konsynski of Harvard Business School. (Note 9-190-022 copyright ©1989 by the President and Fellows of Harvard College.) Excerpts used in this present note with special permission from the authors of the Harvard publication to the case Author.

12

Mrs. Fields'
Secret Ingredient

Part of the late Buckminster Fuller's genius was his capacity to transform a technology from the merely new to the truly useful by creating a new form to take advantage of its characteristics. Fuller's geodesic designs, for instance, endowed plastic with practical value as a building material. His structures, if not always eye-appealing, still achieved elegance — as mathematicians use the word to connote simplicity — of function. Once, reacting to someone's suggestion that a new technology be applied to an old process in a particularly awkward way, Fuller said dismissively, "That would be like putting an outboard motor on a skyscraper."

Introducing microcomputers with spreadsheet and word-processing software to a company originally designed around paper technology amounts to the same thing. If the form of the company doesn't change, the computer, like the outboard, is just a doodad. Faster long division and speedier typing don't move a company into the information age.

But Randy Fields has created something entirely new — a shape if not *the* shape, of business organizations to come. It gives top management a dimension of personal control over dispersed operations that small companies otherwise find impossible to achieve. It projects a founder's vision into parts of a company that have long ago outgrown his or her ability to reach in person.

In the structure that Fields is building, computers don't just speed up old administrative management processes. They alter the process. Management, in the Fields organizational paradigm, becomes less administration and more inspiration. The management hierarchy of the company feels almost flat.

What's the successful computer-age business going to look like in the not-very-distant future? Something like Randy Field's concept — which is, in a word, neat.

What makes it neat, right out of the oven, is where he's doing it. Randy Fields, age 40, is married to Debbi Fields, who turns 31 this month, and together they run Mrs. Fields Cookies, of Park City, Utah. They project that by year end, their business will comprise nearly 500 company-owned stores in 37 states selling what Debbi calls a "feel-good feeling." That sounds a little hokey. A lot of her cookie talk does. "Good enough never is," she likes to remind the people around her.

But there's nothing hokey about the 18.5% that Mrs. Fields Inc. earned on cookie sales of

Written by Tom Richman. Reprinted with permission, *Inc.* magazine, October, 1987. Copyright © 1987 by Goldhirsh Group, Inc., 58 Commercial Wharf, Boston, MA 02110.

$87 million last year, up from $72.6 million a year earlier.

Won't the cookie craze pass? people often ask Debbi. "I think that's very doubtful... I mean," she says, "if [they are] fresh, warm, and wonderful and make you feel good, are you going to stop buying cookies?"

Maybe not, but the trick for her and her husband is to see that people keep buying them from Mrs. Fields, not David's Cookies, Blue Chip Cookies, The Original Great Chocolate Chip Cookie, or the dozens of regional and local competitors. Keeping the cookies consistently fresh, warm, and wonderful at nearly 500 retail cookie stores spread over the United States and five other countries can't be simple or easy. Worse, keeping smiles on the faces of the nearly 4,500, mostly young, store employees — not to mention keeping them productive and honest — is a bigger chore than most companies would dare to take on alone.

Most don't; they franchise, which is one way to bring responsibility and accountability down to the store level in a far-flung, multi-store organization. For this, the franchisor trades off revenues and profits that would otherwise be his, and a large measure of flexibility. Because its terms are defined by contract, the relationship between franchisor and franchisee is more static than dynamic, difficult to alter as the market and the business change.

Mrs. Fields Cookies, despite its size, has not franchised — persuasive evidence in itself that the Fieldses have built something unusual. Randy Fields believes that no other U.S. food retailer with so many outlets has dared to retain this degree of direct, day-to-day control of its stores. And Mrs. Fields Cookies does it with a headquarters staff of just 115 people. That's approximately one staffer to every five stores — piddling compared with other companies with far fewer stores to manage. When the company bought La Petite Boulangerie from PepsiCo earlier this year, for instance, the soft-drink giant had 53 headquarters staff people to administer the French bakery/sandwich shop chain's 119 stores. Randy needed just four weeks to cut the number to three people.

On paper, Mrs. Fields Cookies looks almost conventional. In action, however, because of the way information flows between levels, it feels almost flat.

On paper, between Richard Lui running the Pier 39 Mrs. Fields in San Francisco and Debbi herself in Park City, there are several apparently traditional layers of hierarchy: an area sales manager, a district sales manager, a regional director of operations, a vice-president of operations. In practice, though, Debbi is as handy to Lui — and to every other store manager — as the telephone and personal computer in the back room of his store.

On a typical morning at Pier 39, Lui unlocks the store, calls up the Day Planner program on his Tandy computer, plugs in today's sales projection (based on year-earlier sales adjusted for growth), and answers a couple of questions the program puts to him. What day of the week is it? What type of day: normal day, sale day, school day, holiday, other?

Say, for instance, it's Tuesday, a school day. The computer goes back to the Pier 39 store's hour-by-hour, product-by-product performance on the last three school-day Tuesdays. Based on what you did then, the Day Planner tells him, here's what you'll have to do today, hour by hour, product by product, to meet your sales projection. It tells him how many customers he'll need each hour and how much he'll have to sell them. It tells him how many batches of cookie dough he'll have to mix and when to mix them to meet the demand and to minimize leftovers. He could make these estimates himself if he wanted to take the time. The computer makes them for him. Decision?

Each hour, as the day progresses, Lui keeps the computer informed of his progress. Currently he enters the numbers manually, but new cash registers that automatically feed hourly data to the computer, eliminating the manual update, are already in some stores. The computer in turn revises the hourly projections and makes suggestions. The customer count is OK, it might observe, but your average check is down. Are your crew members doing enough suggestive selling? If, on the other hand, the computer indicates that the customer count is down, that may suggest the manager will want to do some sampling — chum for customers up and down the pier with a tray of free cookie pieces or try something else, whatever he likes, to lure people into the store. Sometimes, if sales are just slightly down, the machine's revised projections will actually exceed the original on the assumption that greater selling effort will more than compensate for the small deficit. On the other hand, the program isn't blind to reality. It recognizes a bad day and diminishes its hourly sales projections and baking estimates accordingly.

Hourly sales goals?

Well, when Debbi was running her store, she set hourly sales goals. Her managers should, too, she thinks. Rather than enforce the practice through dicta, Randy has embedded the notion in the software that each store manager relies on. Do managers find the machine's suggestions intrusive? Not Lui. "It's a tool for me," he says.

Several times a week, Lui talks with Debbi. Well, he doesn't exactly talk with her, but he hears from her. He makes a daily phone call to Park City to check his computerized PhoneMail messages, and as often as not there's something from Mrs. Fields herself. If she's upset about some problem, Lui hears her sounding upset. If it's something she's breathlessly exuberant about, which is more often the case, he gets an earful of that, too. Whether the news is good or bad, how much better to hear it from the boss herself than to get a memo in the mail next week.

By the same token, if Lui has something to say to Debbi, he uses the computer. It's right there, handy. He calls up the Form-Mail program, types his message, and the next morning it's on Debbi's desk. She promises an answer from her or her staff within 48 hours. On the morning I spent with her, among the dozen or so messages she got was one from the crew at a Berkeley, California, store making their case for higher wages there and another from the manager of a store in Brookline, Massachusetts, which has been struggling recently. We've finally gotten ourselves squared away, was the gist of the note, so please come visit. (Last year Debbi logged around 350,000 commercial air miles visiting stores.)

Here are some other things Lui's computer can do for him.

- **Help him schedule crew.** He plugs his daily sales projection for two weeks hence into a scheduling program that incorporates as its standards the times Debbi herself takes to perform the mixing, dropping, and baking chores. The program gives him back its best guess of how many people with which skill levels he'll need during which hours. A process that done manually consumed almost an hour now takes just a fraction of that time.

- **Help him interview crew applicants.** He calls up his interview program, seats the applicant at the keyboard, and has him or her answer a series of questions. Based on the answers given by past hirees, the machine suggests to Lui which candidates will succeed or fail. It's still his choice. And any applicant, before a hire, will still get an audition — something to see how he-or she performs in public. Maybe Lui will send the hopeful out on a sampling mission.

- **Help with personnel administration.** Say he hires the applicant. He informs the machine, which generates a personnel folder and a payroll entry in Park City, and a few months later comes back to remind Lui that he hasn't submitted the initial evaluation (also by computer), which is now slightly past due. It administers the written part of the skills test and updates the records with the results. The entire Mrs. Fields personnel manual will soon be on the computer so that 500 store managers won't forget to delete old pages and insert revised ones every time a change is made.

- **Help with maintenance.** A mixer isn't working, so the manager punches up the repair program on the computer. It asks him some questions, such as is the plug in the wall? If the questions don't prompt a fix, the computer sends a repair request to Park City telling the staff there which machine is broken, its maintenance history, and which vendor to call. It sends a copy of the work order back to the store. When the work gets done, the store signs off by computer, and the vendor's bill gets paid.

That's a lot of technology applied to something as basic as a cookie store, but Randy had two objectives in mind. He wanted to keep his wife in frequent, personal, two-way contact with hundreds of managers whose stores she couldn't possibly visit often enough. "The people who work in the stores," says Debbi, "are my customers. Staying in touch with them is the most important thing I can do."

It's no accident, even if Lui isn't consciously aware of why he does what he does, that he runs his store just about the same way that Debbi ran her first one 10 years ago. Even when she isn't there, she's there — in the standards built into his scheduling program, in the hourly goals, in the sampling and suggestive selling, on the phone. The technology has "leveraged," to use Randy's term, Debbi's ability to project her influence into more stores than she could ever reach effectively without it.

Second, Randy wanted to keep store managers managing, not sweating the paperwork. "In retailing," he says, "the goal is to keep people close to people. Whatever gets in the way of that — administration, telephones, ordering, and so on — is the enemy." If an administrative chore can be automated, it should be.

Store managers benefit from a continuing exchange of information. Of course, Park City learns what every store is doing daily — from sales to staffing to training to hires to repairs — and how it uses that information we'll get to in a minute. From the store managers' perspective, however, the important thing is that the information they provide keeps coming back to them, reorganized to make it useful. The hour- by-hour sales projections and projected customer counts that managers use to pace their days reflect their own experiences. Soon, for instance, the computer will take their weekly inventory reports

and sales projections and generate supply orders that managers will only have to confirm or correct — more administrative time saved. With their little computers in the back room, store managers give, but they also receive.

What technology can do for operations it can also do for administration.

"We're all driven by Randy's philosophy that he wants the organization to be as flat as possible," says Paul Quinn, the company's director of management information systems (MIS).

"There are a few things," says controller Lynn Quilter, "that Randy dislikes about growth.... He hates the thought of drowning in people so that he can't walk in and know exactly what each person does.... The second thing that drives him nuts is paper."

"The objective," says Randy, "is to leverage people — to get them to act when we have 1,000 stores the same way they acted when we had 30."

He has this theory that large organizations, organizations with lots of people, are, per se, inferior to small ones. Good people join a growing business because it offers them an opportunity to be creative. As the company grows, these people find they're tied up managing the latest hires. Creativity suffers. Entropy sets in. Randy uses technology to keep entropy at bay.

He began by automating rote clerical chores and by minimizing data-entry effort. Machines can sort and file faster than people, and sorting and filing is deadly dull work, anyway. Lately he's pushed the organization toward automated exception reporting for the same reason. Machines can compare actual results with expected results and flag the anomolies, which are all management really cares about anyway. And within a few years, Randy expects to go much further in his battle against bureaucracy by developing artificial-intelligence aids to the running of the business.

Understand that it's not equipment advances — state-of-the-art hardware — that's pushing Mrs. Fields Cookies toward management frontiers. The machines the company uses are strictly off the shelf: an IBM minicomputer connected to inexpensive personal computers. It is, instead, Randy's ability to create an elegant, functional software architecture. He has, of course, had an advantage that the leader of an older, more established company would not have. Because Mrs. Fields is still a young enough company, he doesn't have to shape his automated management system to a preexisting structure. Every new idea doesn't confront the opposition of some bureaucratic fiefdom's survival instinct. Rather, the people part and the technology part of the Fields' organization are developing simultaneously, each shaped by the same philosophy.

You see this congruence at corporate headquarters and in the company's operational management organization.

Between Debbi as chief executive officer and the individual store managers is what seems on paper to be a conventional reporting structure with several layers of management. But there's an additional box on the organization chart. It's not another management layer. It transcends layers, changing the way information flows between them and even changing the functions of the layers.

The box consists of a group of seven so-called store controllers, working in Park City from the daily store reports and weekly inventory reports. They ride herd on the numbers. If a store's sales are dramatically off, the store controller covering that geographical region will be the first to know it. If there's a discrepancy between the inventory report, the daily report of batches of cookies baked, and the sales report, the controller will be the first to find it. (It is possible for a smart thief to steal judiciously for about a week from a Mrs. Fields store.) "We're a check on operations," says store controller Wendy Phelps, but she's far more than just a check. She's the other half of a manager's head.

Since she's on top of the numbers, the area, district, and regional managers don't have to be — not to the same degree, at any rate. "We want managers to be with people, not with problems," says Debbi. It's hard, Randy says, to find managers who are good with both people and numbers. People people, he thinks, should be in the field, with numbers people backing them up — but not second-guessing them. Here's where the company takes a meaningful twist.

Problems aren't reported up the organization just so solutions can flow back down. Instead, store controllers work at levels as low as they can. They go to the store manager if he's the one to fix a discrepancy, a missing report, for instance. Forget chain of command. "I'm very efficiency minded," says Randy.

So the technology gives the company an almost real-time look at the minutiae of its operations, and the organizational structure — putting function ahead of conventional protocol — keeps it from choking on this abundance of data.

Some managers would have problems with a system that operates without their daily intervention. They wouldn't be comfortable, and they wouldn't stay at Mrs. Fields. Those who do stay can manage people instead of paper.

If administrative bureaucracies can grow out of control, so can technology bureaucracies. A couple of principles, ruthlessly adhered to, keep both simple at Mrs. Fields.

The first is that if a machine can do it, a machine should do it. "People," says Randy, "should do only that which people can do. It's demeaning for people to do what machines can do.... Can machines manage people? No. Machines have no feelie-touchies, none of that chemistry that flows between two people."

The other rule, the one that keeps the technological monster itself in check, is that the company will have but one data base. Everything — cookie sales, payroll records, suppliers' invoices, inventory reports, utility charges — goes into the same data base. And whatever anybody needs to know has to come out of it.

"Don't enforce this rule, and," says Randy, "the next thing you know you have 48 different programs that can't talk to each other." Technology grown rampant.

Having a single data base means, first, that nobody has to waste time filing triplicate forms or answering the same questions twice. "We capture the data just once," says controller Quilter.

Second, it means that the system itself can do most of the rote work that people used to do. Take orders for chocolate, for instance. The computer gets the weekly inventory report. It already knows the sales projection. So let the computer order the chocolate chips. Give the store manager a copy of the order on his screen so he can correct any errors, but why take his time to generate the order when he's got better things to do — like teaching someone to sell. Or, take it further. The machine generates the order. The supplier delivers the chips to the store and bills the corporate office. A clerk in the office now has to compare the order, the invoice, and what the store says it got. Do they all match? Yes. She tells the computer to write a check. The more stores you have, the more clerks it takes. Why not let the computer do the matching? In fact, if everything fits, why get people involved at all? Let people handle the exceptions. Now, the clerk, says MIS director Quinn, instead of a processor becomes a mini- controller, someone who uses his brain.

The ordering process doesn't happen that way yet at Mrs. Fields, although it probably will soon as Randy continues to press for more exception reporting. You can see where he's going with this concept. "Eventually," he says, "even the anomolies become normal." The exceptions themselves, and a person's response to them, assume a pattern. Why not, says Randy, have the computer watch the person for a while? "Then the machine can say, 'I have found an anomoly. I've been watching you, and I think this is what you would do. Shall I do it for you, yes or no? If yes, I'll do it, follow up, and so on. If no, what do you want me to do?' " It would work for the low-level function — administering accounts payable, for instance. And it would work at higher levels as well. "If," Randy says, "I can ask the computer now where are we making the most money and where are we making the least and then make a decision about where not to build new stores, why shouldn't that sort of thing be on automatic pilot too? 'Based on performance,' it will say, 'we shouldn't be building any more stores in East Jibip. Want me to tell [real-estate manager] Mike [Murphy]?' We're six months away from being able to do that."

The ability to look at the company, which is what the data base really is, at a level of abstraction appropriate to the looker, is the third advan-

tage of a single data base — even if it never moves into artificial-intelligence functions. It means that Debbi Fields and Richard Lui are both looking at the same world, but in ways that are meaningful to each of them.

The hurdle to be overcome before you can use technology to its best advantage — and that isn't equivalent to just hanging on outboard motor on a skyscraper, as Buckminster Fuller said — isn't technical in the hardware sense. Randy buys only what he calls plain vanilla hardware. And it isn't financial. For all its relative sophistication in computer systems, Mrs. Fields spends just 0.4996 of sales on data processing, much of which is returned in higher productivity.

Much more important, Randy says, is having a consistent vision of what you want to accomplish with the technology. Which functions do you want to control? What do you want your organization chart to look like? In what ways do you want to leverage the CEO's vision? "Imagination. We imagine what it is we want," says Randy. "We aren't constrained by the limits of what technology can do. We just say, 'What does your day look like? What would you like it to look like?' " He adds, "If you don't have your paradigm in mind, you have no way of knowing whether each little step is taking you closer to or further from your goal."

For instance, he inaugurated the daily store report with the opening of store number two in 1978. The important thing was the creation of the report — which is the fundamental data-gathering activity in the company — not its transmission mode. That can change, and has. First transmission was by Fax, then by telephone touch tone, and only recently by computer modem.

Having a consistent vision means, Randy says, that he could have described as far back as 1978, when he first began to create it, the system that exists today. But he doesn't mean the machines or how they're wired together. "MIS in this company," he says, "has always had to serve two masters. First, control. Rapid growth without control equals disaster. We needed to keep improving control over our stores. And second, information that leads to control also leads to better decision making. To the extent that the information is then provided to the store and field-management level, the decisions that are made there are better, and they are more easily made. "That has been our consistent vision."

Postscript

Since this case was written, several things have happened at Mrs. Fields Cookies. Specifically, a *Wall Street Journal* headline of January 1, 1989, put it most succinctly: "How the Cookie Crumbled at Mrs. Fields." Several things have recently occurred at the company. During the first half of 1988, the company lost $15.1 million and was expected to report an overall larger loss for the year, compared to a $17.7 million net income in 1987. Further, the company has closed or made provisions to close 95 of its cookie stores.

Why did this rapid turnaround occur? The company suggests that a large part of the problem is the expenses incurred in combining some Mrs. Fields stores with La Petite Boulangeries (a chain of 105 French-style bakeries acquired from PepsiCo in 1987). Under the new name "Mrs. Fields Bakery Cafe," the company will operate a series of combination stores. The com-

pany argues that all of the closed stores were in areas that overlapped with proposed combination stores. These costs, combined with soaring rents in many markets, caused the problems. The company believes that its core business is not in trouble and that the firm will be profitable in 1989 — although well below the impressive 1987 levels.

Several analysts disagree with the company's assessment. They believe many of the problems the company is experiencing stem from its change from a single-product company to a "specialty foods retailer." They argue that the firm was spread too thin in some areas and too saturated in others and did not diversify fast enough. Before the La Petite Boulangerie acquisition, there had been virtually no diversification — a dangerous choice in a trendy market like premium cookies. There is also some question of whether the management structure described in the case could keep pace with the firm's rapid growth and whether the structure was even practical when the company expanded internationally. Since the case was written, the company sold its European operations to a French firm. What else do you think might have caused problems?

13
Acetate Department

The Acetate Department's product consisted of about twenty diferent kinds of viscous liquid acetate used by another department to manufacture transparent film to be left clear, or coated with photographic emulsion or iron oxide.

Before the change: The Department was located in an old four-story building as in Exhibit 13-1. The work flow was as follows:

1. Twenty kinds of powder arrived daily in 50 pound paper bags. In addition, storage tanks of liquid would be filled weekly from tank trucks.

2. Two or three Acetate Helpers would jointly unload pallets of bags into the storage area using a lift truck.

3.   Several times a shift, the Helpers would bring the bagged material up the elevator to the third floor where it would be temporarily stored along the walls.

4. Mixing batches was under the direction of the Group Leader and was rather like baking a cake. Following a prescribed formula, the Group Leader, Mixers and Helpers operated valves to feed in the proper solvent and manually dump in the proper weight and mixture of solid material. The glob would be mixed by giant egg beaters and heated according to the recipe.

5. When the batch was completed, it was pumped to a finished product storage tank.

6. After completing each batch, the crew would thoroughly clean the work area of dust and empty bags because cleanliness was extremely important to the finished product.

To accomplish this work, the Department was structured as in Exhibit 13-2.

The Helpers were usually young men 18-25 years of age, the Mixers 25 to 40, and the Group Leaders and Foremen 40 to 60. Foremen were on salary, Group Leaders, Mixers and Helpers on hourly pay.

To produce 20,000,000 pounds of product per year, the Department operated 24 hours a day, 7 days a week. Four crews rotated shifts: for example, Shift Foremen A and his two Group Leaders and crews would work two weeks on the day shift 8:00 a.m. to 4:00 p.m., then two weeks on the evening shift 4:00 p.m. to midnight, then two weeks on the night shift midnight to 8:00

From "Redesigning the Acetate Department," by David L Hampton, Charles E. Summer, and Ross A. Webber, *Organizational Behavior and the Practice of Management* (Glenview, IL: Scott, Foresman and Company, 1982), pp. 751 - 755. Used with permission.

EXHIBIT 13-1 Elevation View of Acetate Department Before Change

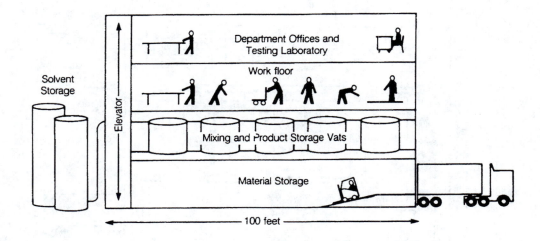

a.m. There were two days off between shift changes.

During a typical shift, a Group Leader and his crew would complete two or three batches. A batch would frequently be started on one shift and completed by the next shift crew. There was slightly less work on the evening and night shifts because no deliveries were made, but these crews engaged in a little more cleaning. The Shift Foreman would give instructions to the two Group Leaders at the beginning of each shift as to the status of batches in process, batches to be mixed, what deliveries were expected and what cleaning was to be done. Periodically throughout the shift, the Foreman would collect samples in small bottles which he would leave at the laboratory technicians' desk for testing.

The management and office staff(Department Head, Staff Engineer, Lab Technician, and Department Clerk) only worked on the day shift,

EXHIBIT 13-2 Organizational Chart of Acetate Department Before Change

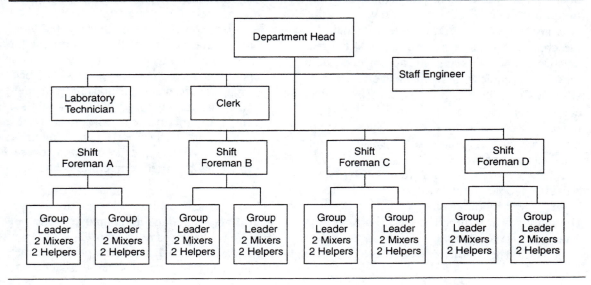

EXHIBIT 13-3 Elevation View of Acetate Department After Change

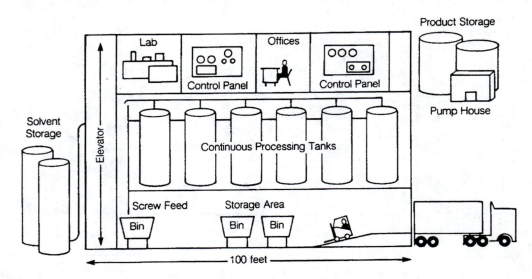

although if an emergency arose on the other shifts, the Foreman might call.

All in all, the Department was a pleasant place in which to work. The work floor was a little warm, but well-lighted, quiet and clean. Substantial banter and horseplay occurred when the crew wasn't actually loading batches, particularly on the nonday shifts. The men had a dartboard in the work area and competition was fierce and loud. Frequently a crew would go bowling right after work, even at 1:00 a.m., for the community's alleys were open 24 hours a day. Department turnover and absenteeism were low. Most employees spent their entire career with the Company, many in one department. The corporation was large, paternalistic, well-paying, and offered attractive fringe benefits including large, virtually automatic bonuses for all. Then came the change....

The new system: To improve productivity, the Acetate Department was completely redesigned; the technology changed from batches to continuous processing. The basic building was retained, but substantially modified as in Exhibit 13-3. The modified work flow is as follows:

1. Most solid raw materials are delivered via trucks in large aluminum bins holding 500 pounds.

2. One Handler (formerly Helper) is on duty at all times in the first floor to receive raw materials and to dump the bins into the semi-automatic screw feeder.

3. The Head Operator (former Group Leader) directs the mixing operations from his control panel on the fourth floor located along one wall across from the Department Offices. The mixing is virtually an automatic operation once the solid material has been sent up the screw feed; a tape program opens and closes the necessary valves to add solvent, heat, mixing, etc. Sitting at a table before his panel, the Head Operator monitors the process to see that everything is operating within specified temperatures and pressures.

This technical change allowed the Department to greatly reduce its manpower. The new structure is illustrated in Exhibit 13- 4. One new position was created, that of a pump operator who is located in a small separate shack about

EXHIBIT 13-4 Organizational Chart of Acetate Department After Change

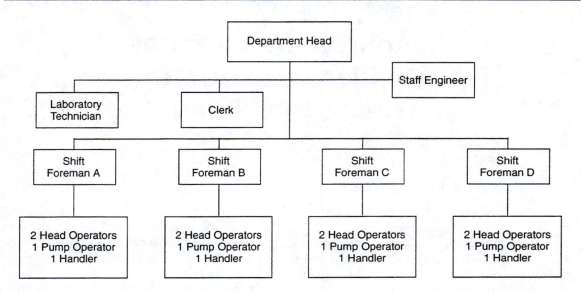

300 feet from the main building. He operates pumps and valves that move the finished product among various storage tanks.

Under the new system, production capacity was increased to 25,000,000 pounds per year. All remaining employees received a 15 percent increase in pay. Former personnel not retained in the Dope Department were transferred to other departments in the company. No one was dismissed.

Unfortunately, actual output has lagged well below capacity in the several months since the construction work and technical training was completed. Actual production is virtually identical with that under the old technology. Absenteeism has increased markedly, and several judgmental errors by operators have resulted in substantial losses.

14

Missouri Campus Bitterly Divided over How to 'Reallocate' Funds

On the campus of the University of Missouri here, the signs of spring came late and were decidedly makeshift: a white sheet bearing the spray-painted legend "SOCIAL WORK IS HERE TO STAY" draped from windows in Clark Hall; a crudely lettered placard taped to a glass door in Memorial Union defiantly announcing, "HELL NO, HOME EC WON'T GO!"

Hasty construction accounted for the home-made quality of the signs, for as the academic year drew quickly to a close, many students and faculty members were surprised to find themselves fighting for their academic lives — the survival of their programs.

In a year in which the campus has had to contend with a host of financial problems — some fabricated, critics alleged — April was the cruelest month. It was on April 2 that proposals to "reallocate" nearly $12 million in operating funds over the next three years were announced. Among them were recommendations to eliminate two of the university's fourteen colleges and to reduce substantially the offerings in five others.

The ensuing controversy divided the campus. "It has set department against department

and colleague against colleague," says one dean. "It's civil war, with everyone trying to gore everyone else's bull."

In mid-April, the faculty voted to call for the resignation of Chancellor Barbara S. Uehling if she did not withdraw the proposals.

By the time graduating students were preparing for last week's commencement exercises, the subject of their conversations — whether or not they had jobs — also seemed to be a prime topic of talk among many members of the faculty and staff.

What led to this course of events was a decision last summer by President James C. Olson to take action "to preserve and even enhance the quality of the university in a time of severely limited resources."

"The university has coped with ten years of inadequate funding by making cuts across the board," he says. "It became clear that a continuation of that policy was a prescription for mediocrity."

Mr. Olson announced last July that the university would attempt to save approximately $16 million over the next three years to finance pay raises as well as library, laboratory, and other improvements. He told the chancellors of the

Written by Paul Desruisseaux. Reprinted with permission of *The Chronicle of Higher Education*, copyright @ 1982.

four Missouri campuses that their first priority was to be the development of an adequate compensation plan for the university staff. His plan was supported by the university's Board of Curators.

President Olson's goal is to bring salaries at the university up to the average of those at member institutions of the Big 8 and Big 10 athletic conferences — institutions that, he says, "are comparable to Missouri in mission." At the start of the 1981-82 academic year, Missouri had the lowest salary average in that comparison group, 8.9 percent below the midpoint.

Mr. Olson instructed the chancellors to find money for salary adjustments "by reducing the quantity of what you do rather than the quality."

That met with approval on the Columbia campus, where Chancellor Uehling has said "the concept of shared poverty is not viable for a competitive university," and where the faculty has been on the record for five years in opposition to across-the-board budget cuts.

The 24,000-student campus, biggest in the system, is scheduled for the largest reductions: as much as $12 million, or about 5 percent of its operating budget.

The curators adopted procedures for the "discontinuance" of programs, and the university established four criteria for reviewing them: overall quality, contribution to the university's mission, need for the programs, and financial considerations. Application of the criteria was left up to the individual campuses.

"On two occasions I identified to the deans the ways in which we might go about this task," says Provost Ronald F. Bunn, who is faced with reducing the budget for academic programs by $7 million.

'A Quality Matrix'

According to Mr. Bunn, most of the deans suggested that he take on the task. The Faculty Council recommended the same. "This was an administrative job," says David West, the council chairman and a professor of finance. "We

wanted the administration to make its proposals, and then we'd take shots at it."

Mr. Bunn reviewed all of the campus's academic programs himself, rating them according to the four criteria established by the president. He compiled what he calls "a quality matrix," which resembles the box score of a baseball game. The programs that ranked lowest he proposed reducing.

Specifically, the provost recommended the elimination of the School of Library and Informational Science and the College of Public and Community Services (with the possible retention of its masters-in-social-work program). He also recommended major reductions in the College of Education, the College of Engineering, the School of Nursing, the College of Home Economics, and the School of Health Related Professions. In some cases the reductions would mean the elimination of one or more departments within those colleges.

All told, campus officials estimated that the cuts in academic programs would affect twenty-five hundred students and as many as two hundred faculty and staff members. Since tenure regulations require the university to give tenured faculty members thirteen months' notice of plans to eliminate their jobs, the reduction proposals would have little effect on the 1982-83 budget.

When university administrators announced their plans on April 2, those in the academic programs predictably provoked the greatest response.

'It Infuriates Me'

An ad hoc committee of faculty members and students was charged with reviewing the provost's recommendations and conducting hearings. Individuals in the targeted programs have been outspokenly critical of Provost Bunn's judgment.

"We are the only accredited library-science program in Missouri, and it infuriates me — as a citizen as much as anything — that this campus, unilaterally, has made the decision to eliminate programs that exist nowhere else in the state," says Edward P. Miller, dean of the library school. "I don't think the provost could have done a worse job of abrogating the criteria for review if he tried."

Bob G. Woods, dean of the College of Education, who supported the idea of programmatic cuts, says he was prepared to reduce his budget by as much as $500,000, but when he learned that reductions of $1.2 million were required, he changed his mind. "I want the process to be refuted as unnecessary at this time," he says.

Officials in the College of Home Economics charge that the recommendations to eliminate two departments there were based on outdated information. "The decision regarding my program was based on a three-year-old internal-review document," says Kitty G. Dickerson, chairman of the department of clothing and textiles, who is in her first year at Missouri. "I was brought here to strengthen this department. There were thirty-five recommendations in that internal review, and we have already addressed all but three. But there was never an opportunity to let it be known that we have made this enormous progress."

Martha Jo Martin, assistant dean of home economics, says that eliminating the two departments would cost the college its accreditation and half of its enrollment.

Opposition was not limited to those in programs proposed for reduction. Says Andrew Twaddle, a professor of sociology, "My main concern is not with the actual targeting of programs but the fact that the administration made these decisions with little input from the faculty, except for a select group of its supporters.

"I honestly don't know what the university's real fiscal situation is — there are so many conflicting figures flying around, and no one is backing them up very well," he adds. "But according to the bylaws of this campus, the faculty is supposed to make academic policy, and when you're talking about what is or is not to be taught at the university, you're talking about policy."

Others are concerned about the impact of the proposals on women and minorities.

"We are assuming that the university is aware of its commitment to affirmative action," says W. L. Moore, an assistant professor of education and chairman of the Black Faculty and Staff Organization. "But we have not been kept informed, and we are very skeptical of all that is being done in this area."

Mr. Moore says his organization has determined that the proposed cuts would affect 63 percent of the black faculty members. The university's Office of Equal Opportunity says the figure is 33 percent. "The discrepancy is due to the administration's inclusion of nonteaching blacks in its figures", says Mr. Moore. "But the precise number doesn't matter, because even 33 percent is too high a price to pay," he adds.

Of the campus's 620 black undergraduates, 255 are enrolled in targeted programs, says H. Richard Dozier, coordinator of minority- student services. "Blacks weren't admitted to this institution until 1950, and they make up only 3.7 percent of the student body," he says. "These cuts would be regressive."

Blacks on the campus have asked the administration for assurances that the university's five-year affirmative-action goals will be met.

There is also some feeling on the campus that faculty salary raises are being used as, in the words of one dean, "a smokescreen" for an attempt to change the institution from a multipurpose university to a research university. One reduction target, home economics, is, according to officials of that college, one of only two areas of study identified in federal farm-bill legislation as being part of the educational responsibility of a land-grant institution.

While some opponents of the proposals were testifying before the review committee, others were mustering support for them. Students, faculty members, and alumni mounted massive letter-writing and phone-calling campaigns aimed at state legislators and the university's curators. Rallies were held, petitions circulated, press conferences staged. The Missouri State Teachers Association expressed outrage. The State Senate's Education Committee held a hearing.

On April 7, the Columbia campus's student senate passed a resolution denouncing the academic review.

On April 19, the faculty voted 237 to 70 to call for the resignations of the chancellor and the provost if the reduction proposals were not withdrawn. The vote, however, has been criticized — by, among others, Chancellor Uehling herself — for not being a true representation of the sentiments of the campus's 2,038-member faculty. Last November, when the faculty voted against mid-year salary increases if they were to come at the expense of campus jobs, more than eight hundred members cast ballots.

The 'Point Man'

The author of the resignation resolution, George V. Boyle, says he believes the vote was representative.

"We should not be cannibalizing ourselves in order to give people raises," says Mr. Boyle, director of labor education, a program not affected by the provost's proposal. "When you encounter heavy seas and the best plan the captain offers is to lighten the load by throwing crew members overboard, I think the crew has to try and come up with something better."

"Our approach to these reductions," says Provost Bunn, "required that I become the 'point man,' and the discussion stage has subsequently become an adversarial one: The source of the recommendations — me — has become as much a subject of debate as the recommendations themselves. It has also become a highly political one, and I think it's unfortunate that the debate has been brought to the legislature and the curators before we have completed the review process on campus."

Chancellor Uehling also came in for some personal criticism when the campus learned that she was among the final candidates for the chancellorship of the nineteen-campus California State University system. She took herself out of the running for that job last week and announced that she was committed to working for policies that would enable the Columbia campus "not simply to survive but to carry into the future even

greater strength than before."

The chancellor says she is not surprised by the demonstrations of hostility. "It's a very frightening and painful process," she says. "I can understand the anger on the part of some, but I still think our greater obligation is to the institution as a whole."

Ms. Uehling says that while she will not review or comment on the recommended proposals until they come to her in their final form, she supports the process and is convinced of its necessity.

"For the past five years, the State of Missouri has provided the university with budget increases that have amounted to only one-half the rate of inflation," she says. "When I came, the faculty was already on the record in opposition to across-the-board cuts to provide salary raises, and we must bring salaries up to attract and retain quality people. We have lost some good people.

"We have no hidden agenda. Our only agenda is our determination to take charge of our own fate. We are trying to anticipate the future so that we won't have to engage in crisis kind of planning. There are enough signs of an impending erosion of our quality to make us want to get ahead and start doing what we do smaller and better."

There have also been signs that the state can't afford to support the university to any greater extent. Missouri voters in 1980 passed an amendment prohibiting the legislature from increasing appropriations unless there was corresponding growth in the state economy. In 1981, Missouri ranked forty-sixth in state-tax- revenue growth, one of the reasons the governor, on two occasions, withheld portions of the university's budget totaling 13 percent.

Nevertheless, some critics charge that salary increases — if they are essential now — could be provided for next year without eliminating programs, since there has been a slight increase in the state appropriation from what was originally expected, and a 17 percent hike in student fees.

"If you take a short-term view, it's possible to conclude that we could have an acceptable level of salary adjustment for the coming year," says Mr. Bunn. "That isn't the case if you're looking ahead. Some on campus feel that it isn't important for us to strengthen our salary structure, but in my judgment that is a very narrow view of the aspirations this campus should have for itself."

To be sure, there is faculty support for the administration. "I think the faculty who approved of this strategy previously ought to be heard from again," says John Kuhlman, a professor of economics. "I don't think we can afford to sit back and watch a few departments create this big fight with the provost."

Adds Sam Brown, chairman of the psychology department, "It would be difficult to find anyone to say they'd favor the cannibalization of their colleagues' jobs for the sake of a salary raise. But ignoring the source of funds, I can say as a department chairman that one of the major problems I face is insufficient salary increments for faculty."

Other Improvements Sought

According to Provost Bunn, when salary raises are given out, they will not be distributed uniformly but will be based on individual merit and the salary market in the particular field.

While salaries will have the highest claim on the "reallocated" funds, the provost also hopes there will be enough money to strengthen equipment and expense budgets — "to bring them back to at least the real-dollar level of three years ago."

The provost said he would consider seriously the advice offered by the committee reviewing his proposals. What is not an option, in his view, is to back away from the $7 million in savings that his proposals would provide.

When it reported to the provost May 6, however, the review committee announced that it had voted to weaken the effect of all but one of the proposed reductions. Mr. Bunn is expected to submit his final recommendations to the chancellor by the end of this week.

The Board of Curators, at meetings on May 6 and 7, conducted lengthy discussions of the reallocation process underway at the Columbia campus. The result, William T. Doak, president of the board, told the press, was that the curators were so divided on the question that had a vote been taken on the proposals, they would have been rejected.

"We are trying to plan for a very uncertain future," says President Olson, "and I'm not sure we've yet found the mechanism for doing that. We are seeking it."

Chancellor Uehling is expected to submit her reallocation proposals to President Olson sometime in June. The curators are scheduled to vote on the proposals in July.

"The board's resistance to any program eliminations has certainly given those who favor such a course of action cause for pause," says the Faculty Council's David West, who has supported the process from the outset. "There has been much more visible and vocal opposition to the process in the past four weeks than there had been support for it up to that time."

On the Columbia campus, faculty members were circulating petitions calling for votes of confidence and of no confidence in the administration. Mr. West says he is advising those faculty members not to call for campus-wide votes at this time. "There has already been too much confrontation, and faculty votes would just prolong it," he says. "I think everyone should try to gather additional information and rethink his position. And try to find some means by which all of this division can be mitigated."

15

School of Education: Case of a Contracting Organization

"How negative do you feel today, Slocum?" inquired Johnson, who was the assistant dean for programs and chairman of the reorganization committee, half in jest and half seriously of the educational administration professor. The school reorganization committee was meeting to discuss problems arising from the recent reorganization of the school.

The school had begun as a Department of Education and Psychology within a small teachers college. In 1964, Psychology became a separate department, followed in 1967 by the Elementary and Secondary Education Departments. Special Education, Educational Administration, and Counselor Education were separated out in 1970. Finally in 1973, the Student Teaching Department was formed (see Exhibit 15-1).

Dr. Anderson had been dean since 1967. Prior to that he was chairman of the Department of Education and Psychology. Having been at the university since 1948, he was now nearing retirement. A man of integrity, he was respected by most of his faculty.

The dean had tried to persuade the School of Education faculty to reorganize in 1972 and 1975. He had proposed combining the departments of Elementary Education, Secondary Education, and Student Teaching to form a Teacher Education Department. The other departments were to remain intact. Both attempts at reorganization failed in the face of considerable faculty opposition.

By 1979, when the dean made his third attempt at reorganizing the school, conditions had changed. Student credit hours (SCH) within the school had decreased by 14 percent since 1975. Full-time-equated (FTE) faculty positions had decreased 6 percent. The Department of Psychology was the only department that was growing. Their SCHs had increased 12 percent and their FTE 32 percent since 1975 (see Exhibit 15-2). If the Department of Psychology was excluded from the School of Education figures, the school decrease in SCH for 1975-80 was 27 percent, and the decrease in FTE was 20 percent (see Exhibit 15-3).

The provost supported the reorganization. The university had originally been a teachers college, but changes in the job market and accompanying changes in student career interests had resulted in the development of a new mission for the university. The education of teachers was no longer the basic purpose of the university.

Written by Mahmoud A. Moursi and Susan K. Smith. Reprinted with permission of Mahmoud A. Moursi, Professor, Central Michigan University.

EXHIBITS 15-1 School of Education Organization Chart, August 1979

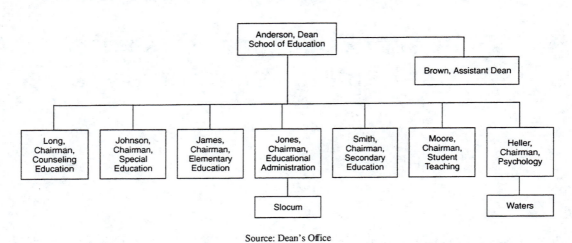

Source: Dean's Office

Rather, the professional education of business men and women was the university's new mission.

Since the university used a "student driven" model, declining enrollment in the School of Education had resulted in a decreased allotment of full-time-equated teaching positions to the school. Under these circumstances, con-tracting the organization from seven to three departments, was an appropriate response from the point of view of the Provost's office.

The decrease in FTE faculty positions was causing problems for the school since 85 percent of its faculty were tenured. Four departments, Counselor Education, Secondary Education, Elementary Education, and Educational Administration, were fully tenured. Most of the faculty had been with the school for many years (see Exhibit 15-4).

In August 1979, the dean proposed a more sweeping reorganization than he had in 1972 and 1975. Not only were Special Education, Student Teaching, Secondary Education, and Elementary Education to be combined into Teacher Education, two of the remaining three departments, Counselor Education and Educational Administration, were to be combined into Educational Services (name changed later to Counseling, Educational Administration, Library Materials,

and Community Leadership). The Psychology Department, as before, was to remain untouched.

The reorganization would require some people to move to different buildings so that members of the same department could be together (see Exhibit 15-5).

An implementation committee, chaired by the dean and consisting of representatives from each of the departments, was charged with developing a proposal on which the faculty could vote on November 9.

The proposal was based on the dean's recommendation, and presented only one reorganization plan. The committee had added a transitional structure, departmental units, to the dean's proposal (see Exhibit 15-6).

The units, corresponding to the former departments, would be headed by unit coordinators. According to the proposal, the continuation of the units depended upon the departmental task forces created to develop departmental procedures. Each department would also be directed to form a program task force charged with reviewing programs and curriculum. The task forces would have time limits within which to complete their work. In addition, an ongoing School Organization Committee would be formed and charged with resolving problems

EXHIBIT 15-2 On Campus SCH[1] Production, FTE[2] Teaching Positions, 1975-1980

	1975-76	1976-77	1977-78	1978-79	1979-80	% Change 1975-80
School Education						
SCH	89,600	87,184	86,229	84,620	77,339	-14%
FTE	141.71	137.71	138.32	134.53	133.28	-6%
Dept. Counselor Education						
SCH	4,758	4,345	3,505	3,432	3,173	-33%
FTE	10.79	8.96	8.47	7.17	7.13	-34%
Dept. Elementary Education						
SCH	12,679	12,401	12,284	11,835	10,707	-16%
FTE	22.20	19.80	20.04	19.47	19.80	-11%
Dept. Education Administration and Library Science						
SCH	6,163	4,11.38	5,092	4,436	3,823	-38%
FTE	10.78	10.78	11.45	10.33	10.14	-6%
Dept. Psychology						
SCH	31,065	33,422	35,689	36,318	34,560	+12%
FTE	37.01	39.92	46.19	47.61	48.92	+32%
Dept. Secondary Education						
SCH	10,324	9,696	7,903	7,623	6,715	-35%
FTE	16.70	15.37	13.10	11.79	11.64	-30%
Dept. Special Education						
SCH	7,200	6,787	6,730	6,405	5,983	-17%
FTE	10.51	10.13	9.98	10.77	10.29	-2%
Dept. Student Teaching						
SCH	17,411	15,622	14,971	14,372	12,210	-30%
FTE	33.22	31.05	28.12	26.26	24.99	-25%

[1] SCH: student credit hours
[2] FTE: full-time-equated
Source: Office of University Planning and Research

that arose out of the reorganization.

The proposal was voted upon in November and passed 61 to 27. Most of the support for the proposal came from the two departments least affected by the change: psychology and student teaching.

Psychology was not really involved since that department was not changed and members did not interact very much with the rest of the school faculty.

Student teaching consisted primarily of off-campus faculty who supervised student teachers in various locations throughout the state. As a result, they were more aware of the need to update the school's curriculum and were supportive of the dean's desire to make programmatic changes in the school. They had attempted to bring about changes in curriculum themselves but had been rebuffed by the on-campus faculty.

Johnson: All right, let's get going. Last week we looked over Wells and Moody Hall to see

EXHIBITS 15-3 SCH[1] and FTE[2] of School of Education, Excluding Psychology Department

Year	1975-76	1976-77	1977-78	1978-79	1979-80	% Change 1975-80
School SCH	89,600	87,184	86,229	84,620	77,339	-12,261
Psych SCH	31,065	33,422	35,689	36,318	34,560	+3,495
School-Psych SCH	58,535	53,762	50,540	48,302	42,779	-15,756
% Decrease, SCH	—	8%	6%	4%	11%	-27%
Psych as % of Total School SCH	35%	38%	41%	43%	45%	
School FTE	142	138	138	135	133	-9
Psych FTE	37	40	46	48	49	+12
School-Psych FTE	105	98	92	87	84	-21
% Decrease, FTE	—	7%	6%	5%	3%	-20%
Psych as % of Total School FTE	26%	29%	33%	36%	37%	

[1] SCH: student credit hours
[2] FTE: full-time-equated
Source: Office of University Planning and Research

where we could put people and I think...

Slocum: Forget it. The people in my department are not going to move out of Wells into Moody Hall. They like the offices they have now; they've been there a long time and they don't want to move in with those guys in Moody Hall. Some of them are even afraid of the rats "Psych" has over there. We didn't want to go in with Counselor Education in the first place. I've been a professor of Educational Administration throughout my career. Now I'm a professor of Counseling, Educational Administration, Library Media, and Community Leadership. The other people in my profession don't even know what that is! Another thing, we don't have anything in common with those counselors. They're all wrapped up in people and their emotions. We take a straightforward, objec-

tive view of problems. We're concerned with systems, not individuals.

Johnson: I know there are problems with putting those two departments together, but each one is too small to continue as a separate entity. With decreasing resources, the Dean had to get rid of the small departments. I'll admit I thought he should have put Counselor Education in with the school psychologists in the Psychology Department. They at least have something in common.

Waters: No way. The school psychologists are in my department and they wouldn't stand for it. The credentials of school psychologists and counselors are completely different. School psychologists have much more extensive training requirements than counselors. Putting those two groups together wouldn't work at all. You know, someone

EXHIBIT 15-4 Faculty Tenure, Fall 1980

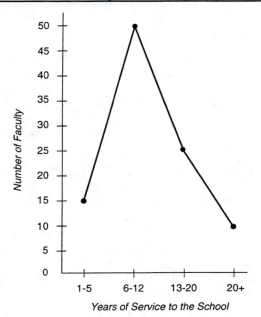

Later on their way across campus, Smith, who was chairman of the new Department of Teacher Education and former chairman of the Secondary Education Department, asked Johnson how the faculty in Special Education felt about the reorganization.

Johnson: They're very concerned. As you know, a lot of them are relatively young and new to the University. Going from a depart- ment of seven to one of fifty-six is quite a change. They are especially concerned about getting tenure. The rest of the faculty in the teacher education department don't know them very well and they are not that familiar with special education. How are the special education faculty going to be evaluated? Also, it's well known that Secondary Education has four more tenured positions than it should have according to the Provost's office, and that when people leave those positions, they won't be replaced. It looks to me as though it's going to be hard for any of my people to get tenure and if anyone has to be laid off, they'll be the first to go.

Smith: Well, I hope it doesn't come to that. Although do you realize that in 1971, 2,300 people were recommended for certification and this year we're only recommending nine hundred? What concerns me are these confounded units. Here I am, chairman of the department, and the unit coordinators are acting like department chairmen. They're signing drop and add cards, approving budgets, and recruiting staff. The units are acting just like mini-departments.

Johnson: That's because this is a year of tran- sition. The units are supposed to fade away after this year, according to the dean. Not everyone agrees with that though.

Smith: That's for sure. Some of my faculty maintain these units can go on forever if the department decides to keep them. To hear them talk, there hasn't been any change at all.

Johnson: Then what's the point of the reorganization?

Smith: Beats me, but keeping these units is a

should have paid more attention to how this whole thing was going to come out. There is a lot more involved in change than just drawing boxes on an organization chart. This reorganization has had a big impact on people: both faculty and staff.

Johnson: Let's get back to the space problems. The dean wants Educational Administration to move into Moody and Special Education to move out of Fenwick into Wells. That way each of the departments will have all their people in the same building.

Smith: Well I hate to break this up, but I have a class at 11 and I have to get back to Wells Hall. It would sure help if we had release time to work on these committees. Some of my people are complaining about the way the departmental task forces are cutting into their class preparation time.

Johnson: OK, we'll meet again next week. Wait a minute, Smith, and I'll walk to Wells with you. I need to stop at the dean's once.

EXHIBITS 15-5 Departmental Locations

Pre-reorganization: Location of Departments

Fenwick	Wells	Moody
Psychology	Student Teaching	Counseling Education
Special Education	Secondary Education	
	Elementary Education	
	Education Administration and Library-Media	

Post-reorganization: Location of Departments

Fenwick	Wells	Moody
Psychology	Teacher Education	C.E.A.L.M.C.L.[1]
	Student Teaching	Counseling Education
	Secondary Education	Educational Administration
	Elementary Education	Library-Media
	Special Education	

neat way to finesse the reorganization.

Johnson: Why do you suppose psychology wasn't touched by any of this?

Smith: Rumor has it that the dean didn't want to do anything that might encourage them to leave the school After all, they're the only department that's growing, and if they went to Liberal Arts, we would lose a lot of FTE.

Meanwhile, two of the Counseling Education faculty were discussing the reorganization over their morning coffee.

Miller: I'm supposed to go to one of those task force meetings again this afternoon. What a waste of time!

Terry: And all for nothing, too. The only money the reorganization saves is a couple of department chairpersons' salaries, and that doesn't amount to anything.

Miller: Let's face it. The real reason the dean wanted this reorganization is so that he can

go out in a blaze of glory!

Terry: That's for sure. We don't have a thing in common with those guys from educational administration. I hope they never do move over here.

Later that day, Johnson, who had become the second assistant dean as a part of the reorganization, met with the dean.

Dean: How did your meeting go this morning, Mike?

Johnson: About the same. Slocum is dragging his feet and we can't seem to resolve the space issue. Educational Administration probably isn't going to move unless you tell them they must.

Dean: It's frustrating to have all this resistance. They don't seem to realize how important this is to the school. We need to cut costs and the reorganization will allow us to reduce administrative expenses. More than that, it will permit us to be more flexible. We have

EXHIBIT 15-6 School of Education Organization Chart, August 1980

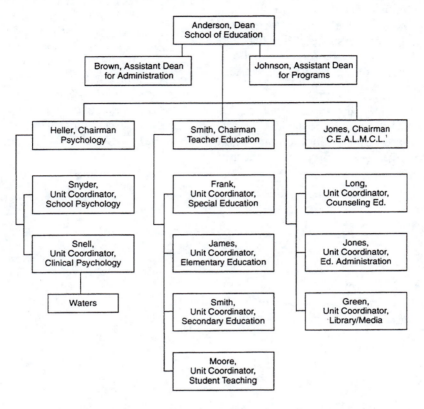

1Counseling, Educational Administration, Library Media, and Community Leadership.

to expand our mission beyond that of educating the classroom teacher. We could be educating people who are training personnel outside the classroom, such as in the private sector. Also, with the emphasis on "mainstreaming," we need to have special education faculty interacting with elementary education and secondary education.

Johnson: I agree with your reasons for reorganizing, dean, but unless you take a stronger stand it's not going to happen. There are many people opposing the change, and unless you use stronger leadership, these committees are going to study it to death.

The next morning the dean met with the other assistant dean, Dr. Brown, who was also a professor of psychology.

Dean: Good morning, Louise. I wanted to speak with you about the reorganization. You talk to a lot of people. How do you think it's going?

Brown: Well, in teacher education it's beginning to come along. The chairman has a nice informal way about him that will bring those people around eventually. Jones, on the other hand, is coming on rather strongly. Most of the people in his department are maintaining their old territorial boundaries and hoping the reorganization will go away.

Dean: What do you think about the relocation of educational administration to Moody at this point?

Brown: Financially, it has to be done. We must reduce some of these administrative expenses. I hope you are successful in persuading them to move. If you force them, however, I am afraid they may bring in the faculty union.

After Dr. Brown left, the dean pondered his options. Should he continue to let the departmental task forces and School Organization Committee try to resolve the problems of the unit structure and the allocation of space, or should he play a stronger role in the process?

He would be retiring in a year or two, and he wanted to accomplish the reorganization before leaving. The dean thought about how he had devoted his entire professional life to the growth and development of the school. Now he had one more task, getting the organization into a stronger position to cope with its changing environment. He needed that reorganization! How could he get it?

16

Planned Organizational Change at the U.S. Naval Air Development Center

Approximately one year after a new Technical Director (TD) was selected for the U.S. Naval Air Development Center (NADC), a new Commander (CDR) arrived. These two individuals quickly developed a good working relationship, operating as a closely knit team from then until the CDR was transferred; all decisions except those limited to military personnel or functions were made jointly, and the two men conferred frequently in their adjoining offices or while on official travel (a frequent occurrence). Within a few weeks of the CDR's arrival, they agreed that there appeared to be a number of opportunities to effect positive change to improve the effectiveness of NADC. They were convinced, however, that inappropriate change or change ineffectively implemented would cause more problems than it solved. Therefore, they needed to determine exactly where the organization was and where it needed to go before beginning any change process.

They were inclined to feel that the primary need was for the development of management skill, probably at the middle level. Consequently, they decided to procure assistance from management-development consultants who had substantial experience in organizational analysis, and who had experience with and understood the Navy laboratory system, to develop a data base. The CDR and TD provided the consultants with background information, discussed their thinking about organizational change, and passed on some of their perceptions concerning the current state of the organization. The consultants were asked to identify specific opportunities for improving managerial effectiveness at NADC and to recommend the means by which these improvements could be made. (They were not asked to identify the strengths and positive aspects of the organization.) Both the consultants and the NADC management expected a management-development seminar would be designed from the data collected.

Initial Organizational Research

The consultants proceeded to collect and analyze organizational data. They reviewed organizational charts and manuals, mission statements, work packages, information systems, and management reports; and they con-

By Harry E. Wilkinson, Robert C. Benfari, and Charles D. Orth. Copyright 1987, Elsevier Science Publishing Co., Inc. Used with permission.

ducted 72 nondirective, one-hour (or longer) interviews with managers at all levels in the organization and from all the major units. All 24 members of the senior executive group were interviewed. The interviews centered on opportunities to improve organizational effectiveness. As the work progressed, it became clear that organizational structure and uncoordinated decision making were critical issues that would have to be addressed before a management-development seminar would be well received by the organization. The data fell naturally into two broad categories: external environmental factors and the evolution of NADC, and significant internal issues.

External Environmental Factors

• *Confederation* Over a number of years, as pressures in the Navy mounted for consolidation, several small organizations were abolished as independent entities and their functions, together with many of their people, were physically moved to NADC. As a result, these organizations lost their former visible autonomy, although they continued to function much as they had before the move. Thus, NADC had evolved into a confederation of 16 quasi-independent entities without much coordination. This situation contributed to the formation of cliques and parochialism along historic lines. People inside NADC expressed concern over how the organization was perceived by their sponsors (the dominant one being the Naval Air Systems Command) and others in the Navy. Rumors that NADC was soon to be closed were not uncommon; morale was low.

• *Trends* Significant trends were changing the fundamental tasks of NADC. The total volume of work was increasing rapidly, and the total funding of NADC had approximately doubled in real terms in the past decade. During this time period, the number of personnel at NADC actually declined, and further reductions were anticipated. Three other trends emerged from the analysis of the initial research:

- Sponsor interest was shifting from technology toward systems-type work, as evi-

denced by shifts in funding.

- The demands for software appeared to be increasing, whereas hardware development was decreasing.

- There was an increasing demand for work to be contracted out rather than done inside NADC due to the political desire of the administration to avoid expanding the federal bureaucracy.

The above trends were placing pressure on NADC to develop more effective ways of managing in order to increase flexibility, cooperation, and integration, and to minimize the use of resources.

The NADC responded to the trend toward systems work by establishing a dedicated organizational unit, the Systems Department, which did all of the work on the various systems. This organization resulted in a high concentration of resources in this department but few procedures or techniques for the transfer or sharing of resources between departments when this would be advantageous. The trend toward software resulted from various technical factors and resource limitations, and the demand for more software created a shortage of good software people. There were not enough people to meet the needs of the various programs, and this created pressure within NADC to cooperate and share resources. The trend toward contracting out had two different kinds of impacts. First, it was necessary to use technical personnel as contract managers; second, there was increased pressure to coordinate with other people, such as procurement and legal specialists, in an effort to integrate work. Collaboration had to be developed and conducted in a relatively parochial environment. Given their choice, the technical groups preferred to do the work themselves rather than contract out.

• *Manpower* With increasing frequency, the Navy was reducing manpower ceilings, average grade levels, and the number allowed in senior grade levels, and it was also imposing a hiring freeze. The authority to classify senior positions was centralized at a level above NADC, at just the point in time where increased flexibility in position management was needed at the Center.

• *Conflicts* The researchers identified three sets of perceived conflicting forces that were acting on NADC. First, the requirements for contracting out and monitoring technical progress of the contractors was perceived to interfere with the desires of NADC engineers to grow technically by performing challenging engineering tasks. Second, civilian managers viewed themselves as providing continuity and long-term technical strength, whereas the military managers were seen as transients, interested dominantly in short-term output. Finally, the CDR and TD felt split between increasing demands for internal management and the critical need to rebuild relationships with the clients and sponsors of NADC.

Significant Internal Issues

• *Organizational Structure* The NADC's organization (Exhibit 16-1) had six support staff departments, four technical departments, the Systems Department, 12 staff assistants, a designated program office, a technology management office, and the Naval Air Facility-Warminster, all reporting directly to top management (the CDR/TD). The size of the organization caused a span-of-control problem, and, in addition, there were five other problems associated with the structure of the organization. First, there was evidence that the "confederated" organization performed those tasks that had been most important in the past (prior to the consolidation) rather than those tasks that were currently the most important. This situation resulted in narrow-minded thinking and empire building rather than cooperation. Second, it appeared as though many individuals did not know how major organizational units were supposed to function, especially the Systems Department, which used a form of matrix management. Third, resource allocations appeared to be based on historical growth patterns rather than the high-priority tasks assigned to the organization at that time. Fourth, many people within NADC felt that there were too many layers of management, and

this interfered with getting the job done and made it more difficult to communicate, let alone coordinate, across organizational lines. And, fifth, it was felt that the technical expertise of NADC was being eroded by the number of people leaving technical work for jobs in management, systems, or contract monitoring.

• *The Decision-Making Process* Five difficulties in the decision-making process were particularly apparent: 1) Too many decisions were being referred to the top of the organization, resulting in top management becoming a bottleneck. The individual organizational units had not developed effective mechanisms for cooperation, and therefore issues involving two or more units were pushed up to the top for resolution. 2) Too many decisions were being referred to committees, which, because of the historical development of the Center, had overlapping responsibilities and were composed of individuals who saw their primary function as defending the position of their organizational unit rather than reaching a decision that would be good for the Center as a whole. 3) The resolution of problems by top management or committee tended to be delayed until a crisis arose. 4) The Center management-information system was inadequate in that individual departments had evolved information systems that were useful to them but were not oriented toward generating the information necessary for Center-wide decision making. 5) Lines of responsibility and authority were felt to be unclear.

• *The Communication Process* Each department's information system was different, making comparisons or integration difficult and resulting in a general lack of information about the functioning of the total organization. This situation was exacerbated by the lack of clarity in the committee decision-making process and the tendency to push things to the top of the organization, thereby overloading top management and not giving them sufficient time to communicate information down adequately. Other groups, especially support groups, tended to isolate themselves and did not communicate to those affected by their work. Hence, people at all levels felt isolated, did not know what was

Exhibit 16-1 Naval Air Development Center Organization

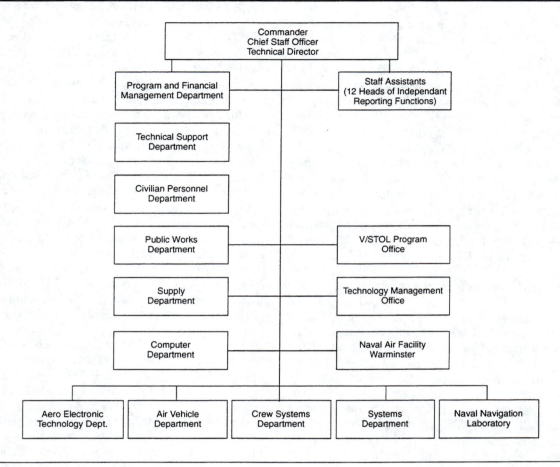

going on, and believed that top management was not only inaccessible but uncommunicative.

- *Goals, Objectives and Priorities* Given the fragmented decision-making process and the ineffective communication system, most people in the organization had little understanding of goals, objectives, and priorities. Individual managers at all levels maintained parochial relationships with sponsors that allowed them to pull work into the Center that interested them or their group, independent of Center goals or objectives, and without informing top management. Given a shortage of resources, especially in terms of full-time permanent employees, it was extremely difficult for top management to do overall, effective, long-range planning. It

seemed to many people that the Center would take on everything but get rid of nothing and that, with declining manpower, the result was self-strangulation, particularly in the areas perceived to be most important to the future of the Center.

- *Planning and Control System* Because of NADC's history and the degree to which it functioned parochially, a short-term time orientation existed that relegated long-range planning to a very low priority. The symptoms of inadequate planning and control manifested themselves in an overhead rate that seemed excessive; poor allocation of manpower resources resulted in mismatches between skills available and those required within organizational subunits, destructive competition among groups, inadequate program reviews, decisions being made without adequate information, and computer reports of questionable accuracy and timeliness.

• *Organizational Climate and Morale* Morale was low, and the organizational climate was not seen as supportive. Some of the environmental trends affecting the Center were driving it in a direction that many people did not like. The increased contracting out, resulting in a need for internal contract management and decreased direct work on technological problems, was a special irritant to many people. These people were required to do work that they found inherently less satisfying, and they felt that the Center would lose its basic technological capability. Because of this shift, people perceived that there was little opportunity for technical advancement and that individuals who made sound technical contributions were not rewarded unless they were willing to leave the technology area and go into management. There was also a perception that the support people, especially in the personnel and contracting areas, had developed a "can't do" attitude, that the last reduction in force (RIF) was badly handled, and that management had failed to remove unproductive "dead wood."

• *Career and Development Training* There appeared to be a widespread perception that promotional opportunities were stifled not only by the ceiling and grade-level constraints imposed on NADC, but by a number of other factors as well, including failure to remove "dead wood," favoritism, poor personnel practices, and no real technical ladder. It was also perceived that managers were not trained to man- age and that they had been selected for the wrong reasons, i.e., solely on the basis of their technical ability. Top management strongly felt, however, that technical ability was and is a critical required skill for a technical manager in a research-and-development environment, but that human and conceptual skills are also required.

Conclusion

Analysis of the data collected in the initial research phase convinced the consultants and the CDR and TD that a management- development program should not be implemented until the critical issues revealed in the data had been addressed. These issues pointed to the need for significant and rather substantial changes to improve organizational effectiveness, and the CDR and TD made the decision to proceed with the necessary changes.

Planning the Change Process

The CDR and TD worked with the consultants to identify objectives of the change process, as outlined below.

Reorganize the structure and management roles to:

1. eliminate parochialism;

2. build in more effective decision-making capability, including decisions involving goals and objectives, planning, resource allocation, and evaluation of the work being done at the Center;

3. reduce the span of control to relieve top management overload; and

4. provide the structure and roles to accomplish realistic long-range planning.

5. open up communication between and among organizational units and between the CDR/TD and the rest of the organization.

The CDR, TD, and consultants agreed on several basic assumptions. First, it was assumed that a change dictated by the CDR and TD would probably be relatively ineffective. Both the CDR and TD had been involved in previous organizational change processes that had been mandated from the top with little involvement of the senior management group, and which they observed had achieved only limited success due to the significant problems of implementation. They recognized that the entire organization needed to perceive that there were significant reasons for change, that all senior managers needed to contribute their thoughts and expertise to the change process, and that all senior managers had to be committed to a different way of doing business in light of the current environment faced by the Center, as well as the environment that was likely to exist over the next several years. Second, much was known about why people resisted change in organizations and the ways this resistance could be reduced if not eliminated. Internal and external change agents could reduce resistance. The CDR and TD were internal change agents, and the consultants needed to become external change agents. Consequently, the consultants' role needed to switch from researchers to facilitators, acting as catalysts and resource persons to help the entire management group implement the change process.

Third, although the change process should take a significant period of time, there were pressures that limited the time available:

- The Center was under pressure from higher-level Navy management to justify its very existence as an organization deserving continued support in the Naval Laboratory community.

- The Commander had only slightly more than two years left of his three-year tour, and he did not want to leave the Center to a new Commander with implementation of the changes incomplete.

Finally, some major effort or step would be needed to create an atmosphere in which the managers of the Center would tend to drop their insular views of their departments and take on a Center-wide perspective. This final step seemed to be especially critical if the resource-allocation decisions required were to be made and if the Center was to develop the organizational flexibility it needed.

Implementing Change

The CDR and TD decided that a carefully planned reassignment process would be an effective first step in dealing with the narrow-minded behavior that pervaded the Center. Accordingly, they advised the top eight managers of the Center that some of them would be reassigned to head up other departments. The technical requirements of the job and their particular backgrounds would, of course, be taken into account, but because of the wide needs of the Center and the breadth of background of the managers involved, most, if not all, of the managers could expect reassignment in time. A few weeks later, three managers were reassigned. Because each of the managers could be moved, no one was secure. All of the managers perceived that their self-interest was better served now by a Center-oriented perspective rather than their former, somewhat parochial view, because if they competed with each other and developed an organization in which one unit was particularly strong and another weak, they might end up managing the weak one.

After several months, some of the executives recognized the acceleration of their own growth and became open advocates of reassignments that took into account the careful matching of technical, human, and conceptual skills with job requirements. This process was, and is, a far cry from the "musical chairs" approach to job rotation that is practiced in other parts of the Navy, and which led the NADC executives initially to resist it.

Involving Managers in the Change Process

The CDR and TD called a meeting of the top 24 managers at NADC so that the data that had been collected and analyzed by the consultants could be presented to them. The group included the eight senior department directors, their deputies, and eight others, including some staff department heads and other staff officers. More than a third of the group were Naval officers (three Captains and six Commanders). The six senior civilians were all SESs; the other civilians were GM-15s, with a few GM-14s. The group agreed with much of the data and decided to follow the consultants' recommendation for a more lengthy meeting. Approximately one month after this discussion of the research information, a three-day meeting was held off- site to examine organizational structure for NADC, particularly matrix possibilities, as well as the problems of decision making by committee. The meeting was facilitated by the consultants, and the CDR and TD adopted the role of "available resource" if requested by the group as a whole, or by any of the subgroups that were formed. In this way, the CDR and TD effectively removed themselves from the discussions in order not to inhibit their managers in a full, free, and open-ended exploration of the issues and possible improvements, while at the same time providing support and input when needed by the group or subgroups.

The charge to the group by the CDR and TD was relatively general: they were to investigate ways of improving NADC's methods of doing business, and they were to review and analyze the organizational structure to determine ways to improve its operation. The consultants acted as both facilitators and as outside experts. They focused on the process the groups were using, attempting to support open communication, and, when requested by the group or sub-groups, provided outside expertise in the two areas being worked on. The group worked 15 or 16 hours a day on the two tasks derived from the research: the role of committees in the decision-making process, and the strengths and weaknesses of the matrix-type structure and its applicability to NADC.

Three different subgroups were formed, each composed of individuals who had sufficient breadth to look at the Center as a whole. Their first task was to look at matrix organizations from three different perspectives: the sponsors, the functional managers, and the top Center management. The three subgroups developed presentations of their findings and fed these back to the total group the following morning. Both the CDR and TD openly expressed their pleasure with the work of the group and their perception of its value.

The second task assigned to the subgroups was to review the functioning and utility of committees at NADC. The groups would look at three different types of decisions: strategic, operational, and tactical; and the value of committees for dealing with them. The subgroups spent the balance of the second day with this task and developed presentations to be given to the total group on the morning of the third day. After these presentations, a general discussion about the outputs of the meeting and its value continued for some time.

Responding to the thrusts of the comments from the managers, the CDR and TD agreed that additional off-site meetings were needed to plan for the redesign of the NADC organization. The CDR and TD agreed to appoint a new ad hoc subgroup to work part-time over the next several weeks to develop a "straw-man" model organization, i.e., one that would provide the basis for further discussion and analysis in the next off-site meeting of the whole group. Certain basic boundary conditions were set for the ad hoc subgroup, but basically they were to have a free hand in developing the straw-man model.

The perceptions of the participants about the first off-site meeting were quite positive. They felt that they had begun to establish more openness, trust, and sharing of power among themselves and had made real progress in identifying opportunities for positive change.

Development of a Proposed Organization

The CDR and TD appointed eight managers to the ad hoc subgroup to develop the straw-man model organization. The eight were selected because of their ability to contribute, their status relative to the rest of the management group, and their openness and breadth of understanding. One of the facilitators was with the ad hoc subgroup at all of their meetings, helping with process problems and providing expert input and current research on organizational design.

The ad hoc subgroup met at least three times a week for over a month to develop an organization that would: 1) reduce the span of control of the CDR and TD; 2) provide a matrix-type operation; 3) improve planning, decision making, and operations; and, 4) include mechanisms for conflict resolution.

Analysis of the Proposed Organization

The organization design that resulted from the meetings was presented to the management group at a second off-site meeting held six weeks after the first. The CDR, TD, and the facilitators assumed the same roles as before, but certain ground rules were imposed: the discussion would initially be limited to clarifying questions, i.e., no critical comments would be allowed until it was clear that everyone fully understood the proposal. It was also decided that the objective of the discussions was to develop an "ideal" organization; modifications addressing individual concerns would be made only after agreement had been reached on the ideal. It was hoped that this process would minimize empire building and parochialism.

After the initial clarifying discussions, three subgroups were formed to analyze the proposals at depth. These subgroups reported their conclusions to the total group, and it was clear that certain aspects of the proposal were acceptable to the entire group. These elements formed the base for an overall design. Some skepticism and hostility was evidenced by a few participants who seemed most concerned with protecting the status quo. It was decided that more intensive work needed to be done over the next two months on the structuring of the systems and functional groups.

Three new ad hoc subgroups were formed.

Their tasks were to refine still further the organizational structure and to develop a plan for implementation, to be presented to the management group at a third off-site meeting. Each subgroup was assigned a part of the total organization. They hammered out the design detail for their specific segment, coordinated with the other subgroups, and developed a rough plan for implementation. The facilitators were available to meet with any or all of the three new subgroups on request, but they were less involved than previously.

A third off-site meeting was held two months later. Two of the subgroups had ironed out the details and had developed firm implementation recommendations. The subgroup working on the functional engineering and systems organizations was less clear and precise, reflecting the lingering insularity and sense of potential "loss" still in evidence in those parts of the organization. A good deal of discussion focused on the third group's report. Well into the evening, specific conclusions were finally reached by the whole group.

The CDR and TD met after the session ended to discuss the conclusions of the total group. They also interviewed individuals who would fill key roles in the new organization. The next morning, the CDR and TD shocked the management group, who had not anticipated immediate action, by abandoning the nondirective roles they had played. First, they accepted the work of the groups and stated that the new organization as designed by the group would be implemented. Then, they specified which individuals would fill key roles. This resulted in several more managers being reassigned to head up organizational elements quite different from those they had previously managed. Finally, they set a date three months away as the ideal time to implement this major organizational change. This time frame ensured a reasonable "shakedown period" before the CDR was transferred.

The balance of the discussion for this meeting focused on problems of implementation. An integrative management group was formed to deal with these specific problems. Christened the Center Management Group (CMG), it was composed of the six SES civilians and three Captains who had been in the original executive group, plus the GM-15 Controller. It was also decided that the new organization should be announced immediately, and that the CDR, TD, and the managers of the CMG would make a series of presentations to the other NADC managers. The CDR and TD accepted the responsibility for securing approval of the new organization from higher-level Naval commands.

Exhibit 16-2 shows the proposed organization that the planning group felt would overcome many of the problems noted earlier and provide a more efficient and coordinated structure. The main features of the new plan were six line departments, four technology groups of roughly comparable size that would work on both advanced technology efforts and projects (though the projects themselves would be managed by a Command Projects Department that had the dollars and a core of managers and monitors but not the people to do the work), and a Systems Engineering group dominantly serving Command Projects in the full range of systems-engineering functions; a Planning, Assessment, and Resources group that would act as staff to the CDR and TD in these areas, making recommendations on such issues as acceptance of work by NADC, resource allocations, and an assessment of opportunities to develop new technologies or drop old ones; a Chief Staff Officer to provide day-to-day supervision of the support groups (to reduce the span of control of the CDR and TD); merger of the Naval Air Facility into NADC; and an Associate Technical Director who would be chairman of the CMG (initially referred to as the "integrator" and now also referred to as the "implementation" group) whose function would be to resolve conflicts and act as an integrator within the organization. It was not envisioned that this group would be a layer of management or would have regularly assigned duties, but rather that two or three members concerned would informally meet to resolve conflicts as they arose, keeping a Center-wide perspective. The major differences between this matrix structure (Exhibit 16-2) and the old organization (Exhibit 16-1) are in four

areas: power distribution, relative balance between units, a thrust toward strengthening the functional engineering groups, and the requirement that the functional groups work for the project groups. Finally, the new organization was designed to allow for the development of centers of technical excellence that could then be used as resources in coordinated efforts for specific products.

The announcement of the new organization and the presentations by NADC management to their suborganizations received mixed reactions. Many of the mid-level managers expressed their frustration at not having had any input in the reorganization and expressed considerable reservations about the proposal. Although some remained skeptical, the functional technical groups eventually became favorably disposed, whereas the systems and project groups became negatively disposed. This was not unexpected as the systems and projects groups would no longer have line authority over most of the resources necessary to get their work done.

This rebalancing of power would, of course, require much greater coordination and cooperation across organizational lines. Most people recognized the desirability of this and of sharing scarce technical talent but expressed concern over priorities and how they would be established, and also whether or not the technical groups could be "trusted" to do the work satisfactorily within budget and schedule constraints.

It became apparent to the senior people involved in the planning for reorganization that they had acquired a considerable amount of knowledge about matrix structures that the rest of the organization did not yet possess. Consequently, during an early implementation meeting of the CMG, it was decided that a short management-development program should be initiated for the next two levels of management to teach them about matrix organizations and to obtain their involvement and help in implementing the change. The consultants designed and implemented this program while remaining available to the CMG and top management as facilitators.

EXHIBIT 16-2 Proposed Organization

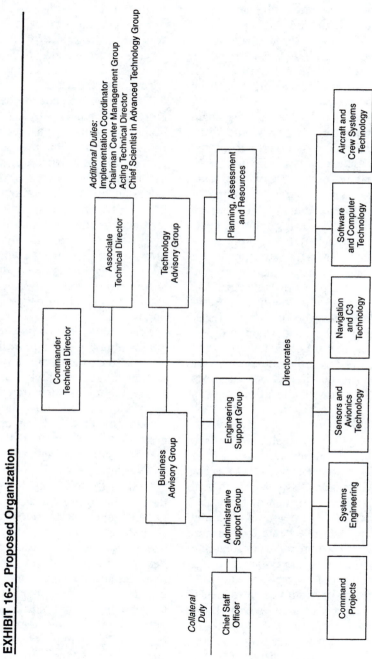

The management-development program began three weeks before the new organization was to be implemented. The first two sessions were devoted to matrix organizations and how they function. Three groups of 25 each were to participate. The first group consisted dominantly of those people who had done the planning for the reorganization, and the other two groups contained a total of 50 mid-level managers from all parts of the organization. At the second meeting of the third group, a number of questions were raised concerning the lack of a modus operandi. The CMG had been assigned this task along with many others but had not yet developed the guidelines for operation of the new organization.

Because the design of the management- development program called for workshop groups to be established to work on implementation problems (to be assigned by the CMG), the CDR and TD assigned the job of preparing the modus operandi to a workshop group of mid-level managers, mostly deputies of the managers serving as the CMG, and asked them to submit a draft within a week. The consultants were asked to assist. The managers on the CMG who felt they were responsible for this task apparently resented the job being given to lower-level people. They told the lower-level workshop group that their task was an academic exercise for the class only. Delays and excuses proved frustrating to the CDR and TD and to the operating groups who needed and wanted adequate guidelines.

This was the first indication that the CMG felt they "owned" the new organization, did not want to share power with lower-level managers, and, indeed, viewed the workshops as usurping their prerogatives. (The CMG refused to assign any implementation problem to a workshop.) The pressures on seminar participants increased when the new organization was implemented. Without the workshops to involve participants in the significant problems of implementation, some participants concluded they had higher priority uses for their time. Attendance in the management-development program declined sharply. The CMG spent a great deal of time working out the details of organizational assignments down to the lowest levels, employee by employee. Indeed, so much time was devoted to this process that other important tasks such as developing the modus operandi were not done, and a resurgence of parochialism and empire building was noted.

Meanwhile, the CDR and TD had submitted the broad plan to higher authority for approval. Only two significant changes were required in order to secure approval, both related to interpretations of regulations or law. Both the Controller and Civilian Personnel groups were set out to report directly to the CDR and TD. A great deal of time was expended in obtaining top-level approval and in "selling" the matrix concept in other parts of the Navy after approval.

The new organization was implemented as planned, on schedule. In the frequent absence of the CDR and TD, who were selling the matrix concept in order to avoid improper downgrading of personnel, the CMG began to function as a layer of management. This seems to have occurred without the people involved being conscious of it, and it led to considerable frustration on the part of the CDR and TD, as well as the members of the CMG. As a result, the CMG decided to hold its own off-site meeting to examine the way it was functioning. Two of the consultants participated in this meeting. After the meeting, additional effort was devoted to the functioning of the CMG and assessment of the new organization. This culminated in the development and use of a questionnaire to be completed by all NADC managers; the results were analyzed, and the data from this instrument, together with the CMG's output from its own analysis of its functioning, were to be presented at a larger off-site meeting of the original top management group to assess the new organization. The consultants and the CDR and TD assumed the same roles as in the earlier meetings.

Several things became obvious as a result of this meeting: the CMG viewed itself as a layer of management, managers below and above the CMG were frustrated, lower-level managers felt they had been prevented from expressing their concerns and problems with the new organization, and a number of implementation problems had not yet been resolved, including the modus operandi. At the end of this meeting, the CDR and TD stepped in and made decisions that effectively put the CMG back into the role originally intended for it, and initiated an off-site meeting of a representative group of lower- level managers so that the unresolved issues could be more thoroughly identified and corrective actions recommended. Names of nominees were to be forwarded to the CDR and TD.

Each level of management reviewed the nominees, and efforts were made to include as many as possible of those who had expressed concern or dissatisfaction. All nominees were notified that attendance was voluntary, and several chose not to participate. Some anxiety was expressed by members of the original top management group and the intervening level of management about their exclusion.

At this lower-level management meeting three weeks later, all the data then available was presented to the group. The consultants assumed the same facilitator role as before, whereas the CDR and TD made data presentations and interacted socially, then returned to NADC. The group formed workshops to define the issues and recommend actions. Presentations by each workshop group were made back at NADC several days later to the CDR and TD directly, with members of the original top management group in attendance. One recommendation was that their bosses, that is, the level between them and the top group, be included in examining the problems and reviewing the recommended actions.

The CDR and TD approved, and two weeks later another off-site meeting was held with the managers at the intervening level in attendance. The consultants again acted as facilitators, and the CDR and TD again made data presentations and interacted socially before returning to NADC. This time the group was asked not only to analyze the output of the last two meetings and develop their own output, but also to develop an action plan for approval by the CDR and TD and implementation at NADC. The group developed the action plan, and it was approved after modification.

Shortly thereafter, however, budgetary re-

strictions and several new tasks were imposed on NADC by the Navy. These factors necessitated a curtailment in implementing some aspects of the action plan, which created some frustrations. It also resulted in the temporary curtailment of the consultants' participation.

Six months later, most managers at NADC felt that most of the significant problems of implementing the new organization had been or were being solved and that the reputation of NADC in the eyes of higher authority had been substantially enhanced. It was also apparent that empire building and parochialism still existed, consciously or subconsciously, at very senior levels. It was suggested that another off-site meeting to reassess progress could help rebuild more elective working relationships.

At this off-site meeting, the facilitators noted considerably greater willingness for participants to be open and confrontational without being hostile. In general, roles and levels seemed to be accepted without inhibition. The group proceeded in a mature, workmanlike manner, dealt with dissent openly, examined the anxieties created by the changes, and pointed out the still-unresolved problems of the new organization, including failure to produce a modus operandi. After listening for three days, the CDR and TD again took charge and made significant decisions where conflict was still unresolved.

Postscript

After the CDR who had been involved in the change process had transferred, a period of consolidation took place. Gradually, the TD was given more and more responsibility for special assignments that kept him away from the Center. The Associate TD (ATD) retired, and another CMG member replaced him, but the frequent absence of the TD resulted in the new ATD, who was also chairman of the CMG, managing the Center and using the CMG as a layer of management, with the Planning Assessment Resources group becoming staff to the CMG. In addition, two former CMG members left to become TDs of other Navy centers, and, of course, all military officers were changed. A new TD was appointed six months after a second new CDR was appointed. Together, they called the consultants back to review the current organization.

The consultants found that the organization was functioning with considerably greater effectiveness than prior to the reorganization, but there were significant opportunities for further improvement, as outlined below.

1. An effective, integrated, Center-oriented management-information system was still not in place and indeed looked several years away.

2. The modus operandi to document the working relationships and procedures for groups and between groups had not been developed, and no effort was being expended to do so.

3. The CMG had become a layer of management with formal weekly meetings, rather than the informal integrator and conflict-resolving group that was originally intended.

4. The CMG was perceived by some to be managing the Center, whereas the CDR and TD were seen to be focused outside the Center.

5. Parochialism, empire building, and self-interest in opposition to Center interest was still in evidence.

6. Mid-level managers appeared very concerned with improving their individual and collective management capabilities and effectiveness for the Center.

7. Managerial paperwork seemed excessive.

8. The decision-making process seemed vague.

9. The strategic-planning process seemed weak.

In short, the organization had improved somewhat, but there was a clear need for team-building activities at the senior-management level and integrated management and organizational development activities at middle-management levels to "fine-tune" the Center.

Some internal team-building activities including strategic planning have been undertaken more recently. It is hoped that integrated management and organizational development activities will be undertaken soon.

17

Special Products Division of Advanced Technologies, Inc.

Introduction

Fred Hazelton spent most of the morning of May 5, 1980, preparing for a 10 o'clock meeting with his staff. The Special Products Division of Advanced Technologies, Inc., had recently received some serious complaints regarding the division's performance. Mr. Hampton, the general manager of the Special Products Division, received this negative feedback through marketing department representatives, who had recently returned from a visit to one of the division's major customers, the U.S. Air Force.

SPD had for many years been a major supplier of portable steam supply systems used for generating electric power at temporary Air Force installations. The division was organized in 1957 in response to the government's need for these types of systems. It had dominated the industry until about five years ago.

The complaints received from this major customer perplexed Mr. Hazelton. He recalled a similar episode just last month with the division's other prime customer, the Energy Research and Development Agency (ERDA). SPD had entered into a contract with ERDA in mid-1978 to design, build, and install a nuclear fusion test unit. An extremely high level of new technology dominated this project, and progress to date had been very limited. Mr. Hazelton scheduled the meeting for that morning to discuss and assess the recent complaints from their two major customers and to develop an action plan.

History of the Division

SPD was a major operating division of the Advanced Technologies Company, a worldwide firm involved primarily in the business of designing, manufacturing, and marketing both component parts and complete package energy systems. Having expertise in engineering and fabricating advanced steam supply systems, the company was approached by the Air Force in the mid-1950s concerning their possible interest in building portable units. In an agreement between the Air Force and Advanced Technologies, the division was established initially to design and fabricate five of those units. From this small beginning, SPD grew into a well-capitalized or-

Prepared by Theodore T. Herbert. Used with permission.

ganization with unique engineering and fabrication capabilities and a strong interest in research and development.

Development of the Market and the Competitive Environment

By 1965, the division's sales to the Air Force had reached $50 million annually. Its success was boosted by the fact that no other company had shown interest in getting into the portable steam system business. SPD had developed a good rapport with the Air Force over the years, primarily because of its outstanding performance in the design, manufacture, and timely shipment of the units. For orders placed by the Air Force, SPD could essentially write its own ticket and often had significant influence on the content of the buyer's specifications. Extensive exceptions to various military specifications were requested by SPD; usually the exceptions were granted.

During the late 1960s, other companies developed the technologies and interest in the portable steam system market. The Air Force and other sources awarded several contracts, apparently for the purpose of developing the infant competition. Three competitors began to mature in the early 1970s, even though, as a result of their lack of experience in the high technology involved, their performance was not equal to SPD's. SPD still dominated the market through the mid-1970s, as contract awards were placed according to an evaluated price. That is, dependability and technical expertise were primary factors, with price being secondary. Several prototype systems were purchased, and SPD continued its dependable performance on those projects.

By 1978, however, the three new competitors had reached full maturity and were bidding on and performing successfully on Air Force and other projects. The product itself had become in general a less risky venture because of several decades of industry design, manufacturing, and plant-operating experience. The technology had stabilized, with design and manufacturing methods remaining fairly constant. Due to the basic, conservative approach encouraged by the Air Force, new design concepts were introduced only where absolutely necessary, and "tried and true" designs were used if possible.

Along with the reduced requirement for technical creativity and the stabilization of design and manufacturing techniques, the Air Force began awarding contracts based on price only. In fact, nearly 90 percent of the orders after 1975 were of a "follow on" (repeats of previously designed components) nature. As a result of changing customer needs, SPD's market share began to drop during the 1970s, accelerating during the last few years of the decade.

New Markets

In 1978, in an attempt to diversify from the Air Force steam systems market, SPD contracted with ERDA to design, build, and test a nuclear fusion reactor. This unit was to be the first test unit actually built to produce electricity in the United States and involved an intense engineering and R & D effort. Fabrication of the unit was to occur in the SPD shops, because the manufacturing and quality-control requirements were very similar to those needed by the Air Force steam systems.

The task was further complicated by a new and unfamiliar customer, necessary interfaces with other companies that served as subcontractors, and the unknowns regarding the future of fusion reactors as dictated by emerging U.S. energy practices and policy. In addition, design inexperience dictated very close coordination among engineering, manufacturing, and the customer. The new and intricate geometries anticipated from this unfamiliar type of energy source, resulting from extremely high operating temperatures and the use of advanced alloys, were likely to cause problems in the manufacturing and assembly process. Developing a design that would be acceptable to the customer and that could be built and assembled economically, and with minimal fabrication risk, requires excellent communication between departments, as well as extreme patience. Although the risks were high, Mr. Hazelton believed that successful completion of this project would give SPD a head start in fusion reactor technology.

With the recent drop in sales to the Air Force, other markets were being explored. Pressure vessels for commercial chemical processors were being considered, and in January of 1979, a chemical company ordered four hydrogenation vessels for a proposed coal liquefaction plant. These vessels were intended for high-temperature and high-pressure use, but the overall quality requirements were not as strict as those for steam systems. Design effort was minimal, with the primary objectives being economical fabrication and prompt shipment. This new product line was extremely price-competitive, but SPD saw the venture as a way to keep the shops active until the Air Force market could be regained. Administration of this new product line took a form similar to the division's established structure for other product lines.

Organization

The division is organized around functional lines, as shown in Exhibit 17-1. This organization was established by the first division manager and has changed only slightly since Mr. Hazelton took the position in 1973.

Interactions between the various departments at all levels are closely controlled by detailed procedures and work standards. Mr. Hazelton has always believed that situations should be well thought out in advance and that action plans should be available for any anticipated happening. For this reason, SPD has a four-volume set of procedures that apply to all functional departments. In addition, each member of the division must write his or her own work instruction, have it approved by the supervisor, and follow it closely. Periodic audits at all levels are performed to ensure compliance

with procedures and work instructions.

Additional departmental tasks and relationships are described in the subsequent sections.

Marketing

As contracts from the Air Force are solicited, the marketing department is responsible for gathering input from all departments and assembling the company's proposal package. Specifications and other related documents pertaining to the particular project are distributed to such areas as manufacturing, engineering, quality assurance, and the contract section. Each individual department plans its execution of the task, estimates costs, and responds to the marketing department. During the early years of the division, when the portable steam system technology was new, close communications existed between the various functional departments. Plans for manufacturing, engineering, quality assurance, etc., were coordinated in the precontract stage to enhance successful overall task performance. However, as the product matured and experience was attained in all departments, less communication existed, and groups began to plan in isolation.

Engineering planning is generally the responsibility of the specific design group that is to perform the task if a contract is received. The manufacturing department, on the other hand, has a special preproduction group that plans the fabrication methods, sequence, schedule, and cost estimates for all projects. It was felt by Mr. Hazelton that, because of the division's past experience, departments already had a mutual understanding of each other's problems and close coordination was no longer necessary.

The marketing department consists of 25 salaried personnel having responsibility for generating proposal packages in response to customer inquiries. For each inquiry, a team from this department is formed to coordinate the proposal activity. SPD has no sales force of its own and depends on Advanced Technology's Corporate Sales Group, located at headquarters, to gather market information. Upon receipt of a

Exhibit 17-1 SPD Organization Chart

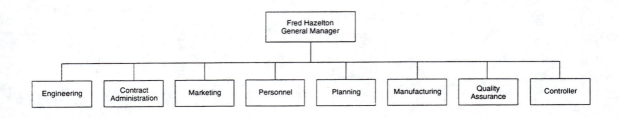

contract, the marketing department's task is complete, and responsibility for performing the task is transferred to the appropriate functional areas. Recent changes in the product line — i.e., entry into the fusion reactor business — has not resulted in significant changes in the operation or organization of the division.

Project Management

The division is organized basically along functional lines, as illustrated in Exhibit 17-1. Operationally, however, each project is coordinated between function groups by a project management section. Each project management section consists of a project manager, a secretary, one or two file clerks, and a number of contract administrators. Each contract administrator is responsible for coordinating the activities of all functions necessary for accomplishing the project tasks.

Dave Roberts is a project manager responsible for three Air Force contracts. His group has one contract administrator for each of his three projects. Dale reports directly to Jim Watts, manager of the contract section shown in Exhibit 17-1. The project management group handles and coordinates all communications with the customer, including distribution of incoming mail and documents to pertinent functional groups. The project manager is basically responsible for success of the overall task.

Lateral communications occur primarily be-tween contract administrators, engineering supervisors, process writers, and production control and quality assurance personnel assigned to the particular task. If conflicts arise, the decision-making role many times is elevated to higher levels in the hierarchy for resolution. Exhibit 17-2 illustrates the type of information flow that exists during a conflict situation.

Dale Roberts recalls several instances during his career with SPD when resolution of conflicts was not possible by "normal" lines of communication. One such incident occurred over an internal piping welding procedure for an Air Force component. The engineering supervisor demanded a high-strength weld with full nondestructive examination (X-ray and penetrant testing). Manufacturing personnel, on the other hand, desired a welding method that would reduce their risk of making a bad weld, which would result in significant repair time. The quality assurance department established the rules for an acceptable result that could be nondestructively examined. Dale got involved early in this dispute as the project manager, attempting to resolve the differences speedily. He was not immediately successful, and the conflict was bumped up the various levels with limited success until the division general manager finally became involved. As Dale describes the incident, he recalls:

As it turned out, there were several acceptable alternatives. The problem was that the optimum alternative relative to effort and risk re-

EXHIBIT 17-2 Information Flow Chart

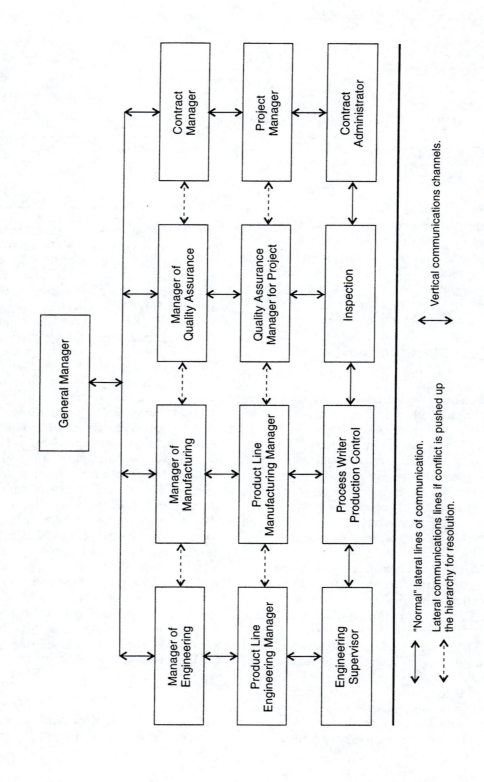

quired, was different for each department Each functional group requested the support of its managers higher and higher in the structure to gain power in instituting its own desired method. Eventually, the problem reached the division manager, who made the final decision, to the betterment of the division as a whole. Furthermore, the decision needed to be reached very quickly, but the whole process took over a month.

Several occurrences of this nature have taken place over the last five years, and Mr. Roberts believes that SPD's performance has dropped as a result.

Another situation occurred on one of Mr. Roberts' contracts just recently that proved to be very embarrassing to SPD. A requirement was included on one particular contract for SPD to verify the material properties of a critical high-strength material to be used in one of the units. The material vendor is always responsible for performing a test on the material prior to shipment, and usually the vendor's test is dependable. However, due to the criticalness of this part, SPD was required to do a verification check in its laboratory within thirty days of material receipt. Parts were scheduled to be machined from these pieces of raw material in about two months after receipt of the material. The verification testing did not happen until after the machining was complete. Subsequent to machining, it was determined that the material was not acceptable. Responsibility for having the testing performed was traced, but no department would admit to having this responsibility. As a result, the division incurred significant additional costs and schedule delays.

Mr. Hazelton believed that the project management approach had been successful during the early years of building Air Force steam systems and decided to continue this approach with the new product ventures.

Manufacturing

The manufacturing department is responsible for economical, high-quality fabrication of the division's products on a timely basis. Often a product of this high quality requires $1\frac{1}{2}$ to $2\frac{1}{2}$ years to manufacture because of the many processes required and the frequent quality checks. Each major product line has a manufacturing manager who directs the efforts of several process writers, production controllers, and shop personnel. Because of the diverse products sold by SPD and the small number of units built for each design, there are normally many different products on the shop floor at one time. Production is done on a job shop basis, and careful scheduling of the various machines is necessary for effective utilization.

Preproduction planning is done by a group in the planning department, which is separate from the manufacturing department. Jobs are planned and quoted by experienced individuals in the preproduction group and are turned over to regular production personnel following a contract award. Often the scheduling and basic methods require considerable modification by the production people, many times to the extent that design changes are requested to facilitate more efficient and economical manufacturing. This situation occurs quite often on "follow-on" contracts that require very little engineering effort. Because each department operates as a cost center, the number of person-hours to complete or support a project are estimated in the proposal stage. Upon contract award, the number of hours quoted are given to the cost center in the form of allocated backlog. Each cost center manager is measured by his or her backlog performance and often resists changes that cause the department more expense.

When changes in manufacturing methods are suggested, a high level of resistance sometimes errupts from other departments. Ed Brutus, a manufacturing manager for ten years in the Air Force product line, put it this way:

Preproduction people are often not as knowledgeable about current methods as they should be and do not ask our advice often enough. Every time a methods change or de-

EXHIBIT 17-3 SPD Engineering Organizational Chart

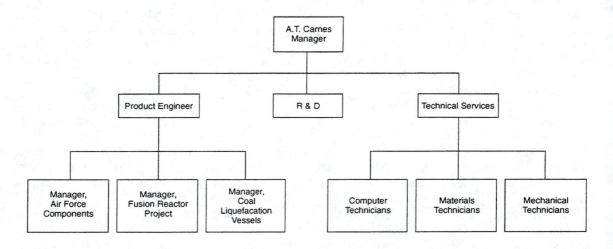

sign change is suggested, engineering and quality assurance yell and scream to high heaven. They don't care whether we save money or not. After all, manufacturing is where this division's money is made or lost. We should get more priority when it comes to cost savings. Engineering is so conservative that they always overpenalize us anyway. When push comes to shove, they can always make the design work on paper. Manufacturing should have more authority in this division.

Engineering

The engineering department is organized into product groups, support groups, and R&D section (see Exhibit 17-3). Mr. A. T. Carnes has been manager of engineering since 1972 and holds more patents than any other employee at Advanced Technologies. Mr. Carnes has organized the engineering department in such a way as to promote a high degree of flexibility. Reorganizations are frequent to meet the needs of changing work loads. Product groups perform design and analysis in direct support of particular contracts, while support groups in the technical services section develop and update the technical tools necessary for contract work.

Considerable use is made of advanced computerized analysis techniques in the Air Force and fusion reactor product groups, while engineering effort on coal liquefaction vessels is limited to manufacturing support and basic sizing using simple design rules.

Over the past years, the department has developed a great deal of technical expertise and has had the opportunity to contribute significantly to the Air Force steam system designs. Recently, however, the engineering task has been limited to analysis of customer-dictated designs, because of product stabilization and much design standardization. Most of the design challenges have come in the fusion reactor project. Many engineers have requested a transfer to this project because of the challenges involved.

The fusion reactor project is engineering centered because of the new technology involved. Close coordination between engineering, manufacturing, project management, and the customer is extremely crucial to this project because of the large number of unknowns. Mr. Carnes agreed with division General Manager Mr. Hazelton that the project management approach would provide these necessary interfaces.

Even though the project promises some future competitive advantages for SPD, it has been plagued with problems since its beginning. Engineers expecting technical challenges have found themselves reviewing specifications and writing work plans. Discouragement and frustration have occurred among the project group members because design progress has gone very slowly. Lack of agreement between engineering and manufacturing functions and the seeming inability to please the customer have resulted in further frustration, confusion, and lack of direction within the group. Mr. Carnes sizes it up this way:

Our biggest problem is that our people lack the experience necessary to handle a new technology project. The mistakes that have been made and the recent customer criticism have come as a direct result of inexperience. George (George Ward, manager of the fusion reactor group J) is a heck of a leader and tries hard, but he lacks sound experience in design. For that reason, I have become intimately involved with this project. I have been helping George out lately by taking some of the load off him. I have directed the work on some key designs and have reviewed them daily. I have also begun weekly design reviews of the entire project.

Regarding the generally slow progress on the project, he said:

Other groups in this division don't pay enough attention to the engineers. Project management rarely understands our problems, and manufacturing hasn't found a quay yet to build any of the designs we have come up with. Take for instance the plasma makeup nozzle. We have sent them five potential designs on this thing and they haven't agreed to any. They said there was no possible way to build the first design, and they said they just didn't like the second one. Nothing in particular; they just didn't like it. Every time, it's back to the drawing board, but they find something that doesn't suit them about each one. All of these could have been built if they had used just a little ingenuity.

Mr. Carnes also added:

The customer has hindered more than he has helped. There seems to be no pleasing those guys, especially when they don't seem to know what they want. Every time we submit a design for their review, it doesn't seem to be what they had in mind.

Conclusion

Fred Hazelton reviewed the criticisms from the Air Force one more time before the meeting began. Those comments reflecting the Air Force's image of SPD are listed below:

- Passive — not aggressive
- Not a problem-solving organization
- Pass problems back to the customer
- Defensive — will not admit poor performance
- No commitment to continued cost reduction and schedule improvement
- Customer is an opponent to be fenced with rather than satisfied

He reflected also on the lack of progress on the fusion reactor project. He wondered why SPD had lost out to competitors last year in the Air Force market. He wondered what could be done to improve SPD's performance.

18

C & C Grocery Stores, Inc.

The first C & C grocery store was started in 1947 by Doug Cummins and his brother Bob. Both were veterans who wanted to run their own business, so they used their savings to start the small grocery store in Charlotte, North Carolina. The store was immediately successful. The location was good, and Doug Cummins had a winning personality. Store employees adopted Doug's informal style and "serve the customer" attitude. C & C's increasing circle of customers enjoyed an abundance of good meats and produce.

By 1984, C & C had over 200 stores. A standard physical layout was used for new stores. Company headquarters moved from Charlotte to Atlanta in 1975. The organization chart for C & C is shown in Exhibit 18-1. The central offices in Atlanta handled personnel, merchandising, financial, purchasing, real estate, and legal affairs for the entire chain. For management of individual stores, the organization was divided by regions. The southern, southeastern, and northeastern, regions each had about seventy stores. Each region was divided into five districts of ten to fifteen stores each. A district director was responsible for supervision and coordination of activities for the ten to fifteen district stores.

Each district was divided into four lines of authority based upon functional specialty. Three of these lines reached into the stores. The produce department manager within each store reported directly to the produce specialist for the division, and the same was true for the meat department manager, who reported directly to the district meat specialist. The meat and produce managers were responsible for all activities associated with the acquisition and sale of perishable products. The store manager's responsibility included the grocery line, front-end departments, and store operations. The store manager was responsible for appearance of personnel, cleanliness, adequate check-out service, and price accuracy. A grocery manager reported to the store manager and maintained inventories and restocked shelves for grocery items. The district merchandising office was responsible for promotional campaigns, advertising circulars, district advertising, and for attracting customers into the stores. The grocery merchandisers were expected to coordinate their activities with each store in the district.

Prepared by Richard L Daft. From: *Organizations: a Micro/Macro Approach* by Richard L. Daft and Richard Steers. Copyright ©1986 by Scott, Foresman and Company. Reprinted by permission.

EXHIBIT 18-1 Organization Structure For C & C Grocery Stores, Inc.

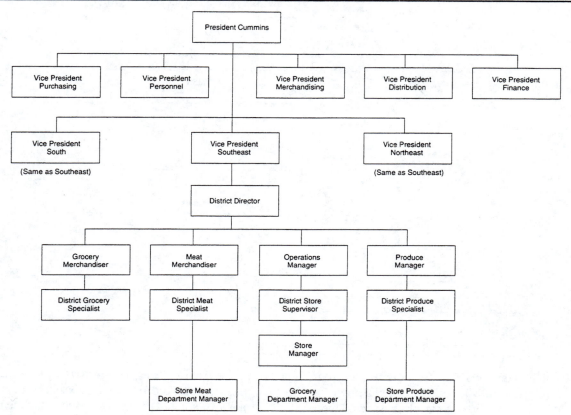

During the recession in 1980-81, business for the C & C chain dropped off in all regions and did not increase with the improved economic times in 1983-84. This caused concern among senior executives. They also were aware that other supermarket chains were adopting a trend toward one-stop shopping, which meant the emergence of super stores that included a pharmacy, dry goods, and groceries—almost like a department store. Executives wondered whether C & C should move in this direction and how such changes could be assimilated into the current store organization. However, the most pressing problem was how to improve business with the grocery stores they now had. A consulting team from a major university was hired to investigate store structure and operations.

The consultants visited several stores in each region, talking to about fifty managers and employees. The consultants wrote a report that pinpointed four problem areas to be addressed by store executives.

1. The chain is slow to adapt to change. Store layout and structure were the same as had been designed fifteen years ago. Each store did things the same way, even though some stores were in low-income areas and other stores in suburban areas. A new grocery management system for ordering and stocking had been developed, but after two years was only partially implemented in the stores.

2. Roles of the district store supervisor and the store manager were causing dissatisfaction. The store managers wanted to learn general

EXHIBIT 18-2 Proposed Reorganization of C & C Grocery Stores, Inc.

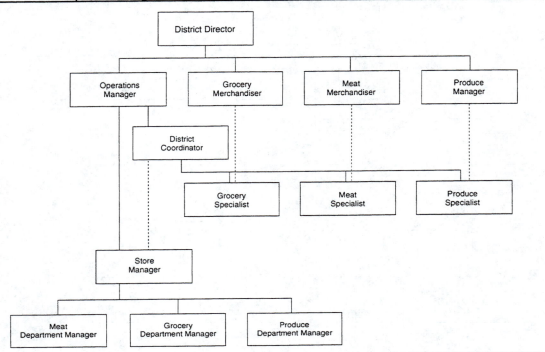

management skills for potential promotion into district or regional management positions. However, their jobs restricted them to operational activities and they learned little about merchandising, meat, and produce. Moreover, district store supervisors used store visits to inspect for cleanliness and adherence to operating standards rather than to train the store manager and help coordinate operations with perishable departments. Close supervision on the operational details had become the focus of operations management rather than development, training, and coordination.

3. Cooperation within stores was low and morale was poor. The informal, friendly atmosphere originally created by Doug Cummins was gone. One example of this problem occurred when the grocery merchandiser and store manager in a Louisiana store decided to promote Coke and Diet Coke as a loss leader. Thousands of cartons of Coke were brought in for the sale, but the stockroom was not prepared and did not have room. The store manager wanted to use floor area in the meat and produce sections to display Coke cartons, but those managers refused. The produce department manager said that Diet Coke did not help his sales and it was okay with him if there was no promotion at all.

4. Long-term growth and development of the stores chain would probably require re-evaluation of long-term strategy. The percent of market share going to traditional grocery stores was declining nationwide due to competition from large super stores and convenience stores. In the future, C & C might need to introduce non-food items into the stores for one-stop shopping, and add specialty sections within stores. Some stores could be limited to grocery items, but store location and marketing techniques should take advantage of the grocery emphasis.

To solve the first three problems, the consultants recommended reorganizing the district and the store structure as illustrated in Exhibit 18-2. Under this reorganization, the meat, grocery, and produce department managers would all report to the store manager. The store manager would have complete store control and would be responsible for coordination of all store activities. The district supervisor's role would be changed from supervision to training and development. The district supervisor would head a team that included himself and several meat, produce, and merchandise specialists who would visit area stores as a team to provide advice and help for the store managers and other employees. The team would act in a liaison capacity between district specialists and the stores.

The consultants were enthusiastic about the proposed structure. By removing one level of district operational supervision, store managers would have more freedom and responsibility. The district liaison team would establish a cooperative team approach to management that could be adopted within stores. The focus of store responsibility on a single manager would encourage coordination within stores, adaptation to local conditions, and provide a focus of responsibility for store-wide administrative changes.

The consultants also believed that the proposed structure could be expanded to accommodate non-grocery lines if enlarged stores were to be developed in the future. Within each store, a new department manager could be added for pharmacy, dry goods, or other major departments. The district team could be expanded to include specialists in these departments who would act as liaison for stores in the district.

19
William Taylor and Associates

"The one thing I can say for certain is that I cannot measure in dollars alone the benefits I derive from running my own business." The speaker was William Taylor, owner of Taylor and Associates. He continued, "Many in business used to say that the impact on the bottom line was all that mattered. But today, even big businesses — or at least some of them — seem to be learning what most small businessmen have known all along — that you frequently are unable to measure total benefit derived from an enterprise on the single scale of profits."

Taylor and Associates was currently a single proprietorship. After considering the possibility that objectives other than profit were important to his overall satisfaction, Mr. Taylor wondered whether the current organizational form was the most appropriate. Mr. Taylor's son, Brian, an MBA student with a master's degree in engineering, had often discussed with him the role of conflicting objectives in the evaluation of his company's performance. Mr. Taylor hoped that, with the aid of his son, he could choose the best structure for his company using a more formal analysis, one which accounted for multiple objectives.

"I agreed to go through with this multi-attribute process for several reasons. First, any formal process which would help me commit to spending some time on my strategic problems seemed to me to be positive. Second, I am an engineer as well as a businessman. For this reason, the formally quantified approach to my problem of which legal form to adopt for my organization has some appeal. I must admit, though, that the business side of me is rather leary of using any magic formula to obtain 'the' answer to such a complex problem. But since my goals and objectives in making this decision were not well formulated, I felt that this process of structuring objectives and measuring alternatives against them would help me to better understand them."

Company History

Taylor and Associates was a twenty-one-year-old engineering consulting firm with its home office in Lynchburg, Virginia. Though it had operated under other forms of ownership, in 1979 it was a single proprietorship operated by William Taylor. During its existence, the firm

This case was prepared by Michael McEnearney, Research Assistant and Samuel E. Bodily, Associate Professor as a basis for class discussion rather than to illustrate effective or ineffective handling of an administrative decision. Names and locations are disguised at the request of the owner of the firm. Copyright ©1981 by the Darden Graduate Business School Foundation, Charlottesville, VA. Used with permission.

had employed design professionals from several disciplines. In recent years, however, the firm had worked primarily in civil engineering, deriving most of its income from work in sanitary engineering design. Its primary market area had included the states of Virginia, Tennessee, and North Carolina.

Operations

The company was a small design firm with a gross income in 1978 of $810,000 and pretax profits of $53,000. The firm had been mildly innovative both in design and in the area of "process" or production. The company's major innovation was its early shift to the use of the computer, having had its own machine installed in 1967. Automated drafting and graphic arts had been used to a much greater extent and started much earlier than even many of the larger engineering firms. Finally, the firm obtained an IBM System 6 word processor in 1978. This processor did for specifications and text in general some of the same things the graphic arts machinery had done for engineering drawing.

Marketing

Taylor and Associates had been heavily involved in the sanitary engineering market segment which, in the 1960's and early 1970's, boomed as a result of the concerns for the environment. It had sought to provide the high level of service which small towns in its market area had needed in dealing with the Environmental Protection Agency and Farmer's Home Administration. Most new clients in this area had come to the firm as a result of its reputation with previous clients.

There had always been a background level of work in other areas of civil engineering —from subdivision work to structural design. However, the degree to which the firm had become primarily involved in sanitary work during the late 1970's is clear from the make-up of the firm's design section. In 1979, all design engineers were civil engineers, and all advanced degrees held were in sanitary engineering. Mr. Taylor

had a dedication to the "marketing concept" which said that the best way to serve the needs of the client was through a multidisciplinary approach, but no specific market segments had been targeted. Due to the company's current industry segment and barriers to entry into the other disciplines, such as architecture, the multidisciplinary approach had never caught on.

While little formal strategic market analysis had been done, the efforts of the two men involved in Project Development had produced some results. In 1979, the two areas in which the most marketing/selling effort was being focused were energy-related work (coal and gas) and the private industrial sector. It was hoped that growth in these new areas would help to counter the effects on the firm of the reduction of demand within the sanitary segment.

Another way in which the company had sought to open markets was based on geographic expansion. The opening of the office in Asheville, North Carolina, had been intended to provide access to North Carolina markets never successfully cracked by the Lynchburg Office. As of 1979, staffing in Asheville would not support engineering, but the surveying practice appeared to have established itself there.

Finance

Unlike any other functional area, the area of finance and accounting had been solely under the purview of the owner-operator himself. Mr. Taylor's computerized accounting and control system seemed to give him the type of control that was critical for a design firm.

In spite of his otherwise conservative financial stance, Mr. Taylor had chosen to use his line of credit as a means of reducing his mortgages and other long-term finances on a regular basis. This had led to relatively high short term debt (in comparison with the industry). Though this policy may have added some expense, it apparently had created little danger of loss of short-term financing because of the firm's record with the bank.

New Ventures

In 1971 Taylor and Associates was one of the three professional firms involved in Freedom Inc., which began putting together a package which was to become the Freedom Ski development in North Carolina. After most of the planning and early development work was finished, the company withdrew from the venture in 1976. However, Mr. Taylor thought the enterprise was an effective way to expand the business and wished to pursue other "new ventures" if possible. In 1979 the company had several opportunities in this area.

In 1979 Taylor and Associates purchased over 700 acres of prime land in and around the city of Asheville, North Carolina. The ultimate plan for the property included an executive park and executive housing areas. The likely first phase, however, would be King's Lodge, a high-quality conference center, overlooking the lake site.

Another opportunity available to the company would be to enter the systems analysis/computer consulting business. The firm's in-house IBM computer and word processor would provide a starting point for a move into this expanding field.

Finally the company could seek other land development projects similar to Freedom Inc. (which the firm participated in but did not control). Such projects would make use of the consulting firm's project management and engineering skills.

Organizational Structure

The firm was a single proprietorship organized along functional lines (see Exhibit 19-1), with one thin layer of reasonably strong middle management. Mr. Taylor's hope was to eventually delegate profit and loss responsibility for projects to project managers although, in 1979, this had not yet occurred. While Mr. Taylor recognized he couldn't separate organizational consideration from business strategy, his main purpose now was a study of the organizational arrangement.

Four general conditions existed which had led Mr. Taylor to consider a possible change:

1. The last two or three years had brought some major changes in the environment. Demand in the sanitary engineering segment was declining while the demand in other areas, such as energy and computer consulting, was growing rapidly. Mr. Taylor questioned whether the firm was well structured to deal with these changes.

2. The owner-operator wished to be involved in new venture activities. Real estate development and management projects appeared to be particularly attractive. Some of the new ventures, however, might not present a good organizational fit with the present structure. Even though they were conceptually related to the business, they would require functional and managerial skills not present in the existing firm.

3. The goals of the middle management of the existing firm and those of the owner seemed inconsistent with one another. Activities Mr. Taylor would take that were beneficial to himself or to the long-term strength of the company might have a negative effect on the managers' profit sharing plan.

4. The question of finances was an area of continuing concern. The form of legal organization adopted by the firm would effect its ability to raise capital. Expansion of new ventures would require large amounts of capital, and it would be easier for a corporation to raise the funds than for a sole proprietarship. In addition, Mr. Taylor could limit his personal financial liability with a corporate organization, whereas with a sole proprietorship he was personally liable for all business debts.

Organization Study

With Brian's help, Mr. Taylor spent a lot of time drawing up concrete statements of his objectives. Though he covered a lot of ground, focus

EXHIBIT 19-1 William Taylor and Associates; Present Organization of the Firm

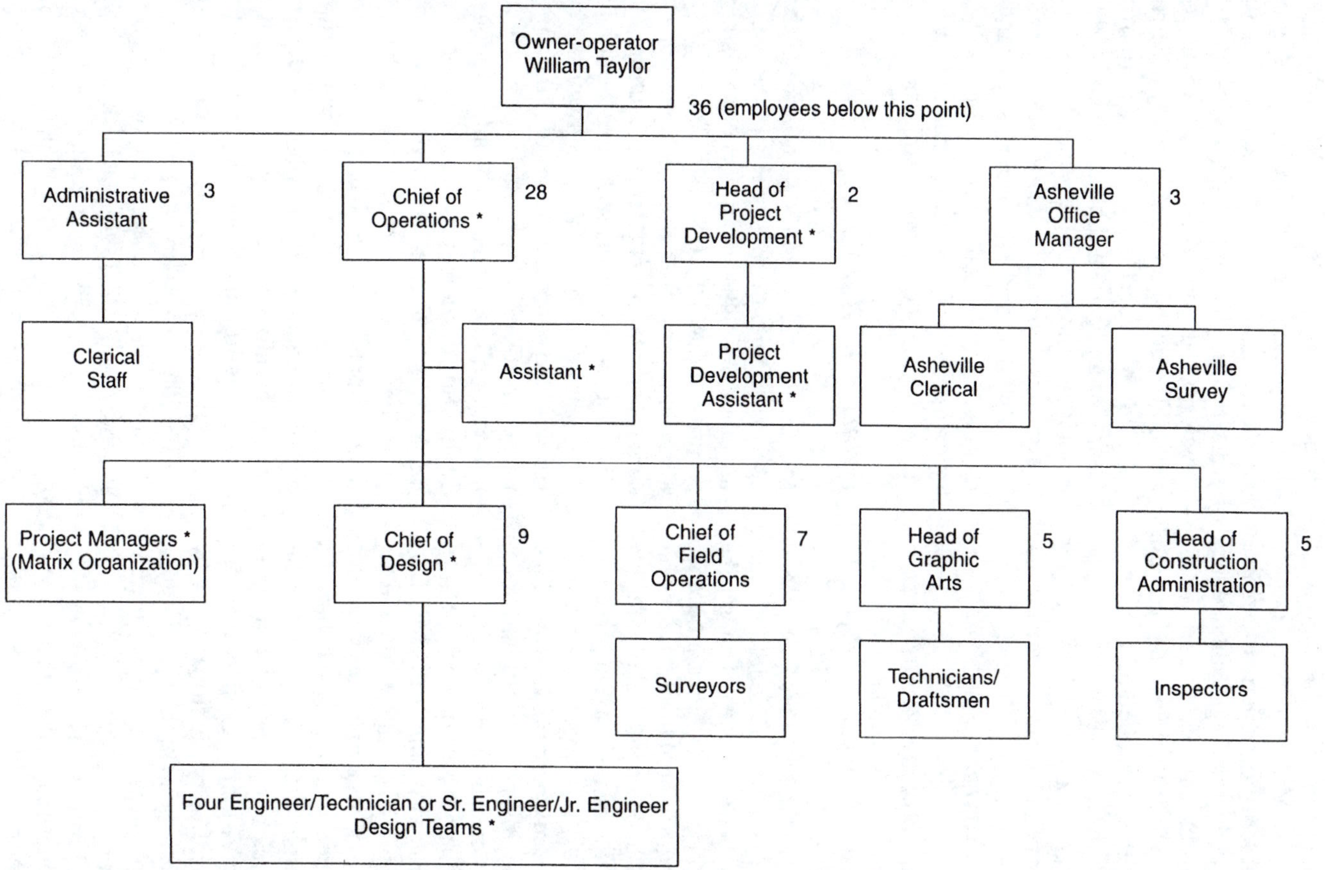

Owner-operator William Taylor

36 (employees below this point)

- Administrative Assistant — 3
  - Clerical Staff
- Chief of Operations * — 28
  - Assistant *
    - Chief of Design * — 9
      - Project Managers * (Matrix Organization)
      - Four Engineer/Technician or Sr. Engineer/Jr. Engineer Design Teams *
    - Chief of Field Operations — 7
      - Surveyors
    - Head of Graphic Arts — 5
      - Technicians/ Draftsmen
    - Head of Construction Administration — 5
      - Inspectors
- Head of Project Development * — 2
  - Project Development Assistant *
- Asheville Office Manager — 3
  - Asheville Clerical
  - Asheville Survey

* These individuals are licensed Professional Engineers. The design section includes six graduate engineers, four of whom are licensed Professional Engineers, and three of whom hold advanced technical degrees. Any licensed engineer could serve as a Project Manager, and in some cases, a licensed surveyor might also. A number of people, including the head of the Asheville Office, are registered Land Surveyors.

was slow in coming. The problem centered on the fact that, as in most small businesses organized as single proprietorships, there was no clear distinction between the owner's personal and business objectives. As Mr. Taylor's attempts at structuring his problem continued, it became increasingly clear that he felt the personal objectives of his employees and his objectives for himself and for the business were in conflict with one another — and that he valued all three sets of objectives. Although the structure of the whole problem remained unfocused, Mr. Taylor decided to center his efforts on these three areas.

Maintaining the Business

Mr. Taylor's primary objective with respect to the business was insuring its stability and future growth even if, for some unknown reason, he should have to leave the firm. His primary means of providing for the business' continued existence had been to carry sufficient life insurance to cover all debts and taxes. Though the majority of this insurance was carried because of the business, the substantial insurance premiums Mr. Taylor paid had to come out of after-tax dollars because of the firm's current structure. Re-organizing the business might not only help insure its future but could also provide an added tax benefit: tax-free insurance premiums (deducted as a business expense) for Mr. Taylor.

Some of the legal aspects of operating a professional organization also concerned Mr. Taylor. The law held a professional responsible for his actions and those of his employees under his supervision. Anyone assuming ownership in a professional firm might assume not only typical business financial risk but professional liability as well. In addition, Virginia state law restricted ownership to 25% of a professional firm by persons not registered in that profession. Finally, the non-professional owner had to be an employee of the company.

Other areas of the business that concerned Mr. Taylor included strengthening the functional areas, finance, marketing, and particularly new ventures, and strengthening the management and control areas.

Employee Welfare

In addition to insuring the income and job satisfaction of his employees, Mr. Taylor was particularly concerned with the strength of his management and their job satisfaction. For several years, the firm had operated a profit-sharing plan which placed a large portion of anything over $50,000 in net income achieved by the firm into investments for the employee's retirement. Geared mainly toward management and senior employees, the amount received by each person was based on relative salary level. Mr. Taylor knew that in order to maintain a strong management group, he had to insure not only their income (i.e. profit sharing) but increase their sense of control over the organization.

Owner's Welfare

Mr. Taylor had to admit that although he was concerned with the business and the welfare of his employees, his major concern was his own security and satisfaction. Mr. Taylor wanted to insure not only his current income but wanted some guarantee of security in the future. He was also concerned that any change in the company's organization would not "give away the store." He expected to remain in control of the company, whatever form it took, and wanted to retain ultimate policy control over all functions. Mr. Taylor did see, however, advantages to limiting his actually "running" the day-to-day operation of the business. Not only could he have more time to spend in areas that interested him (i.e. King's Lodge) but he was anxious to limit his personal financial liability which, under a single proprietorship, was very high. As already mentioned (i.e. life insurance), a change in the organization's structure may also provide personal tax benefits to Mr. Taylor.

After having considered the three major areas in more detail, Mr. Taylor sat back and looked at all his options. The first thing he did was draw up a list of all the organizational arrangements he thought were feasible for his company. Exhibit 19-2 gives a listing of these alternatives and a brief description of each.

Mr. Taylor still was not satisfied that all of his objectives had been clearly stated. He decided to spend some time at a vacation home where he could isolate himself and spend more time on the problem. When he returned, he had a list of twenty-three objectives (Exhibit 19-3) which he felt covered all of his goals with respect to any new organizational structure. Mr. Taylor felt there was still room for improvement. Some of the objectives covered more than one of the three major areas of concern and needed to be broken out further. In addition, Mr. Taylor felt that twenty-three objectives were too many to use. Although he didn't see that any of the objectives could be eliminated, he liked the idea of grouping the objectives into related areas and then dealing with this smaller number of grouped objectives. Then it would be necessary to identify specific attributes and describe how to measure or estimate each one.

The problem of picking a new organization was not a simple one. Mr. Taylor realized, however, that before he could ever consider which organizational structure to pick, he had to place his objectives into a more formalized structure to help him analyze the problem better.

Alternate Organizational Arrangements (Exhibit 19-2)

1. Status Quo

   Mr. Taylor would retain 100% ownership and, therefore, full financial responsibility for the company. Mr. Taylor would still maintain full control over the operations and policy decisions. Growth potential for the company and advancement possibilities for the employees would be limited since Mr. Taylor would be forced to restrict the size of the company to keep it manageable.

2. Single partnership

   Mr. Taylor would enter into a partnership with one other individual, retaining at least 51% interest in the company. A single partnership would provide increased job security for the employees (the company no longer relies solely on Mr. Taylor for continuity), increased financial leverage (the company can borrow against both partners not just Mr. Taylor), and reduced financial liability for Mr. Taylor. Major disadvantages include reduced control over the company's operation for Mr. Taylor, reduced personal income for Mr. Taylor (profits must now be shared with the partner), and reduced personal freedom for Mr. Taylor since the partnership agreement would tie him to the business and limit his ability to change his own working conditions without prior approval of the partner.

3. Multiple partnerships

   Mr. Taylor considered the possibility of breaking the business up into separate operating entities (i.e. surveying and engineering, and various new ventures) and forming a separate partnership for each one. Mr. Taylor would retain at least a 51% interest in each new enterprise. The advantages are the same as with a single partnership only to a higher degree with the added advantages of increased professionalism and growth potential due to specialization within each partnership. The major disadvantages include a reduction in Mr. Taylor's ability to control the different businesses and a reduction in the synergistic benefits of operating a single business (i.e. unified marketing and planning).

4. Professional Corporation + Proprietorship

   A professional corporation would be formed to run the engineering and surveying portions of the business, Mr.Taylor would retain at least a 51% interest, and the remainder of the business would remain a single proprietorship (i.e. new venture, land development and non-engineering consulting). The major advantages include increased stability from the employees' point-of-view, an increase in the professional stature of the business and an increase in personal freedom for Mr. Taylor since he would be free to concentrate on the parts of the business which interest him the most (the segments of the business kept in the sole proprietorship). The disadvantages include a reduction in synergy (as with multiple partnerships), a possible* reduction in tax benefits to Mr. Taylor (who may pay corporate tax in addition to personal tax) and a reduction in the "entrepreneurial" nature of the business.

5. Professional Corporation + One or More General Corporations

   Establish a professional corporation for engineering and surveying and set up one or more general corporations for the non-professional (new ventures, consulting, and land development) aspects of the business. This would combine most of the advantages of the multiple partnerships: growth, professionalism**, and employee satisfaction due to specialization, along with the added protection against personal liability for the financial performance of the company. The major disadvantages would be reduced personal tax benefits to Mr. Taylor (any company income not from subchapter S corporations would be subject to corporate taxes) and reduced control since all of the companies would be publicly owned.

6. Proprietorship with Responsibility Centers

   This form of organization is basically the same as the status quo with the exception that employees at the upper and middle levels of management would become more responsible for the successful operation of the company. Mr. Taylor would retain all of the personal benefits and financial li-abilities of the sole proprietorship he is currently operating but would increase the job satisfaction of his employees.

7. Single Corporation with Employee Stock Option Plan (ESOP)

   A single corporation would be formed with Mr. Taylor retaining at least 51% interest in the company. The remainder of the stock would be owned by employees under a stock option plan. This plan incorporates the benefits of incorporating (reduced personal financial, but not professional, liability) with some of the control of a single proprietorship. Mr. Taylor would remain in control of the operations of the business and the direction the company would take. Major disadvantages include a possible* reduction in the personal tax benefits to Mr. Taylor, a reduction in Mr. Taylor's ownership of the company, a limitation on the company's growth potential due to lack of specialization, and a loss of professionalism** that the formation of multiple partnerships or a professional corporation would bring about.

Source: These alternatives were prepared by the owner-operator during the early part of this study.

Organizational Objectives (Exhibit 19-3)

1. Ample income and retirement security for all employees.

2. A sense of position, or of being part of a moderately-sized organization, for employees (e.g. President, Executive Vice President, etc.). This objective is to see that all employees understand their positions within the organization.

3. Some form of cost-center arrangement whereby profit-sharing can be related to performance and employees will not feel profits from their efforts are unfairly siphoned off

---

*The corporation may be a subchapter S corporation, in which case the taxes to Mr. Taylor would not change.

**By Virginia law, a professional corporation is entitled to practice a single professional specialty and no other form of business. Therefore the professional corporation, like a partnership, is perceived by clients as a source of more specialized and expert professionals than a general corporation.

to other activities.

4. Permanence of organization not dependent on my life, but this need be only to the extent that the employees can see that there is a permanence—not necessarily legal permanence of the ownership entity.

5. Opportunity for employee growth and advancement—as each individual chooses—i.e. along purely technical engineering lines or in areas of business and/or management.

6. A sense of providing input and at least some measure of control by senior employees—related to pride of ownership as opposed to mere employee status.

7. Avoidance of irrevocably "giving away the store," at least in the near term.

8. Maintenance of a professional engineering entity as it is generally understood by organizations like the Consulting Engineers Council (CEC) and our professional liability insurance carrier.

9. Limitation of my personal financial liability.

10. Adequate financing for all resultant organizations and activities.

11. Ability to "sell" each phase of the organization as being large and having adequate support facilities (for use in marketing efforts).

12. Maximum tax shelter benefits for all—myself and employees.

13. Tax-free life insurance premiums.

14. Retention of ultimate policy decision control over all units.

15. Removal of any real or imagined restraints on pursuing "blue sky" projects.

16. Assurance that ultimate benefits of "blue sky" projects accrue primarily to those having capital (or effort) at risk on these projects.

17. Compatibility with King's Lodge development.

18. Compatibility with development of a strong systems analysis/computer consulting capability.

19. Compatibility with pursuit of large land development projects (e.g. Freedom Inc.) with our role being managers as well as engineers and surveyors. This relates primarily to North Carolina.

20. Minimize government interference, particularly I.R.S., to maximum extent possible.

21. Provide for growth in all phases.

22. Compatibility with development of Design Management.

23. Conservation and efficient use of resources (single accounting system, centralized management, etc.).

Source: This list of objectives was prepared by the owner-operator during the early part of this study.

20
Electrolux — the Acquisition and Integration of Zanussi

In recounting the story of Electrolux's acquisition of Zanussi, Leif Johansson, head of Electrolux's major appliance division, had reasons to feel pleased. Through financial restructuring and operating improvements Zanussi had, in only three years since the acquisition, gone from a massive loss of Lit. 120 billion in 1983 to a tidy profit of Lit. 60 billion in 1987*— a turnaround that astounded outside analysts and was perhaps more impressive than the expectations of even the optimists within Electrolux. More important, was the progress made in integrating Zanussi strategically, operationally and organizationally within the Electrolux group, while protecting its distinct identity and reviving the fighting spirit that had been the hallmark of the proud Italian company. Having been the first to suggest to President Anders Scharp that Electrolux should buy financially troubled Zanussi, Johanssom had a major personal stake in the operation's continued success.

*$1 = Lit. 1170 = SEK 5.85 (International Financial Statisitcs, December, 1987)

By early 1988, however, the task was far from complete. Not everything was going well at Zanussi: the company had recently lost some market share within Italy to Merloni, its archrival, which had taken over domestic market leadership following its acquisition of Indesit, another large Italian producer of household appliances. There had been some delays in Zanussi's ambitious programme for plant automation. Moreover, a recent attitude survey had shown that while the top 60 managers of Zanussi fully supported the actions taken since the acquisition, the next rung of 150 managers felt less motivated and less secure. It was not clear whether these problems were short-term in nature and would soon be resoved, or whether they were the warning signals for more basic and fundamental maladies.

Though Leif Jahansson felt it useful to review the integration process, his concerns focused on the next stage of the battle for global leadership. The industry was changing rapidly with competitors like Whirlpool and Matsushita moving outside their home regions. At the same time

This case was prepared by Sumantra Ghoshal and Philippe Haspeslagh, Associate Professors at INSEAD and Dag Andersson, Nicola De Sanctis, Beniamino Finzi, and Jacopo Franzan. It is intended to be used as a basis for class discussion rather than to illustrate either effective or ineffective handling of an administrative situation. The cooperation of the Electrolux company and its executives is gratefully acknowledged. Copyright ©1989 INSEAD-CEDEP, Fontainebleau, France. Revised 1990.
Financial support from the INSEAD Alumni Fund European Case Programme is gratefully acknowledged.

some local European comptitors like GEC-Hotpoint in the UK or Merloni (Ariston) in Italy were making aggressive moves to expand their shares in a relatively low-growth market. The Zanussi takeover and the subsequent acquisistion of White Consolidated in the United States, catapulted Electrolux to the top of the list of the world's largest producers of household appliances.

The challenge for Johansson now was to mold all the acquired entities into an integrated strategy and organization that would protect this leadership role and leverage it into a profitable worldwide operation.

Electrolux

In 1962, Electrolux was on a downward curve. Profits were falling and the company had not developed any significant in-house research and development capability. Compared with other appliance manufacturers such as Philips, Siemens, GEC and Matsushita, it had a limited range of products: the core business was made up of vacuum cleaners and absorption-type refrigerators. These refigerators were increasingly unable to compete with the new compressor-type refrigerators developed by competitors, and sales of the once highly successful lines of vacuum cleaners were rapidly declining.

That same year ASEA, a company in the Wallenberg network (an informal grouping of major Swedish companies in which the Wallenbergs — the most influential business family in Sweden — had some equity shares) sold Electro-Helios to Electrolux for shares and thereby became a major shareholder. Electro-Helios was a technological leader in compressor-type refrigerators and a significant producer of freezers and cooking-ranges. This led to a major expansion of Elctrolux's role in the Swedish household appliance market, but the company found itself in financial difficulty again due to rapid expansion of production capacity during a period of severe economic downturn.

In 1967 Hans Werthen was appointed CEO of Electrolux. In the next two decades he and the other two members of what was known as the "Electrolux Troika", Anders Scharp and Gosta Bystedt, would mange to develop the company from a relatively small and marginal player in the business world into the world's largest manufacture of household appliances.

Growth Through Acquisitions

At the core of the dramatic transformation of Electrolux was an aggressive strategy of expansion through acquisition. At the beginning, Electrolux concentrated on acquiring firms in the Nordic countries, its traditional market, where the company already had a dominant market share. Subsequent acquisitions served not only to strengthen the company's position in its household appliance activities, but also to broaden its European presence and open the way to entirely new product areas. Exhibit 20-1 illustrates Electrolux's major acquisitions between 1962 and 1988.

With more than 200 acquisitions in 40 countries, and 280 manufacturing facilities in 25 countries, the Electrolux Group had few equals in managing the acquisition and integration process. The company generally bought competitors in its core businesses, disposing of operations which either failed to show long-term profit potential or appeared to have a better chance of prospering under the management of another company. In addition, Electrolux always tried to ensure that there were sufficient realisable assets available to help finance the necessary restructuring of the acquired company. Thus, from the beginning of the 1970s up to 1988, the group made capital gains from selling off idle assets of more than SEK 2.5 billion.

At the same time, flexibility had been maintained in order to pick up new product areas for further development. A typical example of this was the chain-saw product line that came with the acquisition of the Swedish appliance manufacturer Husqvarna in 1978. By developing this product line through acquisitions and in-house development, Electrolux emerged as one of the world's leading chain-saw manufacturers with

EXHIBIT 20-1 1987 Turnover by Product Line

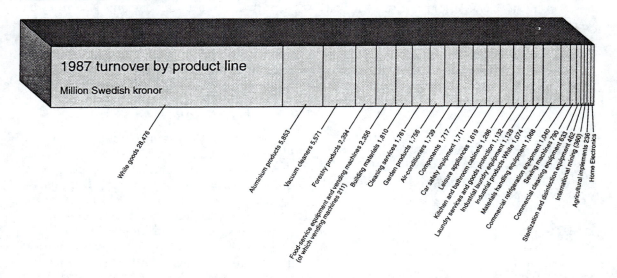

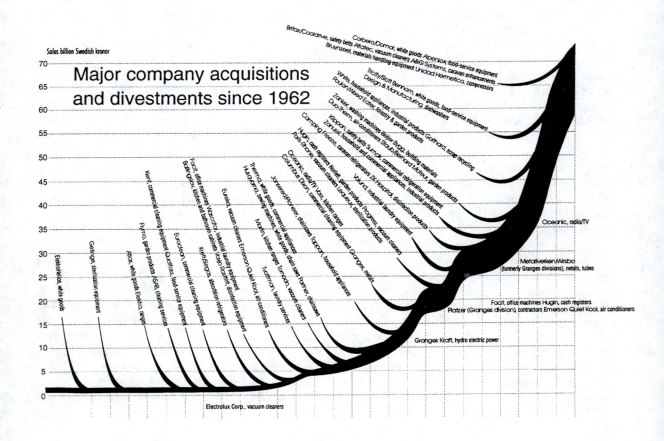

about 30 percent of the global market. Another example was provided by the new business area of outdoor products (consisting mainly of forestry and garden products), which had been grown from the small base of the Flygmo lawnmower business through the acquisition of firms like Poulan/Weed Eater in the US and Staub/Bernard Moteur in France.

The two most notable departures from the strategy of buying familiar businesses had been the 1973 acquisition of Facit, a Swedish office equipment and electronics maker, and the 1980 purchase of Gränges, a metal and mining company. Both companies were in financial trouble. Electrolux had difficulty in fully mastering Facit. After having brought the profit up to a reasonable level, it was sold off to Ericsson in 1983. The borrowing necessary to buy Gränges, combined with the worldwide economic downturn and rising interest rates, pushed Electrolux into a sobering two-year decline (1981-1983) of its profit margin. However, through the Gränges' takeover, Electrolux also acquired new businesses for future growth. An example was the manufacturing of seat belts, now concentrated in the subsidiary Electrolux Autoliv. Nevertheless, the acquisition of Gränges would be the last diversifying acquisition.

Even though Electrolux had dealt with a large number of acquisitions, specific companies were seldom targeted. In the words of Anders Scharp, "You never choose an acquisition; opportunities just come." The company made it a practice to simulate what the merger combination with other companies would result in should they come up for sale. The financial aspects of an acquisition were considered to be very important. The company usually ensured that it paid less for a company than the total asset value of the company, and not for what Electrolux would bring to the party.

Based on their experience, managers at Electrolux believed that there was no standard method for treating acquisitions: each case was unique and had to be dealt with differently. Typically, however, Electrolux moved quickly at the beginning of the integration process. It identified the key action areas and created task forces consisting of managers from both Electrolux and the acquired company in order to address each of the issues on a time-bound basis. Such joint task forces were believed to help foster management confidence and commitment and create avenues for reciprocal information flows. Objectives were clearly specified, milestones were identified, and the first phase of integration was generally completed within 3-6 months so as to create and maintain momentum. The top management of an acquired company was often replaced, but the middle management was kept intact. As explained by Anders Scharp, "The risk of losing general management competence is small when it is a poorly performing company. Electrolux is prepared to take this risk. It is, however, important that we do not change the marketing and sales staff."

Electrolux Prior to the Acquisition of Zanussi

The activities of the Electrolux group in 1984, prior to the acquisition of Zanussi, covered 26 product lines within five business areas; namely, household appliances, forestry and garden products, industrial products, commercial services and metal and mining (Gränges). Total sales revenue had increased from SEK 1.1 billion in 1967 to SEK 34.5 billion in 1984. The household appliance area (including white goods, special refrigerators, floor-care products and sewing machines) accounted for approximately 52 percent of total Group Sales in 1984. Gränges was the second largest area with nearly 21.5 percent of total sales. The third area, industrial products, provides heavy equipment for food services, semi-industrial laundries, and commercial cleaning.

By the 1980s Electrolux had become one of the world's largest manufacturers of white goods, with production facilities in Europe and North America and a small presence in Latin America and the Far East. The Group's reliance upon the Scandinavian markets was still considerable. More than 30 percent of sales came from Sweden, Norway and Denmark. European sales, focusing mainly on Scandinavia and Western

Europe, constituted 65 percent of total Group sales. The United States had emerged as the single most important market with 28.9 percent (1987) of total sales.

Electrolux's household appliances were manufactured in plants with specialized assembly lines. Regional manufacturing operations were focused on local brands and designs and established distribution networks. Sales forces for the various brands had been kept separate, though support functions such as physical distribution, stocking, ordertaking and invoicing might be integrated. With increasing plant automation and product differentiation, the number of models and the volume produced in any given plant had risen sharply. As described by Anders Scharp, "We recognized that expansion means higher volumes, which create scope for rationalization. Rationalization means better margins, which are essential to boost our competitive strength."

One important characteristic of Electrolux was the astonishingly small corporate headquarters at Lilla Essingen, 6 km outside the centre of Stockholm, and the relatively few people who worked in central staff departments. The size of headquarters was a direct outcome of the company's commitment to decentralization. "I believe that we have at least two hierarchical levels fewer than other companies of the same size," said Scharp, "and all operational matters are decentralized to the subsidiaries." However, most strategic issues such as investment programmes, and product range decisions were dealt with at headquarters. The subsidiaries were considered to be profit centres and were evaluated primarily on their returns on net assets as compared with the targets set by the corporate office. Presidents of the diversified subsidiaries reported directly to Scharp, while others reported to the heads of the different product lines.

The Acquisition of Zanussi

In June 1983, Leif Johansson, the 32-year-old head of Electrolux's major appliance division, received a proposal from Mr. Candotti, head of Zanussi's major appliance division in France, from whom he had been "sourcing" refrigerators for the French market. The proposal called for the investment of a small amount of money in Zanussi so as to secure future supplies from the financially troubled Italian producer. The next day Johansson called Anders Scharp to ask "Why don't we buy all of it?," thereby triggering a process that led to the largest acquisition in the history of the household appliance industry and in the Swedish business world.

ZANUSSI

Having begun in 1916 as a small workshop in Pordenone, a little town in northeast Italy where Antonio Zanussi produced a few wood-burning cookers, Zanussi had grown by the early 1980s to be the second largest privately-owned company in Italy with more than 30,000 employees, 50 factories and 13 foreign sales companies. Most of the growth came in the 1950s and 1960s under the leadership of Lino Zanussi, who understood the necessity of having not only a complete range of products but also a well-functioning distribution and sales network. Lino Zanussi established several new factories within Italy and added cookers, refrigerators and washing-machines to the product range. In 1958 he launched a major drive to improve exports out of Italy and established the first foreign branch office in Paris in 1962. Similar branches were soon opened in other European countries and the first foreign manufacturing subsidiary, IBELSA, was set up in Madrid in 1965. Through a series of acquisitions of Italian producers of appliances and components, Zanussi became one of the most vertically integrated manufacturers in Europe, achieving full control over all activities ranging from component manufacturing to final sales and service. It is rumoured that, during this period of heady success, Zanussi had very seriously considered launching a takeover bid for Electrolux, then a struggling Swedish company less than half Zanussi's size.

The company's misfortunes started in 1968 when Lino Zanussi and several other company executives died in an aircrash. Over the next fifteen years the new management carved out a costly programme of unrelated diversification into fields such as colour televisions, prefabricated housing, real estate and community centres. The core business of domestic appliances languished for want of capital, while the new businesses incurred heavy losses. By 1982, the company had amassed debts of over Lit. 1300 billion and was losing over Lit. 100 billion a year on operations (see Exhibit 20-2 for the consolidated financial statements during this period).

Between 1982 and 1984, Zanussi tried to rectify the situation by selling off many of the loss-making subsidiaries, reducing the rest of the workforce by over 4,400 people and focusing on its core activities. However, given the large debt burden and the need for heavy investment in order to rebuild the domestic appliance business, a fresh injection of capital was essential, and the company began its search for a partner.

The Acquisition Process

The process of Electrolux's acquisition of Zanussi formally commenced when Enrico Cuccia, the informal head of Mediobanca and the most powerful financier in Italy, approached Hans Werthn on November 30, 1983, about the possibility of Electrolux rescuing Zanussi from impending financial collapse. It was not by chance that the grand old man of Mediobanca arrived in Sweden. Mr. Cuccia had close links to the Agnelli family—the owners of Fiat, the largest industrial group in Italy—and the proposal to approach Electrolux came from Mr. Agnelli, who wanted to save the second largest private manufacturing company in his country. As a board member of SKF, the Swedish bearing manufacturer, Agnelli had developed a healthy respect for Swedish management and believed that Electrolux alone had the resources and management skills necessary to turn Zanussi around.

In the meanwhile, Electrolux had been looking around for a good acquisition to expand its appliance business. Its efforts to take over AEG's appliance business in Germany had failed because the conditions stipulated for the takeover were found to be too tough. Later, Electrolux had

to back away from acquiring the TI group in the U.K. because of too high a price-tag. Zanussi now represented the best chance for significant expansion in Europe. "It was a very good fit," recalled Anders Scharp. "There were not many overlaps: we were strong where Zanussi was weak, and vice-versa." There were significant complementarities in products, markets, and opportunities for vertical integration. For example, while Electrolux was well established in microwave-ovens, cookers and fridge-freezers, Zanussi was Europe's largest producer of "wet products" such as washing-machines, traditionally a weak area for Electrolux. Similarly, while Electrolux had large market shares in Scandinavia and Switzerland, where Zanussi was almost completely absent, Zanussi was the market leader in Italy and Spain, two markets that Electrolux had failed to crack. Zanussi was also strong in France, the only market where Electrolux was losing money, and had a significant presence in Germany where Electrolux had limited strength except in vacuum cleaners. Finally, while Electrolux had historically avoided vertical integration and sourced most of its components externally, Zanussi was a vertically integrated company with substantial spare capacity for component production that Electrolux could profitably use.

From November 30, 1983, until December 14, 1984, the date when the formal deal was finally signed, there ensued a 12-month period of intense negotiation in which, alongside the top management of the two companies, Gianmario Rossignolo, the Chairman of SKF's Italian subsidiary, took an increasingly active role. The most difficult parts of the negotiations focused on the following three issues:

Union and Work Force Reduction: At the outset, the powerful unions at Zanussi were against selling the company to the "Vikings from the North." They would have preferred to keep Zanussi independent, with a government subsidy, or to merge with Thomson from France. They also believed that under Electrolux management all important functions would be transferred to Sweden, thereby denuding the skills of the Italian company and also reducing local em-

EXHIBIT 20-2 Consolidated Financial Statements For Zanussi Group

Consolidated Income Statements for Zanussi Group (in millions SEK)

	1980	1981	1982	1983
Sales	3826	4327	4415	5240
Operating cost	-3301	-3775	-3957	-4654
Operation income before depreciation	525	552	458	586
Depreciation	-161	-98	-104	-130
Operating income after depreciation	364	454	354	456
Financial income	192	330	284	279
Financial expenses	-407	-489	-647	-627
Income after financial items	149	295	-9	108
Extraordinary items	-53	-228	-223	81
Income before appropriations	96	67	-232	189
Appropriations	-53	-42	-409	-382
Income before taxes	43	25	-641	-193
Taxes	-7	-7	-10	-10
Net income	36	18	-651	-203

Consolidated Balance Sheet for Zanussi Group (in millions SEK)

	1980	1981	1982	1983
Current assets excluding inventory	1559	1987	1811	2108
Inventory	965	1054	999	956
Fixed assets	1622	1539	2366	2902
Total assets	4146	4580	5176	5966
Current liabilities	1590	1832	1875	2072
Long-term liabilities	1273	1441	1864	2349
Reserves	259	301	472	627
Shareholders' equity	1024	1006	965	918
Total liabilities and shareholders' equity	4146	4580	5176	5966

ployment opportunities.

In response to these concerns, Electrolux guaranteed that all Zanussi's important functions would be retained within Italy. Twenty union leaders were sent from Sweden to Italy to reassure the Italians. The same number of Italian union leaders were invited to Sweden to observe Electrolux's production system and labour relations. Initially, Mr. Rossignolo signed a letter of assurance to the unions on behalf of Electrolux confirming that the level of employment prevailing at that time would be maintained. Soon thereafter, however, it became obvious that Zanussi could not be made profitable without workforce reductions. This resulted in difficult re-negotiations. It was finally agreed that within three months of the acquisition Electrolux would present the unions a three-year plan for investments and reduction in personnel. Actual retrenchments would have to follow the plan, subject to its approval by the unions.

Prior Commitments of Zanussi: A number of problems were posed by certain commitments on the part of Zanussi. One major issue was SELECO, an Italian producer of television sets. A majority of shares in SELECO were held by REL, a government holding company, and the rest were owned by Zanussi and Indesit. Zanussi had made a commitment to buy REL's majority holdings of SELECO within a period of five years ending in 1989. Electrolux had no interest in entering the television business but finally accepted this commitment despite considerable apprehension.

Another major concern was the unprofitable Spanish appliance company IBELSA owned by Zanussi. Zanussi had received large subsidies from the Spanish government against a commitment to help restructure the industry in Spain and heavy fines would have to be paid if the company decided to pull out. Once again, Electrolux had to accept these terms despite concern about IBELSA's long-term competitiveness.

Nevertheless, there was one potential liability that Electrolux refused to accept. In the later stages of the negotiations, an audit team from Electrolux discovered that a previous managing director of Zanussi had sold a large amount of equipment and machinery to a German company and had then leased them back. This could potentially lead to severe penalties and large fines, as the actions violated Italian foreign exchange and tax laws. Electrolux refused to proceed with the negotiations until the Italian government had promised not to take any punitive actions in this case.

Financial Structure and Ownership: Electrolux was not willing to take over majority ownership of Zanussi immediately since it would then be required to consolidate Zanussi into group accounts, and the large debts would have major adverse effects on the Electrolux balance sheet and share prices. Electrolux wanted to take minority holdings without relinquishing its claim to majority holdings in the future. To resolve this issue, a consortium was organized that included prominent Italian financial institutions and industrial companies such as Mediobanca, IMI, Crediop, and a subsidiary of Fiat. The consortium took on a large part of the shares (40.6 percent), with another 10.4 percent bought by the Friuli region. This allowed Electrolux to remain at 49 percent. While the exact financial transactions were kept confidential since some of the parties opposed any payment to the Zanussi family, it is believed that Electrolux injected slightly under $100 million into Zanussi. One third of that investment secured the 49 percent shareholding, and the remainder went towards debentures that could be converted into shares at any time to give Electrolux a comfortable 75 percent ownership. An agreement with over 100 banks which had some form of exposure to Zanussi assured a respite from creditors, freezing payments on the Italian debt until January 1987. At the same time the creditors made considerable concessions on interest payments.

One of the most important meetings in the long negotiation process took place in Rome on November 15, 1984, when, after stormy discussions between the top management of Electrolux and the leaders of the Zanussi union, a document confirming Electrolux's intention to acquire Zanussi was jointly signed by both parties. During the most crucial hour of the meeting, Hans Werthn stood up in front of the 50 union leaders and declared: "We are not buying companies in order to close them down, but to turn them into profitable ventures ... and, we are not the Vikings, who were Norwegians, anyway."

The Turnaround of Zanussi

It was standard Electrolux practice to have a broad but clear plan for immediate post-acquisition action well before the negotiation process for an acquisition was complete. Thus, by August 1984, well before the deal was signed in December, a specific plan for the turnaround and the eventual integration of Zanussi was drawn up in Stockholm. As stated by Leif Johansson, "When we make an acquisition, we adopt a centralized approach from the outset. We have a definite plan worked out when we go in, and there is virtually no need for extended discussions." In the Zanussi case, the general approach had to be amended slightly since a feasible reduction in the employment levels was not automatic. However, clear decisions were taken to move the loss-making production of front-loaded washing-machines from France to Zanussi's factory in Pordenone. On the other hand, the production of all top-loading washing-machines was to be moved from Italy to France. In total, the internal plan anticipated shifting production of between 600 and 800 thousand product-units from Electrolux and subcontractors' plants to Zanussi, thereby increasing Zanussi's capacity utilization. Detailed financial calculations led to an expected cost savings of SEK 400-500 millions through rationalization. Specific plans were also drawn up to achieve a 2-3 percent reduction in Zanussi's marketing and administrative costs by integrating the organization of the two companies in different countries.

Immediate Post-Acquisition Actions

On December 14, a matter of hours after the signing of the final agreement, Electrolux announced a complete change in the top management of Zanussi. The old board, packed with nominees of the Zanussi family, was swept clean, and Mr. Gianmario Rossignolo was ap-

pointed as Chairman of the company. An Italian, long-experienced in working with Swedish colleagues because of his position as chairman of SKF's Italian subsidiary, Rossignolo was seen as an ideal bridge between the two companies with their vastly different cultures and management styles. Carlo Verri, who was Managing Director of SKF's Italian subsidiary, was brought in as the new Managing Director of Zanussi. Rossignolo and Verri had turned around SKF's Italian operations and had a long history of working together as a team. Similarly, Hans Werthn, Anders Scharp, Gsta Bystedt and Lennart Ribohn joined the reconstituted Zanussi board. The industrial relations manager of Zanussi was the only senior manager below the board level to be replaced. The purpose was to give a clear signal to the entire organization of the need to change work practices.

Consistent with the Electrolux style, a number of task forces were formed immediately to address the scope of integration and rationalization of activities in different functional areas. Each team was given a specific time period to come up with recommendations. Similarly, immediate actions were initiated in order to introduce Electrolux's financial reporting system within Zanussi, the clear target being to have the system fully in place and operative within six months from the date of the acquisition.

Direct steps were taken at the business level to enhance capacity utilization, reduce costs of raw materials and components purchased, and revitalize local sales.

Capacity utilization: It was promised that Electrolux would source 500,000 units from Zanussi, including 280,000 units of household appliances, 200,000 units of components, and 7,500 units of commercial appliances. This sourcing decision was given wide publicity both inside and outside the company, and a drive was launched to achieve the chosen levels as soon as possible. By 1985, 70 percent of the target had been reached.

Cost cutting in purchases: Given that 70

percent of production costs were represented by raw materials and purchased components, an immediate programme was launched to reduce vendor prices. The assumption was that vendors had adjusted their prices to compensate for the high risk of supplying to financially distressed Zanussi and should lower their prices now that that risk was eliminated. A net saving of 2 percent on purchases was achieved immediately. Over time about 17 percent gains in real terms would be achieved not only for Zanussi, but also for Electrolux.

Revitalizing sales: Local competitors in Italy reacted vigorously to the announcement of Electrolux's acquisition of Zanussi. Anticipating a period of inaction while the new management took charge, they launched an aggressive marketing programme, and Zanussi's sales slumped almost immediately. After consulting with Electrolux, the new management of Zanussi responded with a dramatic move of initially extending trade credit from 60 to 360 days under specified conditions. Sales surged immediately and the market was assured once and for all that "Zanussi was back."

Agreement with the Unions

In the next phase, starting from February 1985, the new management turned its attention to medium and long-term needs. The most pressing of these was to fulfill a promise made to the unions before the acquisition: the presentation of a complete restructuring programme. This programme was finalized and discussed with the union leaders on March 28, 1985, at the Ministry of Industry in Rome. It consisted of a broad analysis of the industry and market trends, evaluation of Zanussi's competitive position and future prospects, and a detailed plan for investments and workforce reduction. The meeting was characterized by a high level of openness on the part of management. Such openness, unusual in Italian industrial relations, took the unions by surprise. In the end, after difficult negotiations, the plan was signed by all the parties on May 25.

The final plan provided for a total reduction of the workforce by 4,848 employees (the emergency phone number in Italy!) to be implemented over a three-year period (2,850 in 1985, 850 in 1986, and 1,100 in 1987) through early retirement and other incentives for voluntary exit. In 1985, as planned, the workforce was reduced by 2,800.

Paradoxically, from the beginning of 1986 a new problem arose. With business doing well and export demands for some of the products strong, a number of factories had to resort to over-time work and even hired new skilled workers, whilst at the same time the original reduction plans continued to be implemented. Management claimed that there was no inconsistency in these actions since the people being laid off lacked the skills that would be needed in the future. With the prospect of factory automation clearly on the horizon, a more educated and skilled workforce was necessary and the new hires conformed to these future needs. Some of the workers resisted, and a series of strikes followed at the Porcia plant.

Management decided to force the issue and brought out advertisements in the local press to highlight the situation publicly. In the new industrial climate in Italy, the strategy proved effective and the strikes ended. In 1987, the company made further progress in its relationship with the unions. In a new agreement, wage increases were linked to productivity and no limits were placed on workforce reductions. Further, it was agreed that the company could hire almost 1,000 workers on a temporary basis, so as to take advantage of the subsidy provided by the government to stimulate worker training through temporary employment. It was clear that Zanussi management benefitted significantly from the loss of union power that was a prominent feature of the recently changed industrial scene in Italy. However, its open and transparent approach also contributed to the success by gaining the respect of trade union leaders, at both the company and national levels.

Strategic Transformation: Building Competitiveness

The new management recognized that in order to build durable competitive advantage, more basic changes were necessary. The poor financial performance of the company before the acquisition was only partly due to low productivity, and sustainable profits could not be assured through workforce reduction alone. After careful analysis, three areas were chosen as the focal points for a strategic transformation of Zanussi: improving production technology, spurring innovations and new product development, and enhancing product quality.

Improving Production Technology: Recalling his first visit to Zanussi, Halvar Johansson, then head of Electrolux's technical R&D, commented: "What we found on entering Zanussi's factories was, in many respects, 1960s technology! The level of automation was far too low, especially in assembly operation. We did not find a single industrial robot or even a computer either in the product development unit or in the plant. However, we also discovered that Zanussi's engineers and production personnel were of notably high standards." As part of a broad programme to improve production technology, Electrolux initiated an investment programme of Lit. 340 billion to restructure Zanussi's two major plants at Susegana and Porcia.

The Susegana restructing proposal foresaw an investment of Lit. 100 billion to build up the facility into a highly automated, high-capacity unit able to produce 1.2 million refrigerators and freezers a year. The project was expected to come on stream by the end of 1988. The Porcia project anticipated a total investment of about Lit. 200 billion to build a highly automated, yet flexible plant capable of producing 1.5 million washing- machines per year. This project, scheduled for completion in 1990, was the largest individual investment project in the history of the Electrolux group. When on stream, it would be the largest washing-machine factory in the world. Both projects involved large investments to build flexibility through the use of CAD-CAM systems and just-in-time production methodology. As explained by Carlo Verri, "The automation was primarily to achieve flexibility and to improve quality, and not to save on labour costs."

Implementation of both the projects was somewhat delayed. While the initial schedules may have been over-optimistic, some of the delays were caused by friction among Zanussi and Electrolux engineers. The Electrolux approach of building joint teams for implementation of projects was seen by some Zanussi managers as excessive involvement of the acquiring company in tasks for which the acquired company had ample and perhaps superior capabilities. Consequently, information flows were often blocked, resulting in, for example, a more than one-year delay in deciding the final layout of the Susegana factory. The delays were a matter of considerable concern to the top management of Electrolux. On the one hand, they felt extensive involvement of Electrolux's internal consultants to be necessary for effective implementation of the projects, since Zanussi lacked the requisite expertise. On the other hand, they acknowledged Zanussi's well-established engineering skills and the need to provide the local engineers with the opportunity to learn and to prove themselves. They also worried about whether the skill-levels of the local workforce could be upgraded in time for operating the new units and looked for ways to expedite the training process.

Innovation and New Product Development: Zanussi had built its strong market presence on the reputation of being an innovator. This ability had, unfortunately, languished during the lean period. Both Rossignolo and Verri placed the greatest emphasis on reviving the innovative spirit of the company, and projects that had idled for years due to lack of funds were revitalized and assigned high priority.

The results were quite dramatic, and a virtual torrent of new product ideas emerged very quickly. The most striking example was a new washing-machine design — the "Jet System" — that cut detergent and water consumption by a third. The product was developed within only 9 months and the new machine was presented at the Cologne fair in February 1986. Through a direct television link with Cologne, Carlo Verri himself presented the assembly line at Pordenone where the "Jet-System" was to be mass produced. By July 1986, demand for the new machine had reached the level of 250,000 per year and the company was facing delivery problems.

While the "Jet System" was the most visible outcome of the new emphasis on innovation, other equally important developments were in the pipeline. For example, the company developed a new rotary compressor to replace the reciprocating compressors that were being used in refrigerators. A major drive was also underway to improve product design and features through the introduction of IC chips. Interestingly, most of these proposals came not from the sophisticated and independent research centre of the company, but from development groups located within the line organizations which produced the products. How to maintain the momentum of innovation was a major concern for Verri, particularly as the company moved into the larger and more complex projects necessary for significant technological breakthroughs.

Enhancing Product Quality: Quality enhancement was viewed as the third leg of the strategy for long-term revitalization of Zanussi. At Electrolux, high quality was viewed as an essential means of achieving the primary objectives of the company: satisfied customers, committed employees, and sound profitability. Zanussi had a good reputation for quality, but the standards had slackened during the turmoil faced by the company for almost a decade prior to the acquisition. Committed to the policy that quality levels must be the same within the group no matter where a product was produced, Electrolux initiated a major drive to enhance product quality at Zanussi and set extremely ambitious targets to reduce failure rates and post-sales service requirements. The targets were such that incremental improvements did not suffice for their attainment and a new approach towards quality was necessary. The technical staff of Electrolux provided requi-

site guidance and assistance and helped set up the parameters for a series of quality improvement programmes launched by Zanussi.

Carlo Verri was involved in these programmes on an almost day-to-day basis. First, he headed the working group that set up the basic policy on quality for the entire Zanussi organization. In accordance with this policy, a Total Quality (TQ) project was started in May 1986 and a series of education and training programmes were introduced in order to diffuse the new philosophy and policy to all company employees. Supplier involvement was an integral part of the TQ project. As described by Verri, "Supplier involvement was crucial. Zanussi's suppliers had to demonstrate their commitment to effective quality control. This meant that all the procedures for quality assurance, for tracking down failures etc., had to be approved by us. In other words, suppliers had to have the capability to provide self-certification for the quality of their products. They had to provide service within days rather than weeks, given that our plants were becoming automated. Our gains in flexibility and quality through new production techniques could be lost if the suppliers did not become equally efficient."

Organizational Revitalization: Changing Attitudes

One of the biggest challenges faced in the turnaround process lay in the area of revitalizing the Zanussi organization. During the troubled years, the management process at Zanussi had suffered from many aberrations. Conflicts had become a way of life, and information flow within the organization had become severely constrained. Most issues were escalated to the top for arbitration, and the middle management had practically no role in decision making. Front-line managers had become alienated because of direct dealings between the workers and senior managers via the union leaders. Overall, people had lost faith in the integrity of the system, in which seniority and loyalty to individuals were seen as more important than competence or commitment to the company.

In addition, the acquisition had also created a strong barrier of defensiveness within the Zanussi organization. In its own acquisitions Zanussi typically eliminated most of the middle management in the acquired companies. As the acquired company, it expected similar actions from Electrolux. Moreover, some Zanussi managers were not convinced of any need for change. They believed that Zanussi's financial problems were caused not by any strategic, operational or organizational shortcomings, but by the practices of the previous owners, including diversion of overseas profits through a foreign holding company in Luxembourg.

Finally, most of the managers were also concerned that both Rossignolo and Verri, with their backgrounds in the Italian subsidiary of a Swedish company, "were closer to Stockholm than to Pordenone."

In an attempt to overcome these barriers, Verri and the entire executive management group at Zanussi participated in a number of team-building sessions that were facilitated by an external consultant. These meetings gave rise to a number of developments that constituted the core of the organizational revitalization of Zanussi.

Statement of Mission, Values, and Guiding Principles: One of the direct outcomes of the team-building meetings was a statement of Mission, Values, and Guiding Principles developed to serve as the charter for change (see Exhibit 20-3). The statement identified the four main values of the company: to be close to the clients and satisfy them through innovation and service; to accept challenges and develop a leader mentality; to pursue total quality not only in production but in all areas of activity; and to become a global competitor by developing an international outlook. Apart from these specific points, the statement also confirmed the new management's commitment to creating a context that would foster transparent and coherent behaviour at both the individual and company levels under all circumstances. As described by Rossignolo, "We adopted the Swedish work ethic — everybody keeps his word and all information is correct. We committed ourselves to being honest with the local authorities, the trade unions and

our customers. It took some time for the message to get across, but I think everybody has got it now."

Management Development Workshops: In order to improve the flow of information among senior managers and to co-opt them into the new management approach, a set of management development workshops was organized. The 60 most senior managers of Zanussi, including Verri, participated in each of three two-day workshops that were held between November 1985 and July 1986. The next tier of 150 middle managers of the company was subsequently exposed to the same programme.

Middle Management Problems: An organizational climate survey in 1987 revealed an interesting problem. The top 60 managers of the company confirmed strong support for the mission statement and the new management style. Conversely, the 150 middle managers, who seemed to feel threatened by the changes, appeared considerably less enthused. Their subordinates — about a thousand front-line managers and professional employees — like the top management, fully approved the change and demanded greater involvement. In response to this problem, it was decided that the 60 top managers should establish direct communication with the 1,000 front-line managers, by-passing the middle management when necessary. The decision was made known within the organization, and a clear signal was sent to the middle managers that they should get on board or else they would risk missing the boat. At the same time, a special training programme was launched for the front-line managers and professional employees in order to broaden their management skills and outlook.

Structural Reorganization: Before the acquisition, Zanussi was organized in five "sectors," with the heads of each sector reporting to the managing director. The sectors, in turn, controlled the operating companies in their business areas. In practice, the sector managers were closely involved with the day-to-day operations of the companies under their charge. Both the managing director at the corporate level, and the different sector managers had strong staff or-

EXHIBIT 20-3 Mission Values and Guiding Principles of Zanussi

Mission

To become the market leader in Europe, with a significant position in other world areas, in supplying homes, institutions, and industry with systems, appliances, components and after-sales services.

To be successful in this mission, the company and management legitimization must be based on the capability to be near the customer and satisfy his needs; to demonstrate strength, entrepreneurship, and creativity in accepting and winning external challenges; to offer total quality on all dimensions, more than the competition; and to be oriented to an internal vision and engagement.

Values

Our basic values, ranked, are:

1. To be near the customer;
2. To accept challenges;
3. To deliver total quality;
4. With an international perspective.

Our central value, underlying all of the above, is transparence, which means that Zanussi will reward behaviour which is based on constantly transparent information and attitudes, safeguarding the interests of the company.

Guiding Principles

1. A management group is legitimized by knowing what we want, pursuing it coherently, and communicating our intent in order to be believable.
2. Shared communication means shared responsibility, not power and status index.
3. The manager's task is managing through information and motivation, not by building "power islands."
4. Time is short: the world will not wait for our "perfect solutions."
5. Strategic management implies:
   - Professional skills;
   - Risk-taking attitudes and the skill to spot opportunity;
   - Integration with the environment and the organisation, flexibility and attention to change;
   - Identification with the mission of the firm, and helping in the evolution of a culture that supports it;
   - Team work ability;
   - Skill in identifying strengths and weaknesses.

Policies To Be Developed

Specific policies were being developed in the following areas to support the implementation of the above mission, values and guiding principles: personnel, image and public relations, administration, purchasing, asset control, legal representation, R&D and innovation, and information systems. Members of senior management were assigned responsibility for developing policies in each of these areas, with completion expected by the end of 1986.

ganizations to support their activities.

Verri abandoned the sector concept, even though the operating companies continued to report to the former sector managers who were now called managing directors. However, staff at the sector level were virtually eliminated and the operating companies were given full responsibility and authority for making all operating-level decisions. Similarly, staff at the corporate level were also reduced very substantially, and the heads of planning, finance and control, organization and human resources, general administration, and legal and public affairs all reported directly to Verri. The four managing directors, the five heads of major corporate staff departments, and Verri constituted the executive management group of Zanussi. As Chairman, Rossignolo concentrated primarily on external relations.

Integration of the Two Companies

As described by Leif Johansson, "With the acquisition of Zanussi, the Electrolux group entered a new era. In several respects we were able to adopt a completely new way of thinking." Much of the new thinking emerged from the discussions and recommendations of the task forces that had been appointed, involving managers from both companies, to look at specific opportunities for integrating the activities of the two organizations. In total, eight such task forces were formed; two each for components, product development, and commercial appliances, and one each for the marketing function and management development. Each of these task forces had met 3 to 4 times, typically for half a day each time. Their recommendations formed the basis for the actions that were taken to integrate the production and sales operations of the two companies, rationalize component production, and develop specialization in product and brand development within the entire Electrolux group. At the level of individuals, a bridge had been built between the top management of Electrolux and the senior management team of Zanussi, and further actions were underway for creating similar understanding and mutual respect among managers lower down in the two organizations.

Electrolux Components Group (ECG)

Following Electrolux's acquisition of White Consolidated in the United States in March 1986, an international task force consisting of managers from Electrolux, White and Zanussi was created to explore the overall synergies that could be exploited within the activities of the three companies (see Exhibit 20-4 for a summary of key group data). The task force concluded that integration opportunities were relatively limited at the level of finished products because of factors such as differences in customer preferences and technical standards, and the high transportation costs. However, at the component level, there were many similarities in the needs of the three companies, implying greater scope for standardization and production rationalization. As a result of this analysis, the Electrolux Component Group was formed at the beginning of 1987 as part of the newly created industrial products division at Electrolux. The group was made responsible for the coordination and development of all strategic components used by Electrolux worldwide. Since over 50 percent of the group's component production came from Zanussi, Verri was appointed head of this group in addition to his responsibilities as managing director of Zanussi, and the group headquarters were located in Turin, Italy. In order to preserve and enhance the competitiveness of the component sector, it was decided that 50 percent of the component group's sales must be made to outside parties and at least 20 percent of the internal requirement for components must be sourced from outside the newly formed group.

Integration of Production

At Electrolux, production, sales and marketing had traditionally been integrated market by market. After the acquisition of Zanussi, all these activities will be reorganised into international product divisions and national marketing/sales companies.

The larger volumes from the combined operations made it feasible to switch to a system in which large-scale specialised plants, equipped with flexible manufacturing technology, would each produce a single product for the entire European market. This new "one product-one factory" strategy was exemplified by the new plants in Susegana and Porcia. Each of the product divisions carried full responsibility not only for manufacturing, but also for development and internal marketing of their products. In order to coordinate long-term development among these 43 divisions, three coordinators were appointed for 'wet', 'hot' and 'cold' products respectively. Based in Stockholm without staff, each of these coordinators would be on the road most of the time.

Integration of Sales/Marketing

Similarly, it was decided to create single umbrella companies over the separate sales/marketing organisations in all countries. Given the long-standing history of competition between the Electrolux and Zanussi organisations, this would turn out to be a difficult and complex process. It was planned that in each country the stronger organisation would absorb the weaker one. This did not mean, however, that the head of the larger organisation in each country would automatically receive the top slot in the combined organisation. A number of complaints arose on both sides over this issue, which became a source of much irritation. For example, it was because of this that Candotti, who had been the first to approach Electrolux for investment in Zanussi, resigned. In what remained a source of considerable frustration, Zanussi continued to operate through directly controlled sales companies in Germany, France, Denmark and Norway.

Coordination among the marketing companies was achieved through an equally lean coordinating structure reporting to Leif Johansson, with an Italian manager coordinating all European countries and a Swedish manager looking after the rest of the world.

To facilitate operational coordination between sales and production, a number of new systems were developed. One, the Electrolux Forecasting and Supply System (EFS), involved the automatic coordination of sales forecasts and delivery orders. By 1988 computer links with EFS would be established in all European Sales subsidiaries and factories. The Zanussi evaluation system was changed to that of Electrolux, in which both sales and factories were assessed on the basis of return on net assets (RONA) rather than on a profit and cost basis. An overall RONA target of 20 percent was set for the Group as a whole.

Brand Positioning and Product Development

One of the consequences of Electrolux's history of international expansion through acquisitions was a proliferation of brands, not only in Europe but also in the US, where the acquisition of White had brought a number of brands. The task of coordinating these brands, some of which were local, others regional, and a few international, would fall to the two marketing coordinators, working closely with Leif Johansson and a task force involving product styling and marketing managers. The challenge was complicated by the fact that even the international brands did not always have the same position from market to market. Zanussi, for example, was not a brand name in Italy itself, where its products sold as 'Rex.' And its image in Sweden was not nearly as upscale and innovative as in other countries like the United Kingdom.

The approach chosen in Europe was to group the brands in four brand-name families, each targeted at a particular customer profile and destined to become a separate design family. Two of these families would be international brands based respectively on Electrolux and Zanussi, and the other two would regroup a number of local brands. The goal was to develop an integrated pan-European strategy for each brand-name family. For the international brands, the strategy would involve high-scale production of standardized products in focused factories and coordinated positioning and marketing across different countries. For the families representing a collection of national brands, the products would again be standardized as far as possible so as to allow manufacturing on a regional scale; but each brand would be "localized" in its country through positioning, distribution, promotion and service.

Mutual Respect and Understanding Among People

Since the acquisition, Anders Scharp, Lennart Ribohn and Leif Johansson had ensured that they jointly visited Pordenone at least once every two months for a two-day review of Zanussi's activities and progress. Hans Werthn and Gosta Bystedt also visited Zanussi, though much less frequently. The visitors would typically spend some time touring one or another of Zanussi's facilities and then move on to pre-planned meetings with Zanussi's top management. Over time these meetings had built a strong bridge of mutual respect between the two groups and helped diffuse some of the early apprehensions. As described by a senior manager of Zanussi, "The top management of Electrolux really understands numbers. They look at a few key numbers and immediately grasp the essentials. That was very good training for us—we had the habit of analyzing and analyzing, without coming to any conclusions.... Besides, the top two or three people in Electrolux have the ability of immersing themselves in a particular problem and coming up with a solution and an implementation plan. They are also so obviously excited by what they do, their enthusiasm is very contagious." For most senior managers at Zanussi these meetings provided stronger evidence than could any words that the top management of Electrolux did not consider the acquisition as a conquest but rather as a partnership. "We have had a lot of exchanges, and have learnt a lot from them, but we have not had a single Swedish manager imposed on top of us here."

At the next level of management the joint task forces had helped build some relationships among individuals, but the links were still weak, and apprehensions remained. "We don't know them, but our concern is that the next level of Electrolux managers may be more bureaucratic and less open. To them we might be a conquest," said a senior manager of Zanussi. "In the next phase of integration, we must develop bridges at the middle, and I frankly do not know how easy or difficult that might be."

Future Requirements

Whereas the acquisition of Zanussi and White Consolidated had catapulted Electrolux into a clear lead in the industry, the race was far from over. After initially failing to reach agreement with Philips in 1987, Whirlpool had come back in early 1988 agreeing to buy out 53 percent of Philips's appliance operations as a first step to taking full control. Upon full completion Whirlpool would have paid or assumed debt totalling $1.2 billion for activities which in 1987 were generating $70 million pre-tax, pre-interest income on sales of $2 billion. The Japanese had started moving outside South East Asia. In the meantime, local European competitors such as GEC and Merloni were ensuring good returns and, more importantly, were gaining back market share.

All of this was taking place in a mature industry highly dependent on replacement demand. Industry analysts expected that even in a moderately growing economy, appliance shipments would be on a downward trend for the next couple of years. Given the concentration of buyers and the shift toward specialised retailers, raw materials price increases were more and more difficult to pass on.

EXHIBIT 20-4 Electrolux Group Key Data

1. Group Sales and Employees World Wide

Nordic Countries	Sales SEKm	No of Employees	North America	Sales SEKm	No of Employees
Sweden	11,128	29,456	USA	19,488	29,750
Denmark	1,735	3,078	Canada	1,580	2,150
Norway	1,505	1,299		21,068	31,900
Finland	1,445	1,563			
	15,813	35,396			

Rest of Europe	Sales SEKm	No of Employees	Latin America	Sales SEKm	No of Employees
			Brazil	302	6,215
Great Britain	6,377	10,589	Venezuela	208	1,032
France	5,098	8,753	Peru	181	750
West Germany	4,045	3,3,317	Colombia	104	1,865
Italy	3,684	15,282	Mexico	66	1,735
Switzerland	1,818	1,814	Ecuador	34	232
Spain	1,445	2,851	Guatemala	24	31
Netherlands	1,238	1,016	Others	443	198
Belgium and Luxembourg	913	1,040		1,362	12,058
Austria	392	958			
Portugal	96	193			
Others	604	41			
	25,710	45,854			

Asia	Sales SEKm	No of Employees	Africa	Sales SEKm	No of Employees
Japan	707	1,175		414	
Saudi Arabia	215	738			
Hong Kong	152	1,340			
Philippines	150	525	Oceania		
Kuwait	147	2,220			
Taiwan	119	2,178			
Malaysia	72	1,833	Australia	497	2,216
Thailand	56	15	New Zealand	114	557
Singapore	50	556	Others	14	-
Jordan	28	137		625	2,773
Lebanon	22	35			
Others	720	1,729			
	2,438	12,481	**TOTAL**	**67,016**	**140,462**

EXHIBIT 20-4 continued

2. Sales by Business Area

	1987 SEKm	1986 SEKm	1985 SEKm	% OF TOTAL sales of 87
Household appliances	39,487	31,378	19,200	58.6
Commercial appliances	5,619	4,250	3,348	8.3
Commercial services	2,893	2,504	2,266	4.3
Outdoor products	4,475	2,909	2,990	6.6
Industrial products	11,784	9,087	9,232	17.5
Building components	3,172	2,962	2,652	4.7
TOTAL	**67,430**	**53,090**	**39,688**	**100.0**

3. Operating Income After Depreciation By Business Area

	1987 SEKm	1986 SEKm	1985 SEKm	% OF TOTAL sales of 87
Household appliances	2,077	1,947	1,589	49.2
Commercial appliances	484	349	260	11.4
Commercial services	169	172	132	4.0
Outdoor products	421	241	373	10.0
Industrial products	910	474	657	21.5
Building components	164	138	126	3.9
TOTAL	**4,225**	**3,321**	**3,137**	**100.0**

21
Indian Iron & Steel Company

The management of the Indian Iron & Steel Co. (IISCO) in 1989-90 were actively planning the modernisation of the production systems of the Burnpur Steel Works. The integrated steel plant was located in the iron and coal mining belt of Eastern India, and was one of the oldest steel making units in the country. The modernisation had been initially proposed in 1966, by the then private sector management. However, its inability to mobilise the funds and technical expertise required for the purpose had led to the takeover of management by the Central Government in 1972. Seventeen years after the takeover, the modernisation proposals were being pushed through the various layers of Government bureaucracy.

Mr. M.F. Mehta, Managing Director, IISCO, was contemplating the changes the proposed modernisation would bring about. Apart from production, the changes appeared to cut across other functional areas as well, for example finance, personnel, marketing and control systems.

Corporate structure of IISCO

Historical Evolution

The Indian Iron & Steel Co. Ltd. was incorporated as a Public Limited Company under the Indian Companies Act, 1913. Registered on the 11th of March, 1918, and promoted by the Managing Agency, Burn and Company, it had an authorised share capital of rupees three crores.[1] IISCO initially operated an iron making plant of 480,000 MT/Yr. capacity, at Hirapur village, near Asansol in West Bengal. Coal was purchased from the collieries run by the Bengal Iron and Steel Co. which operated an iron making unit at Kulti, nearby. The Gua iron ore mines were established in 1919 to feed the Hirapur Works. IISCO commenced iron production in October 1922. (Note: Coal and iron ore are the primary raw materials for iron making).

---

[1] One crore equals 10,000,000 rupees.

This case was made possible through the cooperation of the executives of the Indian Iron & Steel Company. It was written by V. Rangarajan and Sri Ananthanarayana Sarma under the guidance of Dr. B.L. Maheshwari, Centre for Organization Development, Hyderabad, India, to be used as a basis for class discussion rather than to illustrate either effective or ineffective handling of an administrative situation. Copyright ©1990 Centre for Organization Development, Hyderbad, India. Used with permission.

Burn A Co. sold its share in IISCO and its other managed companies in 1924 to the managing agents, Martin & Company. This decision by Burn & Co. was apparently taken due to the financial problems created by the world-wide recession in the iron and steel trade. The new managing agents kept the name of Burn alive by rechristening themselves Martin Burn & Co. Ltd.

The government reported the scope for setting up a second steel works in the country in 1934. (The first was the Tata Iron & Steel Co. Works at Jamshedpur, established in 1907.) Martin Burn & Co. decided actively to pursue this idea. Due to Privy Council litigation in 1921, there was a profit-sharing agreement between IISCO and Bengal Iron & Steel Co. To ensure viability in operations, IISCO absorbed the latter Company in December 1936. IISCO now came to own two iron-making units at Kulti and Hirapur, with an aggregate iron making capacity of 850,000 MT/Yr. and 100,000 MT of castings for pipes. The collieries were augmented by the purchase of the Chasnalla coal mines. There were now also two captive iron ore mines at Gua and Chiria.

Martin Burn & Co, then incorporated the Steel Corporation of Bengal Ltd. (SCOB) on 20th April 1937 to produce steel. The SCOB had share capital of Rs.5.03 crores, and installed a 250,000 MT/Yr. steel making plant at Napuria, adjacent to the Hirapur Works. Steel production commenced in November 1939.

IISCO supplied the entire hot metal (iron) requirements of the Napuria Works. These inputs were provided at cost plus a small profit margin, and in return, IISCO received 20% of the profits made by SCOB. IISCO also subscribed to 11,000 shares (2% of share holding) of SCOB.

The Government of India approached the World Bank in 1952 for financial assistance for making steel. The Technical Mission of the Bank recommended that "the cheapest and quickest way to increase iron and steel production in the country would be to merge IISCO with SCOB and then expand." Further expansions in capacity for SCOB/IISCO were then made conditional upon the merger of the two companies by the Central Government.

The Central Government later promulgated The Indian Iron & Steel Companies Ordinance in 1952, which provided for the amalgamation SCOB with IISCO. The amalgamated company was known by the name of IISCO, all assets/liabilities of SCOB being transferred to IISCO. The Hirapur Works making iron thus merged with the Napuria Works making steel to form the Burnpur Works of IISCO. The Burnpur Steel Works thus became an integrated iron & steel plant, with captive raw material bases. This was the third such in the country after TISCO (1907) and Mysore Iron & Steel Works (1936). The managing agents continued to be Martin Burn & Co., with one Director on the Board being nominated by the Central Government.

The installed capacity of Burnpur Steel Works was expanded to 700,000 MT/Yr. of saleable steel in 1961 (i.e., 1,000,000 MT/Yr. ingot steel). The authorised share capital of IISCO was increased to Rs.14 crores in 1956, and further to Rs.16 crores in 1959. At this time, Kulti Foundry Complex had an installed capacity of 63,000 MT/Yr. castings, and 166,000 MT/Yr. spun pipes.

IISCO and M/s. Stanton & Stevely Ltd. of the United Kingdom jointly promoted the Stanton Pipe & Foundry Co. Ltd. to manufacture spun iron pipes and specials. The company was incorporated in July 1964, with share capital of Rs.3.21 crores. The production unit was located at Ujjain in Madhya Pradesh (central India) with an installed capacity of 60,000 MT/Yr. pipes. Trial production commenced in August 1967.

Nationalisation

IISCO drew up a Rs.23.2 crores plan to develop Chasnalla Collieries in 1964. The authorised share capital was increased from Rs.16 crores to Rs.40 crores in 1967, presumably to fund this project. A proposal to increase steel-making capacity by 300,000 MT/Yr. was accepted by the Central Government in 1966. The proposal costed the scheme at Rs.16 crores, with a foreign exchange component of $16 million. Nine million dollars was budgeted for essential spares and replacements. The World Bank agreed to fund the dollar part. However, the grant of import licences was delayed by the Central Government by three years. As the import licenses had not materialised within the stipulated time, the World Bank cancelled its loan. By 1970, the cost of renovations had increased to Rs.20 crores, and that of expansions to Rs.27 crores.

A takeover attempt of IISCO through purchase of shares in the stock market was attempted by speculators in 1965. They dropped their plans when the income tax authorities began to scrutinise their activities. Another takeover attempt by an Indian industrialist in 1970 (again through stock purchases in the share market) was foiled by government-controlled financial institutions. In the shakeout that followed, under government instructions, these institutions greatly increased their stake in IISCO through open market share purchases.

In April 1970, the managing agency system was abolished, which left IISCO bereft of the support of Martin Burn & Company. Martin Burn then, was the third largest industrial group in the country, in terms of assets, after the Tatas and the Birlas.

In the late sixties, labour militancy became endemic in Eastern India; production declined and labour costs increased for IISCO. The Chasnalla project had a cost overrun of Rs.17 crores. The rupee devaluation of 1967 put an additional burden of Rs.8.4 crores on IISCO. The pricing of steel products was regulated by the Central Government, which did not see such reasons as the basis for price increases. Thus, by 1971-72, the amount of loan repayments stood at Rs.35.04 crores. The Central Government refused to allow rescheduling of debts. The shares of IISCO plunged below par in August 1971.

The Central Government decided to take over the management of IISCO "for a limited period of two years in the public interest to secure the proper management of the undertaking." An ordinance in July 1972 was passed for this purpose. The Union Minister of Steel, while piloting the takeover bill in Parliament, stated the major reasons for the takeover to be:

1. steady deterioration in plant condition;
2. serious industrial relations situation;
3. need for professionalising the management;
4. urgings made by a section of the Board.

The Indian Iron & Steel Company (Taking over of Management) Amendment Act, 1974, allowed for the undertaking of the Company to vest in the Central Government for a further period unto a maximum of ten years. In 1976, the Central Government held that the top management of the Company was guilty of mismanagement of the affairs of the Company, and restoration ... of the management of the affairs of the company to such top management would be prejudicial to the interests of the Company and to public interest. Also, "investment of a large amount is necessary for the maintenance and development of the production of the undertakings of the Company" .... for which ... "acquisition by the Central Government of an effective control over the affairs of the Company is necessary to enable it to make the (aforesaid) investments." The Indian Iron Bc Steel Company (Acquisitions of Shares Act), 1976, was enacted to provide for the acquisition of all shares of IISCO held by the public. In December 1977, the authorised capital was raised from Rs.40 crores to Rs.100 crores.

The Public Sector Iron & Steel Companies (Restructuring) and Miscellaneous Provisions Act, 1978, provided for all public sector steel plants to come under the purview of the Steel Authority of India Limited (SAIL), which was termed as an integral company. All the shares of IISCO held by the Central Government were now vested with SAIL. IISCO thus became a subsidiary of SAIL. However, it continued to retain its status as a separate company under the Indian Companies Act, and had its own Board of Directors. In November 1985 the authorised share capital was increased to Rs.150 crores and further to Rs.550 crores in September 1986. In 1988, the subscribed share capital stood at Rs.273 crores, which was all held by SAIL or its nominees.

The IISCO Stanton Pipe and Foundry Company continued to retain its identity as a separate company after nationalisation. The public sector British Steel Corporation of the United Kingdom acquired Stanton & Stavely Limited, and decided to divest its shares in the Company. The shares were bought by IISCO in 1983-84. The IISCO Stanton & Pipe Foundry Company was now a fully-owned subsidiary of IISCO.

Thus, in 1989, IISCO, a subsidiary of SAIL, had the following units under its control:

1. Burnpur Steel Works, with installed capacity of 1 Million MT/Yr. of Ingot Steel.
2. Kulti Foundry Complex, with installed capacity of 63,000 MT/Yr. castings and 166,000 MT/Yr. C.I. Spun Pipes.
3. A fully-owned subsidiary, Station Pipes & Foundry Company (at Ujjain), with installed capacity of 166,000 MT/Yr. C.I. Spun Pipes.
4. Coal Collieries at Chasnalla, Jitpun, and Ramangore Bc Coal Washery at Chasnalla.
5. Iron ore mines at Gua and Chiria.

Exhibit No.21-1 gives the chronology of the major events in IISCO.

Burnpur Steel Works

Description

The Burnpur Steel Works was the most important unit of IISCO. The fortunes of IISCO had always been tied to that of the Steel Works. More than three-fourths of IISCO's turnover was directly accounted for by the sale of steel, scrap, and by-products of the Burnpur Works—Rs.413 crores on a turnover of Rs.497 crores in 1987-88. Similarly, a little more than half of all employees of IISCO were employed inside the Burnpur Works—around 17,000 out of a total of 35,700. The plant was located about 200 Kms. from Calcutta and was about 10 Kms. off Asansol Railway station on the main Calcutta-Delhi railway line.

The main physical entry to the plant was through a tunnel gate. Immediately on emerging from the tunnel, a visitor could not fail to be overwhelmed by the panoramic setting of the Works. A tree-lined avenue, flanked on either side by the still waters of the cooling pond, greeted the entrant. In the background stood giant cooling towers alongside the various Works units. (Exhibits 21-2 and 21-3 detail the production process and the machinery at the Works).

The Burnpur Works had spawned the Burnpur township—which housed mainly plant employees. The township contained around 900 executive houses and 6,500 non-executive quarters. The township department of the Works maintained five playgrounds, a market, and ran a bus service for the school children. Beyond the township lay the Nehru Park and the aerodrome. There, the aviation department had aviation overhaul shops, which were approved by the Director General of Civil Aviation (the only one to get the approval amongst all the aviation shops of the SAIL steel plants). The township also had a 480 bed hospital, staffed and run by the works.

The highlight of the township was an area named 'The Ridge.' The Ridge contained colonial mansions, which housed top executives. Amidst these houses, nestled the luxurious Burnpur guest house, which was described as the best of the guest houses maintained by the steel plants of SAIL. Alongside the guest house was the Managing Director's office which was previously the Director's bungalow. In Colonial times (when the plant was run by Europeans), as the saying goes, only white-skinned people were allowed to walk along the Ridge roads.

Organisational Analysis

For the analysis of the organisation, the 7-S model, developed by McKinsey & Co, was used. The model assumes that executives have only a limited number of 'levers' to influence complex, large organisations. The model explores the seven major ones: superordinate goals, strategy, structure systems, skills, style and staff. Though there could be more variables than seven, these are presumed to be of crucial importance. The model is to help the executives develop a more effective way of perceiving and cutting through

EXHIBIT 21-1 Chronology of Major Events

1870	- Bengal Iron Works was formed
1872	- Commencement of Iron production
1880-1881	- Bengal Iron Works was taken over by Government of Bengal
1890	- Formation of Bengal Iron & Steel Co.
1892	- Appointment of Martin & Co. as Managing Agents
1916	- Iron ore mining at Chiria
11th Mar.1918	- Indian Iron & Steel Co. was formed
1919	- Gua Iron ore mine was established
1920	- Ramnagore mining started
1926	- Kulti name was changed to Bengal Iron
2nd Dec.1936	- IISCO absorbed Bengal Iron
20th Apr. 1937	- Steel Corp. of Bengal was formed
June-July 1938	- Labour strike at Kulti and lockout for 28 days
1939	- First heat of steel, tapped
1944	- Asansol Iron & Steel Workers' Union was formed (Affiliation to INTUC)
31st Dec. 1952	- Iron & Steel companies ordinance
Dec. 1953	- First Extension, World Bank loan was signed
1955	- United Iron & Steel Workers' Union was formed (Affiliation to AITUC)
30th Apr. 1956	- Industrial Policy Resolution
Dec. 1956	- Second Extension, World Bank loan was signed
13th May 1958	- First mechanised ore mining was started, Gua
1959	- Township was inaugurated at Burnpur
Dec. 1961	- Third World Bank loan was signed
1963-64	- Record production of steel
1967	- Asansol Burnpur, Kulti Metal and engineering workers' union was formed (Affiliation to CITU)
	- Burnpur Iron & Steel Workers' Union was formed (Affiliation to HMS)
1969	- Burnpur Ispat Karmachari Sangh was formed (Affiliation to BMS)
14th July 1972	- Government takeover
4th Sept. 1972	- Indian Iron & Steel Co. Act
1973	- Submission of plant rehabilitation scheme
Dec. 1975	- Chasnalla Mine disaster
July 1976	- Acquisition of shares by the Government
30th Apr. 1978	- IISCO was made as a subsidiary of SAIL
1983	- Russian feasibility report
June 1987	- JICA feasibility report
Nov. 1988	- Agreement with Japanese Consulting Cos. (JCC) for preparation of Basic Eng. Report (BER)
June 1989	- Submission of draft BER by JCC.

EXHIBIT 21-1 cont. Commissioning Date of Plant & Equipment

Plant	Date of Commission	Remarks
Coke Oven		
No. 1 Battery	1922	Closed down in 1950
No. 2	1922	Closed down in 1950
No. 3	1922	Closed down in 1948
No. 4	1922	Closed down in 1948
No. 5	1929	Closed down in 1977
No. 6a 30 ovens	1939	Closed down in 1977
No. 6b 10 ovens	1947	Closed down in 1977
No. 7	1950	Phased out in June 1989
No. 8	1957	Rebuilt in 1987
No. 9	1958	Shut down for rebuilding in 1987
No. 10	1982	
Blast Furnace		
No. 1	1922	Phased out in Apr. 89
No. 2	1924	
No. 3	1958	
No. 4	1958	
Steel Melting Shop		
Bessemer Plant	1946	Phased out in Oct. 1988
Open Hearth Furnace		
A	1939	Equipped with Air Inject facilities
B	1940	Converted to KORF process - July, 1989
C	1940	Converted to KORF process - November, 1988
D	1942	Phased out before Nationalisation
E	1958	Converted to KORF process - July, 1988
F	1959	Equipped with Air Injection Facilities
G	1959	Equipped with Air Injection Facilities
Rolling Mills		
Blooming Mill	1939	
Billet & Sheet Bar Mill	1953	
Heavy Structural Mill	1939	
Light structural Mill	1939	
Merchant Mill	1960	
Sheet Mills	1939	Phased out in June 1989

EXHIBIT 21-2 Burnpur Works Production Flow Chart

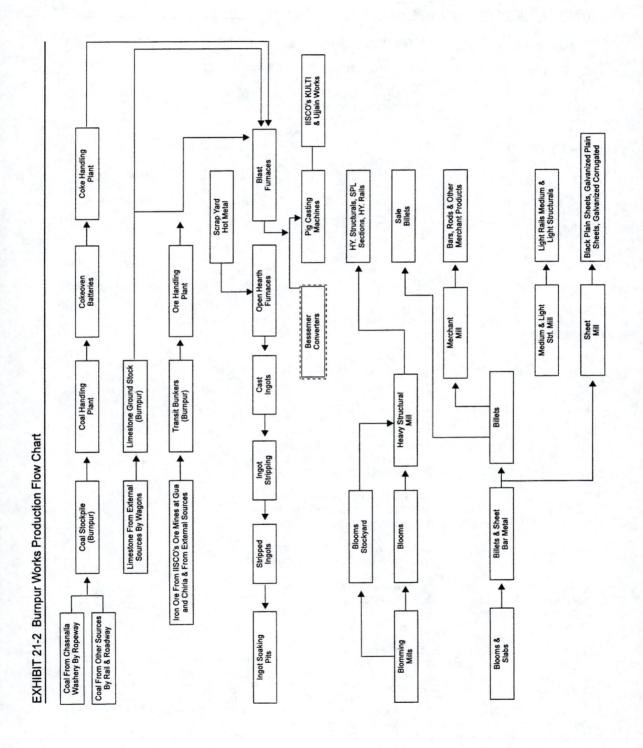

EXHIBIT 21-3 Brief Description of Main Plant

Department	One Million Ingots Tonne Plant
Coke Ovens	4 batteries-306 ovens of 4.45 m height coal (dry) throughput 5,998 tonnes a day
By-product plant	Tar, Naphtha, Benzol and Ammonium Sulphate units

Blast furnace	Hearth dia. (m)	No. of fces	Capacity per day (Tonnes)	Working Vol (cbm)	
	5.2	2	700	434	Yearly capacity
	7.6	2	1200	1041	1.3 million tonnes

Pig casting machine	2 number - 600 tonnes/day each			
		Capacity	Type	Yearly capacity
	3 Bessemer convertors			1.0 million tonnes
	6 O.H. furnaces	225	Tilter	
	1 O.H. furnace	100	Fixed	

Lime shaft kiln	4 numbers - 30 tonnes/day each
Rotary dolomite kiln	1 number - 100 tonnes/day
Rolling Mills	

Soaking pits & Blooming mill	32 number - 40 tonnes each "Sack" 2 Hi-Reversing 42" x 96" size of rolls	Yearly capacity 1.0 million tonnes
Sheet Bar & Billet Mill	"Margan"; No. of stands in Tandem - 10	Yearly capacity 8,000,000 tonnes
34" Stlr. Mill (HSM)	1 2-Hi Reversing roughing stand 1 2-Hi Reversing intermediate stand 1 2-Hi Reversing finishing stand	Yearly capacity 2,500,000 tonnes
18" Strl. Mill	2 3-Hi Reversing roughing stand 1 3-Hi Reversing intermediate stand 1 3-Hi Reversing finishing stand	Yearly capacity 1,200,000 tonnes
Sheet Mills	"Lewis" Two, 3-Hi roughing stands "Hyde Park" Four 2-Hi finishing stands	Yearly capacity 1,200,000 tonnes
Continuous merchant & Rod Mill	2-Hi Morgan-19 stands Edgers - 4 Nos.	Yearly capacity 1,500,000 tonnes

Services

Power Plant	60 MW Installed capacity
Water Plant	Make up - 2,045m 3/hr., including 170m 3/hr. for drinking
Township	23 million litres/day filtered, 9 million litre/day unfiltered
Diesel electric locos	48 numbers - 235/470/670/1100 H.P.

1. One of the Coke Oven Bar (No. 7) phased out in June 1989 and another (No. 9) rebuilt from 1987.
2. One small BF (No.1) phased out in April 1989.
3. Three Bessemer Convertors phased out in Oct. '88 and 100 tonnes stationary O.H. furnace phased out in private sector era itself.
4. Sheet mills had been phased out in June '89 and light structural mill was to be phased out in near future.

Source: Statistics for Iron & Steel Industry in India, 1974, Ranchi.

the complexity of organisations. The framework is illustrated in Exhibit 21-4.

The central point of the model is that the FIT among the seven variables has to be good to get long-term leverage. Addressing oneself to one or two of the S's is generally not sufficient. Even if the manager is aware of the need to work at adjusting the fit of the rest of the S's after a significant change in one or two (say, strategy and structure), it is certain to take effort and time to achieve integration.

Among the 7S's, strategy, structure and systems are perceived to be the hardware—and the rest, skills, style, staff and superordinate goals, to be the software.

The superordinate goals are the lever which integrated the functioning of the other S's. Hence, the presentation of the information relating to the organisation begins with superordinate goals.

Superordinate Goals

Superordinate goals are shared values and aspirations that go beyond quantified objectives, such as profit, ROI, etc. While these might include simple goal statements, the values must be shared by most people in an organisation.

Before the nationalisation, the plant had a "Europeanized" sense of values, with the top management being Europeans. Sons of employees were given preference in employment. This led to three generation linkages from individual families with the Works, enhancing the feeling of "belonging." Stability at the top level led to a team spirit and discipline which contributed to high productivity (consistent achievement of capacity utilisation). Therefore, IISCO had a good corporate reputation. It was the only Indian company quoted on the London Stock Exchange, and it paid 17% dividends in the 60's. However, these shared values were perhaps built on a "fear of authority," and the assumptions of racial superiority. The labour militancy in East India in 1967 overturned these values; anarchic acts of sabotage and personal humiliation which made top executives quit resulted in a sharp deterioration in performance.

Subsequently, the nationalisation brought in a new 'public sector' culture. Senior executives of the Works, who witnessed the transition, explained that with this public sector culture, there was an increase in the number of hierarchical levels, authority was no longer feared, poor work rarely got punished, rules and procedures were given more importance than getting work done, and staff functions like personnel, finance and materials grew in size. Staff functionaries acquired greater power on the 'Control' function.

The high turnover of the top executives (see Exhibit 21-5) appeared to have contributed to dilution of autonomy and uncertainty in decision making. The emphasis had shifted to 'doing things right' from 'doing the right things'.

The Works had been continuously making losses after nationalisation, with low capacity utilisation and improper maintenance.

SAIL (the public sector parent organisation) had initiated the modernisation strategy to reverse this trend. SAIL itself had experienced financial problems until 1985. The new Chairman, Mr. V. Krishnamurthy, introduced a new work culture in all SAIL units, which emphasised better customer service, achieving rated capacity and reducing energy costs. Overtime payments were stopped from 1987. The SAIL plants had reported continuous increase in production (15% for '88-'89) and SAIL expected to wipe out its cumulative losses of Rs.300 crores that year. The Chairman had also initiated a Rs.15,000 crores modernisation programme, to be funded by internal accruals and market borrowings which sought to double steel production and labour productivity. One part of this programme was to spend Rs.3,000 crores to modernise the Burnpur Works, and increase its rated capacity from one million MT/Year to 2.15 million MT/Year.

The SAIL Corporate Planning Director had, in a press interview, expressed the hope that after modernisation "Burnpur could become the model plant for SAIL".

Strategy

Strategy is defined as a distinctive product-mar-

Exhibit 21-4 The 7-S Framework

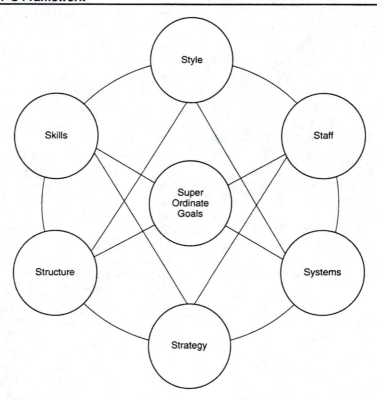

ket-technology choice made by an organisation and the mode of its implementation. This 'set of actions' may be aimed at giving a sustainable advantage over competition (say, providing better service to consumers) or allocating resources.

The initial decision of IISCO to get into steel production was due to the strategic compulsion of finding markets for the iron produced by it. The company (IISCO) had considerable iron production capacity, and stable operation could only be achieved by means of an increase in the off-take of iron within India. In the absence of a large demand to absorb the entire iron output, its conversion to steel and rolled products was considered as the option available. With these considerations in view, the Steel Corporation of Bengal Limited was incorporated on 20th April, 1937, with Burn & Co. as the managing agents.

The depression of the thirties produced a cartel arrangement between the major producers, i.e.

TISCO, IISCO and Mysore Iron Works, to fix prices, regulate output and allocate markets. During the War years (1939-45), the Government exercised informal price control on steel products for war requirement. From July '44, the controls were widened to cover civilian requirements, and prices were fixed by the Government. However, the Government ensured that opportunities were provided for maximising production and profits. The price controls were withdrawn after the war. The steel capacity of the works was increased to 350,000 MT/Year (ingot steel) in 1946 to meet the post-war boom in the market.

The Technical Mission of the World Bank, which visited the country in 1952 at the invitation of the Government, estimated the gap between supply and demand in the country to be around two million tonnes of steel and 400,000 tonnes of foundry iron. One of the strategies

EXHIBIT 21-5

<u>List of Chief Executives - IISCO</u>

1918-36	Sir Rajen Mukherjee	Chairman
1936-72	Sir Biren Mukherjee	Chairman

POST-TAKEOVER

July, 1972 - November, 1972	Shri M.P. Wadhawan	Part-time Custodian
November, 1972 - November, 1974	Shri Arabinda Ray	Custodian
November, 1974 - December, 1975	Shri Hiten Bhaya	Chairman
December, 1975 - June, 1978	Shri V.K. Dar	Administrator/ Managing Director
June, 1978 - March, 1981	Shri D.R. Ahuja	Managing Director
March, 1981 - November, 1981	Shri S. Samarapungayan	Managing Director
January, 1982 - June, 1983	Shri K.R. Sangameshwaran	Managing Director
July, 1983 - Onwards	Shri M.F. Mehta	Managing Director

<u>Burnpur Steel Works - List of Operational Chiefs</u>

May, 1951 - April, 1971	Shri J. McCraben	Chief General Manager
April, 1969 - September, 1972	Shri F.W. Lahmeyer	General Manager

AFTER TAKEOVER

July, 1972 - December, 1972	Shri N.R. Dutt	Chief General Manager
January, 1973 - January, 1975	Shri A. Bajekal	General Manager
December, 1974 - September, 1977	Shri S. Chatterjee	General Manager
September, 1977 - September, 1978	Shri P.R. Mehr	General Manager
September, 1978 - February, 1980	Shri P.K. Rath	General Superintendent
February, 1980 - October, 1981	Shri S.K. Roy	General Superintendent
October, 1981 - January, 1982	Shri K.R. Sangameshwaran	General Manager (Works)
February, 1982 - August, 1983	Shri B.B. Dutta	General Manager (Works)
August, 1983 - November, 1984	Shri C.R. Srinivasan	General Manager (Works)
November, 1984 - May, 1987	Shri K.D.S.	General Manager (Works)
June, 1987 - Onwards	Shri M.S. Chawla	General Manager (Works)

suggested by the World Bank team to meet this gap was to expand the existing units.

As mentioned earlier, the Government then ordered the merger of the steel-making unit of SCOB with the iron-making unit of IISCO, forming the present Burnpur Works and expansion of production capacity of steel. The 1953 expansion increased the capacity of the plant to 700,000 MT of saleable steel and 400,000 MT of foundry iron. The 1955 expansion further increased production capacity to 800,000 MT of saleable steel (1 million MT of ingot steel) and 260, 000 MT of foundry iron .

In the early 1960's, steel production in Burnpur Works touched 90% of the rated capacity. Full capacity utilisation after expansion was reached in 1963-64. This compared favourably with the then prevailing norms in the steel industry, when 60% capacity utilisation was accepted as optimum achievement in the initial year of operation. The period from 1960 to 1967 also saw IISCO consistently outperform TISCO (its major steel-making competitor) in the share market.

As mentioned earlier, a combination of political, financial and labour problems led to the takeover of company management by the Government in 1972 and the subsequent nationalisation. The capacity utilisation that year (1972-73) was only 43%.

One of the reasons for nationalisation given by the Government was to ensure the renovation and modernisation of the Works. The low capacity utilisation was due in part to the fact that foreign exchange required for urgently needed spare parts had not been sanctioned.

However, the Government/SAIL continued to neglect this aspect of ensuring proper maintenance of the plant after the takeover. The Burnpur Works had, since the takeover, never crossed 70% rated capacity utilisation, and had consistently reported losses.

Modernisation of the plant had been the major strategic concern since 1966. The first attempt made by Sir Biren Mukherjee (then Chairman of the Private Sector IISCO) to get a World Bank loan to fund a modernisation programme did not receive support of the Government.

After the takeover, the Government carried out a plant rehabilitation scheme as a temporary solution to the modernisation problem. M/s. M.N. Dastur, steel industry consultants, were appointed in 1977 to carry out a feasibility report. They estimated the modernisation cost to be around Rs.300 crores, with a new sinter plant, shifting from open hearth furnaces to basic oxygen furnaces and using L.D. convertors instead of Bessemer convertors. This report, however, was not followed up.

When the Prime Minister, Mrs. Indira Gandhi, visited the Soviet Union in 1981, she accepted a Soviet offer of a feasibility study for the modernisation of Burnpur Works. The Soviet modernisation report, submitted in 1983, estimated that Rs.933 crores would be required to maintain the plant at one million MT capacity. The second phase was to increase the capacity to 1.6 million MT/Year and the third phase to 3 million MT/Year.

Shortly afterwards, both the Managing Director of IISCO and the Steel Secretary of the Government of India changed, and the proposal was dropped.

The latest attempt at modernisation was initiated when the Prime Minister, Mr. Rajiv Gandhi, visited Japan in 1985. At his request, a Japanese consortium of five major Japanese steel producers came to India and submitted the feasibility report in 1987 through the Japanese International Cooperation Agency (JICA).

The Government/SAIL accepted in principle to plan ahead for modernisation on the basis of this feasibility report. The final cost proposal was expected to be submitted for approval to the Public Investment Bureau (P.I.B.) of the Government in late 1989.

The major highlights of the JICA report were:

1. scrapping of old and building of new blast furnaces and the steel melting- shop
2. building of sintering and continuous casting facilities and one new Coke Oven Battery with simultaneous phasing out of another Coke Oven Battery
3. revamping of some of the existing rolling mills and adding two new bar mills.

The total cost was estimated at Rs.3000 crores, of which Rs.1000 crores was in foreign exchange (to be met through loans from Japan at concessional rates of interest).

The modernisation strategy had become crucial to ensuring the existence of the plant. The Works was operating on vintage technology. A blast furnace installed in 1920 was still in operation. Steel making processes like the Duplex with Bessemer convertors and open hearth furnaces had been phased out by other steel plants in the world a long time ago. Lack of pre-treatment facilities had seen high raw material consumption.

All this had led to financial unviability—the Burnpur Works had continuously reported losses after nationalisation. The comparative cost of saleable steel production for SAIL and for the Burnpur Works was as shown in Exhibit 21-6.

There were four strategic options open for the Burnpur Works at that stage:

1. Shut down the plant.
2. Only renovate the existing units—without adding new equipment.
3. Totally modernise—build a new (greenfield) modern plant and scrap all old facilities.
4. Choose a hybrid route of partial modernisation (bringing in new equipment) and partial renovation of old facilities.

As a senior executive pointed out, the first option of closing down the plant would have meant that the 35,000 odd workers and families who directly or indirectly depended on the Works for their livelihood would have been unemployed. This would have created serious social problems in the township of Burnpur. The Left Front Government of West Bengal would have exerted a lot of political pressure on IISCO/SAIL against this decision. Also, the Works was strategically located in the coal/iron ore mining belt and had in the past been one of the best run plants in Asia. Given SAIL's inherent strength in steel technology, this alternative had not been chosen.

The second option of only renovating existing units would have meant that the Works was stuck with the existing old technology. The blast furnace and steel melting shop equipment was obsolete. The increases in coal and oil prices and in wages had made steel making a loss-making proposition with the existing technology. The Government/SAIL were not prepared to continue underwriting losses of the Works, hence the impracticality of this option.

The third option of building a new plant (of a comparable 2.15 Million MT capacity) would have cost Rs.6000 crores, as opposed to the cost of Rs.3000 crores of updating the existing plant. Two coke ovens had been rebuilt already, and were practically new. It made no sense to throw away such equipment. Also, many of the infrastructural facilities and some of the mills could be run profitably. Thus, this alternative was not pursued.

Therefore, the fourth option of scrapping and rebuilding obsolete equipment and using some of the existing facilities had been chosen, which formed the basic strategy of the modernisation proposal submitted by JICA.

Modernisation programme-Salient features

Marketing

The JICA feasibility report based the modernisation proposal on the SAIL forecast of the steel market in India up to the year 2000. The demand for Bar Mill products was expected to exceed supply in India by 870,000 MT in 1989-90 and increase to 3.63 Million MT in the year 2000. Hence, bar mill products were chosen for capacity expansion; and two new bar and section mills (with a capacity of 1.3 Million MT/Year) were proposed.

The other option of producing hot coils was discarded due to uncertain market and heavy capital investment. Provision for erection of facilities for producing high value-added items like low alloy steel grades was kept for future additions.

SAIL decided that Burnpur Works would con-

Exhibit 21-6 Cost of Production at SAIL & IISCO (Saleable Steel) 1987 - 88

Item	SAIL		IISCO BURNPUR	
	Total Cost (Rs. Crores)	Cost/M.T. (Rs.)	Total Cost (Rs. Crores)	Cost/M.T. (Rs.)
1. Raw materials	1704	2315	196	3612
2. Stores & Spares	788	1071	23	420
3. Salaries & Benefits	715	971	68	1251
4. Power & Fuel	468	636	43	789
5. Freight/Repairs & Maintenance and Misc. Expenses (net of adjustment)	370	503	38	696
	4045	5496	368	6768

Note: Production of saleable steel (including pig iron) in 1987-88 was 7.34 million MT as per Annual Report for SAIL and 0.54 million MT of saleable steel for IISCO.

Source: Figures of annual cost have been quoted from the Annual Report of SAIL for the year 1987-88, as reposed in the *Economic Times*, Bombay May 10, 1989, page five, and the Annual Cost Sheet of IISCO, Burnpur Works for 1987-88.

tinue to produce only long (non-flat) products. Hence, the modernisation package did not envisage new facilities for producing flat products. (Note: Saleable steel is usually classified as long or flat products.)

The steel products after modernisation were expected to be internationally competitive in price and quality.

Production Facilities

Some of the units like coal yards, coal handling plants, two coke ovens (No. 8 & 9) and part of rolling mills were to be retained under the proposal.

The following units were to be scrapped:

(a) Two coke ovens (No. 7 & 10)
(b) The four blast furnaces
(c) The steel melting shop (which uses the Duplex process)
(d) Light structural mill
(e) Sheet mills.

The following units were to be introduced into the works:

(a) One 92 oven, coke oven battery (No. 11)
(b) Two sintering machines
(c) Two blast furnaces
(d) Three basic oxygen converters with oxygen plant
(e) Four continuous casting machines—one bloom caster and three billet casters
(f) Two new bar mills
(g) New captive power generation facilities.

(See Exhibit 21-7 for further details about the current and projected future processes.)

Raw Material

The JICA proposal did not cover the coal and iron ore mines. Modernisation schemes were being taken up to ensure that raw material of specified quality and quantity was available after modernisation.

The coal washery at Chasnalla was being modernised, and the Chasnalla deep mines re-

EXHIBIT 21-7 Comparison Between Present Condition and Condition After Modernisation of Burnpur Works

	Present Condition*	1st Step**	2nd Step***
Coke	4 coke oven batteries (Nos. 7, 8, 9 & 10) (of 228 oven, 127 operated)	No. 8, 9 & 10 batteries	No. 8 &9 batteries and New No. 11 (92 ovens) battery installed
Sinter Plant	None	No. 1 sintering machine ($210m^2$) installed	No. 2 sintering machine ($210m^2$) installed
Blast Furnace Plant	500^3 BF x 2 $1170m^3$ BF x 2	Existing 4 BFs all closed and No. 5 BF ($2250m^3$) installed	No. 6 BF $2250m^3$ installed to make the No. to two BFs
Steelmaking shop	Duplex process in use Bessemer Converters (25T x 3) Open hearth furnaces (225T x 6)	Two BOFs (130T) installed Two units fixed and one constantly in operation. One line calcining plant installed.	One BOF (130T) installed. 3 units fixed & constantly in operation. One more lime calcining plant installed (2-unit operation)
CC Plant	None	Bloom (BL-1) CC installed (3-strand type,300 x 400mm) Billet (BT-1) CC installed (8-strand type)	Two billet (BT-2, BT-3) CC installed (6-strand type, 150mm sq. & 180mm sq.)
Rolling Mills	Bloom mill x 1 billet & sheet bar mill x 1 heavy structural mill x 1 light structural mill x 1 merchant & bar mill x 1 sheet mill x 1 galvanized line x 1	Existing light structural mill closed, but other existing mills such as blooming mill, billet mill, heavy structural mill, merchant & bar mill remodelled & used. New No. 1 bar & section mill installed (600,000 T/Y). Sheet mill operated in 1st step only.	Sheet mill closed. New No. bar & section mill installed (700,000 T/Y)
Self Power Plant	60MW (Achievable capacity 25 MW)	One 60MW unit installed (Existing power plant left as is)	One more 60MW unit installed (two unit operation; output 120MW)
Site Area	2.6 m.sq.m (existing plant)	Site area available for new facilities: 1.5-1.8m sq. m	
Personnel	20,696	15,991	14,134
Productivity	20-30 T/Man. Yr	62 T/Man. Yr	152 T/Man. Yr
Investment		Total Investment: Rs. 12.92 Billion	Total Investment: Rs. 11.57 Billion

*Nominal capacity: 1 million T/Y. 85/86 output: 565,000T.
**Completed at the end of 1992. 1 million T/Y. As per JICA report.
***Completed at the end of 1993. 2.15 million T/Y. As per JICA report.

Note: With the phasing out of units, there have been changes in the "Present Condition."
- Of the four Coke Oven batteries, only two are in operation with 156 ovens. Of the remaining two, one has been phased out and the other is being rebuilt.
- Only three blast furnaces are in operation. One small blast furnace has been phased out.
- At the steel melting shop, duplex process of steel making has been discarded with the phasing out of Bessemer Convertors. Only "KORF" process and "Air Injection Process" adopted in Open Hearth furnaces for steel making. Of the six open hearth furnaces, normally three are in operation.
- Sheet mill has been phased out.

opened for mining in 1992. This was stopped after a mining disaster in 1975 which claimed 375 lives.

The iron ore mines were expected to produce adequate iron lump R fines that would be required for the Burnpur Works after their modernisation. A new coal yard was to be constructed and raw material preparation facilities were to be installed.

Finance

The total cost of modernisation was estimated at Rs.3000 crores. This cost had increased to Rs.3800 crores due to yen appreciation and duty increases from 55% to 80% (duties amounting for 20% of the cost). The foreign exchange part was to be funded by a 20 year loan, with a 10 year moratorium and 5% rate of interest from Japan. The rupee amount was to be funded by SAIL, through its internal accruals, loans from the Steel Development Fund (carrying 8% interest) and sale of bonds.

One of the preconditions that had to be met for ensuring viability of the modernisation programme was that accumulated losses (about Rs.470 crores as on 31.3.89) and expected losses until production commenced after modernisation (1995) were to be absorbed by the Government/SAIL.

Time

The start-up date for the modernisation programme was 21st July 1988. The project was expected to be completed in 7 years and 9 months. By late 1989, the final approval for the programme was expected from the Government. The modernisation was to be carried out on a turnkey basis by the Japanese. The levelling work at the new site was already in progress. (See Exhibit 21-8 for Schedule of modernisation)

The modernisation was expected to be completed in two phases. In step 1, one million MT/Yr. capacity was to be reinstalled, (1993) and in Step 2, full capacity of 2.15 million MT/Yr. crude steel was to be installed (1995).

The existing production processes were to continue operation. A phasing-out programme had been drawn up to synchronise the phasing out of old units and introduction of new ones.

The Major Advantages of Modernisation

1. In the by-product facilities, after modernisation:

   1. Coke oven gas would have been doubled
   2. Coal Tar would increase from 25,000 tonnes to 70,000 tonnes
   3. Crude Benzol would increase from 3200 cubic metres to 12,000 cubic metres
   4. Ammonium Sulphate would increase from 2300 tonnes per year to 4200 T/Yr.

2. In the main iron and steel works:

   1. Manpower was to be reduced from the existing 21,671 to 14,134 employees
   2. The production was to be four times more than the present production
   3. Energy usage would have been reduced from 16 calories to 7 calories per tonne of steel, which would bring down the energy cost
   4. Cost of manufacturing would have been reduced to half
   5. The plant was expected to operate at 100% of its rated capacity.

Exhibit 21-9 reproduces the major features.

The new technology called for new skills. Instead of the 'Duplex process,' the 'Basic Oxygen Furnace' technology would have been used for steel making. The coke rate which shows blast furnace efficiency was 749 Kg per tonne for SAIL. In Japan and South Korea it was around 450 Kg. per tonne. In IISCO after modernisation it was expected to be 589 Kg. per tonne. The total revamping would have meant a quantum jump in steel making technology.

EXHIBIT 21-8 Schedule for Modernisation

Year	1986	1987	1988	1989	1990	1991	1992	1993	1994	1995	1996	Remarks
Annual Production								1MT	2.15MT	2.15MT	2.15MT	

Basic Construction Schedule

Exhibit 21-9 Major Features of Modernisation

	New Plant	Existing Plant
Rated capacity/Annum	2.15 Million tonnes Crude Steel	1 Million tonne Ingot Steel
Power requirement	116 MW.	30 MW.
Production of Hot Metal	Rs. 1593 per tonne	Rs. 2571 per tonne
Consumption of Coke per tonne of hot metal	589 Kg.	1000 Kg.
Slag generation per tonne of hot metal	460 Kg.	700 Kg.
Productivity of blast furnace per cubic meter	1.41 tonnes/M^3/day	0.78 tonnes/M^3/day
Cost of Ingot Steel production	Rs. 2645 per tonne	Rs. 4832 per tonne
Production Process	130 tonnes in 50 minutes with BOF technology	250 tonnes in 10 hours with Open Hearth Furnace
Cost of Production of Saleable Steel	Rs. 3117 per tonne	Rs. 6768 per tonne

Kulti & Ujjain Works

The Kulti & Ujjain works did not figure in the Japanese modernisation programme. A separate modernisation plan was expected to be undertaken for the casting shop in Kulti, by SAIL. The casting unit had evolved into an in-house foundry for the steel plants of SAIL. Its production was 51,749 MT in 1987-88 (80% capacity utilisation).

The production at the spun pipe plant at Kulti was 54,265 MT in 1987-88 (33% capacity utilisation). The production in the Ujjain spun pipe unit was 32,369 MT in the same year (55% capacity utilisation). One of the major reasons for under-utilisation of spun pipe production capacity was the declining demand for the product. The major consumers of spun CI pipes were government and semi-government agencies. These pipes were used for water supply and drainage schemes. The introduction of PVC, asbestos and prestressed concrete pipes had whittled down the share of spun pipes in this market. In view of the uncertain market, the modernisation plans for the spun pipe units were not being firmed up.

Structure

Structure is formally represented by organisation charts. It includes reporting relationships, and details how tasks are both divided up and integrated.

Organisation structure in the 'good old days' as reported in the 'History of IISCO' (page no. 49):

> in the twenties, at the Hirapur Works, (producing iron) ... The works were divided into 13 main departments, each with a departmental manager responsible to the General Manager. Eight were covenanted Europeans, while five were Indians, who managed the 13 departments. Each department had a foreman anchorage and below him were several rungs of labour. Selection of the European staff was by the agent in England, while the General Manager at Burnpur engaged the Indian staff. While no organised training department appears to have existed in the early days, on-the-job training was imparted by European staff and resulted in the development of a very efficient subordinate supervisory staff. Promotion was strictly accorded on merit. Relations between the rank and the file were good. Foremen usually dealt with all labour problems at the shop floor level, though labour could approach the managers, but seldom did. There was no Works Committee. It has been stated that no employee organisation existed to the knowledge of the employer and that there had never been any strike or any dispute." (page No.49)

The General Manager of the Works, in turn, reported to the Chairman of IISCO, who was elected along with other Board members by the shareholders. The day-to-day control of operations at the Works thus rested with the General Manager.

The takeover of 1972 brought the unit under Government control. The staff departments grew in size—the finance department gaining a lot on control functions of other departments. The Government appointed Custodian Chairman to preside over the Board of Directors of IISCO, and continued to leave operational control of the Works to the General Manager (Works).

When IISCO became a subsidiary of SAIL in 1978, the Chairman of SAIL became the Chairman of the Board of Directors of IISCO. A new designation, Managing Director, was created. This position was vested with operational control on all units of IISCO. The M.D.'s office was located near the Burnpur Works, effectively making the Managing Director the operational head of the Steel Works. The Kulti and Ujjain unit General Managers also reported to the Managing Director, instead of the Chairman. The corporate identity of the Ujjain unit (IISCO-Stanton pipe company) was, however, maintained; and the Managing Director of IISCO was made the Chairman of the company. The General Manager (Works) of the Burnpur unit reported to the Managing Director, which saw a dilution of the responsibilities associated with this post.

Exhibit 21-10 illustrates the organisational chart of IISCO in 1989. As can be seen from the chart, all the departmental heads reported directly to the M.D. The Kulti & Ujjain units and the mines/collieries were also treated as departments for operational purposes. The span of consol at the Managing Director level was 16. The top organisation chart looked flat.

The overall control of the functional area was with the functional heads. There were ten levels in the executive cadre, and the hierarchy looked pyramidal. The structure was functional, which had led to specialisation of skills and had not developed people in general management areas. From 1987, the project department had been headed by an Executive Director. Before 1972, it was headed by a project engineer, and then by a General Manager up to 1987. The change had taken place due to modernisation. After the Government takeover, lack of stability was noticed at Managing Director level and at the level of GM (Works), Burnpur.

Before 1972, Sir Biren Mukherjee was the Chairman for almost four decades. Between 1972 - 83 (in a decade), 7 MDs had changed in IISCO. The lack of stability and short tenure of MDs had delayed the modernisation process. The earlier attempts to modernise the plant did not come through because of the lack of stability at the top level. The present MD, Mr. M.F. Mehta, was the first person to have a tenure long enough (from 1983) to carry out modernisation.

At GM (Works) Burnpur level, Mr. J. McCraken was the GM for twenty years, from 1951 to 1971. After 1972, as many as 11 GMs had occupied the same position in less than 20 years with the longest tenure being three years. The short tenure of top executives led them to achieve short-term results, neglecting the plant in the long run.

The organisation structure in 1989 could have been described to be a 'functional' one. Some of the advantages of this structure:

1. allowed specialisation
2. allowed economies of scale
3. minimised duplication of personnel/equipment
4. allowed employees to speak the same language as their peers, which made for comfortable & satisfied employees.

Some of the disadvantages associated with this structure were:

1. sub-unit conflicts (finance/materials/ production, for instance), which led to goal displacement
2. dilution of accountability as no one unit was accountable for end result
3. difficulty in coordinating within units
4. inability to cope with large size
5. failure to develop general management skills.

The alternative methods of viewing the restructuring of IISCO were:

1. Restructuring could bring about changes by divisionalisation. The support functions were then centralised. As part of restructuring, each zone, eg. Coke Oven, Blast Furnace, Steel Melting Shop and Mills, could be made relatively autonomous. This could be done by providing them with full functional support in the areas of personnel, technology, quality, commercial safety, finance, material and maintenance.

In British Steel, this system was called the 'Ship System' where each zone was provided with all the resources and then held responsible for performance. This improved accountability and gave role clarity. Each zone could be considered as a separate profit centre.

The other alternative was that if IISCO was merged with SAIL, the Burnpur Works became one of the units of SAIL. The Collieries and mines could be taken over by the Raw Material Directorate which was taking shape at the corporate level (at SAIL). Kulti and Ujjain could be

EXHIBIT 21-10 cont. Organization Structure of Indian Iron & Steel Company (as of April 1989)

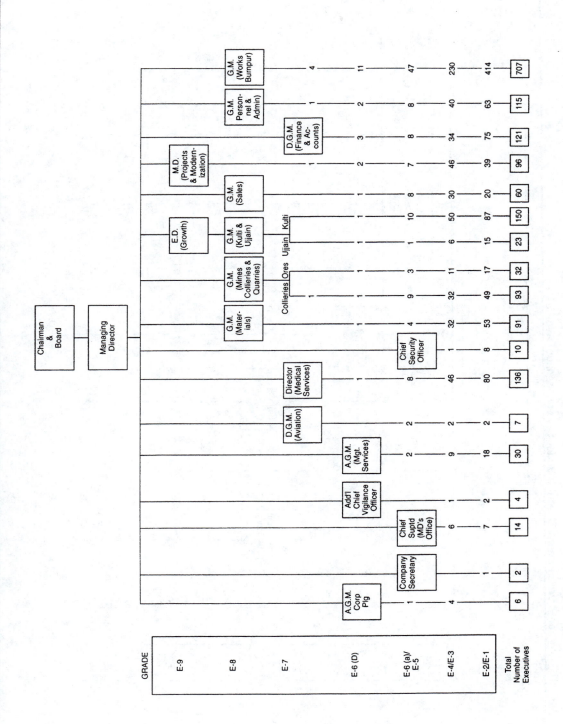

EXHIBIT 21-10 cont. Organization Structure Under General Manager (Works)

GRADE	G.M. (Works) Secretary	Chief Officer (Tech. Div.)	A.G.M. Cost Control	Chief Officer (Contracts)	A.G.M. (Research & Cost Control Lab)	D.G.M. (Iron & Steel Zone)	D.G.M. (Maintenance Zone)	D.G.M. (Mills Zone)	D.G.M. (Service Zone)
E-7						4	3	1	1
E-6 (b)					4	10	17	7	7
E-6 (a)/E-5		2	6	2	11	53	98	28	29
E-4/E-3	2	2		2	51	121	160	25	51
E-2/E-1									

EXHIBIT 21-10 cont. Organization Structure Under General Manager (Personnel & Administration)

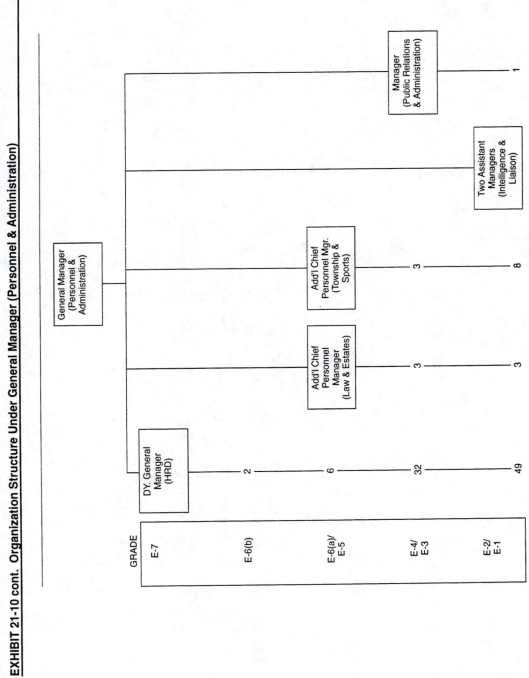

EXHIBIT 21-10 cont. Organization Structure Under D.G.M. (Finance)

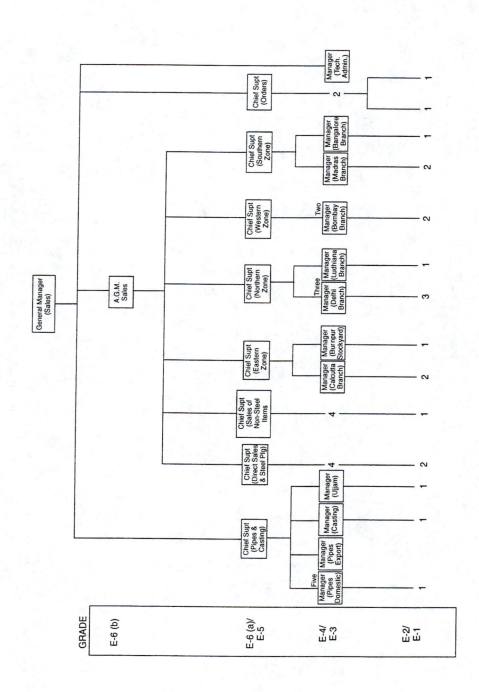

EXHIBIT 21-10 cont. Organization Structure Under General Manager (Sales)

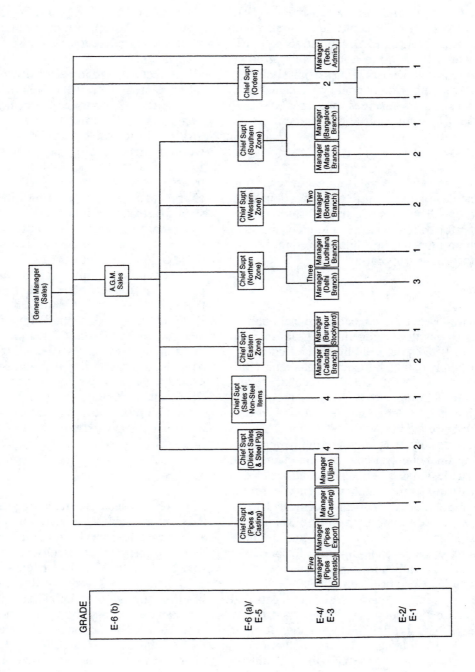

merged together and made a separate unit. The marketing department could be integrated with the Central Marketing Organization of SAIL. This would have led to a lot of new positions being created and existing ones being abolished. The power equilibrium would have changed.

Major structural changes could thus be seen to be a part of the modernisation programme.

Systems

Systems relate to organisational mechanisms that enable organisations to get things done from day to day. They include manufacturing processes, information systems, and other managerial support mechanisms like budgeting systems and performance appraisal.

Finance

The major preoccupation of the pre-nationalization days was the management of the financial systems. IISCO, as a public limited company, had to supply detailed financial statements (Balance Sheet & Profit & Loss Account) to the Registrar of Companies and to its shareholders. The financial systems, hence, evolved to perform these functions. With IISCO continuing to maintain its corporate identity after nationalisation, the financial systems had not changed in the basic design. New financial control systems for ensuring compliance with public sector norms/regulations of decision making had, however, been added (strengthening of audit systems/stricter verification of stock consumption/accounting/tighter tendering rules for purchase decisions). A daily profitability statement for each shop had also been introduced.

Thus, presently, separate Balance Sheets and Profit & Loss Accounts were presented yearly for the IISCO (which included the Burnpur Works, the Kulti Units and Mines/collieries).

The IISCO/Stanton Pipe & Foundry Company at Ujjain presented a separate set of financial statements, having retained its corporate identity. Thus, Ujjain unit accounts were not included in the IISCO financial statements. (Exhibit 21-11 gives a five-year summary of the IISCO financial figures. The financial figures of Tata Iron and Steel Company, the major private sector steel making competitor are also presented for comparison.)

The accumulated losses of IISCO up to 1988-89 were around Rs.709 crores. A Government loan of Rs.239 crores was expected to be converted into a cash grant, bringing down the total loss figure to Rs.470 crores. In practice, the working capital (cash) shortages were funded by SAIL. In a sense, the Rs.470 crores could be treated as a loan from SAIL (depreciation charges amounting to about Rs.226 crores should be excluded for exact figure). A proposal was afoot to convert this loan to equity (with a matching cash grant being made available to SAIL by the Government).

Uneconomical units were being gradually phased out from October 1988, and the loss for the year 1989-90 was expected to be around Rs.70 crores. Of this, the Burnpur Works was expected to contribute 50%. From 1989 to 1995, the annual cash losses (including interest on bank loans, excluding depreciation) was expected to be underwritten by the Government. IISCO thus expected to start with a clean balance sheet after modernisation. IISCO, after modernisation, was expected to produce profits from the first year of operation.

Marketing

IISCO had a separate marketing department—the Central Sales Organization (CSO). CSO had a good customer service record. There had been many instances where steel which could not be sold by CMO/SAIL had been sold by CSO. CSO had 8 stockyards at Burnpur, Calcutta, Madras, Bangalore, Gaziabad, New Delhi, Ludhiana and Bombay. Its products varied in cost from Rs. 6/- a tonne (of air cool slag) to Rs.13,000/- a tonne (of Galvanised Sheet). Selling of scrap was done by Central Sales Organization with its own pricing. It was important to note that the pricing for all other iron and steel items were fixed by the Joint Planning Committee (JPC), which comprised representatives from the Ministry of Steel, Railways (which was

EXHIBIT 21-11 The Indian Iron & Steel Co. Ltd., Comparative Working Results

(Rs. in lacs)*

	1983-84		1984-85		1985-86		1986-87	1987-88	1988-89
	Amount	%	Amount	%	Amount	%	Amount	Amount	(Provl.)
A. Earnings									
Net Sales	27946	83.89	27534	89.72	37156	99.00	48130	44381	46167
Other Revenue/adjustments	5748	17.25	3083	12.39	892	2.38	2850	-1376	411
Stock Accretion (+)/Decretion (-)	-372	-1.12	-649	-2.11	-597	-1.38	-267	1123	-2010
Net Income	33314	100.00	38688	101.00	37531	100.00	41918	44130	44568
B. Expenses									
Raw Materials	17274	51.85	17126	55.81	23104	61.56	26447	27762	26919
Stores & Spares	5673	17.03	5892	16.59	5961	15.88	6362	7986	8633
Employees' Remuneration & Benefits	9441	28.34	10651	34.71	18801	29.78	11336	12488	13699
Power & Fuel	3828	9.09	3913	12.76	4989	13.08	5299	5453	4291
Repair & Maintenance	3363	10.09	2783	8.81	2345	6.25	3141	3215	4017
Other Expenses	3413	10.25	2769	9.82	3125	8.33	3629	5458	3562
Interest	3189	9.57	3581	11.67	1191	3.17	1127	1088	731
Depreciation	1738	3.22	1728	5.63	1311	3.49	1487	1706	1675
Gross Expenses	47119	141.44	47566	155.00	52747	148.54	58748	64588	63747
Loss: Inter A/c adjustment	11399	34.22	8718	28.41	9117	24.29	8639	8883	7794
Net Expenses	35720	107.22	38848	126.59	43630	116.25	50109	55703	55953
Profit (+)/Loss (-)	-2486	-7.22	-8168	-26.59	-6899	-16.25	-8191	-11575	-11385

Note: (1) Other income includes (a) Provision no longer required written back
(b) adjustment pertaining to earlier year (c) interest earned etc.
(2) Percentages have been calculated on earnings
(3) Raw Materials includes purchase of semi-finished steel
(*) One lac equals 100,000 rupees

EXHIBIT 21-11 (cont.) The Indian Iron & Steel Co. Ltd., Summarized Balance Sheet

(Rs. in lacs)

		As at 31.3.84	As at 31.3.85	As at 31.3.86	As at 31.3.87	As at 31.3.88
A.	Funds Employed					
	1. Share Capital	9345	10289	26016	27376	30976
	2. Reserve and Surplus	210	192	203	209	358
	3. Loan Funds	28728	36945	28688	32546	37001
	4. Bank Overdraft	5474	4705	3363	4182	3976
	Total:	43757	52131	58264	64313	72311
B.	Application of funds					
	1. Fixed Assets (net)	15708	16038	18095	21933	25145
	2. Investments	331	531	331	316	315
	3. Current Assets	31425	32511	36043	33792	31882
	4. Less: Current Liabilities	29149	30330	35885	39624	44960
	5. Net Current Assets	2776	2181	158	(58321)	(13078)
	6. Misc. Expenditure	-	-	-	25	483
	7. Profit & Loss Account	23442	33581	39688	47871	59446
	Total:	43737	52131	58264	64313	72311

EXHIBIT 21-11 (cont.) The Indian Iron & Steel Co. Ltd., Statement of Working Capital

(Rs. in lacs)

	83-84	84-85	85-86	86-87	87-88
Current Assets					
A. Inventories					
1. Stores & Spares	6504	6594	6880	8273	8117
2. Finished Goods	4460	3948	3445	3174	3884
3. Goods in Process	615	478	464	465	904
4. Raw Materials	2553	2905	3278	3036	2733
5. Loose Tools	-	-	-	-	-
Total:	14132	13925	14067	14948	15638
B. Sundry Debtors					
1. Debts outstanding over six months	2725	3355	4854	3126	2933
2. Other Debts	4330	3504	4662	4095	4835
Total:	7055	6859	9516	7221	7768
C. Cash & Bond Balance	1984	2688	1153	1030	1563
D. Loans & Advances	8324	9830	11298	10389	6905
E. Others (including Security Deposit)	10	9	9	82	6
F. Grand Total	31425	32511	36003	33792	31882
Current Liabilities					
G. Sundry Creditors					
1. For Goods	16058	20267	24927	29073	36562
2. For Expenses	2593	3870	3479	3220	2717
3. For other Liabilities	6661	2426	3496	3562	2431
Total:	25312	26563	31902	35855	41710
H. Advance Payments	2916	3037	3483	3176	2882
I. Other Liabilities	660	395	457	437	324
J. Interest on Overdraft & PRG Loan	261	335	123	162	124
K. Grand Total	29149	30338	33885	39624	44960
L. Working Capital	2276	2181	156	(5832)	(13078)

EXHIBIT 21-11 (cont.) The Indian Iron & Steel Co. Ltd. (Burnpur Works), Earnings of Employees

	Unit	83-84	84-85	85-86	86-87	87-88
Salary & Wages	Rs./lacs	4965	6864	6454	639	7441
Number of Employees	Number	25184	24791	24323	23528	227385
Average earning per Employee per Month	Rs.	1643	2839	2210	2245	2727
Labour cost per tonne of Ingot	Rs.	914	1365	1142	1281	1364
Labour cost per tonne of saleable steel	Rs.	1119	1591	1298	1206	1373

Note: Figures relate to Burnpur Works only.

EXHIBIT 21-11 (cont.) The Indian Iron & Steel Co. Ltd., Cost of Raw Materials Purchased

(Rs. per Tonne)

	1979-80 Basic Rate including Levies & Taxes	1979-80 Freight	1979-80 Total	1983-84 Basic Rate including Levies & Taxes	1983-84 Freight	1983-84 Total	1984-85 Basic Rate including Levies & Taxes	1984-85 Freight	1984-85 Total	1985-86 Basic Rate including Levies & Taxes	1985-86 Freight	1985-86 Total
Cotine Coal												
Washed	258	13	171	418	32	450	486	31	517	608	40	640
Unwashed	141	16	157	251	38	28	389	31	420	477	39	511
Chasnalla (Own)	252	16	263	463	16	479	466	16	482	524	37	561
Iron Ore												
Gas	47	29	76	75	60	135	67	60	127	64	60	124
Man Changes	78	29	93	103	59	162	114	59	173	121	57	178
Purchases	42	36	72	61	62	123	75	64	139	86	62	148
Limestone												
B.F. Gr.	58	37	95	88	75	163	98	79	169	118	75	193
S.M.S. Gr.	43	78	121	48	160	268	59	168	219	71	188	251
Bolcaite												
B.F. Gr.	59	37	96	181	75	176	106	79	185	110	75	185
S.M.S. Gr.	58	37	93	91	75	166	106	75	181	114	75	189
Ferro-Manganese	3820	130	3150	6021	201	6222	6432	285	6637	7072	225	7297
Ferro Silicon	6218	245	6463	8385	626	9005	12668	460	10528	11965	672	12637
Aluminum	16835	-	16035	19925	-	19925	24817	-	24017	24226	90	24316
Zinc Spelter	13098	238	13336	24319	90	24489	27267	90	27357	26566	90	26655
Boiler Coal	110	13	123	234	29	263	292	28	320	304	30	334
Fernace Oil	1135	52	1187	2592	153	2745	2578	155	2733	2961	282	3243

EXHIBIT 21-11 (cont.) Summarized Financial Analysis of Tata Iron & Steel Company

(Rs. in Crores)

	1987	1986	1985	1984
ASSETS				
1. Fixed Assets	1299.84	1115.76	911.55	843.64
2. Depreciation Reserves	591.75	538.35	460.00	390.18
NET FIXED ASSETS	708.09	577.41	451.55	453.46
INVESTMENTS	130.12	144.54	103.12	20.22
3. Cash	38.77	37.37	52.85	28.00
4. Receivables	139.72	129.40	112.26	109.44
5. Inventories	244.77	346.16	241.59	232.54
6. Other Current Assets, Loans & Advances	278.61	129.63	84.45	29.87
TOTAL CURRENT ASSETS	701.87	642.56	491.15	399.85
TOTAL ASSETS	1540.08	1364.51	1045.82	873.53
LIABILITIES				
7. Equity Capital	82.63	82.74	72.02	72.02
8. Reserves & Surplus	401.05	334.19	230.24	160.61
NET WORTH	483.68	416.93	302.26	232.63
9. Secured loans	304.83	343.06	334.97	296.42
10. Fixed Deposits	86.49	73.56	61.84	69.67
11. Unsecured Loans (others)	126.51	30.81	1.71	14.53
TOTAL DEBT	517.83	447.43	398.52	380.62
12. Current Liabilities	433.46	412.33	316.44	246.40
13. Income Taxes	74.45	67.22	113.48	1.64
14. Dividends	20.66	20.60	15.12	12.24
TOTAL CURRENT LIABILITIES	538.57	500.15	345.04	260.28
TOTAL LIABILITIES + NET WORTH	1540.08	1364.51	1045.82	873.53

EXHIBIT 21-11 (cont.) Year Ending 31 March

(Rs. in Crores)**

	1987	1986	1985	1984
Sales/Services	1347.68	1224.51	1057.52	853.25
Gross Profit/Loss	157.12	206.96	166.69	63.15
Depreciation	57.60	49.28	54.90	43.14
Provision for Taxes	12.00	50.00	12.00	-
Net Profit/Loss	87.52	107.68	99.79	20.01
Dividends	20.66	20.66	15.12	12.24
(a) Debt-Equity ratio	1.07	1.07	1.32	1.64
(b) Current ratio	1.30	1.29	1.42	4.54
(c) Net Worth per equity	582.75	503.91	323.01	223.01
(d) Net Profit - Total Assets %	5.68	7.89	9.54	2.29
(e) Net Profit-Sales %	6.50	8.79	9.44	2.35
(f) Receivables to sales days	38	39	39	47
(g) Inventories to sales days	49	52	39	45

FUNDS PROVIDED BY	1987	1986	1985
1. Internal Generation	137.12	161.16	139.64
2. Inc. in Borrowings	70.40	48.91	17.90
3. Inc. in Reserves	7.89	12.67	0.01
4. Dec. in Working Capital	-	3.70	-
5. Dec. in Investments	14.42	-	-
6. Share Capital/Share App. money	-	10.72	-
	229.83	237.76	157.55

FUNDS USED FOR			
1. Capital Expenditure	188.28	175.14	52.99
2. Inc. in Investments	-	41.42	82.90
3. Inc. in Working Capital	28.89	-	6.54
4. Dividends	20.66	20.60	15.12
	229.83	237.16	157.55

also a major customer), and representatives from SAIL/TISCO, and mini steel plants. The saleable steel sold during 1988 was 412,000 tonnes, and was expected to be 310,000 tonnes during 1989. The CSO sold coal and other by-products also. They helped in purchasing raw materials from outside and also marketed Kulti and Ujjain's products. The sales were done either directly to the major customers or through the stock-yards.

There was to be a reduction in the sale of saleable steel as production was to decrease at the Burnpur Works till modernisation was completed. CSO was also to undertake the purchases of construction steel for modernisation (500 varied sizes of 100,000 tonne lot size).

There was a possibility that restructuring of the marketing system would be carried out to accommodate the changes during modernisation and after. The CSO was to be made to report to the Central Marketing Organization of SAIL (instead of the M.D. IISCO). The CMO had 46 sales outlets all over the country and was a larger organisation with a bigger turnover. An Act of Parliament which would merge the two organisations was being contemplated. Problems of suitably integrating the marketing personnel of CSO within the CMO/SAIL structure had stood in the way of such a merger.

Production System

Steel-Making Process at Burnpur Works

The Steel Industry used process technology. The inputs—raw materials such as coal, iron ore, dolomite, and limestone—were transformed into outputs, which were either semi-finished like ingots or fully finished products like Structural rails, etc.

Coal from the collieries was fed into the coke ovens, and various gases were removed from the coal. Heat was provided by the batteries, and the metallurgical coke was removed. This was the first stage in the process. From raw coke oven gas, vital coal chemicals were recovered for manufacture of a number of by-products like Ammonium Sulphate, Benzol products and

crude tar. Crude tar was used within the plant as a fuel for open hearth furnaces. The clean coke oven gas was used as fuel for various units in the plant including coke oven batteries.

The major inputs for the Blast Furnace included metallurgical coke, iron ore, limestone, dolomite, manganese ore, etc. Hot metal produced through smelting was either sent for steel making or poured in pig casting machines for use at Kulti or Ujjain, or for sale to other customers. Slag produced in the process was supplied to cement manufacturers. The by-product blast furnace gas served as an important gaseous fuel for the plant.

The conversion of molten iron into steel was effected through the Duplex Process of steel making, a combination of Acid Bessemer Converters and Basic Open Hearth Furnaces. In October 1988, the Bessemer Converter was removed from operation. The energy requirement was industry coke oven gas, furnace oil and crude tar.

Steel was conventionally teemed into ingots and supplied to the Blooming Mills where it was rolled into blooms and slabs. The blooms and slabs were converted to billets or sheet bar and fed to finishing mills. Some amount of blooms/billets were also sold to re-rollers.

Style

Style is what the top management of an organisation does (as opposed to what it says). It includes tangible evidence of what management considers important by the way it collectively spends time and attention and engages in symbolic behaviour.

The Burnpur Works was initially manned by European managers. Their benevolent and patriarchical style saw a bustling township emerge with schools, a park and residential quarters for the officers.

The Management style of IISCO was personified by its Chairman, Sir Biren Mukherjee, for nearly four decades. The obituary of Sir Biren in the IISCO Newsletter 'Yours Faithfully' (Dec. 1982 issue) described his style in the following words:

An era came to a close with the passing away of Sir Biren Mukherjee, on November 4, 1982. It was an era of entrepreneurial leadership, result-oriented approach and authoritarian management. Sir Biren was more often mentioned and referred to than seen or heard at Burnpur. His direct involvement with Indian Iron lasted for just a year short of four long decades, but his association with the managing agents of the company was older by nearly a decade. He led IISCO to the pinnacle of its glory. He did not court the establishment, which cost him dearly.

Sir Biren Mukherjee had the distinction of arranging the first private sector loan for any industry in India from the World Bank. This was a US $31.5 million loan in 1953 to cover the foreign exchange requirements of the expansion of the steel plant to 700,000 MT/Yr. This was perhaps a measure of his stature in the country then.

There was a feudal streak in this style, which was revealed in the low housing level (below 17% in 1972) provided for the workers and staff. Only accommodation for officers was provided for fully, most of these officers being foreigners.

Due to rapid turnover of top executives since nationalisation, no discernible personal style could be noticed. However, the advent of Mr. V. Krishnamurthy as Chairman-SAIL in 1985 had created a new style of management. Mr. Krishnamurthy was a "great helmsman" of the public sector of India. He had been credited with the successful establishment of the Maruti Udyog Limited (the premier automobile manufacturing organisation in the country). He had also been responsible for successfully transforming the Bharat Heavy Electricals Limited (BHEL), into an internationally competitive power equipment manufacturer.

Business India (May 1-14, 1989) in an article headed "Reanimating a giant," credited Mr. Krishnamurthy with presiding over an organisational metamorphosis in SAIL. His stewardship was reported to have resulted in labour overtime costs being cut to almost nothing from Rs.40 crores earlier, inspite of having 240 unions to contend with. This was done by taking the workers in confidence at every stage.

He had in his four years in SAIL wiped out cumulative losses of Rs.300 crores and had initiated a capital spending programme of Rs.15,000 crores over seven years to double steel production and labour productivity (to be funded only by internal accruals). The Burnpur modernisation was one part of this programme.

A distinct feature of Mr. Krishnamurthy's managerial style was the regular meetings he held with shop floor managers, supervisors and trade union representatives in all the steel plants. In one such meeting at Burnpur, held in November 1988, he emphasised that:

> What is required here is the determination to succeed ... you must learn to swim against the current, ... or get washed away.

The Managing Director of IISCO, Mr. M.F. Mehta, had the longest tenure since nationalisation (six years). A veteran steel technologist, with more than thirty years of experience in the steel industry, he moved to Burnpur from the Bokaro Steel plant of SAIL (Bokaro records for production of steel were set under his leadership). Mr. Mehta spent most of his time on the Burnpur Works. He made two/three trips a month to Kulti and five/six trips per year to the collieries and mines. The Ujjain unit was visited twice a year.

Mr. Mehta in an interview with the case-writers, explained his style of decision-making thus:

> My day starts at 6 a.m. when I receive the previous day's production figures on the phone. Around 7 a.m. there is a teleconference between various G.M.s from their homes. I tune into it at my residence. I visit the plant around 9 a.m. I don't believe in meetings (for decision-making). I meet people individually. I have allowed time to various functionaries throughout the day. Pending problems are solved on the spot during this period. The evening is devoted to paper work. No work is taken home.

Mr. Mehta was scheduled for retirement from service in 1990.

SAIL had a poor record in project implementation. The successful completion of the modernisation programme at Burnpur (and in SAIL) appeared to depend to a large extent on the quality of leadership and decision-making at IISCO and SAIL after Mr. Krishnamurthy/Mr. Mehta had retired.

Staff

Staff relates to human resources (i.e, the people in an organisation) and its related dimensions - morale, attitude, motivation, and behaviour. Corporate demographic details rather than individual personalities are included in this variable.

As of 01-06-89, all units of IISCO together employed 37,210 people, comprising 1,503 executives and 35,707 non-executives. The breakup of non-executives in various units was as follows:

There were about 3,000 contract workers. The Industrial Relations culture was described by the Personnel Manager thus:

There has been no problem for the last three years. Plant personnel are looking forward to modernisation. Though we changed duty timings and stopped overtime, there has been no protest. The workers have been told that the only alternative to modernisation is shutting down the plant.

We have five functional unions—INTUC, CITU, HMS, AITUC, BMS. Though INTUC is the recognised Union, negotiations have been undertaken with all the five unions. A common agreement is signed with all unions. We do not ascertain the actual numbers supporting each union, as this would be construed as interference. Yes, the numbers given to the Labour Authorities (on Union strength) are fictitious. There have been no strikes and lockouts since I have joined the plant. The State Government usually calls for a bandh three days in a year—special passes are issued to 3000 workers who are allowed to come inside. We have not retrenched anyone after the takeover in 1972.

The manpower strength at the time of takeover (in 1972) was 36,604, of which 35,740 were non-executives and 864 executives. After 1972, there was addition to the manpower, and it reached the high of 43,597 in 1984. Between 1984-1989, manpower had been planned and brought down through a voluntary retirement scheme and by natural separation with not much addition to the employees, strength. After modernisation, the projected requirement of manpower according to the JICA report was 14,134 at Burnpur Works. The present strength of 20,696 non-executives had to be trimmed down. The new technology would call for new skills. The modernisation, apart from bringing about technological changes, called for changes in attitudes and skills of the employees, for which employees had to be retrained. Around 1500 new recruits would have been added to the existing workforce by 1995.

Voluntary Retirement Scheme

A voluntary retirement scheme, which was implemented first by SAIL, was extended to IISCO in October 1986. The retirement age, which was 60 years at IISCO, was changed to 58 years for non-executives who joined after 06-01-79 and executives who joined after 01-06-73. The eligibility for the voluntary retirement were employees with 10 years of experience above 40 years of age, for those who retired at 58 years of age; and above 42 years for those retiring at 60 years. By March, 1989, 1,783 employees had gone on voluntary retirement. The distribution of voluntary retirement by year and status is shown in Exhibit 21-12.

A task group had been appointed to identify the eligible employees and to counsel them to take voluntary retirement. At Burnpur Works, 1837 non-executives and 156 executives who were in the age group of 56-60 would have retired by 1993. The employees between 40-55 years of age were the target population to be

Exhibit 21-12 Voluntary Retirements By Year and Status

Years	IISCO (Total)	Non-Executives	Executives
1986-87	325	319	6
1987-88	940	916	24
1988-89	518	507	11
Total:	1,783	1,742	41

Exhibit 21-13 Agewise Distribution of Employees

Age group	Non-executives	Executives
42-49	4,991	356
50-55	3,390	244
56-60	1,837	156

counselled for voluntary retirement. (See Exhibit 21-13 for the age distribution of the employees.)

Redeployment

With impending changes, the concerns of staff related mainly to their status after modernisation. "The letters from the Managing Director's desk," in the IISCO Corporate Newsletter, tried to assuage these concerns. The Sept. '88 issue read:

> ... While it had been repeatedly emphasised that permanent employees would not be retrenched and that on redeployment an employee's employments would be protected, it is essential that employees earnestly take up whatever work they are offered. A sizable portion of our employees would have to be redeployed in various activities of modernisation and later absorbed in the new plants. Some of our employees would also have to be redeployed within the existing plant.

With the assurance that no retrenchment was to be carried out, redeployment had become a major issue.

Redeployment Plans

The excess manpower, the less skilled employees above 48 years of age, were to be redeployed in areas like projects for construction work and laying 46 kms. of railway track at the site. Employees were also to be used for dismantling the machinery which was being phased out. Redeployment was also to be done in the areas where contract labour was being used. For instance, there were 900 contract labourers in the coal handling area alone. Contract labour jobs were to be abolished. Union agreement had been obtained on this issue.

The manpower distribution in the major areas is illustrated in Exhibit 21-14.

The manpower requirement after modernisation (as per JICA report) is in Exhibit 21-15.

The redeployment exercise had to be carried out in a manner that the future requirement was met from such present manpower—who needed to be suitably trained for their new jobs.

Skills

Skills are those dominating attributes or capabilities which demonstrate what the organisation does best. Skills are those capabilities that are

Exhibit 21-14 Manpower Distribution in Major Areas of Burnpur Works (as of 1/6/89)

Area	Non-Executives	Area	Executives
Coke Oven	1530		1530
Blast Furnace	1124	Operation	1124
Steel Melting Shop	981	Maintenance	981
Rolling Mill	2015	Service	2015
Sheet Mills	1257		1257
Maintenance & Service	8023		8023
Total of Burnpur Works	16387	Total of Burnpur Works	16387

Exhibit 21-15 Manpower Requirement After Modernisation

DIVISION	Manpower Estimates NUMBERS REQUIRED PRESENTLY (figures in parentheses show requirement after step 2)
1. Personnel and Labour Relations	305
2. Finance & Accounts	82
3. Administration	133
4. Purchase	50
5. Technical Control	237
6. Production Control	349
7. Iron Making	1,326 (1,605)
8. Steel Making	561 (777)
9. Rolling	2,953 (2,390)
10. Equipment Maintenance	4,725 (5,224)
11. Energy	391
12. Transport	4,569 (4,201)
13. Laboratories	189
14. Engineering Centre	121
Total:	15,991 (14,134)

Productivity: First Step: 62 MT/Man Year
Second Step: 152 MT/Man Year

possessed by an organisation as a whole as opposed to the people in it. It could be viewed as a derivative of the other S's.

At the Burnpur Works, skills in the pre-nationalization days were in the area of project implementation and production. For instance, the 'History of IISCO' (page no. 44) claimed that "the iron-making plant in the 1920's was more up-to-date than any average European plant and the management was as efficient as in Europe."

The erection of the steel plant and its three expansions were all done within the scheduled time-limit and within the stipulated costs. The last expansion (in 1955) was completed 13 months ahead of schedule and saved foreign exchange due to import substitution. One of the Works' Indian managers received the prestigious Carnegie Silver medal in 1958 from the Iron & Steel Institute London for his contributions to the steel making process.

The post-nationalization era saw a distinct dilution in technical skill which was held as one of the causes for poor production performance. However, some of the Works' shop floor managers claimed that operating and maintaining the vintage machinery was itself a technical feat.

The productivity of the Blast furnaces (two of which were established in the 1920's and two in the '50's) was said to compare favourably with those of even the Bhilai or Rourkela steel plants of SAIL (which had more modern machinery) in spite of poor raw material quality.

Marketing was another function where corporate skill was evident. An Indian Market Research Bureau (IMRB) "customer-satisfaction survey" ranked IISCO along with TISCO and ahead of CMO of SAIL. The Chairman of SAIL and IISCO, Mr. V. Krishnamurthy, had publicly praised the marketing department's performance: IISCO's CSO had sold products of other plants of SAIL at 2.5% commission, when CMO could not deliver the service.

A crucial skill for successful modernisation was the ability of the Burnpur Works to complete the project within stipulated cost and time limits.

SAIL's records in this area had been poor. (See Exhibit 21-16).

Retraining

The new technology to be adopted after modernisation required new skills for operation. The learning of these new skills entailed attitudinal change—the plant, after modernisation, was to operate at four times the existing production level with two-thirds of the manpower. For example, the testing time in the laboratory, which was presently 48 hours, had to be cut down to eight hours.

A comprehensive two-year training programme had been drawn up. As phasing out of operations were to be started, planning had to be done to ensure that 50 percent of the employees below 48 years of age were withdrawn for training. The withdrawal of workers for training was being planned for synchronisation with the phasing out of units. The training of employees for the future technology was to be in the respective areas of work. The training was to be given on the job in other steel plants where such technology was already available. The summarised training plan is shown in 21-17.

Case Closing

The Burnpur Steel Works had been regarded as a model steel-making unit, perhaps of all Asia, for much of its existence. The last twenty years had seen its performance and reputation dramatically slide downwards. A stage had been reached where the possibility of the Works being shut down was being considered as a possible strategic alternative. The Managing Director, Mr. M.F. Mehta, realised that the Burnpur modernisation was a complex task. The "infusion of technology" solution could not alone suffice. Mr. Mehta was also acutely aware that the restructuring decisions that had to be taken could either rebuild the works as a model steel plant, or push it towards the path of getting wiped out of existence.

Exhibit 21-16 SAIL's Sad Legacy: Project Cost and Time Overruns

Project	Capacity	Month of Govt. Approval Original (Revised)	Approved Cost (Rs. Crores)	Final Cost (Rs. Crores)	Cost overruns (Rs. Crores)	Time overrun (months)
Alloy steel plant expansion	100,000 tpa	July '81	66	113	47	32
Bhilai expansion	1.19m tpa	Mar. '76 (Dec. '86)	938 (2,263) *	2,262	1,324	73
Bokaro expansion	1.17m tpa	Mar. '73 (Dec. '82)	947 (1,638) *	2,072	1,125	131
Captive Power Plant, Bokaro	3x60 MW	Sept. '78 (Dec. '82)	76 (120) *	145	69	51
Captive Power Plant, Durgapur	2x60 MW	Sept. '78 (Oct. '81)	55 (82) *	125	70	54
Captive Power	2x60 MW	Jan. '81	80	210	130	30

* Revised cost estimates (figures rounded to the nearest crore)

Source: Ministry of Programme Implementation Report 1987-88. *Business World*, March 1-14 Issue, p.50.

Exhibit 21-17 Training Plan in Man Days

Field		Training given by Indian Trainers in India	Training given by Trainers dispatched by Eqpt. & Tech. Manafacturers at Burnpur	Training given by countries giving Eqpt. & Tech.
1. Sintering:	-Ore Yard	0	1,037	122
	-Sintering	0	1,403	122
2. Blast Furnace:	-X	0	1,500	1,056
3. Basic Oxygen Furnace:	-B.O.F.	750	1,600	750
	-Line calcining	110	0	110
4. Continuous Casting:	-Blooms CC	378	158	189
	-Billets CC	378	158	189
	-Rolling Bar	0	530	1,050
5. Maintenance:	-Machine Assembly	0	30	0
	-Forging	0	50	0
	-Central Maintenance	0	1,650	3,256
	-Local	0	1,650	3,960
5. Power:	-Receiving & Distribution	0	0	120
	-Oxygen	480	120	0
	-Blast Furnace	0	120	240
	-Gas	0	120	240
	Grand Total:	2,096	10,126	1,404

22
Ferox Manufactured Products

November 1989, the Velvet Revolution

It was unusually cold for that time of the year, and the several hundred employees of Ferox Dêcín who gathered in the yard could see their breath. Facing them, standing on an unloaded railroad wagon, was the managing director, Radek Malec.[1] The time was exactly noon. Millions of people in Czechoslovakia stopped working that noon. Just as in Decín, people gathered in meeting rooms, corridors, cafeterias, classrooms, and factory yards and went into the streets with one thing on their minds: making this the very last week of Communist rule in Czechoslovakia.

But few managing directors shared this goal, and even fewer were able to face their subordinates at this critical moment. Many of this elite group knew that it would be better not to show up. However, Radek Malec did face the volatile crowd at Ferox. After decades of mistrust between workers and managers, Malec knew that

what he was going to say would be decisive for his own future, as well as for the future of Ferox.

October 1991

Radek Malec, managing director of Ferox, a gas and chemical company, has just read the Czech Republic's public announcement of Ferox's proposed privatization plan. Before proceeding with his plans, Malec had to wait for the U.S.company Air Products and Chemicals (APCI) to purchase controlling interest in Ferox and to allow for competing proposals to be brought forward. Although he has had little time to marvel at the monumental changes he and Ferox have experienced, he has devoted considerable energy to planning for the acquisition of Ferox by APCI.

Background

Ferox is located in Decín, a northeastern industrial city near the German border. The company was founded during World War II to produce chemicals and chemical equipment for the military. At the end

---

[1] The names of all of the individuals in this case have been changed.

This case was prepared by Professor Jone Pearce of the Graduate School of Management, University of California, Irvine, and Dr. Michal Cakrt of the Czechoslovak Management Center. It was supported by a U.S. Agency for International Development grant. The material is intended for discussion purposes and is not intended to serve as an example of either good or poor management practices. Reprinted from *Managing in Emerging Economies: Cases From the Czech and Slovak Republics*, Dan Fogel (ed.) 1994, By permission Westview Press, Boulder Co.

EXHIBIT 22-1 Functional Departments at Ferox

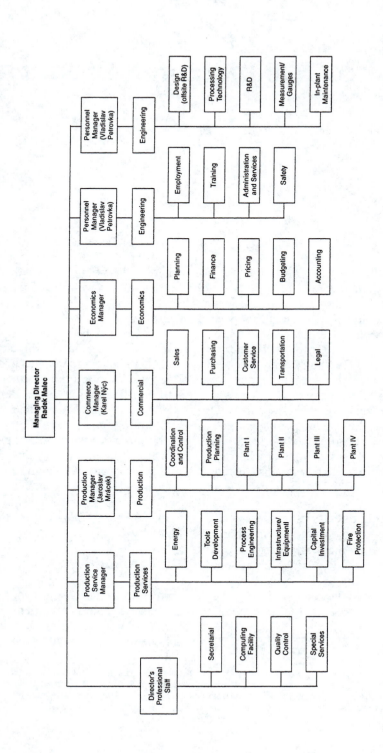

of the war it was confiscated as Nazi property by the Czechoslovak government and began to produce simple agricultural chemical products.

Until 1989 Ferox was a component of one of the biggest Czechoslovak industrial trusts. In 1991, as a result of the first phase of the privatization process, it became a separate joint-stock company with stock held by the government. By October 1991, Ferox was governed by an operating board that included people from the company (the chairman of this board was the deputy director for engineering), from other companies, and also from the government ministries. It was anticipated that in the second phase of the privatization the state would offer its shares to potential buyers.

At the time of this study, Ferox had three main product lines: cryogenic equipment, chemical equipment, and air-cooling systems for the chemical industry's long-distance pipelines. In January 1991, Ferox began selling gas, and this line was assumed by its joint venture with APCI. In 1991, the company was working with APCI on a new gas-manufacturing joint venture.

Ferox's customers have been many and varied. Before the 1989 revolution, 40-45 percent of the company's market was dependent, either directly or indirectly, on the Soviet market. In 1991, only 1.5-2 percent of their sales came from that market because their former Soviet customers did not have the convertible currency to pay for Ferox purchases. In October 1991, Ferox had 1,350 employees organized into six functional departments: production services, production, commerce (included purchasing and sales), economics (accounting), personnel, and engineering (see Figure 22.1). Ferox had annual sales of approximately $15 million.

In October 1991, Ferox formally submitted a privatization project to the Czech Republic Privatization Ministry and awaited approval. In accordance with the law, the proposal stipulated that 3 percent of the shares would be set aside for a reserve fund for restitution to the original owners of companies. In addition, Ferox's proposal reserved 3 percent of the shares for employee purchase and 52 percent for purchase by APCI, with the remaining 42 percent of the shares allocated for purchase by Czech citizens through the government's voucher program. Shares purchased through vouchers must be held by the original purchasers for two years, until after the privatization of the entire economy is completed, before they can be traded. Revenue from the 55 percent of shares to be purchased by employees and by APCI would go to the National Property Fund.

Several Ferox employees were interviewed regarding the changes as a result of Ferox's joint venture with APCI. Some excerpts from these follow.

Radek Malec, Managing Director

In other companies, the whole management was changed after the revolution, and those companies have had a lot of difficulties. Oftentimes they put researchers and design engineers in charge who are smart but don't really know how to run a company. They believed that all of the old contacts and relations would be useless, that people needed to be replaced because they could not change their behavior. The people expected big changes. We changed the government. Why not change the management? They wanted to see blood. We at Ferox devoted a lot of energy to this transition. There was strong opposition to retaining top management, but people recognized quickly that we were playing an honest game. I believe our continuity was well chosen, and we have been able to change.

Since the very beginning of the revolution, I had close contact with the Civic Forum committee, the umbrella antiregime movement in this plant, and we agreed to share information with each other. I kept emphasizing that we didn't want the different political factions fighting here. We have to cooperate at work. If two individuals who must work together in the production process are fighting, the work cannot go on. After the purges following the Soviet invasion of 1968, working relationships were disrupted for nearly ten years and cooperation was damaged. I knew that the company would bear the most unpleasant results for years to come if we had fighting here. I met frequently with the

Civic Forum and emphasized the damage that would be done by the clashes here. I met often with the company's branch of the People's Militia, and I tried to persuade them to remain calm and to accept that the situation had changed. I emphasized that everyone needed to respect that we were here for production and that the political changes should not destroy the company on which we all depended.

Certain people tried to use the political changes to advance their own positions. They really didn't care about the political changes or the company, only themselves. They tried to take advantage of the situation. Because the Civic Forum was a broad umbrella movement, anyone could say they were a member. We agreed to involve the Civic Forum in the operation of the company by giving it a seat on the operating board of the company and by inviting its representatives to trade union-management meetings, but because the Civic Forum was participating in the running of the company, it had to be responsible for the behavior of its members. In this way we were able to prevent these opportunists from taking over the company. We even had a bulletin board that the Civic Forum could use. It once posted a notice that was very critical of management, and a foreman took the notice down. I put it back up; I felt that if we agreed to let them have a bulletin board, we had to live with whatever they put there. Later, we banned the participation of all political parties in the company. So, when the Civic Forum itself broke apart into political parties, it eventually lost its seat on these management committees too.

Even during the most uncertain period of the revolution, we were able to keep production going with relatively little loss. People would start work a little later because they were busy exchanging news with each other when they arrived at the plant, and their breaks were a little longer for the same reason. But we had to be reasonable and couldn't take a hard line with them.

Not once have we in top management been caught lying. That was very important. People saw that management was working to protect the company from attacks. We had to show our people that we are here to protect their future. No one had to leave the company, and with the exception of one of my deputies, no one has left. I have had a job offer for more than double my salary here, but we all have a sense of responsibility to the company. When we had a problem with an order about one year ago, many people worked extra hours to save the good name of the company even though the problem was not their fault.

I first brought in CAPA Consulting back in 1988 because I wanted to change two attitudes in my managers: The system is perfect and problems are only created by people failing to carry out their jobs, and things don't change. I wanted them to know that the structure may change. Thanks to this cooperation (between CAPA and Ferox), we were able to anticipate, well before the revolution, the changes now being required of all companies.

Under our old system, the scope of responsibilities for a company's managing director were much wider than in the West, but the authority was much narrower. We have different tasks to do every day. We are a typical Czech company: We have a kindergarten; we own and maintain apartments for our employees; we have canteens. Up to five years ago, we were also responsible for our seventy-ton quota of dry hay.

Ten to fifteen years ago, the local authority discovered a shortage of hay. All companies in its region were made responsible for a quota of hay. Our assigned meadows were inaccessible for heavy mowing equipment, so we had to select those people from Ferox who understood how to work hand scythes. Our managerial problem was how to choose people who knew how to cut hay. Which employees were needed least that day? Who knew how to use scythes? Even our lawyer went out to cut hay. We had to provide lunches and transportation for them. Then the local authority decided that yields were too low, so we were invited to purchase a quota of fertilizer each spring. Later, the local authority decided that because we were contributing something of economic value to the agricultural cooperative, they should "pay us" for this work. So they paid us 40 koruny per ton[1] — but our own cost was over 150 koruny per ton. After that, we bought a specialized machine to cut on these steep hillsides. A couple of years ago, this responsibility ceased, so now our problem is, who do we sell this equipment to?

Now we can laugh at it. It is the same as looking back on your experience as an army draftee: You look back and only see the comical aspects; you remember the amusing things. It was too crazy. We are here to produce chemical equipment. But then it was different — it was impossible to quarrel about it. It was horrible.

We have to spend a lot more energy to find new customers now. Someone from your system really cannot understand us. Five years ago, this was a strictly planned economy. The main problem was to organize production under conditions in which we were overloaded. The sales forecast was known two years in advance because the only customer was the state. The major problem was to meet the state's special requests for exports — through which the state hoped to make some extra hard-currency profits. Now, we have to find our own customers. Before, we had to take gifts to our suppliers in order to secure deliveries; now, we take gifts to our customers. The procurement problem was much bigger than the sales problem. It was a dictatorship of the suppliers; now, this system is gone. We need to increase our sales department by two or three times, and we lack sales methodology and experience. At present, the situation in our country is still very unstable. Even trying to understand all of the information that comes out each week is hard. Nobody knows what will happen tomorrow. But we are firmly committed to the belief that this company will survive. We believe in our capability to find solutions to our problems. This belief has three pillars.

The first pillar is improvisation. Every day brings new information. One example of how we have improvised is our management of the internal debt problem. Today, we owe our suppliers

about 60 million koruny, and our customers owe us 150 million koruny — this latter is the value of over three months of our production. Most of our suppliers retire their debt within the ninety-day period. We have only about five customers who have not paid us within ninety days. They are all big state-owned companies. One is the national railroad. It is impossible to know whether these are bad debts. We cannot imagine that the country will let the state-owned railroad go bankrupt. But we do not know whether a Western partner will come in and help any of these companies to become profitable. Everything is uncertain right now. Recently, we invoiced about 77 million koruny but received only 37 million koruny. Compared to the rest of Czechoslovak industry, we are in good shape.

Another example of how we have learned to improvise started with one of our suppliers. Our stainless steel supplier wrote us a letter saying, "You owe us five million koruny, so we have decided to postpone your next delivery for two months because you haven't paid us." When this letter arrived, we had to solve that problem immediately. So we discovered that we have knowledge of which companies owe money to other companies. We discovered that the steel mill is a supplier of pig iron to the stainless steel manufacturer, and the steel mill is one of our customers. We found a complete circle of debt. So we got all of the economics deputies for all three companies together and we agreed to simultaneously cancel as much of this circle of debt as possible. Each controller crossed the debt off the ledger and sent a fax to confirm.

This was so successful that we have tried to find other complete debt circles — some involve four parties, some even more. We have now hired one person whose sole responsibility is to try to clear debts in this way. But if there had been a computer network connecting us with all our customers and suppliers — which is not the case yet — we could be much more efficient. It is estimated that the entire Czechoslovak industry has 100 to 150 billion koruny of this internal debt, equal to one-third of the country's gross domestic product.

The second pillar is privatization. There are

---

[1] As of August 1994 the exchange rate was approximately $1.00 equals 28 koruny.

several reasons we believe privatization is the most important precondition for reaching our long-term goal. First, we need investment money, and it is simply not available from local sources. We need new technology to modernize and to reach European technical standards. We need to improve our physical infrastructure to be more efficient.

Second, we need know-how. What I mean by know-how is how to organize. We need information about how to conduct successful sales activities, to overhaul the financial and accounting systems, and how to manage. The smallest difference between us and the West is the difference between our shop floor workers. Our welders are highly skilled. We need injections of knowledge, but we don't want to copy the West thoughtlessly. The West is the source of information, but it is up to us to use the information properly to reach our goals.

I feel that the biggest difference is in sales activities. Before, I thought it was just a matter of selling. Now, after working for a year with APCI, I see that it is much more than that. The main thing is to get customers who will be able to pay, and help potential customers find the means to pay.

The third pillar for our survival is our long-term strategy. Our long-term goal is to become one of the most prosperous companies in the country by European standards. Privatization is our next objective but not our ultimate goal. It is not why we are here. It is a conduit, a tool to help us reach our goal. Privatization has taken a great deal of our time and attention, and we hope it will end soon. Now, we must wait for final approval. We don't want any agitation that might disrupt or slow down the government's approval of privatization.

At present, there is a coalition government and there is a great deal of political jockeying, as well as uncertainty, about future political stability.

We have an interim postrevolutionary parliament to guide the nation through the immediate postrevolutionary turmoil and develop a new constitution. Because we are a government-owned company, there is always the risk that the politicians will want to use us for political purposes. However, we are not very worried about this because we are in relatively good shape economically and have a good privatization plan, and they have enough other things to worry about. We are trying to get away from political interference and be fully independent as quickly as we can, and we must be privatized to do that. Until we are privatized, we cannot do anything — we cannot sell property or reorganize.

As part of our privatization agreement, we have had numerous discussions with APCI about what we should do to reach our long-term goals. The agreement covers the training they will provide for our people in their facilities, know-how transfer, and so on.

We found APCI two years ago, before the revolution. As part of our 1988 strategic plan developed with a consulting company, we began to look for Western companies with which to form a joint venture. Of course, we were too modest and vague at the beginning. We were just looking for someone to talk to us. We didn't know enough then. You can't create big plans without information. Before that, we had a bad experience trying to make contact with a Russian company, so we began to look for a Western company. We contacted the major companies in the industry. Only APCI was willing to sit with us then. During a conference in the United Kingdom, several of our researchers had an initial confidential discussion with several people from APCI. We offered them certain opportunities.

Then the revolution arrived and we realized very quickly that we would be facing economic reforms. We have been a monopolist supplier for most of our customers. We felt that this monopoly was neither sustainable nor desirable. Now we could see that the currency becoming convertible would not only allow foreign competition here but would also allow us to go international. We saw that we would soon be facing a normal market, and we did not have the know-how.

Of all the major companies we approached, APCI seemed the most flexible. About January or February 1990, we started our first real discussions. One of APCI's Western competitors had formed a joint venture with one of our customers. APCI expressed its interest in our gas separators and cryogenic units. In April 1990, I visited the company, but still not openly; it would have been dangerous to release information at that time.

In July 1990, we signed a letter of intent for the first joint venture, scheduled for the second quarter of 1991. This joint venture involves the new business, gas production, as well as the transfer of our existing cryogenic business to APCI.

In January 1991, we began our own gas business. We wanted to show APCI that we could get it started without them. We have only about 10 percent of the market, but because many of the customers who depended on us for necessary equipment also buy gas, we thought we would be able to influence more of them to do business with us in the future. Because our containers are 30 percent cheaper than any they can get elsewhere and are just as good, we hoped to retain and even increase our market share for both gas and equipment.

After more months of discussion we created the joint venture with APCI, which came into formal existence in April 1991. APCI owns 51 percent, and Ferox 49 percent. The joint-venture agreement also covers the distribution and sales of cryogenic equipment and liquified gases in Central and Eastern Europe, over which the joint venture has exclusive dealership.

Now we are working on the second joint venture, a large refinery that the first joint venture will need to produce the gas. It is a $70 million project that involves Ferox, APCI, and another Czechoslovak company. We signed the letter of intent in March 1991.

Finally, we agreed to the marriage of Ferox with APCI through the privatization program. They have controlling interest because they like to control what they are paying for. We had to show APCI that we were a good prospect. We have established markets. There is some synergy in the cryogenics area.

Sometimes they don't understand how it is here. I was describing to Heinz Hoffman, the European vice president, and Bill Stoughton, the U.S. chief engineer, how we would use the de-

pendence of our tank customers to influence them to buy gas from us. Stoughton put his head in his hands; he was horrified by the rough way we do business here. But Hoffman, who fled East Germany years ago, said, "Good, good." He understood the situation and got the point right away. You in the West have developed an excellent system for yourselves over the years; you are used to shooting with a silencer on your guns. But we live in the real Wild East during this period here. You Americans can afford to be all polite and honest. If you act like that in this environment today, you won't get anywhere. It's a lot of trouble to explain.

Right now, neither APCI nor Ferox can pull out. It is a marriage with no possibility of a divorce. We are proud that we were able to get a company from the West, that we found the right worm for the hook. U.S. companies often appear too lazy and afraid. The Germans are the most aggressive here; they know the market, the territory, and our mentality.

APCI feels that we are a large company; Ferox will be its biggest manufacturing facility. APCI has 250 people in its U.S. plant and 250 in its UK plant. Its target is to increase our efficiency. We wonder what will be the effect on the other parts of our company, where APCI has no product expertise. Our agreement with APCI says employment will be kept at a reasonable level based on profit in all of the product lines. There is also another uncertainty: After privatization, what will we do with our service work? Some of it may be more efficiently provided by us, but each case has to be examined in detail. APCI wanted me to hire a security service. We have them now in Czechoslovakia, but they usually have only lazy, young people. These pensioners we have now are the cheapest, best solution for us.

For each of these services, I will want to review options such as retaining it or leasing it. After privatization, I want to create a steering committee made up of high-level managers from APCI and Ferox to study these areas — people with sufficient knowledge to go through it all and to indicate our weak points. The chief of APCI's manufacturing facility told me, "Don't copy us."

APCI managers are very slow and careful.

They evaluate projects step-by-step. They evaluate, then they estimate the finances; they check and check again. I can see how deeply interested the Americans are in the finances, so that even if an order is canceled it will still make money. Before, Ferox was a core manufacturing facility. All of the other kinds of tasks were done by others, for example, the foreign trade companies handled foreign sales. Now we are free to do this work ourselves, but we don't have anyone who understands how to write these contracts, issue letters of credit, conduct currency transfers, and so on. Today, we know about 50 percent of what it takes to make a good deal.

Now, I can see that a successful company is cautious, and why. What is the customer's ability to pay? Sometimes I have been disappointed in the cautious, slow progress in negotiations with APCI. It is their natural style. They must be sure of success. APCI has an entire system of making offers: stages one, two, and three. They protect their power and capability. Even after a U.S. group said that our second joint-venture plant was financially sound, the European Bank for Reconstruction and Development (to whom we have applied for a loan) requires yet another group of Western financial experts to examine the project. This project will have a firm base. Before the 1989 revolution, getting investment money was a grammar exercise. Who could paint the rosiest future? Or an important minister might have a pet project, and then after it was built, someone had to find a market for its production.

To inform the employees about the privatization program, we had to respond to their natural reaction: What will be the future of the company? In the spring, we started to organize meetings of employees, and we explained it to them — all that we knew and our intentions. We have been lucky to retain the trust of our people. We don't have any problems with public disobedience like they sometimes do elsewhere. Of course, the people here have mixed feelings about the relationship with APCI. Many are afraid of losing their jobs. APCI expects us to strictly reduce our staff because productivity is very low here.

There are different levels of employee interest in the privatization program. Some employees would like to talk about it all night. When we had our April meeting to explain the privatization project, we filled our largest canteen to overflowing. We always have our meetings right after the first shift. This was a very good turnout, almost a third of those who were not required to be at their stations.

Many employees still take things lightheartedly. Management's job is to see that employees give 105 percent (the 5 percent is overtime for some extra income; employees don't want more overtime than that because it would cut into their free time). Many believe their only job is to show up at the start of the shift. Quality? Well, everyone makes mistakes. But most here have a sense of responsibility. If they are caught stealing or drinking on the job, they are fired immediately. The trade union supports this policy. APCI agreed to respect the trade union in the privatization agreement.

We are confident that we will have our approval for privatization by the end of 1991. Then we can begin to implement our privatization plan: restructuring the company and selling the support services and equipment we don't need. We need to provide a stable environment in the next three months. We want the image of a smoothly running company. The next couple of months is going to be decisive for many years to come.

Karel Nyc, Commerce Manager

In the past, we negotiated only delivery date and price. Now we negotiate much more. For example, we have added penalties for late payment. One of the ways I try to tell whether we are going to have trouble collecting payment from a potential customer is if they want to negotiate over the penalties. In addition, if it is a customer I don't know well, I ask our economics department to use its good connections with the banker to find out whether the company is in a good financial position.

Now, we have some completely new customers, but Ferox is unknown in the West. One new customer, a Japanese company, is making a purchase from us. Its representatives have just made their ninth visit to the plant in four months; they come twice a month. This Japanese company has very detailed rules for technical requirements. They require sixteen different checks on a flange. They require more detailed production plans and want these plans to be provided very rapidly. I have to put more pressure on the technical department to get us information quickly to make a proposal. Western customers want a quote back in ten days and will not even look at it if it comes in after that. Pressure from my department affects all areas. There is more pressure on the pricing department to provide information more rapidly. For this big Japanese project, after we had a firm order, I called a meeting of all of the directors. Previously, this was completely unheard of. I wanted them to know that this was an important order.

We have not made these same changes for our old customers — we treat their orders as we always have. So far, we are closely tracking new accounts only because this still requires a lot of effort. But these new customers force us to make gradual changes in purchasing, planning, production, and control. We are not as computerized as APCI; we have many workers in purchasing and only two terminals. They must do their spreadsheets and economic analyses by hand. Due to these changes, other departments are under more pressure. There are lots of new activities emerging; many people have to do new things to change their jobs, and they complain. Under the old system, everything was petrified; everything was done the same way for decades. People do not know how to change, and they are reluctant. I know very well that they should get some training, but for the time being, we have to change on the go. Later, perhaps when APCI gets in, there will be more opportunity to work in a more structured fashion.

Another difference is that we have to make our own sales directly. Before the revolution, for foreign sales we went through one of the foreign trade companies. You know, before there was this almost insurmountable barrier between us and the outside world. In about six months we

are going to have to establish a Ferox office in Prague because we cannot get people with foreign-trade skills to move here. For some sales business, it is easier for customers to fly into Prague and for us to meet them there.

All of these changes take time and money. I have to find a real manager for each activity. It's not easy to ask a fifty-year-old to learn German and to master a computer. Before, we were so overloaded with orders that the customers came to us. Now, the sales people have to visit the customers, and they don't like to travel. All of that has to change.

We cannot know what our focus should be in three years. Nowadays our best customer can change into our worst customer in six months. For example, Poland has changed its customs duties six times in the past year. Even the banks do not know what is really happening in the companies. For the next few years, the winners will be those who survive.

Jaroslav Mracek, Production Manager

We have one goal: to survive the next two years. We sacrifice everything for this goal. There are multiplying pressures for quality of production, especially for the blue-collar workers — the exempt workers were already working at a high standard. I will need two or three more managers in production. Some of my managers held party posts and were members of the so-called People's Militia. The new law forces me to remove them from management positions for the next five years.

Unfortunately, production has traditionally had a lower status than other areas; therefore, it has always been difficult to attract good people. It's a high-pressure job; managers have to resolve conflicts every day. They would rather escape to the laboratories.

The blue-collar workers are often so naive. They don't understand that if they want the same living standards as the Germans, they have to accept the whole package. The way I let them know that standards are higher now is by fully supporting the head of quality control. This is a big change. Previously, quality control was the enemy of the production department. I really need to support the quality-control manager because his people are even worse. Quality is the production supervisors' responsibility; they have the ultimate responsibility for quality. Now, the pressure on them is more accentuated. I have been in this job for a year, and my first and most important goal is to improve production quality.

Many of the employees understand, but some do not; it depends on their maturity. Some are much too self-confident. They agree, in general, that they need to improve themselves, but they want to start with someone else. They are used to comparing their work to that done in other companies in Czechoslovakia, and our work has always been good. Now that we are exposed to the West, we see poorer comparative results. The skill levels are high, but there is a lot of complacency.

We have been introducing the International Standards Organization Program for quality improvement that we received from APCI. It involves monthly meetings run by the production unit manager. Before, the meetings were always focused on party politics, but the employees now recognize that the accent has changed. I have asked the personnel manager to add more information on quality to the new-employee training programs. I approached the local technical college to work with them [the college] to change their curriculum — we cannot wait for the Education Ministry.

The union has been flexible and supportive so far, although sometimes it can be unreasonable and want to have influence without responsibility. The union doesn't protect employees who are doing a bad job.

Our progress on quality improvement was reviewed by the chief APCI quality man the last time he was here, and he was not happy with our progress. He lives in quite another world. People who have spent some time here have adjusted better. We were given thousands of pages of English text to process. He says we are too slow; he has doubts about whether we are committed to change.

APCI managers have voiced their dislikes. Our technical procedures are inadequate, our product line is too broad, and we need to focus. But in choosing which products to drop, we cannot make an error because it would involve the loss of many millions of koruny of revenue. APCI itself could be more diversified. There is no reason they cannot sell various equipment as we do. Different products would help them cope with instability in other lines. Not all in APCI have the same opinion. Some see far ahead and want the long-term prosperity of the company.

It's clear that whatever benefits APCI brings to us, it will also take care of itself. There are many completely new situations here. APCI managers have problems knowing who they can trust here. They will face the problem of picking the right people to run Ferox their way, people who have enough energy to turn it around. It will be an enormous amount of work for domestic people. We know that we are all being tested by them. They have been coming here for more than a year and are working around here freely, looking to see if the pace is fast enough. They are evaluating me and the commerce director in particular.

I am convinced that APCI was the right company to make a deal with. We want to enter this marriage without debts and with no liabilities. We want our performance level as close as possible to APCI's even though that is almost impossible. As soon as we achieve that level, it will be easier for us.

We must manage ourselves. But APCI should tell us our goals — so we are moving in the right direction. I'm glad APCI is a U.S. company because I am uncomfortable with the way German businesspeople behave here; the Americans have a milder style. I did not hesitate to support the choice of APCI, because the U.S. market is larger and more dynamic and the United States is the technical leader in many respects.

When APCI management gets control of Ferox, we will learn a lot of things we don't know now. I fully understand that APCI cannot tell us everything freely yet.

Vladislav Petrovna, Personnel Manager

Everything in this department will be affected by APCI's involvement. This is because we have never had a real human resources department in Decín. Recruitment, performance evaluation, professional development, career planning, civilized ways of handling retirement — all are undeveloped here. I can see hardly any area that will be unaffected.

In this department, we are responsible for all of the support activities — canteens, kindergartens, company flats, company-provided health care — as well as for building maintenance and office supplies. At present, compensation and benefits are in the economics department, but we really feel they should be our business.

My biggest headache is dealing with the serious blow to the personnel department's staff in the aftermath of the November revolution. This department was a stronghold of the Communist party and despised by many. Here were stored the secret files on employees; the employees were not supposed to be able to see them. This department was a refuge for many incompetent workers for whom the party found comfortable positions. Several people were removed in this department after the revolution. It was no tragedy that some of them left, given their attitudes and orientation.

The worst effect has been in the minds of the people: the assumption that we in personnel are dispensable. Many people think we are still doing the same political activities, for example, keeping secret files on people. Our real work — supervising the support activities — is less visible, and they don't see our role in those tasks.

With the exception of the managing director, the supervisors and managers are not interested in using this department effectively. If a supervisor needing a blue-collar worker comes in here, he tells us to get one and "don't you dare deliver one I don't like." But supervisors will not provide any details about their requirements. The delivery system must work, but quality isn't important to them.

It is a difficult task to teach every manager how to be more effective. Some supervisors mistreat their subordinates, so the best people sometimes leave. Some go to other companies, some decide to start their own businesses. Many bosses have no concept that they should take care of their employees' continuous development.

The burden of the past forty years is on our backs. Personnel policy is still something of a dirty word. There would be an uproar if I developed a succession plan — it would be seen as the restitution of the old "cadre reserve system" by which the party controlled positions. In that system, the party looked first for the most loyal people, then within that group, they tried to find the most suitable person for the position. Those in the personnel department were the party's mouth. The stink of the party's dead body is all over us.

Air Products and Chemicals, Inc.

Background

Air Products and Chemicals, Inc. (APCI) is an international gas products corporation of 15,000, headquartered in the United States, in Allentown, Pennsylvania, with $3 billion in annual sales. The APCI acquisition of Ferox was negotiated by a team of U.S., German, and British APCI executives. Initially, Nigel Chandler, a British APCI executive, was appointed as managing director of the new Ferox-Air Products joint venture. In the following interview, Chandler shares his experiences and observations on the challenges Western companies face in acquiring and forming joint ventures in the new Czech and Slovak Republics.

Nigel Chandler, Joint-Venture Managing Director

I think you can see that Malec really runs Ferox. Last year in APCI there was a great deal of debate about the direction we were moving in forming this relationship with Ferox. You can imagine that it was a difficult decision. I genuinely believe it was the right decision. We will bring several important contributions to Ferox.

First, we bring know-how, which is a lot more than sheer technical knowledge. We bring specific know-how about the gas business. We know how to sell it commercially and where to make changes. We are a large successful gas company. Management skills that we bring are important also, but they're more difficult to define.

Second, we bring financial and accounting skills. Quite clearly, the free market accounting system needs to be adopted — particularly pricing and costing systems, which barely exist now. Everything was done by rules under the old system. We are setting up our accounting systems with the hope that they will be in accordance with the new Czechoslovak tax laws, which are due in January 1993. But at this point we don't even know what kinds of business expenses will be deductible in computing taxes.

Third, regarding the privatization, APCI brings technological skills, as well as marketing skills. Ferox brings local knowledge and a low-cost manufacturing base. It also has an existing customer base. We want to be able to manufacture our products here and also to export our products from this plant to the West. Compared to our other plants, we can make the product more cheaply here.

It is important to us that any acquisitions are made with the full support of local management. We need tremendous mutual cooperation. We think it is a good agreement, but we didn't undertake it lightly. It's not just the money, but the time. Heinz Hoffman, our European vice president, is spending a great deal of his time on this project, and our senior legal people are spending a lot of time on it as well. It is a tremendous investment of our most valuable managerial resources. The senior managers are very involved.

Of course, we have had to sell ourselves to Ferox. Ferox had choices — we're quite aware of that. We want to drive it, but it's important to work together. The engineering staff at Ferox are very good. It was important that we bring our best engineering people out to talk to them.

After privatization we are clearly going to have to bring in a Western accounting person, a manufacturing person, and other staff. Probably they will need to be single, as it would be very difficult to move a Western family to Decín. There are no English schools here in Decín.

We will also move key individuals from Ferox into jobs in our Western plants for six months to a year. We will actually place individuals in jobs for which they will be held responsible. We will be interchanging people.

APCI has been in most countries in Western Europe for up to thirty years and has more recently developed businesses in the Pacific Rim. We have experience in starting businesses in developing countries, but we have no experience in a former Communist country. It is very important that a company such as ours understands that this is not a third world country. It is a developed, heavily industrial area that has been dormant for many years but that still has employees with high educational levels and well-qualified engineers. The industry is old, but there is a lot of production capacity.

It appears to be quite difficult to recruit the people we want. There are many good jobs in Prague, and people with the skills we need are unhappy to move to Decín. It is partly cultural. People in Europe just don't move like Americans, and they value their leisure time more.

It is also important to a large multinational company to understand any extra liabilities that are taken on in the acquisition of a large manufacturing company here. For instance, any liability for previous environmental damage must be fully assessed and minimized by such actions as taking soil samples.

An apparent problem here is the lack of depth in managerial talent. Czech companies are very compartmentalized and are not very good at recognizing young talent; they don't think laterally.

One great concern to any Western company acquiring a Czech manufacturing facility is a general level of overstaffing compared to the West. This is particularly apparent in the administrative areas.

The employment ethic is amazingly harsh here compared to the Western standard. Of course, you know that the remuneration is very much lower and there have been no meaningful pay differentials. A welder may have a higher monthly salary than a salesperson. It is likely that Czechs with commercial and language skills will begin to command higher salaries as they gain experience.

Another example of the harsh personnel practices here is that a supervisor has the authority to cut an employee's bonus pay for what we would consider to be trivial things. At the end of the month he decides the employee didn't do a task he thought should have been done, and he cuts the bonus by 10 percent. Management here is based much more on fear as a motivation. Managers do not know how to motivate without fear. There is no concept at all of carrots, just of sticks. They have the concept of working hard but not the concept of achievement. However, we have built a fantastic commitment on our joint-venture team.

One thing that any Western manager who comes here will have to understand is the cultural differences. I've learned that some aspects of the culture you have to keep.

For one thing, I sign a lot more paper here in Czechoslovakia. This is definitely a holdover from the old Communist system, where all commands were written. It is very difficult to travel here on business; you need written forms and permission to travel. If there is not prior written permission for a trip, the insurance company will not reimburse if there is an accident. Salespeople cannot just get in their cars and call on customers. I have tried to get rid of forms and to just talk to my employees.

The Czech government must first approve the privatization plan, which is expected in the near future. Then, the Ferox and APCI managers will be free to begin to make the changes necessary to meet their strategic objectives, and the process of carrying out the acquisition by APCI will begin.

There are adjustments and changes in store for both companies in the future, but we are sure that Ferox will make a good partner.

III

Organization Design
Processes

Conflict

23
Weirton Steel Corporation

"I think it is by no means an understatement to say that the future of all companies may very well lie with how well they handle the people side of their business. And a notion that I like to keep in mind is that people must be led, and not driven."

— *Robert L Loughhead*

At the end of March 1985, Robert Loughhead, president and CEO of Weirton Steel Corporation, sat in his office looking over the copy of preliminary first quarter results that his secretary had just left on his desk. In his mind, he began roughing out the contents of his quarterly letter to the Weirton employees. He knew that he had a number of different issues to review in this letter, several of which were related to the figures in front of him. He wanted to make sure that he presented the employees with the facts about Weirton's recent performance. But he also wanted to touch on a few things that he knew were on the employees' minds: profit-sharing, foreign competition, projections for the future.

Loughhead believed very strongly in the need for and power of open and effective communication. In speeches, he cited Lee Iacocca's words, "The ability to communicate is every-thing," usually adding, "and he is absolutely right." In the Hot Mill Office at Weirton, a sign read, "The greatest illusion of communications is the illusion that it has been achieved." At Weirton, a manufacturer of general steel products (located in Weirton, West Virginia, in the upper Ohio Valley), communication took on a special importance. Over the past year, Loughhead had been leading Weirton Steel from the brink of economic ruin to a level of profitability superior to that of the top American steelmakers. But Weirton's turnaround was not just a simple economic revival of an ailing corporation. It was a special case — a unique transformation of an old-style company — that involved changes in how everybody in the company thought about themselves and their jobs.

At Weirton, the phrase "people side of the business" took on new meaning, for the Weirton Steel Corporation was the nation's largest and best known 100 percent employee-owned company. Under a program known as the Employee Stock Ownership Plan (ESOP) that went into effect in January 1984, every one of the company's employees — hourly workers and managers alike — was also an owner and a stockholder of Weirton Steel. But with these titles

---

This case was prepared by Gregory Roux under the supervision of Gary Shaw, Assistant Professor of Business Administration.

came burdens and responsibilities as well as privileges. The key to the spiritual "New Beginning," so vaunted in press coverage of the Weirton ESOP, was to be found in the concern and personal commitment exhibited by every one of these "employee-owners."

Loughhead called this crucial component a combination of "employee participation and participative management." He explained further: "Employee participation at Weirton Steel means groups of people with common work interests being trained in problem identification, problem solving, making recommendations for solutions and getting commitments from management to implement recommendations. And what is it all about? It is about change — changing the way we do things — changing the way we treat each other and work together. It means bringing mutual respect and dignity and trust into relationships." Participative management, added Loughhead, also requires an intensely time-consuming and personal commitment on the part of top management: "Persons who lead successful companies are finding the really critical success factors are listening to employees, listening to customers, and listening to suppliers. Believe me, there is a healthy dose of change in all that."

But if active participation by employees and management was the mainspring of Weirton's recent successes, effective communication provided the key to wind it regularly. Even before the ESOP was officially underway, the new Weirton was beginning to reap benefits from a communications program that was probably one of the most comprehensive and systematic corporate communication efforts launched by an American company. The emphasis on regular information flow was in itself as radical a departure from old Weirton managerial policy as the concept of employee ownership.

Weirton under National Steel

For many years, the Weirton mill was an operating division of the National Steel Corporation, one of the United States' largest steel manufacturers, based in Pittsburgh, Pennsylvania. National Steel, like the other industry giants, had enjoyed a number of very prosperous years during the 1960s and 1970s. They got through the lean recession years by living off the profits of the fat ones. But during the early 1980s, permanent changes in the industry rendered this strategy obsolete. By the time business activity took a nosedive in the second half of 1981, steel had become a global commodity. As steel consumption dropped by 25 percent in the crippled economy, U.S. steelmakers found their business eroding even further in the face of able foreign competitors who could compete successfully both on price and quality. Domestic steel producers suffered $7 billion losses in three years.

The market for tin mill products was particularly hard hit. Even before the latest economic downturn, major changes in packaging technologies had caused demand for tin/steel cans to shrink considerably. This trend was expected to continue. National Steel produced virtually all of its tin plate at the Weirton mill, and that product made up nearly half of the plant's output. The Weirton Division had been strongly profitable for years until a gradual slide began during the late 1970s. (Exhibit 23-1 shows a statement of operations and shipments of products of 1973-1982.) This decline accelerated sharply in 1981, and the plant suffered heavy losses until becoming employee-owned.

The hostile economic climate had an acute effect on National Steel. The corporation was operating further in the red during early 1982 that it had in over fifteen years. Overexposed, National Steel began looking for a way to pare down its operations. At the time, Weirton appeared to be a large liability with little potential for improvement. On March 2, 1982, in a carefully worded surprise release, National Steel announced its intention to divest itself of the facilities at Weirton.

The news exploded upon the town of Weirton with the force of a small atomic bomb, and the shock waves spread out from there. The town drew its economic and spiritual lifeblood from the Weirton plant. Without it, said a local leader, "this place will become a ghost town." Furthermore, the Weirton mill was the primary employer in the entire region. National's decision to phase down and eventually phase out the steel-making activities would eliminate almost eight thousand jobs. The majority of these workers were facing the prospect of unemployment in a region that couldn't absorb them in new jobs. The state of West Virginia stood to lose its largest private source of tax revenues.

The way the announcement was handled by National Steel caused almost as much anger and resentment as the decision itself. While everyone had known that National, like all the other industry giants, was having difficulties with poor corporate results, the employees at Weirton had had no idea that their jobs would be cut as a consequence. The company did nothing to prepare them for the blow. The workers found out about the planned divestiture when it was announced in the media.

This closed-mouth approach to communications within the company long had been the rule rather than the exception at Weirton under National Steel. The flow of information was very restricted. In management's view, knowledge was power, and they had no interest in sharing it with the rank-and-file. Top management alone reviewed financial information. Hourly employees were told nothing about Weirton's profitability or operational performance. In fact, the workers didn't have even basic knowledge about who the plant's customers were, what Weirton steel products were used for, or why things were done the way they were. The relationship between National Steel and Weirton employees was fraught with mistrust. "There was a very deep bitterness on the shop floor," admitted one company director. The men even believed that management kept two sets of books to keep them from catching on to anything. The Independent Steelworkers Unions (ISU) received strong support from the workers, and contract negotiations were always highly adversarial. Company management had been forced over time to sweeten salary and benefits packages, which put Weirton workers considerably above the industry average.

Founding the ESOP

In the March announcement, National Steel offered only one alternative to shutting down the Weirton division: the employees could band together and buy the plant under an ESOP arrangement. Within three days, the division management and the unions had formed a joint study committee to consider the proposal. The path from this initiative to the eventual adoption of the ESOP eighteen months later surmounted many obstacles.

First, the committee hired a leading consulting firm to do a feasibility study. Its findings were not entirely encouraging. Weirton's ability to increase sales dramatically was limited by its equipment, its location, and its markets. Prices could not be raised quickly because competition from imported steel and from domestic steelmakers with excess capacity would continue to depress prices. Weirton would have to reduce costs substantially to become profitable and to have cash for capital improvements. At least one billion dollars in capital expenditures would be necessary over the next ten years to modernize the mill facilities and allow Weirton to become fully competitive. But the consulting team concluded that the ESOP could work if Weirton could achieve a 32-percent reduction in employment costs: "an independent Weirton could be successful — but only with deep wage cuts and a better product mix."

Next, the joint committee retained an internationally known banking firm and a law firm to help structure the financing of the ESOP and assist in negotiating the terms of the buyout with National Steel. In coming to the bargaining table, National Steel technically enjoyed a position of advantage. If an agreement couldn't be reached, National would incur the cost of shutting down the plant as well as a substantial pension fund liability; Weirton stood to lose everything.

The costs of the professional services needed by the joint committee to structure the buyout were too great to be covered by the union strike

EXHIBIT 23-1 Weirton Steel Division-Operations and Shipments

Statement of Operations, 1973-1982 (dollars in millions)

	1973	1974	1975	1976	1977	1978	1979	1980	1981	1982
Net Sales	$685	$881	$719	$884	$921	$1,088	$1,179	$1,185	$1,284	$904
Cost of goods sold(a)	561	717	628	799	856	962	1,046	1,053	1,133	829
Gross profit	124	154	91	85	65	126	133	132	151	75
Operating expenses										
Mill overhead	27	31	34	35	39	43	49	54	61	61
Selling, general and administrative	19	17	17	17	20	16	18	20	22	19
Corporate expenses	5	6	6	7	7	19	21	21	21	22
Total	51	54	56	59	66	79	89	95	103	103
Net operating profit (loss)	74	110	35	25	(1)	47	44	37	48	(28)
Other income (loss)	2	1	1	1	1	1	1	3	1	(1)
Other expenses (b)										
Depreciation	22	23	25	27	26	27	28	31	32	30
Other	4	1	7	6	6	5	6	6	0	45(c)
Earnings (loss) before tax	$50	$87	$5	$(6)	$(33)	$16	$11	$2	$11	$(104)

Totals may not add due to rounding.
(a) Includes inventory adjustments and amortization of blast furnace lining expense.
(b) Does not include interest expense, because National did not allocate charges for capital employed on a divisional basis.
(c) Includes non-recurring charge for write-off of coke plant.

Shipment of Products, 1973-1982 (thousands of net tons)

	1973	1974	1975	1976	1977	1978	1979	1980	1981	1982
Hot roll	310	304	189	238	206	244	266	167	178	103
Hot roll bands	40	40	31	26	31	86	87	96	86	76
Cold roll	410	431	265	365	328	372	397	269	249	143
Galvanized	541	530	282	414	402	481	478	383	430	334
Tin plate	1,240	1,271	1,011	1,032	1,078	1,037	1,008	1,063	916	767
Other	227	152	56	110	37	14	7	49	2	—
Subtotal	2,760	2,728	1,834	2,185	2,072	2,234	2,243	2,026	1,859	1,423
Inter-division sales (a)	585	379	299	345	369	526	449	357	595	169
Secondaries (b)	190	109	99	148	198	181	159	124	123	85
Total	3,534	3,217	2,231	2,678	2,640	2,941	2,852	2,507	2,577	1,678
Total excluding secondaries	3,344	3,107	2,133	2,530	2,442	2,760	2,692	2,383	2,454	1,593

(a) Sales to other National divisions.
(b) Aged or off-specification products, which are generally sold at cost.

fund and employee contributions. The entire community pitched in to help. A massive fundraising campaign was run under the slogan, "Share Our New Beginning." Townspeople, businessmen, steelworkers, and their families played donkey basketball, organized fairs and art shows, ran contests and raffles — all to push their new communal dream closer to reality. A Weirton telethon on cable TV — broadcast only in the upper Ohio valley — alone netted $150,000. The cause attracted national media attention, as well as the political support necessary to obtain the tax relief and other agreements crucial to the economics of a buy out. The governor of West Virginia even opened a satellite office down the street from Weirton headquarters. Overall, the New Beginning fund drive raised more than $1.2 million to help defray the consulting and legal fees.

Ultimately, the Weirton negotiating team and National Steel arrived at a complex $386 million deal. National was to received $74 million in cash and hold two promissory notes worth $120 million, while the new Weirton Steel Corporation would assume $192 million of the old division's liabilities. Among the more important terms of the sale was National's continued responsibility for pension liabilities accrued through May 1983. One manager at National lamented that his company had been too accommodating and had "given away the store." A spokesman for Weirton limited himself to saying, "Weirton struck a hard bargain and got a good deal."

Other terms provided for the establishment of an Employee Stock Ownership Trust that would acquire 6.5 million shares of Weirton's authorized common stock in return for a $300 million note. As the Weirton Steel Corporation made annual contributions to the ESOP trust, the trust would return funds to be credited against the trust's note, thereby increasing the owners' equity in the corporation. This new equity, in turn, would be allocated to accounts established for individual employees on the basis of their salary (as a portion of total employee compensation). When all the shares were distributed, union members would control approximately 80 per-

cent of the stock. The agreement would also required that Weirton's board have eight outside directors until 1989. As one of the architects of the deal explained, "This is not industrial democracy, it's worker capitalism. Just like any other company, stock-holders do not make day-to-day decisions." Before the deal could become valid, however, a majority of Weirton's employees had to vote for acceptance of all the terms, including the ratification of a new collective bargaining agreement containing the recommended wage reductions.

The final task of the joint committee was to orchestrate the companywide voting procedures. September 23, 1983, was set as Vote Day, when Weirton's unionized employees would express their approval or disapproval of the ESOP. The timing gave the joint committee only about a month to educate the rank and file about the complex issues involved in the ESOP agreement. By now, Loughhead had been offcially hired (temporarily as president of National's Weirton division until the acquisition was closed), and he played an active role in selling the deal. In a huge communications push, involving open meetings, telephone hot lines, official disclosure statements, company publications, and other supplementary material, each worker had carefully explained to him what it meant to be an owner as well as an employee.

When Vote Day arrived, much of the city gathered at the community center. The purchase agreement and new labor contract were approved by the steelworkers by a margin of 8 to 1. The whole town of Weirton celebrated with a noisy, spontaneous parade.

The New Communications Program

Now offcially the CEO of the Weirton Steel Corporation, Loughhead was faced with the challenge of leading the new enterprise from mere feasibility to a concrete and successful reality. But he found that, in spite of the general jubilation over the ESOP agreement, the relationships between management and the workers were anything but ideal. Some friction and misunderstanding still remained, a troublesome legacy from the days under National.

Loughhead moved quickly to break down these barriers. One of his first major projects was a concentrated effort to improve communications. His plans included frequent interviews, regular press announcements, and corporate advertising to enhance the company's external image. But the primary focus was on radically improving internal communications. In an open letter that went to all Weirton employees even before the formal signing of the agreement with National in early January 1984, Loughhead laid out the details of the new communications program. Common to every element of this program was the underlying belief that the best employees were those who understood the company's business well and appreciated their role in it. Information was to be accurate and unvarnished. The new plant newspaper, *The Independent Weirton*, typified this philosophy: directed by a joint union-management editorial board, it went far beyond the usual limits of a plant newspaper in that the company didn't sanitize its content.

Over the course of the year, all the pieces of the new communications program were put in place. Employee reaction was extremely favorable, and feedback from the workers was plentiful. Based on these responses, the communication channels were refined and expanded. One idea, for example, led to establishing a new opportunity for communication—hourly employees began visiting customer plants to see first-hand how Weirton steel was being used and why quality concerns were of such vital importance.

Loughhead believed that direct contact between himself and the workers was an especially important component of the communications program. He realized that, as the leader of the new Weirton, his actions took on symbolic status; for the hourly worker, he personified the ideas and methods that offered Weirton its hope for the future or its link to the past. Loughhead carefully cultivated an air of approachability and candor in his weekly "face to face" meetings with employees in the various work areas. Together with the president of the labor union, he would talk about the state of the business, listen to comments by the workers, and answer questions. The atmosphere of these sessions was informal; employees found they could ask tough questions and get equally frank responses. Reactions to these meetings were extremely positive.

Since Loughhead could meet with only a relatively small part of Weirton's employees in any given week, he felt that his open letters to the other workers were practical and important extensions of this direct contact. These letters to each "employee-owner" varied in their contact from in-depth discussions of the importance of quality consciousness at Weirton to more general reviews of quarterly results. The quarterly review letter was, by now, an entrenched tradition. Loughhead aimed at fleshing out the results in a personal way for the employees—before the offcial news release went out to the public, or even before the results were published in *The Independent Weirton*, as was the usual practice.

December 8, 1983

Dear Fellow Employee:

In one of my recent letters, I told you that we were developing a program of employee communications that would keep everyone informed about what was happening in our new company. That communications program is now well along, and this is a report to you on what you may expect in the near future.

The program has been discussed with the I.S.U. and I.G.U. leadership as well as key people throughout our company. I'm happy to report that these people have been enthusiastic about the idea of increased communications and the way we plan to go about it.

Here is what is in the works:

New employee publication — This will be a monthly tabloid and will bring you a wide variety of news and opinion about all phases of Weirton Steel's activity — changes, improvements, sales success, production records, new equipment, stories about our employees, our involvement in the community, special problems we must solve—and a lot more. One special section will be employee feedback — a "man-in-the-street" feature that will carry your response to an important and timely question.

Two current publications, "Independent Weirton" and "Current Events" will become part of the new employee publication. The type of articles usually found in those publications will now be regular features in the new tabloid.

By absorbing the two publications, we'll be able to have expanded communications without greatly expanding the cost.

On-stream date: First issue in late December or early January.

Employee Mailings — This will be a series of mailings to your home on those subjects you want to know about. In addition, these mailings will be used to bring you news about important developments that are too "hot" to hold for an upcoming issue of the employee tabloid.

In the beginning, these mailings will come from me. Later on, you'll also be hearing from other people in our organization.

An important part of our communication program will be your feedback. So that you can give me your reaction and your ideas and opinions, almost every mailing will include a reply form. One of these reply forms is part of this mailing.

Bulletin Boards — We will have a bright, clean, well-lighted and well-maintained bulletin board in at least forty-five locations. If you would like to see a board installed where one does not now exist, let us know. (Use the appropriate space on the enclosed form.)

On-stream date: Renovation of boards to begin no later than January 1.

"Face to Face" — This part of our communication program will be a continuous series of meetings in which I'll visit work areas and office areas to give you a chance to ask questions and voice your opinions and concerns face to face. In turn, I'll try to bring you the latest news and developments at Weirton Steel.

On-stream date: Already underway; meetings have been held in the Central Machine Shop, Sheet Mill, and the Blast Furnace. A schedule of subsequent meetings is included with this mailing.

Pipeline — We're revising this telephone "hot line" to make it more useful to you and more responsive. First, we'll eliminate the one-minute "commercial" you hear when you call in. Second, we'll answer the phone "live" as often as we can (rather than use a tape recorder exclusively). Third, we'll acknowledge all calls within twenty-four hours. Fourth, we'll get back to you with answers promptly and directly.

On-stream date: "Pipeline" is now operating; by December 15 we'll be answering "live" part of the time and will acknowledge all taped calls within twenty-four hours.

Internal TV Network — We now have thirty TV monitors and the same number of tape decks throughout our facility. We believe we can add just a few more and create a "network" that will enable us to do many good things with our communications. Some examples are training, news that "won't wait," in-depth discussions of important issues by the heads

of I.S.U., I.G.U. and myself, customer stories (so we can all see where and how our products are used), successful new applications — and a lot more.

On-stream date: Full network by February 28; thirty operational units by January 30.

The items above are just seven of the communication vehicles we are preparing for you; there are several more in the planning stage, and I'll be telling you about them in the coming weeks.

I can promise you one thing for certain: our communications with each other are going to be the very best they can be.

But — communications won't work if they are just oneway. And that's why we need your help. We need to know your ideas, your opinions, your concerns. The communications must be two-way. In other words, input from you and your fellow employees is vital.

I'll provide the means if you provide the input. We can start with the reply form and envelope enclosed with this letter; you can give me your reaction to the communications program and tell me what else you would like to hear about.

With your input and your interest, communications can be one of the driving forces behind our success. Let's make Weirton Steel not only the largest, successful employee-owned company in the world, but also the company with the best informed, most communicative employees.

Sincerely,

Robert L. Loughhead
President

Enclosures

Mr. Loughhead:

Here are my reactions to the planned program of communications at Weirton Steel:

_____ I like the idea of more communications
_____ I don't like the idea

Here's why:

_____
_____
_____

I believe we can improve communications by doing the following:

_____
_____
_____

Here are subjects I would like to know more about:

_____
_____
_____

EXHIBIT 23-2 Weirton Steel Corporation: Financial Statements (dollars in thousands)

Year/Quarter	1984/1	2	3	4	1985/1
Net Sales	$283,127	306,276	256,110	229,614	295,562
Cost and expense	267,019	276,638	233,677	211,733	279,607
Operating profit	16,108	29,638	22,433	17,881	15,955
Interest expense	6,433	6,884	6,595	5,528	5,766
PBT *Profit Before Tax*	9,675	22,754	15,838	12,353	10,189
PBT (% of sales)	3.42	7.43	6.18	5.38	3.45
Tons shipped	572.7	610.8	485.2	439.0	592.4

Here's where I think a new bulletin board should be located:

_____

_____

_____

Name _____

Department _____

Address _____

City/State _____

The Quarterly Letter: March 1985

Loughhead thought he would try to present the results from the latest quarter in the context of Weirton's operations since the establishment of the ESOP at the start of 1984. (Exhibit 23-2 shows financial statements from 1984 and first quarter of 1985.) He had been generally pleased by the successes that Weirton Steel had achieved during the last year, and he knew that the workers had been pleased as well. The company's healthy performance, contrasting sharply with the losses and marginal profits under National, validated the new ways of working together and the many sacrifices that had been made. Loughhead wanted to reinforce the positive aspects of what had been accomplished, but at the same time, he aimed to present a balanced and realistic picture of exactly how far Weirton still had to go.

Weirton had slated an ambitious capital spending program that would be creating tremendous future cash flow requirements. The need to continue rebuilding and modernizing the plant was urgent. It was anticipated that another $300 million to $400 million in capital would be needed over the next five years just to stay competitive. In 1985 alone, $65 million in expenditures had been planned for pollution control, to build blast furnaces, revamp a galvanizing line, and improve a continuous casting machine. These improvements could lead to improved product capabilities and considerably lower costs, but such benefits would be realized only further down the line.

The profit-sharing mechanism, almost surely to be triggered during the 1985 fiscal year, was creating yet another strain on the corporation's cash flow. The ESOP agreement had provided for the allocation of one third of earnings to the employees in the form of cash to begin when the company's total equity exceeded the $100 million mark. Loughhead knew that the workers would be particularly interested in hearing that preparations were being made for disbursements. After sacrificing pay and benefits to get the Weirton Steel Corporation off the ground, employees were anxious to see tangible returns. Already this quarter, the company had begun to provide for the liability so that the impact would be spread over several quarters.

To meet these cash demands, Loughhead knew that earnings levels higher than those of the first quarter would have to be maintained. Steel prices showed no sign of lending a hand. Selling prices remained very depressed, putting great pressure on margins. U.S. steelmakers, operating at low capacity levels, were discounting heavily in the marketplace. Import levels remained very high despite efforts by the Reagan Administration to negotiate voluntary import restraints with foreign producers. In short, Loughhead realized that despite the uplift in the economy, competitive conditions continued to be exceptionally severe. Weirton Steel would have to look instead to stringent cost reduction measures, productivity gains, quality improvements, and higher yields as the best means for relieving the margin squeeze and freeing up additional cash.

Loughhead didn't want to forget to mention, however, that Weirton's bookings for the second quarter were good in all areas. The company had succeeded in gaining forty-eight new customers in the first quarter. Combined with the two hundred customers gained in 1984, these new clients would help keep up operating and employment levels.

24
FMC Aberdeen

Kenneth Dailey, site manager for FMC Corporation's Green River, Wyoming, facility, leaned back in his seat in the conference room near his office. He was listening to a team of employees tell him about their visit to FMC's Aberdeen, South Dakota, plant and the unusual operating procedures they had observed there. Dailey was intrigued with the results that Roger Campbell, plant manager at Aberdeen, and his predecessors had been able to achieve at the plant, and he had sent this team to see it and make recommendations about whether or not it would work at Green River. He wondered if the Aberdeen system would work for his operation as a whole, in part, or not at all; if there were parts that might work, he wondered what they were and how to implement them.

Dailey knew that his operation was different from the Aberdeen plant in a number of significant ways and that these differences would make his deliberations difficult. First, Aberdeen had only a single customer, while Green River had over 100 and distributed its products worldwide. Second, the Aberdeen facility employed only 100 people, while Green River, with 1,150 on the payroll, had more than 10 times that number. Third, Aberdeen produced basically a single

product, while Green River had several product lines. Fourth, Aberdeen had been a new start-up five years ago, while the first of the several Green River plants was begun in 1948. Dailey was supervising the start-up of three new plants in his complex this year, though, and recognized that similarity. Fifth, the two units functioned in very different industries—Aberdeen in defense and Green River in chemicals. Finally, Aberdeen had no union, while the Green River site worked with the United Steel Workers of America.

Despite these differences, there were several features of the Aberdeen management approach that were either appealing to Dailey or suggested that the Aberdeen approach might fit his operation. Operating under FMC corporate guidelines, both management teams enjoyed, along with the other 87 FMC North American sites, considerable flexibility in how they ran their businesses. Both units also had a common link to the FMC corporate image and objectives and thus had some similar operating values and systems. Dailey also knew that productivity in the Aberdeen plant had grown dramatically since its opening and that costs had continued to drop. Finally, Dailey felt that the principles and values upon which the Aberdeen system were built

Prepared by James G. Clawson. Copyright ©1990 by the Darden Graduate Business School Foundation, Charlottesville, VA. 11/8/90.

aligned well with his own. As Dailey listened to his team describe the Aberdeen system, he continued making mental notes and questions about the system and its applicability to the situation in Green River.

Aberdeen

When FMC's Naval Systems Division (NSD) won a secondary sourcing bid with the U.S. Navy to supply them with surface-ship missile launching canisters, many factors pressed NSD management to consider a new plant to fill the contract. Headquartered in Minneapolis, Minnesota, NSD was a large facility, with over 40 acres under factory roof and more than 3,000 employees. Its primary product was naval surface-ship gun mounts, large systems that were produced at the rate of about 1 per month. The smaller (2' x 2' x 20') missile canister could be produced at the rate of about 2 per day and was viewed by NSD as a volume product that required a different production approach from the gun mounts. NSD executives also noted that since the canister contract was a fixed-price one, the new operation was much more like a "commercial" operation than the cost-plus government contract under which NSD usually worked. Furthermore, recent investigations of the local business environments suggested that the tax regulations, community support, and available labor pools and wage rates were more favorable in nearby South Dakota than in Minnesota.

With these factors in mind, NSD's director of manufacturing, Ron Weaver, chose Bob Lancaster as the new plant manager. Lancaster had been plant manager in FMC's construction equipment division's Bowling Green, Kentucky, plant when Weaver had been director of manufacturing for divisional headquarters in Cedar Rapids, Iowa. While in Bowling Green, Lancaster had captured Weaver's attention with his unorthodox managerial style and ability to raise plant productivity some 10 to 15 points higher than the parent Cedar Rapids facility. In the fall of 1984, Weaver and Lancaster chose Aberdeen from among many aggressive offers as the site for the new facility. Aberdeen was a town of about

30,000 people located 90 minutes flight time southwest of Minneapolis. The Aberdeen Development Corporation had offered to build a building to FMC specifications, to give FMC favorable tax status, and to assist in whatever way possible in return for the selection. FMC negotiated a 7-year lease on the new building, with options to renew annually thereafter.

FMC and the Vertical Launch Missile Canisters

FMC Corporation was a Chicago-based conglomerate with $3.4 billion in 1989 sales spread over five major businesses: Industrial Chemicals ($975,000,000), Performance Chemicals ($566,000,000),Precious Metals ($190,000,000), Defense Systems ($900,000,000), and Machinery and Equipment ($783,000,000). The company's products included military equipment (including the Bradley Fighting Vehicle), a variety of industrial chemicals, gold and other precious metals, agricultural chemicals and a variety of specialty chemicals, and a broad range of specialized machinery and equipment for the material-handling, petroleum, and food industries.

Although NSD had seen the missile canisters as a natural extension of its work with other naval surface-ship weapons systems, the new product was different in many ways and surprisingly complex. First, the canisters had to be strong enough to withstand the tremendous heat and explosive force of the ignited rocket engines that propelled the missiles. A structurally failed canister could endanger the entire ship and the lives of its crew. The missiles used were powered by solid-propellant engines that, once lit, could not be shut down. If a missile failed to launch, the canister would have to contain and control the engine until it burned out. For this reason, the canisters were fitted with a controllable fire extinguisher system that could flood the entire canister. The tubes were also fitted with launching electronics that armed the missiles' warheads and ignited the engines. The insides of the tubes were lined with a system of rails and flanges that guided the missiles out of the tubes on a straight course and allowed their folded guidance fins to extend properly. The inside of the top part of the tube was also covered with a shock-absorbing material to ease the impact on the warheads of any inadvertent bumps from loading or the rigors of sea passage. The entire canister had to be clean and relatively free of dirt to minimize the possibility of malfunction. The tubes were also fitted with an anti-electromagnetic shielding system that shielded the missiles and their launch electronics from any disruptive electromagnetic force. The top of the canister had to have carefully designed tearable membranes to keep the tube clean and yet allow free and easy passage once the missile was ignited. Also, amid the extremely corrosive conditions of sea life, the canisters had to be completely rust proof. Pinpoint-sized holes in the rust-proofing paint on the canisters would begin to run and wear through in as little as two weeks at sea. The canisters were designed and built to fit in eight-tube modules in large holes in the decks of missile cruisers and frigates. Consequently, they also had to have armored, water-tight, and carefully synchronized sections of decking with a hatch for each tube to be secured in place after the loaded tubes were lowered into the decks of the ships.

NSD also knew that modifications of the present tube design were coming soon. New prototypes would probably include stronger structural components, heat-sensitive and flame-retardant paint materials that would immediately swell to 32 times their normal size in case of a fire, and more sophisticated electronics subassemblies. Consequently, if the new facility was to survive, it would have to have the capacity of responding to and contributing to these new designs as they came along.

Bob Lancaster

Lancaster was known throughout FMC as something of a maverick. As the plant manager at Bowling Green, he had tried several new approaches to management, most of which were based on principles of participative management, trust of production workers, and respect for the individual. One Lancaster story originated when he worked where they built cranes in Bowling Green. One young man from a poor family came and asked for the blueprints to the company's crane. He said he was going to build a scale model, sell it, and then go to college. Lancaster gave him the blueprints. Several months later, the boy returned with a remarkable scale, working model of the crane. Lancaster asked him how much it was worth. The boy said $5,000. Lancaster paid him $20,000 and installed it in front of the office building as a marketing tool. The divisional controller expressed serious concern with Lancaster's action. Lancaster persisted, though, knowing that he was paying for the boy's college education.

Stories like this about Lancaster circulated through the company. One time, Lancaster had told his employees that they knew what needed to be done and he expected them to do that without bothering him. If they needed something they couldn't get, he remarked offhandedly, then steal it. The next morning as Lancaster arrived in his office, he noticed that his water cooler was gone; he later found it in the welding bay. Recognizing this as a test of his commitment to his ideas, he left the cooler where it was and did without himself. Another time, Lancaster had a customer who was complaining about late delivery of parts. When another order for a small part came in, Lancaster had a parachutist carry the part and jump into the customer's back yard. Then he called to see if that was fast enough service. Once he had been pressing divisional leadership for a new retractable factory door that would accelerate the flow of materials. The division had balked at the cost and refused. Lancaster then began encouraging an employee to drive his fork lift truck through the wall, saying that it was the only way they could get through the bureaucracy. At first, the employee resisted but finally gave in and destroyed the wall in question. Lancaster got his retractable door.

Roger Campbell, the first quality manager at Aberdeen and later plant manager, explained one of Lancaster's central beliefs:

He had a saying, "What's the worst they can do to me?" And then he'd sit and tell you the worst. "The worst they could do is kill me, right? And as long as I'm OK with dying, I'm OK. I've made my peace with dying. What is it that's gonna stop me?"

In his negotiations with Ron Weaver, Lancaster had said that at Aberdeen he wanted to build a participative-management system on the principle of trust, involving self-directing work teams that would eliminate fear from among all employees. In January 1985, Lancaster began to assemble a team to build and manage the new plant. He wanted people who were open to new ideas, who had a history of participative-management interests, who were dedicated to serving the customer, and who were not only willing but eager to create something new, something outside the mainstream of current management practice. He chose five men, four of whom had grown up in the South Dakota area and who therefore wanted to live in the Aberdeen area for more than professional reasons. During this recruitment period, Lancaster also began to formulate the basic principles that would govern the new plant. He printed these up for all to read and to use in training his new team (see Exhibit 24-1).

Lancaster's desire to create a new management system at Aberdeen presented something of a problem for the plant's only customer, the U.S. Navy. Navy contracts required adherence to MIL-Q-9858, which specified inspection systems, supervision, and other quality-control processes that would not be manifestly visible at Aberdeen. Roger Campbell explained that Bob Lancaster was a master at sitting down with other human beings and talking about what it is that's important and what isn't. He spent a lot of time with the local NAVPRO [U.S. Navy purchasing department] folks telling them that he considered them his customer, and that he was going to do what was necessary to make sure that he kept them satisfied with what was going on there. He convinced them that participative management and the quality standards were not mutually exclusive. He spent a lot of time doing just that. This is the "commercial mentality" we were trying to get. Commercial people are business-men.

Having selected his leadership team and cleared the way with the Navy, Lancaster began organizing his staff and teaching them the principles that would govern the plant. The entire organization would be built on trust of every employee: they would eliminate fear altogether; they would eliminate supervisors and foremen by organizing self-directing work teams; they would expect people to assume and exercise responsibility; they would pay everyone a salary based on their ability to contribute; and they would maintain high standards of quality and service. Lancaster began meeting with his staff every night after work in Minneapolis for extended dinner discussions about how they should organize the plant. These sessions often lasted for three hours and extended over a three-month period. Out of these meetings and Lancaster's values statement, the group developed the initial concepts that were to become the Aberdeen Credo shown in Exhibit 24-2.

Employee Selection

Employee selection for the Aberdeen plant became a rigorous process that focused on a four-hour assessment-center activity. Lancaster hired a consultant to lead his team through a two-day seminar that identified the kind of employee that would thrive in the new environment. Their underlying philosophy was that technical skills were more easily trained than personal and interpersonal attitudes and skills. Once the group had agreed on what those skills were, the consultant developed four group exercises for use in identifying those skills. The skills and attitudes targeted by the workshop were group skills, communications skills, personal skills, problem-solving skills, results orientation, and leadership skills. These were the same criteria that the company determined to use in performance evaluations.

The recruiting assessment centers were typically conducted on Saturday mornings. During the morning, 12 applicants were divided equally into 2 groups, each with 2 assessors. As the groups worked on the various problems and

**Exhibit 24-1 Aberdeen Plant Philosophy
and Policies**

Robert F. Lancaster
Plant Manager
01 Jan 85

The Aberdeen plant will operate on policies and procedures that come from a foundation of "TRUST." This is in line with modern American business practices and certainly encouraged by FMC Corporation. For clarification, I quote from "Building Trust in the Workplace" by Gordon F. Shea:

America is undergoing a social revolution as profound as its technological one. The transformation, as far-reaching as any in history, is as fundamental as the emergence of democracy and self-government, the growth of public education, or the rise of capitalism.

This benign overturning is in the way people interact with one another for mutually beneficial ends. And the business community has positioned itself at the forefront of the revolution, though sometimes unknowingly.

Never before have we seen such a pervasive interest in participative management, quality circles, union-management committees, work teams, quality of work life programs, and the like. At their core, each of these innovations draws on the power of mutually beneficial interaction.

And this unleashing of the human potential, a great resource indeed, will continue to shape our future. Across America, individuals are increasingly searching out, informally, through their churches, schools, and institutions of higher learning, human relations skills to improve the quality of their personal, family, and organizational lives. These efforts to become more effective, to develop problem-solving skills, and to operate more productively in organizations signal a new era of human growth.

How do you identify these "budding revolutionaries?" As Caesar's spies knew when ferreting out early Christians, you note the words they use, the deeds they do, the ideas they express, the locations they frequent, and with whom they associate. From these, you can ascertain their beliefs and guiding philosophy. As with those earlier, gentle revolutionaries, many of our "new breed" have chosen the inner way and are therefore difficult to discern.

During the past 10 years with FMC I have explored many of the concepts and practices of working together, with common goals, in an open communications environment. I have found these concepts to be much more productive than our historical "win-lose" approach which invariably results in "lose-lose" outcomes.

Quality

Product quality is everyone's concern! The plant is to function with a total quality concept where each piece part is to be known to meet specification and each operation is performed in a manner known to produce the specified result. Defects (which can cause expensive rework and scrap) are to be prevented by focusing on process control inside the plant and vendor manufacturing techniques for buy parts.

Design Engineering, Manufacturing Engineering, Production employees, and Quality Control employees are to work as a team to identify and solve quality problems. Responsibility for documentation and follow-up of these activities rests with the Quality organization.

Customer Relations

Customers (the U.S. Navy) are not adversaries—they are the people we intend to please. We will interface openly, with integrity. We will provide all appropriate information in an accurate and timely manner. We will assume that the customer is the final authority on what is required and make every effort to accommodate his wishes.

Community Relations

This Plant is a corporate citizen of Aberdeen, South Dakota. It is concerned about the environment and will take appropriate action to assure its preservation. It will financially participate in community activities, and its employees will be encouraged to take active leadership roles in civic, charitable, political, social, educational, and religious activities.

Employee Relations

All employees will be on the salary payroll and will share the same benefit programs. A highly productive, disciplined work environment will be maintained. All employees will be treated fairly, thereby making unions unnecessary.

Health and Safety

FMC is particularly concerned about the physical and mental well-being of its employees. Every employee will be asked to participate in maintaining a safe, healthy and pleasant environment.

Cost Containment

This Plant represents a large investment by FMC Corporation as well as the city of Aberdeen. The product for this Plant was competitively bid, and fu-

Exhibit 24-1 cont. Aberdeen Plant Philosophy and Policies

ture contract awards depend on our ability to remain competitive.

Opportunities for product cost reductions should be sought and cataloged so that proposals can be made at the appropriate time. Individual productivity must be maximized to reduce labor and overhead costs. All expenditures should be tested for their value added to the business.

Systems
Systems are to be kept simple! Current technology makes it possible to handle large amounts of infor-

mation very efficiently. Since our plant is quite small we will emphasize the use of micro-computers using commercially available software. All personnel will need an understanding of these devices in order to effectively participate in the business.

Organization
Job titles and labor grades will be developed to accurately reflect the unique circumstances at Aberdeen. Because of the size, each job title will have a broad job description which may include the combining of functional responsibilities in nontraditional manners.

Exhibit 24-2 The Aberdeen Credo

Quality: Everyone is responsible for quality in everything we do.

Customers: We will willingly satisfy our customer through honesty, integrity, cost and quality.

Community: As citizens of Aberdeen, we will actively promote and participate in community activities and work to protect the environment.

Employees: Employees are treated fairly and trusted to actively participate and communicatein achieving objectives.

Health and Safety: Safety and health is everyone's responsibility to each other and must not be taken for granted.

Cost: All employees continually strive for the most productive use of labor, money and materials to ensure our future.

Systems: Systems will be kept simple and understandable while remaining efficient and effective.

Organization: Broad jobs necessitate nontraditional, creative methods. All employees creatively define their responsibilities and work beyond job title and salary grade boundaries.

tasks given them during the morning, the assessors would observe and rate each applicant on the key dimensions. Each assessor used a 1-7 rating scale where 4 was the average acceptable level of that skill in that assessor's view. After each task, the assessors and applicants would rotate to give the assessors each a chance to observe all of the applicants. When the applicants had been dismissed at noon, the assessors would remain to compare notes and ratings, to generate a composite score for each applicant, and to make hiring decisions. Typically, only 4 of the 12 applicants would meet the assessors' minimal standards. The opportunity for assessors to review hiring criteria and values and to reach consensus on what they looked for in candidates was a significant culture-building aspect of the assessment center.

All of the exercises in the assessment center were designed to highlight aspects of group-ver-

sus-individual behavior. The goal of the first exercise was to have each and every member of the team construct a completed square from parts of squares given to each team member. The second was a survival exercise where team members had to rank the importance of a list of items left to them in the midst of a life-and-death emergency (like being shipwrecked at sea, crash landed in the subarctic, or stranded on the moon). The third exercise was a hiring decision that had to be made by a leaderless group. Many of the "candidates" were minorities. The fourth exercise was a problem-solving situation where each of the team members had important but disparate clues to the solutions.

By 1990, this recruiting-and-selection process had produced 100 Aberdeen employees, 74 of which worked in production. The administration manager commented that they had 30 percent women plantwide, and about 8 percent minorities, primarily American Indians. He noted that the goal of the plant was to have 50 percent women.

Training

Lancaster and his staff expected that, in order to make the experiment work, employees in the facility would need to have introductory and ongoing training. They began with an orientation to the philosophy of the Aberdeen plant in which the idea that everyone was responsible for the success of the facility was presented. If this were to work, management noted, there could be no game playing and no withholding of data in plant relationships. Lancaster and his team told the new employees that they were to be included in the decision-making process and they were to be trusted with all relevant management information. Furthermore, employees were taught how to give and receive information about each other as data rather than as judgments or criticisms.

Fear of every kind, especially fear of failure, Lancaster noted, also had to be eliminated. Failure was sometimes the result of taking good risks and usually had a positive effect on learning and growth. People should not be held at risk for making honest mistakes and for learning from them. He stressed that the usefulness of any innovation was limited to the time that a better idea came along and that every employee should be seeking new innovations constantly. The management team taught that the "invented here" mentality caused people to stop looking for and accepting new solutions. They stressed that there were no job definitions in the plant, and that therefore everyone was responsible for making top-quality canisters profitably. The management team also discussed their own willingness to share power and to include all employees in the decision-making process. Fear and trust, they said, could not survive in the same environment. People had to be free to do the right thing and to make decisions without fear of reprisal and arbitrary anger and dismissal. Lancaster knew from his previous experiences that the new employees would test these ideas before

accepting them fully.

Lancaster and his staff retained a consultant from New Jersey to conduct three nine-day seminars divided into three-day segments on topics like personal growth, accepting responsibility, interpersonal skills, nurturing fellow employees, giving clear and descriptive feedback, causation, a sense of "family" at work, and team management skills. These sessions were called "Mastery Training" and included the idea that people were perfect as they were, and therefore employees had no need to try to change others. In Mastery Training, useful feedback consisted of relating data and facts, including how one felt about those facts. The sessions were intended to point out that these ideas were not simply nice, abstract ideas, but the values upon which Aberdeen would operate. By 1990, three groups of fifteen employees had been through the full nine days of Mastery Training. They had been encouraged to pass on what they had learned to those who had not yet gone. At least one employee interviewed claimed that these seminars changed her entire outlook on life and work.

In the emerging Aberdeen culture, criticism and allegation were replaced by direct feedback. Campbell explained:

> We talk about feedback being neither positive nor negative; it's only feedback. That's an important piece of what we do in the evaluation system. When you're giving somebody feedback, you're saying this isn't negative or positive; it's just feedback. For example, "I notice you were late three days last week. When you were late, that caused me to work harder; I noticed I was pretty irritated about that." People talk about how this training helps them in their families. We talk about the plant being a family. As a result of being here, people should be doing better with their lives and taking more responsibility for their lives.

Team Organization and Management

The fundamental work unit of the Aberdeen organization was the work team. Teams ranging in size from 3 to 16 managed virtually every aspect of the plant's work and reporting. Teams scheduled work hours, purchased materials and tools, planned work schedules, coordinated with other teams, evaluated team members' performance, recommended salary increases, generated reports, and dealt with virtually every problem that arose in the running of the plant.

Every employee at Aberdeen was assigned to a team. A team leader was chosen by the team from among volunteers. The team decided how long team leaders would serve; this tenure varied from a few weeks to two or more years depending on the team leader's willingness and perceived competency. Each team also selected a supply person, a safety person, and a quality person to pay particular attention to those areas. Teams met as needed to discuss and resolve issues that confronted them. A team member of the Deck and Hatch team (responsible for assembling the decking and hatches that covered a pod of 8 canisters) who had been with the company 5 years and in manufacturing environments for 19 years, commented:

> We have 13 on our team now. When we have problems, we don't wait for a meeting. If our leader met with [the plant manager] about a schedule or something, he'd come back and holler, "Come on over! We need to talk for a few minutes." And we would get things ironed out right away. That really helps. We do not wait for pay evaluation time to talk. If we have problems, we take care of them right away. It is so much easier that way. If you have something on your mind that you are going to talk to this person about it, go see them now. If you do, a month from now, that person might have realized what he was doing and have changed it. The problem is, if you don't get it out and talk about it, it just keeps getting worse and worse. Our people have learned that.

Each employee's work schedule at Aberdeen was administered by his or her team. One team member outlined the system:

> On a normal week, our average hours are 6:00 to 4:30. We say you have to call in if you're not there by 8:00. Eight o'clock is late, but unless it really disrupts the function of another station or another team or something, anything between 6:00 and 8:00 is okay. We work 40-hour weeks, 4 or 5 days a week. If our schedule is good, some of the teams may work 4 10-hour days and then they have Friday, Saturday, and Sunday off. Then the rest of us use Friday for any kind of catch-up paperwork or updating manufacturing procedures or anything like that that has to be done. Working 50 hours a week is pretty normal out here. This year we have cut down a lot compared to the last few years. We work the overtime to insure our jobs. We'd rather work overtime than to have more people hired so that we were working an even 40 hours and then sometime in the future have a layoff. Now, we would just cut back to 40. It helps keep our jobs secure.

The plant manager added:

> The interesting thing is that the teams will make it OK for people to work different hours. Mothers out here with young children are allowed to work around baby-sitting schedules. When people have baby-sitter problems or things like that, the team will figure it all out and still get the work done. I couldn't administer that. Nor could anybody else. They can administer that so much better than anything I could do.

Team leaders were an important part of the Aberdeen team organization. Donna Cwikla, a former team leader for over two years, described the role:

> Team leaders facilitate. If you see a problem, you call them together. If someone comes to me and says, "I have a problem," you don't solve it. You say, "Okay, let's get a meeting." You keep things going if meetings get side-tracked. If they get into personal fights or just talking, the team leader has to get them back on track. Team leaders

are responsible. You've got to make schedule, so you can suggest this and that. But it is up to the whole team what your schedule is, what your hours are, and what we do. Team leading is facilitating mostly.

I think the hardest thing for me [as a team leader] was to step back and stop taking responsibility. If the team failed, I would take it as if I had failed. That was really hard to get over. But once I realized that it was going to be the team's responsibility, whether I was a member or the team leader, it took a lot of the pressure off.

The importance of selecting the right kind of people to fit the system was highlighted by this team member:

One thing that works against us is people who withhold from actually involving themselves or people who just don't want that responsibility. There are very few of those people. Most people enjoy the fact that they can be responsible and take responsibilities easily. But there are a couple of people that I have worked with who said, "I don't really need this job; I don't really have to participate and be responsible; my husband has a better job and we get by; or I am just working here because xyz." That makes it hard.

The team will sit down and counsel that person, if they are like late for work, if their quality is bad, or whatever the problem may be, just their attitude, or getting along with other people. At any given time, your team or a team member can ask for an evaluation of you. If the team feels that it is necessary to have it documented and put it into your personnel file, they will bring in Sheila [human resources manager] and sit down and go around the room and say, "This is what I feel, and I don't think you are living up to what the expectations are of this place, and we either feel that you should conform or else find another job." They are usually given a choice and a time limit to how long they think that it should take a person to

come around. Usually people react fairly well. There have been a few people who have just left; they just didn't like it. And they just didn't fit in. Some people who just didn't like working indoors.

One team member talked about program innovations that teams made:

We are responsible to keep our own area clean. There for a while, it had gotten so that production was really heavy, and the people weren't caring about the way the place looked as much as what they had when I had started. I have always been kind of picky about that, because I knew how good and clean the place can look, where other people if they come in and it is halfway dirty they never realize that. So, I went out and purchased two signs that said "Cleanest Area in the Plant," one for the plant and one for the office. We rotate them on Mondays. The last team to receive it will go around, survey the plant on Monday morning before the 8:00 plant meeting and then come in and give it to another team to keep for a week. It's an honor and lots of fun. We used to have a Pig Pen award, but the negative began to outweigh the positive. We usually concentrate heavily on the positive. Negative just shows up. You don't have to try to find it. And people bring it from other plants, other jobs, their home life, whatever. You don't have to work to make negative feelings happen.

Information

Managing at Aberdeen required individuals who were willing to share information. Campbell held plantwide meetings Monday and Thursday mornings involving all 100 employees; these meetings were a primary means of communication in the Aberdeen plant. Roger Campbell described these meetings:

We talk about schedule; we talk about quality; we talk about customer questions and what's going on with the competition.

About costs, about our new budget, about overtime, productivity—all those things. We talk about the contract: "Here's the contract, and here's the contract delivery requirement. Here's how we think we have to smooth this work to make this factory work and help the contract schedules. Here's how each team has to interface with each other team in order to get this flow going so that it gets through the assembly in the time it's supposed to. Here's when we are going to start ordering materials and tooling." We run that meeting as a group. Then people go off in their teams and talk about whether or not this makes sense, and can we live with this schedule, and maybe we ought to move this to there, and so on. So, when they're done, it's their schedule; it's not mine.

On Monday, we open it up; we talk about everything. We talk about the company picnic, about the fishing trip, personal sorts of things that go on. We talk about anything that anybody wants to know about—softball games and who went fishing last week. We make that a time when people get together and talk about what needs to be talked about. See, my perception is that it'll happen anyway. I'd just as soon have it done there where you aren't asked six different times to tell the story over and over. Observers who just spend a day in the plant won't see that time savings. They'll just say, "Gee, you guys spend a lot of time in meetings." Thursday's meeting is more focused towards the plant, the schedule: Who needs help; what are we going to do about this weekend?

Two large charts in the cafeteria provided focal points for these discussions. One was a diagrammatic layout of the plant with movable stickers showing each canister's location in the manufacturing process. The second was a large table showing productivity measures for each department in the plant. Since these charts were updated weekly, anyone in the room could easily see what was going well and what needed further attention.

With regard to management information, Campbell described the custom-built Aberdeen system:

We built a customized dBase system in this plant. The neat part of it is that it fills the demands of the new government requirements, material-handling requirements, and accounting system, including the 10 key elements. We think that $200,000 systems don't do the things that ours does. We tie in and integrate shop-floor control systems with the purchasing and quality system. And we run all that off the master schedule. For $30,000. That was a part of our credo. We keep things simple.

Rewards

The Aberdeen reward structure was unusual in a number of ways. First, all employees at the Aberdeen plant were referred to as technicians and were paid on a salary basis. Those who were production technicians were also paid overtime for any hours worked beyond 40 per week. There were no annual bonuses, no profit-sharing plans, no stock-option plans. Elaine Jensen, a team member, described one reward the teams had in addition to salary:

We do have a thing going right now where if we can keep four or five factors, including productivity, sick time, our downtime, and our absenteeism, at certain rates, we get a day off around the 4th of July. So, it's sort of like a bonus or an incentive type day.

The evaluation system included a continuous peer-review process. Team members were expected to give accurate and timely feedback to their team members on their work on an ongoing basis. When evaluation time came around, the team decided whether or not a team member had learned enough and contributed enough to deserve a pay increase.

Qualification Standards

At Aberdeen, team members were expected to learn all of the jobs associated with their team so that, if one person was gone, others could fill in.

This was done on a voluntary basis at a self-determined pace through a certification process. Team members who were certified on each set of tasks assigned to the team were expected to respond to requests by other team members for coaching, training, and eventual certification.

People were paid according to the number of skills, called "qualification standards," in which they were certified. Each skill had a number of points assigned to it according to the contribution it made to the plant's work. The more jobs members could do, the more valuable they were as employees, the more they were paid. The plant had guidelines for how long a person had to work with a particular skill before being eligible for that pay level. Overall, though, a person could move to the top of the five-step pay scale within two years. An outline of the pay system and the related qualification standards appears in Exhibit 21-3.

Certification for each of the qualification standards involved four basic, agreed-upon steps. First, an employee had to find a coach who was willing to teach the set of skills to him or her. Second, the aspirant would observe the certified coach perform the task to see how it was done correctly. Third, the person would perform the task under the supervision of the coach until the coach was satisfied that the person had learned the skills. Finally, the person would perform the tasks alone for subsequent review by the coach. When the coach was satisfied that the person could perform the task in the skill set independently and properly and with high quality, he or she would sign a certificate indicating that the person was "certified" in that skill set. Roger Campbell described this as "watch while I do it; do it while I watch; do it alone; follow-up." Elaine Jensen described her experience learning new skills:

When I came out here, the only thing I knew about welding was that you weren't suppose to look at it because you would go blind. We lived on a farm, and my dad told me. I went into receiving, but I wanted to learn to weld. I worked hard on those certifications. To me, it was like going to trade

school. That's what this whole shop is. People are not hired on their technical skills, they are hired on their behavioral factors. We make our salary and are still being taught a skill that we can take with us the rest of our lives. I think it is fantastic!

Every Monday and Wednesday, we had a class, on our own time. We came out here, and we welded. They've changed that now to get more people certified because of the demand for welders. So they pay them during the regular hours now. I learned how to weld machine parts and to paint. Some of those skills you can take with you no matter where you go. Once you learn them, it's great.

Layoffs, Turnover, and Morale

There had been only two forced terminations at Aberdeen in recent history. In both cases, the employee's team members concluded that the individual did not fit temperamentally with the management concepts at Aberdeen. One individual, described by several Aberdeen employees, simply wanted to be told what to do and not have to accept responsibility to find out what to do.

Turnover at the Aberdeen plant, at 5-10 percent annually, was not unusually high or low. Most people who left the plant did so because they did not like the independence of the working culture, because they had found better paying work elsewhere in the country, or because they were going back home.

A team member noted:

We've had maybe 5-percent turnover since I started, I think. I think that is fair to say. I have been working on the [company] newspaper lately and, on the last three issues, I have gone back through all the people who had started out here and the people who have left, trying to track down everybody who has moved on to other things. What I have found is that everybody has really done great with their lives. Everybody

Exhibit 24-3 Skill-Based Pay System

The Aberdeen FMC employee skill-based pay/evaluation system is based upon two criteria: a) technical competence and b) social/interpersonal skills. The employee attaining the subsequent step in pay must complete both criteria.

Technical Competence
Technical competence is demonstrated by means of a series of qualification standards. Qualification standards have their roots in the "Nuclear Navy" and are based on demonstrated skill in particular areas of plant operations. For example, an employee would have to demonstrate competence in operating a forklift (including safety and maintenance requirement), slinging, lifting, etc., to be qualified in material handling. These skills are demonstrated by a plant employee who has been identified as qualified in that particular area. Completion of a qualification standard is indicated by the qualified "signer" signing off on demonstration indicating satisfactory completion.

At the Aberdeen plant there have evolved approximately 70 qualification standards. These standards range in length from several sign-off lines to as many as 30. Each qualification standard, when complete, indicates attaining skills in a particular area of plant operation.

Generally there is a qualification standard for each work area in the plant, mandatory areas such as safety, hazardous materials, material handling, etc., and "elective" qualification standards such as Lotus, dBase, Multi-Mate, Assessing, etc.

A point value is assigned for each elective and plant work area qualification standard. This plant value is based upon complexity, skills required and duration to complete. At the Aberdeen plant a group of Shop Technicians and Office support personnel review the standards and establish point values. This group will generally meet annually for this purpose. At that time any requirement for new standards will be established, if necessary.

The point designation is used as a basis to determine when an employee is eligible to be considered for a pay increase. At Aberdeen, the employee review group is integral to the process of determining what the point requirement is in order to be eligible to progress to the next pay level. For example, there are approximately 700 points available, 400 points required to reach the top of the pay scale (5th step) and 40 points to be eligible for the 1st pay evaluation.

Social/Interpersonal Skills
Upon completion of the technical requirement the employee will petition the team he/she is working with for a pay evaluation.

In this process the team members and any plant employee who has input will evaluate the employee. All data is acceptable with certain "ground rules" being observed:

- Whatever is said with the employee out of the room must be said with the person in the room.

- Employees giving input must speak for themselves and in the first person. Ex: "I notice that you are very competent in your grasp of the first station assembly requirements."

- Give straightforward feedback. Use examples to illustrate points. State facts and tell how you choose to feel about the stated action. Ex.: "I noticed that you were late coming back from break 3 times last week. That causes me to work harder to make schedule and I feel angry when that happens."

- Do not attack the human being. Follow the precept that all human beings are perfect and there may be behaviors that the person may choose to alter. Come from the position that everyone wants to work and do a good job.

- Establish eye contact.

- Keep the comments serious. Joking causes confusion about whether you mean what you say.

- Feedback is neither positive or negative. Data given is merely data and the person may choose how he/she interprets the feedback.

- Demonstrate care and concern for the employee.

Based upon completion of technical requirements and acceptable social/interpersonal skills, the team members determine by consensus if the employee is entitled to the pay increase.

Most pay evaluations end positively. The session is training in the art of feedback and straightforward talk. The pay increase is often secondary to the feedback session. That gets everyone on the team "flat" with each other and gives a forum to get personality and habit differences on the table before they get out of proportion. It also establishes the legitimacy of an evaluation or feedback session whenever it is required.

It will typically take 18-30 months for an employee to get through the five pay steps. In order to accomplish this the employee will have to pass through 4 of the 7 teams.

Exhibit 24-3 cont. Skill-Based Pay System

A monthly point system was established for positions in the plant that did not allow for completion of qualification standards or where longer time in the job is desirable. Examples would be maintenance and the receiving area. At Aberdeen, we determined that 10 points per month for a maximum of 24 months was a norm for those positions.

The employee acceptance of this pay/evaluation system has been extraordinary. They have a stake and responsibility in the pay system and an influence in the outcome. The feedback sessions generally have a positive outcome, and the employees normally are relieved to hear honest comments from their peers.

At Aberdeen, we incorporate the same evaluation system for office support and staff personnel. Employees have the opportunity to evaluate the plant manager in the same fashion as their peers.

Positions Earning Points by Month
The following positions are treated as exceptions to the Pay Progression System.

Since these team members are expected to stay in these positions for a minimum of one (1) year (and more than likely longer), they will accrue qualification points per month at the rate listed below. The maximum number of points that can be acquired by working in any of the jobs that have monthly points is 240. Once 240 points have been earned, through one or more of the jobs listed below, no additional monthly points are earned.

Points Per Month	Position	Team
10	Material Coordinator	ASSY
10	Material Coordinator	CCA
10	Material Coordinator	D&H
10	Material Coordinator	WELD
10	Machining Expert	MACH
10	Maintenance	WELD
10	Maintenance	FINISH
10	Category H	CCA
10	Category D	CCA
	Total People	9

Pay Progression Criteria

FIRST STEP

- Accumulate 40 qualification points.
- Complete all mandatory qualification standards.
- Obtain team consensus in formal meeting that pay increase is warranted.
- Complete 1 welding certification or a soldering certification.

Note: All Shop Technicians are expected to progress to the 1st step in 3-12 months after hire. Shop Technicians will be counselled by their respective team and management if they take longer than 6 months.

SECOND STEP

- Accumulate a total of 95 qualification points.
- Complete 1 elective qualification standard.
- Complete 1 weld certification and 1 soldering certification, or 2 welding certifications.
- Obtain team consensus in formal meeting that pay increase is warranted.

Note: All Shop Technicians are expected to progress to the 2nd step in 6-24 months after hire. Shop Technicians will be counselled by their respective team and management if they take longer than 12 months.

THIRD STEP

- Accumulate a total of 205 qualification points.
- Complete 2 weld and 1 solder certifications, or 3 welding certifications.
- Complete a total of 3 elective qualification standards.
- Obtain team consensus in a formal meeting that pay increase is warranted.

Note: All Shop Technicians are expected to progress to the 3rd step in 12-36 months after hire. Shop Technicians will be counselled by their respective teams and management if they take longer than 18 months.

FOURTH STEP

- Accumulate a total of 300 qualification points.
- Complete a total of 5 elective qualification standards.
- Obtain team consensus in formal meeting that pay increase is warranted.

FIFTH STEP

- Accumulate a total of 400 qualification points.
- Complete a total of 7 elective qualification standards.
- Obtain team consensus in formal meeting that pay increase is warranted.

Note: The team consensus meeting required at each pay progression step is an opportunity for the team and management representatives to give that individual

Exhibit 24-3 cont. Skill-Based Pay System

feedback both positive and negative on their performance.

The individual desiring a pay increase will ask his/her team leader to schedule the meeting. At this point, the team leader should check with the Human Resources Rep to see if all requirements have been met (# of

points, mandatory and elective quals, certs). Schedule the meeting with Human Resources Rep and Plant Manager or designate.

The team and management representatives will meet prior to inviting the individual to join them to develop a consensus as to whether the individual should receive a pay increase based on that individual's performance and behavior.

Qualification Standard Listing

Qual #	# Points	Description	Type
10	15	Assy Station 1	A
12	10	Safe & Arm Drilling Station 2A	A
45	10	Assembly Inspection	A
54	15	Assy Station 5	A
79	0	Blue Print Assembly Mk14	A
11	15	Assy Station 2	A
42	20	Final Acceptance Test	A
46	10	Safe & Arm Assembly	A
78	0	Blue Print Assembly MK13	A
9	95	Totals	
48	10	Soldering Cable Conduit Assembly	C
56	15	Test and Wrap Station	C
58	10	TB2/J2/JI Assembly	C
60	10	J3 MK14 CCA	C
62	5	Box Build-Up Mk14	C
34	5	Pre-Assemble Box MK13	C
55	5	J-1 Kit Assembly	C
57	10	W2-W3 Sub-Assembly	C
59	10	PI MK14 CCA	C
61	5	P2 MK14 CCA	C
63	10	Final Box Assembly MK14	C
11	95	Totals	
70	15	Hatches Sub Assembly	D
72	20	D&H Assembly I	D
74	15	D&H Test	D
81	20	D&H Assembly IV	D
83	15	Elevator Door/Cyl Brack/Adjust	D
93	10	Inspection/Close Out	D
71	15	D&H Assembly II	D
73	20	D&H Assembly III	D
75	5	D&H General	D
82	10	Mechanical Sub Assembly	D
84	5	Deluge	D
11	150	Totals	

EXHIBIT 24-3 cont. Skill-Based Pay System

Qualification Standard Listing

Qual #	# Points	Description	Type
16	0	Receiving Plant	E
22	0	First Aid	E
25	0	Computer-DBase III	E
29	0	General-Assessment Center	E
32	0	General-Public Relations	E
37	0	General-Group Facilitator	E
39	0	General-Consensus Building	E
98	0	Station Training Requirements	E
9	0	Gage Calibration	E
17	0	Just in Time	E
24	0	Computer-Lotus	E
26	0	Computer-Word Processor	E
30	0	General-Career Development	E
35	0	General-Group Problem Solving	E
38	0	General- Training	E
99	0	Misc	E
16	0	Totals	

Qual #	# Points	Description	Type
7	20	Finishing-Ablative/Autoclave	F
14	15	Finishing Inspection	F
36	10	Finishing-Interior Paint	F
47	5	Finishing Receiving Inspection	F
77	0	Blue Print Finishing MK14	F
6	10	Finishing-Exterior Paint	F
8	10	Finishing-Surface Prep	F
23	10	Finishing-RTV-Baseplate	F
44	15	Flame Spraying	F
76	0	Blue Print Finishing MK13	F
10	95	Totals	

Qual #	# Points	Description	Type
15	20	Machining Inspection	K
49	25	MK13 Machining	K
51	10	Tool Set Up	K
80	0	Blue Print Machining	K
66	55	Launcher Cable Prints	K
5	15	Deburring	K
31	20	Machining-Cincinnati	K
50	25	MK14 Machining	K
53	10	De-Grease	K
8	125	Totals	

EXHIBIT 24-3 cont. Skill-Based Pay System

Qualification Standard Listing

Qual #	# Points	Description	Type
65	40	Launcher Cable Manufacturing	L
67	5	CCA & L. Cable Safety/Quality	L
68	5	CCA & L. Cable Hand Tools	L
69	5	CCA & L. Cable Automatic Tools	L
5	110	Totals	
			M
13	0	Quality Program	M
19	0	Manufacturing-Material Handling	M
21	0	Manufacturing-Safety	M
33	0	General-Employee Orientation	M
18	0	Shop Floor Control	M
20	0	Manuf-Hazardous Material	M
28	0	General-Plant Security	M
64	0	Employee Expectations	M
8	0	Totals	
1	10	Longeron Fabrication	W
3	15	Shell Fabrication	W
27	5	Weld-General	W
41	15	Leak Check/Path Weld	W
52	15	NCI Inspection	W
2	15	Panel Fabrication	W
4	15	End Casting Welding	W
40	15	Pad Welding	W
43	15	Welding Inspection	W
9	120	Totals	

Type Codes

(E) - Elective
(M) - Mandatory
(W) - Welding
(K) - Machining
(L) - Launcher Cables
(F) - Finishing
(A) - Assembly
(D) - Deck & Hatch
(C) - Cable Conduit

Source: FMC Aberdeen internal document.

seems to be really happy, really content with what they have done and feels leaving FMC was a good decision for them. FMC does not discourage that.

Roger Campbell also commented on turnover:

I don't want you damaged when you leave here. If it doesn't look like you fit into this organization, then it's time now for you to go find a job someplace else where you'll be happier and more comfortable. There's a lot more responsibility here than at most places. Are people going to stay here for money? No, probably not. They stay because they are in control of their lives, their destinies here. The idea of having people walk around with smiles on their faces while they're doing their job seems like it's foreign to many people. And you spend half of your life here [at work]! People at work ought to be happy.

Morale was consistently high. People commented on how much they appreciated being trusted by management, having management's help in times of need, having a management who listened to their concerns, and having control over their work environment, pace, and structure.

Managerial Style and Organizational Culture

Dailey's team noted that a key balance in self-directed systems was the amount of upper level involvement in planning and implementing such systems. For some, this was a paradox. Mark Scherschligt, manager of administration, commented on the importance of the business leader in making a system like the one at Aberdeen work:

I truly believe that this has got to come from the guy at the top. You could pronounce that, "yeah, there is no fear; everything's on trust." But if you don't act like that and really have a commitment to it, it won't

work. It is a commitment. You've got to let people make mistakes. We see that when people from other FMC plants come to visit, that the guy at the top says, "yeah, I want this to happen, but I'm not willing to give up any of the power that I've got to make it happen." I see that so much when people come visit here. That's the thing that's got to be changed, that unwillingness to give up their so-called power.

Given this emphasis on the leadership of the operating officer, Dailey's team had asked Campbell about his managerial style:

I am not going to run off and fire you or take disciplinary action against you for telling me how you feel about something. Now, if they can tell me how they feel, it also follows that I get to go out and tell people how I feel about what they're doing. One of the rules we've got here, and we've got damn few of them, is you don't attack the human being. We try to run this place like a family. Once people come in here, they're OK like they are. We don't go around trying to change human beings. And what the heck, I'm too tired and too busy to go off and try something impossible like changing human beings anyway. So, I'm OK with people being like they are. Once in a while, there are some things that I point out to them and ask them to consider changing.

Now, this isn't a democracy. There are certain things that we do here, and we decide as a group, as a plant, what's unacceptable behavior. I usually sit and talk to every person who gets hired here and spend some time with them. I tell them that I don't want them to lie, cheat, or steal, and I want them to understand that they're responsible for their own actions in this place. Once I get people to nod their head that they agree with that, that's about the only rule we need to put into place. Lancaster expanded it and said that you could run an entire plant based on The Ten Commandments. That's probably true, but I've got it down to you can't lie, cheat, or steal. That's what we ask people to do when they come to work here. Don't lie, cheat, or steal, and be responsible for your own behavior.

I tell them, "I want you to run this like it was your own business; I want you to help me manage it. If you know the right thing to do, by all means, do it." We give the team leaders, for instance, purchasing authority to $500. You hear horror stories about people who need six signatures to get a wrench. We tell them to go to the store and buy a wrench, and we sign the invoice when it comes through. New employees always test us on this. They'll come in without exception and ask about buying something. And I ask them, "Is it something you need for the business? Would you do this if this were your business?" If the answer to that is yes, then I ask them, "Why are you asking me about it then?"

We allow for some mistakes. We consider it a learning experience. I could tell an example about myself. We have to vacuum out these canisters about four times, and it is hard on vacuum cleaners. I came up with the idea that a sump sucker [a large machine used to clean out the sumps of oil-cooled machine tools] would work like a huge vacuum cleaner and cut the vacuuming time in half. It was a good idea in theory; however, a sump sucker doesn't work very efficiently if you don't have it in liquid. And the hoses are really bulky and hard to haul around. So, I went out and bought one of these things for $12,000, and it didn't work well. So, I sent it back, and I took some pretty good ribbing from people. People don't walk around saying, "I wonder if I'm going to lose my job" about things like that. They don't wonder if they're going to get sat down and hear the riot act. We tolerate honest mistakes all the time here.

There were a variety of social activities that also helped build the family culture at Aberdeen. The plant sponsored softball teams, basketball teams, fishing tournaments, and an annual all-employees meeting. Donna Cwikla explained:

They make a point of it. When the plant started, family activities were everything. They had swimming parties, roller-skating parties; the whole point wasn't how many canisters you were going to get off that week; it was—we are going to be a family. We are going to do things together. And it is still that way; that's as important as anything else.

The annual off-site, all-employees meeting provided another example of employee involvement. Before 1990, these meetings were often seen by employees as boring and dry, filled as they were with overhead transparencies, charts, statistics, and long recitations of the past year's events. In 1989, the employees came to management and asked if they could plan the day. Given the chance, a team took responsibility for the entire event. They planned the day around the credo, dividing the group up into teams who made presentations and led cheers on each element in the credo. Six months later, photos of the event still hung in the main corridor of the plant and people still talked with enthusiasm about what a good experience it was.

When asked if they thought the Aberdeen system was a durable one, Dailey's team reported that Campbell expressed confidence that the Aberdeen system was well in place and that, even if a more traditional, authoritarian manager were to replace him, the system would carry on. "I don't think you could change it if you wanted to. It's down the path now," he had said. He also expected that he would have some say in who the next plant manager would be and that he would try to make sure that a person with values consistent with the Aberdeen culture would be selected.

Aberdeen Structure and Organization

The organizational structure at Aberdeen was simple. The plant manager had a staff of four: a quality and engineering manager, a purchasing manager, a production manager, and an administration manager. None had a secretary. One office technician answered the phones and greeted people at the front door. Campbell commented that if you wanted a letter typed, you learned how to use a word processor (listed, by the way, as one of the skills on the qualification-standards list).

It was clear at Aberdeen who the plant manager was, but the usual trappings of executive title were missing. Campbell usually wore boots, jeans, and an open-necked shirt to work. He parked in whatever slot was left open. He did have a nice, new, expensive lap-top computer on his work counter in the plant manager's office, but he noted that anyone who needed it could come in and use it.

Aberdeen and FMC

The Aberdeen facility was a cost center for accounting purposes within FMC. Initial engineering and product designs came out of NSD in Minneapolis, as did sales and marketing support and government liaison. At the same time, Campbell noted, the plant's products were built, tested, inspected, shipped, and invoiced from Aberdeen, so that the Navy began to look at the plant as its primary contact for the canisters. Aberdeen did not maintain its own general ledger but consolidated with NSD. In absolute terms, the Aberdeen plant was not a major contributor to FMC. FMC's defense segment was about 30 percent of overall sales, and Aberdeen's part was only 3 percent of the defense business.

The plant manager reported to two people at NSD: one a dotted-line relationship to the program director for vertical launch systems and the other a solid-line relationship to the site manager at NSD. This was a change from recent history when the Aberdeen plant manager reported directly to the vertical launch system's program director. The plant manager was evaluated on meeting production schedule, on controlling costs, and on the quality of the product. Human resource activities for the plant were managed locally.

Management Succession

After two years, Bob Lancaster had established with great care and consistency the operating culture outlined here. At that time, he returned to NSD headquarters in Minneapolis, where he began teaching similar principles to the larger installation. Then one day, he complained to his wife of chest pains. She called an ambulance and, when it arrived, accompanied her husband to the hospital. As she stepped out of the ambulance at the emergency room, she collapsed and died. Lancaster passed away two days later. When Lancaster had left Aberdeen, he was replaced by Jeff Bust.

Jeff Bust

From the description by those who worked for him, Bust, who graduated from the U.S. Naval Academy and had an M.B.A. from the Amos Tuck School at Dartmouth, really lived the Aberdeen philosophy. Sheila Quinn, the human resources manager, described his style:

> He would try to get you to think about things differently. He would go around to the plant and spend a lot of time just talking with folks trying to get them to see things a little differently. Jeff actually lived it. He would go out and actually work in an area. He would go out and work with the welders, and he lived there and learned how things were going by actually spending time with the teams. Even as plant manager, he would go weld. Both he and Bob would get to where they wanted to get you to go. Bob would talk about it a lot longer; Jeff wouldn't. Bob would bend your ear for 2 hours, where Jeff would take 30 minutes. Roger's more easygoing than both of them.

Elaine Jensen, a member of the Cable Conduit team, added her description:

> Jeff Bust was always in here with his worn-out, steel-toe work boots on. He always wore these shabby, shabby coveralls that we always begged him to get rid of, but he would spend more of his time, I would say

he spent 60 percent of his time if not more, out on the shop floor. He would weld, he would grind, whatever awful job needed to be done. He would walk around and say, "Well. So, where are you having a problem in your team today?" It meant a lot to the people out on the floor, because here was the plant manager—this was the guy that was our role model—and he was coming out here. Nine times out of ten he got the real rotten jobs, the jobs that everybody would kind of leave to the last, or the dirtiest, or, you know, the heaviest. That meant a lot.

Roger Campbell

Roger Campbell became the third Aberdeen plant manager in 1988. He had received his bachelor's degree from South Dakota State University in mechanical engineering and gone to work for FMC directly out of school. He had worked in the construction-equipment division and observed Bob Lancaster as he managed the Bowling Green plant. When he heard that Lancaster was putting together a team to start a new plant in Aberdeen, South Dakota, he had contacted Lancaster and convinced him to let him join the team. Although he knew that Lancaster's approach was not his own style, he was intrigued by Lancaster and welcomed a chance to live near the area in which he grew up. He started out as the quality manager for Aberdeen, then went to manage production and finally, plant manager. By 1990, he was 41 and had 2 children.

Campbell wasn't sure how people would describe him, but offered that he was pretty easygoing about most things. The thing that made him angry was:

Dishonesty is probably the biggest one. People not taking responsibility. And people who quit without giving me notice.

With regard to his future, Campbell mused: I'd like to go run another plant someplace; maybe start one up again. If I went to work in Chicago [at company headquarters], I'd probably have to get an M.B.A. before I did

that. My challenge is to go find another place to work and let somebody else come in here. That's a responsibility I've got to the folks in a plant this size.

If I went to another plant, I'd do the same thing I'm doing here. It would take longer. There's a magic number in the world someplace, and I haven't found it, that says this is the optimum size of factories. Maybe it's 200, maybe it's 500, I don't know. It's not 2,000, I don't think. It's easier if you've got fewer numbers of people because you can sit everybody down in one room and talk to everybody at once. They all get the same story; they all get a chance to get out what they've got on their minds.

I came out of a traditional UAW shop with the yelling and screaming, "Do it this way," and all that. It doesn't really work. If you're desperate, for a short term, you could get 10 more points out of this plant in productivity. You go around and rant and rave and scream and fight. But it doesn't last. Here we "benchmarked" the standards. We work on learning curves. We're working on a 79 percent learning curve here on decks and hatches. We think that's about 6 points better than Minneapolis was doing.

Mark Scherschligt, the manager of administration, described Roger:

I've known Roger for a long time. I knew him back in a previous life in Cedar Rapids, and he's changed a lot. Roger's changed an awful lot. He was kind of authoritarian, and he's changed into a people-type person now. In fact, when he first started, he had a lot of doubts about this philosophy and how this thing would work. Through his involvement and just working on it over time and since becoming plant manager, he's switched 180 degrees from where he was before. He really believes in it, really feels that it's important to push responsibility down to the lowest level, and he supports it all the way through. I think the swing for Roger took a couple of years, to really sign up for it and to live it.

Elaine Jensen commented on the change in management:

I had a lot of problems dealing with the change in management. Bob was like my father. He was the man who gave me all the encouragement and support and the nurturing that my own father hadn't given me in a completely different adult life relationship. And then Jeff Bust, he was a young, highly intelligent, brother type of a guy, and when he left and Bob left, I felt really alone. A lot of the people I had started with have left. When Roger came, he was okay, but he was very traditional—up until last November, when Roger finally just kind of got it. He realized he was more empowered by releasing his powers than by dictating. It really empowers the people to release your power. He had no idea, I think, how powerful he really became after that.

Career Development at Aberdeen

The topic of management succession stimulated Dailey to ask about career development at Aberdeen. He could see how the rotating training was a career development of sorts, but with a flat organization, there wasn't much room to move up. On the rotating assignments, the team reported on Elaine Jensen's experience:

I started out here in November 1985, right after the grand opening, doing a little bit of receiving. That was before any teams were really born. Then I became a member of the Weld team. Then I went into the Finishing team and was team leader there. Then I went into assembly. I worked there for quite a long time, and finally into the Cable Conduit team. I am still a member of the Cable Conduit team, but I work outside of the team as a material coordinator for the cables and the Cable Conduit teams doing a lot of receiving of their supplies and what nots. So, I have kind of circled the place and come back to receiv-

ing, which has changed a lot.

What about quiet people? Some people when they come into a team are quiet. But the more you get to know people, the more they come out of their shell. They do open up. They do take responsibility. On every one of the teams, we have a supplies person, a safety person, a quality person, and we have a team leader. Everybody gets a chance to take on one of those responsibilities. So, being a team member responsible for an area encourages that person to grow. I have seen massive growth in people that before would have had a real tough time just speaking in front of a group. We do that, too; we take turns. In the Thursday plant-wide meeting, we take turns standing up and conducting the meeting.

Visitors to Aberdeen

The unusual nature of the Aberdeen operation had, as Bob Lancaster predicted, made it something of a model to be studied by others. In fact, interest was so high that observation teams, like the one from Green River, came through at the rate of about two per month. Roger Campbell commented:

People come to visit and walk away from here a little disappointed because I don't give them a cookbook about how you do this. There is no magic to it. If you really believe that people want to do a good job, and that's a well-worn thing, but if you believe that and that they're intelligent, sensitive human beings, and if you just get out of their way, they'll do the job for you; then I guess it's all pretty easy.

It's the middle managers that are stopping this whole thing from going on in the whole country. They're the ones that don't understand about sharing their power. For years, you were taught: when you get promoted, you've got a little more authority. Then, the game is to go collect all the authority you can and all the power you can, and keep it. Try it the other way. Go get all the authority you can, then walk around and give it away to people, and see how it works. It's amazing how it works.

We've got folks that offer, and they've done it, to get in a car, drive to Indiana, and pick up 10 gallons of adhesive because we're out of it, and we couldn't figure out how to get it here any faster. No one told them to do that. And if you would have, they'd have thought you were crazy. They wanted to do it because that's how you get the product out of the door. They come up with stuff in this place on a monthly basis that amazes me. All this by just saying, "Now, if this was your business, what would you do?"

There are some people in the world, a few of them—two that I can think of—that came through here, that leave because they don't like this management style. They want to come in here in the morning and be told what to do, be watched, make sure they did it right, and then go home with their minds shut off. They are absolutely miserable here.

One team member who had been at Aberdeen for 5 years and working in manufacturing for 19 years before that reflected on one visiting team meeting he had participated in:

I have talked to people out of a Wyoming plant, out of an Idaho plant, out of a West Virginia plant. I have talked to people out of San Jose and all over who came here and looked at our system. They come thinking "It ain't going to work, it ain't going to work!" and by the time they leave, they're convinced. They go out and see how happy and cheerful the people are that are working here. The best part is we are building quality product, and we are moving it fast. So they say, "Maybe this will work." By the time they leave, they have gotten an idea. And lo and behold, they get back and start talking about this to other people.

But to take it into a union? I shouldn't say it, but I got my foot in my mouth one day. I was in a meeting of some men who worked in the

soda ash plant in Green River, Wyoming. I was saying to them, "I don't think I have worked in a union job before." I said, "I don't think that you could take this kind of a management system into a full-blown union shop." My team member kicked me under the table, and I told the other person, "I don't care. I want everybody at the table to hear it." I didn't know who they were. It was the union president.

They were opening new sections to their plant, but it was still management against workers. The union president called me back approximately a month later, and said, "I took this idea back, and I think we are going to be able to lighten up the union in this plant." He said, "I don't think it will work in a union shop in the traditional way."

Sometimes Aberdeen employees were invited elsewhere to explain the system to others. In one such trip to another FMC facility in Minneapolis, Elaine Jensen explained the plant and then fielded questions. One listener, referring to Roger Campbell's trips to Washington, said:

"Well, if you guys are so equal, why is Roger in D.C. and you're here?" They had asked me so many questions, I felt like I had really been prosecuted by noon. They were asking me all these questions, and I answered them basically as honest as I could, and when Roger came back from Washington at noon, this man asked Roger the same questions. It was as if Roger and I had sat down and had planned this all out, had it all written down, 'cause his answers were almost word for word what I had said. It was funny. And people had actually come up to me afterwards and apologized for being rude and disbelieving. I think it is a philosophy that we truly believe in. We have the credo that we have written and we work by it; we live by it. I think if you ask anybody out there [in the plant], they all know. It's a way of life; it's nothing special, we just do it. It is easy to have the same answer to come out of 20 people, because that's just the way it is. It's nothing special to us. It's a way of life.

Results

The results of the Aberdeen experiment through the end of 1989 were dramatic. Productivity had been increasing steadily at a fast rate, costs had been decreasing consistently, and employee morale continued unabatedly high. Employees were learning a variety of new skills that they could use, enjoyed a variety of tasks and assignments, were listened to in all employee and team meetings, and felt and behaved as if they were colleagues with the management group.

Pride in the plant's work and in being a part of the team was high among employees. Campbell relayed one incident in which some used canisters came back to the plant for refurbishing. The Navy said that they didn't want them cleaned up, just made functional again for further test launches. The factory employees could not tolerate returning the canisters in their dirty state. Unasked, they vacuumed, scrubbed, and touched up the old canisters so that they went back looking almost as good as brand new ones. That kind of pride in quality and reputation, Campbell noted, came along with giving employees all the business data so they knew who their customers were and so that they realized they were part of the success or failure of the plant.

Campbell said he also often sent shop technicians ["hourly workers," in the usual parlance] to visit dockside at the naval yards so they could talk to the sailors and get the real story on how their canisters were performing. Campbell thought that they learned more from those conversations than from the managerial-level discussions. This policy also contributed to the high level of employee morale.

Enthusiasm for the Aberdeen way was perhaps best exemplified by this team member's comments:

I love everything about this place. It's hard for me to get that across to people; I haven't worked that many places. I am so young, but it's just when people ask me about this place, it's like I just can't tell them enough.

I mean, it's the most incredible thing! I can't believe it works. I guess the hardest thing to think is it works without supervisors and stuff, but the thing I like about the plant most, I guess, is what it does for the person. Everything you get done is going to be self-motivated. I think that every person that works here, even if they didn't come in growing or self-motivated, that's the way they are going to get around here. It took me a while to realize when I first started. I was so happy to get the job, because I went from a minimum-wage job working in a jewelry store to this, and it was all completely new. I was getting a lot of money, and they trust me! I have been here a year and a half, and the money doesn't even impress me any more. In a way, that's not why I am here. I'd give up everything; I'd give up the great benefits and everything to be able to work in a place like this.

FMC Green River

As Ken Dailey listened to his team present the major features of the Aberdeen system, he outlined in his mind the major characteristics of the Green River facility. The large underground mine employed 400 people and produced about 5 million tons of trona ore (a mixture of bicarbonate of soda and soda ash) a year. The first plant, begun in 1948 and completed in 1953, produced about 1.3 million tons of various grades of soda ash a year. The second refining plant, completed in 1970, turned out 1.5 million tons of a single grade of soda ash; Green River also had the largest sodium tri-polyphosphate plant in the world. The power plants for the complex relied on the coal and natural gas that were abundant in the high Wyoming/Utah/Idaho basin. The refineries were organized by the steel workers' union. Dailey was supervising the construction of three new, smaller plants, one each for 60,000 tons annually of sodium bicarbonate, 30,000 tons of sodium cyanide used in refining precious metals, and 60,000 tons of caustic sodium hydroxide.

Dailey had been in Green River for 18 months.

Previously, he had been an operating supervisor at another FMC chemical plant, the plant manager of FMC's coke plant, manager of the environmental compliance project at the company's Pocatello, Idaho, facility, and most recently, development director at the Alkali Division headquarters.

The Green River complex was a part of the Alkali Chemicals Division of FMC that supplied sodium-based chemicals to the detergent industry, the glass industry, and large commercial chemical plants. Each day, the complex would send out an 80 to 100-ton hopper car train full of product. Much of the bicarbonate went out in 50- or 100-pound bags. Green River sent about 10 percent of its products by truck to different railheads in an attempt to spread out its distribution costs to different railroads. For most of these products, freight composed 25 percent of the final cost. Some 25 percent of Green River's revenues came from overseas. FMC competed against Texas Gulf, General Chemical, Rhone-Pulanc, and Tenneco (owned 20 percent by Japanese interests) in these markets. Dailey believed that the market for his products was strong over the next 10 years.

Dailey had recently reorganized the facility. Historically, there had been separate managers for the mine and for the surface plants. Now, he had a manager for the soda ash business in both below-surface and surface facilities, one to oversee the three new plants under construction and one to look after all of the services required by the plants.

Recruitment in Green River was surprisingly easy. Green River itself was a town of only about 15,000, but for the last 10 openings that FMC had advertised, over 300 applicants, from as far away as Colorado and Alaska, had applied.

Dailey thought that his management style was very interactive, with a high level of trust for people; he was relatively open, was willing to pass out information, and was eager to drive decision making down into the organization. He believed that the company's ability to share information was limited by its computer systems.

Dailey thought that the union was a progressive one that yet labored under old standard job descriptions. He believed he would receive their support in seeking more flexibility in applying those job descriptions. He also noted that the Green River force earning $18 per hour was the highest paid among all FMC employees. Mine productivity, too, he noted, had doubled in the last 8 years, despite a decline in the size of the work force.

As he thought about the Aberdeen system and whether or not it would work at Green River, he wondered about the huge infrastructure already in place in Green River and did not know if he could change it quickly. He also realized that the plants, built 20 and 40 years ago, contained isolated work stations with little opportunity for groups of people to interact.

As Dailey wondered if the special characteristics of the South Dakota plant were what made it possible for the Aberdeen system to work so well, his team reported the comments of one Aberdeen team member:

I personally feel that you can do this any place in the country. I know we have had groups from all over the country in here. I think the biggest factor that you will find is the trust level. You can initiate trust simply by eliminating fear. When I started up here, there were only six of us technicians out here. Bob Lancaster was our plant manager, and he told us to do what we needed to do. I wasn't used to having freedom to just do whatever I wanted: If you need it, go buy it. It just amazed me, and I still had a lot of fear about that. He says, "How about if I tell you this? No matter what you do," he says, "as long as you don't perform an unsafe act toward yourself or a fellow employee, I promise you you won't lose your job. You do what you want to; you do what you need to, to get this product produced at this set time. But other than that, however you want to go about getting it done, just go do it."

25

General Electric TSBO: Purchasing and Just-In-Time

In mid-1982 John Yates, Manager of Purchasing at General Electric Company's Transportation Systems Business Operations (TSBO) in Erie, Pennsylvania, was facing several crucial decisions involving procedures and policies in his purchasing function. The necessity for these decisions arose as a result of the proposed expansion of a "Just-In-Time" materials management program at the Erie facility. Full implementation of the Just-In-Time (JIT) approach by the Purchasing function would require a sharp break with policies traditionally followed in purchasing. Certain of these policies, such as the utilization of multiple competing vendors for a purchased part wherever possible, had been pursued with renewed vigor at TSBO in recent years and had been responsible for significant cost savings. However, the Just-In-Time approach seemed to call for fewer, not more, vendors.

In one particular decision facing Yates, a potential long-term supply contract with a single vendor for a critical diesel engine part had been proposed to replace short-term contracts with the two vendors currently supplying the part. While this contract was only one example, it carried potentially significant ramifications for

TSBO operations. Also, Yates knew that pursuit of this same philosophy on a broader scale would ultimately result in a significant reduction in the number of TSBO vendors, possibly by as much as 50 to 60 percent. The prospect of this reduction was troubling, and Yates was unsure to what degree the Just-In-Time approach should be attempted, if at all, in Purchasing.

Background

The TSBO group produced complete railway locomotives and electric drive motors for application in off-highway vehicles, rail transit vehicles, and oil and other drilling equipment. Many different types of railway locomotives were manufactured, including diesel-electric, electric, and switching and mining locomotives for both the domestic U.S. and export markets.

The manufacture of rail locomotives was a complex, time-consuming procedure. Each locomotive was a custom-designed product built to the unique specifications of the customer. The variety of end products was large relative to the total number of units produced each year. Thus, because of the relatively small customer orders

EXHIBIT 25-1 Material Flow in Locomotive Production

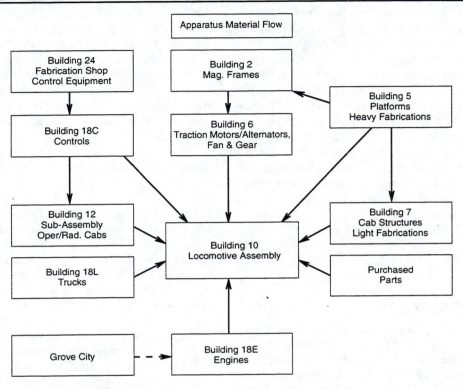

for each model, the fabrication and procurement of locomotive parts was typically conducted in small lots, often no more than five to ten each. Standard lead time from order receipt to locomotive shipment was about one year, of which only a few weeks were required for the actual manufacturing build cycle once parts and raw material were on hand. The various steps in manufacturing a locomotive were conducted in ten separate buildings, as illustrated in Exhibit 25-1. Parts, materials, and semi-finished components moved among and within these buildings as required.

The period from 1970 through 1976 was one of severe decline for the Erie operation. General Motors' locomotive manufacturing division, located in LaGrange, Illinois, had traditionally dominated the domestic U.S. market for rail locomotives; it succeeded in capturing almost the total U.S. market during these years. For example, of the 28,000 rail locomotives estimated to be operating in the U.S. in 1976, ap-

proximately 24,000 were built by G.M. and only 4,000 by G.E. In the 1970-76 period, G.E.'s new locomotive market share was extremely low, and according to one G.E. top manager, "We didn't even deserve that." He agreed with other observers that G.E.'s locomotive product image in the marketplace was one of generally low quality and high operating costs. Small orders were reportedly given to G.E. by major users to maintain a second source of supply, "just in case" of major need. The absolute low point was reached in 1976, when TSBO received not a single new order for locomotives.

In 1977 C. J. (Carl) Schlemmer, Vice-President and General Manager of TSBO, appointed M. S. (Rick) Richardson General Manager of Locomotive Operations; they, with the support of other members of the Erie top-management team, convinced corporate management that TSBO could be a viable, successful business. Their arguments were so successful that corporate heads subsequently authorized a $300 million expansion program, which represented the first major "retrofit" of an existing G.E. operation in a mature industry in the Northeast. New programs were begun to upgrade product quality, improve manufacturing productivity, and reduce costs. Automation of manufacturing processes was a major component in these programs, and plans called for the introduction of robotics and numerically controlled equipment in the welding and metal fabrication shops, the use of a new flexible machining center in motor-frame manufacturing, and several new computer-controlled stacker-crane storage-retrieval systems for raw material and work-in-process control. A new, highly automated facility for the manufacture of locomotive diesel engines was also planned, to be built 60 miles away in Grove City, Pa.

Purchasing at TSBO

Traditionally considered a support function to manufacturing, purchasing activities at TSBO were complex, involving about 6,000 suppliers, 50,000 parts, over 100,000 drawing numbers, and approximately $300,000,000 in annual procurement value. Until 1978 purchasing operations were divided into four independent "product-oriented" units: locomotive and diesel, propulsion, control, and transit cars. A total of 80 buyers and expediters (in a ratio of about 1 to 1) handled purchases.

In terms of manufacturing process, TSBO was an enormous job-shop complex, with great variety in day-to-day activities. Purchasing activities reflected this variety, with an extremely high volume of typically small-lot "buys." The number of purchase orders processed annually was in the tens of thousands; lead times on these orders were often short, and purchasing personnel worked on tight deadlines under high pressure. As one purchasing manager noted, "Running a purchasing operation in a business like TSBO is a high-pressure affair. Thirty percent of our items are needed in two weeks or less from order placement. Manufacturing is always pushing us to get the parts in so they can meet

their delivery deadlines." Buyers and expediters frequently cited a normal 50-to-60 hour workweek as proof of the rigors of the purchasing function, and also expressed pride in their ability to meet Manufacturing's deadlines. As a manager in Contract Administration noted, "I don't think the locomotive line has ever been stopped due to lack of purchased parts; that's rule number one around here; we will never knowingly hold up the line."

Materials Management Improvements, 1977-79

In the period 1977-79, a number of cost-reduction and productivity-improvement efforts in the materials management area were undertaken at TSBO. E. R. Woods, currently Manager of Materials at TSBO, came to the Erie operation in 1975. He commented on the situation that existed prior to 1977 as follows:

> Materials management was out of control. The sales forecasts given to us were insufficient; we had no capacity planning; production schedules were revised every month, and we couldn't react fast enough; the number of new parts, products, and engineering changes were driving us crazy; and there were continual delays in new-product introductions. We had tried MRP [material requirements planning] a couple of times, but it failed because we didn't involve the workforce and they didn't support it. Every building had its own separate purchasing and materials staff; some buildings reported to the Production Control Manager, some to the Materials Manager. The business was so fragmented; everyone was looking out for his piece of the total. There was no overall plan. Oh, we had a systems plan, but it wasn't integrated across the whole business. We left it up to Finance [their systems people] to implement things; there was no one in Manufacturing to coordinate materials systems with other functions.

In 1979 total responsibility for materials in all buildings was given to the Manager of Materials,

Ed Woods. Under his direction the first-ever Materials Operating Plan was drawn up, a total systems plan was developed, and a new Production Control Manager to coordinate it was appointed. Over the next two years, a number of major projects were begun, including a new MRP education program for the workforce, the establishment of building-by-building inventory-reduction plans, and improved inventory record accuracy and stockroom discipline. Also, a manufacturing-cycle analysis was begun to facilitate the systematic establishment of inventory goals. The locomotive diesel engine was selected for this study because of its importance in the process. As Woods noted of this project,

"This was a massive effort. There were so many different possible engine variations. We knew what we wanted to do, but the job was immense. So we got some help from Corporate Consulting. We did a generic engine-manufacturing and procurement cycle analysis for each of the basic model families we had, about eight to ten different models. We formed study teams for every line on the chart and went in and asked, "How can we reduce the cycle? How can we reduce buffer inventories?" We found out what really went into each of the products and how to manage them, how to cut cycle times. It took us two years to do it all, but we knew we had to have those facts."

By December 1979, the MRP system was operating, with a high degree of employee support, and significant improvements in materials operating performance were beginning to be realized. For example, locomotive material availability increased from 60 percent in 1977 to 85 percent in 1979 and locomotive parts stockroom accuracy from 75 percent to 85 percent. Also, significantly lower inventory goals were set for the next two-year period. Commenting on these improvements, George Sauerwine, Manager of Inventory Programs, felt that "the most important step for us was first understanding the manufacturing cycle. You have to understand the cycle before any big adjustments to inventory can be made." He also credited the ready acceptance of the new inventory goals by all parties involved to the careful analysis of manufacturing cycles that had been conducted.

Purchasing Improvements, 1980-81

In 1980 the first of a series of major reorganizations and consolidation steps in Purchasing were implemented. Plans for these changes had been formulated during the previous two years when the Materials Management function was restructured. A new Advanced materials organization was created, which included consolidation of three of the four independent purchasing operations into one unit. Propulsion was combined with locomotive and diesel (over a one-year period). The transit-car operation was dissolved because of declining sales. The duplication in buyers, expediters, and other personnel that had previously existed with the separate organizations was eliminated. The new organization used only one head buyer for each major commodity group (steel, rubber, etc.), with specialty buyers for sub-groups such as steel castings, plastic injection moldings, etc. Because of these and similar efficiencies, manpower was reduced from 80 to about 55, and the new ratio of buyers to expediters was on the order of 2 to 1. Exhibit 25-2, showing the material management organization under Ed Wood, indicates the revised Purchasing organization.

The Purchasing reorganization efforts were part of what some observers termed a "new era" for Purchasing at TSBO. This era had its origins in the new directions set by the Richardson management team in 1977. As Ed Woods noted,

"Up through the mid-1970s our cost-containment and productivity-improvement concerns here, like most other U.S. manufacturers, were primarily focused on direct labor. But after we backed off and looked at it from a fresh perspective, we began to see the increased importance of purchased materials. The purchased-parts content of our end product was up to over 50 percent,

EXHIBIT 25-2 Materials Management Organization

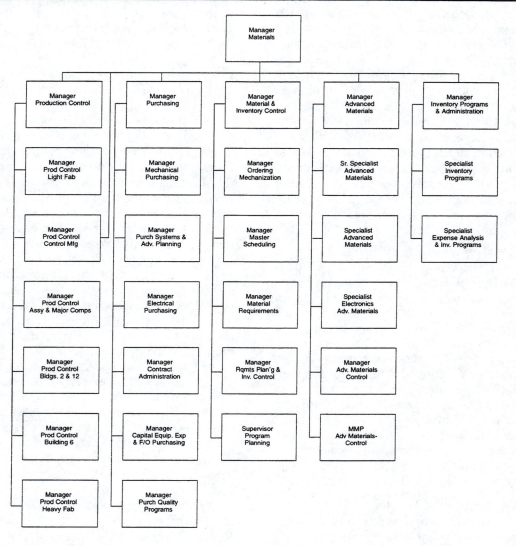

and our inventory carrying charges alone were about equal to the direct-labor content of the product. So that motivated us to look harder at Purchasing, to intensively examine everything we were doing."

The new efforts in Purchasing included the appointment of John Yates as TSBO Manager of Purchasing and the creation of three new vendor-oriented programs aimed at improving quality and reducing the cost of purchased materials.

The PACE ("Product Application and Cost Evaluation") program was one of these new programs. Focusing on TSBO's major dollar-volume suppliers, it called for new levels of cooperation between TSBO and the vendors and, in the words of John Yates, was intended to offer the vendors more than the traditional cost-cutting "philosophies and platitudes." As Yates noted,

"In the past, whenever there was a big push on controlling purchased parts, TSBO would rent a conference room, invite 100-200 vendors in and lecture to them. But that was essentially a one-way conversation." PACE was something entirely different; it involved our bringing the vendors in one at a time. First, Richardson or C. M. [Chuck] Watland [General Manager of Manufacturing] would have breakfast with them, then we'd give them a complete tour, show them what we were doing, ask their opinions on how we could make improvements, cut costs. After they visited Erie, we'd send a team into their facility, which often included people from Engineering and manufacturing, in addition to Purchasing. We'd work with the supplier's people on ways to improve their business: new manufacturing techniques, new equipment, better financial controls, new quality-control procedures. Sometimes both Ed Woods and I would go on these visits, which could last one or two days.

Another goal of PACE was to see if our better vendors might be able to increase the number of products they supplied to us. We thought this could result in a higher quality product and also reduce the total number of vendors we had to deal with. We were at 6,000 vendors in 1979 and increasing. So when we took them through our business, we didn't just talk about what they were already doing with us; we'd show them other parts, other applications of their own products, and encourage bids on them, too. We were after quality improvements with PACE as much as after cost savings. But we also got cost savings, sometimes in unexpected ways. For example, one of our suppliers of a precision-machined part asked, after he saw how we were using the part, "Why do you require those polished surface-finish tolerances in these non-interfacing areas?" We didn't really know; our engineering department said, "That's always been our spec for that type of part." It turned out we didn't need that finish, so we eliminated the spec and saved money with absolutely no loss in performance quality. There were many examples like that. Right from the beginning one of our major rules was never criticize a vendor's idea, no matter how silly it seems at first." And it paid off for us. Another reason the PACE program was so effective was that for the first time the suppliers heard right from the top of our organization what our problems and concerns were, and we heard from their top people the same kinds of things ... and everybody involved heard it all at the same time; they all heard the same thing. Before this, whatever was said often got twisted up in being passed around.

According to Yates, a key factor in the success of the PACE program was the direct support it received from top management. He noted that, over a two-year period, Richardson or Watland never missed a PACE meeting at Erie. He felt such support was responsible for the steady growth of the program, in spite of the amount of time and effort required in working with each vendor, which effectively limited potential participation to fewer than 50 vendors a year. By the middle of 1982, over 90 vendors had been involved who accounted for more than 60 percent of the annual dollar value of purchased parts, with estimated total savings to G.E. in the neighborhood of $4 million.

The focus of the PACE program was the relatively few suppliers who accounted for the majority of purchased-parts dollar volume. Another program, the SOS ("Supplier Originated Savings") program, was established in mid-1981 to involve the remaining vendors in TSBO's productivity improvement efforts. This program was based on a similar earlier program at the Ford Motor Co. and provided incentive bonus awards, prizes, and added business for supplier suggestions and ideas that led to improvements. The program had an announced goal of reducing TSBO purchase costs by 6 percent. To initiate this program, special announcements were distributed to approximately

4,500 suppliers. Meetings with individual vendors were also held as the need arose, but not on the same scale as with the PACE program. The program was well received, and by mid-1982 savings were estimated to be in the neighborhood of $1 million.

Another improvement program undertaken in the 1980-81 period was the Dual Source Savings (DSS) program. Competitively sourced parts accounted in 1979 for a total of about 51 percent of purchased-parts dollar volume. The majority of single sources were due to engineering specifications/approvals and vendor tooling limitations. The DSS program sought to reduce both the number and dollar volume of single-sourced items by opening as many as possible to competitive vendor bidding. TSBO would then benefit, it was argued, from having the lowest possible item cost as well as from having multiple sources of supply, as specified by traditional Purchasing doctrine.

The DSS program also included cross-functional review teams to analyze Purchasing performance measurements, set vendor evaluation criteria, and establish budgets for vendor tooling, samples, and prototypes. Competition among vendors was encouraged through the program by requesting bids from new vendors, evaluating and approving multiple vendors, and actually placing orders with new vendors. These changes were undertaken with the realization that the DSS program presented some risks, including possibly higher prices (if the current single vendor turned out to have been supplying the part at an unrealistically low price), increased tooling costs, more vendor startup problems, and additional engineering costs.

Savings from the DSS program turned out to be significant. While these savings were slow to develop, it was estimated that cumulative total savings in the third full year after program inception would amount to about $3 million. As a result of this program, TSBO vendors had become increasingly more competitive, and frequent changes in sources of supply resulted as first one vendor, then another, reduced prices.

Just-In-Time Movement, 1982

The application of Just-In-Time concepts had originated in the course of efforts to reduce inventory carrying costs. In early 1981 Chuck Watland had challenged the entire manufacturing team to optimize inventories not only by eliminating excess inventories of work-in-process parts within the shops, as they were in the process of doing, but also by implementing a JIT system for delivery of parts to TSBO. Raw material and parts were typically ordered by TSBO on a monthly, quarterly, or even semi-annual basis; upon delivery to Erie, the material was placed in inventory and held until required for use. In addition to the usual problems of occasional late deliveries, material was often delivered earlier than required; this practice had gone unopposed at Erie for years, for a variety of reasons. A Just-In-Time delivery system, with weekly or even daily deliveries, would theoretically minimize unneeded inventory. However, under this approach early deliveries were as undesirable as late deliveries. There had been a great deal of discussion among TSBO production control and purchasing personnel about this problem. All agreed that better control of the timing of vendor deliveries of parts and material was needed, but there was great uncertainty about how to accomplish this objective. There was also general reluctance to attempt any type of JIT approach before significantly better control was achieved.

In October 1981, Ed Woods had participated in a G.E. management seminar that had involved a trip to Japan and visits to several Japanese manufacturing companies. His experience there caused him to rethink the JIT concept. He began to consider seriously the possibilities of applying the JIT approach not only to the external delivery of parts to the factory, but also to the flow of materials and components among the ten buildings within TSBO that comprised the major work centers for locomotive manufacturing. The application of JIT concepts to these work centers would require that all work in process not required for a particular day's use at a particular work center be returned to the location from whence it came. If all of this excess work in process were pushed further upstream in the manufacturing process, all excess material would eventually be returned to raw-material inventory or fabricated- and purchased-parts storage. As inventory would build up at these storage locations, it would in turn be pushed back on the supplier. This process would theoretically eliminate all excess raw material and purchased-parts inventory held at TSBO.

When these JIT ideas were presented to the shop foremen and production control supervisors in early 1982, they encountered some strong, but not unexpected, concerns and doubts. The general reaction was that, if JIT worked in Japan, it was due to the unique conditions there, and it was not suitable for the TSBO environment. There was some agreement among this group that work-in-process inventories had in the past been too high, and it was acknowledged that the shop floors were often cluttered with parts and material awaiting work, to the point of confusion. But as they pointed out, these problems were already being attacked with the new MRP system and other programs, with good results. The dominant concerns about JIT revolved about the potentially serious effects of not having sufficient supplies on hand to keep lines operating and workers active. Under the JIT approach, buffer stocks would be essentially eliminated, with greatly increased risks of a major work stoppage if parts or material problems occurred.

As the JIT concepts were studied more closely over the next few months, other constraints on implementing them within TSBO surfaced. For example, it was learned that the MRP system that had been operating so successfully for only a couple of years would have to be redesigned to permit scheduling in daily intervals rather than the weekly periods being used. It was also estimated that much higher levels of MRP data accuracy would be required, as well as higher service levels on all parts provided, if manufacturing schedules were to be maintained, with much shorter intervals of time for correcting problems and essentially no room for error in quantities or schedules. Another problem recog-

nized early on with JIT was the more severe impact of poor quality. As one foreman commented, "What good does it do to get the material in right on time if it's no good, and we don't have any buffers to cover our tails?" The proponents of JIT argued that, for fabricated parts, the quality problem could be addressed by intensive educational and motivational programs oriented towards the unionized hourly work force. For purchased parts, they felt that the infrastructures that had been established by the PACE and SOS programs could be capitalized upon to include still higher quality levels as another goal.

In spite of these initial concerns, implementation of JIT concepts in the shops was pursued further in the early months of 1982, primarily through intensive discussions and study sessions by teams of supervisory and middle- management personnel. The diesel engine was selected as a test case: the study teams were charged with determining the feasibility of applying JIT concepts to achieve significant inventory reductions and cost savings on this important component. These concepts would, if shown feasible, be applied at the highly automated engine plant under construction at Grove City.

JIT in Purchasing

The initial focus in Purchasing was to pursue Watland's original ideas about delivery frequency. The broad geographic distribution of TSBO suppliers and the distance involved (see Exhibit 25-3) created great skepticism about the feasibility of these ideas. However, with some diligent effort, the Purchasing study team was able to identify 300 of about 1,000 purchased diesel engine parts that were currently on monthly or quarterly deliveries but were potential candidates for weekly deliveries because of proximity, method of delivery, size, weight or other factors. The total dollar value of these 300 parts was more than 75 percent of the total. However, it was unclear how many of these could be converted to weekly deliveries. Furthermore, the earlier-mentioned question of how to gain better control over the timing of deliveries had yet to be answered.

EXHIBIT 25-3 Geographic Distribution of TSBO Suppliers

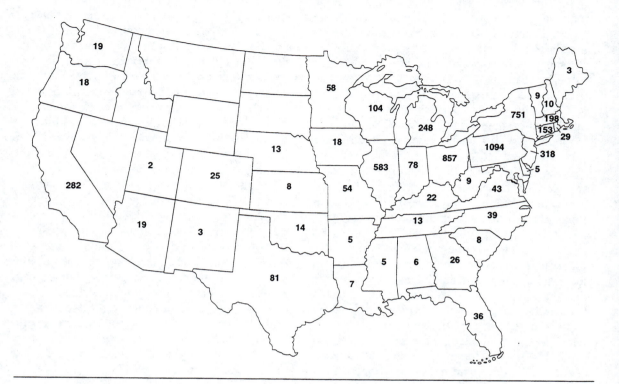

As John Yates and his management team dug deeper into the details of applying the JIT approach in Purchasing, they discovered that it involved much more than simply requesting more frequent deliveries from the suppliers. They found, for example, that Japanese companies had far fewer vendors than similar U.S. companies. This situation was due at least partially to the Japanese concept of "vendor co-destiny," which treated the supplier as an extension of the company. Relations between supplier and user company were much closer than was common in the U.S. and were characterized by more sharing of information, longer term relationships, and a greater number of parts supplied to one user by a given vendor. Also, in contrast to U.S. practice of pitting vendors against one another through competitive bidding, single-sourcing was widely practiced by many Japanese companies. The efficiencies gained in dealing with fewer vendors and the open sharing of such information as production schedules, long-term demand forecasts, and engineering and design information were apparently important factors in the JIT approach that contributed to the very high reliability of vendor deliveries as well as extremely high quality levels.

In a review of these facts, it became apparent to Yates' team that serious pursuit of the JIT approach would require reductions--possibly significant--in the number of suppliers doing business with TSBO and an increase in the number of single-source vendors. The latter prospect was particularly troubling, since it ran directly counter to traditional Purchasing doctrine in general and the Dual Source Savings program in particular.

The idea of single-sourcing critical engine components was a major barrier to many individuals in the TSBO study team. After much discussion it was decided to select one such test case for thorough evaluation before making any conclusions or recommendations to higher management. The diesel engine crankshaft was subsequently chosen for this analysis.

Single-Sourcing: The Crankshaft Decision

Because of the critical nature of the crankshaft in TSBO's manufacturing process, at least two sources of supply had always been required by TSBO purchasing procedures. The company's primary supplier, providing a majority of TSBO's needs, was Vendor A, located a few hours' drive away in another part of the state.* In the past Vendor A had maintained prompt deliveries and excellent quality. TSBO's second supplier was Vendor B. While Vendor B prices were slightly lower than those of Vendor A, there had been problems in the past of missed delivery dates and occasional below-spec quality. These two companies were the only U.S. vendors considered for supplying the crankshafts, as the product was one of the locomotive's highest priced parts and required many intricate machining operations and expensive special-purpose machinery to manufacture.

Vendor A had already participated in the PACE program because of the importance of the product it supplied. This fact, plus its past performance record, made Vendor A a logical candidate for single-source supply. John Yates and Ed Woods requested a meeting with Vendor A's top management to discuss this possibility. During this initial meeting, the TSBO team that visited Vendor A's plant investigated its manufacturing capabilities and fabrication processes and determined the "critical path" for crankshaft manufacturing.

Vendor A was eager to become the single-source supplier of crankshafts. In addition to increased business with TSBO, other benefits would result. For example, A's management pointed out that by being a single source with a

long-term contract, Vendor A could better plan its capital investments for all crankshaft manufacturing, including non-G.E. business. The equipment used in A's operations was custom-built, with a 2-1/2 year lead time. With knowledge of its crankshaft requirements 2 to 3 years down the road, A would be more likely to invest in equipment to reduce its costs of operations and lower its prices to TSBO. Vendor A's management stated that this investment would not occur if current TSBO purchasing procedures were continued.

With single-sourcing of crankshafts at Vendor A, it was likely that the overall quality level and reliability of deliveries would be improved. On the other hand, if crankshafts were not available or were defective, the manufacturing process for the engine stopped in its second work center, upsetting the entire manufacturing operation. Proponents of single-sourcing at TSBO felt there was little chance of such a calamity. They pointed out that Vendor A's record showed them to be essentially riskless as a source of supply; the quality of the crankshaft was nearly 100 percent perfect, and deliveries were reportedly always on time. Vendor A also had its own steelmaking capabilities in the event the raw-material supply was interrupted, while down time for its equipment was negligible. Furthermore, although A was unionized, the union was an independent one, with only one strike in its history, which had occurred during contract negotiations just at the time President Nixon came out with his wage-price freeze. A also kept a small inventory of crankshafts in its finished goods inventory as a precautionary measure against unexpected problems and seemed willing to increase this inventory if selected as sole source.

In addition to questions of risk and safety of supply, there were also issues relating to contract terms and pricing. For example, if TSBO decided to single-source crankshafts at Vendor A, a contract explicitly stating all terms and conditions of the agreement was needed. An important question was how long should this contract extend? Clearly, Vendor A wanted as long-term a commitment as possible (for equipment pur-

---

*The name and location of both companies have been disguised to preserve confidentiality.

chasing, etc.), while TSBO wanted a shorter commitment as a hedge if single-sourcing did not work out. Another contract issue was whether single-sourcing of crankshafts should be explicit or implied. Also to be resolved was the procedure for setting prices.

Finally, an issue of great concern to TSBO was how much finished goods inventory would be carried by Vendor A. Typically, each current TSBO order constituted about a 12-week supply.* This amount, with a few extra crankshafts as safety stock, would usually be produced by Vendor A shortly before the required delivery time. Thus, A typically carried very little finished goods inventory for TSBO. The issue was what level of inventory would be appropriate for the new long-term, single-source contract? The TSBO purchasing staff felt that at least 12 weeks supply should be required at all times, while A's management thought that this would be excessive.

The issue of single-sourcing generated much argument at TSBO, since it opposed traditional purchasing philosophy and notions of competition. Some argued the crankshaft would become overpriced very quickly due to the lack of vendor price competition. Also, under the JIT approach, quantity discounts would be lost because of smaller order lots, and there was concern expressed about the possible ethical problems arising from too much familiarity with the vendor. It was argued that this could lead to legal problems such as being viewed as restraint of trade or price-fixing. There were also fears that this part was simply not the correct one with which to attempt single-sourcing, given its criticalness in the manufacturing process. Finally, there were fears that the supplier would take advantage of the situation and "put it to G.E.," since suppliers had previously been played off against one another.

Other Unresolved Issues

In addition to the single-sourcing issue, a problem that had to be addressed before the JIT concepts

*At current production rates, TSBO placed approximately eight new crankshafts per week into the manufacturing process.

could be implemented further in Purchasing was that of vendor delivery schedules. Because of the emphasis given in Purchasing to meeting manufacturing deadlines and the skills built up in the expediting group, late deliveries had become a relatively small problem. However, the practice of early deliveries of material had gone unopposed for years and had slowly been increasing in the past year or so. There were several alternatives which TSBO could take to solve this problem, none of them particularly attractive to everyone involved. They could, for example (1) return the non-required material to the vendor and either charge the vendor for transportation or absorb it themselves, (2) keep the excess material on a consignment basis and either hold the vendor's invoice without payment or re-invoice the vendor for the non-required portion, or (3) find another vendor who would stick to the required delivery schedules.

Finally, important issues of managing quality of vendor-supplied parts under a JIT approach had not yet been resolved. As noted earlier, quality was of much greater significance under the JIT approach than before. Finding vendors who could consistently meet the new quality standards and maintain the close vendor contacts required by JIT was a task that would put considerable strain on the TSBO purchasing organization. Also, even if suitable vendors could be found, the tighter discipline and greater workloads imposed upon them could lead to higher prices for the material supplied. Under a JIT system, vendors could be expected to experience increased costs due to additional set ups, packaging, freight, and financing, while the receiving company (G.E./Erie in this case) would experience savings in such areas as inventory carrying costs, material handling, storage space, insurance, etc. While it could be argued that it was unrealistic to expect the vendors to absorb all of these extra costs, there was unfortunately no previous experience to use as a guide.

It was clear to John Yates as he considered these issues that the JIT approach, if implemented fully, would have tremendous impact upon his purchasing operations. It was also clear that his handling of these issues could influence the success of the entire JIT program at Erie.

26
The Bank of Boston

Introduction

The chilly February morning became colder as Bostonians heard the news reports and read the headlines: "Bank of Boston Guilty in Cash Transfer Case." In a plea bargaining arrangement with the Financial Investigation Task Force unit of the Justice Department, the bank agreed to pay a $500,000 fine after pleading guilty to federal charges of "willfully and knowingly" failing to report $1.2 billion in cash transfers with nine foreign banks. The bank had violated the Bank Secrecy Act which stipulates that all cash transfers over $10,000 made through financial institutions be reported to the Internal Revenue Service. The allegations came quickly:

- The bank was involved in businesses with criminal overtones.

- The bank laundered drug money.

- Bank employees were "on the take."

Less than one week later, one of the allegations appeared to be true. The bank had placed two companies controlled by a reputed organized crime figure on a list which exempted their cash transactions from being reported to the Fed.

That information started an avalanche of events. Two local communities withdrew their funds from the bank; and, of greater magnitude, the city of Boston was considering withdrawing its funds. Bills to remove state money from the bank were filed in the state legislature. Both houses of Congress scheduled hearings, and approval of two pending mergers of out-of-state banks was deferred.

Stories about the bank dominated the news media until early March, when two events signified a turning point:

- Two other Boston banks disclosed reporting violations.

- Merrill Lynch announced that the bank would retain its quality rating.

Meanwhile, the congressional hearings continued; and at the bank's annual meeting, the stockholders were told that an additional $110 million transfer had not been reported. This time the cash was transported from the bank's international banking subsidiary in Miami to banks in Haiti.

This case was prepared by David Breyer, Ph.D. Assistant Professor of Management, Suffolk University, as the basis for class discussion rather than to illustrate either effective or ineffective handling of an administrative situation. Copyright ©1986.

Despite all the troubles, the chairman of the board, William L. Brown, was able to announce to the stockholders a 70 percent projected increase in earnings.

Narrative of Events

In an effort to aid law enforcement officials in the detection of criminal, tax, and regulatory violations, Congress passed the Bank Secrecy Act in 1970. By requiring that banks report large cash transactions to the IRS, Congress intended that "money laundering" (a method by which criminals attempt to funnel illegal funds through a legal institution) be abated. Banks were given until July 1, 1972, to establish a list of customers who, in the normal course of business, have currency transactions in excess of $10,000. This "exempt" list precluded the necessity for those customers to file large currency reports. The bank complied with this request and submitted its exempt list to the government, thereby alerting the authorities to those customers normally dealing in large amounts of cash.

In 1976, the branch manager of the North End branch of the bank placed Huntington Realty Co. on the exempt list and in 1979 added Federal Investments, Inc. These companies were owned and operated by the Angiulo family, customers of the bank since 1964 and allegedly involved in organized crime in New England. The bank's records show that between 1979 and 1983 representatives of the Angiulo companies purchased with cash 163 cashiers checks totaling $2,163,457.50.

In 1980, new regulations narrowed the scope of the exempt list to operators of retail-type businesses, such as supermarkets and restaurants, whose receipts involved substantial amounts of cash. But when the bank submitted a new list, Huntington Realty and Federal Investments were still included.

In 1982, the Department of the Treasury, with help from the Organized Crime Strike Force, began investigating organized crime activities in Massachusetts. This investigation brought to light the bank's unreported overseas currency transactions. On June 8, 1982, investigators asked the Banking Offices Administration unit of the bank to provide additional information concerning certain customers on the exempt list. With that request, the Treasury enclosed a copy of the bank's exempt list with two types of notations:

1. check marks beside customer names requiring additional information (taxpayer number, address, etc.);
2. an X beside names of depositors that did not appear to be types of establishments that a bank is permitted to put on its exemption list without prior approval of the Treasury Department.

Because the bank's Coin and Currency Department was responsible for its own exempt list of customers (some of whom the Treasury was investigating), Banking Offices Administration referred the June letter to that department. The Coin and Currency Department did not respond to the Treasury's request until several months later.

After reviewing the information provided by the bank, the Treasury announced that several items on the list did not meet the requirements of the regulations. The Treasury requested further information which the bank supplied. Because the Treasury's request was interpreted by the bank as a request for information rather than as a requuest to remove the questionable customers from the list, the list remained intact at that time. However, in May 1983, the bank received subpoenas relating to its lack of compliance with the Act. At that time, the bank conducted a more thorough review of the exempt list and removed the Huntington and Federal companies.

In 1984, a grand jury probe into organized crime activities was begun in Boston. That same year, action was initiated by the Justice department's newly formed Financial Investigative Task Force, comprised of representatives from U.S. Customs, the IRS, and the Organized Crime Strike Force. As a result of both investigations, Bank of Boston on February 2, 1985, pleaded guilty to large currency reporting violations. The specific charge focused on cash transfers of $1.2 billion to Swiss banks without the filing of large currency reports. A $500,000 one was assessed. However, given the nature of the plea, criminal overtones were unavoidable; and on February 13, local papers reported that the Angiulo businesses had been on the exempt list, thereby loosely linking the foreign cash transfers to money laundering. An onslaught of accusations followed.

William L. Brown, chairman of the bank's board of directors, called a press conference at which he blamed the violations on "systems failure" and made the point that the international money transfer business is a legitimate banking function.

Another damaging report was released on February 27: the Treasury announced that federal bank examiners had informed the bank of international reporting failures in 1982, at which time the bank had promised to take corrective action. The bank issued a swift denial, stating that the 1982 report had referred only to domestic violations, which the bank had corrected. The Treasury later retracted its statement and admitted it was mistaken. This strengthened the bank's assertion that it did not know of the international reporting violations until the summer of 1984. Nonetheless, by the end of February, five independent investigations had been initiated by the following groups: the United States Senate, the United States House of Representatives, the Securities and Exchange Commission, the New England Organized Crime Strike Force, and the bank's special committee (comprised of five outside directors). The probe into reporting compliance extended even to brokerage houses, as reported in a *Boston Globe* spotlight report on money laundering channels.

Throughout this period, Chairman Brown asserted that criminal activities had not occurred at the bank; he emphasized that international transfers were legitimate and entirely unrelated to the Angiulo exemptions. He acknowledged, however, that the bank used "poor judgment" in placing the Angiulo companies on the exempt list. To restore confidence in the bank, he charged the special committee to evaluate the bank's overall state of compliance, not only with the act, but with other regulations, including Regulation E, which governs electronic funds transfers, and Truth-in- Lending.

Over the next several months, the bank continued to be the target of a highly critical media barrage which included coverage of banking activities well beyond the scope of the reporting failures. In one case, as a result of a negative news report, a pending merger with Rhode Island Hospital Trust was called into question and put on hold by the state legislature. The news media also questioned the bank's decision to relocate its credit card operation to New Hampshire.

The reporting violations became a national issue as other banks came forward with admissions of similar failures. On March 9, the Shawmut Bank of Boston made public its failure to report over $200 million of large currency transactions. Shortly thereafter, similar reports were released by Wells Fargo Bank, Chemical Bank, Bank of America, Manufacturers Hanover Bank, Irving Trust, and the Bank of New England. In all cases, officials at these banks claimed that the reporting failures were unintentional, due either to a failure to note the changes in the Bank Secrecy Act, or to a misinterpretation of those changes. The Bank of Boston was the only one to plead guilty to "willfully and knowingly" violating the regulations.

The special committee appointed by the bank's directors to conduct an internal investigation made its findings public on July 25, 1985. The report acknowledged that the "level of non-compliance at the bank with the [Bank Secrecy] Act was extensive" and that bank employees exhibited "wide-spread laxity and poor judgment." The committee concluded, however, that no one had profited from the reporting violations.

On July 28, 1985, the *Boston Globe* ran an editorial entitled "Finale at the First." The closing sentence captured the prevailing feeling among many bank employees and customers: "The First's world will never be the same as before, but it has won the right to get back to its main line of work."

The Special Committee

On February 25, 1985, the board of directors appointed a special committee to review the bank's efforts to comply with the Act. The special committee consisted of five outside directors: George R. West (chairman), chairman of the board, Allendale Mutual Insurance Company; Samuel Huntington (vice chairman), president and CEO, New England Electric System; Martin R. Allen, chairman of the board, Computervision Corporation; Thomas A. Galligan, Jr., chairman of the board, Boston Edison Company; and J. Donald Monan, S. J., president, Boston College.

The mandate of the special committee was to review the adequacy of the record compiled by management on matters relating to the reporting of large currency transactions as required by the Act; to determine who was responsible for the failures of the bank to comply with the Act; to recommend disciplinary action if deemed appropriate; and to review management's policies, procedures, and systems to ensure future regulatory compliance. During the next four months, the committee conducted a rigorous investigation which included holding over 100 interviews, reviewing files, consulting legal experts, and conducting audit tests.

The committee's findings were reported to the board of directors on June 27, 1985. The report confirmed that the level of noncompliance at the bank was extensive. Failure to comply with the act went beyond the immediate situation and extended into other operations of the bank and its affiliates. Further, when the government began its investigation, management failed to realize the seriousness of the situation or to take corrective action.

The investigation uncovered the fact that although the requirements of the act received widespread distribution throughout the bank, there was no concerted follow-through to see that the new reporting requirements were implemented. As a result, no one caught the mistake for four years. The Coin and Currency Department which handled the cash transfers misun-derstood, and therefore neglected to implement, the amended regulations. At the same time, many personnel in other departments and divisions, including Staff Services (Corporate HRD), the Law Office, and the Internal Audit Department, failed in their staff responsibilities. (Exhibit 26-1 shows the organization of the bank.) The committee found no evidence that the cash transfers involved "tainted" money.

The problems at the North End branch concerned a modification in the act which narrowed the circumstances under which domestic transactions must be reported. Prior to July 1980, the regulations provided that transactions with established customers whose business regularly involved large currency transactions could be exempted from reporting. Therefore, having the Angiulo's real estate businesses on the bank's exempt list prior to 1980 did not violate any express provision of the regulations. The amendment clearly disqualified the Angiulo businesses from the exempt list, but the manager of the North End branch kept them on the list. Although the decision to do so was questioned by the Banking Offices Administration (Retail Banking Division), it was not overruled.

Although numerous transactions went unreported and personnel in the North End branch were aware of the Angiulos' reputed ties to organized crime, there was no evidence of collusion between any employee of the bank and the Angiulos to violate any requirement of the act. The Angiulos, like some other customers, occasionally gave small gifts to branch personnel. There was no evidence, however, that such gifts were related to the improper maintenance of their accounts on the exempt list.

Much more serious was the Bank's failure to respond promptly when a Treasury official questioned the appropriateness of certain customers on the list, including the Angiulos. Some 13 months passed before the bank responded to the Treasury, during which time the bank's Coin and Currency Department failed to report transactions for those customers.

In concluding the findings, the special committee found an unsatisfactory overall level of compliance with the act by the seven inde-

EXHIBIT 26-1 Bank of Boston Corporation, 1984-85

```
                              ┌──────────────┐
                              │  Chairman's  │
                              │    Office    │
                              └──────────────┘

┌────────┐  ┌──────────┐  ┌───────────┐  ┌──────────┐  ┌──────────┐  ┌────────────┐
│ Audit  │  │  Loan    │  │ Strategic │  │ Finance  │  │  Law     │  │   Corp.    │
│        │  │ Review   │  │ Planning  │  │          │  │  Office  │  │   HRD      │
│        │  │          │  │           │  │          │  │          │  │ (CorpComm) │
└────────┘  └──────────┘  └───────────┘  └──────────┘  └──────────┘  └────────────┘

┌───────────┐  ┌──────────────┐  ┌────────────┐  ┌─────────────┐  ┌───────────────┐
│ Corporate │  │  Treasury    │  │ New England│  │ Real Estate │  │ International  │
│  Group    │  │ Investment   │  │   Group    │  │   Group     │  │    Group      │
│           │  │Banking Group │  │            │  │             │  │               │
└───────────┘  └──────────────┘  └────────────┘  └─────────────┘  └───────────────┘

              ┌───────────────┐        ┌──────────────┐
              │ Credit Policy │        │ Dewey Square │
              │ & Loan Review │        │  Investors   │
              └───────────────┘        └──────────────┘

┌─────────────┐  ┌─────────────┐  ┌───────────┐  ┌────────────┐  ┌──────────┐  ┌──────┐  ┌──────────┐
│ N.E.        │  │Massachusetts│  │ Operating │  │ Systems and│  │ Casco    │  │ RIHT │  │ Colonial │
│ Integration │  │  Banking    │  │ Services  │  │Data Proces.│  │ Northern │  │      │  │ BanCorp  │
│ Management  │  │             │  │           │  │            │  │          │  │      │  │          │
└─────────────┘  └─────────────┘  └───────────┘  └────────────┘  └──────────┘  └──────┘  └──────────┘

┌───────────┐  ┌─────────┐
│ Fiduciary │  │ Staff   │
│ Policy &  │  │ Support │
│ Review    │  │         │
└───────────┘  └─────────┘
```

Boston Region*	Facilities Management	Shareholder Svcs. & Corporate Trust	Deposit Operations	Mutual Funds	Correspondent Banking	Monec

- Commercial
- Middle Market
- Private Banking
- Retail Banking

Deposit Operations:
- Cash Letter & Collections
- Check Collections
- Checking Accts. & Rec. Control
- Money & Wire Transfer
- Coin and Currency

Correspondent Banking:
- Corresp. Banking Credit
- Corresp. Banking Marketing

pendent banks which the Bank of Boston Corporation had acquired during 1974 through 1981. Also, there was evidence of unsatisfactory compliance by the bank's Suffolk County branches and by certain branches of the Casco Northern Bank, a Maine based affiliate acquired by the bank in 1984.

Conclusion

After careful review of the special committee's report, on July 24, 1985, the bank's board of directors made public its conclusions in a news release:

The policy of the bank is and always has been to comply with all governmental regulations. Thus, the bank had written procedures regarding the Treasury department's currency reporting requirements since their inception in 1972. However, the bank failed to put in place systems and controls adequate to ensure that regulatory changes would be incorporated promptly and correctly into that policy, and to ensure that the policy would be understood and fully implemented throughout the organization. These failures led to widespread misunderstanding and misapplication of the currency reporting requirements, especially after the change in the regulations in 1980.

The Staff Services Department circulated to a number of the bank's other departments the Bulletin received by the bank in July 1980 from the Office of the Comptroller of the Currency. Neither Staff Services nor any of the recipients of the Bulletin, however, requested appropriate action by Information Systems and Services, the department which prepares and publishes the bank's operating procedures. As a consequence, the operating procedure on currency reporting which the bank had had in place since 1972 was not amended to reflect the new requirement of reporting transactions with foreign banks and the new standards for exemption for retail customers.

Even those units of the bank's operations which were in fact informed of the 1980 changes did not in all cases properly interpret and apply them. Although Banking Offices Administration sent a detailed memorandum to all branches under its jurisdiction explaining the changed standards for exempting bank customers from reporting, it did not exercise sufficient supervisory control over the exempt list to remove the ineligible customers from the list.

Similarly, as previously noted, the Coin and Currency Department of the bank received notice of the 1980 regulatory changes but failed to understand them to require reporting of transactions with foreign banks. Because the 1980 changes were not highlighted in any subsequent operating procedure or other directives to Coin and Currency, this serious error of interpretation went uncorrected until it was discovered in mid-1984.

In addition, the bank failed to adequately audit its operating units for compliance with the act's requirements. As a result, opportunities were missed to correct the misapplication and violation of those requirements which in fact occurred. Although the bank's internal auditors conducted periodic branch audits, which included a cursory review of compliance on a periodic basis, neither the North End Branch nor Coin and Currency was audited for compliance after the change in the regulations in 1980. Moreover, even prior to 1980, the Internal Audit Department failed adequately to test the bank's administrative controls relating to compliance with currency requirements.

27
Making of A Bad Cop and Roleplay

What makes a policman go sour? I can tell you. I was a Denver policeman until not so long ago. Then I quit so I could hold my head up.

Don't get me wrong. I'm not trying to shift the burden of responsibility for the burglaries, break-ins, safe objects and that sort of thing. That is bad, very bad. But I will leave it to the big shots and the newspapers and the courts to say and do what needs to be said and done about that.

My concern is about the individual officer, the ordinary, hard-working, basically honest but awfully hard-pressed guy who is really suffering now.

Young fellows don't put on those blue uniforms to be crooks. There are a lot of reasons, but for most of the guys it adds up to the fact they thought it was an honorable, decent way of making a living.

Somewhere along the line a guy's disillusioned. Along the way, the pressures mount up. Somewhere along the way he may decide to quit fighting them and make the conscious decisions to try to "beat" society instead.

But long before he gets to that point, almost as soon as he dons the uniform, in fact, he is taking the first little steps down the road that does, for some, eventually lead to the penitentiary.

Let me back up a little. I want to talk about how you get to be a policeman, because this is where the trouble really starts.

Almost any able-bodied man can become a policeman in Denver—if he is within the age brackets, if he is a highschool graduate, if he has no criminal record, he is a cinch.

There isn't much to getting through the screening, and some bad ones do get through. There are the usual examinations and questionnaires. Then there is the interview. A few command officers ask questions. There is a representative of civil service and a psychiatrist present.

They ask the predictable questions, and just about everybody give the predictable answers: "Why do you want to become a policeman?" "I've always wanted to be a policeman. I want to help people." Five or ten minutes and it is over.

Five or ten minutes to spot the sadist, the psychopath — or the guy with an eye for an easy buck. I guess they weed some out. Some others they get at the Police Academy. But some get through.

Along with those few bad ones, there are more

The text material is reprinted by permission of *The Denver Post*. The Roleplay materials were developed and are copyrighted by Jack Brittain, School of Management, University of Texas at Dallas, Richardson, Texas 75083-0688. Used with permission of the author.

good ones, and a lot of average, ordinary human beings who have this in common: They want to be policemen.

The job has (or had) some glamour for the young man who likes authority, who finds appeal in making a career of public service, who is extroverted or aggressive.

Before you knock those qualities, remember two things: First, they are the same qualities we admire in a business executive. Second, if it weren't for men with these qualities, you wouldn't have any police protection.

The Police Academy is point No. 2 in my bill of particulars. It is a fine thing in a way. You meet the cream of the Police Department. Your expectations soar. You know you are going to make the grade and be a good officer. But how well are you really prepared?

There are six weeks at the academy — four weeks in my time. Six hectic weeks in which to learn all about the criminal laws you have sworn to enforce, to assimilate the rules of evidence, methods of arbitration, use of firearms, mob and riot control, first aid (including, if you please, some basic obstetrics), public relations, and so on.

There is an intangible something else that is not on the formal agenda. You begin to learn that this is a fraternity into which you are not automatically accepted by your fellows. You have to earn your way in; you have to establish that you are "all right."

And even this early there is a slight sour note. You knew, of course, that you had to provide your own uniforms, your own hat, shoes, shirts, pistol and bullets out of your $393 a month.

You knew the city would generously provide you with the cloth for two pair of trousers and a uniform blouse.

What you didn't know was that you don't just choose a tailor shop for price and get the job done.

You are sent to a place by the Police Department to get the tailoring done. You pay the price even though the work may be ill-fitting. It seems a little odd to you that it is always the same establishment. But it is a small point and you have other things on your mind.

So the rookie, full of pride and high spirit, his head full of partly-learned information, is turned over to a more experienced man for breaking in. He is on "probation" for six months.

The rookie knows he is being watched by all the older hands around him. He is eager to be accepted. He accepts advice gratefully.

Then he gets little signs that he has been making a good impression. It may happen like this: The older man stops at a bar, comes out with some packages of cigarettes. He does this several times. He explains that this is part of the job, getting cigarettes free from proprietors to resell, and that as a part of the rookie's training it is his turn to "make the butts."

So he goes into a skid-road bar and stands uncomfortably at the end waiting for the bartender to acknowledge his presence and disdainfully toss him two packages of butts.

The feeling of pride slips away and a hint of shame takes hold. But he tells himself this is unusual, that he will say nothing that will upset his probation standing. In six months, after he gets his commission, he will be the upright officer he meant to be.

One thing leads to another for the rookies. After six months they have become conditioned to accept free meals, a few packages of cigarettes, turkeys at Thanksgiving, and liquor at Christmas from the respectable people in their district.

The rule book forbids all this. But it isn't enforced. It is winked at on all levels.

So the rookies say to themselves that this is OK, that this is a far cry from stealing and they still can be good policemen. Besides, they are becoming accepted as "good guys" by their fellow officers.

This becomes more and more important as the young policeman begins to sense a hostility toward him in the community. This is fostered to a degree by some of the saltier old hands in the department. But the public plays its part.

Americans are funny. They have a resentment for authority. And the policeman is authority in person. The respectable person may soon forget that a policeman found his lost youngster in the park, but he remembers that a policeman gave him a traffic ticket.

The negative aspect of the job builds up. The majority of the people he comes in contact with during his working hours are thieves, con men, narcotics addicts, and out and out nuts.

Off the job his associations narrow. Part of the time when he isn't working, he is sleeping. His waking, off-duty hours do not make him much of a neighbor. And then he wants to spend as much time as he can with his family.

Sometimes, when he tries to mix with his neighbors, he senses a kind of strain. When he is introduced to someone, it is not likely to be, "This is John Jones, my friend," or "my neighbor"; it is more likely to be, "this is John Jones. He's a policeman."

And the other fellow, he takes it up, too. He is likely to tell you that he has always supported pay increases for policemen, that he likes policemen as a whole, but that there are just a few guys in uniform he hates.

No wonder the officer begins to think of himself as a member of the smallest minority group in the community. The idea gradually sinks into him that the only people who understand him, that he can be close to, are his fellow officers.

It is in this kind of atmosphere that you can find the young policeman trying to make the grade in the fraternity. But that is not the whole story.

A policeman lives with tensions, and with fears.

Part of the tensions come from the incredible monotony. He is cooped up with another man, day after day, doing routine things over and over. The excitement that most people think of as the constant occupation of policemen is so infrequent as to come as a relief.

Part of the tensions come from the manifold fears. I don't mean that these men are cowards. This is no place for cowards. But they are human beings. And fears work on all human beings.

Paramount is the physical fear that he will get hurt to the point where he can't go on working, or the fear that he will be killed. He fears for his family.

There is the fear that he will make a wrong decision in a crucial moment, a life-and-death

decision. A man has been in a fight. Should he call the paddy wagon or the ambulance? A man aims a pistol at him. Should he try to talk to him, or shoot him?

But the biggest fear he has is that he will show fear to some of his fellow officers. This is the reason he will rush heedlessly in on a cornered burglar or armed maniac if a couple of officers are present — something he wouldn't do if he were alone. He is tormented by his fears, and he doesn't dare show them. He knows he has to present a cool, calm front to the public.

As a group, policemen have a very high rate of ulcers, heart attacks, suicides, and divorces. These things torment him, too. Divorce is a big problem to policemen. A man can't be a policeman for eight hours and then just turn it off and go home and be a loving father and husband — particularly if he has just had somebody die in the back of his police car.

So once again, the pressure is on him to belong, to be accepted and welcomed into the only group that knows what is going on inside him. If the influences aren't right, he can be hooked.

So he is at the stage where he wants to be one of the guys. And then this kind of thing may happen: One night his car is sent to check on a "Code 26" — a silent burglar alarm.

The officer and his partner go in to investigate. The burglar is gone. They call the proprietor. He comes down to look things over. And maybe he says, "Boys, this is covered by insurance, so why don't you take a jacket for your wife, or a pair of shoes?" And maybe he does, maybe just because his partner does, and he says to himself, "What the hell, who has been hurt?"

Or maybe the proprietor didn't come down. But after they get back in the car his partner pulls out four $10 bills and hands him two. "Burglar got careless," says the partner.

The young officer who isn't involved soon learns that this kind of thing goes on. He even may find himself checking on a burglary call, say to a drugstore, and see some officers there eyeing him peculiarly.

Maybe at this point the young officer feels the pressure to belong so strongly that he reaches over and picks up something, cigars perhaps.

Then he is "in," and the others can do what they wish.

Mind you, not all officers will do this. Somewhere along the line all of them have to make a decision, and it is at that point where the stuff they are made of shows through. But the past experience of the handouts, the official indifference to them, and the pressures and tensions of the job don't make the decision any easier.

And neither he nor the department has had any advance warning, such as might come from thorough psychiatric screening, as to what his decision will be.

Some men may go this far and no further. They might rationalize that they have not done anything that isn't really accepted by smart people in society.

This is no doubt where the hard-core guy, the one who is a thief already, steps in. A policeman is a trained observer and he is smart in back-alley psychology. This is especially true of the hard-core guy, and he has been watching the young fellows come along.

When he and his cronies in a burglary ring spot a guy who may have what it takes to be one of them, they may approach him and try him out as a lookout. From then on it is just short steps to the actual participation in and planning of crimes.

Bear in mind that by this stage we have left all but a few policemen behind. But all of them figure in the story at one stage or another. And what has happened to a few could happen to others. I suppose that is the main point I am trying to make.

Making of a Bad Cop Roles

Instructions

The instructor will assign you a role to play during the "Making of a Bad Cop" case discussion. You will caucus with other members of your role group prior to the discussion to come up with some suggested solutions to the problems outlined in the case. The following newspaper story discusses each of the groups partici-

pating in the meeting that is going to be held to tackle the police corruption issue. The following paragraphs describe the generic perspective that each role group operates under.

THE CITY — Yesterday the Mayor announced a task force charged with solving the police corruption scandal that recently shocked The City. At the news conference called to announce the task force, the Mayor was adamant: "We must do something about the crime wave that has swept over our police force. And we will do something about it. No excuses." The Mayor announced that the task force will have representatives of The City's taxpayers, the Downtown Chamber of Commerce, the Police Force, the Public Employees' Union, and the City Council. Each of these groups sees the problem differently and brings a different agenda to the task force.

City Council. The Mayor appointed the task force to make sure the City Council understands the police corruption problem and hears a variety of suggestions for addressing it. Responsibility for the corruption scandal ultimately resides with the Council, which is in a difficult situation. They face a public outraged by the scandal and unwilling to pay higher taxes, corrupt police that cannot readily be identified, a Public Employees' Union that is seeking to protect the salaries and job security of other city employees, and a mandate to control crime. If the Council fails to solve the police corruption scandal, several members could be out of a job. And this scandal also has the potential to completely disrupt the functioning of city government. It is an explosive situation and the future political careers of all the Council members are on the line.

Citizens (and Taxpayers). The Mayor has asked a group of citizens to represent the community on the task force. Citizens generally feel they are overtaxed by city government and under protected by the Police Department. And now a scandal has erupted in the Police Department that goes well beyond petty corruption. The citizens want the Police Department cleaned up, better police protection, and a more effective use of their tax dollars. And they are prepared to throw the city council out in the next election if necessary to get this scandal resolved.

Police Force. At the request of the Mayor, the Chief of Police selected a group of "good cops" to represent their fellow officers on the task force. The officers on the police force are concerned that the citizens of the community do not understand police work and will advocate solutions that will make policing more difficult and dangerous. As a result, one of the top priorities of the police representatives is making sure that all involved parties understand the average officer's life on the beat. The police representatives would also like to see working conditions and pay improved. The perception among most officers is that corruption is not the only injustice in this case. The pay officers receive for performing a necessary and dangerous service that benefits the entire community is outrageously low.

Public Employees' Union. The City Public Employees' Union has also been asked to select members to serve on the task force. The Union represents all city employees and must make sure that no employees — including the police officers — are hurt by the corruption scandal. So, even though officials agreed off the record that the police are woefully under funded and the officers are shamefully under paid, the Union cannot support any alternative that takes money from other public employees. And Union representatives are apparently prepared to pull all public employees out on strike, a move that would be an illegal work stoppage, to protect employee interests. Representatives announced that "any solution that plays one set of city employees against all city employees is unacceptable."

Downtown Chamber of Commerce. Representatives of the downtown business community were chosen from the membership of the Downtown Chamber of Commerce. The downtown business community is very concerned about crime, but is even more concerned that the police corruption scandal is going to get blown out of proportion, resulting in police reticence in dealing with criminals, reluctance on the part of citizens to shop downtown, and increased insurance premiums for downtown businesses. The Chamber wishes the powers that be in the city would just handle this problem so downtown can get back to business as usual.

The Mayor will chair the first meeting of the task force. This meeting is restricted to members of the task force only, a move the Mayor justified by saying, "Let us figure out what we think. Then we will open up the process to anyone who wants to participate."

28

Private Inc.
The New Substance Abuse
Policy

Jeff Kotter had just arrived in Sarasota Florida to take over as the President of Private Inc., a growing manufacturer of printed circuits. One of his first jobs was to continue the implementation of Private Inc.'s new policy on substance abuse testing. He wasn't sure how he wanted to go about dealing with the policy in the future. He had been hired by Steve Alderwood (the CEO and majority shareholder in this family owned business). Alderwood was very concerned about drug and alcohol abuse among his employees. While there hadn't been many overt drug or alcohol abuse cases among the employees, he believed the company should take decisive action because it was the right thing to do. Alderwood strongly believed that family values should be incorporated in the workplace. An entire wall in the entrance to the administrative offices is devoted to biblical or scriptural references and quotations. A further insight into the company culture is their refusal to sell to Communist countries as it is believed that such sales would be a violation of Private's belief system.

On the subject of substance abuse testing, Alderwood said, "We look at drug screening as the moral thing to do for our employees. It is our duty and we are committed to drug screening. Industry must play a role in society's drug problem. By checking our employees, we can make an impact on drugs."

His attitude was that Private Inc. is a family-run business, and all employees are part of the family. Therefore, when one person has a problem, the entire family or group suffers. Private uses a disciplined approach in that employees are expected to come forward voluntarily if they have a drug problem. An employee must do this 24 hours before the random testing begins in order to qualify for company-paid rehabilitation. Otherwise, they are terminated immediately upon failing the drug test. (Positive tests were confirmed.) There is no suspension period and no rehiring after clean-up. However, Private does not protest claims for unemployment compensation. (See Appendices I and II for the specifics of the policies.)

Jeff was not sure what he thought of the policy so he held meetings with several senior staff. As was his custom, he had taken notes from the meeting. He decided to review these notes:

This case was written by Teri Beals, Mansoor Khaleeluddin, Leslie Lambert, Todd Schatzman, Danny Smith and Mark Sharfman. It was written as a basis for class discussion rather than to illustrate effective or ineffective handling of an administrative decision. All rights are retained by the authors. Used with permission of the authors.

Exhibit 28-1

Notes From Meeting With Nancy Redear, Personnel Manager, on Friday, 4/22

Nancy reported that Private had their second random drug testing yesterday 4/21/93. St. Anthony's conducted the exam on all 175 employees at the Sarasota location. There are an additional 85 employees at the plant in Blacksburg. They will be tested at another time. Only three people knew that the drug tests were scheduled: Nancy; Tom Adams, the Exec. VP; and Harvey Black, the plant manager. It took two St. Anthony's people all day to do the tests. They decided not to witness each employee. Instead they were using temperature vials that measured body temperature so that there was no way someone could carry in a baggie of urine. Toilets have blue water in them and all other water is turned off the day of the testing. They test for all drugs, .04 alcohol content and as little as 20 nanograms of marijuana.

The first test cost 7 people out of 230 employees. Yesterday's tests detected no illegal substances. She believes this happened because the workers know that employees who test positive at the time of the random test are terminated. If an employee comes in at least 24 hours before a random test and admits to a problem, the company will pay for inpatient and outpatient rehabilitation, which can cost as much as $10,000. This rule was added after an employee who failed the first test asked to be rehabilitated instead of terminated. They drug screen all workers' compensation/accident claim injuries automatically.

Nancy mentioned three reasons why Private implemented their drug testing program: high accident ratio, at the suggestion of employees who responded to the "suggestion box," and at the request of a significant other who reported an at-work drug use problem of an employee.

Beginning Monday, May 29th, no smoking will be allowed in most of the plant areas. For the last five years, no smoking has been allowed in the office areas.

Exhibit 28-2

Notes From Meeting With Harvey Black, Sarasota Plant Manager 4/25

Harvey was not certain, but he believed the program was started because:

1. employees were complaining about individuals coming to work impaired, and
2. the owners of the company do not believe employees should take drugs or drink alcohol.

Harvey did not believe the direct costs were very substantial. Employees are rotated from their jobs to the testing areas whenever a test is being performed. This reduces the downtime associated with the testing of the employees.

Harvey stated that absenteeism has been reduced while quality has improved. In addition, rework and scrap have been reduced. He believed the morale of the employees has improved. The improvement was attributed to the discipline associated with the drug program. Prior to drug testing, an employee would realize that a coworker was impaired. The employee would become frustrated because they knew the impaired individual was being paid by Private and the impaired individual was probably not performing his or her job adequately.

Harvey believes the manner in which the plan has evolved is fair. Before the initial tests were performed, the employees with drug problems were asked to come forward. The company was prepared to pay for a rehabilitation program and pay the individual sick leave during the period. The company still allows individuals to come forward prior to a drug test when they have a problem.

I had asked him if he knew of employees who had quit because they felt the drug tests violated their rights. He said he didn't, but some individuals who are still with the company have complained; and Harvey believed some individuals had discussed the testing with their attorneys, but to date no one had challenged the program.

Exhibit 28-3

Notes From Meeting With Tom Adams, Executive V.P. 4/26

I asked him what prompted Private to initiate its random drug testing program.

He had difficulty answering this initially, but after considering the question, responded that Mr. Alderwood was the impetus behind the program and wanted a drug free environment. He did not mention that employees suggested the program or wanted it. However, as the Exec. V.P., he may not have had enough contact with the production employees to know this, if in fact it is the case. Tom believes that Mr. Alderwood's primary reason for the program is based on his values.

He does not know the costs of the program and they have never really looked into the monetary costs, because costs are not a factor in their decision making on this issue. He suggested that other than the direct costs of the individual tests, the only other costs would be the lost productivity when people are being tested. He does not feel this cost is significant.

In short, he believes in the program and is not going to let costs change that. He said the following benefits have resulted from the program:

- Morale and productivity have increased.

- Workmen's Comp. claims, liability insurance, and cost of group health insurance have decreased.

- Personnel who were not maximizing their productivity have been weeded out.

- Private is close to having a drug and alcohol-free environment, as evidenced by fact that there were zero failures on the last test.

- Profitability has also increased since implementation.

Asked if he was satisfied with the policy of immediate termination for testing positive to the drug test, Tom responded "yes" because he felt the employees had been warned and given opportunity to come forward and get help. To summarize discussion on this issue, he believes there is need for this discipline for the benefit of the firm and individuals.

Regarding anticipated problems, he was concerned about legal suits, but did not have any. Also, he expected an initial backlash from the employees and did get that. However, there does not seem to be a problem with backlash anymore, or at least nothing is said by the employees. Tom has never requested anyone submit to a random test because of probable cause. He mention that any accidents or injuries, other than eye, did have to submit to a test.

Jeff didn't feel very comfortable yet about this new policy. He figured that he better get some background—especially on the legal side. He remembered a handout he received at that Executive Seminar he had attended in 1990. He knew it was a bit out of date now (see Appendix III) and that new developments were occurring rapidly, but he knew it was pretty good for the time. After he reviewed the handout, he wrote a memo to his student intern asking her to do some research to see what had developed in the last 3 years.

Jeff was comforted a little by the care the company had taken in setting up its testing procedures. Alderwood's confidence in the propriety of the drug testing program was enhanced by his belief in the quality of St. Anthony's testing procedures. The first step in the drug screening process is the collection of the urine sample, documentation of the specimen contributor's identity, and testing for adulteration of the specimen. Initial screening tests are performed on an automated instrument. If all the tests are negative for a given specimen, then a negative report is generated and sent to Private. If one of the tests is positive, additional confirmatory testing is performed to assure the correctness of the screening results. This involves extraction of the drug from the specimen, concentration and chemical treatment of the extracted drug, and its identification and quantification using a gas chromatograph/mass spectrometer. When both the screening and confirmation tests are positive, and the supervisor and director have reviewed them, the final result is declared to be positive.

St. Anthony's program is supervised by Susan Spencer, Ph.D., associate director of toxicology; Sam Beckett, M.D., director of clinical pathology and associate director of toxicology; and James Southern, M.D. St. Anthony began offering drug screening for companies in 1987. By 1993, they were performing 27,000 employee drug screens and pre-employment screens per year. The program is certified by the College of American Pathologists for Forensic Drug Testing and the National Institute of Drug Abuse. NIDA has only certified some 38 labs, and the process is expensive and complicated. It was the first successful industrial drug testing program in Florida.

In tailoring their program to meet Private's needs, St. Anthony's uses their on-site mobile unit for random testing. Observation of the specimen collection is no longer required due to the use of temperature controlled vials that measure and compare the temperature of the specimen to that of the employee's body. Water at the plant is turned off or tinted to avoid any opportunity to tamper with samples. Employees individually arrive at the mobile unit where they sign an authorization form which asks for a list of any medications currently used by that employee. Before pronouncing a test positive, St. Anthony's supervisor and director will compare this list to the test results for possible overlap. According to industry surveys, marijuana is the drug abused most often by employees. Therefore, Alderwood requested a 20 ng/ml level of testing instead of the National Institute of Drug Abuse's recognized level of abuse of 100 ng/ml. The U.S. Armed Forces uses this 20 ng/ml level, but some experts argue that such a low level does not differentiate between passive exposure to marijuana smoke and actual use. The lower level is in keeping with Private's philosophy because Alderwood's goal is to help eliminate all illegal drug use in society.

Jeff knew that drug and alcohol use is potentially a major problem for a business. He understood that workers abusing drugs or alcohol cost money and sometimes lives. He glanced back at the Executive Education materials. He saw data that indicated up to $100 billion in annual business productivity was lost not the least because drug and alcohol users were twice as likely to miss work or be fired and had almost four times as many accidents. He knew he had to have a policy. He was just not sure he wanted this policy.

APPENDIX 1

Notice of New Drug Policy

January 30, 1992

TO: All Employees
FROM: Steve Alderwood, Chief Executive Officer
SUBJECT: Announcing Policy Concerning Alcohol & Drug Use

Private, Inc. realizes the importance of providing a safe, healthy work environment for all employees and visitors.

The Company is aware that the use and consumption of alcohol and drugs by employees while performing their jobs or while outside the scope of employment will detrimentally affect their job performance, the safety of the employees and their co-workers, as well as employee productivity, morale and efficiency.

The Company is aware from both direct and indirect contacts that alcohol and drug abuse problems exist within our company and include the illegal use, consumption and sale of drugs as well as the abuse of alcohol.

In order to maintain a safe working environment and insure quality workmanship and maximum productivity as well as the reputation of the Company, it has become necessary for the Company to initiate a program designed to eliminate alcohol and drug abuse by its employees. The program will become effective 60 days from the date of this notice, or March 30, 1992.

This notice is designed to make each employee aware of the position of the Company as it relates to drug and alcohol abuse and the actions employees can expect to be taken on the effective date of the program.

I. Company Assistance in Obtaining Treatment

Our first effort will be to assist employees in obtaining proper treatment for alcohol and drug abuse problems. We also assure any employee who requests assistance in obtaining treatment that no employee will jeopardize his or her job by requesting such assistance from the Company. The confidential nature of such problems will be preserved in the same manner as all other medical records.

II. Prohibition of Use, Possession and Sale of Alcohol and Drugs

A. The use, possession, concealment, transportation, promotion or sale of the following items or substances is strictly prohibited from all Company properties, facilities, lands, buildings, structures, installations, trucks and all other work locations while in the course and scope of Company employment: Alcohol, illegal drugs, controlled substances, look-alikes, designer and synthetic drugs and other drugs (with the exception of prescription drugs as limited by Part C below) which may affect an employee's senses or motor functions.

B. It shall be a violation of the Company policy for any employee to report for duty, come on Company premises, or work while under the influence of alcohol or while having alcoholic beverages in his or her possession.

C. Prescription drugs may be used at work only as prescribed by authorized medical professionals and used only by the person possessing such prescription under the proper dosage and only after employee's supervisor has been informed.

III. Searches, Inspections and Screening:

Private, Inc. reserves the right, at all times while employees are on the Company premises and properties described in Part IIA above, to conduct searches and inspection of employees, work areas, and containers to determine the possession, use or concealment of any of the prohibited items or substances. Inspection may be conducted by managerial and supervisory personnel.

IV. Substance Screening. Urine Testing

The Company reserves the right to perform substance screening, which includes urine testing, under circumstances such as:

1. Pre-employment examinations.
2. When an employee or person is found in possession of suspected or illicit or unauthorized drugs and/or alcohol.
3. When an employee exhibits signs of being incapacitated or unable to work due to possible intoxication, use or influence of drugs or alcohol.
4. When an employee suffers an occupational on-the-job injury.
5. When a serious or potentially serious on-the-job accident has occurred.
6. Excessive tardiness or absences.
7. When it determines that the screening of one or more employees is in the best interest of the Company.

V. Disciplinary Action:

Any employee having possession on Company premises of any of the above-mentioned items shall be subject to disciplinary action up to and including discharge from employment. In the event that the result of any substance screening test, including urine, is positive and indicates the presence of drugs or alcohol with respect to any employee, that employee shall be subject to discharge from employment. All positive tests will be confirmed before discharge actions are taken.

This policy is being implemented in good faith for the purpose of achieving the maximum safety and well-being of all Private, Inc. employees and other personnel. Your assistance and cooperation in achieving this goal are vitally important.

APPENDIX 2

Details of the New Policy

March 30, 1992

TO: All Employees
FROM: Steve Alderwood, Chief Executive Officer
SUBJECT: Clarification of Issues in the Drug/Alcohol Policy Effective March 30, 1992

1. PURPOSE

1.1 The purpose of this Policy is to help insure a safe, healthy, and productive work environment for the employees of Private, Inc. (hereinafter referred to as "Company") and others affected by the Company's operations, to protect Company property and assets, and to assure efficient operations.

1.2 This Policy restricts certain items and substances from being brought in or being present on Company premises, and it prohibits Company employees and others working or present on Company property from having detectable levels of certain drugs and other substances.

2. PROHIBITED SUBSTANCES OR DRUG PARAPHERNALIA

2.1 The use, possession, transportation, or sale of prohibited substances (as hereinafter defined) or drug paraphernalia by any employee while on duty, while on Company premises or in any Company vehicle, or while on any job site of a customer is prohibited.

3. INTOXICATING BEVERAGES AND/OR ALCOHOL

3.1 The use, possession, transportation, or sale of intoxicating beverages and/or alcohol while on duty, while on Company premises or in any Company vehicle, or while on any job site of a customer is prohibited unless specifically authorized by Management.

4. REPORTING TO WORK WITH DETECTABLE LEVELS OF PROHIBITED SUBSTANCES, INTOXICATING BEVERAGES AND/OR ALCOHOL

4.1 Reporting to work with detectable levels of prohibited substances, intoxicating beverages and/or alcohol in the body fluids is prohibited.

5. SEARCHES, INVESTIGATIONS, TESTS, AND DISCIPLINE

5.1 In order to accomplish the purpose of this Policy, the Company reserves the right to carry out a reasonable search of any employee and his/her personal effects when such employee is on duty, or while any such employee is at a job site of a customer. Personal effects of employees include, but are not limited to, clothing, purses, personal vehicles, baggage, lockers, tool boxes, and lunch pails.

5.2 Reasonable searches by the Company may be initiated without prior notice and conducted at times and locations deemed appropriate by the Company.

5.3 Any employee while on duty, while on Company premises or in any Company vehicle, or while on any job site of a customer may be directed to cooperate in a urinalysis test at any time.

5.4 Employees have the right to refuse to be searched, to have their personal effects searched or to cooperate in the directed tests; however, refusal by any employee to permit such searches or to cooperate in such tests will be just cause for discharge.

5.5 Violation of this Policy will be just cause for discharge.

5.6 The Company may take into custody any illegal, unauthorized, or prohibited items and may turn them over to the proper law enforcement agencies.

6. SAVINGS CLAUSE

6.1 If any part of this Policy is held invalid by a competent authority, such part shall be invalid and the balance of the Policy shall continue to be valid and in full force and effect.

7. DEFINITIONS

7.1 PROHIBITED SUBSTANCE   Prohibited substances include marijuana, narcotics, illegal drugs, controlled substances, mood or mind-altering substances. Prohibited substances shall not include over-the-counter medications used in accordance with manufacturer's recommended dosages, properly reported and properly used prescription drugs prescribed by a licensed physician as medication for use by the person possessing such substance, or nicotine in tobacco products and caffeine contained in beverages (such as coffee, tea, and soft drinks).

7.2 ILLEGAL DRUGS   Illegal drugs include drugs which are not legally obtained and drugs which are legally obtainable but have been obtained illegally.

7.3 CONTROLLED SUBSTANCE   Anything that one can eat, drink, inhale, absorb, and/or inject into one's body but cannot legally purchase.

7.4 DETECTABLE LEVELS   Laboratory evidence of the presence of a drug, intoxicating beverage, alcohol, or prohibited or controlled substance in the body fluids at levels of detection above the lowest cut-off level established in the procedure used by the testing laboratory.

APPENDIX 3

Executive Education Handout on Drug Testing
10/90

LEGAL STATUS OF DRUG TESTING

The Harrison Narcotics Act of 1914 was the beginning of the federal prohibition on drugs. Many believe that the ensuing 76 years have been a costly and abject exercise in futility.[1] In 1971, President Nixon signed an Executive Order to begin random drug testing in the military. This order was in response to the large number of Viet Nam veterans who were returning home addicted to heroin. In 1981, a Marine Corps Prowler jet crashed while attempting to land aboard the USS Nimitz. The accident caused 14 deaths and 48 injuries. Subsequent tests revealed that some of the carrier crew had traces of marijuana in their systems. As a result of this disaster, the military implemented mandatory drug testing in all branches of the service.

In September, 1986, President Reagan signed Executive Order 12564, mandating random, mandatory drug testing for federal employees, declaring that "Persons who use illegal drugs are not suitable for Federal employment."[2] Drug-related accidents combined with increasing drug use in the United States prompted the government and various government agencies to take an active role in creating rules and regulations for both public and private employers. This uncoordinated effort has created a variety of inconsistent rules and regulations for employers to consider. Even after the aforementioned 1987 Commission on Organized Crime report requested the help of business, employers were faced with the problem of determining what type of plan to implement.

In 1987, a Conrail-Amtrak accident killed 16 and injured over 100 passengers. A subsequent drug test found that the engineer had drugs in his system.[3] This accident and others eventually led the Department of Transportation (DOT) to implement drug testing regulations for 4 million transportation workers. DOT requires testing of private company applicants and mandates 5 types of testing procedures. The requirements preempt state laws and labor agreements.[4]

The Department of Defense (DOD) has implemented a drug testing plan for their contractors as well. This plan gives private companies the authority to test applicants, and it requires the testing of employees in "sensitive positions," a designation which is not defined. These requirements differ from the DOT's in that they do not preempt state laws and labor agreements.

The Drug-free Workplace Act was passed in 1988 and took effect March 18, 1989. This Act requires any company with a federal government contract of at least $25,000 to certify that they will maintain a drug-free workplace. The Act does not require mandatory implementation of a drug testing program, but it focuses on employee awareness, a drug-free policy and drug rehabilitation.[5]

In addition to federal requirements, employers must determine if they are constrained by state or local laws. A few states (California, Arizona, New York, Florida, Montana, and Alaska) have constitutions which provide privacy protection, and some (Massachusetts and Rhode Island) guarantee protection against unreasonable search and seizure.[6] Some people do not realize that the U.S.

---

[1] George J. Church, "Thinking the Unthinkable," Time, 30 May 1988, 12.

[2] Marick F. Masters, "The Negotiability of Drug Use in the Federal Sector: A Political Perspective," Journal of Collective Negotiations in the Public Sector 17 (1988): 309.

[3] Robert H. Elliott, "Drug Testing and Public Personnel Administration," Review of Public Personnel Administration 9 (Summer 1989) 15-31.

[4] Yvonne Kidd, "The Drug-Free Workplace Act of 1989: A Brief Guide," Inform 3 (May 1989): 8-9.

[5] Michael R. Carrell and Christina Heavrin, "Before You Drug Test...," HR Magazine 35 (June 1990): 64.

[6] Michael A. Verespej, "Death Blow For Random Testing," Industry Week, 2 July 1990, 47.

Constitution guarantees apply only to intrusions by the government. While this prohibition covers government employees, it can be extended to companies which act as "agents" of the government.

The fourth, fifth and fourteenth amendments are most often cited as being applicable to drug testing. The fourth amendment provides the most protection for government employees. It protects them from unreasonable searches and seizures, but this protection can be limited by the courts in the public interest. The Supreme Court ruled in Amalgamated Transit v. Suscy, that in cases of either a serious accident or suspicious behavior, drug testing would not constitute an unreasonable search. The court has also held that under normal circumstances a drug test would be considered an unreasonable search.

The fifth and fourteenth amendments do not provide as much protection as the fourth amendment. The fifth amendment protects individuals from self-incrimination, while the fourteenth amendment provides individuals due process and equal protection. The courts have held that if a search is not unreasonable under the fourth amendment and the major purpose of the test is to protect the public, the individual's fifth and fourteenth amendment rights are not violated by a drug test.[7]

So far, only a few cases have been decided by the United States Supreme Court. In National Treasury Employees v. Von Raab, the Court upheld the decision that certain employees have diminished expectations of privacy when balanced against the social and governmental need for safety.[8] They said that jobs which required drug interdiction or the use of firearms could be tested, but not necessarily those which merely handled classified material. In Skinner v. Railway Labor Executives Association, the Court held that testing was justified after an accident even if an individual does not show signs of impairment.[9]

Federal constitutional provisions do not apply to private sector employers. The courts have ruled that a search performed by a private individual for purely private reasons falls outside of the fourth amendment. Private employees must look for protection in federal civil rights laws, union contracts and grievance procedures, or state and city statutes. Private employers could be impacted by these laws if their testing programs are considered discriminatory. Some states have extended handicap-discrimination laws to include AIDS. It is conceivable that drug use (or at least addiction) could one day be considered to be a handicap.

Another issue that employers must consider is the potential liability associated with negligence. An employee can assert negligence against a private employer if a drug-test was not performed in a reasonable manner.[10]

Private employers must be concerned with the legal environment that exists in the states and cities they operate in. Even in states which have constitutional provisions concerning privacy, the public interest of safety and health can prevail (*Luedtke v. Nabors Alaska Drilling Company*).[11] The California Supreme Court has upheld the state privacy provision. The court upheld the appellate court decisions in *Semore v. Kerr-McGee and in Luck v. Southern Pacific*. The appellate court ruled that the state privacy provision not only guarantees the right of privacy for individuals when they are dealing with the government but more importantly for employers, they extended this provision to include individuals when they are dealing with private entities.

Private sector employers must consider the legality of the drug test that is implemented. The Semore ruling stated that random testing violated public policy. That is, the test is illegal even if the employee

---

[7] Sami M. Abbasi, Kenneth W. Hollman and Joe H. Murrey, Jr., "Drug Testing: The Moral, Constitutional, and Accuracy Issues," Journal of Collective Negotiations 17 (1988): 221-235.

[8] Terry Halbert and Elaine Ingulli, Law and Ethics in the Business Environment (St. Paul: West Publishing) 1990, 87-93.

[9] Michael W. Skulnick, "Key Court Cases," Employment Relations Today 16 (Summer 1989): 141-146.

[10] Sami M. Abbasi, Kenneth W. Hollman and Joe H. Murrey, Jr., "Drug Testing: 'Be Moral, Constitutional, and Accuracy Issues," Journal of Collective Negotiations 17 (1988): 221-235.

[11] Terry Halbert and Elaine Ingulli, Law and Ethics in the Business Environment (St. Paul: West Publishing) 1990, 65-71.

consented to it. This ruling opened the door for tort claims of punitive damages against the employer.[12] The potential for monetary damages can exist when you have an invasion of the statutory and common law tort of right to privacy. This invasion can be established if two criteria are met:

(1) the means used to gain access to the private information is abnormal, and
(2) the defendant's reason for obtaining the information is questionable.

Logically it has been argued that a mandatory taking of bodily fluids is an invasion of privacy and therefore meets criteria 1. In *Satterfield v. Lockheed*, the employee was terminated after testing positive during an annual company physical. The court ruled that criteria 1 was not met because a urine test was a routine part of a physical. In *O'Brien v. Papa Gino's of America*, the court ruled that the employee had been improperly terminated when the employer used the results of a polygraph test to prove the employee used drugs. In that case the court ruled that criteria 1 was met because it was not normal for this type of test to be administered. A logical implication of this case is that a urine drug test, which is arguably more abnormal than a polygraph test, would also meet criteria 1. The case also examined the reason for performing the test. If the test was randomly given with no correlation to job performance, the employer testing could be liable for monetary damages.[13]

By 1988, eleven states (Connecticut, Iowa, Louisiana, Minnesota, Montana, Oregon, Rhode Island, Utah, Vermont, Nebraska and Tennessee) had passed some drug testing legislation. At least as many more are considering it. San Francisco and Berkeley, California, have city ordinances. This is legislation in addition to the states which have made constitutional inferences about drug testing. These laws affect test restrictions, procedural requirements and post-test issues such as rebuttal and termination.

How have employers reacted to the complex situation surrounding drug testing? A survey conducted on selected subscribers to Personnel magazine conducted by the American Management Association chronicles drug testing by employers from 1986 through 1989. Prior to the 1987 Organized Crime Committee Report, drug testing was performed on a fairly limited basis. Since the report was issued, the percentage of companies testing for drugs increased dramatically. It appears, however, that the uncertain legal environment surrounding drug testing has caused the number of companies testing to stabilize.

The most significant information discovered from the surveys is as follows:[14]

1) the percentage of companies testing from 1988 to 1989 stabilized at about 50%;

2) 67% of manufacturing firms test as compared to 38% of service firms;

3) manufacturers focus on testing new hires (90%), while only testing 69% of their current employees. Service firms focus on testing current employees (81%), while only testing 69% of their new hires;

4) only 1 company in 5 dismisses a current employee who tests positive for illegal substances.

---

[12] Michael A. Verespej, "Death Blow For Random Testing," Industry Week, 2 July 1990, 48.

[13] Robert J. Aalberts, "Drug Testing - Walking a Legal Tightrope," Business, January-March 1988, 52-56.

[14] Eric Rolfe Greenberg, 1990 and 1989 AMA Surveys, Personnel (July 1990 and May 1989).

29
The Merck Finance Organization

The Merck Culture:
Leading Edge with a Hard Edge

At Merck, the competitive team orientation is cast in the language of leading edge professionalism. The current strategic plan for Merck's financial organization starts with the following mission statement.

> The mission of Merck's financial organization is to improve the Company's profitability through astute financial and tax planning, accounting, reporting and performance evaluation. An important objective is to extend our reputation as one of the most professional and progressive financial staffs in the industry. To do this, Merck is committed to achieving excellence in all aspects of its financial organization, with special emphasis on recruiting and developing top-flight individuals.

In itself, the emphasis on developing a leading-edge financial organization is not terribly distinctive. A random selection of financial function plans would probably turn up many similarly worded statements. What is distinctive about Merck's financial function is that the rhetoric of leading edge is underwritten by a very coherent vision, that is, backed by a strategy for bringing that vision into reality with measurable results.

The CFO, Frank Spiegel, is committed to developing a group of team-oriented financial professionals. Frank Spiegel has a vision of the type of financial professional that Merck needs: an individual who brings sophisticated analytic tools to the decision table and who makes substantive contributions to solving management problems. Sophistication includes a solid grounding in the logic of risk and return, and a sound understanding of the business.

Merck hires high-impact individuals from top business schools and provides them with ample resources and an open, flexible working environment. In return, Merck's financial executives expect these individuals to create innovative financial tools and products to produce a measurable impact on the bottom line. Openness and flexibility are essential. Financial executives at

---

Written by Patrick J. Keating and Stephen F. Jablonsky. This case was written as part of a project sponsored by the Financial Executives Research Foundation. The final version of the case appears in *Changing Roles of Financial Management: Getting Close to the Business*, published by the Financial Executives Research Foundation copyright 1990. Used with permission of the authors and the Financial Executives Research Foundation.

Merck, moreso than at any of the other four industrial firms studied in this research, stressed their impatience with narrowly defined job responsibilities. Traditional specialist distinctions such as accounting and finance, treasury and control have no place in Frank Spiegel's vision.

Given Merck's commitment to measurable results, it is fair to say that leading edge is not simply a cliche. Leading edge has a hard edge. Financial products and analytic tools are deemed leading edge only if they have at least one of the following properties:

1. They result in a measurable improvement in the firm's profitability.
2. They represent innovative practices either introduced into the industry by Merck's financial staff, or are found in only a limited number of firms.
3. They represent practices which outside financial experts (found in banks, consulting firms, or universities) have stated to be highly progressive.

As Al Smith, the current Vice President of Finance put it:

Success of (the financial) organization really depends on being able to demonstrate that you have contributed in some major way to financial success of the firm.

Frank Spiegel is rather direct when it comes to the commitment to making a tangible contribution to the firm's profitability:

I won't put anything on this list (going to the CEO) that you can't put a buck on.

Apparently, there have been enough successes to report, since the financial organization has been the only corporate staff to receive top management's excellence rating for the last two years. The shift in financial function orientation from command and control to competitive team has played an important role in improving the status of the financial organization.

The Shift From Command and Control to Competitive Team

The emphasis on leading edge financial management belies a shift in posture and position within the firm. Consider the following comments by Stanley Fiddleman, the current Vice President for Research Administration.

I think there's been a tremendous change in the financial area—probably in the last 5-7 years. [Historically,] I would look at the financial people, and it didn't matter whether we were making drugs or shoes or anything else. Financial people did financial things. They didn't perceive themselves as being part of the company in decision making, even at the top of the company. They didn't consider themselves to be an integral part of management; at the divisional level they too were divorced.

The biggest single change I found as of late was their participation in the area that they're involved with... more substance and more caring and more trying to understand what it is... what the client is about.

These comments are significant in that they come from a top member of the research organization in a firm where research is king. These comments are indicative of the basic shift in orientation that has occurred over the past five to seven years, most notably the last two to three years. The shift has been away from arms-length monitoring and control to customer service and involvement in the business.

In making this shift, the financial organization has become more influential in shaping competitive decisions. Possibly, the most tangible evidence of the importance of the financial point of view within Merck is the increased involvement and influence of the current CFO, Frank Spiegel, as a member of Merck's top management team, the Operating Review Committee (ORC). Again, Stanley Fiddleman notes:

You put your money where your mouth is.

Frank's recent promotion says he is more than a financial guy doing a traditional financial role.

If you look at Frank Spiegel's role in the company today and even his role 2-3 years ago, it was more than a just a financial person. By being part of the management team he not only was a member by designation, but he was a member by doing... in our history that was not considered part of their [finance's] job description—it may be a philosophy, it may be the people, it was sort of "that's not my area, I shouldn't have to get involved.

The shift in orientation toward greater involvement and influence has not been as dramatic as the shifts found in the financial functions at firms like AT&T, Citicorp, and Ford. Rather, the shift appears to be one of movement away from a **muted command and control orientation** to a very **visible competitive team orientation**. We use the term "muted" for two reasons. First, the interview comments do not surface a historically strong or distinct financial culture at Merck. Certainly there are clear references in the interview comments to tensions between financial and line management that are indicative of a traditional command and control approach to financial control; however, these references are not extensive.

In referring to the previous orientation of the financial function, the Vice President for Research Administration offered the following comment.

If you lined up people in every operating area, they'd tell you financial was a big pain in the ass and did stifle things. Whether they did or not, that was their perception.

There were also shades of confrontation and second guessing. Charlie Cosgrove, Assistant Controller, makes some very eloquent statements in this regard.

Interviewer: This shift to a service orientation. That's something divisions see as a definite change?

Charlie: Absolutely. You should get the same type of vibes from everybody you talk to. We certainly have changed from lunging forward at people to the point of walking along with them for a while. (But) you know you will be fired... if you are so comfortable in bed with these people, that you start doing it the wrong way.

On a similar note, Charlie Cosgrove recalled the confrontational style of a previous Corporate Controller.

It was a contentious issue for a while. As division controller I was expected to give the [corporate] controller a list of questions... that would expose the fact that they [operating divisional management] were asking for too much. The second year I gave a copy to [the controller] and the division head. He [the controller] went into orbit. To me it was the classic culture being established that you were there, but you weren't there to work and smooth things over. (You were) there to say, "I wouldn't have done that."

Merck did not have a strong financial culture. The financial organization only played a limited role until recent times. In explaining the increased involvement of the financial organization in the management of the firm, Judy Lewent, Vice President and Treasurer, argues that sophisticated financial management was not needed in years past when Merck was smaller and the pharmaceutical industry was stable and well-protected.

(Merck was a) tiny company with a few good drugs, no therapeutic competition, patent protection, anti-substitution laws which effectively outlawed generics. Productivity of research was slow thereby giving product life cycles of 7-8 years. (In this environment) what do you need a financial person for?

In a relatively simple and non-threatening environment, strategic decision making is not intimately tied to financial or economic considerations. Why waste resources where they are not needed?

It can be argued, and Merck staff do, that as the environment in the pharmaceutical industry has become more complex and risky, the need for sophisticated financial analysis has increased. It is a well established fact that the research pipeline was running dry for the entire industry pipeline in the 1970's. Financial strategies were needed to ride out the dry years. The dry years also coincided with the repeal of anti-substitution laws across the U.S. (which had effectively outlawed generic drugs). Product sales can now drop by as much as 50% in the first year after a drug goes off patent. Merck anticipated more intense competition leading to reduced margins and returns on R&D and capital. This perceived environmental threat was reflected in Merck's 1988 corporate strategic plan.

The strategic plan identifies a number of strategic issues and action plans of a directly financial nature, including issues concerned with 1) managing a complex organizational and capital structure stemming from Merck's growth and worldwide marketing and manufacturing presence, 2) managing Merck's stated external growth strategy, and 3) coping with potential regulatory constraints on pricing freedom. On the last issue, Merck is concerned that claims of excess profits could lead to regulatory restrictions on the freedom of pharmaceutical firms to set product prices, thereby reducing economic returns.

In addition to issues of environmental complexity, managing growth, and responding to increased regulatory pressure, two specific changes initiated by the financial organization have played an important part in the shift to a competitive team orientation.

Key Financial Organization Initiatives

Merck's current CEO, Roy Vagelos, believes in having a strong measurement-based performance evaluation system. And the current CFO, Frank Spiegel, has been intimately involved in integrating the financial organization into Merck's measurement-oriented culture . Two initiatives are particularly significant in this regard:

1) In 1982, Merck made their product managers full resource managers and the financial organization supported that move by developing a comprehensive ROA-based measurement and performance evaluation system, and

2) The financial organization also developed an R&D planning model to improve the strategic management of Merck's substantial R&D investment process.

Through its success in these two ventures over the past five to seven years, the financial organization has demonstrated its commitment to a competitive team concept and has demonstrated that it can make a measurable difference in the financial performance of the firm. The financial organization is now involved in business decision making to an extent unequalled in its recent past. As the earlier comments by Stanley Fiddleman indicate, the value of the financial organization's stock and its status within the firm have risen substantially.

The ROA-based Performance Evaluation System

In the early 1980s Merck was experiencing, by its own historical standards, underpar profit margins, asset turnover and return of assets (ROA). Merck had fallen into the bottom half of the pack compared to the other twelve leading pharmaceutical companies.

One of the reasons for the decline in financial performance can be traced to John Horan, former CEO of Merck during the late 1970s and early 1980s. Horan made a tough, but ultimately very wise decision, to invest heavily in R&D. Merck is now reaping the rewards from that investment. The lower (by pharmaceutical industry standards) profits margins, asset turnover and ROA reflected the lag between making the investment decision and realizing the benefits of the investment through increased sales. In retrospect, the investment in R&D paid off; however, at the time, Horan decided to take the risks with only a hope for the return. The language of risk/return and the increased importance of the financial organization within Merck started during the Horan years.

Frank Spiegel talks about the contribution of the financial organization during this period.

> When we turned the corner in the 1980s, which is normal in this high risk business, we had a dearth of products and we had dollars going the wrong way... our returns were going in the wrong direction and our cost of capital was going in a counter direction. So we had to change the cultural thing to get people thinking about asset management... The changes that we've made in a couple of years are absolutely unbelievable in terms of redirecting assets. At a strategic meeting in 1982, I introduced a couple of concepts about return when I was in the planning function... that bit into the system. Then we moved it into the annual measurement system. So its really bitten. And people are now full resource managers as opposed to being quasi-marketing people. So there's a big drive if you have an asset that is not making its cost of capital and is never expected to, to do something different with that... My guess is that our success story in the last three years is better than anything you read about in the papers.

In terms of ROA, Merck has moved from the bottom half to the upper quartile of the twelve leading pharmaceutical companies. Merck is shooting for the number one rank in 1989. As Merck has improved its ROA, the market has responded with a substantially appreciated stock price. Merck has successfully integrated traditional financial measures into its management performance evaluation system. The financial organization provides a valuable support service to the line managers who are responsible for achieving the business objectives.

The R&D Planning Model

Merck's financial organization has made a major, innovative contribution to improving the sophistication of the R&D planning process. In addition to implementing a fully-integrated ROA-based performance evaluation system, the financial organization has developed an extremely sophisticated R&D planning model that introduces a financial discipline into the R&D planning process. The researchers and scientists at Merck are the company's most important assets. The management challenge is to maintain and improve the productivity of the investment in R&D. The financial organization has translated this challenge into the development of the R&D planning model. In partnership with the research division, the financial organization has developed a planning model which uses the financial logic of portfolio theory to analyze the projected economic payoff of new R&D projects proposed for the pipeline. The model incorporates a comprehensive array of marketing, R&D, and manufacturing variables that influence the ultimate profitability of each R&D projects. Using Monte Carlo techniques, the researchers and financial analysts can forecast the profitability of alternative research portfolios up to twenty years into the future.

An unanticipated, but critically important benefit of the model, has been its role in improving communications among the individuals in different organizational units. The model integrates all the actions and interdependencies that must be managed over the entire product life cycle—from basic research, through development, testing, FDA approval, and ultimately to market. The "R&D planning model" is the financial organization's exemplar of analytic sophistication, innovative professional work, and bottom-line payoff. The model is the hallmark of the competitive team philosophy. The R&D

planning model will be discussed more fully later in the Merck story.

It could be argued that adding analytic sophistication to the strategic management of Merck's R&D programs was a natural extension of the strong measurement-oriented culture of the R&D group. Yet the financial staff members who initiated the project, faced the same skepticism any outsider faces in coming into an organization under the pretense of providing help. Within the operating divisions of many American corporations, fear of "Trojan horses," not to say corporate spies, runs deep. At Merck, performance must precede legitimacy and credibility.

As it turns out, the head of the R&D division at the time the R&D planning model was being developed was Roy Vagelos, the current CEO. The support of Vagelos was critical to overcoming the fears among the research staff that members of the financial organization were intruding within their rightful domain.

The Influence of the CEO

The interview comments indicate that there has always been a long standing relationship between the CEO and the financial organization at Merck. Tom Osterbrink, Corporate Controller, commented on the current, centralized, financial organization:

We are highly centralized. We were that way the day I started with this company. A lot of this follows the philosophies of your CEO. Henry Gadsen was a very control-conscious guy. He wanted to know what was going on in this company. If you want that kind of information in that kind of depth you can't have a decentralized organization—even within your own function of a controller... you'd go out and get nothing but noise... It got extremely difficult for people to pull together data without a lot of grief and argument and convincing that that's what you wanted. Gadsen changed the reporting relationship (at the initiative of the VP for Finance).

The other driving force you have here is

what does your Chairman think of your financial area? Does he want the information... Gadsen was a strong user of financial data and wanted a lot of detail. Vagelos uses this data to measure their (managers') performance. In his first year in company, he decided to adopt the philosophy that we are going to enhance stockholder value—through growth and profitability—and divisions are measured by it. That enforces the financial role.

While there is some difference of opinion within the financial organization about the strength of the commitment of previous CEO's for the financial organization, Vagelos is a particularly strong advocate and supporter of financial management. As a noted research scientist, Vagelos comes from a culture of measurement and numerical analysis. Judy Lewent, who served as Controller of Merck's Division of Research when Vagelos headed that unit, explains the impact that an individual such as Roy Vagelos can have on a financial organization.

[The sophistication of the financial function has] dramatically accelerated over last 3 years because of Vagelos' support, insight, and understanding; and hopefully what [we] did for all those years when he was listening for the first time to financial people and had a positive experience instead of others who have had negative experiences.

Referring to the changes in the company's size and environment, Ms. Lewent remarked:

Roy (the CEO) has a willingness to accept change; and we have a responsibility to figure out how to do it right and be a contributor instead of a god damn ball and chain on the operating divisions and research division to get the job done. If we prove our value, we'll get the resources we need and have an exciting environment, attract good people and do the job we need to do.

Vagelos is a strong supporter of the financial

organization and a strong user of financial information. The Corporate Controller spoke of Vagelos' personal Executive Information System (EIS), and the increase in financial assessments of the firm's performance.

> [The EIS reports on] the performance of every market in the world—plan vs actual vs prior year—graphic display of products—providing a series of 50 charts. Vagelos accesses [the EIS] every month. He has used it to call up divisional heads. He is a strong user of financial information.

> (Regarding business forecasting) It's becoming a very big thing in the company with Vagelos. We've imposed forecasting on top of our total reporting system. Because at mid year, he is following the practice of wanting to reassess where he's going... I give the presentations to the ORC (Operating Review Committee)... we do a risk analysis... and Vagelos, when I go up there, will ask, "How confident are you in this?"... [and in responding to this query] I've accepted a responsibility.

"I've accepted responsibility." This statement by Tom Osterbrink should not be overlooked. Merck's culture of leading-edge professionalism that underpins the competitive team orientation is a very people-centered management philosophy. At Merck, terms such as "personal contribution," "individual expertise," "training and development" replace terms such as "task," "specialization," and "function" which pervade the interviews at some of the other firms in the study. This culture of leading-edge professionalism is described in the next section.

The Heart of Merck's Competitive Team Orientation: Participation, Sophistication and Communication

Tom Osterbrink's comment embodies the core elements of the competitive team orientation at Merck. First, the Controller's role in the mid-year assessment is not passive, not one of simple number crunching. The controller is a key **participant** in the management process and he is expected to exercise his **business judgment, for which he is accountable**. Second, members of the financial organization are expected to perform **comprehensive and sophisticated analyses** of business problems using the logic of risk/return, informed by a thorough **understanding of the business**. Finally, the **communicative aspect** of financial analysis is every bit as important as the sophistication underpinning the conclusions. The financial professionals within Merck are expected to make positive contributions to business decisions by being analytically sophisticated, communicatively competent, and accountable for their recommendations.

The credibility of the financial organization is defined not only in terms of expertise and competence, but trust and communication as well. Sophisticated analysis that befuddles or back bites, that fails to address the issues or support the communicative process, is not credible. To be successful, sophisticated analysis must support the communicative process of the management team, and the financial professionals are held accountable for the quality of the analysis. They are no longer impartial, third party, commentators on the successes and failures of other members of the organization.

The team metaphor at Merck is an explicit one. Frank Spiegel, the CFO, stressed the team orientation at Merck as the starting point for fulfilling the corporate financial control responsibilities.

> I think it's more the whole team atmosphere [as opposed to check and balance]. We're all pulling oars in same direction.

In Merck, being a member of the team means that the financial organization must bring more than a financial perspective to the decision table. The financial professional must, first and foremost, be a business person who exercises sound business judgment. The importance of being a business person, of grounding financial analysis in a sound knowledge of the business, is a fundamental expectation at Merck. Tom Osterbrink alluded to this in discussing the factors critical to the success of the controller's operations.

I could be measured on how well I train and develop my people to be good business men, not just bookkeepers... The guys in the divisions have to be business men. They've got to be able to get up there and say, "Hey, here's the way I look at this, and this is what's happening, and I think you ought to consider doing these kind of things." That's where their role can be most effective.

To have credibility the divisional controller must:

1) bring a distinctive competence and business perspective to the decision making process that can make a difference in the decision outcome and

2) effectively manage the joint imperatives of corporate accountability and participation as part of the divisional unit team. This latter requirement is especially challenging in Merck because divisional controllers report on a solid-line basis to the Corporate Controller, not the divisional unit managers.

Judy Lewent argues that the divisional controller must manage this tension by building credibility based on expertise, not position. The stewardship role is an important and necessary one, but taking a stand on control issues, when necessary, should be based on credibility founded on competence, not fear based on position within the organization.

My view of the divisional controllers is that they should be considered confidants and members of the team, not selling their soul, but respected for their credentials and their judgment. Credibility built on expertise permits you to take a stand on controls... without being perceived as a policeman... If you have respect for your business acumen, and they know you have concern for corporate assets, there can be mutual respect.

At Merck, the distinct competence that the

financial person brings to the decision making table is the logic of risk and return. The framework of risk/return and the array of decision making tools grounded in risk/return logic provide a basis for disciplining the decision making process and improving communication among members of the management team. In commenting on the recent criticisms of "managing by the numbers," Ms. Lewent discussed her image of the finance person.

[This gets to my] vision of a finance person— and I don't believe it's a beancounter and a policeman...The superficial attack on finance not being receptive to modern technology, and to modern management and to short sightedness is also a lot of bunk... [following principles of finance such as returning the cost of capital, factoring in uncertainty and risk] doesn't mean... that you sit there in the financial area and say, "No, you can't do that."... In fact, I think economics and finance are very enlightened. We've been working quite a bit on the use of option theory and Monte Carlo analysis to enlighten [management] about what risk is and what acceptable ranges are. We do not say that you have to make this number or we won't take this project.

The language of risk/return is used extensively throughout the interview comments. The Corporate Controller, Tom Osterbrink, also makes reference to the divisional controller as an evaluator of business risk.

My people have got to step into the business. I want them to tell me how confident they are in it... he should know what's going on in that business. And he should know where the exposures are. And we ask him to do a risk analysis. We ask him at the profit plan time... where are the major risks with this plan?... All of this is based on analysis, on their knowledge of the markets, what kind of introductions we have, what kind of market share do they have in those markets?... Then we come down to what we call a confidence kind of schedule. Do we think we can achieve this for the year?

Most of my guys today have an excellent reporting relationship with their divisions... the idea is to put together the risks on [the division's] behalf... put the risks on the table... all this is good intelligence and input into Vagelos... It's just a vehicle "to get it up on table."

The financial organization contributes to the management team by insuring that all aspects of the business problem are 'put on the table' and analyzed within the framework of risk and return. The meat of the Osterbrink quote allows us to come full circle to the particular qualities that make up the team orientation at Merck— participation, competence, and communication. 'Putting the risks on the table' aptly characterizes the qualities of participation, competence, and communication that are expected from the financial professionals within Merck.

At this stage in the story, we will return to a more complete discussion of the "R&D planning model" to expand on the logic of risk/return and show how the financial professionals contribute in a measurable way to Merck's success.

The R&D Planning Model: An Exemplar of Leading-Edge Financial Work at Merck

The concepts behind the R&D planning model are not new; Merck has always thought in terms of 10-20 year planning horizons. What is new is the actual, operational, computer-based planning model. The financial organization, under the direction of Frank Spiegel and Judy Lewent, has developed and implemented the highly sophisticated planning model to support management, not second guess their decisions. The R&D planning model provides management with a tool to explore alternatives with greater sophistication and in greater detail than has been possible in the past. The decisions made with the help of the model are then integrated into Merck's capital budgeting process.

As a project which he has championed, Frank Spiegel extolls the model's virtue, and the professional and technological sophistication required to make the model a reality.

We have a planning model that is the envy of any company in the world...It's become a living document that's part of the total planning system and in resource allocations in research. We couldn't have done that without getting the people and the technology.

The model contributes more to the decision making process than just analytic sophistication. As the Vice President of Research Administration hastens to emphasize, the model is seldom used to make go/no go decisions with respect to particular research programs. Rather, the principal value of the model lies in improving communications among all the members of the management team. The productivity of an R&D program is dependent upon a complex array of factors. Just understanding what all these factors are and communicating this information to individuals from marketing, R&D, and manufacturing is no small challenge. Judy Lewent, who actually developed the model under Frank Spiegel's direction, argues that the model has provided a common set of terms and provided a common foundation upon which the communicative process at Merck has now been built. The model offers a comprehensive framework for understanding all of the interrelationships that must be managed. The model is where all the numbers have to come together even when people do not agree about the implications of the numbers.

The numbers talked to each other even if people didn't. You could put something on table and then say, "All right let's discuss what this says."

In the following interchange on the topic of the R&D model, Ms. Lewent reiterated the more general communicative function of finance.

Judy Lewent: It [the model] is the only thing

they will agree on... their numbers. That is the only thing that has caused a truce. They all accept that. They gave input. We've had consensus time after time.

Interviewer: The model serves as an intermediary...

Judy Lewent: I think Finance does that everywhere.

The Vice President of Research Administration confirmed the value of the model in supporting the communications process.

... That's true, that's fair. In this way ... at least we're all speaking the same language... the other thing is that we are putting [things] in the same frame of reference... forces definitional issues... It does structure that relationship [of research with marketing]. So we both know we're talking about the same thing—it forces everyone to think a little more...to commit. Those are the major gains of model.

The success of the R&D planning model has demonstrated the value-adding potential of the financial organization in the management of the research enterprise. The model exemplifies the vision that the CFO, Frank Spiegel, is attempting to implement—**servicing the internal business customer and being a partner in the decision making process through knowledge of the business and through the application of innovative financial tools that help frame decisions and facilitate communication.**
The Vice President for Research Administration comments on the proactive role of the financial organization:

[It is] also clear that someone within finance wanted it to happen because Judy was the first one at a higher level who came to do the job ... somebody came in... not only with a job to do but the job was done... From that time on, the financial person who comes in is clearly a member of research. We treat them as part of the research management

operation... which says you're a partner. They [finance] showed that they were useful and could understand... I feel that it was a great change in the concept of participation.

Clearly then the team orientation at Merck, as articulated in the preceding analysis and as exemplified in the R&D planning model, represents a distinct operating philosophy and pattern of relationships with other organizational units.

Building a Leading Edge Financial Organization at Merck: The Human Resource Strategy

A revealing aspect of Merck's commitment to being a leading-edge financial organization is evidenced by its expenditures per employee in the area of financial planning and analysis. While Merck had the lowest ratio of financial function costs to company sales of all the pharmaceutical firms that reported this figure in a recent study conducted by the Pharmaceutical Manufacturer's Association, it had the second highest cost per financial employee in the financial planning and analysis area. This latter figure is consistent with Merck's strategy for building a leading-edge organization: namely, investing in high-impact individuals who possess the skills and talent to produce financial innovations that enhance the profitability of the firm. As Al Smith, Vice President of Finance, put it:

We want to go out and find really bright people to do these things. That's where true productivity increases come from. Getting good people gives you good hitting power... We're trying to get more of those people built into our organization and figure out a way to challenge them.

Merck's strategy is to hire individuals with the drive and capacity to do leading-edge financial work. Management's responsibility is to establish a professional environment that explicitly values and encourages creative behavior. Then, given the resources, tools, and technology to support these individuals, top management expects a financial chemistry to take place similar to the chemistry that occurs in the R&R labs.

Another revealing indication of Merck's commitment to investing in top notch individuals is that Merck establishes a <u>target</u> for the amount of training that each staff person must undertake. In calculating year-end management incentive compensation, a certain amount of bonus points are given to those managers who reach the <u>floor</u> for training and development. Additional bonus points are awarded up to a <u>ceiling</u>. Compared to the pre-Vagelos days, even the <u>floors</u> are stretch goals for most organizational units. Between 1986 and 1987, the financial organization increased its budget for training and development by over 20%.

To complement its professional development strategy, Merck is attempting to establish a climate of challenge and creativity. As Judy Lewent explained, the aim is to:

"get that atmosphere, the bubbling up of ideas, of looking to outside, encouraging a willingness to read; it [the ethic of creativity and innovation] is critical."

But true to the hard edge on Merck's leading edge culture, the atmosphere is only a means to a very concrete desired end: namely, the creation of specific innovations that impact the bottom line. Financial innovation is defined as either:

1) the development of financial tools and analysis that help give answers to business questions and stimulate management actions that get the right financial results; or

2) the development of financial products that directly impact the bottom line.

The R&D planning model is an exemplar of the first type of innovation. Merck's financial executives also point to a whole laundry list of financial products that have increased cash flows, such as the exploitation of the safe harbor leasing regulations and use of option theory to restructure executive stock options. Thus, Merck's financial organization assesses its own performance in terms of its success in creating value, not simply maintaining the value created by other organizational units.

Financial innovations are the work of creative individuals and teams of financial professionals. As a staff person, you are given the resources and moral support to perform, but you are evaluated on the basis of the measurable difference that you make. In the following comment, the Vice President and Treasurer reinforces the financial organization's penchant for innovation that is on a par with their peers in research and manufacturing.

You don't get a good rating for doing your job... You get a good rating by doing something way beyond your job. Something really tangible, something new.

Interview comments also stress the vision for a culture of financial professionalism. As the CFO, Frank Spiegel, put it:

"My three words are creativity, challenge and professionalism. Professionalism wraps everything up as far as I am concerned... It gets you into doing your own R&D, increasing your training and development programs internally; into going outside [to interact with knowledgeable professionals]."

Interviewer: "The management philosophy is more cultural than structural...

No two ways about it—lean, mean and in front technologically. That's what we're trying to do with people and technology."

In the next section, we discuss the key financial organization strategies for designing a culture of leading edge professionalism.

Building a Leading Edge Financial Organization at Merck: Some Key Design Strategies

In addition to strong recruiting and development policies, and efforts to foster professionalism, there are three explicit organizational strategies that figure centrally into Merck's overall leading edge posture:

1) an emphasis on financial R&D which complements the strong scientific R&D culture at Merck;

2) management leadership that attempts to provide focus for financial innovations through a strong issues orientation tied to the competitive and financial strategy of the firm; and,

3) the breakdown of traditional boundaries between treasury and control roles within the financial function; the creation of a new role model: that of financial advisor capable of integrating the traditional disciplines of tax, financial analysis, and control.

Emphasis on R&D

In discussing the functions of the financial organization, Al Smith, Vice President of Finance, identified three broad sets of activities that are analogous to those of a complete business—the production shop (financial operations), the marketing effort (corporate and divisional controllers), and the R&D function. He referred to the latter as the function that is at the heart of the change in the financial organization.

The third function of finance is analogous to R&D. It's the new product development within the finance function... the thinking side of the finance function in terms of what's going on now, where we should be going strategically, how we are going to get there... There's no central core of staff set aside for this...This is really the challenge and the thing that's changing, and the future of the financial function.

This notion of financial R&D was touched upon in other interviews. Frank Spiegel refers to the notion of financial R&D within the context of his vision of a leading edge financial function.

.. Excellence in finance, recruiting, challenge, creativity, communications, [and training and development]; I really think those are six key things, all under this professionalism—which really says that you've got to do your own R&D, have some training—that you've got to really stay out in front of all the literature—and be searching for new products and that kind of thing.

As noted by Al Smith, the R&D function is not specific to an organizational unit, but rather is an attitude to be adopted by everyone within the organization. Innovation is supposed to be part and parcel of everyone's job. Frank Spiegel elaborates on the creation of an atmosphere conducive to learning and innovation.

So I see people, technology, issues, analysis as really [the key]—challenge and creativity too—we're trying to create an atmosphere where you do not get your head handed to you. Challenge is another big piece of it. It's a mindset. Issue management is a mindset.

The R&D mindset is reflected in specific programs within Merck's financial organization. For instance, the financial organization has undertaken a series of institutional studies to address the issue raised by regulators regarding excess profits in the ethical pharmaceutical drug industry. This effort also includes the development of a retrospective R&D model which examines the historical financial performance of new compounds introduced in the past. The model documents the risk involved and the historical reliance of the industry on a relatively few "block buster" products that carry the majority of the other products that do not earn back their cost of capital.

As a second example, staff members are encouraged to use outside consultants to stay apprised of new financial products and to assist with the development of new financial tools. Judy Lewent, who spearheaded the development of the R&D planning model, describes the value she places on access to outside expertise and reaching out as a basic management philosophy. I would say the most important factor beyond that [good financial systems]... is access to the experts outside this company... to know what the new products are, what best pricing is, to know what the competitive environment is outside... Merck is a very small user in a very big system. And if we're going to be cost effective, and really smart and have the best products, the only way we're going to do that is by constantly reaching out to see what's going on... go to conferences to find out what others are doing... get out in to the world by meeting regularly with investment and commercial bankers to find out what they're doing.

Ms. Lewent also described studies underway with faculty at leading universities to examine the use of option theory, and to study Merck's real cost of capital in relation to that of Japanese firms. The latter study is part of the effort to address regulatory concerns about industry profits.

We have a little mini-economics shop trying to do some studies with outside universities to elucidate our point intelligently—hopefully to get enlightenment on part of regulators and Congressmen, the EEC, and Japan.

Emphasis on Issues

To insure that innovative behavior addresses the needs of the business, the entire financial organization operates under a strong issues orientation. All analyses produced by the staff members must be issue focused. Frank Spiegel, the current CFO, brought this orientation over from a brief stint as director of the Merck's strategic planning unit. In that job, he developed an appreciation of the value of an issues orientation for coalescing management action, or as he put it, "ringing bells."

Once you get through people and technology... it's an analysis function and an issue function that really makes the thing work.

Good hard analysis, laying out the facts as best you can... but then issues. .. we're big on issues... We've identified ten key issues in the company. That's all we want to have. And we rang bells like the Salvation Army guys making people address issues, to come up with strategic action programs to deal with those issues. And we feel if that's successful, we're going to be successful.

Merck's top financial executives meet routinely to formulate and monitor the strategic direction of the financial organization, including making an assessment of the most fruitful areas for new financial "product development." The CFO holds monthly strategic issues sessions. A different issue is addressed at each meeting with different people attending, depending on the issue. These sessions have dealt with issues such as R&D productivity, asset utilization, capital structure, and manufacturing cost control. The meetings serve as brainstorming sessions which result in new ideas and proposals for product and decision tools innovation; they foster communication among staff members that might otherwise not come into contact with each other; and they reinforce in a regular and highly visible way the strong issue orientation. Frank Spiegel comments:

The idea of those (strategic issues) meetings—they're helpful in getting everyone together and just preparing for them—but then we have them very wide open, so [together] there's a lot of challenge and no bruised egos; we can use it [the meeting] to challenge and to deal with strategic issues, and also to communicate... Some neat issues come out of there. It seems to me that part of the "new product" kind of thing and leading edge of technology, because that's what we're trying to drive for, staying ahead and trying to tie that into identifying issues that will get us out in front of people.

Breaking Down Boundaries

Finally, in an effort to foster individual initiative

while recognizing the need for integrated approaches to problems, Merck's financial management has made an effort to tear down the boundaries associated with traditional jobs and roles within the financial organization (such as treasury and controller, or accounting and finance), while making greater use of individual participation in problem-oriented task forces.

As Ms. Lewent, Vice President and Treasurer, put it, the emphasis on individual initiative consists of job flexibility coupled with a "show me" philosophy of recognition and reward for creating value-adding financial tools and products.

> The culture that I personally take to heart and try to disseminate is, there are no boundaries on your job description, and the only thing I'd ask is for someone to come up with an idea. Anything you want to do, we'll do if it's worth doing... If you do something, it'll be there. But you've got to get people to understand that the culture is [to] come forward, do things. Don't tell me you don't have resources. Look beyond that, figure that they'll come if you've added value and there's something worth doing. You'll get them, but you've got to give something first. Maybe that's the research side too. It's sort of test it, show me why it's worth doing, prove yourself, expend a little extra effort if you think it's so good, and in the end you will be rewarded and you'll also get the support.

The elimination of traditional boundaries extends beyond individual job descriptions. Judy Lewent is vociferous about her impatience with the constraints imposed by traditional boundaries within the financial organization.

> I have this very specific view of what a division controller should be. And I see all of it as almost nondifferentiable in function, and I see the financial person as a business partner who happens to have expertise in finance and accounting and so on.

Merck's financial organization is pursuing a variety of approaches to integrate traditionally separate functions. Referring to the importance of integration, Ms. Lewent discusses the issue of career movement.

> A very important strategy [to foster intrafunction integration]... where it counts most in my opinion is... where you have people who have always been in treasury. They have a treasury view and a bias. People in the controller's area have a controller's bias. And you're not going to get rid of that unless people experience the other side. And there's been a conscious effort, but it's going to take time... to move people... in a funny sort of way, to dislodge these tree trunks that have been in these areas for years...

A very concrete, if not innovative step taken by the current CFO to foster this cross-fertilization, has been to create an organizational unit with responsibilities encompassing the traditional boundaries of treasury and control. The individual placed in charge of this unit, called Financial Evaluation and Analysis (FEA), was given "dual but interlocking responsibilities." These responsibilities include 1) evaluating all capital requests, 2) evaluating business acquisitions and divestitures and prospective licensing of new products, 3) developing the firm's product cost allocation methodology, and, in addition, 4) has responsibility to the controllership of the two major capital intensive divisions, manufacturing and research. There were multiple objectives involved in the establishment of the FE&A, as the following comment by the current CFO suggests.

> When I came back to the financial area, I created that function [FE&A] to encourage asset utilization) and for the economics. And economics came into play because we are looking at our strategic plan... it was clear... we were in for exciting times to break away from the competition. And the chances of justifying our profits, prices and patents versus anyone else... So we had to

get our story together.

The day that I came back to the financial area was the day of consolidation, not necessarily the addition, of what I then called Financial Evaluation and Analysis, to give that [analysis] purpose, to give it focus, to let it serve ORC and the Board. The main thing we wanted to do there is get away from the single bullet type of financial evaluation, and get into a range of possibilities... get the issues out so that it wasn't incumbent upon management and the Board of Directors to sift through a ton of paper... that's a major difference in the Board's sophistication, I think.

The CFO also used FE&A as a mechanism to signal his intent to break down the traditional boundaries within the financial organization, boundaries which he perceives to be barriers to innovative financial work. Referring to the chimney problem and the CFO's move to create FE&A, the the Vice President and Treasurer commented:

The controller's area is on one side, the treasurer's area is on other and there's an imaginary line there. So [the CFO] said, we're going to solve this. I'm gong to give you [FE&A] to force communication.

In the following interchange, Frank Spiegel confirms this commitment to FE&A as a signal of his desire for his staff members to begin to think beyond traditional intra-function boundaries.

Frank: "FE&A incidentally was just the conglomeration of various departments. That drove the [divisional] controllers crazy because in their mind financial services for

manufacturing should be with the controller. I now have it in treasury."

Interviewer: "You're trying to break down those distinctions rather than reinforce them."

Frank: "Someday I would like to get away from even having controllers and treasurers. There's something else. I mean something completely wild, as long as its effective."

This strategy has been taken a step further with the promotion of Judy Lewent, who originally headed up FEB A, to Vice President and Treasurer.

FE&A has served as a vehicle to implement two key organizational changes:

1) The development of issues-oriented, sophisticated, financial analysis, that

2) Cuts across the disciplinary boundaries of finance and accounting traditionally found within the financial organization.

Hopefully, the foregoing analysis of the interview comments has conveyed the soft as well as the very hard edge of the "leading-edge" culture within Merck's financial organization. Hopefully as well, we have shown how Merck's financial organization represents an embodiment of the competitive team orientation, as that concept has been developed in this study. Consistent with the notion that each firm has its own conception of the competitive team orientation, as a function of its history and the unique contingencies it currently faces, we have seen that Merck's competitive team orientation has shades of similarity and difference in relation to the competitive team orientations articulated in the other cases.

30
That's Easy for You to Say

It all began on labor day weekend in 1982. Allan A. Kennedy was sitting in a low beach chair on the shore in front of his cottage on Cape Cod. Next to him was his friend and fellow consultant Tony Merlo. As they relaxed there, watching the sailboats drift across Cape Cod Bay, drinking beer, and listening to a Red Sox game on the radio, Kennedy turned to Merlo and, with the majestic eloquence suited to great undertakings, said, "Gee, Tony, you know, we ought to start some kind of business together."

This identical thought has, of course, passed between countless friends ever since the discovery of profit margins. Coming from most people, it would have fallen into the general category of loose talk. But Kennedy was not most people. For one thing, he was a thirteen-year veteran of McKinsey & Co., the management consulting firm, and partner in charge of its Boston office. More to the point, he was the co-author of a recently published book that offered a startling new perspective on corporate life — one that challenged the whole way people thought about business.

The book was entitled *Corporate Cultures*, a term that was itself new to the language, and it dealt with an aspect of business that, up to then,

had been largely ignored. Broadly speaking, that aspect involved the role played by a company's values, symbols, rites, and rituals in determining its overall performance. Citing examples from some of the country's most dynamic companies, Kennedy and co-author Terrence E. Deal showed that these "cultural" factors had a major effect on the attitudes and behavior of a company's employees, and were thus of critical importance to its long-term success.

By any measure, the book was a groundbreaking work, challenging, as it did, the rational, quantitative models of corporate success that were so popular in the 1960s and '70s. But its impact had as much to do with its timing as its content. Published in June 1982, during a period of economic stagnation — with unemployment at 9.5 percent, the prime over 16 percent, and trade deficits soaring to record levels — *Corporate Cultures* offered a welcome antidote to the doom and gloom that was abroad in the land. Like *In Search of Excellence*, which appeared a few months later, it suggested that Japan was not the only nation capable of producing strong, highly motivated companies that could compete effectively in the international arena. America could produce — in fact, was

Prepared by Lucien Rhodes. Reprinted with permission, *Inc magazine*, June 1986. Copyright @ 1986 by Goldhirsh Group, Inc., 38 Commercial Wharf, Boston, MA 02110.

already producing — its own.

What the book did not detail, however, was how corporate cultures were actually constructed. The authors could describe a particular culture and demonstrate its effects, but they offered few clues as to how a company might develop a culture in the first place. So the news that Allan Kennedy was going into business was greeted with more than passing interest among the followers of corporate culture. Here was an opportunity to find out how a living, breathing culture could be created, and the creator would be none other than the man who wrote the book.

After an extensive survey of business opportunities, Kennedy and Merlo decided to develop microcomputer software for sales and marketing management. They felt this was their most promising option, given the anticipated growth of the microcomputer market and their own experience as consultants. Acting on that assessment, they resigned from McKinsey and, in February 1983, formally launched Selkirk Associates, Inc. with four of their friends.

Kennedy had lofty ambitions for Selkirk. More than a business, he saw it as a kind of laboratory for his theories. He wanted it to function as a society of professional colleagues committed to building a culture and a company that would stress collaboration, openness, decentralization, democratic decisions, respect, and trust. In this society, each individual would be encouraged to devise his or her own entrepreneurial response to the challenges of the business.

For Kennedy, this was not a long-term goal, something that would evolve naturally in the fullness of time. On the contrary, it was a pressing, immediate concern. Accordingly, he focused all his attention on creating such a culture from the start. "I spent lots of time," he says, "trying to think about what kind of values the company ought to stand for and therefore what kind of behavior I expected from people." These thoughts eventually went into a detailed statement of "core beliefs," which he reviewed and amplified with each new employee. In the same vein, Kennedy and his colleagues chose a "guiding principle," namely, a commitment to "mak-

ing people more productive." They would pursue this ambition, everyone agreed, "through the products and services we offer" and "in the way we conduct our own affairs."

And in the beginning at least, Selkirk seemed to be everything Kennedy had hoped for. The company set up shop in Boston in an office that consisted of a large, rectangular room with three smaller attachments. Each morning, staff members would pile into the main room and sort themselves out by function — programmers and systems engineers by the windows; administrators in the middle; sales and marketing folk at the other end. In keeping with Kennedy's cultural precepts, there were no private offices or, indeed, any physical demarcations between functions.

It was a familial enterprise, informed with the very qualities Kennedy had laid out in his statement of core beliefs. The work was absorbing, the comradeship inspiring. Most mornings, the staff feasted on doughnuts, which they took to calling "corporate carbos," as a wordplay on "corporate cultures." They began a scrapbook as an impromptu cultural archive. Included among the memorabilia was "The Ravin'," an Edgar Allan Poe takeoff that commemorated Selkirk's first stirrings in earlier temporary headquarters:

Once upon an April morning,
   disregarding every warning,
In a Back Bay storefront,
   Selkirk software was begun:
True, it was without a toilet,
   but that didn't seem to spoil it.

To strengthen their bonds even further, the staff began to experiment with so-called rites, rituals, and ceremonies — all important elements of a corporate culture, according to Kennedy's book. Selkirk's once manager, Linda Sharkey, recalls a day, for example, when the whole company went out to Kennedy's place on Cape Cod to celebrate their common purpose with barbeques on the beach. "The sun was shining, and we were all there together," she says. "It was a beautiful day. That's the way it was. We didn't use the terms among ourselves that Allan uses in the book. With us, corporate culture was more by seeing and doing." Sharkey remembers, too, Friday afternoon luncheons of pizza or Chinese food, at which everyone in the company had a chance to talk about his or her accomplishments or problems, or simply hang out.

Kennedy was pleased with all this, as well he might be. "We were," he says, "beginning to develop a real culture."

Then the walls went up.

The problem stemmed from the situation in the big room, where the technical people were laboring feverishly to develop Selkirk's first product, while the salespeople were busy pre-selling it. The former desperately needed peace and quiet to concentrate on their work; the latter were a boisterous lot, fond of crowing whenever a prospect looked encouraging. In fact, the sales-people crowed so often and so loudly that the technicians complained that they were being driven to distraction. Finally, they confronted Kennedy with the problem. Their solution, which Kennedy agreed to, was to erect five-foot-high movable partitions, separating each functional grouping from the others.

In the memory of Selkirk veterans, "the day the walls went up" lives on as a day of infamy. "It was terrible," says Sharkey. "I was embarrassed."

"It was clearly a symbol of divisiveness," says Kennedy.

"I don't know what would have been the right solution," says Reilly Hayes, Selkirk's twenty-three-year-old technical wizard, "but the wall certainly wasn't. It blocked out the windows for the other end of the room. Someone [in market-ing] drew a picture of a window and taped it to the wall. The whole thing created a lot of dissension."

Indeed, the erection of the walls touched off a feud between engineering and marketing that eventually grew into "open organizational warfare," according to Kennedy. "I let the wall stand, and a competitive attitude developed where engineering started sniping at marketing. We had two armed camps that didn't trust each other."

As if that weren't bad enough, other problems

were beginning to surface. For one thing, the company was obviously overstaffed, having grown from twelve people in June 1983 to twenty-five in January 1984, without any product or sales — to show for it. "That was a big mistake," says Kennedy. "We clearly ramped up the organization too fast, particularly given the fact that we were financing ourselves. I mean, for a while, we had a burn rate of around $100,000 per month."

Even more serious, however, was the problem that emerged following the release of the company's initial product, Correspondent, in February 1984. Not that there was anything wrong with the product. It was, in fact, a fine piece of software, and it premiered to glowing reviews. Designed as a selling tool, it combined database management, calendar management, word processing, and mail merge — functions that could help customers organize their accounts, track and schedule sales calls and follow-ups, and generate correspondence. And it did all that splendidly.

The problem had to do with the price tag, a whopping $12,000 per unit. The Selkirk team members had come up with this rarefied figure, not out of greed, but out of a commitment to customer service — a goal to which they had pledged themselves as part of their cultural mission. In order to provide such service, they figured, a Selkirk representative might have to spend two or three weeks with each customer, helping to install and customize the product. Trouble was, customers weren't willing to *pay* for that service, not at $12,000 per unit anyway. After a brief flurry of interest, sales dropped off.

"We just blew it," says Kennedy. "We were arrogant about the market. We were trying to tell the market something it wasn't interested in hearing. We took an arbitrary cultural goal and tried to make it into a strategy rather than saying 'we're a market-driven company and we've got to find out what the market wants and supply it.'" Unfortunately, six months went by before Kennedy and his colleagues figured all this out and began to reduce Correspondent's price accordingly.

By then, however, Selkirk's entire sales effort

was in shambles, a victim of its commitment to employee autonomy. Sales targets were seldom realized. Indeed, they were scarcely even set. At weekly meetings, salespeople would do little more than review account activity. "If a salesman said each week for three weeks in a row that he expected to close a certain account, and it never happened," says Merlo, "well, we didn't do anything about it. In any other company, he would probably have been put on probation." As it was, each of the participants entered the results of the meeting in a red-and-black ledger book and struck out once again to wander haphazardly through uncharted territory. "The mistake we made," rejects Merlo, "was using real money in a real company to test hypotheses about what sales goals should be."

Finally, in June 1984, Kennedy took action, laying off six people. In July, Correspondent's price was dropped to $4,000 per unit, but sales remained sluggish. In September, Kennedy laid off five more people, bringing the size of the staff back to twelve.

One of those laid off was the chief engineer, a close friend of Kennedy's, but a man whose departure brought an immediate ceasefire between the warring factions. That night, the remaining staff members took down the walls and stacked them neatly in the kitchenette, where they repose to this day. "We felt," says Sharkey, "like we had our little family back together again."

With morale finally rebounding, Selkirk again cut Correspondent's price in the early fall, to $1,500. This time, sales responded, and, in November, the company enjoyed its first month in the black.

But Selkirk was not yet out of the woods. What remained was for Kennedy to figure out the significance of what had happened, and to draw the appropriate conclusions. Clearly, his experiment had not turned out as he had planned. His insistence on a company without walls had led to organizational warfare. His goal of providing extraordinary service had led to a crucial pricing error. His ideal of employee autonomy had led to confusion in the sales force. In the end, he was forced to fire more than half of his staff, slash

prices by 87 percent, and start over again. What did it all mean?

Merlo had one answer. "We're talking about an experiment in corporate culture failing because the business environment did not support it," he says. "The notion of corporate culture got in the way of toughminded business decisions." He also faults the emphasis on autonomy. "I don't think we had the right to be organized the way we were. I think we should have had more discipline."

Kennedy himself soon came around to a similar view. "Look in [the statement of core beliefs] and tell me what you find about the importance of performance, about measuring performance or about the idea that people must be held accountable for their performance," he says. "That stuff should have been there. I'm not discounting the importance of corporate culture, but you have to worry about the business at the same time, or you simply won't have one. Then you obviously won't need a culture. Where the two come together, I think, is in the cultural norms for performance, what kind of performance is expected of people. And that's a linkage that wasn't explicit in my mind three years ago. But it is now." He adds that, if the manuscript of *Corporate Cultures* were before him today, he would include a section on performance standards, measurement systems, and accountability sanctions.

On that point, he might get an argument from his co-author, Terrence Deal, a professor at Vanderbilt University and a member of Selkirk's board of directors since its inception. Deal does not disagree about the importance of discipline and performance standards, but he questions the wisdom of trying to impose them from above. The most effective performance standards, he notes, are the ones that employees recognize and accept as the product of their own commitment, and these can emerge only from the employees' experience. "One of the things that we know pretty handsomely," says Deal, "is that it's the informal performance standards that really drive a company."

In fact, Kennedy may have gotten into trouble not by doing too little, but by doing too much.

Rather than letting Selkirk's culture evolve organically, he tried to impose a set of predetermined cultural values on the company, thereby retarding the growth of its own informal value system. He pursued culture as an end in itself, ignoring his own caveat, set down in his book, that "the business environment is the single greatest influence in shaping a corporate culture." Instead, he tried to shape the culture in a vacuum, without synchronizing it with the company's business goals.

In so doing, Kennedy reduced corporate culture to a formula, a collection of generic "principles." It was a cardinal error, if not an uncommon one. "There are a lot of people," says Deal, "who take our book literally and try to design a culture much as if they're trying to design an organization chart. My experience across the board has been that, as soon as people make it into a formula, they start making mistakes." By following the "formula," Kennedy wound up imposing his own set of rules on Selkirk — although not enough of them, and not the right kind, he now says. The irony is that a real corporate culture allows a company to manage itself *without* formal rules, and to manage itself better than a company that has them.

Deal makes another point. Kennedy, he observes, might be less concerned with performance today if he had not hired so many friends at the beginning. "Friends are nice to have around, but it's often hard to discipline them, or subject them to a company's normal sanctions. Over the long run," Deal says, "their presence at Selkirk probably undermined the development of informal performance standards."

Kennedy himself may have played a role in that, too. He estimates that, over the past year, he has spent only one day a week at Selkirk. The rest of the time he has been on the road as a consultant, using his fees to help finance the company. In all, he has sunk some $1 million of his own money into Selkirk, without which the company might not have survived. But it has come at a price. "Nobody had to pay attention to things like expenses, because there was a perception of an infinite sink of money," Kennedy says.

The danger of that perception finally came home to him last summer, when three of Selkirk's four salespeople elected to take vacations during the same month. The result was that sales for the month all but vanished. Kennedy had had enough. "I told the people here that either you sustain the company as a self-financing entity, or I will let it go under. I'm unwilling to put more money on the table."

And yet, in the end, it was hard to avoid the conclusion that a large part of Selkirk's continuing problem was Allan Kennedy himself — a thought that did not escape him. "I've got a lot to learn about running a business successfully," he says, "about doing it myself, I mean. I think I know everything about management, except how to manage. I can give world-class advice on managing, but — when it comes right down to it — I take too long and fall into all the traps that I see with the managers I advise."

Whatever his shortcomings as a manager, there is one thing Kennedy can't be faulted for, and that is lack of courage. Having drawn the inevitable conclusion, he went out looking for someone who could help him do a better job of managing the company. For several months, he negotiated with the former president of a Boston-based high-tech firm, but the two of them were unable to come to terms. Instead, Kennedy has made changes at Selkirk that he hopes will achieve the same effect. In the new structure, Merlo is taking charge of the microcomputer end of the business, while Betsy Meade — a former West Coast sales representative — has responsibility for a new minicomputer version of Correspondent, to be marketed in conjunction with Prime Computer Corp. As for Kennedy, he will concern himself with external company relations, product-development strategies, and, of course, corporate culture.

Kennedy is full of optimism these days. He points out that despite its checkered history, Selkirk has emerged with a durable product and an installed base of about 1,000 units. In addition, the company will soon be bolstered with the proceeds from a $250,000 private placement. Meanwhile, he says, some of the company's previous problems have been dealt with, thanks to the introduction of a reliable order-fulfillment process, the decision to put sales reps on a straight commission payment schedule, and the establishment of specific sales targets for at least the next two quarters. "I think we have much more focused responsibility," he says, "and much more tangible measures of success for people in their jobs."

Overall, Kennedy looks on the past three years as a learning experience. "There are times when I think I should charge up most of the zigs and the zags to sheer rank incompetence," he admits. "But then there are other times when I look back

and say, 'Nobody's that smart, and you can't do everything right.' In life, you have to be willing to try things. And if something doesn't work, you have to be willing to say, 'Well, that was a dumb idea,' and then try something else." Now, he believes, he has a chance to do just that.

In the meantime, he is in the process of writing another book. He already has a proposal circulating among publishers. In his idle moments, he occasionally amuses himself by inventing titles. One of those titles speaks volumes about where he has been: *Kicking Ass and Taking Names.*

31
Lands' End

Lands' End, Inc. (LEI) was founded in 1963 by Gary C. Comer, an avid sailor and an award-winning copywriter with the advertising agency of Young & Rubican. LEI was founded to sell equipment to racing sailors by direct mail. Its unique name was the result of a mistake in its first printed mailing piece. Lands' End was meant to be Land's End, the name of a famous English seaport. The error was left uncorrected and the firm was off and running. Comer has said, "For me, Lands' End is a dream that came true. I always wanted to create a company of my own and here it is."

From its founding until 1976, LEI emphasised the sales of sailing gear while gradually adding related traditional recreational clothing and soft luggage to its product line. The clothing and luggage became so popular among the firm's upscale clientele that by 1976, LEI had shifted its focus entirely to these more popular items. In 1979, having outgrown its Chicago location, LEI moved to its current headquarters in Dodgeville, Wisconsin. The Chicago facility, which once housed the whole firm, was retained as the location of its marketing creative staff of thirty-five people.

In its first twenty-five years, Lands' End has grown to sales of over $335 million, making it one of the nation's largest merchants selling entirely through the medium of the direct mail catalog. In the five years between 1982 and 1987, LEI's sales more than tripled, and the firm set a goal of doubling fiscal 1986 sales by 1991. LEI went public in October 1986, achieving listing on the New York Stock Exchange in late 1987. LEI's 20,040,000 shares had a market value of $560 million in September 1988. For the fiscal year ending in January 1989, Lands' End is expected to circulate 72 million catalogs, achieve sales of $388 million, and earn profits of $26 million, or $1.30 per share.[1] Further financial information is presented in Exhibits 31-1, 31-2, and 31-3.

Business and Customers

Lands' End is a clothing retailer serving the market by direct mail through its extensive catalog of traditional clothing and related items. The main types of products sold include men's dress

This case was prepared by Peter G. Goulet and Lynda L. Goulet of the University of Northern Iowa and is intended to be used as a basis for class discussion rather than to illustrate either effective or ineffective handling of an administrative situation. The authors thank Julie Coppock, a UNI graduate student, and Stephen Ashley of Blunt, Ellis, and Loewi for their help in the preparation of this case. Presented to and accepted by the refereed Midwest Society for Case Research. All rights reserved to the authors and to the MSCR. ©1988 by Peter G. Goulet and Lynda L. Goulet. Used with permission.

shirts, slacks, ties, and accessories, as well as sport clothes, such as sweaters, shoes, jogging suits and "sweats," and a myriad of styles of knit shirts. The women's line includes similar sport clothing, as well as traditional natural-fiber shirts, skirts, and slacks, shoes, and accessories. The firm also offers a limited, but growing, line of children's clothing in styles similar to the adult lines. Finally, the firm manufactures and sells a line of soft luggage products and has recently introduced a line of linen and bedding.

The Lands' End customer is reasonably affluent. Sixty percent have incomes in excess of $35,000. Most have been to college and are employed in professional or managerial jobs. Exhibit 31-4 compares the typical Lands' End customer to its counterpart in the population as a whole. In 1986, LEI estimated that there were 23 million households in the United States that met its typical customer characteristics. Moreover, this group was growing more than three times as fast as the population as a whole. Further, it typically spends a larger proportion of its income on apparel than the average for the population.

The Direct Marketing Association (DMA) estimated that 10.1 percent of the total female population and 5.4 percent of the male population ordered at least one item of clothing from a catalog or other direct mail merchant in 1986. On average, between 9 percent and 10 percent of all the people with incomes over $30,000 made a direct mail clothing purchase. In addition, DMA has estimated that 10.7 percent of the college graduates and 10.5 percent of the professional/managerial households made such a purchase. Overall, it would appear that about 10 percent of the group Lands' End considers to be its prime customers can be expected to make a direct mail clothing purchase from some firm in a given year. Out of the base of 23 million customers, this would imply an average of 2.3 million active customers per year. In fact, LEI estimates that in the thirty-six months preceding February 1988, it had made at least one sale to 3.4 million different persons (see Exhibit 31-4).

Industry Environment

Lands' End is part of the catalog apparel industry that accounts for approximately 10 percent of all apparel sales. Recent data for these markets is shown in Exhibit 31-5. In 1988, the firm held about a 4 percent share of the catalog apparel market, making it the seventh largest direct market or catalog apparel retailer (see Exhibit 31-6 for a list of selected competitors). This market has enjoyed recent growth of 8.6 percent per year and is expected to continue to grow at 10 percent per year through 1991. Lands' End has grown roughly two to three times as fast as the market since calendar 1985.

Though catalog retailing is expected to grow faster than retailing in general in the next three to five years, there are some clouds on the horizon. The prospects for growth have caused a sharp increase in the number of catalogs directed to the buying public. In 1985, a total of 10 billion catalogs were mailed, rising to 11.8 billion in 1987. In addition, poor service on the part of some catalog merchants may help create a negative image for the segment in general. *Consumer Reports* has recently published ratings of catalog retailers to help consumers determine the relative service quality of many of the larger firms, including Lands' End. Lands' End was beaten only by L. L. Bean in these initial consumer ratings.

Another threat to catalog retailers is the rising cost of shipping goods and mailing catalogs. Early in 1988, the U.S. Postal Service raised postage rates for catalogs 25 percent and UPS raised surface shipping costs as well. In addition, catalog production costs are also rising, as are catalog sizes. The typical cost for a catalog the size and quality of that published by Lands' End can run as high as $750 thousand to $800 thousand, exclusive of mailing and handling costs. A typical sixty-four-page catalog in two or four colors costs around $350 thousand to $400 thousand. To partially offset these rising costs, some catalog retailers such as Bloomingdale's, for example, have begun to sell their catalogs in major chain book stores and sell advertising

EXHIBIT 31-1 Lands' End Income Statements for the Fiscal Years Ended January 31 (thousands of dollars)

	1988	%	1987	%	1986	%	1985	%
Net sales	$336,291	100.0%	$265,058	100.0%	$227,160	100.0%	$172,241	100.0%
Cost of sales	190,348	56.6%	152,959	57.7%	135,678	59.7%	101,800	59.1%
Gross profit	145,943	43.4%	112,099	42.3%	91,482	40.3%	70,441	40.9%
Operating expense	104,514	31.0%	80,878	30.5%	67,781	2.9%	55,431	32.2%
Depreciation	3,185	1.0%	2,576	1.0%	1,867	.8%	1,435	.8%
Operating income	38,244	11.4%	28,645	10.8%	21,834	9.6%	13,575	7.9%
Interest expense	(1,357)	- 0.4%	(1,488)	- 0.6%	(1,579)	- 0.7%	(1,697)	- 1.0%
Other income	1,441	0.4%	1,329	0.5%	1,329	0.6%	938	0.5%
Income before tax	38,328	11.4%	28,486	10.7%	21,584	9.5%	12,816	7.4%
Income tax (1)	15,523	4.6%	13,881	5.2%	10,314	4.5%	6,076	3.5%
Net income	22,805	6.8%	14,605	5.5%	11,270	5.0%	6,740	3.9%
Per share (2)	$1.14		$0.73		$0.56			
Catalogs mailed	63.5 mil.		50.0 mil.		44.0 mil.		29.0 mil.	

Quarterly percents	Sales	Gr.Pr.	Sales	Gr.Pr.	Sales	Gr.Pr.		
Feb-Apr	18.0%	17.6%	17.8%	16.7%	19.1%	19.5%		
May-July	19 0%	18.8%	19.9%	18.7%	19.4%	18.1%		
Aug-Oct	23.8%	24.1%	24.5%	25.3%	23.7%	24.4%		
Nov-Jan	39.1%	39.4%	37.8%	39.3%	37.3%	38.0%		

Lands' End was a Sub-chapter S corporation through part of 1987. Therefore,
(1) Income taxes from 1985-1987 are estimated to react a normal corporate structure.
(2) Earnings per share are estimated based on shares outstanding in 1988.

space in the catalogs.

Finally, most states do not require catalog retailers to charge sales tax on catalog sales outside of the states in which the firm operates. Recently, however, states are beginning to view this practice as a significant source of lost revenue. In 1988, Iowa was added to a small, but growing list of states that will require catalog firms to remit sales tax on all purchases made from catalogs by residents of the state, regardless of where the catalog firm is located. If all states move to this type of policy, it will reduce one of the key advantages to catalog retailers and could create significant overhead expenses for keeping the records required to satisfy each state.

A segment of the direct market retailing industry outside of the catalog segment may also pose a threat to the catalog retailers. Home shopping through cable television was expected to generate an estimated $1.75 billion in sales in 1987. The companies in this segment, of which the largest is the Home Shopping Network, Inc., were estimated to have reached over 40 million households in that year. Further, though some view the cable shopping phenomenon as a fad, the DMA estimates that by 1992, this industry segment could be generating $5.6 billion in sales and be reaching nearly 80 million households. If this is true, it represents a 26-percent average annual growth rate for the period. Given the growth of retail sales in general and forecasts for direct market retailing, this would seem to be growth that could easily come at the expense of other direct marketers.

Though entry into direct marketing does not require the same level of investment required to generate similar sales in the normal retail market, the costs may still be significant. To provide sufficient service requires expertise and may involve a large equipment investment. To develop a mailing list is also important and expensive. Name rental may run anywhere from $60 to $100 per thousand names annually, or upwards of $100,000 for a million quality, proven names. As the established firms such as Lands' End and L. L. Bean become large, economies of scale and learning-curve effects may make it difficult for new firms to enter the business in all but small niche markets.

EXHIBIT 31-2 Lands' End Statement of Changes in Working Capital for Fiscal Years Ended 1985-1988 (thousands of dollars)

	1988	%	1987	%	1986	%	1985	%
Sources:								
Operations (1)	$25,668		$21,804		$23,451		$14,251	
Long-term debt			264		316			
Sale of stock			22,584				520	
Fixed assets, net	776		38		243		205	
Total sources	$26,444		$44,690		$24,010		$14,976	
Uses:								
Dividends (2)	$4,008		$28,000		$13,775		$11,755	
Fixed assets	5,862		9,595		6,631		2,658	
Reduce long-term debt	1,918						478	
Other			40		24			
Total uses	$11,788		$37,635		$20,430		$14,891	
Net increase in working capital	$14,656		$7,055		$3,580		$85	

(1) Cash flow from operations consists of net income, depreciation, and additions to deferred taxes.
(2) Lands' End was a Sub-chapter S corporation through part of 1987. Therefore, dividends from 1985 to 1987 are sub-chapter S distributions.

Pure catalog retailers have a number of significant advantages over conventional retailers. The most obvious of these is that they have no stores to operate and have, therefore, lower costs. Passing on some of these cost savings can create a competitive advantage. In spite of this inherent advantage, however, several of the major catalog competitors do operate store locations in addition to their catalog operation, thus offsetting the advantage. What these firms have attempted to do is improve their performance as traditional retailers by using higher profit catalog sales as an adjunct to normal store-based selling. The Limited, Eddie Bauer, Talbots, J. C. Penney, and Sears, for example, operate anywhere from several dozen to several hundred stores each.

In addition to having lower costs and prices, catalog retailers give the customer the advantage of convenience. Being able to shop through a catalog and call in an order, even in the middle of the night, may be of great benefit to households where both spouses are working outside the home, for example. Further, using a catalog means the consumer may think about the purchase and compare alternate sources without costly transportation and sales pressure. Finally, catalog shopping is also a convenience for people who live in smaller communities where a variety of upscale goods, especially, is typically not available and obtaining such goods from a conventional store would be even more inconvenient than purchasing through a catalog.

The biggest weaknesses of catalog shopping involve the inability to see an item before buying it and the cost and inconvenience of having to return an unsatisfactory purchase. In spite of these issues, however, a Gallup poll reported by the DMA in 1987 shows that two-thirds of the population would consider making a direct mail/catalog purchase even if the item were available in conventional stores.

Lands' End's Strategy

Catalog retailers must adhere to most of the principles that govern traditional store-based retailers. Merchandise must be fresh, varied, and of satisfactory quality. By maintaining itself as a retailer of traditional clothing, Lands' End does not have the concerns with fad and fashion faced by such combination in-store and direct mail retailers as the Limited and Bloomingdale's, for example. However, the firm does have to offer

EXHIBIT 31-3 Lands' End Balance Sheets for the Fiscal Years Ended January 31 (thousands of dollars)

	1988	1987	1986
Current assets			
Cash & marketable securities	$28,175	$16,032	$3,578
Receivables	274	238	319
Inventories	46,444	40,091	31,057
Other	3,363	1,299	733
Total current	$78,256	$57,660	$35,687
Plant and equipment			
Land and buildings	15,114	13,809	9,499
Equipment	21,974	19,667	13,266
Leasehold improvements	908	661	584
Other	674		1,250
Total	38,670	34,137	24,599
Depreciation	9,947	7,315	4,758
Net fixed assets	28,723	26,822	19,841
Total assets	$106,979	$84,482	$55,528
Current liabilities			
Current portion			
Long-term debt	$1,918	$ 321	$ 193
Accounts payable	21,223	16,791	13,927
Order advances	453	449	193
Accruals	7,226	4,394	2,589
Profit sharing	2,646	1,707	830
Taxes payable	5,394	9,258	
Total current	38,860	32,920	18,002
Long-term debt	8,667	10,585	10,321
Deferred income tax	2,778	3,100	
	50,305	46,605	28,323
Stockholders' equity			
Common stock	200	100	95
Paid-in-capital	22,308	22,408	73
Retained earnings	34,166	15,369	27,037
Total equity	56,674	37,877	27,205
Total debt and owners' equity	$106,979	$84,482	$55,528

new merchandise regularly. Its most recent introductions have been its line of children's clothing and linens. Other featured items include its knit shirts and rugby shirts, the latter having been chosen by the U.S. National Rugby Team as its official jersey.

All Lands' End merchandise carries the firm's own private label. All catalog items except luggage are produced by outside vendors. The luggage is manufactured by the firm at its plant in West Union, Iowa. Product quality is assured by frequent inspections of goods, both at the manufacturer's facility and at the company. The firm even maintains a Lear jet to fly its staff of quality

assurance personnel to the factories of domestic manufacturers to direct production according to Lands' End specifications. Further, 10 percent of every shipment received at Dodgeville is inspected to assure continuing quality. Critical products are purchased from more than one vendor, and consistency between them is maintained by strict specifications. To further assure quality and service from vendors, officers of these companies are regularly brought to Dodgeville to see the Lands' End operation.

Lands' End understands that catalog retailing is a difficult business in which to create a competitive advantage. Its catalogs, therefore, are

EXHIBIT 31-4 Lands' End Customer Analysis

	Median Household Income	Women, Percent Employed	Percent Aged 25-29	Growth 25-49 $30K*	Percent Employed Profess.
LEI	$46,000	75%	69%	3.2%	70%
U.S.	24,500	<50%	50%	<1.0%	<25%

*Annual growth expected from 1985-1995 for population group with incomes over 530,000 aged between 25-49.

EXHIBIT 31-5 Retail Sales Data (dollars in billions)

	1985	1986	1987E	1988E	Growth Rate**
Retail sales	1374.00	1454.00	1541.00	1633.00	5.9%
Retail apparel	74.00	81.00	86.70	92.80	7.8%
Catalog sales*	26.00	27.50	29.70	32.10	7.3%
Catalog apparel*	7.50	8.20	8.90	9.60	8.6%
Lands' End	.23	.26	.34	.39	19.2%
Share catalog apparel	3.1%	3.1%	3.8%	4.1%	

*Estimated
**Average annual growth 1985-1988
Source: U.S. Commerce Department

produced with what the firm calls an "editorial" approach. Goods are not merely described in short, dry sentences. Rather, key product lines are given large half- or full-page descriptions that are designed to be interesting, appealing, and original. In addition, the catalog often contains several pages devoted to editorials, essays, and witty commentary dealing with a variety of subjects of interest to the firm's clientele. Two pages in the April 1988 issue described glass blowing. This kind of content is not unique to Lands' End. The catalog issued by the trendy Banana Republic also employs a similar approach. However, because different writers and subjects are involved in each catalog, Lands' End's catalogs can still be differentiated and are difficult to copy.

In addition, the quality and presentation of the Lands' End catalog is tightly controlled, and merchandise is presented in life-style settings designed to appeal to the firm's clientele. Merchandise is grouped in "programs" to promote multiple item sales. This "magazine style" approach is further supported by the use of product teams. New items are studied by a team consisting of a writer, an artist, and a buyer to make certain that each item is presented properly in the catalog.

To interest prospective customers, Lands' End uses print advertising. The cost of this national campaign in selected upscale publications, such as the *Wall Street Journal* and the *New Yorker*, is approximately 1 percent of sales. The campaign is designed to be compatible with the arm's editorial catalog structure and contains copy in a similar style.

Lands' End considers itself a "direct merchant" and summarizes its marketing and operations strategy as:

1. Establishing a strong, unique consumer brand image.
2. Placing an emphasis on product quality and value.
3. Identifying and expanding an active customer base.
4. Creating a continuous relationship with active customers.
5. Building customer confidence and convenience through service.

Service

At least part of the success of Lands' End has been attributed to its customer-oriented marketing philosophy. This customer orientation is rejected in a number of ways. Prompt service is supported by rapid response and personal attention. The firm claims its twenty-four-hour-a-day 800 number, which is the source of 73 percent of all incoming orders, rarely requires more than two rings before it is answered. In addition, 99 percent of its orders are shipped within twenty-four hours of receipt. This level of service is facilitated by a dedicated staff, a sophisticated computerized operating system, and a distribution center just doubled in size to 275,000 square feet. The DMA reports in its 1987 survey of customer attitudes that 83 percent of all direct. mail customers have some sort of complaint about direct mail purchasing. Though the most common complaints are that one cannot tell what one is likely to receive or that one will have been deceived by the merchandise, a significant percentage are either about poor service (20 percent) or inconvenience of some kind (16 percent). In addition, over half of the consumers surveyed by the DMA say they would buy more from direct marketers who provide prompt delivery.

Lands' End deals with customer complaints with the same commitment they have to customers placing orders. This is essential if the firm is to retain its strong group of dedicated customers. The DMA reports that though a high proportion of customers may have some complaint with mail order, 73 percent will remain as repeat customers if the complaint is satisfactorily handled, compared to 17 percent if it is not.

Lands' End sums up its marketing and service philosophy through its "Principles of Doing Business." These principles have been published in the catalog, annual reports, and advertising copy produced by the company.

PRINCIPLE 1. We do everything we can to make our products better. We improve material and add back features and construction details that others have taken out over the years. We never reduce the quality of a product to make it cheaper.

PRINCIPLE 2. We price our products fairly and honestly. We do not, have not, and will not participate in the common retail practice of inflating markups to set up a future phony 'sale.'

PRINCIPLE 3. We accept any return, for any reason, at any time. Our products are guaranteed. No fine print. No arguments. We mean exactly what we say: GUARANTEED. PERIOD.

PRINCIPLE 4. We ship faster than anyone we know of. We ship items in stock the day we receive the order. At the height of the last Christmas season, the longest time an order was in the house was thirty-six hours, excepting monograms which took another twelve hours.

PRINCIPLE 5. We believe that what is best for our customer is best for all of us. Everyone here understands that concept. Our sales and service people are trained to know our products and to be friendly and helpful. They are urged to take all the time necessary to take care of you. We even pay for your call, for whatever reason you call.

PRINCIPLE 6. We are able to sell at lower prices because we have eliminated middlemen, because we don't buy branded merchandise with high protected markups, and because we have placed our contracts with manufacturers who have proved they are cost conscious and efficient.

PRINCIPLE 7. We are able to sell at lower prices because we operate efficiently. Our people are hard working, intelligent, and share in the success of the company.

PRINCIPLE 8. We are able to sell at lower prices because we support no fancy emporiums with their high overhead. Our main location is in the middle of a forty-acre cornfield in rural Wisconsin. We still operate our first location in Chicago's Near North tannery district.

Operations

The heart of any catalog retailing operation is, of course, the catalog itself. Lands' End currently mails thirteen 140-page (average) catalogs a year to its proven customers. In all, the firm circulated a total of 50 million catalogs in fiscal 1987. That number is expected to rise to 63.5 million in 1988 and 72 million in 1989, up from 18 million in 1984, the firm's most productive year in terms of sales per catalog mailed.

Another key to effective catalog retailing is the mailing list. Firms the size of Lands' End commonly maintain lists of five million or more names. LEI maintains a proprietary list of 7.8 million names. Although many catalog retailers obtain names from mailing list brokers and even competitors, Lands' End has attempted to build its list internally as much as possible as a source of competitive advantage. It has also reduced its participation in the mailing list rental market.

Catalog retailing also depends on order fulfillment and service. Merchandise is stored in and distributed from the firm's 275,000-square-foot distribution center. In spite of the size of this facility, however, it is only expected to be able to satisfy the firm's needs through 1989, when a 250,000-square-foot addition is expected to be completed. Through this center, Lands' End processed approximately 31,000 orders per day in 1987, with a high of 75,000 orders on its peak day. The center has the capacity to process 35,000 orders per nine-hour shift.

To facilitate the function of the distribution center, manage inventories, and minimize shipping costs, the firm uses an optical scanning sorting system. Orders are processed through the firm's mainframe computer system, based on three very large Series 3090 computers by IBM. Through this computer system, management can obtain real-time information on any part of its current operation status. In addition, during 1987, the firm installed a new computer- controlled garment-moving system and inseaming system as part of $6 million in capital expenditures. Finally, an automated receiving system installed during 1987 has increased the firm's receiving capacity to ten thousand boxes per day from four thousand.

Phone service is maintained through company phone centers. This service was recently enlarged by the addition of an auxillary center designed to handle seasonal overload traffic. This phone system now operates on a fiberoptic cable system to increase communication quality. Through the computer system, each operator has access to customer records and past sales history as well as a fact file on each catalog item. It is not unusual for this system to handle seventy-five calls at a time, around the clock, in normal times, with a much higher load in the Christmas season.

Though 95 percent of all sales are through the catalog and Lands' End operates no retail stores, it does maintain nine "outlet stores" at various locations in Chicago and Wisconsin. The firm also uses a "Lands' End Outlet" section in its catalog to help dispose of overstocks.

As the firm has grown, so has the number of employees. The firm now employs more than 2,200 people, with as many as 1,200 more added to handle the extra load during the busy fourth quarter. Both the founder and the current president have extensive advertising experience as well as considerable experience with the company. New additions to the list of top managers include experts in catalog merchandising, quality assurance, and other related specialties.

Lands' End realizes the importance of a quality work force. It has worked with the University of Wisconsin, Platteville, to set up an extension in Dodgeville to help workers increase their skills at company expense. Part-time workers earn full-time benefits after they work 1,040 hours in a year. All workers receive the right to an employee discount on the firm's products and

EXHIBIT 31-6 Direct/Catalog Sales, 1985: Largest Direct Mail/Catalog Apparel Firms

Firm	Direct/Catalog Total 1985 Sales
Fingerhut Corp./Cos.	$1,485 million
Spiegel	847 million
Sears	695 million
The Limited/Lane Bryant	612 million
J. C. Penney	510 million
New Process	330 million
Combined International	227 million
Lands' End	227 million
L. L. Bean	220 million
Hanover House	212 million
Avon Direct Response	205 million
Bear Creek	130 million
General Mills	104 million
CML Group	55 million
Popular Services	40 million

Source: *Inside the Leading Mail Order Houses,* Colorado Springs, CO: Maxwell Sroge, 1985.

share in the firm's profits. The firm also plans to provide a $5-million employee fitness center in 1988. Overall, wage levels in this industry average approximately $5.75 per hour.

Competitors

Dozens of catalog retailers sell apparel, even in the market dominated by Lands' End. However, in its specific target market, LEI has apparently become the market leader. LEI's competitors may be classified into several basic categories. There are firms, such as the J. Crew unit of Popular Services, Inc. (men's clothing); Talbots (women's clothing), formerly owned by General Mills; and The Company Store (linens), that compete directly with a product segment served by Lands' End. Other firms, such as Hanover House, produce multiple catalogs serving a wide variety of customer product and demographic segments. Some of these segments may overlap with those served by LEI. Major retailers, such as Sears, J. C. Penney, and Spiegel, produce large, seasonal, full-line catalogs selling a wide variety of merchandise, of which apparel is only a part. These large firms, as well as other smaller catalog retailers that also operate retail stores, tend to compete more closely with traditional retailers. Exhibit 31-6 identifies a number of major catalog retailers and competitors for LEI. Exhibit 31-7 describes and contrasts several op-

EXHIBIT 31-7 Lands' End Competitor Characteristics, 1985

Company	Catalog Sales ($ millions)	Catalogs Mailed (millions)	Sales per Catalog	Active Buyers (millions)	Stores and/or Notes
Lands' End	$227	44	$5.16	3.43	9 outlets
Hanover House	212	250	0.85	4.00	20 catalogs
L.L. Bean	221	68	3.25	2.15	1 store
Popular Services					
J. Crew	30	7	4.29	.45	
Cliff & Wills	10	2	5.00	.20	
CML Group	55	25	2.20	.49	5 catalogs 100 stores
General Mills (1985)					
Talbots	47	38	1.25	.47	59 stores
Eddie Bauer	57	25	2.28	.72	39 stores
General Mills (1987)					
Talbots	84	60+	<1.40	.65+	109 stores
Eddie Bauer	76	N/A	N/A	1.00	39 stores

erating characteristics of LEI's closest competitors.

Performance

Since 1984, when Lands' End achieved sales of $123.4 million and net profits of $7.3 million, the firm's sales and profits have grown at 22.2 percent and 25.6 percent annually, respectively. Sales and profit growth in the first half of fiscal 1989 were 33.7 percent and 64.6 percent higher than the same period in 1988, respectively. Gross margins have improved steadily and may be compared to a level of approximately 42.5 percent, typical for apparel retailers in general. Net profit margins have also improved and may be compared to a recent level of about 3.5 percent for large retailers. The percentage of debt to equity has declined steadily throughout the period. The net profit to total assets measure of return on investment has averaged 21 percent over the last five years, compared to 4.4 percent for the nation's thirty-three largest-value retail firms (including LEI) in 1988 and approximately 7.5 percent for all retail establishments. LEI's return on stockholder's equity has averaged 40.4 percent since 1984, having earned 40.2 percent in 1988, compared to 15.4 percent for the thirty-three largest firms. Financial results for Lands' End are presented in Exhibits 31-1, 31-2, and 31-3.

Although Lands' End's recent performance is spectacular and far exceeds industry standards, it remains to be seen how long its growth and margins can be maintained. As the catalog market becomes increasingly competitive, new products and marketing methods will have to be developed.

Endnotes

[1] All financial data in this case comes from Lands' End annual reports and analytical reports prepared by Stephen Ashley of Blunt, Ellis, and Loewi, Inc. (August 4, 1987, and November 23, 1987).

[2] A. Hagedorn. " 'Tis the Season for Catalog Firms." *Wall Street Journal*, November 24, 1987, p. 6.

References

Major sources of other information include:

1987 Supplement to the Fact Book. Direct Marketing Association. New York: DMA, 1987.

Inside the Leading Mail Order Houses, 3d ed. Colorado Springs, CO: Maxwell Sroge Publishing, 1987.

Lands' End Annual Reports, 1987 and 1988.

1988 Industrial Outlook. U.S. Department of Commerce.

32
Meadville State Prison

Introduction

Meadville State Prison is one of four major correctional facilities in the state. Until recently, it operated strictly in a custodial role, making very little effort to rehabilitate the inmates.

The organization of the prison consists of three departments reporting to the warden. An administrative staff, consisting of the purchasing, maintenance, health care, and recordkeeping departments, is considered as being apart from the mainstream of prison activities. A rehabilitation director heads a staff responsible for the training and counseling of inmates in preparation for their re-entry into civilian life. The deputy warden is in charge of the guards and is responsible for the security of the prison.

Meadville has experienced a change and is presently in a state of conflict. Before describing this conflict, it is essential that the personalities involved and the prior state of affairs be explored.

Background

Warden Aaron Hunsacre has been an administrator of Meadville for fifteen years, the first five of which were spent as a deputy warden and the last ten as warden.

On completing his high school education, Hunsacre immediately enlisted in the Marines, where he hoped someday to become a high ranking officer. Although he completed Officer Candidate School, he became bitter when he did not rise above the rank of major. Finally, in 1963, after thirteen years in the service, he decided to accept the deputy warden position at Meadville. Several motives prompted his acceptance of this job, but foremost the implicit understanding that the warden's job would be his when the present holder retired in five years. The thought of being head honcho at a large prison was very appealing; he felt that the several years he had spent as an MP (military policeman) in the Marines had adequately prepared him for the position.

This case was prepared by Becky Fox, Steve Hardy, Jim Kreiner, and Kitty Putzier under the supervision of Theodore T. Herbert. The case is not intended to reflect either effective or ineffective administrative or technical practices; it was prepared for class discussion. Reprinted by permission of Theodore T. Herbert.

From this point on, events seemed to fall neatly into place for Aaron: he moved into the vacated warden's position at the end of five years and influenced the hiring of an old Marine buddy, Eugene Halter, to fill the deputy warden spot. Aaron was very content with his job, feeling that he had achieved a secure position of power and prestige in society as well as in the organization—after all, he was responsible directly to the governor of the state!

Aaron interpreted his job as warden as one of maintaining firm control in managing inmates. He had to punish and keep those people who threatened society out of sight. With this orientation, he hired employees who advocated strict enforcement of the rules and tolerated little misbehavior on the part of the inmates. He was very suspicious of younger, college-trained persons and held most of their theories in contempt. Whenever it could be avoided, he refused to hire college graduates.

Deputy Warden

Eugene Halter, the deputy warden, was supposed to take care of the daily operations of the prison, having the responsibility of supervising the guards who controlled the prisoners. He was to report any problems to the warden, as well as keep him informed of daily occurrences.

After Eugene had completed his stay in the Marines, he returned to school and received a two-year technical degree in criminology. It was at this point that he went to work at Meadville, a decision based on the encouragement of his friend Aaron. He felt that this institution offered him the opportunity to rise someday to the top. Consequently, he took his job very seriously and was careful not to rock the boat in matters affecting Aaron's perceptions of the way he executed his job. After seven years with Meadville, Eugene had become Aaron's "yes man"; Eugene always avoided telling Aaron things that might upset him.

The deputy warden took his lead from Aaron and became an almost tyrannical enforcer of order. (In response to his commands, it became a standing joke for the prisoners, as well as some guards, to salute behind his back and garble his last name to sound like Heil Hitler!) The prisoners held Eugene in contempt; most of the guards regarded him with awe. It was felt that his actions to carry out his responsibilities bordered on being sadistic and that overall he was extremely power hungry.

The Captain of the Yard

Jeb Slatka was responsible for the guards and inmates in one of four sections of Meadville. He had been captain of the yard for five years, working his way up through the ranks by advancing from guard through sergeant, to watch officer, and finally to captain. He was now fifty-two with twenty-one years of service at the prison. Most of Jeb's earlier work experience had been in the military as an army noncom. After his combat tour of duty in Korea, the peacetime army no longer had an appeal for him. He had decided not to "re-up" and was looking for a job when an opening for a guard at Meadville came to his attention. The job seemed to suit his temperament, and he took it.

Jeb's office acted as the center for all yard communications. As a result of the custodial goals of the institution, primary interest was placed in the hour-by-hour reports on the location and movements of the prisoners. In addition, all orders, assignments of men, requests, and reports had to pass through his office and communications center. The line work supervisors, under these conditions, although equal in rank to the guards, had lower status and were obliged to take orders from the guards. This situation had evolved because the custodial goals of order and control were of prime importance. Meaningful work and rehabilitation were insignificant in the eyes of the warden and, therefore, to his guard staff. Other activities that might interfere even slightly with security just were not allowed.

The Guards

Although all other functions in the prison had operated under authoritarian and narrowly defined limits, much discretionary authority had been given to the guards insofar as their relationship to the prisoners was concerned. The guards had almost always been backed by their supervisors. This condition, in fact, had given the guards, as a group, more power than the line work supervisors and other rehabilitative personnel. The inmates recognized this power and considered it in all of their actions. The guards' position of power over the prisoners was enhanced by the psychological domination arising from the regimentation, frequent head counts, assemblies, and imposed silence during all supervised activities. Hence, the use of punishment was infrequent and usually unnecessary.

When imposed, punishment for control had few rules and was based on the individual guard's determination of insubordination. This created a situation wherein the accused had no rules, no forewarning, and no recourse for appeal. The uncertainty of the infliction of punishment as a means of control, not justice, produced an underlying and everpresent terror in the prisoners, especially at the lower hierarchical levels. Any of the very infrequent rewards were made only for prisoner conformity.

The Inmate Society

The authoritarian, custodial nature of the Meadville prison operation had created a no-frills environment, with few privileges available to the inmates. Under these conditions, one might have expected the men to become coequals and ready to rebel against the system at any chance. This was not the case. A highly structured inmate society, aimed at adjustment rather than rebellion, had developed. This society was led, rather surprisingly, by the least violent and aggressive men.

Although the inmate society, like the prison authorities, demanded that all prisoners be treated alike, interpersonal relations founded on dominance and subordination were the rule. The ability to exercise coercion was highly valued, not for the power, but because it was a means to achieve the goals common to all inmates: integrity and safety from official sanctions. As it currently existed, the inmate society had a static, sharply defined structure and power hierarchy aimed at attaining these goals. The society enforced member conformity through punishments usually more severe than those used by the prison officials.

When a new inmate or "fish" (just caught) arrived, he wasn't given a book of regulations defining his position. The shock of entering the prison, the capricious nature of discipline, the secrecy, and the regimentation all made the new man very dependent on any veteran inmate to whom he could attach himself. He needed an experienced man to teach him about the undefined and uncertain tolerances of the guards and to give him any insights vital for making life even the slightest bit more pleasant.

The new man was, in time, introduced to the prison grapevine. The grapevine was usually inaccurate, but it created and circulated the myths that helped to explain satisfactorily otherwise inexplicable (to the inmates) events. It helped the new men to adjust to prison life. The grapevine also helped, through the myths that held the prison officials in contempt, to create and maintain a degree of dignity and group unity.

The new, not yet accepted fish found himself lumped together at the bottom of the inmate society with those inmates whose prison jobs, behavior, or outside ties created suspicions that they might act as informers to the officials. The least a new man had to do to gain, or a current member to retain, membership in the society was to conform to the group norms. These included rejection of the outside world and taking any punishment without talking. A man who had gained seniority and the confidence of the membership and was able to explain, predict, or control in part the circumstances that others could not, and would probably emerge as a leader. These leaders, because they had power, were mediators between their inmate followers and the officials. They were allowed to talk to the guards, which was not permitted for men in lower positions.

When conditions were stable, as things had been for the many years of the warden's custodial stewardship, the inmate society actually acted as a support for the authoritarian, custodial system. The inmate leaders had responsible contacts with the guards and had a voice in the assignment and distribution of privileges. This interaction between the officials and inmate leaders helped both sides achieve common, mutual goals of peace, order, and adjustment. In this way, each hierarchy was able to maintain its position of power and advantage.

The Rehabilitation Staff

The rehabilitation services department at Meadville is directed by Polly Hoover. Polly has her master's degree in social work. Before beginning graduate school, she worked for several years as a counselor in the State Detention Center for juvenile delinquents. Polly was an outstanding student during her graduate work, and at thirty-one, she is quite a bit younger than any of the previous directors. Polly has been at Meadville for almost two years now, and her staff is still making adjustments to her rehabilitation plans.

Polly is quite an idealist and believes strongly in the modern goals of therapy, treatment, education, and rehabilitation. She espouses the belief that if discipline is absolutely necessary, it must be administered in such a way as to preserve the dignity of the inmate.

The rehabilitation staff is made up of one full-time psychologist, a librarian, a part-time art instructor, two full-time vocational instructors, and another social worker (besides Polly).

Sam Fall, the prison psychologist, is fifty-three years old and quite comfortable with his position at Meadville. He is much more comfortable than he was fifteen years ago when he was still struggling to make a go of his private practice. When this position opened up twelve years ago, Sam jumped at the chance to, for once in his

life, have a steady income he could count on, without the worries and responsibilities he faced when he was self-employed. Sam looked forward to spending the next twelve years waiting out his retirement.

Sam's formal responsibilities included scheduling private counseling sessions with inmates, which took up most of his time. He was also to conduct group therapy sessions, keep certain office hours for visitation by inmates, and maintain each inmate's file, updating it as to treatment and progress. He also served in an advisory capacity to the rest of the rehabilitation staff as well as the custodial staff.

The librarian, art instructor, and shop teachers were responsible for their own areas only and planned and coordinated their curricula with the advice and approval of the director. If Polly thought it necessary, Sam was called in for consultation.

The resident social worker was responsible for placing inmates in jobs within the prison in such areas as the kitchen, the laundry, and the library. He also directed prison recreational and social activities and assisted the director, Polly, in maintaining supportive relationships between prisoners and their families and friends and between prisoners and supportive volunteer organizations.

Polly was quite enthusiastic about getting outside groups more involved in the prison and trying out some of the rehabilitation techniques that she had researched during her graduate work. However, most of her staff had a less optimistic view of rehabilitation than she. Most of their efforts were directed toward keeping peace among the inmate society, rather than toward rehabilitation.

It was no secret that most of the inmates regarded the whole idea of rehabilitation as a joke. They played the game because they knew that, if they didn't, parole was a virtual impossibility. Sam Fall was not one of the most perceptive people when it came to human behavior, but even he had begun to realize that during personal counseling sessions, the inmates' responses had begun to follow predictable patterns.

Polly had become frustrated with the lack of

support her rehabilitation efforts were receiving at Meadville. In fact, she was considering looking for a job elsewhere, where the attitudes of the administration were more enlightened. However, a riot at neighboring Roland State Prison brought the need for prison reform to light, and Polly felt that maybe now her ideas would be considered seriously.

The Change

The news was full of the explosive situation at Roland State. No one knew exactly how the riot started; accidently caught in the middle was a group of college freshmen from the local university who happened to be touring the facility as a field trip in psychology. Six of the group, four males and two females, had been held hostage along with four guards and a clerk from the prison's administrative staff.

The confrontation lasted for four long days with the prisoners demanding improved treatment in exchange for the hostages. The state police were prepared to attack the prisoner-controlled area and regain control by force. The fact that innocent bystanders, not a part of the prison system, were involved generated national public interest. People realized that the activities within a prison system can affect the general public and became very interested in the situation that led to the riot.

Jay Cole supplied the desired information and is considered the man most responsible for settling the riot and obtaining the release of the hostages unharmed. Cole is a local TV personality with a late-night talk show. Several months before, Cole and his station filmed a documentary on prison conditions at Roland State and conducted interviews with inmates. The show went relatively unnoticed when first aired, but during the riot the program was repeated nationwide during prime time. Cole's program and his genuine concern about prison conditions convinced a large segment of the public that reform was overdue and that the prisoners had legitimate complaints. Governor Wendell, well tuned to political pressures, saw a way to end the riot

and take the initiative for reform. He selected Jay Cole to negotiate with the prisoners and offered to establish a state commission for prison reform in exchange for the hostages. The prisoners trusted Cole and agreed to the governor's terms. Cole promised the prisoners that he would keep the activities of the commission in the public eye to assure that real action would be taken.

The newly formed state commission visited Meadville and informed the warden that rehabilitation must be emphasized. A portion of the commission's findings states that:

consequently, it has been determined by our investigations that the 70 percent recidivism rate and the increase in severity of crimes committed by those released from prison indicate that prisons should take a more active part in attempting to rehabilitate inmates. Prisons must be made into something other than breeding places of hate-filled and vengeful individuals if we expect these individuals to one day re-enter our society.

The governor has also visited Warden Hunsacre and made it clear that prison reform is one of his major goals. He wants specific actions that the voter can relate to for use in his re-election campaign next year. He reminded the warden that Jay Cole will keep this issue alive and will insist on real action, not just paper plans and programs.

The State Commission for Prison Reform presented all prison staff with a copy of the newly-developed guidelines for achieving the desired changes in the state's prison system. Most of the guidelines are aimed at assuring more humane treatment of inmates and providing more opportunities for rehabilitation. The prison staff is to be responsible for maintaining a separate file on each inmate. Reports are to be filled out by both custodial and rehabilitative staff and are to be updated weekly. Each report is to include descriptions of all rehabilitation programs and efforts in which the inmate is involved, the results of the program and progress of the inmate's attitudes and behaviors, and an evaluation of custodial cooperation.

These reports are sent to the rehabilitation director, who evaluates them and summarizes the progress of the inmate population in reaching the goals set forth by the commission. These summaries will be sent to the State Commission for Prison Reform, and all inmates' files will be made available for the commission's examination.

Also, the rehabilitation staff was increased by the addition of two full-time counselors to assist in implementing the new guidelines.

Aaron realized that he had no choice other than to accommodate the wishes of the State Commission for Prison Reform. Although he felt that these new goals of the governor had their basis in political vote rallying and were not expected really to accomplish anything, he knew he would have to make a pretext of implementing them or else lose his job. He confided the following to Eugene:

Listen, I'm not about to let that Wendell and his commission come in here and tell me what to do. As far as I'm concerned, these new rehabilitation goals are nothing but a lot of hogwash! I'm only putting up with this rehabilitation director and her division because there's no way around it—but I'll tell you—they're really out in left field when it comes to understanding what a prison system is all about. They must think we're running a day care center here instead of a prison. Thieves, murderers, and no good bums!— that's what we've got here, and there's no way anyone's going to make upstanding citizens out of that lot. Give these guys an inch and they'll take a mile. I'm sure I've made my point and you know what I mean—don't give them that first inch!

Eugene transmitted Hunsacre's sentiments to the guards and let it be known that under no circumstances were security and control over the prisoners to be lessened. In turn, the guards were expected to remind the prisoners of exactly who was in charge and that nothing had changed.

On the other hand, Polly could not have been happier. She felt that with the governor and the commission behind her, she was finally going to have some clout in implementing her rehabilitation strategies. She expressed these beliefs in a discussion with her newly enlarged staff:

I've been waiting a long time for this kind of backing and finally we've got it. Now maybe we can make the warden see the kind of progress we can make with the prisoners if they're just treated like respectable human beings. Warden Hunsacre has told me I'm free to do whatever I want with this program and I'm sure we've got his full cooperation.

Various programs were created for the prisoners in the hopes that their self-improvement would be forthcoming. Participation in vocational education classes was encouraged, as well as participation in the formal therapy and rap sessions.

After several months of organizing and establishing these programs, Polly felt that she wasn't making as much progress as she had hoped. She felt that her social workers were facing a subversive resistance from the guards. Although the guards always seemed to listen to the rehabilitation staff, often their actions were inconsistent with the advice. Behind the staff's backs, guards apparently continued to belittle the inmates and exercise control in the way they felt necessary. The rehabilitation staff learned this through the complaints of some of the prisoners. At first, Polly could not understand why the guards were being so uncooperative, but then attributed it to laziness and unwillingness to exert the effort to interact decently with the prisoners.

The guards viewed their situation differently, as is evidenced by this conversation between two of them:

This rehabilitation stuff is for the birds. I don't know about you, but I'm getting a little tired of listening to their preaching about how we should respect these hooligans. "Try to get to know them better," they say—ha!—I know all I care to know and that's too much. I know who signs my paycheck, and if he wants the cons to toe the mark, that's what he's going to get.

Yeah. Things ran a lot better around here before rehab got so high and mighty. These social workers are always siding with the inmates and believing their accounts over ours. You should hear some of the stories I've heard prisoners tell—sheesh! Those rehabs are a gullible bunch; they fall for any sob story.

During the ensuing months, problems between the rehabilitation staff and the warden's group increased drastically. Minor occasions for interaction between the two groups seemed to assume more importance, and tensions increased. Guards complained that the rehabilitation staff was too lax in their dealings with the inmates, which endangered security. One guard confronted a rehabilitation teacher with the following:

Three times last week I had to confiscate weapons from inmates that they got from your class. You may think they're only harmless tools, but in the hands of most of these fellows, they're as lethal as any gun or knife. You just don't understand that these guys can't be trusted, do you?!

Oftentimes, a guard would, as a form of punishment, not permit a certain inmate to attend a class or self-help session. Conflicts then arose because teachers and social workers felt that the classes were too important for inmates to be arbitrarily denied.

The inmates were caught in the middle of the situation. Those in the top level of the prisoner hierarchy knew that their best course of action was to stay on the guard's best side and avoid any siding with the rehabilitation staff. Taking their cue from the facade used by the guards, those prisoners would go through the motions of "being rehabilitated," when in fact they thought it was a joke. However, in the lower echelons of the ranks of prisoners were those inmates who were trying to get the best deal for themselves by playing the staff against the guards. They could covertly "squeal" to the rehabilitation workers and gain sympathy without much fear of reprisals or sanctions from fellow inmates. It was these individuals, because they didn't conform to the main prisoner group, who wanted compliance and safety from prison sanctions, who increased the conflict between the warden and guards and the rehabilitation staff.

It became evident to Polly that the warden was not really being very cooperative in helping her to meet her rehabilitation goals. One day, the two confronted each other in the explosive argument that follows:

Polly: Listen here, Hunsacre! I get the impression you don't care at all about what I'm attempting to do with these prisoners. You tell me one thing, and the next time I turn around you're doing the opposite. I can't get anywhere with your guards either, and I need their cooperation. It looks like I may have to go to the state commission if you don't make a few changes.

Aaron: What have I been trying to tell you all along!? Get your head out of the clouds and return to earth, will you? Don't try and put the blame on me because your program is a flop. Sometimes I think I'm the only one around here who's living in the real world. You're so blind you can't see what a mess you're making of everything. The only way to handle prisoners is with firm control and the sooner you realize that, the better off we'll all be. I wouldn't be so anxious to broadcast this mess to the commission if I were you; you just might be cutting your own throat!

33
Masters of Innovation

It was 1922. Minnesota Mining & Manufacturing inventor Francis G. Okie was dreaming up ways to boost sales of sandpaper, then the company's premier product, when a novel thought struck him. Why not sell sandpaper to men as a replacement for razor blades? Why would they risk the nicks of a sharp instrument when they could rub their cheeks smooth instead?

The idea never caught on, of course. The surprise is that Okie, who continued to sand his own face, could champion such a patently wacky scheme and keep his job. But unlike most companies then — or now — 3M Co. demonstrated a wide tolerance for new ideas, believing that unfettered creative thinking would pay off in the end. Indeed, Okie's hits made up for his misses: He developed a waterproof sandpaper that became a staple of the auto industry because it produced a better exterior finish and created less dust than conventional papers. It was 3M's first blockbuster.

Through the decades, 3M has managed to keep its creative spirit alive. The result is a company that spins out new products faster and better than just about anyone. It boasts an impressive catalog of more than 60,000 products, from Post-it notes to heart-lung machines. What's more, 32 percent of 3M's $10.6 billion in 1988 sales came from products introduced within the past five years. Antistatic videotape, translucent dental braces, synthetic ligaments for damaged knees, and heavy-duty reflective sheeting for construction-site signs are just a few of the highly profitable new products that contributed to record earnings of $1.15 billion in 1988.

At a time when many big U.S. corporations are trying to untangle themselves from bureaucracy, 3M stands apart as a smooth-running innovation machine. Along with a handful of other companies that might be called the Innovation Elite — Merck, Hewlett-Packard, and Rubbermaid among them (see exhibit 33 — 1 at the end of the case) — 3M is celebrated year after year in the rankings of most-respected companies. Business schools across the country make 3M a case study in new-product development, and management gurus trumpet 3M's methods. Peter Drucker's Innovation and Entrepreneurship is peppered with 3M tales. A star of the bestseller *In Search of Excellence*, 3M remains a favorite of co-author Thomas J. Peters. "It is far more entrepreneurial than any $10 billion company I've come across," he says, "and probably more entrepreneurial than a majority of those one-tenth its size."

The publicity has attracted representatives of dozens of companies from around the world to tour 3M headquarters near St. Paul, Minn., in search of ideas and inspiration. While such companies as Monsanto Co. and United Technologies Corp. have adopted some of 3M's methods, it's hard to emulate a culture that has been percolating since the turn of the century.

Lose Some

So how does 3M do it? One way is to encourage inventive zealots like Francis Okie. The business of innovation can be a numbers game — the more tries, the more likely there will be hits. The scarcity of corporate rules at 3M leaves room for plenty of experimentation — and failure. Okie's failure is as legendary among 3Mers as his blockbuster. Salaries and promotions are tied to the successful shepherding of new products from inception to commercialization. One big carrot: The fanatical 3Mer who champions a new product out the door then gets the chance to manage it as if it were his or her own business.

Since the bias is toward creating new products, anything that gets in the way, whether it's turf fights, overplanning, or the "not-invented-here" syndrome, is quickly stamped out. Divisions are kept small, on average about $200 million in sales, and they are expected to share knowledge and manpower. In fact, informal information-sharing sessions spring up willynilly at 3M — in the scores of laboratories and small meeting rooms or in the hallways. And it's not unusual for customers to be involved in these brainstorming klatches.

Peer Review

That's not to say that corporate restraint is nonexistent. 3Mers tend to be self-policing. Sure, there are financial measures that a new-product team must meet to proceed to different stages of development, but the real control lies in constant peer review and feedback.

The cultural rules work — and go a long way toward explaining why an old-line manufacturing company, whose base products are sandpaper and tape, has become a master at innovation, and a highly profitable one at that. Earnings spurted 25 percent in 1988 from a year earlier. However, it wasn't always so. The company hit a rocky stretch in the early 1980s. But stepped-up research spending and some skillful cost-cutting by Chairman and Chief Executive Allen F. Jacobson have revived all of 3M's critical financial ratios.

A 3M lifer and Scotch-tape veteran, Jake Jacobson took over the top job in 1985 and laid out his J-35 program. That's J as in Jake, and 35 as in 35 percent cuts in labor and manufacturing costs — to be accomplished by 1990. 3M is well on its way to reaching those goals, and the push has already improved the bottom line. Last year return on capital climbed almost three points, to 27.6 percent, and return on equity had a similar rise, to 21.6 percent. Jacobson has clamped down on costs without harming his company's ability to churn out new products one whit.

Motley Crew

3M was founded not by scientists or inventors but by a doctor, a lawyer, two railroad executives, and a meat-market manager. At the turn of the century, the five Minnesotans bought a plot of heavily forested land on the frigid shores of Lake Superior, northeast of Duluth. They planned to mine corundum, an abrasive used by sandpaper manufacturers to make the paper scratchy. The five entrepreneurs drummed up new investors, bought machinery, hired workers, and started mining. Only then did they discover that their corundum, alas, wasn't corundum at all but a worthless mineral that the sandpaper industry wanted no part of.

The company tried selling its own sandpaper, using corundum shipped in from the East, but got battered by the competition. How perfect:

The company that tolerates failure was founded on a colossal one. 3M was forced to innovate or die. Most of the original investors got swept out of the picture, and the remaining 3Mers set about inventing. First, the company introduced a popular abrasive cloth for metal finishing. Then Okie struck gold with his Wetordry sandpaper. They drew inspiration from William L. McKnight, who is revered to this day as the spiritual father of the company. He started out as an assistant bookkeeper and worked his way up through sales. His approach, unusual for its day, has stuck with the company. Rather than make his pitch to a company's purchasing agent, McKnight talked his way onto the factory floor to demonstrate his products to the workers who used them. After he became chairman and chief executive, he penned a manifesto that said, in part, "If management is intolerant and destructively critical when mistakes are made, I think it kills initiative."

Loyal Lifers

That kind of thinking breeds loyalty and management stability. The company rarely hires from the outside, and never at the senior level. Jacobson, 62, a chemical engineer, started out in the tape lab in 1947. And all his lieutenants are lifers, too. The turnover rate among managers and other professionals averages less than 4 percent. "It's just not possible to really understand this company until you've been around for a long while," says Jerry E. Robertson, head of the Life Sciences Sector.

Don't let 3M's dull exterior fool you. The St. Paul campus, home of company headquarters and most of the research labs, is an expanse of brick buildings with a high-rise glass tower that could have been designed by a kid with an Erector set. But inside is an army of engineers and technical experts and platoons of marketers just raring to innovate.

Here's how it typically works: A 3Mer comes up with an idea for a new product. He or she forms an action team by recruiting full-time members from technical areas, manufacturing, marketing, sales, and maybe finance. The team designs the product and figures out how to produce and market it. Then it develops new uses and line extensions. All members of the team are promoted and get raises as the project goes from hurdle to hurdle. When sales grow to $5 million, for instance, the product's originator becomes a project manager; at $20 million to $30 million, a department manager; and in the $75 million range, a division manager. There's a separate track for scientists who don't want to manage.

Many Paths

As a result, 3M is big but acts small. There are forty-two divisions, so ladders to the top are all over the place. Jacobson reached the pinnacle by cleaning up old-line operations, while his predecessor, Lewis W. Lehr, invented a surgical tape and then rode the company's burgeoning health care business all the way to the chairman's post.

So what are the corporate guidelines? A prime one is the 25-percent rule, which requires that a quarter of a division's sales come from products introduced within the past five years. Meeting the 25-percent test is a crucial yardstick at bonus time, so managers take it seriously. When Robert J. Hershock took over the occupational health division in 1982, it was utterly dependent on an aging product category, disposable face masks. By 1985, his new-product percentage had deteriorated to a mere 12 percent.

That set off alarms. He and his crew had to come up with plenty of new products — and they had to do it in eighteen to twenty-four months, half the normal time. Using technology similar to the division's facemask filters, Hershock's action teams created a bevy of products. One team came up with a sheet that drinks up the grease from microwaved bacon. Another devised a super-absorbent packing material that was widely welcomed by handlers of blood samples. The idea came from a team member who had read a newspaper article about postal workers who were panicked by the AIDS epidemic. The division's new-product sales are back above 25 percent.

Then there's the 15 percent rule. That one allows virtually anyone at the company to spend up to 15 percent of the workweek on anything he or she wants to, as long as it's product related. The practice is called "boot-legging," and its most famous innovation is the ubiquitous yellow Post-it note. Arthur L. Fry's division was busy with other projects, so he invoked the 15 percent rule to create the adhesive for Post-its. The idea came out of Fry's desire to find a way to keep the bookmark from falling out of his hymn book. Post-its are now a major 3M consumer business, with revenues estimated at as much as $300 million.

Cultural Habits

A new-product venture isn't necessarily limited by a particular market's size, either. Take Scotch tape. It was invented in 1929 for an industrial customer who used it to seal insulation in an airtight shipping package. Who could have known that it would grow into an estimated $750 million business someday?

Another recent example: The market for 3M chemist Tony F. Flannery's new product, a filter used to clean lubricants in metalworking shops, was a mere $1 million. But Flannery got the go-ahead to dabble with it anyway. He hooked up with a customer, PPG Industries Inc., which sells paint-primer systems to auto makers. The filters they were using to strain out impurities weren't doing the job. Flannery made prototypes of filter bags using a fibrous 3M material. They not only turned out to be bang-up primer filters, but the new bags are also being used to filter beer, water, edible oils, machine oil, and paint. Flannery figures that the filters could become a $20 million business in a few years.

Getting close to the customer is not just a goal at 3M — it's an ingrained cultural trait. Back in the 1920s, 3M inventor Richard G. Drew noticed that painters on automobile assembly lines had trouble keeping borders straight on the two-tone cars popular at the time. He went back to the lab and invented masking tape.

In-House Grants

Even with 3M's emphasis on innovation, new ideas do fall through the cracks. In 1983, some employees complained that worthwhile projects were still going unnoticed despite the 15 percent rule. Guaranteed free time doesn't guarantee that there will be money to build a prototype. So the company created Genesis grants, which give researchers up to $50,000 to carry their projects past the idea stage. A panel of technical experts and scientists awards as many as ninety grants each year.

One recipient was Sanford Cobb, an optics specialist at 3M. In 1983, a bulb went on in his head at a scientific conference when he ran across something called light pipe technology. Plastic is inlaid with nearly microscopic prisms so it can reflect light for long distances with little loss of energy.

Cobb knew the heavy acrylic used in the original invention was impractical because it would be difficult to mold, but he figured he could use 3M technology to make a light pipe out of a flexible plastic film. Because 3M isn't in the lighting business, though, Cobb couldn't find a division manager willing to fork over prototype money. So he applied for a Genesis grant. He got it, and made his idea work.

City Lights

3M licensed the basic technology from the inventor, and now its light pipes are used in products offered by several divisions. One use is in large highway signs. The new ones feature two 400-watt bulbs, replacing sixty to seventy fluorescent tubes. Manufacturers of explosives use light pipes to illuminate their most volatile areas. And the top of One Liberty Plaza, the new office tower dominating Philadelphia's skyline, is decorated with a light-piping design. Cobb's development is part of a major new technology program at 3M, with potential annual revenues amounting to hundreds of millions of dollars.

It's a surprise, given 3M's strong predilection

toward divisional autonomy, that its technology gets spread around. But 3M is a company of backscratchers, eager to help fellow employees in the knowledge that they'll get help when they need it in return. For example, when the non-woven-fiber experts got together with the lab folks at abrasives, the result was Scotch-Brite scrubbing sponges. A Technology Council made up of researchers from the various divisions regularly gets together to exchange information.

The result of all this interconnection is an organic system in which the whole really is greater than the sum of its parts. It's no coincidence that 3M is never mentioned as a possible breakup candidate. Bust it apart, sever the interconnections, and 3M's energy would likely die. Even if a raider decided to leave it intact, an unfamiliar hand at the helm might send the company off course. The possibility of a raid on 3M was taken a bit more seriously in the early 1980s, when financial performance slipped as the result of a strong dollar and skimping on R & D in the 1970s.

Jacobson's cost-cutting has done wonders for 3M. But his next challenge is formidable. The company's fortunes tend to track the domestic economy, so with a slowdown on the horizon, he must now find ways to spur growth. For one, he wants to expand internationally, boosting overseas sales from 42 percent of revenues to 50 percent by 1992. It may be slow going, however. Just as Jacobson was about to win a beachhead for a plethora of 3M products by buying the sponge unit of France's Chargeurs, the French government blocked the sale on antitrust grounds.

Jacobson is also starting to insist that 3M's divisions develop bigger-ticket products. The company has been taking core technologies and coming up with hundreds of variations. But those market niches can be pretty skinny — often only a few million dollars or so. Now the company's strategists are focusing on forty-five new product areas, each with $50 million in annual sales potential three to five years out. One example: A staple gun that replaces pins for broken bones. A 50-percent new-product success rate would contribute $1.2 billion in sales by 1994 from this program alone.

Sincere Flattery

Jacobson's latest achievements have yet to be reflected in 3M's stock price, which has been hovering in the 60s since the 1987 crash. Analysts are concerned that despite the company's diversification into health care, it still makes about 40 percent of its sales to the industrial sector, so it could get socked in a recession. And 3M is still considered vulnerable in floppy disks and videotape and related media, which account for about $800 million in sales. The unit has been locked in a bruising battle with the Japanese for years and lost an estimated $50 million in 1987. While those products finally became profitable in last year's fourth quarter as a result of cost-cutting and wider distribution, the area could remain a trouble spot. "It's a fragile turnaround," says analyst B. Alex Henderson at Prudential Bache Securities Inc.

Other companies would love to have 3M's problems if its successes came with them. Indeed, 3M constantly finds itself playing host to companies trying to figure out how to be more creative. Monsanto has set up a technology council modeled on 3M's, and United Technologies has embarked on an effort to share resources among its not-so-united operations. Eight years ago, Rubbermaid Inc. began insisting that 30 percent of its sales come from products developed in the previous five years.

While other companies may pick up ideas piecemeal from 3M, it would be impossible for any big corporation to swallow the concept whole. "We were fortunate enough to get the philosophy in there before we started to grow, rather than trying to create it after we got big," says Lester C. Krogh, who heads research and development. 3M has a simple formula: Find the Francis Okies, and don't get in their way. But for managers of other companies, large and small, that's often easier said than done.

EXHIBIT 33-1 Corporate Innovators: How They Do It

3M Relies on a Few Simple Rules...

Keep divisions small. Division managers must know each staffer's first name. When a division gets too big, perhaps reaching $250 to $300 million in sales, it is split up.

Tolerate failure. By encouraging plenty of experimentation and risk-taking, there are more chances for a new-product hit. The goal: Divisions must derive 25 percent of sales from products introduced in the past five years. The target may be boosted to 30 percent.

Motivate the champions. When a 3Mer comes up with a product idea, he or she recruits an action team to develop it. Salaries and promotions are tied to the product's progress. The champion has a chance to someday run his or her own product group or division.

Stay close to the customer. Researchers, marketers, and managers visit with customers and routinely invite them to help brainstorm product ideas.

Share the wealth. Technology, wherever it's developed, belongs to everyone.

Don't kill a project. If an idea can't find a home in one of 3M's divisions, a staffer can devote 15 percent of his or her time to prove it is workable. For those who need seed money, as many as 90 Genesis grants of $50,000 are awarded each year.

... While Other Companies Have Their Own Approaches

RUBBERMAID Thirty percent of sales must come from products developed in the past five years. Looks for fresh design ideas anywhere; now trying to apply the Ford Taurus-style soft look to garbage cans. A recent success: stackable plastic outdoor chairs.

HEWLETT-PACKARD Researchers urged to spend 10 percent of time on own pet projects; twenty-four-hour access to labs and equipment; divisions kept small to rally the kind of spirit that produces big winners such as its Laser Jet laser printer.

DOW CORNING Forms research partnerships with its customers to develop new products such as reformulations of Armor-All car polishes and Helene Curtis hair sprays.

MERCK Gives researchers time and resources to pursue high-risk, high-payoff products. After a major scientific journal said work on anticholesterol agents like Mevacor would likely be fruitless, Merck kept at it. The drug is a potential blockbuster.

GENERAL ELECTRIC Jointly develops products with customers. Its plastics unit created with BMW the first body panels made with thermoplastics for the carmaker's Z1 two-seater.

JOHNSON & JOHNSON The freedom to fail is a built-in cultural prerogative. Lots of autonomous operating units spur innovations such as its Acuvue disposable contact lenses.

BLACK 8 DECKER Turnaround built partly on new-product push. Advisory councils get ideas from customers. Some new hot sellers: the Cordless Screwdriver and ThunderVolt, a cordless powertool that packs enough punch for heavy-duty construction work.

Data: Company Reports

34
Banco Del Duero

Avelino Gonzalez hung up the phone and went storming into the office of Berta Martinez, the Marketing Director.

Avelino: This is ridiculous! Do we really want to specialize in an industry and be the best, or not? It doesn't look that way! Every single time that I ask Data Processing for something, they tell me the same: that it's either impossible, or that it's going to take them two years to do it, which in the end is the same thing! Is this how we want to compete with the big banks?

Berta: Calm down, Avelino. Have a seat. What happened this time?

Avelino: The usual. After I worked so hard to design a new product, the first answer I get from Data Processing is that they can't prepare the programs that we need to put it in place. And then we'll be the ones who won't meet our objectives[1] at the end of the year, not the people in Data Processing.

Background

Avelino had recently received an MBA from a prestigious business school in Barcelona, and had been hired by the Banco del Duero just under a year ago. He had joined the Marketing Area in order to pursue marketing activities in the area of retail banking. He was a creative and efficient person, but he was also a bit impetuous. Thanks to his style of tackling problems head on, he had also managed to come up against almost everyone in the bank. The Data Processing Department had been one of the first areas with which Avelino experienced repeated confrontations. Berta still believed that she could help Avelino solve this problem.

The Marketing Department had recently done a study of the bank's competition, in an effort to identify which products were well-positioned, and which were not. As a result of this study, the bank had begun a process involving the design of new products, aimed at improving Banco del Duero's positioning with respect to these products. Berta tried to calm Avelino down and assured him that she could follow up on the negotiations with Data Processing.

---

(1) As a result of the company's latest reorganization, a management by objectives system had been introduced.

This case was prepared by Nuria Casaldaliga, under the supervision of Professor Rafael Andreu. June 1989. ©Copyright 1989, IESE. Instituto De Estudios Superiores De La Empresa, Universidad De Navarra, Barcelona-Madrid, Spain. Used with permission.

Berta: At any rate, I hope that you've set up an appointment with them...

Avelino: Yes, next week. I don't know what good that'll do...

Berta: O.K. Make sure my secretary makes a note of it in my agenda. I'll go to the meeting too.

Banco del Duero

Banco del Duero was a regional bank with a solid base in a small geographic area, most of it rural. For reasons that remained unclear, the local savings banks had had little success in this area, where Banco del Duero enjoyed a notable reputation and degree of presence. Through its network of 120 offices, it covered the area well, and the majority of its clients were small investors and farmers (cooperatives, etc.). The large, national banks also operated in this region, although their activity was basically limited to urban centers; none of them had the same presence as that of Banco del Duero.

The bank had recently undergone an internal reorganization, mainly the result of the recommendations that an international consulting firm had formulated in response to management's concern about indentifying "a specific focus in our present financial environment, which was as dynamic in this region as well." The strategy recommended by the consultants was that the bank, given its size, should specialize in two areas: retail banking and agriculture. This specialization strategy seemed to be coherent with the conditions of the financial environment; the new strategy was supposed to be in the introductory phase by the end of 1986.

A clear objective of this strategy was to continue being the top bank in the region. A specific bench mark figure had been set for growth, along with specific objectives aimed at expanding into neighboring regions. This figure called for the opening of 8 to 10 new offices per year and for 10% annual growth of deposits for the next 3 years.

In order to achieve this growth in deposits, two very different lines of action had been proposed: one that was meant to increase the bank's relationship with its already existing clients, and another aimed at capturing new clients. Although there were no conclusive data at hand, it was well known that the majority of Banco del Duero's clients also dealt with other institutions, which had led to the conclusion that it was necessary to improve customer service in the bank's offices so that its clients would decide to do more business with "the Duero." Improving services meant, among other things, making sure that the client could carry out all of his or her paper work through one single employee, therefore avoiding the typical pilgrimage from window to window that was presently all too common at the bank. It was also understood that in order to achieve more activity on the part of existing clients, improving service would not be enough; certain clients dealt with other institutions simply because Banco del Duero could not offer them certain products. For this reason, the bank had initiated a program for the development of new products and services that would emphasize personalization. For example, the bank was considering making up individual, comprehensive reports that reflected a client's entire asset and liability status, and that summarized their activity in any one group of different products.

The effort to capture new clients focused on opening new offices in the areas in which Banco del Duero's presence was weakest, supported by direct marketing activity, both by mail and by telephone. In addition, the bank planned to extend a pilot program that it had already tested, consisting of an agreement with a chain of household appliance stores to facilitate the financing of the store's products. To do this, they managed to facilitate the paperwork involved in granting the corresponding loan; if the client had his or her paycheck deposited directly to the bank, the loan was granted almost automatically (if not, the paperwork continued to be bothersome).

Other aspects of the specialization program in retail banking and in the agrarian sector had to do with a certain specialization in personnel, since the problems and the services offered in each of these areas were substantially different.

Finally, the bank planned to initiate relationships with other regional banks. This would facilitate client operations at Banco del Duero when its clients traveled away from the region, although the most basic operations, such as checking an account balance or withdrawing money, could already be done through the 4B system, which the bank had joined some years earlier.

The Use of Computers at Banco del Duero

Banco del Duero had been a pioneer in the use of computers. The previous president, who was now retired, had enthusiastically supported the introduction of technological innovations, and as a result the bank had been, for example, one of the first to install teleprocessing.

After this intial impetus, computer services had continued to grow according to the bank's needs; however, this growth had always come after certain needs had arisen, as the department never took the initiative to lead. The recent reorganization had also brought in a new Data Processing manager, Ramon Prieto, who came from a mid-sized insurance company, where he had held the same position for 4 years. His predecessor, who was more of a banker than a computer person, had recently become very unpopular with the different departments within the bank, and he had decided to accept an offer at a local savings bank in another area of the country. All of this had created an atmosphere of expectation for Data Processing at the bank.

Historically, computer applications had been developed over time as needs arose. There had been little time for keeping the existing applications up to date, both technologically as well as functionally; as a result. these applications on many occasions needed "urgent updates" — or, as the employees called them, "patches" — on a regular basis. One of the first steps taken by the new Computer Services manager was to undertake an in- depth review of the existing applications.

As for the equipment itself, the story was the same. It had also been upgraded in response to the demands of each moment, but rarely had the department made an overall plan concerning its needs for infrastructure. The equipment that was currently in use did not allow for much upgrading, which meant that it would therefore be necessary to start thinking about new equipment in the near future. In fact, the department was already drawing up a request for an investment in new equipment, which, in the words of the new manager "would allow for a major advance in machine capacity, so that we will be able to respond better to the requests that we continually receive from the different departments within the bank."

Again, in the words of the Data Processing manager:

Changing our computer equipment will not be traumatic at all. The new systems are completely compatible with the present ones, so that our investment in applications will be safe in this area. Also, this means that we will also be able to begin using them immediately after the change.

Although the new equipment would allow for more capacity, this did not necessarily mean that it would be able to respond more quickly to all of the requests of the different departments.

When the requests have to do with changes in existing applications, there is another problem. Our programs are very poorly documented, especially the ones that perform basic transactions, which were designed earlier on. This means that any change that we undertake will have unforeseeable consequences. Also, we have a problem with the data files, which are different for each application. This means redundancies, integration problems. etc. Our next in-depth review must focus on establishing a serious data base... Otherwise it will be difficult for us to be able to integrate all of the information we have on a certain client, for example.

In responding to the requests that Data Processing received from the rest of the departments in the bank, the Operations Department also had an important role, since it actively participated in the meetings that were held periodically (or that were called each time that an important conflict arose, such as the one called by Avelino). It was the Data Processing manager who, in the end, assigned priorities to the different requests, together with the Operations manager. Both communicated the result of their decision to their respective departments.

The New Services

In preparing for the following week's meeting, Avelino did not plan to discuss with Data Processing all of the changes that he was planning, but instead he intended to negotiate only those that were most likely to be introduced without problems and that would also require little work time on the part of Data Processing. He believed that in this way he would manage to create a positive atmosphere which could later be used to his advantage when he began to discuss the more fundamental changes that he had in mind.

> After all, he reasoned, something is better than nothing. We can always include the improvements that are possible in a good advertising compaign that emphasizes personalized attention toward the client. At least we'll being taking some steps in the right direction.

The list of proposals that he prepared for the meeting in the end were are follows:

- Give clients the opportunity to choose how often they want to receive information concerning activity in their current accounts (each time that a transaction occurs, every week, every two weeks, etc.)

- Allow maximum limits to be assigned to automatic payments from any type of account. This meant not accepting payment for certain bills without first consulting with the client if these bills exceeded a limit that had previously been set by the client himself.

- Offer clients an annual summary of their account activity, classified by concepts. Several banks were already offering this service on a routine basis.

- For clients with investment portfolios, provide periodic summaries of their account status, evaluated according to the past Friday's closing prices, for example. Also, consider the possibility of allowing the client to choose the frequency of this report, as well as including in this report portfolio activity for the most recent interval. This service was seen as an important complement to investment services, which was experiencing considerable growth in recent times. For this reason, this request seemed particularly coherent with the bank's general strategic plan.

Avelino felt that his list was modest enough so as to not provoke problems in the meeting with the people from Computer Services. He also planned to propose the development of a new product, which was called Customized Loan, which he believed would be attractive not only for the bank's existing clients, but also for people who did not yet have a relationship with the bank.

The idea for the Customized Loan had come about as a result of findings that, although the tendency in the market was on the rise in the segment of consumer lending, the bank's participation in this sector was not growing at the general rate. In the context of the bank's strategic planning, this situation was extremely unsatisfactory.

Taking into account that the causes of this problem could have to do with the length of the lending process for this type of loan at Banco del Duero, and also with the inflexibility of the loan's conditions, Avelino had come up with this new product. In order to facilitate the lending process, it was necessary to automate it as much as possible, and this included using a credit scoring system. Avelino believed that this could be subcontracted out to a company that specialized in this process, although making this decision was not within his responsibility.

Making lending conditions more flexible concerning the length of a loan, frequency of payments, pay schedules with not necessarily uniform, payments, exclusion period, etc., meant preparing a sufficiently open program. With respect to the upcoming meeting with the people from Computer Services, the idea of discussing such an open program was what worried Avelino most.

Some of the bank's competitors were already beginning to offer loans of this type, although with less potential for flexibility than what Avelino foresaw for the Customized Loan at Banco del Duero. The most common practice was to permit a lack of homogeneity in payment schedules, so that the client could adapt the rhythm of loan payments to his or her personal situation (for example, paying back more when earning a bonus, etc.), within limits established at the time that the contract was drawn up.

The Meeting

In addition to Avelino and Berta, the following people attended the meeting: Ramn Prieto, Data Processing Manager; Juan Prez, head of Development and Maintenence in Data Processing; and Julio Gutirrez, Assistant Manager of Operations (see Exhibit 34-1). The following transcript summarizes what transpired at the meeting:

Berta: As you all know, the reason that we are having this meeting is to discuss the introduction of a series of new services and products that Avelino, as the person responsible for marketing for Retail Banking, has proposed. There is also a proposal for a completely new product, the Customized Loan, which may help us improve our position in this market and with which the people in Finance have already agreed to, in principle. The objectives that we have set for the next few years are ambitious, but nevertheless attainable if we can manage to work as a team. In this respect, I believe that meetings such as this one should be more frequent. Avelino, tell us what you've been thinking.

Avelino: You already know that the bank has decided to emphasize the area of Retail Banking, and also that its focus is on personalizing our products and services as much as possible. I have prepared a preliminary list of steps that we could take in this direction, and I believe we should try to offer our clients these services as soon as possible. They do not involve significant changes, but still can help us achieve some of the differentiation that we are seeking. There is one single idea that underlies all of the changes that I am proposing: Personalized Attention to the Client.

Ramon: We've already done a superficial analysis of these requests. Juan, who has an in-depth knowledge of our applications, can comment briefly on our first impressions of each one of them.

Juan: O.K. We'll go in the order that they were proposed. The first suggestion consists of giving clients information about their accounts, with the frequency that they desire. This is currently infeasible. We have a process that produces reports every two weeks for all clients, whether there has been activity or not. Considering the way we have our data structured, you're asking us, first, to add a new field to our main account file, and then to check every account every day to determine what type of information the client wants, and to produce a transaction report if there is activity and the client asks for it. This would mean developing a new application, with at least 3,000 lines of program, as well as more computer time (we're already saturated), and higher costs for paper and mail. I don't think it's worth it to undertake a change of this magnitude. And I don't think that this will make life easier for our clients either.

Avelino: This is a great way to begin. If something as trivial as this isn't feasible...

Berta: Avelino, please. Let Juan continue.

Juan: Let's go on to the second proposal. This refers to the ability to specify limits for automatic payments made from accounts. If we had known about this 6 months ago, it would have been easy... We've just finished revising this application, and the new version has already been in place for a month.

Avelino: We didn't know that you had revised the application. Do you people just make the changes that you want, when you want to?

Ramon: Not exactly. We have one list of pending changes, and another of new applications solicited by Operations and other departments. Depending upon the priorities that have been assigned to each of them, our resources and the expense that would be incurred from undertaking these developments, we do one or the other.

Juan: This is what we always do. At the end of the day, it's the Operations Department that determines the operations of each branch. This time we've incorporated a series of changes that will facilitate the handling and reconciling of receipts. It is my understanding that this will help us to significantly reduce our operational costs.

Julio: And we hope that this procedure doesn't change. Otherwise, we'll run into additional operational costs. Flexibility doesn't come free of charge. Frankly, so much emphasis on flexibility worries me. We may end up being a lot more flexible, and a lot less profitable...

Avelino: There is another possibility... Reducing our costs to zero by ending up with no clients...

Juan: The third proposal, which refers to preparing an annual summary, presents no real problem. By the end of the year we can have it ready. The only foreseeable problem might be a lack of processing capacity at year end.

Avelino: Come on! At least it's a start! Even though I can see that it isn't exempt from potential problems... Don't you people know how to begin a response without using "no" or "but"?

Juan: O.K., I'm going to put it in the affirmative for you: The new securities application is also just a dream at this point.

Ramon: However, this seems like a good idea to me... We're thinking about revising the securities application by the end of next year. Perhaps we could revise the overall plan and address this matter a few months earlier. What do you think, Julio?

Julio: It's possible. Maybe by exchanging it with the foreign application, which we have scheduled for next quarter...

Avelino: All together, we're talking at least a year and a half before we have something. How will we improve services for our clients in the meantime? This makes me think of a great jingle that rhymes with BanDuero for the next advertising campaign. Computer Services at the bank's service! It's unbelievable.

Ramon: I understand what you're saying, Avelino, but you could try to understand me, also. We're short on personnel. They don't allow me to hire good professionals unless they're for highly specialized, technical positions. The rest has to be covered internally, with people from other areas, who don't reach an acceptable level until 7 or 8 months have passed, and that's if they decide to stay on at that point. And on top of all this, our computers are saturated... And I'm not so sure that this proposal for change works... I sense somewhat of a conflict with other investment proposals that the Operations Department is going to make. Don't think you're the only one with problems! As always, this is a question of allocating limited resources!

Julio: Our investments are rather modest. But the fact is they are clearly justified: The Automated Teller Machines save on personnel, allow us to open more offices without increasing staff, and they also give us the image of being a progressive bank.

Avelino: I'm going to lose my mind. Installing the new ATM's won't cause problems with computer saturation?

Ramon: No. In this case, the bottleneck would be communications, but last year we upgraded the controllers. We won't have capacity problems in this area. It must be the only area where we won't have problems.

Avelino: I don't know why, but it seems I am simply unable to propose something that needs surplus capacity. I must be a jinx. So what do I do with my proposals? Hold onto them until you people tell me in writing that you finally have capacity?

Ramon: Come on, we can at least give you a few suggestions. After all, we're the ones who know what the applications are like... We can suggest things that are easy to do. Then you can decide if they make sense from a marketing standpoint.

Avelino: This is insane. Everything is upside-down. But, as they say, half a loaf is better than none... Go ahead.

Ramon: Listen to this, for example. Given the way we have designed the application that issues the checks, it would be relatively easy for us to speed up requests for checkbooks from our clients by keeping track of the amount of checks they are using... Couldn't you also sell this as "Personalized Attention to Clients?" More than a few people would welcome the fact that their checkbook was ready as soon as they put in their request... don't you think?

Avelino: Of course. I had already thought about that, but I thought it would be a lot more complicated than the proposals that I decided to bring to the meeting today. And in the end, I haven't scored on a single one!

Ramon: That's because you didn't have enough information. Everything depends on how each application is designed. I understand that this is not the best way to operate, but until we have the new computer and a good data base...

Avelino: I don't know what our competitors must have. Maybe new computers and data bases, and everything else. Or maybe not. Maybe they're just smarter than we are. But they're bringing out new products, they're being innovative, they're gaining market share, and sooner or later they're going to eat us alive. Either we get going, or they're going to get us. We still have to talk about the Customized Loan. I sent you a preliminary outline (see Exhibit 34-2). Do we launch it or not?

Juan: No, we don't launch it. It's more of the same, Avelino. And also, with this one we have the additional problem of the teleprocessing terminals. They can't give more than they're capable of either...

Avelino: This must be my fate! Yet another technology interfering in my path! There's no longer any doubt. I'm seeing ghosts. Ghosts do exist. They're computer ghosts. And they've been plotting against me. Didn't you say that you needed people? Well, I'm signing on. This way, at least I'll be part of the problem, like everyone else.

Berta: I don't know what the rest of you are thinking, but I'm very worried. We need to do something. This is a serious problem, and we absolutely must find a solution, however unattractive it may be. We won't introduce the new strategy without the right technology. Ramon and Julio, I think we should speak with the technical director about this, and if necessary, with the managing director. Immediately.

EXHIBIT 34-1 Banco Del Duero Organizational Chart

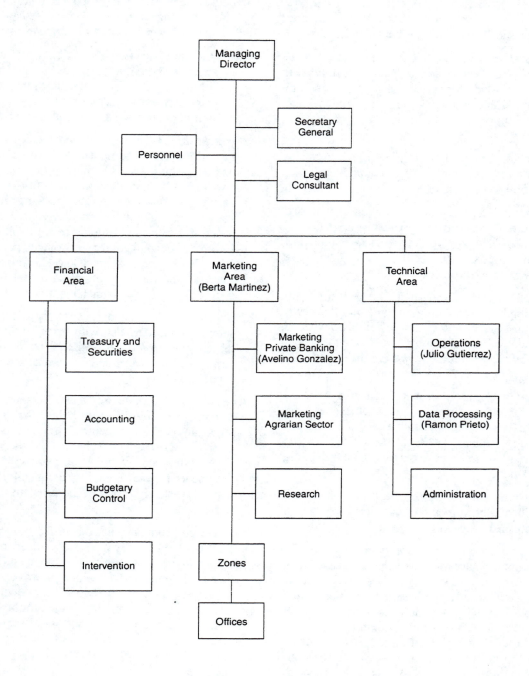

EXHIBIT 34-2 Banco Del Duero Characteristics of the Customized Loan

Customized Loans include Housing, Consumer and Personal loans.

By default amortization payments will be constant and on a monthly basis, including principal and interest.

At the client's request, however, a totally "customized" payment plan may be designed, with payment schedules that vary both in frequency and in amount. The minimum frequency will be monthly and the maximum, annually.

Independently of the payment plan that is initially determined, principal payments may be paid in advance at any time, and the resulting payments will then be recalculated in a new plan.

For Housing loans, two years of non-payment will be allowed. During this period, the interest rate will be a half point higher than the rate in effect at the time that the loan is granted. Also during this period, interest will be paid at intervals determined by the client (at least one payment per quarter).

In order to facilitate office work, each office will have available, through their own computer equipment, a program that allows them to carry out the simulations that the client desires, calculate the total interest to be paid, and prepare a detailed and personalized profile of the resulting payment plant.

35
Company A:
The CIM Decision Process

The Resurgence of Technology

Company A is a large mature corporation with several business units, all of which operate in a basic industry. In the late 1970s, a number of people within Company A began to feel that technology was not being taken seriously by the corporation. While this idea was expressed in different ways by different people, it centered around the perception that the company was overly concerned with finance and marketing, and that these disciplines had replaced technology as the driving force within the firm. "Technologists" were not occupying key vice-presidential positions, their statements were discounted, and technologically risky decisions were not being made. In the period between 1978 and 1982, a number of efforts arose spontaneously, in disparate parts of the corporation, to try to combat this trend.

Steven Robinson, at the Corporate Research Center (CRC), had become increasingly frustrated with the type of R & D planning that was going on in the business units. R&D projects were funded by the business units, and the General Managers of the business units also chaired the committees that allocated funds to research projects. Over time, it became clear that long-range, fundamental, "blue sky" projects were not getting funded. Instead, the business units were funding research which would generate quick returns in terms of existing product lines.

Robinson and others became concerned about the long-term effects of this type of planning on the corporation. In order to address the problem, an R&D planning group was formed at CRC. The focus of this group was to assist the committees in developing long-range R&D plans. They experienced some success in getting the business units to think in a more long-term and strategic manner about research.

At about the same time, Thomas Kidwell was transferred from CRC into corporate planning. He soon became concerned about the harm done to technology by the strategic planning process. He expressed it as follows:

Corporations, not just this one, but corporations as a whole are getting increasingly into technological and business problems because

---

Prepared by James Dean Jr., the Pennsylvania State University. Reprinted with permission from James W. Dean's *Deciding to Innovate: Decision Processes in the Adoption of Advanced Technology*, Copyright ©1987, Ballinger Publishing Company.

there's an inordinate financial emphasis in the strategic planning process. Strategy is more than finance. Strategy expresses itself ultimately in finance, but it does not capture technology unless it asks, for a moment, "What could technology substantively do for us?" You do that in the language of technology, and then, you can fold it into a financial plan. But if you don't do that carefully, you'll miss it.

While Kidwell tried to express this problem to the top management, he was unsuccessful in doing so, at least during this period. He was hampered by his place within the financial organizations, and the fact that he had three new bosses in the two years he was in the position. As Kidwell tells it, "Each time I got some awareness in the Vice President, he moved and I got a new boss." So Kidwell's message limitedly got beyond corporate planning.

The third, and probably the most significant, initiative in the resurgence of technology at Company A began in the hills outside the city where Company A's headquarters are located, on a Sunday afternoon in 1982. Geoffrey Munson, who had one year to go before retirement as Vice Chairman of Company A, was having dinner with his daughter-in-law at a local country club. He noticed at a nearby table a man who was a former vice president for a steel company. Something clicked for Munson. He said, "You know it's beginning to haunt me that those men, instead of being able to enjoy this country club, should be punished for the way they've destroyed an industry." He wondered if the management of Company A could be guilty of this as well. At that moment, he made a vow to himself that he would not be in a position to be accused of the same thing after he retired.

As a result of this experience, Munson felt that he really needed to do a better job of incorporating technology into the business plans than was being done at the time. He was thus instrumental in creating a new entity within Company A: the Strategic Technology Group. Thomas Kidwell was named Director of Strategic Technology and reported to Munson. As Kidwell describes it:

[Munson] knew he had to make it so that technology could rise to the top of the corporation without passing through finance. That meant that corporate planning and technology planning had to be parallel. I could not report into corporate planning. It had to rise to the top of the corporation in parallel.

The R&D Planning group that Robinson had started at CRC now reported to Kidwell, and their scope was broadened from R&D to include the whole corporation.

The main task of the Strategic Technology Group was to assist the business units in preparing their plans, so that they would seriously include technology. Nate Charles, who had worked in the R&D Planning group and then in Strategic Technology described the impact of the group:

It's reached a point that in the forthcoming planning cycle, when the businesses bring in their annual five year plans... they have been instructed by the President that they must deal explicitly with technology... [they must] give explicit examples of what their targets are, how much it's going to be worth once they reach those targets, and how they are going to get there. No broad-brushed stuff any more. No more glib words like "we're going to put in robots"... He said that you've got to be much more explicit than that.

Shortly after the formation of the Strategic Technology Group, Company A's "Office of the Chairman" changed en masse. The former chairman retired, and was replaced as Chairman and CEO by Peter Chandler, who had been President. Geoffrey Munson also retired, and Howard Ruskin assumed roughly similar duties under the title of Executive Vice President of Science and Technology. Chandler was replaced as President by Ralph Fredericks. Paul Jamison remained as Vice Chairman, with the financial organization reporting to him.

Howard Ruskin, the new Executive Vice President for Science and Technology, had the following comment on the situation at that time:

I would suspect that the technical effort wasn't getting the proper coordination or push; it would be pretty easy for whatever came up to be washed away.

I suggest that [when the top level changes] is the best time for change... It is certainly a time in which you can make changes that the top guys won't block. Whether the rest of the organization will block it or not depends on how good the top guys are.
Also, it's a time that creates an awful lot of turmoil. Folks are jockeying for position... Everyone is nervous.

Many aspects of Ruskin's sentiment were in fact borne out by subsequent developments at Company A.

With the creation of the Strategic Technology Group, and the turnover of the senior officers, the seeds which Munson and others had planted began to grow and bear fruit. First, the new Executive Committee drafted a Statement of Direction for Company A. The process by which the statement was drafted was significant because both Corporate Planning and Strategic Technology were involved. The content of the document also provided some direction for technology within the corporation:

We will strengthen our core by focusing our resources where Company A can improve our competitive advantage... enter new areas and expand existing businesses that build upon our strengths... In all our endeavors we will continue to be an innovative technological leader...

While such statements can be dismissed as boilerplate, this one was taken as a serious statement about technology and competition by people within Company A. As Bruce Lindsay, the Director of Management Information Systems (MIS) put it:

I think there's a total commitment at the policy level of this company to have a rallying point... we are going to plant a flag, we're not going to abdicate our business to foreign com-

petition, and we're not going to sit and atrophy the way steel did. Here's where we stand and fight. That implies we're going to do things differently, because [what] steel did was a formula for disaster.

One school of thought could be that basic industry is a lousy business... we should get out of it, let the third world have it, and start building semi-conductors or something. We've said, "No, we'll change, this is our business. It's going to be our business ten years from now. Instead of looking for an easy solution, we'll do what we've got to do, to be here ten years from now, and hand off a healthy company to somebody else."

Subsequent to the executive turnover and the Statement of Objectives, a number of tangible outcomes of the resurgence of technology emerged. The budget for CRC was increased, with the expectation that it would not be the first thing cut back in the event of an economic downturn. A science advisory group, consisting of top people in various fields, was formed, and its reports are presented to the Board of Directors. Another new group, called the Technology Council, was formed with Howard Ruskin as Chairman. This group includes the Director of CRC, the Vice President of Engineering, the Vice Presidents of the business units, and Kidwell. Its mission is to oversee the total portfolio of technology activity.

Thus, there have been a number of outcomes of the resurgence of technology at Company A. The outcome on which the rest of this case report will focus, however, is the development of Computer Integrated Manufacturing (CIM).

The April 1983 Meeting

The Strategic Technology Group was formed in the fall of 1982. As indicated above, its primary role was to assist the businesses in developing a technological context and strategy as an integral part of their business plans. In addition to coordinating this activity, Thomas Kidwell had taken on another task. With input from the executive level, he had developed a list of words or terms, each of which denoted a technological option which might be open to Company A. As he started his new job, he began to explore the words on his list. The word that quickly rose to the top of the list was "computer."

Kidwell had not had a great deal of prior involvement with computers, and he was immediately fascinated with them. While most of the technologies he was exploring had price/performance ratios growing at a yearly rate of two or three percent, computers were growing at 25 to 100 percent, with no limit in sight.

In order to explore this technology, Kidwell and Helen Evans, a member of his group, spent the early months of 1983 visiting other firms. Many of the firms they visited, such as IBM, DEC, and GE, were both producers and users of computer equipment. Kidwell and Evans quickly noted that the emphasis on computers in the firms they visited was quite different from the emphasis at Company A: while Company A was emphasizing business applications (e.g., accounting, payroll), others were emphasizing manufacturing applications (e.g., process control) and the integration of manufacturing and business systems. They were quite struck by this discrepancy.

In order to further Company A's involvement in the technology of computers (which Kidwell had dubbed "low-cost information management"), he decided to have a meeting of those people within the firm who were most involved with computers. Three groups would be involved: MIS, which is in the financial organization; the process computing group, which at this time reported to the Chief Electrical Engineer; and CRC, which reported to Ruskin. The meeting was planned for April 1983.

In discussing his plans for the upcoming meeting, Kidwell indicated that he had gathered data on the wisest use of low-cost information. This broke down into two areas: the technology itself, and the organizational arrangements necessary to support it. On this latter point, he noted that, for example, Company A would need a higher ratio of engineers to accountants than was currently the case.

At this point Kidwell began what was to become a long and frustrating campaign to keep consideration of computer technology from being overwhelmed by organizational or "turf" considerations. It soon became clear that at Company A, the notion of computers, and particularly of computer integration, was intricately entangled with the notion of what organizational arrangements would support this technology.

The initial impact of this entanglement was that Kidwell was explicitly directed to exclude discussion of organization from the meeting. As Kidwell put it:

They told me, "How can you even bring up the subject? Don't you know how sensitive it is in the organization?" So this part got killed off. Organization was illegal... We narrowed the subject area to say that even though we've learned some things about how the human system responds to computerization, that's not going to be dealt with in those three days at all.

As the meeting approached, Kidwell and Evans decided that it should be limited to high-level people in the three computer-related areas. Bruce Lindsay, who had recently become Director of MIS, but had an extensive background in operations, represented the MIS group. Sanford Turner, the Chief Electrical Engineer, represented process computing. Donald Joyce, an Assistant Director at CRC, represented the computer-oriented research part of the company. Each of the three was accompanied by two others from their area. Finally, two people from the business units were present, and Kidwell and Evans participated as facilitators.

It was amazing to many in the company that the meeting could be held at all, given the fact that MIS and the process computing group had a long history of ignoring one another. They were located in two different buildings separated by a river, which was seldom crossed:

Our human system began as completely separated. Four hundred and fifty MIS people degreed in business, accounting, and computer science. One hundred fifty [in process comput-ing] with electrical engineering degrees, and no mobility between them. Nobody from here ever went there, and nobody from there ever came here. They don't even know who each other is... they've never met each other before; it's a human problem. (Kidwell).

The meeting was held on April 11-13, 1983. As promised, the guidelines distributed to the participants were to "deal with what Company A should do with computers, not what organization best enables us to do it." The Company A participants spent the first one and a half days of the meeting listening to presentations made by representatives from IBM, Digital Equipment Corporation, Arthur D. Little, and General Electric. These representatives were asked to say what use a manufacturing company like Company A should be making of computers. The mechanism for doing this was to distribute 100 points among the various types of potential computer applications: business computing, office automation, CAD, process computing, and so on. Kidwell and Evans did this to allow the participants to experience directly the gap they had perceived in their visits, between Company A's (de facto) computer strategy and the thrust of state-of-the-art computing. All of the presenters stressed the need for Company A to emphasize process computing and computer integration, or CIM.

The agenda item that followed the consultants' presentations was a description of Company A's current deployment of computer resources. This presentation was made by Helen Evans, who had spent several months performing an audit of Company A's use of computers. This completed the picture of a problem with Company A's current strategy that had been begun by the consultants: while they had advised that Company A emphasize process computing and integration, Company A was placing two-thirds of its resources on business computing, one-third on manufacturing/process computing, and virtually no resources on the integration of the two.

Faced with this information, the meeting participants were next asked to enumerate potential computer strategies for Company A in the next decade, and to arrive at a consensus as to which strategies were most appropriate, and would therefore be pursued by the group. The three strategies around which consensus emerged were the idea of using computers as a tool to differentiate Company A from the competition, the need to increase computer literacy within Company A, and CIM, which quickly rose to the top of the list. The draft of the key strategies arrived at by the group at the meeting went beyond mere endorsement of CIM to advocating the immediate selection of a demonstration site:

- Formulate/implement an integrated information system for Company A.

- Select a location and immediately implement the integrated system (including CIM) at a plant or business unit of manageable size, such that feasibility and benefits can be effectively demonstrated.

- Recommend that the upcoming modernization embody state-of-the-art CIM.

So in the space of a three-day meeting, the top computer professionals within Company A came to an agreement as to computer strategies for the next decade, and how they could be initially implemented. All the participants agreed that there was a high degree of consensus on these strategies. The next major step would be to obtain approval for these strategies from the Executive Committee of the corporation.

What actually happened at the April meeting? First of all, what apparently did not happen is that the Company A participants learned about CIM:

Tom felt more strongly than the rest of us about the consultants being there. They didn't say anything that anyone who reads Datamation wouldn't know themselves... a lot of hype, no real insights (Lindsay).

Sanford Turner also noted that everyone pretty much knew what the experts were going to say. Lindsay, Turner, and Tony Joseph (a member of Turner's group) all had some previous interest/experience with CIM.

If the meeting was not primarily an educational experience for the participants, why was it universally seen as important? Several things were apparently accomplished. Sanford Turner felt that the big contributions of the meeting were the buffering of the participants from their pressing day-to-day concerns, and the establishment of a direction:

In an operating entity, the problem is today's business, and that's where you gravitate all the time. You have to get off and think about new and innovative things, which is very difficult. So we were looking for approval of a direction that would allow us to go off and worry about CIM ... keep ourselves out of the mainstream of daily problems.

In addition, while the ideas that were presented by the consultants were not seen as a big revelation, the fact that several respected outside sources would agree did seem to have an impact. As Lindsay put it:

What they lent is a catalyst. Four different perspectives all with a common theme without rehearsing... made people feel a little bit better... Any one of a dozen [Company A] people could have gotten up and said it, but I don't think it would have carried the same weight.

Finally, in spite of, or perhaps because of, the proscription against discussion of organization, some organizational barriers were overcome. Bruce Lindsay commented:

I think Tom really threw a spotlight on the need to work together. You've got four computing communities in Company A: the research group, the business computing group (MIS), the process computing group, and the plants. To get anything done, those four end up having to coordinate and work together. The overlap had been minimal, and the interfacing had been only when necessary. The thing that's getting increasingly apparent to everyone is that... we've all got a vested interest in [CIM],

let's work on it together.

Perhaps the real significance of the April meeting can best be captured by an exchange that took place between Helen Evans and Thomas Kidwell when the meeting was over. Evans told Kidwell that she was disappointed with the outcome of the meeting, because the strategies that had been adopted were obvious before the meeting took place. Kidwell responded:

Wait a minute, there's a difference between you having made up your mind [on the strategies] as a result of spending four months outside and the corporation forming consensus and commitment around this word 'computers.' In a sense, the meeting was to develop the backdrop, the common commitments, and the working relationships to do something about it.

Evans, after reflecting on the meeting, concluded:

Out of everything that happened out of this meeting, this was the most valuable thing. These guys closed ranks. They put away politics for a while, and said, "Hey, there's a technology out there that we ought to be grasping.

As subsequent events would show, the closed ranks, common commitments, and working relationships would be absolutely necessary to survive the challenges ahead.

The Executive Committee

Following the April meeting, the team of Sanford Turner and Bruce Lindsay, with the help of Tom Kidwell, tried to schedule a presentation before the Executive Committee to obtain top-level corporate support for the computer strategies they had devised. However, the Secretary of the Committee did not feel that this was an appropriate agenda item for the committee, so the presentation was made to only some of its members, as well as other key individuals in the senior management of Company A.

The presentation was not very well received. Descriptions of the reaction to it included "a bloody nightmare," "great abuse," "blown out of the water," and "thrown out." In fact, it did not even end with the presentation itself. As one of the presenters mentioned, "we were beat up all week long."

Why this reaction? The participants were unanimous in concluding that, once again, technology had been defeated by organization. At a time when Company A was undergoing a major push toward decentralization and business unit autonomy, the officers thought that Lindsay, Turner, and Kidwell were advocating recentralization through computers. The timing, the wording and even the identity of the presenters were all problems:

The first thing that happened was that it was a political thing. It was not a technological argument, it was an organizational argument; and this kind of slowed things down a lot. It was turf: who was going to do what... I think that just clouded things... At the time, we were doing all of this reorganization... and the word organization came up, and it kind of worried them (Ruskin).

The subject of centralization/decentralization had gotten confused with the subject of networking and architecture. Those of us who had considered computerization had never dealt with the question of whether or not computers should be used in a centralized or decentralized corporation ... You can draw the corporate lines either way ... But when we were talking about words like architecture and networking and so on, people thought that meant centralization at a time when they were trying to be decentralized (Kidwell).

At the time we did this, we were in the throes of decentralizing... they wanted no inference whatsoever that the integration effort was going to centralize [the corporation]. They had just committed their souls and a lot of people's livelihood [to decentralization], and they couldn't segregate the two. Maybe, if we

would have had a representative from the two or three major business units with us as presenters, the officers would not have read what they read into it. But here were Bruce and I... both of us corporate, making this presentation on computer strategy... It came across that these strategies were going to be corporate mandated (Turner).

The computer spokesmen did not back down in the face of this reaction, a fact which did not go unnoticed by the senior management. They (Turner et al.) felt that there was nothing substantive in what they had heard that would change their minds, and they concluded that the problem was "basically semantics." Thus, they tried a number of related tacks to recover from the presentation debacle.

First, anything that even hinted at organizational issues was deleted. Second, they removed any language in the strategies that sounded, even remotely, like computer jargon. They were concerned that the uncertainty created by this language may have been threatening to the officers, none of whom were experienced in computing. Third, the strategies got "softened" a little.

In order to defuse any further misinterpretation of what they had in mind, Turner, Lindsay, and Kidwell held a number of one-on-one meetings with the senior officers. Kidwell met with Ruskin, his boss, as well as Jamison and Fredericks. Turner spent an hour with Chandler, at Chandler's request. Lindsay talked with his boss, Warren Ernest, Company A's Controller.

After a week or two of this sort of activity, the officers were convinced that at least Kidwell et al. did not think of this as an organizational issue. With this in mind, another meeting was scheduled to discuss the strategies. The revised strategies were explicit in their recognition of business unit autonomy:

Emphasize the technological importance of the following key elements in business unit computer strategies... CIM.

Work with the business unit managers to select a location of manageable size, and immediately begin implementing a computer inte-

grated manufacturing system.

The wording changes and explanations in one-on-one meetings had the combined effect of swaying the officers: at the second meeting, the strategies were approved. With this approval, however, came more evidence of the officers' commitment to decentralization. The computer spokesmen were directed to go to the business units, and try to sell them on the strategies: "Get your story together and then go talk to the businesses. If they support it, then we support it."

The Business Units — Issues

The arena for the CIM initiative had now shifted to the business units. Rather than soliciting corporate consensus on broad strategies for computer utilization, the computer spokesmen would now have to convince the Vice Presidents/General Managers of Company A's three major business units to spend money on CIM. The next hurdle would be funding for demonstration sites, which presented a new set of issues.

One set of related issues was the long time it would take for the business unit managers to see any return, the intangibility of the short-term products of their investment, and the large amounts of money that would need to be spent. As Bruce Lindsay put it:

What's just alien to a lot of management is that we [want to spend] at one location a million and half dollars to do nothing but a general design. That still hasn't dawned on the operating folks. They expect to spend a million and a half dollars and get a 50 percent ROI next year... It's just how we are conditioned to go at things. I think that's one of the more fragile dimensions of the whole process. Some folks are going to spend a million and a half dollars, and what they are going to get is four thousand sheets of paper that tell them they have a real bear to take on, versus a product.

Then, you say to carry it through the detail designs, it's going to take ten years and $20 mil-

lion or whatever it is. When you get into those kind of numbers, rather than being a nicety in the corner, it is going to be center stage, because now you are starting to compete with major capital. There's going to be a lot of people saying, "Wait a minute. When I buy a cold mill, I know what I get. When I buy this, all I know is I got a bunch of computer types running around saying this is the right thing to do. I don't grow up with it, I don't understand it, and I'm not really sure what the hell I'm going to get out of it." I think we still have to cross that bridge before we are really off and running.

Another issue that would have to be addressed is the criteria to be used in evaluating investments in CIM. Due to intense competition for corporate capital, Company A's hurdle rate for cost reduction projects (which would include computer projects) had been increased from 50 to 100 percent. It became clear that CIM would have a very dificult time meeting these hurdle rates, so there was something of a mismatch between the computer strategy and the finance policy. It was perhaps another sign of Company A's technological resurgence that the issue was resolved in a way generally favorable to CIM:

These projects have to be justified to some extent, but there's a little bit of the rigor removed from the intensity of the justification... Once the corporation begins to lean toward computer integrated manufacturing, then the individual proposals have a better chance of passing the guidelines (Kidwell).

[Years ago] the technical people said we don't really need computers. You can't justify them... They held back the development of the computer for a long time. In these kinds of technologies, you have to get ahead, and do some degree of testing it out. Get it out of the conversational stage, get a critical mass in there, move it... There's hardly any way you can IE it or MBA it to really find out. You've just got to try it (Ruskin).

I'm financial and quantitative and analytical

by nature, and I don't think that [ROI] is the right question to be asking. I think the question is, "Do you want to be in the business?" What does it take to be successful at that? If this is one of the things that it takes, I don't think you have an option not to do it...

Our controllers today have a very heavy [operations] kind of background. They use accounting as... one of many tools... It's usually false precision when you start reducing things to columns and rows anyway. They'll run through that to make sure they're in the general ballpark, but within that I think they agonize with the general manager about the market and the risk, and the technology... Ultimately, I don't see [the numbers] driving our decisions. I think that's very healthy (Lindsay).

A third issue that had to be addressed before CIM could proceed was, inevitably, organization. Put simply, who would do the work? The reorganization had included a substantial downsizing of corporate engineering, in which a large number of engineers had been relocated to the plants, given early retirements, or had quit. Thus, corporate handling of the projects was made difficult by a lack of engineering resources, as well as the obvious clash with the pervading spirit of decentralization.

Many felt, however, that the plants did not possess the resources to do CIM either. And, even if they did, could a truly "integrated" system be created by a set of autonomous plant-level groups? If corporate were to develop an architecture at one plant that would then be used at others, who would pay for it? And so on. Perhaps the most daunting organizational issue was the likelihood that to "create" CIM at Company A would require some combination of technical support from Electrical Engineering, MIS and CRC. This was a coalition which simply had never before existed in Company A.

To emphasize the importance of the CIM initiative, the process computing group was elevated one step in the corporation. Rather than reporting to the Chief Electrical Engineer, it now reported to the Vice President of Engineering. Sanford Turner was chosen to head this group,

and, to underline the move, was given the title of General Manager.

In spite of the difficulties to be overcome, Bruce Lindsay was optimistic about the business units' response. He felt that what was most necessary was an initial success with CIM:

I would guarantee that the business and plant managers, if you demonstrate to them the ability to meaningfully change their ability to compete, they'll go through the hammers of hell with you. Their staying power is greater than that of a functional person when they believe there is something at the end of the road.

In the second half of 1983, Turner, Lindsay, and Kidwell began to approach the business units to talk about CIM.

The Business Units' Response

The Northwestern plant, which is part of the Midstream business group, had been mentioned by name in the strategies adopted at the April meeting. Those attending that meeting had felt that the size of the plant was appropriate for a demonstration project, and there was also some interest from the technologists within the plant.

In July 1984, Scott Varano, VP/GM for Midstream, approved $900 thousand to be spent on a requirements definition for CIM. This work was to be done by Sanford Turner's group, with the help of some MIS personnel, and was to be completed by late 1985 or early 1986. To date, there has been good support and enthusiasm from personnel at Northwestern. Some have credited Tony Joseph, a member of Turner's group with responsibility for Northwestern, with solidifying process computing's relationship with that plant's production management.

The response of the Downstream business unit has been more problematic. When CIM emerged from the April meeting and the Executive Committee as an area of emphasis for Company A, Downstream was already in the midst of a complete modernization effort involving three plants. The Midwestern plant was chosen as a demonstration site for CIM over the Southern plant (the other likely candidate), both because it was smaller, and because there was a greater volume of technical skill present within the plant.

Once personnel at Midwestern began to talk to Sanford Turner about how the job would be done, however, tensions arose. Midwestern has always seen themselves as an independent plant, and they felt that Turner was telling them that it would be done his way. A falling out occurred between the plant and the process computing group. The type of bond that had been formed between the corporate group and Northwestern never materialized, and the relationship came to be characterized by "a fair degree of animosity."

The culmination of this was that Midwestern decided that, rather than utilizing corporate services, they would engage an outside consultant, and hired one to begin work. This firm had never done a CIM job outside of their own facilities, and most corporate computer personnel were convinced that their approach to the Midwestern project was much too narrow. This effort is still in process at Midwestern.

The third and final business unit which showed interest in CIM was Upstream. Following the April meeting, Kidwell, Patrick Broadbent from CRC, and Michael King, the Chief EE for the business unit held a similar meeting in October, just for personnel from the business unit. Some of the same outside presenters were used. Broadbent and King both had some prior interest in CIM, and Broadbent had participated in the April meeting.

As a result of these efforts, the Upstream group approved $350 thousand for the development of some CIM capacity for the Foreign plant. This project was also to be undertaken by an outside group. Turner and others were again disappointed with the scope of the Foreign effort. It was, however, clear that the corporate group did not have the resources to pursue this project.

Ironically, the Foreign initiative in CIM had to be discontinued altogether. There was such a world oversupply of its product that, in early 1985, the Foreign plant was shut down.

Postscript

In the early months of 1985, the Science Advisory Board, which had been formed by Howard Ruskin, began to look at Company A's computer strategies. In their feedback to the company, they stressed the fragmented nature of Company A's computer initiatives, and the unevenness of the progress being made toward CIM. They described the company as "fragmented," "a set of baronies," and "lacking focus." Thomas Kidwell, who substantially agreed with the Advisory Board, said that the situation reminded him of a passage from scripture: "In those days there was no king in Israel; every man did that which was right in his own eyes" (Judges 21:25).

36
Catlin College

Catlin College, located in Zenith, a town in the state of Polis, is a city with a population of 52,500 according to the 1980 census. It was founded in the early thirties as Ivy University Junior College (a two-year division of Ivy University) to meet the need for higher education in Zenith and the Sullivan Valley of Polis. The college became chartered as Catlin College, a four-year institution, in the late forties after WW II. It became a fully independent, accredited, non-sectarian institution, with no formal ties with Ivy University in 1951. The first graduate programs were added in the late 1960s.

Over time, Catlin College increasingly widened its scope beyond Zenith and the Sullivan Valley. By 1989, 40% of its student body was living on campus, and the college was drawing more of its student body, from other states in the eastern U.S. Under the administration of President Rosalyn Dresser, which began in the early eighties, the college has continued to work hard to improve its reputation and increase its academic quality. By 1990, 60% of the full-time faculty had earned doctorate degrees, and 75% had terminal qualifications (earned doctorate or the equivalent). The library collection was 250,000 volumes (books and bound journals).

Exhibit 36-1 is a copy of the College's Organization Chart. Exhibits 36-2 and 36-3 comprise financial data on the college.

Although the board of trustees, the president, administration, alumni, and faculty were all committed to achieving a strong national reputation for the college, some of the trustees, faculty, administration and many of the alumni believed that the local needs of Zenith and the Sullivan Valley should be given priority over other needs. Others on campus and some alumni believed that the College should give first priority to building a reputation as one of the top liberal arts colleges in the Eastern U.S.

President Dresser had had a typical event-filled day today. She started her day by attending a fund-raising breakfast at 7 a.m. at a local hotel to benefit the local United Way organization. She arrived on campus at 9 a.m. and answered her correspondence until 10 a.m. when her staff meeting with her Cabinet of key administrative advisors began. The staff person in charge of enrollment management again raised the question of whether the College should apply to the Polis State Department of Education for designation as a university and change its name to Catlin University.

This case was prepared as a basis for class discussion rather than as an illustration of either effective or ineffective handling of an administrative situation. By Philip Baron and Donald Grunewald, Iona College. Used with Permission.

EXHIBIT 36-1 Catlin College Organizational Chart

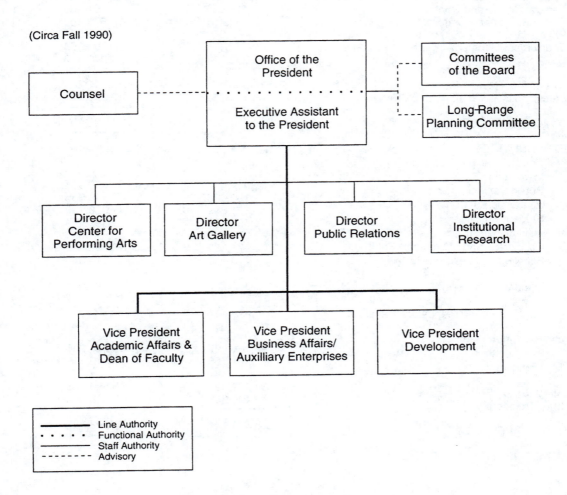

(Circa Fall 1990)

Office of the President

Executive Assistant to the President

Counsel

Committees of the Board

Long-Range Planning Committee

Director Center for Performing Arts

Director Art Gallery

Director Public Relations

Director Institutional Research

Vice President Academic Affairs & Dean of Faculty

Vice President Business Affairs/ Auxilliary Enterprises

Vice President Development

——————— Line Authority
· · · · · · Functional Authority
——————— Staff Authority
- - - - - - - Advisory

EXHIBIT 36-2 Catlin College Statement of Current Unrestricted Fund Revenues, Expenditures and Other Transfers for the Years Ended May 31, 1990, 1991

	Fiscal 1991	Fiscal 1990
REVENUES:		
Educational and General:		
Tuition and Fees	$17,141,024	$15,663,481
Federal Grants and Contracts	113,526	51,736
State Grants and Contracts	698,418	572,409
Private Gifts/Grants/Contracts	799,050	810,227
Endowment Income/Similar Funds Income	572,116	703,553
Other Sources	283,917	240,378
Total E & G Revenues:	$19,608,051	$18,041,784
Sales and Services of Auxiliary Enterprises	$4,116,053	$3,692,023
TOTAL REVENUES:	$23,724,104	$21,733,807
EXPENDITURES:		
Educational and General:		
Instruction		
Public Service	$8,002,517	$6,858,054
Academic Support	159,628	149,935
Student Services	1,301,861	1,050,738
Institutional Support	1,559,702	1,399,424
Operations and Maintenance of Plant	3,779,895	3,812,391
Scholarships/Fellowships	2,971,885	2,992,465
	1,718,953	1,516,003
Mandatory Transfers	371,796	321,964
Total E & G and Mandatory Transfers	$19,866,237	$18,100,974
Auxiliary Enterprises:		
Expenditures	$3,001,497	$3,274,206
Transfers	321,102	316,319
Total Auxiliary Enterprises	$3,322,599	$3,590,525
Other Transfers (net)	$495,268	$2,308
TOTAL EXPENDITURES:	$23,684,104	$21,693,807
NET INCREASE IN FUND BALANCE	$40,000	$40,000

EXHIBIT 36-3 Catlin College

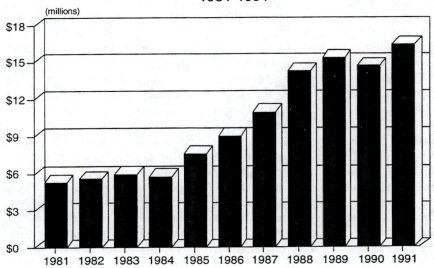

Market Value - Endowment Fund
1981-1991

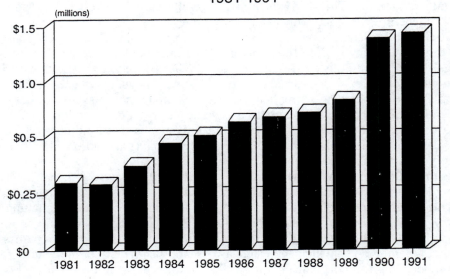

Institutional Financial Aid
1981-1991

Whether it should be called a college or a university involved more than mere nomenclature. It would likely have a major effect on the recruitment and evaluation of faculty, administration, and students. And it would certainly have an impact on the posture of the College and its future. Some on campus believed that there were broad differences in the mission of a college compared with the mission of a university. In Polis, a college is legally an institution "which offers four-year post-secondary educational programs or the equivalent and which grants primary baccalaureate or first professional degrees" [(Title 38 Education, Chapter 42 General Provisions, Subchapter A, Section 26.3, Public School Code of 1951 as amended through January 30, 1992)]. It would likely have a major effect on the recruitment and evaluation of faculty, administration, and students. And it would certainly have an impact on the posture of the College and its future. Some on campus believed that there were broad differences in the mission of a college compared with the mission of a university. In Polis, a college is legally an institution "which offers four-year post-secondary educational programs or their equivalent and which grants primarily baccalaureate or first professional degrees" [(Title 38 Education, Chapter 42 General Provisions, Subchapter A, Section 26.3, Public School Code of 1951 as amended through January 30, 1992)]. A University is legally defined in Polis as "A multi-unit institution with a complex structure and diverse educational functions including instruction, promotion of scholarship, preservation and discovery of knowledge, research and service." Changing the name from College to University would imply to some on campus, a change in the mission of the institution from a main emphasis on teaching to a more diverse mission with more emphasis on research and publication.

It was foreseen that competition among institutions for students would intensify in the 1990s as a result of demography which indicated a smaller number of high school graduates (at least through 1995) than were available in the 1980s. This predicted increased competition for fewer students would probably lead the more prestig-ious private and stronger state universities to accept students with weaker academic qualifications to fill their classes. This would force less prestigious institutions such as Catlin College, desirous of increasing its academic standards and reputation, toward difficulties in this external environment to increase the academic quality of entering students. Additionally, Zenith is in an area experiencing both economic and population declines, accentuating the problem of survival and growth. Accordingly, remaining an essentially regional institution would not be sufficient to assure viability.

Changing the designation of the institution from college to university was one possible way to help attract more highly-qualified students. The conventional wisdom was that many prospective students perceive a university to be more prestigious than a college. This belief was particularly true for international students, especially those from many British Commonwealth nations (except Canada) where the word "college" was used either primarily to denote secondary schools such as Eton College or as a subset of a university, (Balliol College, Oxford). Post-secondary or higher educational institutions in many British Commonwealth nations were generally called universities or polytechnic institutes.

Other major European, Asian, African and Latin American nations also often designated higher educational institutions, when using the English language, as universities.

Although the reasons are not clear, it is believed by some fund raisers for colleges and universities that a number of foundations and other donors are more willing to donate to institutions called universities than to those called colleges. However, it is not always clear what the term "university" connotes.

Increasingly, state and municipal-operated higher educational institutions throughout the United States changed their names from normal schools at the turn of the century to college and, more recently, to universities. For example, in New York State, the Albany Normal School became Albany State Teachers College and ultimately the State University of New York at

Albany. Many states, such as California, changed the designation of virtually all their state colleges to universities. Sometimes this change even included two-year community colleges. For example, the City University of New York Hostos Community College refers to itself in its catalog as a university.

In Polis, most smaller institutions, with some exceptions, such as Ivy University, had historically been called colleges. Examples are Polis College, Grunewald College, Baron College, and Catlin College. Large independent institutions such as the University of Polis, Carnegie-Smith University, and Burgoyne University were historically referred to as universities. In Polis, schools such as Polis State University, and others among state-owned and state-assisted institutions, were designated historically as universities. But in 1980, the entire state college system in Polis, including some small (primarily teaching-oriented) institutions were renamed as universities. In addition, another independent institution applied to the Department of Education and was given permission to change its name. Again, this raises questions regarding the substantive content supporting the term and the matter of what inferences should be drawn from the term "university."

Nonetheless, sentiment on campus and among alumni about designation of Catlin College as a university was divided. Some believed that changing the name to Catlin University would bring more prestige to the institution as well as help lead to improved admissions and fundraising results for the institution. Some faculty, who believed that research should receive more emphasis, were especially supportive of the change, in the hopes that the mission of Catlin would be changed to emphasize more research and scholarship with possibly lower teaching loads for those who published frequently. Townspeople and some members of the board believed that a university would enhance the image of the city, giving people more pride in the community and making it more attractive to non-residents.

Others in the College community were opposed to any change in designation. Some opponents believed the cost of a change in signage, literature, stationary, etc., could exceed $100,000. Some believed that the total cost would be even higher as changing a name would require advertising the new name extensively so that it would become recognizable, and no commensurate return was assured. When Standard Oil of New Jersey changed its major brand name in the United States from ESSO to EXXON, it spent millions to achieve name recognition for the new name.

Many alumni were opposed to any change in name. Catlin College was a familiar name and they did not want to change it.

Some on campus were proud of being a college. They believed that Catlin should stay a college and model itself on the likes of Amherst College, Union College, and Williams College. They pointed out that some universities had poor reputations. They believed that there was no advantage and some disadvantages to changing the name.

Some of those on campus who supported the primacy of teaching students as the major mission of the College were afraid that a change in name would ultimately lead Catlin into the publish or perish syndrome. Some of the business faculty, who were appalled by the American Assembly of Collegiate Schools of Business's rigid emphasis on publications at the possible expense of teaching were involved in a nationwide effort to set up a second national accrediting agency for business schools that would place much more emphasis on quality of teaching than research, and they were afraid this effort would be compromised by university status.

Many of those opposed to changing the name cited Dartmouth College. In 1819, the State of New Hampshire tried to take over Dartmouth and change it to a university. In a celebrated United States Supreme Court case (Dartmouth College v. Woodyard, 4 Wheat. 518), Daniel Webster argued that Dartmouth was a little college, but there were those who loved her. The Court, under the leadership of Chief Justice John Marshall upheld the college, and Dartmouth to this day is designated as a college.

No consensus was reached at the Cabinet

meeting on the issue of seeking university designation. The president had to leave the meeting early to go back to the same local hotel where she had breakfast to attend a board meeting of the local chamber of commerce.

She returned to the campus for a series of meetings after lunch, including one with an alumnus who had ideas on how the college could improve its banking relationships by shifting its accounts to a bank whose board the alumnus has just joined, a meeting with buildings and grounds officials over a persistently leaky roof that might have to be suddenly replaced at an unbudgeted cost of over $500,000, a meeting with a brilliant student who wanted the president's personal recommendation to accompany her application to law school, a meeting with a faculty member who believed he deserved a better office than the department chair had assigned him and the dean had approved, and several other meetings.

At four o'clock the president left campus with the Director of Development to make several fund-raising calls on local alumni. At seven o'clock the president returned to the local hotel for the third time that day to her second straight meal of chicken, baked potato, salad, green peas, and parfait for an honors dinner for the science national honorary society, which was inducting several students from the college. She spoke to the group and their parents as part of the ceremonies. Afterwards, she remained to greet each student and each parent personally and to commend each parent for his or her offspring's academic success.

After leaving the dinner, the president returned to campus one more time to ride around the campus and see what was going on. Satisfied that all appeared well (it wasn't raining and the roof was not leaking) she returned home and spent a quiet hour with her family before going to bed.

As the president lay in bed, her thoughts returned to the issue of the name of the college. Should the college decide to apply to change its name to Catlin University, it would first have to secure internal approval from several key constituencies at the college and formal approval from the College's Board of Trustees. The alumni association's support would also be crucial.

Since the president had decided she would not proceed without consensus, it would be useful for the entire College Community to study the issue of university status. The Academic Affairs Cabinet of the college, which includes the deans of the four academic schools and the officers responsible for admissions, student affairs, and the library would organize deliberations. Each school's faculty would discuss the issue at a faculty meeting. The Academic Affairs Cabinet would synthesize the results of the discussions and prepare a report for the Long Range Planning Committee of the college. This is a Joint faculty-administration-trustee-study body which advises the president on issues of structure and long term goals.

The Long Range Planning Committee would review the financial implications of the proposed change, would organize student discussion of the issue, and would poll alumni and donors for their views. The Committee would then make a recommendation to the President of the college. The President, in turn, would make her recommendation to the College's Board of Trustees.

The college would also have to comply with all the requirements of Polis law to be designated as a university. (See Appendix A).

The only provision of Polis law that might be difficult for the College to meet is the requirement that a university offer at least one doctoral program in the arts and sciences. The college currently offered no doctoral programs. Exemption from this requirement could be made if it could be demonstrated that the market is saturated and that there is no need for an additional doctorate program.

As this president drifted off to sleep, she knew what she would recommend be done on campus about the name of the college upon her return to the college in the morning.

Appendix A

Taken from section 42 of Article 38 of Public

School Code of Polis: University — A multi-unit institution with a compilex structure and diverse educational functions including instruction, promotion of scholarship, preservation and discovery of knowledge, research and service. A university complies with the following:

(i) Consists of a minimum of three units.

(A) The first unit—college, school, division—provides for study of the arts,and sciences at the undergraduate level.

(B) The second unit provides advanced degree programs through the doctorate in the arts and sciences, with an adequate number of majors in the various disciplines.

(C) The third unit provides a minimum of five professional programs at the graduate level.

(ii) Has a broad cultural basis from which undergraduate and graduate units draw upon the arts and sciences for basic courses whether or not these are an integral part of the programs provided in the unit.

(iii) Provides access to cultural facilities and opportunities to the community and at the same time utilizes similar assets of the community.

37

The Robotics Decision

Goals

I. To help participants understand the issues involved in major technological changes.

II. To help participants understand the opposing needs of the various stakeholder groups in a technological change.

Group Size

Groups should not exceed four to six members.

Time Required

Approximately 75 minutes.

Materials

I. A copy of the Robotics Decision Case History for each participant.

II. A copy of the appropriate role play sheet for each group member.

III. Blackboard space or flipcharts and markers for each group.

Physical Setting

A room large enough so that groups can work without disturbing each other. Movable chairs should be provided.

Process

Step I. Introduction (10 min.)
The facilitator explains the purposes of the activity and leads a short discussion of the idea of stakeholders and their differing needs and agendas. Groups are given their assignment of coming up with a solution to this dilemma.

Step II. Role Play (30 min.)
Participants assume their roles and attempt to resolve the dilemma. Participants are encouraged to come to consensus about whatever choice that they make.

Step III. Processing (20 min.)
Participants are asked to identify the agenda(s) that they were promoting. The group should be able to answer the following questions:

Prepared by Mark Sharfman. "The Robotics Decision Case History" is from *The 1989 Annual: Developing Human Resources*, University Associates, Inc., San Diego, CA. Used with permission.

1. What were the issues involved in implementing this new technology?

2. What was each participant's agenda in regard to the new technology?

3. What were the conflicting agendas and how did they conflict?

4. How did each person's agenda affect the technology change?

Step IV. Large Group Discussion (15 min.)
All of the small groups reconvene and discuss the questions in Step 3. A general discussion should include a discussion of the relationship between human resource issues and productivity/ profitability issues in the adoption of new technology.

The Robotics Decision
Case History

Elmire Glass and Plastics, Inc., is one of the nation's leaders in the production of glass and plastic for industrial use. The company has just received a proposal from United Robotics for the automation of its main production facility in Elmire, Pennsylvania. The change would entail full conversion from human operation to robotic production lines in the Plastic Components Division plant. This plant is the company's principal facility for the production of plastic components, which are used primarily in electronic equipment.

Elmire Glass and Plastics has been an innovator in the plastic components industry, and its components division has consistently yielded a 30 percent pre-tax return on investment. Although the demand for the company's component products appears to be strong, many of its competitors have recently switched to robotic production operations. This shift toward robotics is a source of concern to the company. Some industry analysts believe that robotics will transform the industry and will be a critical success factor in the future. Other analysts warn that robotics is a temporary solution, that it diverts

attention from productivity and morale problems, and that the high capital investment required is not warranted because robotic tooling is not flexible enough to adjust to changing plastic product needs.

United Robotics claims that the pessimism of some industry analysts is totally unwarranted and that its products contain built-in design features that will ensure adaptability. The management at United argues that although the risk of obsolescence might naturally be high over a long period — say twenty years — the robotic equipment will have paid for itself five times during that period in terms of labor savings. Financial analysts at Elmire concur with this claim, estimating that the incremental rate of return from the equipment can reasonably be expected to range from 25 percent to 40 percent (pre-tax). This estimate is based on an expected capital investment of $50,000,000 and the generation of yearly savings between $12,500,000 and $20,000,000. The savings computations are based on current labor costs that will be eliminated by the changeover and do not include the cost savings due to increased efficiency. Although efficiency-related savings could be substantial, the components division at Elmire Glass and Plastics is noted to be a highly efficient operation with low defect rates and minimal employee absenteeism and turnover.

In addition to financial considerations, there are numerous other factors involved in the investment decision. This morning local representatives of the union (to which all of the company's manufacturing workers belong) met with top management. They voiced concern, resentment, and their strong opinion that even considering the robotic transition was inconsistent with Elmire's history and reputation as a family organization. They noted that although the transition might bring a substantial return in the short term, it would have an overwhelmingly negative effect on the entire company in the long term. The union leaders pointed out that other Elmire Glass and Plastics divisions, located both in Elmire, Pennsylvania, and in other locations throughout the United States, would not stand for the changeover. They noted that the interdependent divisions that make up the company rely on many unionized skilled craftsmen and technicians and that these workers would be mobilized to strike if the robotic operation were implemented. The union leaders said that the integrity of the entire company was being threatened. Interestingly, middle managers and the secretarial staff were recently overheard in the cafeteria voicing the same concern and questioning the ethics involved in the changeover.

Other pressures are being placed on the company from the local community. The town of Elmire, with a population of 50,000 and located in an already-impoverished anthracite mining area of northeastern Pennsylvania, has been hurt recently by other plant closings. The prospect of five hundred more layoffs as well as the possibilities of strikes by other workers and layoffs from future robotic implementations are bringing many strong reactions. Several members of the town council and the Chamber of Commerce have phoned Elmire Glass and Plastics to express their concern, as have several congressional representatives and a number of local businesspeople. For the past two days, picketers from Citizens Against Corporate Irresponsibility (CACI) have been in town, organizing demonstrations in front of the components division offices and carrying signs with slogans like "Another Step Toward Greed," "Your Choice: Robots or Food for Elmire's Children," and "Robots or Responsible Management?" Although the CACI is viewed as a moderate group and advocates nonviolent protest, a number of more threatening protesters, believed to be part of an organized radical group that has used sabotage in some upstate New York manufacturing plants, jeered at managers and office employees who were entering and leaving the facility.

Three-year union contract negotiations come up for the components division in one year, just about the time the robotic operation could begin if a contract were signed now. At this point the top managers are divided regarding the best way to proceed. All agree that Elmire Glass and Plastics has survived through its years because of dedicated employees and that it has maintained a commitment to caring for its employees like family members. Layoffs have occurred in the past during difficult economic periods, but none of the magnitude of the one that would ensue with the robotic transition. The industry competition has never been so intense, and there is a fear that missing the opportunity to go with robotics and gain further competitive advantage would be disastrous and an injustice to Elmire's stockholders. A gradual transition to robotics would yield significantly lower returns in at least the next five years; also, replacements of retiring workers by automation would have its own unique set of problems, possibly acting like salt in a wound.

The need for a solution to this dilemma is critical.

38

The Department of Residence Life and Housing Western State University

PART A

The central management staff of the Department of Residence Life and Housing met regularly on Friday mornings for the weekly staff meeting. This Friday's agenda included several items, but none as unsettling as the topic of Organizational Review. Dr. Jim Wellan, the Director of the Department, carefully broached the topic with his central staff members: Frank (Assistant Director-North Campus), Joe (Assistant Director-South Campus), Susan (Coordinator for Residence Life-North Campus), Rob (Coordinator for Residence Life-South Campus), John (Coordinator for Fraternity Affairs), Lynn (Coordinator for Sorority Affairs), Shauna (Leadership Education Coordinator), Sheri (Director-New Student Orientation), Terry (University Apartments Manager), Maggie (Custodial Supervisor), and Jean (Administrative Assistant to the Director).

Jim shared with the staff his observations regarding the present structure of the Department. Although most of the staff were familiar with the fact that some type of evaluation of the present structure would take place, it was at this meeting that Jim clarified the procedure and shared his choice for who should coordinate the organizational review. A few sidelong glances were shared when Jim announced that Lynn would be assuming responsibility for the new Organizational Review Committee. This committee was designed to function much like an ad hoc task force of diverse representatives from the entire Department. The charge to the committee was to serve as an information gathering group that would make an initial effort to formalize the diverse opinions held by departmental personnel.

Discussion on the subject was brief during the staff meeting; however, several clarifications were solicited regarding the exact authority and responsibility delegated to the committee. Although not challenged publicly at the meeting, several staff also wondered how much authority and responsibility had just been handed over to Lynn, considering the fact that she had only been a member of the staff for seven short months and was regarded by some as simply a junior staff member. Lynn was also the youngest member of the staff by more than five years.

Prepared by Linda Elkin. Used with permission of the author. The author wishes to acknowledge the contribution of Dr. Douglas Baker, Washington State University in the development of this case.

EXHIBIT 38-1 The Division of Student Services after 1988

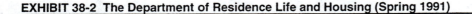

The Present Organizational Structure

The Department of Residence Life and Housing was a self-sufficient division of Western State University. It generated revenue from the rental of its residence hall space, University owned apartments, and lodging for summer camps and conferences. The Department had endured several administrative, functional, and personnel changes in its recent history. Once organized as two departments, Housing and Food Service and Residence Life, the organization was restruc-

tured in 1988 (see Exhibit 38-1).

At that time University Dining Services, Student Services Maintenance, and Financial Services were spun off to operate as separate entities, each with its own director. Thus, the resultant Department of Residence Life and Housing functioned according to the following Organizational Chart (see Exhibit 38-2).

The Central Management

The central management staff included the fol-

EXHIBIT 38-2 The Department of Residence Life and Housing (Spring 1991)

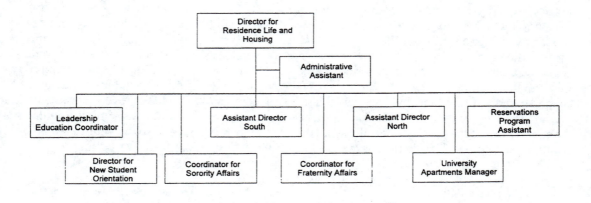

EXHIBIT 38-3 Department of Residence Life and Housing, North Campus

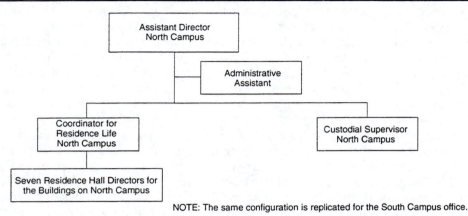

NOTE: The same configuration is replicated for the South Campus office.

lowing cast of players: The Director served as both the internal leader of the entire Department and as the Departmental representative to external campus agencies and divisions. The Director's time was split approximately 40/60% internally and externally, respectively. The 40% spent internally was further eroded by the number of one-on-one meetings the Director maintained weekly with the staff reporting directly to him. The intention was to provide a formalized vertical communication linkage with his staff. The communication flow in these meetings was one or two-way depending upon the staff member. For instance, Jim maintained open dialogue with the staff of Special Programs and Greek Affairs. However, in communicating with the Residence Hall staff, he tended to be more directive.

As the Director, Jim was extremely service oriented and driven by positive results. Although very kind and gentle, he pushed hard to move ahead with objectives and implementation strategies. This tenacity frustrated some employees who were more concerned about staff development and enrichment, and less concerned with implementation.

The two Assistant Directors to the Department actually worked strictly for the residence hall system. Neither one had a particular interest in the other living options or programs contained within the Department. Each was strictly focused on carrying out responsibilities and opera-

tions for his particular geographic area, either North or South Campus (see Exhibit 38-3). Furthermore, neither Joe nor Frank was willing to commit to evening engagements requiring a Departmental representative. The result was that Joe and Frank seemed unable to maintain broad administrative perspectives; and this frustrated Jim as he could not depend upon his Assistant Directors. Therefore, Jim refrained from delegating departmental responsibilities to either Assistant Director and continued to work late evenings, often four nights per week.

As the Assistant Director for South Campus, Joe was very low-key. He prided himself on maintaining a relaxed, open atmosphere in the South Campus satellite office. However, Joe was very hard to read; and although he was unofficially considered second in command, many questioned his motives.

Conversely, Frank, as the Assistant Director for North Campus, was extremely predictable and basically dysfunctional in his position. Frank could not grasp the "big picture." Rather, he would continually get bogged down in tiny details that increasingly diminished his productivity. Frank was also extremely theoretical, and yet had difficulty applying his theories of management to the day-to-day operations of the North Campus office.

Joe and Frank, as Assistant Directors, devoted the majority of their time collaborating with their staff: the Coordinators for Residence Life and the front line group of Residence Hall Directors. They valued the opportunity to be mentors to their developing younger professionals. However, because the residence hall system was organized geographically, there was duplication of responsibility at the Assistant Director, Coordinator, and Custodial Supervisor level for both North and South Campuses.

The delineations for North and South Campuses were artificial boundaries as the configuration of residence halls in each area was altered from year to year depending upon resident populations, building maintenance and renovations, and personalities of Residence Hall Directors.

The Coordinators for Residence Life, Rob and Susan, were originally hired to coordinate residence hall programming within their geographic area; however, both demonstrated an affinity for simply serving as a sounding board for their staffs: the Residence Hall Directors. Rob and Susan spent a disproportionate amount of time in one-on-one meetings with Residence Hall Directors. The time was generally wasted as neither one was very adept at communicating professional expectations and providing constructive feedback to their Residence Hall Director staffs. As a result, the Coordinator positions added to the height of the organizational structure while simultaneously diminishing the effectiveness of communication between the front line staff and the central management.

The effectiveness of the vertical linkage was further eroded by Rob and Susan's personal frustrations in their positions. Both felt devalued as professionals and isolated from the Director, as he was not their immediate supervisor. Furthermore, both were so driven by their own personal agendas that they became easily disillusioned with the conservative nature of the Department and the conservative University community. At one in- service session, both Rob and Susan said they were tired of being treated like children. However, neither one had taken the initiative to pursue new programs consistent with the Department's Long-Range Plan. Rather, each maintained an extensive personal agenda for redirecting the priorities of the Department and Western State University. For in-

stance, Rob and Susan were interested in promoting diversity of all kinds in the work-place, co-ed living options, and environmental recycling programs that would eliminate all synthetic materials within the Department. Finally, both acted like political victims and spent a disproportionate amount of time feeling sorry for themselves. Both Rob and Susan were extremely dissatisfied.

The personal frustrations of the Coordinators did not go unnoticed. The Director sensed that communication and accessibility to front-line staff were obstructed by the Coordinators for Residence Life. The poor communication channel would probably hinder the eventual implementation of the Department's Long-Range Plan by the Residence Hall Directors. Thus, at the time of the organizational review, the Coordinator positions were privately considered to be disposable by the Director and some of the central staff.

The Residence Hall Directors functioned as the primary administrators in the residence hall buildings. These staff members were responsible for programmatic, administrative, and maintenance activities within the respective buildings. The Residence Hall Directors often felt isolated from the central office and yet did not fully understand their role as an integral component to pursuing Departmental objectives at the grass roots level. Currently, there were sixteen Residence Hall Directors on staff, although consolidation was considered a viable alternative in the near future. A certain type of personality was required to be a Residence Hall Director. One had to be extremely self-reliant and independent. Because they lived in undergraduate student populations, the Residence Hall Directors also had to be accessible, accepting, and tolerant of the unexpected.

The independence and self-reliance exhibited by the Hall Directors in their respective buildings did not facilitate the cohesiveness of the aggregate Hall Director group. The Residence Hall Director staff met weekly with Rob and Susan. The meetings were not very productive, as many Residence Hall Directors did not see the need for large group meetings when they consid-

EXHIBIT 38-4 Department of Residence Life and Housing, North Campus

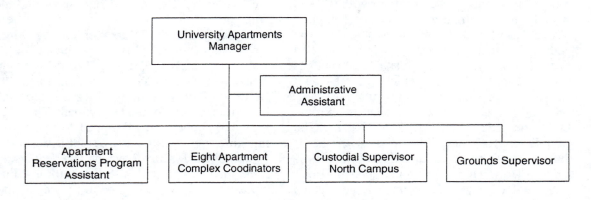

ered themselves to be independent building administrators. Furthermore, it was increasingly difficult to monitor their implementation of objectives outlined at the central management level because of their dispersement across campus and the failure of Rob and Susan to communicate clear expectations and control mechanisms.

As the Apartments Manager, Terry also reported to the Director. This person was responsible for supervising all aspects of University-owned apartments including selection of staff, supervision of custodians, and implementation of new programming initiatives (see Exhibit 38-4). Although the apartments were University housing, the amount of staffing was much less than that for the residence hall system. This was due to the older student population attracted to the apartment living option. Terry was an extremely likeable man. He maintained an excellent rapport with the clerical assistants in the central office and with his staff. He seemed to relate better to women than to other men. He became insecure and fumbled with his words when talking with the Director. Terry also had the most longevity of the group with over twenty years experience as a University employee.

Terry supervised a relatively small staff of ten. Staff members reporting directly to the Apartments Manager included among others, an administrative assistant, a program assistant responsible for reservations, and six apartment

coordinators (one for each apartment complex). This group administered all functions of property management for the apartment units. The apartment coordinators were sometimes compared to Residence Hall Directors due to commonalties within their respective positions. For instance, both implemented programs designed to build community relations within the living environment. However, the Residence Hall Directors took offense with the comparison because they were nationally recruited professionals while the apartment coordinators were selected from an on-campus pool of applicants. Apartment Coordinators did not receive a salary or benefits, although their housing costs were covered by the Department.

As the Reservations Program Assistant, Marcia reported directly to Jim. She was responsible for making room and roommate assignments throughout the residence hall system. The operations for this position were routine and highly cyclical. Late Spring and Summer were the peak seasons. Marcia therefore functioned in isolation from the rest of the central management. She did not attend the weekly central staff meeting; however, she maintained frequent contact with the Assistant Directors and the Residence Hall Directors on an informal basis. The autonomy inherent in the Reservations Program Assistant position suited Marcia very well. She was another employee with significant longevity. She seldom liked change and frowned upon others' suggestions for improved efficiency. She did not enjoy one-on-one meetings with Bill and would quickly retreat to her isolated computer terminal as soon as the uncomfortable meetings ended. The entire reservations operation had been targeted by the central management staff as needing attention and evaluation. Marcia would certainly be resistant to such an initiative.

Greek Affairs was also contained within the Department of Residence Life and Housing. The Coordinator for Fraternity Affairs and the Coordinator for Sorority Affairs both reported directly to Jim. They maintained good informal horizontal communication among themselves and with the students they advised. As the Coordinator for Fraternity Affairs, John executed his responsibilities with little thought. He was burned out and desperately hoped to finish his doctoral degree in an effort to leave the Department. Nevertheless, he often had an opinion for just about everything. The other staff members had conditioned themselves to become detached from the conversation when John spoke.

As the Coordinator for Sorority Affairs, Lynn was fairly autonomous. No one else in the Department understood or took an interest in student sorority activity. Newly hired, Lynn was enthusiastic and motivated to improve her functional area. Although she enjoyed the autonomy, Lynn frequently became frustrated with her co-workers who did not value her position as a central staff member. Lynn and John worked well together; but the disparity in age and position longevity between the two made for challenging teamwork. Throughout her first year, Lynn slowly assumed more Departmental responsibilities in an effort to bridge the gap between her functional area and the rest of the central management.

Greek Affairs was considered the black sheep of the Department. Other staff members did not care to be involved or informed of its daily activities, programs, and administrative operations. Some people felt that Greek Affairs could be staffed by one central staff member utilizing two graduate assistants. As Director, Jim supervised this area at arms' length, trusting his staff and participating when time allowed.

Conversely, Jim was heavily absorbed with the Leadership Education Coordinator and the Director of New Student Orientation. Both were new additions to the Department by the Director's encouragement. Shauna's position as Leadership Education Coordinator had been newly created that year in an effort to implement the Leadership Programming component of the Long-Range Plan for the Department. The leadership component was designed to match living/housing options on campus with the opportunities for involvement and leadership development for students. Furthermore, this functional area was designed to provide a centralized program for students in 1500 residence hall leadership positions. Additional benefits of the program were to recruit students to a university with living options that offered educational leadership experiences, to retain students longer in the residence hall system, to improve the effectiveness of student organizations, and to strengthen the network of alumnae leaders willing to assist with career placement and mentoring. As such, the leadership program was fairly ambitious in its objectives; however, total implementation was considered difficult in light of the absence of assistants and clerical support for Shauna, the Leadership Education Coordinator.

Furthermore, during the year, Shauna assumed several of the staff selection and training responsibilities previously assigned to the Coordinators of Residence Life. Balancing many responsibilities was certainly challenging for one person; however, Shauna thrived on adversity and being percieved as an over-achiever. She also maintained good informal communication and horizontal linkages with other staff during her initial months in the position. A problem surfaced though as not all co-workers were convinced that Leadership was a significant component in the overall mission of the Department.

Finally, the Director of New Student Orientation was added to the Department during mid-year. Originally contained within another University Division, it was believed that student orientation had a natural connection to Residence Life and Housing. In other words, both programs were designed to help students adjust to a university environment. New Student Orientation was an extremely large program that attracted droves of people from all over the state each summer. As the program gained popularity, it became increasingly obvious that more office space and support staff would be necessary to maintain such a quality program. Although New Student Orientation was added to the Department, not all staff were supportive of the move. The new functional area also increased Jim's internal Department commitments as Director. At the time of the organizational review committee, the Director of New Student Orientation, Sheri, was fairly new as a central staff member and therefore did not have much personal impact on the process.

The Department was thus a mixture of poor structure, weak coordination and poor staffing. Furthermore, these problems were not being properly addressed because of Jim's selective involvement and his lack of control. The result was unclear departmental objectives that lacked specificity and demonstrated a failure to plan collectively.

The Need to Reorganize

The organizational chart was therefore a hybrid of geographical and functional departments. Although several positions were designed to execute functional responsibilities at the central staff level, the staff responsible for the residence hall system was organized geographically according to North and South Campuses. Some thought that this type of delineation was inherently at odds with the Department's Long Range Planning Document that targeted functional initiatives in the form of accomplishing overarching goals. These included the following:

- Providing the highest quality housing facilities for all students attending the University at the lowest possible cost.

- Providing educational opportunities and support mechanisms for all University housed students which would complement the learning received in the classroom.

- Developing residential communities which promote an appreciation for individual and cultural differences.

- Developing high quality involvement opportunities for students to actively participate in the functioning of the Department and the University to ultimately enhance their leadership and citizenship capabilities.

- Collaborating with a variety of agencies to provide the highest quality service and interaction between the University and University housed students.

Although these overarching goals were quite vague and ambiguous, the Long-Range plan was nevertheless developed to provide direction for the Department of Residence Life and Housing as it prepared to move into the next decade. In order to move forward, eight specialized functional areas were selected to serve as parameters for organizing the Department in order to prioritize initiatives, resource allocations, and program development strategies. These eight areas were categorized as the Freshman Year Experience, the Upper Level Experience, Leadership Education, Greek Affairs, Internationalization of the Residential Experience, University Apartments, Information Access and Technological Advancement, and Facilities Enhancement. Actual implementation of objectives stemming from these eight areas would take place in the near future; however, the formula for implementation was as yet undetermined. Furthermore, although there was significant potential for crossover of all targeted initiatives for each division within the Department, the majority of activity within the first year of implementation of the Long-Range Plan would most likely be directed toward the Residence Hall system.

Furthermore, although the concept of a long-range plan was positive, the tremendous ambiguity likely contributed to the current discontent within the Department.

The central staff met weekly for three hours to discuss issues and handle tasks as they arose. A review of the items covered in the Spring of 1991 would indicate that although representatives from all functional areas of the Department were required to attend, 95% of the items covered related directly to operations and initiatives for the Residence Halls.

Part B

Beginning the Organizational Charge Process

It was at that April meeting of the central staff that the topic of organizational review was formally highlighted as a significant area needing attention. Issues related to structure included the following: Geographic versus functional organization, the amount and effectiveness of horizontal and vertical linkages, the staffing patterns in each functional area, and the applicability of the structure to the Long-Range Plan.

In addition to the breadth of issues facing the Organizational Review Committee, the challenge of building a cohesive committee loomed large for Lynn, as the committee chair. Several key players within the Department required cooptation or encouragement to contribute to the work of the committee. Furthermore, the progress of the committee would be tempered by the different values and interests of various members. Lynn understood that whoever served on the committee would bring varying levels of commitment to the task at hand, as well as hidden agendas and conflicting processes.

Strategies for Change

Returning from the staff meeting, Lynn sat at her desk and considered the different strategies she could pursue as chair of the committee at her organizational review. The mood of uneasiness surrounding the staff meeting that had just ended was a significant indication of the tremendous uncertainty clouding the issue of reorganization. Although most staff members were secure in their positions as state employees, the possibility of demotions, additional responsibilities, or revisions in pay augmented the uneasiness of the Depart-

ment and added to the level of uncertainty.

Understanding the Sources of Power

A fundamental goal of the organizational review process was to understand the sources of power within the Department and to use political power to achieve the outcomes outlined in the Long-Range Plan for the Department of Residence Life and Housing. By understanding these dynamics, Lynn hoped to facilitate decision making and consensus building.

The strategic selection of task force members would serve to inherently provide clashes of opinion; however, over time and through cooptation, the committee could ultimately be proud of the finished product: the report of its findings to the Director. Lynn also sought to maneuver the ultimate consensus of the committee by monitoring the dominance of certain players on the task force or by the strategic absence of others from the committee. For those employees that would not be asked to serve on the committee, Lynn still included them on an informal basis by soliciting their opinions while cautiously offering alternative viewpoints. For example, Lynn purposely did not include either Susan or Rob on the committee as their duplicated positions of Coordinator of Residence Life (North, South) were contributing to the excessive verticality of the current structure. Furthermore, their personal values and political power over the Residence Hall Directors (the front-line management staff for the Department) were considered detrimental by the Director and other central staff members. Therefore, Lynn decided that their input was necessary to the work of the committee, but not at the expense of filibustering any initiatives for change. Thus, although Susan and Rob were deliberately kept from serving on the committee, the essential timing of their visit to the committee in late May served the dual purpose of giving them the opportunity to express their dissenting views while confirming within the committee the need to streamline positions and operations within the Residence Halls staff.

The process of building informal power was not without its challenges. Lynn was aware of uncooperative factions within the Department. A group of five influential staff members were particularly challenging. Joe (Assistant Director, South Campus), Frank (Assistant Director, North Campus), Susan and Rob (Coordinators for Residence Life), and Bridget (Residence Hall Director) continually rubbed against the grain of the committee. As the committee was beginning to advocate a centralized functional structure, this group verbally criticized the impending reorganization as unnecessary, inappropriate, and unsubstantiated. Joe and Rob were particularly loyal to the North-South configuration, Susan believed that the committee did not have enough empirical evidence to substantiate a reorganization, and Bridget shared that not all of the Residence Hall Directors concurred with the adopted Long-Range Plan for the Department. By its own vocal dissention, this group served a dual purpose. Although they had significant influence over several other staff members (particularly the Residence Hall Director and Clerical Staff support), their resistance to the initiatives proposed by the Director did not send a positive signal to the Residence Life and Housing staff at large. Over time, the Director's dissatisfaction with this group became common knowledge to the rest of the central management staff.

The Next Phase of Reorganization

As June turned into July, the Organizational Review Committee was concluding its meeting schedule. Lynn extended a final invitation to all staff members. The intent was to provide one last opportunity for input from the Departmental staff. The entire committee process had been very participatory up to that point, and the intention was to conclude in just such a manner. Two staff members accepted the opportunity to come to the last committee meeting, including Rob. He wanted to make his points one more time. This was helpful for him in order to feel valued, but was even more helpful for the committee to reaffirm in their minds the outcomes that were truly desirable. Needless to say, Rob's opinions

would not correspond well with the majority of the committee.

By August 1, the final report of the committee was handed to Jim Wellan, the Director. The report included a synopsis of the significant themes generated during the course of the investigation. These themes included the ineffectiveness of the existing organizational chart, the issue of geographical versus functional structure, the need to streamline departmental operations, and the notion of separate islands working independently and at cross purposes within the Department. The committee concluded its report by providing ten suggestions for alternative organizational structures to Dr. Jim Wellan for addressing the issues contained within these four themes.

1. Reduce the number of staff reporting directly to the Director.
2. Develop a flatter organizational chart.
3. Switch from a geographic to a functional structure.
4. Eliminate the South Campus office.
5. Use the South Campus office suite for student programs.
6. Fit the organizational structure to be compatible with the the functions outlined in the Long-Range Plan.
7. Streamline operations within the organizational structure.
8. Create Associate Director position(s) to coordinate functional areas.
9. Adopt one of the alternative organizational structures developed by individual committee members.
10. View the organizational structure from a broad perspective but keep change simple.

The next step in the organizational review process was as yet undetermined. At the summer in-service retreat for the central management staff, Lynn was asked to present the work of the Organizational Review Committee. She was excited about the opportunity to share the information, but was more anxious to note the reactions of her co-workers to the proposed suggestions for reorganization. Lynn concluded by asking for questions and comments. Initially no one spoke. Finally, Rob spoke slowly and deliberately: "Lynn, although I have some reservations about what is included in this report, I appreciate the time and effort given by the committee. I'll be curious to see what transpires in the near future."

39
Political Processes in Organizations

The purpose of this exercise is to analyze and predict when political behavior is used in organizational decision-making and to compare participants' ratings of politically-based decisions with ratings of practicing managers.

Politics is the use of influence to make decisions and obtain preferred outcomes in organizations. Surveys of managers show that political behavior is a fact of life in virtually all organizations. Every organization will confront situations characterized by uncertainty and disagreement, hence standard rules and rational decision models can't necessarily be used. Political behavior and rational decision processes act as substitutes for one another, depending upon the degree of uncertainty and disagreement that exists among managers about specific issues. Political behavior is used and is revealed in informal discussions and unscheduled meetings among managers, arguments, attempts at persuasion, and eventual agreement and acceptance of the organizational choice.

In the following exercise, you are asked to evaluate the extent to which politics will play a part in eleven types of decisions that are made in

organizations. The complete exercise takes about one hour.

Step I. Individual Ranking (5 minutes)

Rank the eleven organizational decisions listed on the scoring sheet below according to the extent you think politics plays a part. The most political decision would be ranked 1, the least political decision would be ranked 11. Enter your ranking on the first column of the scoring sheet.

Step II. Team Ranking (20 minutes)

Divide into teams of from three to seven people. As a group, rank the eleven items according to your group's consensus on the amount of politics used in each decision. Use good group decision-making techniques to arrive at a consensus. Listen to each person's ideas and rationale fully before reaching a decision. Do not vote. Discuss items until agreement is reached. Base your decisions on the underlying logic provided by group members rather than on personal preference. After your team has reached a consensus, record the team rankings in the second column

Thanks to Don Hellriegel for suggesting the idea for this exercise. The scoring sheet is based on Jeffrey Gandz and Victor V. Murray, "The Experience of Workplace Politics." *Academy of Management Journal* 1980, 23, 237-251. Prepared by Dick Daft.

on the scoring sheet.

Step III. Correct Ranking (5 minutes)

After all teams have finished ranking the eleven decisions, your instructor will read the correct ranking based on a survey of managers. This survey indicates the frequency with which politics played a part in each type of decision. As the instructor reads each item's ranking, enter it in the "correct ranking" column on the scoring sheet.

Step IV. Individual Score (5 minutes)

Your individual score is computed by taking the difference between your individual ranking and the correct ranking for each item. Be sure to use the absolute difference between your ranking and the correct ranking for each item (ignore pluses and minuses). Enter the difference in column 4 labeled "Individual Score." Add the numbers in column 4 and insert the total at the bottom of the column. This score indicates how accurate you were in assessing the extent to which politics plays a part in organizational decisions.

Step V. Team Score (5 minutes)

Compute the difference between your group's ranking and the correct ranking. Again, use the absolute difference for each item. Enter the difference in the column 5 labeled "Team Score." Add the numbers in column 5 and insert the total at the bottom of the column. The total is your team score.

Step VI. Compare Teams (5 minutes)

When all individual and team scores have been calculated, the instructor will record the data from each group for class discussion. One member of your group should be prepared to provide both the team score and the lowest individual score on your team. The instructor may wish to display these data so that team and individual scores can be easily compared as illustrated on the bottom of the scoring sheet. All participants may wish to record these data for further reference.

Step VII. Discussion (15 minutes)

Discuss this exercise as a total group with the instructor. Use your experience and the data to try to arrive at some conclusions about the role of politics in real-world organizational decision-making. The following questions may facilitate the total group discussion.

1. Why did some individuals and groups solve the ranking more accurately than others? Did they have more experience with organizational decision-making? Did they interpret the amount of uncertainty and disagreement associated with decisions more accurately?

2. If the eleven decisions were ranked according to the importance of rational decision processes, how would that ranking compare to the one you've completed above? To what extent does this mean both rational and political models of decision-making should be used in organizations?

3. What would happen if managers apply political processes to logical, well understood issues? What would happen if they applied rational or quantitative techniques to uncertain issues about which considerable disagreement existed?

4. Many managers believe that political behavior is greater at higher levels in the organization hierarchy. Is there any evidence from this exercise that would explain why more politics would appear at higher rather than lower levels in organizations?

5. What advice would you give to managers who feel politics is bad for the organization and should be avoided at all costs?

SCORING SHEET

Decisions	1. Individual Ranking	2. Team Ranking	3. Correct Ranking	4. Individual Score	5. Team Score
1. Management promotions and transfers					
2. Entry level hiring					
3. Amount of pay					
4. Annual budgets					
5. Allocation of facilities, equipment, offices					
6. Delegation of authority among managers					
7. Interdepartmental coordination					
8. Specification of personnel policies					
9. Penalties for disciplinary infractions					
10. Performance appraisals					
11. Grievances and complaints					

	Team Number						
	1	2	3	4	5	6	7
Team scores:							
Lowest individual score on each team:							

40

Dover Municipal Hospital

I knew the hospital either made money or lost it based on its professional services. And I knew that you came in contact with the whole hospital through those services; so I said that's what I want to run. I also knew that professional services was filled with the biggest prima donnas on the staff — radiologists, biochemists, cardiologists — each more difficult than the others and that my predecessor, at age twenty-eight, had developed a bleeding ulcer and left.

Chuck Graham, Assistant Administrator
Dover Municipal Hospital

So thought Chuck Graham when he had accepted responsibility for professional services at Dover Municipal Hospital in Delaware. The past few months had given him a much better insight into just how difficult it was to manage those prima donnas, and now he had to decide whether or not, how, and how tightly to put the lid on this business of sending tests to outside laboratories.

The Dover Municipal Hospital

The Dover Municipal Hospital (DMH) was a complex of five buildings located in one of the poorest sections of Delaware's capital city. Constructed mostly in the 1930s, the physical plant was drab, and security was tight. After five o'clock in the evening, heavy chains and padlocks secured the doors to passageways leading from one building to another. Nearly all of DMH's patients arrived via the hospital's emergency room, and most of the remainder came through its ambulatory care unit. The Dover Police Department brought DMH most of the hospital cases it picked up, and other hospitals sent their "dump jobs" — indigent, uninsured patients that these hospitals were "too full" to accommodate.

Throughout its history, DMH had been a teaching hospital and was currently affiliated with Delaware University's medical school. The

This case was prepared by Professor John R. Russell of Boston University's Public Management Program with the help of Terrence Briggs, research assistant. Funds for its development were provided by a grant from the National Training and Development Service. The case is intended to serve as a basis for class discussion, not to illustrate either effective or ineffective handling of a managerial situation. Revised December 1977. Used with permission. Names and locations have bc;en disguised.

hospital was staffed entirely by residents and interns who worked under a salaried senior medical staff that provided both teaching and supervision. No physicians in private practice had staff privileges. All the senior medical staff committed only one-quarter to one-half of their time to the hospital. They were paid an "administrative" salary by the city, which was all that third-party reimbursers would pay for and which was only a fraction of what a doctor could earn in private practice or from a full-time job at a private hospital. Most of the physicians augmented their DMH salaries with teaching stipends from the university, salaries received as principal investigators on research grants, jobs managing outside laboratories, and other means. In addition, a special physicians' billing corporation culled the hospital's records to identify patients with third-party reimbursement resources, such as commercial medical insurance, that could be billed for the doctors' services. According to one observer, these arrangements created friction:

The city wants to pay for clinical care for indigent patients. It doesn't want to pay for research or teaching or try to make DMH a great research center. The medical staff, on the other hand, are the kind who are willing to give up the money available in private practice because they are researchers. And this is where they expect to do their research and their teaching.

The breakdown of billing for inpatient care was Medicare, 20 percent; Blue Cross, 3 percent; Medicaid, 40 percent; commercial insurance, 5 percent; and "self-pay," 35 percent. In practice, the hospital sent all its patients a bill, but did not expect to recover from any of the self-payers. Each year, DMH estimated the cost of the services it would deliver next year, subtracted the amount of third-party and self- paid reimbursements it expected, and submitted the remainder as its annual budget proposal to the city. The city usually cut several million from this proposal, and it was up to the hospital to determine how to absorb the cuts. The current city share of hospital expenses was about $10 million.

At one time, the hospital's capacity had been about 750 beds, but demand for its services had slackened when the advent of Medicaid and Medicare gave many indigents the option of going to other Dover hospitals. Eventually, over half of DMH's beds had been "delicensed." The staff currently numbered about 2,000, of whom approximately 150 were interns, residents, or senior medical staff, and the remainder were nurses, technicians, clerical help, maintenance people, messengers, orderlies, and so forth.

The *medical* staff was organized into two major departments — medicine (which included pediatrics, cardiology, gastro-intestinal, hematology, pulmonary, and other internal medicine subservices) and surgery (which included obstetrics/gynecology). There was also an outpatient department. The hospital's *administrative* staff reported to an associate director and three assistant directors — one for medicine, one for surgery, and one for professional services. The assistant director for professional services had administrative responsibility for the laboratories and other diagnostic services as well as various support services, such as medical records, admitting, social services, messenger, pharmacy, and transportation. (In a few instances, such as the biochemistry laboratory, these professional services subdepartments reported on medical matters to the department of medicine and on administrative matters to the assistant director of professional services.) Both the associate director and the heads of the two medical departments reported to the hospital director, who was hired by the city. The relative influence of the director, the associate director, and the medical staff depended on the individuals who occupied the various positions at a particular time.

Chuck Graham

In the spring of 1975, the old director of DMH retired and was replaced by Donna Breen. The two were a study in contrasts. Whereas her predecessor has been described as a wily and cautious civil servant who had managed, nevertheless, to alienate city hall, Breen was young, active, and had excellent relations with the city manager and his staff. She had just completed three years as Delaware's assistant commissioner for social services. Breen was without experience in medicine or the health system, but believed firmly that a hospital could be managed well by people who were good managers, but who were not necessarily doctors. She also believed in change and innovation. Good ideas should be tried and mistakes tolerated. Within a few days of Breen's arrival, the associate administrator resigned, and Breen, herself, decided to occupy the position until a suitable replacement could be found. In the weeks that followed, a great many junior administrators left DMH and others were shifted to new responsibilities. One of the latter was Chuck Graham.

Like Breen, Graham had no medical background. As an undergraduate, he had been a summer intern at DMH and decided he liked "working in health." After three years as a Peace Corps volunteer in South America, he returned to DMH, this time as unit coordinator for three wards and the intensive care unit. In this capacity, he was responsible for "administrative operations" — that is, making sure the units were properly stocked with supplies, dealing with the demands and complaints of the physicians and nurses, supervising the secretaries, and handling other administrative chores. Graham characterized the work as "middle management," which to him meant solving whatever problems came up in the wards and "doing what head nurses used to do but don't want to do anymore." After six months, he had been promoted to assistant manager for the unit coordination department and after a year, to head of the department. In a few months, he had been promoted again, to junior administrator in charge of twelve support service departments, including messenger, transportation, housekeeping, mail, central supply, laundry, and kitchen.

During the fall of 1975, Breen offered Graham any of the three assistant administrator slots, and Graham elected professional services:

I went from managing twelve departments to managing over twenty. They said I could give up transportation and messenger, but I decided to keep them. I knew if I wanted to make the labs work, I'd have to control the process from the time a specimen was drawn to the time the results were delivered back to the doctor.

The main additions to Graham's responsibilities were five large decentralized clinical laboratories and several small research labs that performed one or two tests of clinical importance to the hospital. The five were hematology, biochemistry, bacteriology, pathology, and the blood bank. They employed about two hundred people. A physician had medical responsibility for each of the labs, and as administrator, Graham would "more or less," as he put it, be in charge of personnel and budget.

If a lab wanted to buy a new piece of equipment, I'd have to sign off on it. On the other hand, if I wanted a lab to do a particular test, the doctor could say, "No, I won't do it." Or, he could say, "I'll do it, but it will cost you two technicians and $100,000 in equipment." In other words, the doctors controlled what went on in the labs. And I had to avoid practicing medicine.

Since the lab chiefs were there only part time, the day-to-day operations were run by chief technicians who ordered supplies, signed documents, scheduled work, and trained other technicians. Bringing outside work into the labs (except under a contract to which the city was a party) was against the law. While the lab chiefs had the final say on hiring technicians, Graham theoretically could fire anyone, including the lab chief himself. In practice, this was difficult, because replacing a lab chief for $15,000 to $20,000 meant finding someone in the area who had enough other activities to augment his DMH salary, but who still had enough time left to work one-quarter time for the hospital.

The Test List

During his early days on the job, Graham was plagued by his own ignorance of the labs and by a barrage of complaints from the doctors:

The physicians, when they're unhappy with the administration, think their best leverage is to complain. Donna (Breen) was moving strongly to shift the balance of who ran the hospital — from the physicians to the administration — and the physicians were fighting it. One thing they did was to complain about the service they were getting from the labs and other support departments. What really was bothering them was Donna's demands that they devote more time to clinical work and less to their research and teaching. She didn't want to support those activities with public funds.

One discovery Graham made was that no one in the hospital knew every test that was offered by the laboratories. His predecessor had tried to compile a list, but failed. Graham decided to try for himself and visited each lab chief:

They all said, "All we've got is a partial list." I said "May I see it?" and they said, "Sure but it's outdated. We've added a few tests and dropped a few others. Also, I'm short a few people because of layoffs, and I really don't have time to put a list together for you now." I began to think that most of the lab chiefs didn't want the administration to know what tests they could perform. It gave them more flexibility.

After two months of trying, Graham had virtually nothing of any value from biochemistry, pathology, or hematology. Bacteriology and the blood bank, on the other hand, had provided him with lists that he thought were complete.

What I did was design a form (see Exhibit 40 — 1). Then I said, "I want a completed form for every test you do. It's getting close to budget time; and if you give me ten tests, that's what I'll base your budget on. If you do fifty more on the sly, you'll have to find the funds on your own". Suddenly, I began to get a little cooperation, and the number of tests that everyone was doing began to go up.

I also began to call the chief lab technicians into my office and deal with them because the physicians were only there part of the time.

It took almost six months, but at the end of that time, Graham believed he had a collection of forms that represented quite accurately the tests currently being performed. He had also developed the following impressions of the five labs:

Hematology

The lab consisted of two units: the main hematology lab, where a staff of thirty technicians, blood drawers, and clerks provided round-the-clock service and performed the bulk of hematology testing, and an outpatient laboratory that ran simple tests on ambulatory patients. Little or no research was done in the lab.

The lab chief, who also ran the hematology lab at another Dover hospital, was extremely independent. Said Graham:

If he feels like doing a test, he does it. If he doesn't feel like it, you're out of luck. He's very dificult to get along witb, but he's a very skillful hematologist, and be runs a quality lab. No matter what you want, though, it's push, shove and toe-to-toe, and there's always a price attached to it.

He runs the lab like a dictator, and the techs do what he tells them to. But he sends them home two hours early if he thinks that's good for them. And he won't let his techs help with some of the chores that all the other lab techs share.

I've been told that be asks only for new equipment in his budget request, even when he

EXHIBIT 40-1 Dover Municipal Hospital: Sample of Completed Test Inventory Form

LAB: Central Hematology

1. Lab test name:
    White Blood Count (WBC)

2. What it does (what is its purpose? What does it test for? What sample (blood, urine, etc.)? Is it a common test?):
    Very Common Test
    Blood Sample
    Test for:
           Infection — Leukemia — Surgical conditions

3. How many tests are done per year?:
    85,000

4. Is it part of a larger test (i.e., CBC, SMA 12)?:
    Yes (CBC) — Usually done on Coulter Counter

5. Charge of this test as of 8/25/76:
    Manually — $4.00
    Coulter — $10.00

6. Cost of the test as of 10/1/76:
    $0.50

7. Automated or manual test (batches or individual)?:
    Either —   Automated = 95%
                  Manual = 5%

8. How long does it take to perform?
    Coulter — 45 seconds
    Manually — 10 minutes

9. Emergency nature or routine (how quickly is it needed)?:
    Either

10. What reagents and equipment are used to perform this test?:
    Reagents: 2% Acetic Acid - Manually (unopette)
           Isoton — Lyse S — Coulter
    Equipment: Microscope — coverglass — counting chamber — tally counter (manually)
           Coulter models

11. The hours the test is offered (What is the turnaround time)?:
    24 hours
    STAT Turnaround Time — 30 minutes or less

12. Procedure used to perform the test (i.e., radioimmunoassay, etc.):
    Manual unit count by hand
    Particle count on Coulter

13. Who takes the specimen? What container is used? How is it transported?:
    Phlebotomist — Lavender Top Tube (EDTA)
    By hand by tech — messenger service - pneumatic tube

14. Amount of sample required:
    At least half-filled Lavender Top Tube

knows some of the most vital older equipment will probably break down soon Then when it does, you have to add money to his original budget so he can go on performing the tests.

Biochemistry

Staffed twenty-four hours a day, seven days a week, biochemistry was the largest producer of tests in the hospital. It was also the biggest money maker and the best equipped. Daily operations were supervised by a Ph.D. in chemistry who presided over a staff of about forty- five technicians and support personnel. There was also a consulting biochemistry lab that consisted of two people, on a normal forty-hour week, working on research grants and doing a few sophisticated clinical tests.

The chief of biochemistry was new at DMH. He had come to Graham with several requests from his technicians concerning longer lunch hours or shorter work days — all of which Graham had refused. He spent almost all his time either teaching or working on his research in the consulting biochemistry lab. The Ph.D. in chemistry appeared to run the laboratory.

Bacteriology

From a technical viewpoint, this was the showpiece laboratory. More than in the other labs, the work in microbiology — which involved planting specimens in culture media — was an art form. While the output of the hematology and biochemistry labs was sometimes criticized, the quality of microbiology's output was never questioned. The forty technicians and bacteriologists worked a five-day week, and because bacteriologists would not read anything that someone else had planted, delays sometimes developed over weekends.

The lab had a degree of fiscal independence that the other labs did not. Almost two-thirds of its budget came from a local foundation and another 15 percent from contracts to perform work for Memorial Hospital. DMH paid for only that part of the lab's budget that was not supported by these outside sources.

The lab chief was one of the DMH's medical "statesmen." He stayed out of hospital politics and hospital administration, seemed always to have a good word for everyone, and made few demands of his own. When he did ask for something — such as a new piece of equipment — the request was invariably reasonable.

Pathology

Pathology, with about ninety people, was concerned with the analysis of disease. Its lab chief, who was to retire at the end of 1976, had earned a national reputation in anatomical pathology research. His fund-raising efforts had paid for most of the equipment in the building where the lab was housed, and his continuing success at acquiring research grants kept more than a dozen physicians working at the hospital, providing services for which the city did not have to pay. In return for these benefits and the high quality of his work, he expected to be given a budget and then left alone. No one on the Dover University medical staff, except the senior surgeons, ever set foot in the laboratory. Graham visited the area once, but discovered that most of the doors were locked and that keys were not available.

Blood bank

The blood bank managed DMH's inventory of blood and performed the simple tests necessary to dispensing that inventory properly. Nominally, one of the staff surgeons was the lab chief, but the bank was actually managed by a very pleasant and capable nurse.

The Free T-4 Incident

As he was developing the list of tests and becoming more familiar with the laboratories, Graham learned that almost $150,000 in testing (10 percent of the total DMH lab budget) was being sent to labs outside the hospital. After securing a breakdown of these outside tests from the DMH accounting department (see Exhibit 40-2), he noted that over $20,000 was being spent annually just to perform Free T-4 tests at Memorial Hospital, Dover, where the biochemistry lab was run by a doctor who had recently left DMH. He asked several doctors why this was being done:

Their answer was something like, "Well, young man, this is a superior methodology being used by a superior laboratory. We've done it that way for three or four years, and it's really none of your business".

Rather than let the issue drop, Graham asked other doctors about the Free T-4 test. He discovered that there was a more advanced method of doing the test that could be set up in the DMH biochemistry lab for an initial cost of about $20,000.A

So, I went to my laboratory advisory committee (the group of doctors who advise me on the technical and medical aspects of the labs) and asked them if they thought it would be all right to switch to the new method. They said "No". Then I went to biochemistry since Free T-4s are basically biochemistry tests — and asked if he'd be willing to do them inhouse. I was told that it was none of my business, that I wasn't a physician, that Memorial's method was much better, and that biochemistry reported to the department of medicine anyway.

I didn't buy it. I called an out-of-state friend who was a hospital administrator and talked to his clinical pathologist, and he convinced me that the new method was not only better, it was cheaper. He also said the Memorial Hospital method cost a lot less than they were charging us, which made me think our money was being used to support teaching and research over there.

I went back to biochemistry and said, "Will you do it?" But he wouldn't. So I talked to hematology, and he said he'd do it provided I gave him another S15,000-a-year technician.

The Outside Testing Issue

In the midst of his efforts to resolve the Free T-4

issue and to compile a complete list of tests, Graham received a phone call from the city's auditor. The auditor, too, was concerned about the amount of outside testing. What was even more disturbing to him, many of the outside labs that DMH used were receiving more than $2,000 in business. The law required that dealings of this amount be covered by a contract and that these contracts be awarded on the basis of competitive bidding. None of DMH's outside sources were under contract.

In response to the auditor's prompting, Graham set out to learn, in detail, how the process worked. He found that physicians who wanted a test performed by an outside laboratory filled out a four-part form and delivered it (together with the specimen) to the secretary of one of the medical staff. (About ten or twelve secretaries throughout the hospital processed these requisitions.) The secretary sent a messenger, with one copy of the requisition, to the invoice once where the requisition was assigned an invoice number, authorizing payment for the test. The invoice number was filled in on the remaining three copies, the secretary obtained a cab voucher, and the messenger delivered the specimen and two copies of the requisition, via cab, to the outside lab. The remaining copy stayed with the secretary and was eventually filed in the patient's record. When it had performed the tests, the lab returned the results and one copy of the requisition to the DMH secretary (who transmitted the results to the doctor) and retained the second copy for its records. Periodically, the lab submitted a bill to the DMH invoice once, listing all the tests it had performed by invoice number. The invoice office matched the numbers with its copies of the requisitions, paid the outside lab, and sent the requisition copies to the hospital's billing office, so the costs could be billed to patients and third-party reimbursers.

The system seemed to work reasonably well except for several problems. First, messengers from the outside labs who delivered test results (and sometimes picked up requisitions and specimens) often got lost in DMH and delivered material to the wrong location. Second, the invoice office's copy of the requisition frequently

EXHIBIT 40-2 Dover Municipal Hospital: Summary of Outside Laboratory Tests for January 1976

Test	Number of Tests	Price	Total
Ag Titer to Crystococcus	3	$20.00	$60.00
Alcohol Level*	42	16.00 **	672.00
Alkaline Phosphatase — Fractionated*	2	10.00	20.00
Alpha Fetoglobin	2	11.00	22.00
Amino 8 Organic Acids	1	10.00	10.00
Aminophylline Level	1	23.00	23.00
Analysis of Kidney Stone	2	9.50	19.00
Analysis of Urinary Calculus	2	9.50	19.00
Anti-Mitochondrial Antibodies	1	16.50	16.50
Anti-Smooth Muscle Antibodies	1	16.50	16.50
Anti-Toxoplasma Antibodies	1	18.00	18.00
Australian Antigen (H.A.A.)	77	4.75	365.75
Barbiturate Level	3	16.5	49.50
Calcium*	64	6.50	416.00
Carcinoembryonic Antigen	11	30.00	330.00
Catecholomines	1	16.00	16.00
Chromosomes	1	100.00	100.00
Cortisol*	12	20.00	240.00
CPK — Fractionated*	1	8.00	8.00
CPK — Isoenzymes*	22	19.50	429.00
Digitoxin Level*	1	25.00	25.00
Digoxin Level*	19	21.00 **	399.00
Dilantin Level*	20	25.00 **	500.00
Dilantin & Phenobarb Level	1	25.00	25.00
Drugs of Abuse	1	35.00	35.00
Elavil & Thorazine Level	1	20.00	20.00
Estradiol Level*	13	38.00 **	494.00
Fats*	1	6.00	6.00
Febrile Agglutinins	1	10.00	10.00
Fluorescent Treponema Antibodies	1	9.00	9.00
Free T-4	90	18.00	1,620.00
FSH*	15	22.00 **	330.00
Gamma Glutamyl Transpeptidose	1	10.00	10.00
Gastrin Level	5	22.00	110.00
Histoplasma Compliment Fixation	1	29.25	29.25
Immonoglobulin E	1	15.00	15.00
17 — Ketogenic Steroids*	1	18.00	18.00
17 — Ketosteroids*	1	12.00	12.00
Lap Stain*	1	5.00	5.00
Latex Fixation*	1	11.00	11.00
Leucine Amino Peptidose	1	5.00	5.00
LH	15	22.00 **	330.00
Lithium Level	1	9.00	9.00
Luteinizing Hormone	1	19.50	19.50

Mercury Level*	2	$6.00	$12.00
Metanephrine	1	20.00	20.00
Myoglobin	1	10.00	10.00
Mysoline Level*	2	18.00 **	36.00
Parathyroid Hormone	13	49.50	643.50
Phenobarb Level*	2	16.50	33.00
Phenothiazine Screen	1	3.50	3.50
Phosphorus*	2	4.40	8.80
Pregnanetriol	13	23.00 **	299.00
Progesterone* 17 — OH	15	24.00 **	360.00
Progesterone	3	25.00	75.00
Prolactin Assay*	13	30.00	390.00
Protein Analysis*	1	38.50	38.50
Protein Electrophoresis	1	24.00	24.00
Rast Profile	1	70.00	70.00
Renin Level*	16	25.00	400.00
Rubella	18	8.00	144.00
Salicylate Level*	1	5.00	5.00
Semen Analysis	1	10.00	10.00
Sensitivity to 5 FC	1	15.00	15.00
Sub B Unit Level	1	21.00	21.00
Sweat Test*	1	35.00	35.00
Tegretol	1	18.00	18.00
Testosterone*	16	32.00 **	516.00
Testosterone Doxycortisol	1	20.00	20.00
Theophylline Level	10	12.00	120.00
Toxic Screen (blood)	70	13.00 **	910.00
Toxic Screen (urine, gastric)	35	13.00 **	455.00
Valium Level*	2	15.00	30.00
Zarontin Level	1	15.00	15.00
	690		$11,634.30

*Can be performed at DMH.
**Average cost.

did not arrive in the billing office until long after the patient had been dismissed. Finally, there was no way for the invoice office to know if a test for which it was billed had actually been performed. It was standard practice for the invoice once to pay outside laboratory bills even if the invoice number could not be matched.

When a physician wanted a test done by one of the DMH labs, he obtained the specimen and filled out one of several different in-house, four-part requisition slips, depending on which lab did the test and what test it was. He then "stamped" the requisition with the patient's name and hospital number. One copy of the requisition stayed in the doctor's department for inclusion in the patient's record, and three copies, together with the specimen, were sent to the laboratory where the test was performed. The lab kept one copy of the requisition, sent one back with the test results, and sent the third to the DMH billing office so the patients and third-party reimbursers could be billed. (Instead of doing the work themselves, physicians could simply ask that a test be performed. In that case, a technician drew the specimen and a secretary filled out the requisitions.) The only substantial problem in this procedure occurred when a physician failed to provide the patient's name and number, or did so illegibly, so that subsequent billing was impossible.

Graham discovered several reasons why physicians sent tests to outside labs:

Sometimes the senior staff just decided that it made sense to use tests we couldn't or hadn't been performing. We also had some senior staff who ran laboratories outside DMH, and they might say to the house officers, "When you need an Australian antigen, send it to my lab, because I know they do it the way I like it done." They might even ask — as they made their rounds with the house staff — why Australian antigen tests hadn't been ordered for some patients and direct that they be ordered.

A lot of other tests went out because the physicians thought our labs did poor work or because they'd had a fight with the lab chief. The head of hematology had chewed out a lot of interns and residents for criticizing so they tried to avoid his lab. Sometimes a fleeb (the person who draws the blood sample) would mix up specimens, so a physician would get wildly

fluctuating results and conclude it was because the lab wasn't testing properly. Some of the newer interns and residents just didn't know what tests our labs could do.

Graham also discussed with several house physicians and lab chiefs the issue of contracting for outside laboratory services. They were all adamantly opposed to the concept.

City Hall had suggested that we give all the outside work to one laboratory, but there were some reasons why this didn't make sense. If you go to the lowest bidder, you may get someone with poor quality control. Then, once they've got your contract, they may begin to cut comers or reserve their fastest service for other customers. We also were using some small specialty labs that were doing work for us almost as a favor, and the price at a big lab under contract would almost certainly be much more.

I told all this to the auditor, but be wouldn't budge. He wanted everything over $2,000 under contract. He didn't care about the diffculties, and he didn't care if it cost more money. Those were my problems. He just wanted to satisfy the legal requirements for a contract.

41
DCI

In early 1979, DCI, a major telecommunications company in the Southwest, faced a shrinking market share in certain of its product lines due to increased competition. Top management at DCI was extremely concerned over this turn of events and was certain that this trend would continue and affect many of its other products. In response, top management at DCI decided to restructure and expand their marketing management division in the hopes of regaining their dominance in the market place.

DCI's new marketing strategy revolved around new product development and technological improvements which could be used to upgrade and modify their existing products. This strategy was prompted because of the rapid influx of many new and smaller competitors into DCI's market as a result of federal deregulation. These companies had some competitive advantages over DCI. They were smaller and could respond more rapidly to changes in the market place. They were also able to exploit new technology by buying state-of-the-art equipment from others and packaging this equipment in their own unique constellations. They were also able to vary price structure more than DCI be-

cause of lower capital investment costs.

In June 1979, the entire Marketing Management Division of DCI was expanded and restructured (see Exhibit 41-1), with many current employees promoted or transferred and new people hired. Jim Roberts, a former marketing manager with ten years experience at DCI, was designated as Vice President and head of Corporate Marketing. Roberts quickly determined that DCI's diversity of clients required that a market segmentation strategy was necessary in order to understand and serve each major market. Therefore, a unit was created within the division to study and service the hotel/motel industry.

The new manager of the hotel/motel unit was Debbie Drater. Drater was hired from a high-technology, non-direct competitor with a reputation for sophistication in market strategy.

In December 1979, Debbie Drater and Jim Roberts announced the development of a new product targeted specifically for the hotel/motel industry. The product was a Property Management System (PMS) designed to monitor the usual hotel/motel functions, such as check-in, check-out, housekeeping, wake-up, etc., and additionally, to perform such novel functions as

1981 copyright John Aboud, Ph.D., President, Organization Dimensions, Inc., Richmond, VA, Virginia Commonwealth University; Joseph Weintraub, Ph.D., Babson College; Neal Thornberry, Ph.D., Babson College. This case is meant to be used in class discussion only. It is not meant to illustrate either effective or ineffective management or administrative techniques.

EXHIBIT 41-1 Partial DCI Organizational Structure

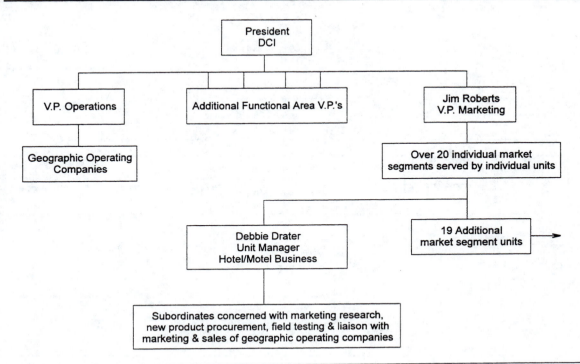

local call registration, energy control in all parts of the hotel, and front-desk accounting. The corporate objectives of offering such a property management system from Jim Roberts' point of view were:

a. The development of a turn-key concept in communications (i.e., one-stop shopping for all of a client's communication needs).
b. A desire to meet the needs of the hotel/motel industry.
c. An introduction of a technologically advanced product that would broaden the base of DCI's offerings.

Since the Property Management System (PMS) was new, and DCI had no experience along this line, a field trial was set up to "debug" the PMS system. From Debbie Drater's perspective, the field trial would provide the following information:

a. A data base for making appropriate changes in the product and/or the techniques of introduction.
b. The development of a marketing plan for the new system.
c. An identification of the successes and failures associated with the introduction of a new computer system.
d. An assessment of the behavioral impact of a new high technology system on the hotel staff and guests.

The PMS was developed by DCI in collaboration with Techni-Lab, a computer hardware and software manufacturer as well as one of the world's largest communications organizations. The PMS consisted of a Techni-Lab computer system integrated with standard DCI manufactured equipment.

The field trial began in February 1980 at The Carlton Hotel in San Antonio, Texas (see Exhibit

EXHIBIT 41-2 Partial Organizational Chart: The Carlton

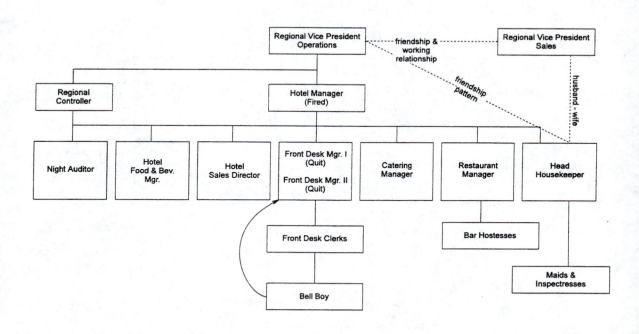

41-2). The Carlton was part of the Ripley organization, one of the world's largest hotel chains. The Carlton was chosen by DCI as its test site since its existing telecommunications equipment could adapt easily to the new technical hardware. From The Carlton's management viewpoint, the field trial allowed the hotel to test, without financial cost, an innovative system that would give the hotel a marketing edge over its competition as well as save energy at a time when energy costs were skyrocketing. The field trial at The Carlton was to take place in two phases starting in February 1980 and ending in June 1980 (see Exhibit 41-3).

The run during Phase I was not uneventful. The most serious problems were the down time during occasional "crashes" of the system and resistance of some of the hotel staff. Nevertheless, the trial was considered to be successful, and Phase II began. Unfortunately, the experience with Phase II was even more difficult.

The computer system was often down, requiring The Carlton to allow guests to leave with bills deferred for later billing because the old manual system for posting the bills had been completely removed and there was no way to extract them from the new system. Additionally, the hotel staff were not always sufficiently familiar with the operation of the system to use it effectively, and the manuals were poorly written and of little help.

Even more serious were the personnel changes at The Carlton during the field trial. At the beginning of Phase II, The Carlton's manager, who was supportive and knowledgeable about the PMS, was fired. This firing occurred because the hotel was overbooked by 40 percent and several flight attendants from a large airline were among the many who could not be accommodated. Inasmuch as their airline had booked and paid for these rooms in advance, the flight attendants requested help in finding alternative arrangements. Because of a convention in town, the hotel found many unaccommodated, grumbling

EXHIBIT 41-3 Field Trial at The Carlton

1. Background

The installation took place in two phases that had the following features:

Phase I Features (February-March)

This part of the Property Management System (PMS) provides a modular computerized data collection and display system integrated with the hotel PBX to perform the following basic hotel/motel functions:

1. *Room Status Management*

   Provides information on the status of each room in the property and assists the hotel personnel in the performance of the room management function.

2. *Housekeeping*

   Updates and displays housekeeping information to provide instantaneous status on the housekeeping conditions of the rooms in the hotel. The system also includes provisions for monitoring the assignment of maids and provides the means for reporting the housekeeping data.

3. *Automatic Wake-up*

   Operating automatically through the telephone lines, this feature will wake guests at a predesignated time with a prerecorded wakeup message.

4. *Night Audit*

   Audit displays are available for local telephone charges, wake-up summaries and house summaries to assist the night auditor in the performance of his/her functions. The audit can also be printed by the journal printer, providing hard copy.

Phase II Features (March-June)

Expansion is possible through the addition of optional features that enhance the basic system. Each of these features is modular and can be added to the system to provide additional operational and management control of the hotel/motel, such as:

1. *Guest Directory*

   A list of the current guests and their respective rooms occupied at the hotel is provided by this feature.

2. *Guest Ledger*

   The Guest Ledger/Charge Collection feature permits the collection of guest charges at revenue collection areas such as restaurant, pool, pro shop, etc., for allocation to the guest folios. This information is instantly posted electronically on the guest folio.

3. *Energy Control*

   Energy Control consists of a number of remotely located control units under control of the PMS System. The control units can turn off any power-consuming device capable of being electrically controlled. Once certain operating parameters are selected at installation, operation is completely automatic. Intervention is necessary only when the innkeeper elects to alter one of the initial operation conditions.

---

guests milling about the lobby. Since it was also running thin on staff, the hotel was unable to help them. The flight attendants called their airline headquarters in New York for help, reaching the vice president of personnel, who in turn called the hotel manager at 7:00 p.m. The hotel manager, who had been harassed and verbally insulted by stranded guests in the lobby, assumed that the vice president speaking to him was another flight attendant and hung up on her. She, in turn, immediately called the regional operations vice-president of the Ripley chain and demanded that the hotel manager be fired. Within a half an hour of the phone call, the hotel manager was discharged and was last seen loading his personal furniture on a rental truck the next day. Upon hearing the hotel manager was fired, the front desk manager, who was a friend of the hotel manager and also a supporter of the PMS, quit his job.

The next day, the bell captain was promoted to front desk manager and the regional operations vice-president assumed control of the day-to-day operations of the hotel. After two days, the newly-appointed front desk manager quit, citing the pressure of the new job. He took a job in another hotel as a bellhop. One Carlton employee referred to these frequent changes as reflecting "soap opera management."

Other dynamics at The Carlton proved important. The head housekeeper of The Carlton was married to a vice president of the Ripley organization and lived on the property, as did the regional operations vice president, who was now running the hotel. During Phase I, the head housekeeper was given a CRT (visual display) to allow her to enter and audit housekeeping data in the system. Noticing that she could also monitor the activity of the front desk on her CRT, she used it in her long-standing conflict with front desk personnel. She would call the front desk each time the front desk took an action she did not approve of, especially when a room was rented before she punched in that it had been completely cleaned, even though it was known to be ready. She also stormed the front desk from time to time, yelling and berating them for their incompetence.

Due to complaints from the front desk personnel, her CRT was taken away in Phase II and replaced by one with limited ability to monitor non-housekeeping functions. She complained vociferously to her husband and the regional operations vice president. Her full-function CRT was returned the next day.

As a result of her negative feelings, she decided not to inform her maids to leave the fans of the individual room heating/airconditioning units in the "on" position. The computer system required this setting if the heating/airconditioning unit was to be controlled remotely from the front desk and thereby achieve energy savings. Further, the head housekeeper did not make an attempt to maintain the work standards of her maids, who had slowed down in anticipation of a "speed up" due to the PMS. Design problems were also evident. The billing keyboard of the PMS at the front desk was the reverse of standard calculator keyboards. This resulted in slowed punching and errors when the front desk was under pressure to speed up at busy times. The night auditor/night manager who was undertrained on the system was hostile to it and badmouthed the system because she no longer felt important, as the system would do her auditing job. She also had fears that she might be dis-

charged as no longer being needed. This was not true, but her fears were real to her. No one told her this was a field trial and that it might be a long time before a system was operational. Nor was she told that the regional operations vice president had made a commitment to DCI to keep her regardless of the system's capability, as she was needed to run the hotel at night and to use the system to prepare daily summary reports for him.

A further difficulty came about because the assignment of responsibility for maintaining the system was not clear. DCI expected their local office to provide training for the hotel staff and maintain the system with the help of Techni-Lab. The local office had received a transfer of funds from the corporate office for this purpose; however, once it was expended, the local office refused to commit its own resources to the project. Also, they lacked the expertise to deal with the frequent hardware problems. Techni-Lab was most reluctant to expend any effort to support the system as it was (unknown to DCI) in the process of phasing out of the computer business. The problems became so severe that after contact at the top levels of both companies and the commitment of more funds from DCI, the team of Techni-Lab engineers responsible for the development of the system's hardware and software were flown to San Antonio for the remainder of the field trial.

When the Techni-Lab engineers arrived at The Carlton, one hotel employee who had experienced all of the changes associated with the new PMS was heard remarking, "I don't know why everyone is so concerned with this system since it's never going to work here."

42

Space Support Systems, Incorporated

Space Support Systems, Incorporated (SSS) is a small but growing corporation located in Houston, Texas, adjacent to NASA's Manned Spacecraft Center. The corporation was founded four years ago with the objective of obtaining government contracts for research studies, for preliminary development in space suit technology, and for studies in other areas of environmental systems connected with space flight. At present, twenty-five people are associated with Space Support Systems.

The company was founded by its current president, Robert Samuelson, for the specific purpose of bidding on a study contract for an extravehicular hard suit (a special type of space suit) with lunar, and possibly Mars, capabilities. At the time of the company's inception, Samuelson, James R. Stone, and William Jennings comprised the entire Space Support Systems company.

Mr. Samuelson, the president, is forty-seven years old, holds a B.S.E.E. degree from a large southern state university, and prior to forming Space Support Systems, was a senior engineer with North American. He has worked for several large aircraft corporations since his graduation from college twenty-five years ago. The present venture, however, represented a technologically new slant for him.

James R. Stone, vice-president and director of Technological Research, is thirty-eight years old. He has a Ph.D. in physiology from a leading West Coast university and had, prior to the inception of Space Support Systems, taught for six years at a leading university. He also has degrees in the field of aeronautical engineering. He worked for two years in the aeronautics industry before returning to school to work toward his doctorate in aerospace applications. Dr. Stone's reputation among his colleagues in both the theoretical and creative aspects of aerospace environmental control is quite good.

William Jennings, vice-president and director of Technology Applications, is forty-two years old. After graduating from high school, he attended college for three years before a shortage of funds forced him to quit school and seek employment in the then-lucrative aircraft industry. While in college, he majored in mechanical engineering. For three years prior to joining SSS, Mr. Jennings worked on an air force contract that involved the development of high-altitude flight suits. His particular specialty was in the development and construction of functional

Chapter 13, "Space Support Systems, Incorporated" (pp. 59 -- 67) from *Organizational Behavior: Cases and Situations* by B. J. Hodge, Herbert J. Johnson, and Raymond L Read, Copyright ©1974 by Harper & Row, Publishers, Inc.

EXHIBIT 42-1 Organizational Chart of Space Support Systems, Incorporated

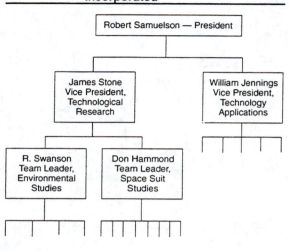

flight suits for initial testing, but he also showed considerable insight in new developments and changes in designs that were submitted to him prior to final construction. His reputation was such that Mr. Samuelson had been prompted to seek him out to join SSS four years ago.

The current organization chart for Space Support Systems is shown in Exhibit 42-1. There are two branches under Dr. Stone—the Environmental Studies Team and the Space Suit Studies Team. The Environmental Studies Team is primarily concerned with studies on environmental and physiological systems in spacecraft and modular structures for lunar (and other planetary) habitation. At present, there is no hardware output from the company along these lines. The team leader is Roger Swanson, and there are four men under him. Roger is thirty- three years old and has a master's degree in biology. He is highly respected by his peers and well thought of by Dr. Stone.

The Space Suit Studies Team works on study contracts investigating either hard or soft space suits used primarily for extravehicular use. Its members have also worked on suits for wear within the spacecraft. Composed of bright men, the Team is led by Don Hammond, who is twenty-eight years old and has a master's degree

in physiology. He has had many opportunities to return to school to work on a Ph.D. but has elected to stay with the company each time. He is considered extremely bright and, while not as old as most of the men on his team, he is unanimously accepted as the leader. On occasion, Don and Dr. Stone have had differences of opinion, and while the two do not seem to like each other personally, they respect each other's professional abilities and qualifications.

Much of the actual management and leadership of both these teams comes from Dr. Stone. The team leaders serve as depositories for information and as spokesmen for their groups, rather than as centers of responsibility and authority. These teams are, for the most part, college-educated and well qualified technically. The average age of the fourteen men under Dr. Stone is thirty-one years, and the average number of college degrees per man is 1.6.

Bill Jennings's area is responsible for actually developing and building suits for testing and presentation to NASA. This function is a logical extension of the work of the Space Suit Studies Team and requires a close coordination between the two groups. The five men under Jennings are all skilled technicians who are actually the craftsmen who build the technological systems. None of them has a college degree, although two of the men completed junior college. The average age of these men is forty- three years. They work together well and have formed a close-knit work unit. Jennings may often be found in the middle of the group working on some aspect of building mockups of functional space suits. The group is quite autonomous and functions with little direction from Mr. Samuelson.

Mr. Samuelson had never had any managerial problems in SSS that he knew of. The work had always run along fairly smoothly and, being very project-oriented, the company's employees seemed to be constantly busy with one job or another. Mr. Samuelson had to be engaged in the work of obtaining contracts and serving as a liaison with the government once a contract was secured. As a result, he knew that he might not have as thorough knowledge as he should regarding the inner workings of the SSS organization. He particularly realized that he had little feedback from personnel in the firm, but since he had experienced no apparent difficulties, he felt that all must be going well.

One afternoon, Jennings came in to see Mr. Samuelson. Jennings seemed upset and it was apparent that something was on his mind.

Samuelson: What's on your mind, Bill?

Jennings: Bob, I have worked for you for four years and I have always enjoyed my work and, in particular, working under you. But I don't think I can continue to function much longer with Jim Stone's group hanging like an albatross around my neck.

Samuelson: I don't understand. What kind of problem are we talking about?

Jennings: Well, my group does its job, and does it well; now, we could do it much better if Don Hammond, in particular, would keep his nose out and let us work once a plan is submitted to us for building. I mean—that crew from Space Suit Studies think they are supposed to supervise our work. My men are proud of their jobs and of their work. But we are going to lose some of our best guys pretty soon if this meddling isn't stopped.

Samuelson: Have you discussed this with Stone?

Jennings: No. Jim's difficult to talk to. He looks down his nose at my group because we are not eggheads. One other thing—whenever I make a change that improves the suit, Hammond's crew gets upset, particularly when it is an obvious improvement.

Samuelson: We'll straighten this problem out, Bill, I promise. But what bothers me is that your group and Don's are supposed to work together.

Jennings: Yes, I know. But it has never worked out that way. They simply look over our shoulders and don't think we are competent to work with their precious designs — even when we can make them better—which is almost always.

The conversation was terminated when Sa-

muelson told Bill that he would look into the problem thoroughly. Bill seemed relieved that Samuelson was taking action.

The first thing the next morning, Mr. Samuelson asked Dr. Stone if he would drop by for a chat. Upon Dr. Stone's arrival, Mr. Samuelson asked him to be seated and opened the conversation.

Samuelson: Jim, how are things in your area? Any problems with the X-2B suit design?

Stone: No, we are working primarily on the breastplate design right now. I think we are ahead of our target schedule.

Samuelson: Bill mentioned some friction between his men and Don Hammond's group.

Stone: [Thinking a moment] Well — you know we have never gotten the support and cooperation from Bill's team that we need to do our job. Don's team has to have a significant amount of cooperation from Applications in order to do its job. We need to be able to work with Bill's group, to be there to make changes and alterations as needed. Their job is to build to our specifications and let them go from there. We have to provide continuing guidance, and Bill just won't accept it. On top of all this, Bill seems intent on putting his personal touch on each piece of hardware they build.

Samuelson: I don't understand.

Stone: He makes changes on his own, which alter the specs. His group often comes up with a different product from what we asked for. We can't do anything about it because he won't allow cooperation between our groups.

Samuelson: Are his changes worthwhile?

Stone: Oh, I suppose he has some good ideas. Yes, some of his changes were very imaginative and worthwhile. But the point is that his function is to build and ours is to create designs. His suggestions are sometimes worthwhile, but he should consult me before making any changes. That's why he is there and we are here. Otherwise, why don't we simply change the structure of the organization?

Samuelson: Are there any other problems that you have experienced?

Stone: No, otherwise things are fine. All in all, we don't really have any major problems. As long as everybody does his job and stays within bounds, everything functions fine. As I said before, only when someone usurps another's authority does a problem arise.

Samuelson: Well, thanks, Jim, you've been very helpful. Do you mind if I talk with Don about this problem?

Stone: No, go right ahead.

Mr. Samuelson immediately called in Don Hammond and opened the conversation.

Samuelson: Don, I'll get right to the point. How is the working relationship between your areas and Bill's?

Hammond: What relationship? Those guys won't do anything we say. We don't get along at all.

Samuelson: Why is this?

Hammond: I don't know. Maybe it's a defense mechanism.

Samuelson: Meaning what?

Hammond: Well, Mr. Samuelson, I think they resent us because we are educated. They want to do our jobs and don't seem to realize that they are not qualified. They want to do more than build suits; they seem to want to do our design function. They just aren't qualified. I really think they resent our superior knowledge. I have tried to get Dr. Stone to talk to them or you about this, but he seemed somewhat indifferent. I guess he finally did something though. Anyway, something has got to be done. We can't do our jobs if we can't give them guidance in the building of our suits.

Samuelson: Are their changes ever worthwhile?

Hammond: No.

Samuelson: Never?

Hammond: Oh, I suppose so ... sometimes. *[Hesitation]* But that's not the point. It's not their job. They just aren't qualified to tinker with our designs. Don't they realize that is why we spent all those years getting our degrees? Did I waste my time? If a bunch of guys with no education can do my job, maybe I'd be better off uneducated.

Samuelson: Of course not, Don. You and your team are top notch. But you must, by the very nature of the work, have a working relationship with Bill's group. If they can suggest improvements, all the better.

Hammond: Yes, I guess so. But we can't seem to work together. They don't clear their changes through me or Dr. Stone.

Samuelson: Well, we've never made a definite statement about the arrangement for changes, as far as I can remember.

Hammond: Mr. Samuelson, I think all their recommendations should come through me. I can then study their merits and decide on which ones should be accepted. However, they are just not qualified to design this type of equipment. They should stick to their jobs of building.

Mr. Samuelson closed the conversation by thanking Don for his frankness and promising to take action when he had all the facts.

Left alone, Robert Samuelson pondered this new turn of events. He had thought everything was just fine. The work seemed to be getting done — and now this.

He realized that after four years of the successful operation of Space Support Systems, he was faced with the first real test of his managerial abilities.

43
O Canada

Introduction

The Public Service Commission of Canada (PSC) is responsible for the provision of a comprehensive human resources management service to the fifty-two departments and agencies of the federal public service. In 1978, the commission operated through six branches. One of these, the Staff Development Branch (SDB), is the focus of the present case. The case examines the SDB in 1978 as it began to experience problems of financial restraint. The SDB was responsible for the provision of:

1. regularly scheduled courses in a variety of professional, technical, and general subjects;
2. regular and special courses for senior and executive managers;
3. specialized, custom-designed courses on a consulting basis as needed;
4. a research and development service on federal adult educational needs.

Created in 1967, the SDB had grown steadily. Its members were highly qualified professionals in their specific fields, and the SDB provided them with extensive training in adult education methods. The SDB served the federal government on a cost-recoverable basis. That is, it had to market courses and cover all of its costs, including overhead. Courses were sold to client departments at prices comparable to those charged for similar programs available on the open market. Prior to 1978, SDB enjoyed more business than it could handle. It had an excellent reputation, and there was no lack of funds within departmental training budgets.

In 1978, the SDB had about 250 members and was organized as shown in Exhibit 43-1. Each of the five directorates was a cost center, responsible for forecasting its own revenues and costs. Although the SDB technically operated on a "branch break-even" basis, each directorate operated on the assumption that it should cover costs.

The two largest directorates within the branch were the Directorate of Staff Development and Training (DSDT) and the Regional Operations Directorate (ROD). These provided the bulk of the regularly scheduled courses offered by the branch. The primary division of responsibility

Prepared by Bonnie J. Lovelace and Royston Greenwood, Department of Organizational Analysis, Faculty of Business, University of Alberta. Used by permission. This case was prepared as a basis of classroom discussion. The events portrayed are not meant to reflect on good or bad managerial practice.

EXHIBIT 43-1 Staff Development Branch

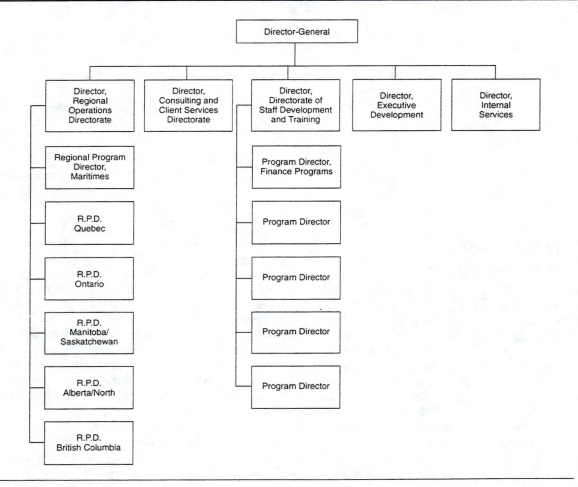

between the DSDT and the ROD was that the DSDT serviced the Ottawa region, where the vast bulk of the public service was located, and the ROD serviced the rest of Canada. The six regional units of the ROD and the DSDT operated the same courses, but in different locations.

Directorate of Staff Development and Training

The DSDT was organized in terms of six programs, each headed by a program manager and staffed by up to fourteen people (including two clerks). Each program had its special field and provided a full range of courses within that field.

Trainers within a program did most of their own course design and teaching and would hire outside consultants only for very special courses offered on a limited basis.

The client group of the DSDT included any public servant in the Ottawa region who was not a senior manager or an executive. The latter groups were serviced through the Executive Education Directorate. The DSDT trainers worked singly or in teams, depending on the course and their experience. Each trainer generally was responsible for one or two courses that would be taught ten to fifteen times a year.

Consulting and custom design work in the Ottawa region was not handled by the DSDT.

Such work would be handled through the Consulting and Client Services Directorate (CCSD). If a client department wanted a regular course to be run in-house and for itself alone (as opposed to sending participants to the DSDT's courses), the DSDT would "sell" an appropriate trainer to the Consulting Directorate. Regional units of the ROD also could use (and be charged for) DSDT trainers.

Marketing and registration for Ottawa courses were handled through the Internal Services Directorate. Program units within the DSDT concentrated on the provision of high-quality, regularly scheduled courses in Ottawa, leasing out trainers to consulting or to regional operations when time permitted and as need demanded.[1]

Essentially, the task facing the DSDT was reasonably straightforward: develop and teach courses in one city for a very large population. The directorate was large and operated through four levels of management providing a heavy schedule of repeated courses. Each of these levels of management had controls and pressures that affected the next.

Regional Operations Division

The ROD had a small headquarters group in Ottawa, headed by the director. The six regional offices were located in Halifax, Montreal, Toronto, Winnipeg, Edmonton, and Vancouver. Each regional office was headed by a regional program director and staffed by two or three full-time trainers, supported by a secretary, a registry clerk, and a student from Waterloo University who administered the Open Learning Systems Correspondence courses.

Regional offices catered to federal public servants in the regions and handled most SDB business within their area. The basic role of the ROD was to provide the same spectrum of

courses for the regions as was offered in Ottawa by the DSDT. However, because of the lower volume of demand, regional trainers were generalists and were required to teach and manage a variety of courses that in Ottawa were divided between the six program areas. The regional trainers were responsible for all administrative support services. They would design and advertise courses, prepare necessary materials, set up the classroom, teach, and assess the course. In addition, the regional trainers would administer, but not teach, a wide range of other courses. These courses would be taught by local consultants or Ottawa trainers (from DSDT) hired by the regional trainer.

The director and the trainers in the regions spent a considerable amount of time visiting clients, advertising programs, and putting out newsletters. The registry clerk spent most of her time contacting departmental training officers, looking for course participants. She also ensured that administrative letters and details were put out on time by the trainers. In addition, the trainers and director actively sought out consulting work, which they set up and discharged themselves.

The regions carried high overhead and travel expenses and had smaller clients with smaller budgets. The trainers were conscious that every penny counted. At the same time, quality had to be maintained. In times of trouble, most rules were set aside, and people within the regional offices worked together to generate new ideas for courses. The regional offices were small enough to encourage considerable face-to-face interaction.

Relationships between the DSDT and the regional offices of ROD were good before 1978. Many of the regional people had worked in the DSDT earlier in their careers. Two regional directors had worked through the ranks of the Otttawa division. Minor skirmishes had often occurred over the years, generally relating to problems with a few DSDT trainers who tended to head for the regions and demand that everyone from the director down should cater to their every whim. These few were well known, however, and avoided when possible. The Regional

[1]The regional trainer would monitor registration, provide all the pre-course counseling and advice, and administration. The Ottawa trainer could walk into a regional course ten minutes prior to commencement, secure in the knowledge that all would be in readiness. Often, the two would collaborate on some of the teaching and evaluate the course together. The regional trainer would provide all postcourse administration and follow-up.

Operations Directorate, however, deliberately sought persons who preferred smaller working groups, diverse tasks, and a great deal of autonomy. The DSDT tended more towards individuals who had a particular specialty and taught it, leaving their senior managers to handle the "paperwork." There was no question that Ottawa trainers felt strong ownership of "their" courses and, given the opportunity, wanted a say in the regions. The regional people taught "everyone's" courses, depending on the schedule, and were just as happy to find local people who could do the others with a little guidance.

From Boom to Bust

Prior to the spring of 1978, the SDB had enjoyed a booming business. There was no lack of funding in departmental training budgets, and the branch had all the business it could handle. Although the economy seemed to be slumping, it did not appear serious. Rumors, however, were circulating about cutbacks as the full force of the economic downturn began to make itself felt. The Treasury Board demanded thorough reviews of departmental budgets, and one of the first areas cut by most departments was training. The SDB, on full cost recovery, found its market suddenly less affluent.

In June 1978, the regional directors were in Halifax for their semi-annual meeting. They usually met in one of the regions during September for a general meeting and again in January in Ottawa for a budget meeting. This year, however, they were meeting in June because a major educational conference was taking place for two days at Dalhousie University, at which some of the top experts in the field were featured speakers. The regional directors had agreed with their boss, George Hudson, that they would work Sunday through Wednesday to handle regular business, leaving Thursday and Friday for the conference.

On Tuesday afternoon, the group was discussing what the ensuing months might hold....

I'm worried, mused Herb Aiken of Halifax. My registrations are dropping off, and we're looking at cancelling courses. You know what that means: trainers sitting around on the overhead with nothing to do.

Sarah Wilson from Edmonton concurred. She had just received a telex from her office informing her that a three-day course set to start the next day had just suffered seven last-minute cancellations.

That only leaves eight people; we can't do it, financially or pedagogically. And we've sunk training time and administrative costs into it. I'm going to have to call and tell my staff to contact the other participants and try to postpone. This is very bad for business though and we can't keep it up.

She left to make her call. Thomas Russell from Vancouver picked up the ball:

The funny thing is, our clients are willing to lose the one-third late cancellation penalty, rather than pay the whole course fee. Forecasting revenues is becoming impossible and we're barely keeping our heads above water. Where is this taking us?

George Hudson tried to soothe everyone's fears, saying everyone in Ottawa was still doing okay and was optimistic. The directors looked at one another, each silently thinking that it was always the regions that got hit first. It was easier for the Ottawa mandarins to make cuts where the pain wasn't staring them in the face every morning. At that moment, Sarah returned and told George there was an urgent phone call for him. He left, and the others continued to discuss the future. Hudson returned about ten minutes later, his face grim.

There's very bad news, he said flatly. Treasury Board issued a directive this morning stating that all nonessential training is to be reviewed and cancelled whenever possible. The phones are ringing off the wall and everything on our books is on hold until October or November.

The situation worsened during the summer. Regional trainers were out visiting their clients constantly, trying desperately to drum up business, selling a day's consulting here, working on a problem there. It was difficult. Many clients were in offices located significant distances from the regional centers. Regional directors, however, were on the rampage over travel costs and telephone bills. But, as one Toronto trainer said to her boss one day:

A letter a day just won't do it! We need to talk to them, get them to spend whatever money they've got on our courses rather than buying on the private market.

Alice Waters knew this was true, but she had to keep costs trimmed to the bone. The Treasury Board had told departments to trim training costs. Given their smaller budgets, many departments preferred to provide their own training or use consultants.

By late summer, a few courses were beginning to pick up registrants as people began to sort out their budgets. Some Ottawa courses were rescheduled, but there was still a lot of slack.

One morning, Sam Wisler of Winnipeg called Vancouver.

I just had a long talk with Mike White, the Financial Management Program manager. He wants to negotiate with us about having his trainers do all the resourcing on our regional financial courses from now on. Did a lot of talking about how we should be saving branch funds by keeping the money inside wherever possible.

Thomas Russell, listening carefully, said:

Well, in the past, we could never get their trainers, unless somebody wanted to visit his relatives and made a deal with us. All the regions hire local consultants for courses we don't teach ourselves. Saves all those travel costs. However, it's worth thinking about. What did you tell him?

Wisler replied:

Just that. We should all think about it. The way I see it, things are getting better, but we may never see those good times again. If we can get Programs to do some of our courses (which are the same ones being done in Ottawa), and for less than our local consultants can do it, we'll be helping each other. They've got a lot of trainers with expensive time on their hands, and we've got courses our own staff can't do, especially in EDP, Finance and Personnel. Maybe we can help each other. I think I should talk it over with Hudson, and see about putting out a telex to all regions on it. We could discuss it on our next teleconference.

By November 1978, both Ottawa and the regions had managed to reschedule most of their courses, but at drastically reduced registration levels. This meant costs were more or less the same, but revenues were way down. Even though the branch had an official policy that break-even was calculated on the branch level, everyone knew that cost centers losing money were vulnerable. And each program, each region, was a cost center. They closed ranks. People who had worked well together for years with colleagues in the other directorate suddenly discovered negative characteristics of which they had previously been unaware. ROD jealously defended its right to hire local resources; the DSDT stubbornly insisted that course manuals were their property. Each group saw the other as untrustworthy, and open communication virtually ended. This was on everyone's mind as the regional directors held a conference by phone one morning. George Hudson opened the discussion:

I've been getting feedback from all of you by telex on progress with Programs. My assessment so far is that they want to sell you their trainers' time to cut their overhead, and you're willing to buy it as long as charges are comparable to what it costs when you resource these programs locally. However, it appears that what they want to charge exceeds your local costs. Not only that, but each of you is negotiating separate agreements.

Thomas Russell broke in angrily:

You can say that again. Mike White wants to send me two trainers to do the four-day "Fundamentals of Budget Formulation and Control" course, and he wants a total of nineteen days of time plus travel costs to do it. But he offered to do it for Sarah with one trainer and fewer days of time. What's going on here?

Sarah's reply was consistent with what everyone had been experiencing.

The month my course is scheduled is one where most of Mike's trainers are booked. He gave me whatever time was left. It seems that they want to dump all their excess time on us. Well, our budgets won't take it.

Evelyn D'anjou in Montreal continued:

We've got to negotiate standard charges. And they must be reasonable ones, or we'll go to local, as we've always done when we had to rely on ourselves.

George Hudson, sensing that feelings were heating up and deciding a teleconference was not the best medium for this discussion, told everyone to sit back. He promised to meet with the DSDT Director, Bob Smythe, and talk things over as soon as possible.

The next day a furious Alice Waters was on the phone to George Hudson.

Things are getting totally out of hand. I phoned Mike this morning to tell him we couldn't accept the charges he wants for our next financial course, so I had hired the Jameson people to do it. He tells me that's just fine, but all those new regulations for budgeting are being worked into the course, and his people are the only ones who can do it. And he refuses to release the new course manual be-

cause he claims it's not in its final form. George, you know we can't do outdated courses in the regions. I have to have that course book. Those manuals are branch property, not DSDT property! The Programs develop them because that's part of their responsibility, but it's policy that they must be made available to the regions, because we have to offer the same course out here. Mike as much as hinted that we will all be having trouble getting manuals for the Programs from now on. He says when things were slack over the summer, they revamped many of our courses, but the changes are still being tested. We're being blackmailed!

Alice stopped, having run out of breath. George questioned her, giving her time to cool off a bit, but he was concerned. Alice was one of his best managers, a skilled trainer herself, and one who was more than able to negotiate solid agreements with her colleagues. If her problem-solving skills were not helping, they were in trouble.

Have you considered training some of your own staff to do the more specialized courses, Alice? Maybe we can reduce our dependence on the Programs that way.

Alice was not mollified:

George you know what our trainers do. Everything... teach, administer, market, consult, clean up classrooms, weekends in airports. They just don't have time for more. Besides, why train them to do a course that's only offered twice a year in their own region.... We have others that run frequently both on our regular schedule and on an in-house basis. But the Ottawa trainers only have their one or two little courses to think about. No marketing, no consulting. Even big training centers with everything done for them! They walk out of our classrooms on Friday night and don't clean up a thing! They say that's our job, not theirs. Well, we don't have big staffs catering to our small offices and it's our weekend, too.

But I'm getting off the topic... What about those course books? I've already telexed the other regions to warn them about what's happening.

Inwardly, Hudson groaned. Every one of his directors would be up in arms by the end of the day. He promised Alice he'd go to Bob Smythe, the director of DSDT, to talk matters over, and hung up. Glancing at his telephone, he could see the lights coming on; it was starting already. Thankful it was Friday, he told his clerk to hold the calls and left to find Bob Smythe.

A half hour later, Hudson returned, and dictated a telex: everyone was to sit tight. Smythe was meeting with his managers Monday morning to discuss the matter.

The following Tuesday, Hudson picked up the teleconference phone to address his regions. He wondered how much he'd get through before the protests began.

I just had a meeting with Bob Smythe. His managers claim we're doing outdated courses and that they should be given control of course content. They also believe we should hire their resources before any consultants to help minimize branch downtime. Smythe agrees with them, and they'd tabling the matter with the Director General at the next management committee meeting.

There was silence as the six listeners digested this news, each realizing the potential consequences. Then Sam Wisler in Winnipeg spoke angrily:

This is incredible They mant to make money at our expense! Are we working for the same place or aren't we? What the hell is going on here? We won't let those bastards get away with this!

Herb Aiken's language was much stronger, but the message was the same. Hudson listened to the chorus of angry voices for a while and then asked for everything in the way of financial ammunition, details of travel costs, local costs,

and Programs charges. Then he ended the call.

The SDB Management Committee came to the conclusion that branch resources should be used whenever possible to teach branch courses. The regions and the Programs were instructed to work out standard charges to be used in the January budget exercise for the 1979-80 fiscal year. The point was noted that the regions had to provide up-to-date courses; and if that involved using the DSDT resources, that was the way things had to be.

In January 1979, two of the regional directors came to Ottawa to meet two representatives from the DSDT. The objective was to settle standard charges for all courses. Preparation time, teaching time, travel time, and administrative responsibilities would be fixed. Ratios were to be agreed upon and used as formulas for all courses in the future. Alice Waters and Sarah Wilson had canvassed the other regional directors on acceptable alternatives and had full authority from them to act. They had requested that the two DSDT representatives come with the same authority, as time was running out. The group met for a full day on the Monday; and by the end of it, the two regional directors were exhausted and frustrated. The DSDT representatives were demanding costly ratios, were not giving an inch, and had to take back any proposals to their own director for his approval. And he was away until Wednesday.

That night Alice and Sarah paid a late night visit to Hudson, venting their anger openly. The regions could not survive the charges being imposed by DSDT. It seemed that the SDB had some fundamental decisions to make about its internal affairs, decisions that were beyond the authority of Wilson and Waters. Those decisions had to be made before the new budgets were drafted.

Despite meeting again on Tuesday and Wednesday, the DSDT and ROD representatives failed to agree on standard charges. The matter was again put to the Management Committee. The committee reiterated its position that in-house resources had to be used and decided that the regions would have to live with the Program demands.

In March 1979, the Regional Operations Directorate tabled its budget for the 1979-80 fiscal year. It showed a substantial projected loss. The DSDT tabled its budget, showing a substantial projected profit.

Epilogue

The conflict that began between the ROD and the DSDT eventually spread to all directorates in the SDB as profits continued to decline for the next two years. The management issues were not resolved. Eventually, the director general of the SDB left to assume new responsibilities, and a new director general was appointed. He made sweeping management changes and restructured the objectives of the branch and most of its divisions. Courses were to be completely standardized, printed, and made available to all trainers. Breaking even financially became mandatory at the cost-center level (where it had always, in reality, been). The DSDT and ROD were joined together under one director. A massive study of the regions was undertaken to determine profitability in the face of continued economic problems. Eventually, all four western provinces were combined into one region for financial reporting purposes. The entire staff of the branch was technically laid off (achieved through a complicated process of wiping out everyone's position and then reinstating these positions in slightly modified form), and then all were invited to compete for any job in the "new" branch. In the face of so much uncertainty, morale had sunk and many competent people left.

Some of the outcomes described above may possibly have resulted even if the branch had been able to resolve the issue and ROD and DSDT had worked out their differences. The drastic decline in revenues would eventually have demanded changes. Nevertheless, the bitterness that arose between the two directorates provided a lesson to all managers who had been involved, and the present management holds frequent meetings where problems are aired and solved by the parties involved where possible.

However, a strong current of bitterness remained for a long time.

44
Datatrak: Dealing With Organizational Conflict

Goals

I. To illustrate the types of conflict that can arise within a work group.

II. To provide the participants with an opportunity to experience and deal with organizational conflict.

III. To help the participants to identify effective and ineffective methods of resolving conflict.

Group Size

Twenty-six to thirty participants.

Time Required

Two to two and one-half hours.

Materials

I. One copy of the Datatrak Background Sheet for each participant.

II. Seven or eight copies of the Datatrak Accounting Department Sheet (one for each of the six department members and one for each of the department's observers).

III. Six or seven copies of the Datatrak Purchasing Department Sheet (one for each of the five department members and one for each of the department's observers).

IV. Six or seven copies of the Datatrak Operations Department Sheet (one for each of the five department members and one for each of the department's observers).

V. Seven or eight copies of the Datatrak Marketing Department Sheet (one for each of the six department members and one for each of the department's observers).

VI. One copy each of the following role sheets (a different sheet for each of the twenty-two participants who are designated as department members):

1. Datatrak Accounting Role Sheets 1 through 6;

2. Datatrak Purchasing Role Sheets 1 through 5;

3. Datatrak Operations Role Sheets 1 through 5; and

4. Datatrak Marketing Role Sheets 1 through 6.

Prepared by David J. Foscue and Kenneth L. Murrell. Reprinted from: J. William Pfeiffer and Leonard D. Goodstein, (Eds.), *The 1984 Annual: Developing Human Resources*, San Diego, CA: University Associates, Inc., 1984. Used with permission.

VII. One copy of the Datatrak Observer Sheet for each observer.

VIII. A name tag for each participant. Prior to conducting the activity, the facilitator completes twenty-two of these tags with the job titles appearing on the role sheets and each of the four to eight remaining tags with the word "Observer."

Physical Setting

A room with movable chairs and plenty of space to accommodate four separate groups as well as a group-on-group configuration (see Process, Step VII).

Process

Step I. Assigning Roles

After announcing that the participants are to be involved in an activity that deals with organizational conflict, the instructor forms four groups and designates them as follows:
1. The Accounting Department (seven or eight participants);
2. The Purchasing Department (six or seven participants);
3. The Operations Department (six or seven participants); and
4. The Marketing Department (seven or eight participants).

Each group is seated at a separate table.

Step II. Distributing Background Sheets

Each participant is given a copy of the background sheet and a copy of the appropriate department sheet. The participants are instructed to read these handouts, beginning with the background sheet.

Step III. Selecting Roles

Within each department, the instructor distributes the appropriate role sheets and gives each remaining member a copy of the observer sheet.

All participants are asked to read their sheets, but are cautioned not to share the comments.

Step IV. Distribute Name Tags and Explain Activity

Each participant is given a name tag that identifies his or her role. The instructor has the participants put on their tags. The instructor emphasizes the importance of maintaining roles during the role play and then elicits and answers questions about the task. After telling the department managers that they have thirty minutes in which to conduct their meetings and their decisions, the instructor tells the groups to begin.

Step V. Announce Decisions

At the end of the thirty-minute period, the instructor stops the group meetings and asks the managers to spend five minutes announcing their decisions to their subordinates and explaining their rationales.

Step VI. Conclude Roles

The role plays are concluded. The observers are asked to provide their groups with feedback, and the remaining members within each group are asked to share their reactions to the feedback.

Step VII. Process Roles

The four managers are instructed to form a circle in the center of the room, and the remaining participants are asked to form a circle around the managers. The instructor leads a discussion with the managers, requesting that the remaining participants listen but not participate. The following questions form the basis of the discussion:

1. How did the details of your role affect the way in which you directed the department meeting? How did these details affect your decision?
2. How might your decision have been differ-

ent if you had not been required to play a role?

3. How did you deal with the conflicts that arose?

4. How effective were your methods for managing conflict?

Discussion Questions

After the managers have completed their discussion, the instructor leads a total-group discussion by eliciting answers to the following questions:

1. What were the consequences of your role behavior during this activity?

2. How did you feel about the constraints that your role placed on you?

3. How did the roles in your group affect the interaction of the members?

4. How might you have behaved in the same situation if you had not been required to play a role?

5. In your back-home work group, what methods does your supervisor use to manage conflict? How effective are these methods?

6. What steps can you take in the future to help to manage conflict in your own work group?

EXHIBIT 44-1 Datatrak Background Information

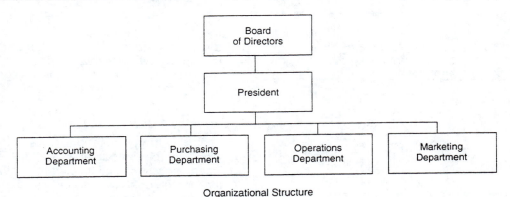

Organizational Structure

Products

Datatrak manufactures computer hardware and software designed to meet the specific needs of individual customers.

Organizational Objectives

The company's objectives are as follows:

- To manufacture computers designed to meet the specific needs of individual customers.
- To accomplish manufacturing in a manner that is cost effective to customers and that generates substantial revenue for the company and its stockholders.

Present Situation

The country is currently in the worst recession that it has ever experienced. Unemployment has reached 30 percent and is rising. The Stock market has closed each day for the past several months in a downward trend that, some economists fear, may lead to a stock-market crash.

Datatrak, your employer, is feeling the effects of the recession and is presently trying to cope with a reduction in sales and profits. An outside auditing firm has audited the company's books and determined that if the company is to survive the recession, it must reduce expenses. Consequently, the board of directors has just announced that, as a cost-reducing measure, each department must lay off one employee. Each department manager has been asked to meet with his or her subordinates in order to elicit input and opinions regarding which position should be terminated; then the manager is to make the ultimate decision. The department meetings are to take place in a few minutes.

EXHIBIT 44-2 Datatrak Accounting Department Background Information

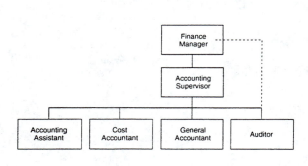

Job Descriptions

Finance Manager

Responsible for managing the Accounting Department and for presenting pertinent financial data to the president and the board of directors to facilitate timely and sound business decisions.

Accounting Supervisor

Responsible for directly supervising the accounting personnel and establishing and monitoring departmental budgets. Also responsible for other duties as assigned by management. Reports to the finance manager.

Accounting Assistant

Responsible for typing reports, providing assistance to the accountants and the auditor when necessary, and helping to put together the monthly operating report. Also performs a monthly bank reconciliation.

Cost Accountant

Responsible for accurately recording and classifying the cost of materials and properly accounting for work in progress, finished goods, and the cost of goods sold. Also responsible for providing the general accountant with this information for the preparation of the monthly operating report.

General Accountant

Responsible for preparing the balance sheet, the statement of income and retained earnings, the statement of changes in the financial position, and the monthly operating report.

Auditor

Responsible for ensuring that all departments

comply with company financial policies and procedures. Also responsible for conducting periodic audits of inventories as necessary. Reports to the accounting supervisor for routine matters, but has the authority to consult the finance manager or to report directly to the president regarding significant matters.

Rumors About the Department

1. The accounting supervisor has no real work other than to report weekly to the finance manager and then to communicate the manager's wishes to others.
2. The accounting assistant habitually arrives late, frequently socializes in the other departments, and often calls in sick.
3. The cost accountant is rumored to be interviewing for positions with several competing companies.

EXHIBIT 44-3 Datatrak Purchasing Department Background Information

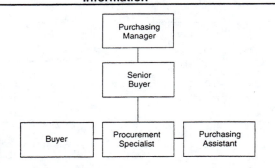

Job Descriptions

Purchasing Manager

Responsible for planning and supervising the effective procurement of materials and supplies requested by all departments within the company. Also responsible for ensuring that such items are bought after firm but fair negotiations and are delivered on a timely basis at the requested place and in excellent condition.

Senior Buyer

Responsible for planning and supervising the procurement of material and supplies re-

quested by all departments within the company. Also responsible for ensuring that such items are bought after fair negotiations and are delivered promptly and without damage.

Buyer

Responsible for procuring materials, equipment, and services at the lowest possible cost consistent with the requirements of sound company operation. Also responsible for selecting vendors through an evaluation of price, availability, specifications, and other factors.

Procurement Specialist

Responsibilities are the same as those of the buyer.

Purchasing Assistant

Responsible for providing stenographical and other services necessary to maintain and support the functions of the Purchasing Department. Duties include transcribing material from handwritten or typed copy to final form through the use of word-processing equipment and operating terminal equipment to transmit and store textual and statistical information.

Rumors About the Department

1. The buyer is receiving kickbacks from vendors.
2. The senior buyer is eligible for early retirement, but wants to work for a few more years to build a larger retirement fund. This person frequently arrives late and leaves early, apparently without regard for the consequences.
3. Although the company has a policy against nepotism, the procurement specialist has a close relative in upper management.

EXHIBIT 44-4 Datatrak Operations Department Background Information

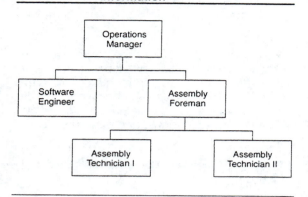

Job Descriptions

Operations Manager

Responsible for the final design, assembly, and packaging of all computer hardware and software. Also responsible for keeping assembly costs to a minimum while maintaining maximum quality and ensuring that all orders are completed on time. Supervises two people, a software engineer and an assembly foreman.

Software Engineer

Responsible for providing the software to meet each customer's needs. Also responsible for providing customers with manuals and training sessions on computer use and user language. Designs software diagnostic programs for troubleshooting the software packages. By virtue of experience and training, is the software expert in the company.

Assembly Foreman

Responsible for ensuring that computer parts are stored and assembled properly. Also responsible for checking each computer after assembly to ensure that it is operational, properly packaged, and sent to the warehouse. Makes sure that the proper tools and equipment are available to assemble each machine. Supervises assembly technicians I and II.

Assembly Technicians (I and II)

Responsible for assembling and packaging new computers and any spare parts required for existing computers, performing maintenance

on tools and equipment necessary for assembling, and delivering packaged computers to the warehouse for shipping. Strong background in electronics required for both positions.

Rumors About the Department

1. The assembly foreman is given to back stabbing and to frequent verbal outbursts that upset people throughout the organization.
2. The assembly technician II is a free spirit who is often late to work and frequently calls in sick.
3. The operations manager, who was the software engineer before being promoted, spends a lot of time helping the present software engineer.

EXHIBIT 44-5 Datatrak Marketing Department Background Information

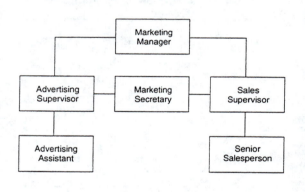

Job Descriptions

Marketing Manager

Responsible for effectively coordinating the delicate balance between the national coverage of advertising and sales. Exercises control over both the advertising supervisor and the sales supervisor in order to maintain this balance. Tasks include implementing budgets passed on by superiors, effectively reporting department sales to superiors, and informing superiors of advertising needed to maintain proper market coverage.

Advertising Supervisor

Responsible for managing all company advertising, maintaining a close relationship with the Operations Department in order to promote product lines, and advertising as effectively as possible within the limits of the budget. Works directly with the marketing manager.

Advertising Assistant

Responsible for preparing all advertising layouts and coordinating all advertising efforts with various media. Good art background required.

Marketing Secretary

Responsible for processing all paperwork for the department; answering all phone calls; and effectively managing all office equipment, such as copiers, typewriters, teletypewriter devices, and so forth.

Sales Supervisor

Responsible for setting all sales quotas, covering major accounts, and solving any and all major sales problems. Must be sensitive to market needs and must maintain a close working relationship with the Operations Department so that each sale can meet the customer's time requirements.

Senior Salesperson

Responsible for covering existing accounts in an assigned territory and acquiring enough new accounts to meet a quota.

Rumors About the Department

1. Although the company has a policy against nepotism, the sales supervisor is related to the president. Also, sales have been deteriorating since the sales supervisor has held this position.
2. The marketing manager spends many work days playing tennis.
3. The marketing manager shows favoritism toward the marketing secretary.

EXHIBIT 44-6 Datatrak Observer Instructions

During the department meeting, you are to listen and observe carefully and make notes regarding answers to the following questions. After the role play has been concluded, you will be asked to share these answers with the members of your department.

1. What types of conflicts arose?

2. What methods did the manager use to manage these conflicts?

3. How did the other department members respond to these methods?

4. How did the manager gather information from the subordinates?

5. How did he or she use that information to make the ultimate decision?

6. How would you describe the mood of the department at the beginning of the meeting?

7. How did this mood change as the meeting progressed?

IV
Organizational Decline, Turnaround and Design

45
TQM Implementation
at IS Pacific

Information Systems Pacific (IS Pacific) provides information systems (IS) support to the West Coast offices and facilities of a defense contractor, Apex Aerospace. Eighty percent of IS Pacific's services go to a single customer, Rotary Company. IS Pacific has a sister company, IS Atlantic, that supports the east coast offices of Apex—including the head office. IS Pacific, IS Atlantic and the organizations they support are all units of Apex.

In the late 1980s, anticipating defense industry downsizing, Apex senior management sought to achieve more efficient use of its resources. They focused on improving and enlarging Apex's non-defense businesses. Senior management anticipated that entering these markets, Apex would face increased competition, on the basis of price, product quality and customer service. To meet these new challenges, Apex senior management decided to restructure the entire Apex organization and then implement Total Quality Management (TQM).

At the same time that Apex senior management considered TQM implementation, Apex information resource managers planned a reorganization of all its information systems (IS) organizations, including IS Pacific. They considered off-loading some of the responsibility for programming to the IS organizations' customers. The application programmers—responsible for designing and maintaining software specific to each customer's business—were to become employees of each customer's organization. For IS Pacific, this produced a fifty percent reduction in headcount. The remaining 834 IS Pacific employees supported customer requirements for system programming and operations, hardware maintenance, network management, and computer skill training.

In February 1989, IS Pacific leadership started implementing the programs mandated by Apex management. The organization moved application programmers to its customer organizations and reorganized from a seven-level hierarchy to a five-level one with teams on the bottom level. The IS Pacific Organization Chart depicts this new organization (see Exhibit 45-1). The level 4 and level 3 managers comprised the leadership team. Aside from managing strategic issues, this team was responsible for developing TQM strategy and overseeing the implementation of that strategy.

Transition teams designed each level of the new hierarchy. These teams brought together individuals possessing the knowledge and experience to inform the design of each level of the

Prepared By Malu Roldan, Anderson Graduate School of Management, University of California, Los Angeles. Used with permission.

hierarchy. These individuals included highly experienced members of the department being designed, employees and managers from other IS Pacific divisions, and representatives from IS Atlantic, Rotary Company and other Apex units. Sheryl, a Quality Division level 2 leader, describes her experiences as a member of a transition team*:

> We had a transition team even at level 2 to look at the business management organization, to determine how the teams would be formed and which functional groups would go together to form a team. I think that was probably where we had problems because we have a wide variety of functions done in this area. And they're not real similar so it's hard to mix functions.

> I would say we had the most trouble with the role of the team leader. There was a lot of discussion whether or not they could survive without a level 1 leader, and many of people on the transition team were concerned about loss of a career path. There are a lot of people, especially young ones, who have been here just a few years and logically want to move on to the next step, perhaps supervisor. Then it seemed those positions didn't exist. That was an issue and also the issue of whether it was a team representative or team leader, not a level 1 supervisor. What would the functions be that that person would perform? How would they do that in addition to the regular workload and would they be compensated? Also, at that time we had the same questions that teams have now. Will they hire, will they fire, what will teams be responsible for? How much authority would they have, how far would they be able to go, how self-empowered would they really be? And I really think we kind of compromised in the end and realized that we were not gonna solve all those problems. We should just go ahead and organize and start working in teams and

some of the other things might [work themselves out].

> I think even though we had a list of concerns, the benefits that we saw outweighed those. I mean, in the same breath that someone would tell you they were very concerned, they would also tell you that they wanted to go ahead and try the team concept. I think that people were to the point where they wanted to work on a team and just get going, you know. It may not have really been that long if you look back on it, but you know we had been selecting level 4 leaders, level 9 leaders, level 2 leaders; and that's a long time to kind of be in a chaotic state and not know who you work for or what you do or where you'll end up.

Terry, Quality Division level 3 leader, discussed his regret that they did not provide enough guidance to the transition teams designing the work teams that comprised the lowest level of the IS Pacific hierarchy:

> The department leaders formed transition teams, and they let their transition teams recommend how to organize underneath. How to split out into teams, how to design the teams. One of my biggest regrets is we didn't at that point, as it was happening, we ourselves did not know how to design teams and still don't. So what we were essentially doing was our people were learning by trial and error.

After the work of the transition teams, the hierarchy ended up with essentially only three layers of management. The IS Pacific leadership team, deviating from IS Atlantic policy, decided to staff the layer just above the teams (level 1) sparingly. The official explanation was that teams were intended to eventually become self-managing, making level 1 managers superfluous. IS Pacific leaders thought it best not to establish a layer that they expected to remove eventually. IS Pacific level 0 employees were concerned about this policy since it differed from IS Atlantic's policy and meant that there

---

*To make quotations easier to read and to save space, ellipses are not used for every word omission.

EXHIBIT 45-1 IS Pacific Organization Chart

Organization member pseudonyms start with letters that signify their position in the 5 level IS Pacific organizational hierarchy: F for fourth (top level); T for third; S for Second; Z for zero.

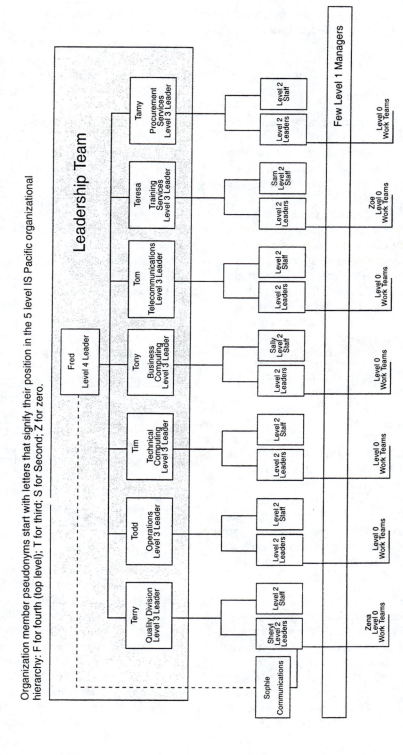

would be fewer management jobs available. Zena, one of the level 0 employees in the Quality Division, described her concerns over the reduction in management positions:

> When we started to form the teams, my most negative thought (and I was very negative on this) was, "Well, I'm going to have to completely rethink the way I think because if I'm not going to be in upper management—To me management was gone, okay?" There were few opportunities, basically only Sheryl's job. That would now be the job that I was desiring. Well, about 300 people will be desiring that job too. So, in other words, management is completely gone. That has always been everybody's drive. Basically, unless you wanted to be a technical person or whatever, that was the desire. For American people in general that is what everybody is working towards and it's more money. That is how I am compensated for my work, is money, and that is how I see that I'm gonna get money.

Furthermore, some level 2 managers felt that the nature of the work done in their department warranted an extra layer of management. Sheryl expressed her concerns:

> I was of fairly strong opinion that we needed to have level 1 supervisors in this area because of the wide variety of functions. The work is very important, and it's financial data. I was very concerned and still am that a level 2 leader with responsibility for so many functions is not going to be able to know all that detail and still spend time leading and providing coaching.

Despite these concerns, the IS Pacific leadership team remained committed to the policy of having no level 1 managers. The only exceptions involved areas that worked shifts during periods when no level 2 managers were present.

In October 1989, as transition teams were forming IS Pacific work teams, TQM implementation commenced. An in-house designed training program included off-the-shelf films and publications on TQM. Managers held sessions with their employees to discuss TQM principles. Outside consultants provided training on group dynamics at all levels of the organization. The leadership team also used outside consultants to facilitate its discussions of strategic issues.

Managers throughout IS Pacific applied a variety of implementation strategies but lacked a unified plan to coordinate their efforts. In December 1989, several level 2 employees, fresh from a TQM conference, pressed for the development of a unifying TQM implementation plan. On their suggestion, the leadership team and several cross-functional teams started developing a plan in January 1990. The plan was to spell out the implementation steps to be followed in the next five years. The goal was to define and establish a "supportive" organization culture, self-managing teams, procedures for identifying and managing quality improvement projects, and a customer service orientation.

Two months later, Apex senior management instituted cost-cutting measures to further counter the effects of defense cuts. From this point on, IS Pacific's leadership team became preoccupied with cost-cutting issues. The team delegated many strategic issues to cross-functional teams of employees from level 2 and below. These issues included the development of the implementation plan, design of a supportive culture, definitions of team empowerment, and the design of career paths. Unfortunately, leaders and employees seemed to differ in their perceptions of the purpose of the teams. Fred, IS Pacific level 4 leader, talked about this conflict:

> In my mind [the cross-functional teams] were created to maximize participation, to make organization members feel they have been listened to and are part of the implementation. I also wanted wide-ranging participation so that the members would go back to their work areas and talk about their experiences at these various teams and generate excitement about TQM and communicate that management was serious about making changes. Whether the teams produced a great product or not was not impor-

tant; the involvement process was the most important. I know that other people thought that horizontal teams were focused towards producing something and were disappointed when some of them did not come up with anything.

[For example] the Culture Team chose to work on a survey of employee concerns. I had visualized a different role for the team since the determination of employee concerns is provided for by a company-wide team. I wanted the Culture Team to be the eyes and the ears looking out for organization signals that are counter to the culture we are trying to develop. They said they didn't want to do that; they wanted to work on the employee surveys. We did very little with the surveys, we mainly used it as information for input to the corporate-wide surveys. Why did the team not want to be the vanguard of the new culture? I had not communicated this idea very well to them. They felt that they would be tattletales on their manager. I saw it more as people looking at a memo I send out, finding it maybe a little too heavy handed, and people on the culture team feeling free to call me and tell me so. The team members took the term "supportive culture" to mean more of the day care, flex-time issues.

Because leaders did not value the team's outputs, culture team members felt that leaders were reneging on their commitment to empowering their employees. Sophie, communications officer and a member of the Culture team, describes a typical reaction:

Fred did not believe the results of the survey; said that people did not really think the way the survey showed they did. This made people really doubt that management "walks like it talks." They ask for your input and then refuse to believe it when you give it.

A cross-functional team of level 2 employees completed the implementation plan in May 1990. The leadership team was impressed with the plan and the amount of work that went into it. The plan was very detailed, breaking down the manpower requirements of the TQM implementation by department and year. However, it did not have much impact on the TQM implementation effort. In retrospect, leadership team members said that the plan was too detailed and that it was not flexible enough to stay relevant given the scarcities and uncertainties brought on by defense cuts. Sam, a quality training specialist and TQM advocate, pointed out the problems with the plan and some of the reasons behind them:

We did not get much participation from senior management. The people writing the plan were not involved in strategic planning. The plan had no relevance to the business plan—a business plan that did not exist. People [on the implementation plan team] came from strong structured, technical backgrounds and what they came up with was more like a systems planning document. Very detailed—planned out to 5 years and at 5 levels of detail, with timelines and identifying people by name for roles, etc. There was no flexibility in the plan, no room to grow, to adapt to changing circumstances. They treated the plan as they would a computer systems design project. Here are the specifications, now go do it. However, TQM is not that kind of effort. The plan needs to be generic, tied to the business plan and driven from the top. Follow-up on items by the managers is needed as well.

In spite of the plan's faults, Fred made an effort to implement the plan. This effort was ill-fated, particularly because Fred started it right after a 25% reduction in IS Pacific's headcount. Sophie, IS Pacific's communications officer, chronicled Fred's futile attempt at following the plan and its recommendation that the leadership team should establish a separate TQM office:

After the September 1990 layoff, Fred said we were still going ahead with the plan and that we were going to have a TQM office. People were outraged because they couldn't believe he was hiring people after all the layoffs. So they interviewed people internally; and out of 5, they picked 2 from here to become co-chairs, Sally being one of them. Well, even then Fred was getting flak for setting up the office, so he did not really give Sally any power to do anything; he kept the office really low-key. She got resources but really no ability to call meetings; Fred did not play up the value of the office. Sally was mostly involved with training follow-ups. It turned into a nothing position. Sally had no place to present her implementation efforts, but she kept trying. When the new layoffs were announced, she felt that her job was probably in jeopardy, so she quit. Sam (the other person chosen to chair the office] is still involved in training, and during the time the office was in place, he was mostly involved in TQM team training.

In retrospect, Fred summed up the plan's value in the following way:

Even though the plan has not been used fully, to my mind its value is that it made us plan. The value of the planning process is that you think about where you are and where you are going and develop a statement and agree on where you are going and why. It was very pragmatic—we wanted to improve quality, with less effort, less people, less cost. This is difficult to achieve though. The plan was more like an over-all conceptual model of where we are going, but we have had to become less ambitious. Some people think that we should have gone with smaller, more specific steps rather than the complexity and detail provided for in the plan. I, however, found that it is useful to have the detail; but after seeing all that, we should have said that it was too much and that we should take the changes in smaller steps. We had to do it anyway because of circumstances, not due to our wisdom.

The September 1990 lay-offs were especially devastating to IS Pacific employees because Fred had assured them that layoffs would not occur within IS Pacific in 1990. Additionally, three level 3 leaders resigned from IS Pacific to take positions in Apex. This resulted in further restructuring within IS Pacific—including the integration of two functions into a single one. Again, there were conflicts between the perceptions of managers and employees regarding the effects of the lay-offs. As Sam assessed it:

The layoffs destroyed many teams because they lost members. It had a negative effect on morale. People tended to work less, especially when we had a reduction in workforce (RIF). Productivity is low, people say "Why bother?" It fluctuated. Generally, it's at its worst when there is a RIF. There's a lot of concern now about more layoffs, and are we going to be integrated first and then there will be a layoffs. Mostly people come to work, do their job, unsure why they do it, something like a habit. I don't really have an idea of how management is dealing with all this because I don't have access to them; I don't see how they work day to day. Management has always been pretty invisible. They just work among their own level.

Fred focused on the positive side of the layoffs and how they served as an opportunity to apply TQM concepts like teamwork and working across functions:

The downsizing and austerity has helped in a way. It has made it clear to the people that they have to work together to get the job done. It encourages horizontal linkages that create efficiencies in the completion of tasks.

All throughout the rest of 1990 and early 1991, IS Pacific leaders continued their cost-cutting activities. This was done through a second wave of lay-offs in April 1991, shutting down services to their customers, and leasing out excess equipment. Lay-offs reduced IS Pacific headcount to 650. At several points during this period, Apex senior management ordered studies to determine the pros and cons of merging IS Pacific with either IS Atlantic or with Rotary and the other west coast clients. Each study resulted in the conclusion that it was most efficient to have IS Pacific function as a separate organization. These circumstances made it difficult for leadership team members to maintain their strategic focus and continue with TQM implementation activities—strategic planning was put on hold, communications suffered, and employees lost trust in the leadership. Employees doubted that managers ever had any commitment to TQM. Sophie described how Fred withdrew from communicating with employees and how employees took this to mean that Fred had only a superficial commitment to TQM:

> I was doing communications, so I was trying to be with Fred all the time to develop some communications items to send out. There was a month when Fred would not send anything out. I would write something and he would hold up on it.

> I would say it's been a month since your last memo, and he would say write something up; and then I'd get back to him with something, and he would say let's wait on it. He was getting really isolated then and now—he is not really walking around and talking to people either.

> People used to like Fred—he would walk around, talk to them—but people feel that was all PR only. They have lost faith in Fred because he would not make a stand for IS Pacific, particularly in the issue of remaining a separate organization.

Sam pointed out the problems that he felt kept leadership team members from fully embracing the TQM philosophy:

> Fred needs to be more directive. He is basically a hands-off manager; he is opposed to planning and following through on those plans. The Level 3s are the same, no follow through. Plus, they are all focused on defending their turfs, their fiefdoms. They're

used to operating on the policy of we'll do what we have to do and get back to you to tell you what we've done. They deal with their customers this way and they deal with their people this way. And I saw little effort to change this.

Leadership team members acknowledged these problems but felt that they had made progress with surmounting them. However, they did not attribute their difficulties with TQM and strategic planning to these problems. Instead, they identified issues that distracted them from the TQM effort—including cost-cutting and the low value placed on their services by their customers. Tony, Business Computing level 3 leader, provided the following assessment of the leadership team's performance:

> Now I think we [level 3 and 4 leaders] are better at following up on our tasks and have solid personal relationships with each other, although we still have trouble with following up on things and are still in the reactive mode due to circumstances we face. A breather would really help the team. We are so very focused on reducing costs, headcounts, budgets that we have developed a reactive frame of mind. We are, however, dealing with things better; before we would work things out individually; now we are working together on issues. We are also not working with our customers—particularly with the executive management. Specifically, they do not understand our services, how they use them, how important they are. Their focus is on reducing costs; and due to a communication breakdown, they see IS Pacific as a place to reduce those costs.

Fred underscored the difficulties that the leadership team was facing:

> The leadership team talks about long-term issues but also focuses a lot on the cost-cutting aspects. As it is, we cannot cut usage. There is not one system you can cut, or a group of systems you can cut that will allow you to shut down an entire main-

frame. So the other option is to cut people and other expenses so as to lower rates. There is no way to reduce it by shutting down applications because Rotary is not willing to live without CAD or its inventory system and the like. As of yesterday, the VP of Finance at Rotary asked me to cut another $4 million from our charges. This could mean more layoffs but there's very little I can cut out now, maybe some from human resources, some accountants, very little left.

Mid-year 1991 leadership team members and their employees had conflicting perceptions of IS Pacific's progress with TQM. Leadership team members felt pretty good about their progress given all the obstacles they faced. Tony assessed it as:

We have done pretty well with TQM implementation. We can build on and continue with the progress we have made so far. We have gone through a lot of education in the past year, particularly with TQM team training. We have implemented teams, with varying levels of success. I would say that in 1990 we took a good step towards implementing TQM.

Fred thought that they had made "tremendous progress" and was heartened to find that IS Pacific met milestones he had laid out in a 1990 document:

As far as TQM progress is concerned, I think that Apex, if you look at the entire corporation, it is not going well. If you look at the west coast, it has regressed in Rotary; and IS Pacific has made tremendous progress. I say we have made tremendous progress given that we had to deal with so many difficulties.

I wrote this document early in 1990 (I wish I had dated it) and just discovered it recently while I was cleaning out my desk drawers. I wrote out what kind of organization I expected us to be 3-5 years from now, what

is our desired future stage. Some of the ideas are naive. I also wrote out where I thought we should be in 2-9 years, in 1-2 years. I looked at it just recently when I found it, and found that we have actually achieved some of these 1-2 year targets. Some of them have become irrelevant. But for example, our customer ratings are well known and understood—not at all levels but certainly at the organization-wide level they are pretty well known. We have had almost 60% of our people complete TQM team training, which is pretty close to the percentage I planned for in this document. I was thinking if I showed this to people a year ago, they would have thought I was smoking pot!

But employees saw the TQM effort as another in a long series of failed attempts at improving IS Pacific. Comments from Sam and Sophie echoed this sentiment.

Sam:

Some individuals still see value in TQM and are hoping that we will still implement it. But many people just see it as another "program of the year," and TQM was last year's program.

Sophie:

There is a lot of cynicism about TQM. People feel it is just another program, another cover for business as usual.

In January 1993, confirming most employees' fears, Apex outsourced IS Pacific. For security reasons, critical, proprietary software applications and the programmers responsible for their design and maintenance remained part of Apex. The rest of IS Pacific, including computer operators and systems software programmers, became a unit of Business Data Systems, a third-party information systems services provider. Based on the outsourcing contract, TQM and the work teams would remain intact for a year but no one knew what would happen after that. Fred feared that possible lay-offs and a move out of state could result in the break-up of the teams. However, Business Data Systems agreed to maintain a commitment to TQM, to sharing of scientific knowledge with Apex, and to participation in Apex's Malcolm Baldridge Award assessments.

Fred did not join the outsourced organization. He remained with Apex, heading a team of 6 people in charge of administering the outsourcing contract.

46
Sole Survivors

There were around 350 of them, and only one of him. But Tommy Hewitt was ready for battle.

He didn't have to wait for long. By the time he started speaking, there were plenty of angry faces among the employees of Servus Rubber Co. Most of the workers were older than the thirty-five-year-old Hewitt, and some had been making boots since before he was born. Yet here he was, an outsider dressed in khaki pants and leather moccasins, asking them to make concessions so that he and a partner could buy the company.

Drowned out at times by boos and hisses, Hewitt got only halfway through his presentation. "You're just trying to take things away from us," yelled one worker, challenging Hewitt's claim that Servus's parent company had plans to shut it down. Then came a long volley of questions. Why should we give up a week's vacation? What are you going to do with the salary you want to defer? "We can't support our families now," shouted one man. "How can we give all this up?"

Hewitt didn't get a chance to answer. "Do you want to work?" yelled the union vice- president. "We have to help them. We don't have a choice Do you want to be out on the street?"

It was 1982, and the streets of Rock Island, Ill., were just starting to get crowded with people out of work. At International Harvester, Deere, and J. I. Case, production was shrinking. And the smaller manufacturers were losing business as subcontracting work winged overseas. Now, it was Servus's turn.

That night at the Rock Island Moose Club, a local fraternal lodge, the workers approved Hewitt's plans by a decisive vote. "It was the only future we had," says one worker, shrugging. Nobody could have predicted what the new owners had in mind. Maybe Hewitt and Michael Cappy would continue trying to compete at the low end of the market against cheap Korean boots. Or maybe they would even padlock the factory and become a marketing group. In any case, Servus would never be an industry leader again.

Or would it?

A presidential candidate might well come to Rock Island, a living symbol of America's industrial decline, to highlight his commitment to competitiveness. On a quick tour of Servus Rubber, he might promise to fight for American jobs.

There is no kind of government intervention, though, that could have rescued a company like

Written by Joshua Hyatt. Reprinted with permission, *Inc magazine*, October, 1987. Copyright © 1987 by Goldhirsh Group, Inc., 38 Commercial Wharf, Boston, MA 02110.

Servus. A tariff on Korean boots wouldn't have helped. Nor would a more favorable foreign-exchange rate. Servus fell into dire straits because it was poorly managed. Challenged by foreign competitors, the company decided to compete on the Koreans' terms. It lost touch with its market and, worse still, with its own strengths.

Servus first began drifting off course about ten years ago. Swamped by cheaper imports, the company got winded trying to match the numbers on the Koreans' price tags. It suffered steep losses. "The only question was 'When would we go?' " recalls Leon Goold, a Servus employee for thirty-five years.

Servus had seen much better days. From its 1921 beginnings, Servus had been distinguished by the quality of its boots and the splendor of its annual picnics. The all-day outings were glorious family affairs—especially packed during the 1940s, when the company employed 1,100 workers—complete with popcorn and ice cream. From Rock Island, which is about midway between Des Moines and Chicago, people had to take three buses to get to the state park in Moline, Ill. One family owned the business back then, and many families worked there: fathers brought their sons into the company to work side by side on the assembly line.

Foreign competition became a factor in the late '60s, when cheap sneakers from the Far East overran the market. Servus, which at one time was producing 25,000 tennis sneakers a day, closed its sneaker operations and successfully crept into smaller niches. It produced, for instance, a plastic galosh called the Hustler, which was popular among farmers, construction workers, and electricians. And it made special overshoes for military and industrial workers.

In 1972, the $25-million business was sold to a division of Chromalloy American Corp. Chromalloy installed new chiefs at Servus and left the strategizing to them. As the Koreans challenged more of its markets, Servus panicked. The new executives forgot what Servus did best — produce quality boots — and instead initiated a decade-long process of competing with the Koreans on price. "I don't think they even understood the reasons for Servus's success," says one observer.

To keep prices low, the company began stripping down its products. It bought rubber, zippers, buckles, and cloth from the cheapest suppliers it could find. What were once quality boots were fast becoming low-quality "me too" products. For example, the lining in one of its most popular farming boots, the Northerner, was changed to a more loosely netted fabric. That saved about $60,000 a year. At the same time, companywide returns rose to about ten percent, undoubtedly because of such problems as the netting, which tore easily. Those returns were adding substantially to shipping and labor costs; never mind the disgusted customers who left for good.

Servus stopped investing in its business. "We didn't deal with them, unless they took things away from us," says Jack Miller, the industrial-relations manager who in 1971 started as a night "cracker man" in the mill room, grinding up used rubber. Even though employees were fainting on the job, management refused to install an adequate number of fans. A minor disagreement over health insurance turned into a seven-week union strike and a one-week wildcat strike in 1978.

Equipment was also neglected. One example was the Banbury mixer, a giant machine that stirs rubber like an electric eggbeater. Servus decided not to spend $60,000 to keep an extra reconditioned body at hand. When one broke down, so did the factory.

By 1981, Servus was losing more than $1 million on $14 million in sales — and this after starting a decade earlier with a profitable company *twice* as big. No wonder; customers were fed up. "I would have bet you $1,000 that I would never buy another Servus boot," says Mary Grilliot, vice-president of Morning Pride Manufacturing Inc., which makes and distributes protective clothing for fire fighters. Customers in Servus's other markets — industrial, farming, and sporting boots — felt the same way.

A major consulting firm, called in to diagnose the company's ailment, looked at the production costs of Servus and the Koreans. It issued a half-inch-thick report. This company is terminally ill, the consultants said. Might as well shut it down. Soon, unless a buyer appeared, there would be an additional 350 unemployed people wandering the streets of Rock Island.

Michael Cappy spent about six years wandering through the corridors of corporate America—such big names as Peat, Marwick, Mitchell; Booz, Allen & Hamilton; and General Electric. At thirty-three, though, what he really wanted was to run his own manufacturing business. Tommy Hewitt, whom he had known at GE, had heard about Servus through a consultant.

So Cappy traveled to Rock Island to have a look. He met with workers and was impressed by their commitment. "They had a lot of pride," he recalls. "They talked about the history of the company, the history of the company, and the history of the company." They also voiced concerns about the *future* of the company. Chromalloy had recently liquidated a boot company it owned in Chicopee, Mass. Is the same fate in store for us? they wanted to know. Can you get us out from under them?

Maybe, Cappy thought. Back in Louisville, he and Hewitt buried themselves in industry data. Little by little, Cappy's enthusiasm grew. Here was a company that had been sorely neglected, its brands milked and run into the ground. Yet the brand names still meant something to customers. Take the Northerner line of boots, for instance. Despite being stripped of most of its value, the name still attracted customers. "That sucker deserved to be dead with what they did to it," says Cappy. "Yet it demonstrated uncanny resilience."

Servus's problem, as Cappy eventually diagnosed it, could be summed up in a word: positioning. It was competing in the wrong end of the market; it had blindly followed its Korean competitors into a market that played to the Koreans' greatest advantage, low labor costs. Servus had turned its back on its own strengths. "If the basis on which Servus competed in the marketplace was price, and there's a lot of labor content in what it makes, it doesn't take a genius to figure out that the business is going to die,"

Cappy says. "We found Servus playing under rules by which it could not win."

Would it be possible, he wondered, to boost the company's margins by finding small niches where customers would buy quality? Everything he read convinced him that it would be. Well, *almost* everything. Just as Cappy and Hewitt were getting close to making a deal, the consulting group's report landed with a thud across Cappy's desk. "It gave us indigestion," he recalls.

Not a chronic case, though. The report didn't change Cappy's analysis of Servus's basic strengths. It still had a solid name, some promising markets, and strong internal spirit. "Buried in every $20-million dog," Cappy says, "is a $10-million gem." And, perhaps best of all, Cappy could buy this dog at a substantial discount. CIT Commercial Finance, now a division of the New York City-based Manufacturers Hanover Corp., agreed to finance the $5.7-million buyout. The United Rubber Workers and salaried employees made some concessions that eased the bleeding. In return, Cappy gave workers about twenty percent of the business through an employee stock ownership plan. And he gave the union president a seat on the board of directors.

The first challenge was fixing the company's production and quality problems. All the marketing genius in the world wouldn't help if Servus's boots were leaking. To boost quality, Cappy brought in consultant Behrooz Jalayer, who had recently fied Iran.

But who would run the company? For the first few months, Cappy had left most of the existing management in place, including the president that Chromalloy had installed. Jalayer contended that the president had to go, in large part because he had a terrible relationship with employees. When Jalayer started "quality sessions" between managers and workers every morning, the president hesitated to sit at the same table as the union chief. On the other hand, Hewitt argued that millions of dollars would follow the president out the door. "The more careful you want to be," Jalayer countered, "the more you are dragging your feet on the recovery of this company."

Cappy finally fired the president. The day it was announced, Servus workers went wild. Somebody took the keys to the president's company car, threw them on a table, and shouted, "Anybody want to drive the president's car?" Another employee knocked down the nameplate on his desk. Says Leon Goold, who once got into a scuffle with the president in the men's room: "There wasn't an unhappy face in the building."

Soon there was a new face in the corner once. Marc Caparrelli, the new Servus president, had spent thirteen years at Campbell Soup Co., six of them in marketing-related jobs. He and Cappy had been buddies since high school. Jalayer stayed on as a consultant, later rising to vice-president of operations and, eventually, president. All three of them own stock in Norcross Cos., the holding company that includes Servus and some ten other small businesses. Cappy owns a controlling interest in Norcross, which has revenues of nearly $135 million.

What Servus needed was "to take a consumer-marketing approach to the business," Caparrelli says. Every product is, in some ways, a consumer product. The safety director who buys a fire boot is similar in many ways to the shopper deciding on a dish-washing liquid. So, Caparrelli argued, we have to ask the same questions that a consumer marketer would ask: how can we differentiate ourselves? People purchase products that represent the best value, a mix of quality and price. How do we make ourselves a better value?

The sales staff thought that it had the answer: slash prices even more to help them open new accounts. Cappy disagreed: a price decrease, he felt, would have a negative long-term effect. Customers might try a product once, but they wouldn't stick with something inferior.

So Cappy moved ahead, positioning the company as a quality leader. Along with Hewitt, who left the company in mid-1983, he visited potential customers and assured them that Servus was returning to the top-notch quality they remembered. They played on their fond memories of the company. *You guys are still around?* the potential customers would respond, wide-eyed. Why, heck, I haven't seen a Servus sales rep in, oh, it must be *five years.*

And the salespeople brought something new with them: cut-up samples of Servus boots. We have boots, they began, with six-gauge felt lining, a high abrasion index, and total imperviousness to fatty acids. Waterproof and seamless too, with rust-resistant buckles. Never mind that other boots have some of these characteristics as well; they had never been described in such detail. "Part of what we did," says Cappy, "was to be the first to state the obvious."

The company got a surprisingly good reception. "People remembered Servus as being a good, solid company," notes Caparrelli. "Brand images die hard." If those memories weren't enough to sway them, Servus had other means. Sometimes during a visit to a potential customer, for instance, Jalayer might talk about his flight to the United States from Iran. "I get a lot of mileage out of my life story," he says. But more often he would talk about Servus: sixty- year-old company on its last legs, 350 people just barely getting by on some $6 an hour. We are trying to save these jobs, Jalayer appealed. And then there were the practical advantages of buying from Servus instead of the Koreans: you didn't have to tie up your money for nine months or take the product as is. And the new owners offered delivery within seventy-two hours.

Later, as Servus grew more surefooted, it used hardball tactics. One Servus salesman took a foreign-made boot to an independent lab. The test results showed that its steel toe crushed under the weight of seventy-five pounds, violating the federal standard. That became part of the usual pitch to customers. Servus also had tests done on a foreign fire boot. Salesmen took the less-than-impressive results to state purchasing agents and to distributors. If, heaven forbid, there's an accident, Jalayer would warn distributors, these inferior boots could land you knee-deep in liability problems. "We put a push on the liability, and that there are a lot of weirdos in this country who will sue over anything," says sales manager Julie Dolter.

By mid-1983, Servus had picked up some major accounts. A few months later, it raised prices about three percent. The company, Cappy felt, had demonstrated its commitment to quality. "You want to increase the price to be consistent with the positioning," says Cappy. "Nothing confuses a consumer more than to get something that looks like it could cost more, and doesn't." It was also consistent with the new slogan its ad agency had suggested: Servus Sets the Standard.

Servus now had a foothold. But only through innovation could the company's sales grow in mature markets.

To make that happen, Caparrelli took a cue from his former employer, Campbell Soup: wherever possible, create a flagship product. At Servus, these would be leading-edge boots that stood at the top of each line. "They create an umbrella under which the enhanced image rubs off on the other products," says Cappy, who had seen the same strategy work at General Electric. Not all consumers would be able to afford the flagship product. But they would assume that Servus brought the same know-how to its other lines of boots.

To find ripe niches, they did what any good marketers do: they got in touch with their customers. They scrutinized every possible market segment and sub-segment. The sales staff played a key role. "New-product ideas don't come from people in the labs," Cappy says.

Cappy assembled the entire sales force in Winter Park, Colorado. The first day, he listened to complaints about service, delivery, and pricing. Then he talked about his plans. "Everybody was skeptical," says Cappy. "But they can detect the difference between sincerity and BS." We've never been asked about the direction of the company, the salespeople figured, so what do we have to lose? Some came up with new products, others had ideas about material, and some contributed packaging suggestions.

Potential customers were another good source of ideas. Jalayer went to trade shows and talked with boot distributors. What niche are you after? he would ask. How do you appeal to your customers? What new products would you like to see? They were mining for sizable markets where price wasn't the decision factor.

The fire-boot market was one. Customers would happily pay for quality. And it was easy to find the nation's fire fighters. They read industry magazines and attend trade shows. Just a mildly improved fire boot, backed by targeted marketing, could create sparks. "Fire boots had gotten stagnant," says Mary Grilliot, the boot distributor. "And this is a market that will pay for an improvement, since lives are at stake." And Grilliot, who had sworn off Servus forever, was impressed. At a trade show, Jalayer dragged her to the Servus booth. There she saw a fire boot with more supple rubber, melded design lines, a beefed-up sole, and a better fit and feel. Could this be the same *Servus Rubber?*

It wasn't. But if that didn't convince her, the company's next step would. Jalayer had started thinking about how to differentiate Servus's fire boot. One night at a trade show, a customer asked him, "Why isn't the lining up to the same technological level as the rest of the boot?" That got Jalayer thinking, Why not create a fire boot with a flame-retardant lining? Not just any flame-retardant lining, mind you, a *Kevlar-Nomex* lining. Sounds impressive, doesn't it? And that's just the point. No matter that the fire is outside the boot. Fire chiefs and safety directors appreciate technological improvements. Servus created the boot, then doubled its advertising budget for such magazines as *Fire Chief* and *Fire House*, the most efficient way of reaching the fire fighters. "We had so many calls and inquiries that it forced the distributors to start carrying this boot," says Dolter.

Servus worked hard to convince users to shell out the extra 15 percent. Jalayer sent free samples of the boots, which retail for around $80, to a number of fire chiefs to use and evaluate. The Chicago Fire Department, for example, was using Korean fire boots. When a fire fighter was injured, Jalayer used the opportunity to visit the fire chief and explain Servus's edge. He not only won him over, but the chief also agreed to recommend the Firebreaker line to suburban fire departments. Before a major trade show in 1986, Jalayer sent letters to 23,000 fire chiefs urging them to stop by and see the boot. About 4,000 visited Servus's booth during the first three days.

This year, Servus expects to sell 30 percent more fire boots than it did last year. Since 1982, sales of the fire boots have more than doubled. And among Servus's major customers is Mary Grilliot, who returned, she says, because "Servus was willing to innovate."

And not only in fire boots. Servus's line of dielectrics was very limited when Cappy bought the company. Some competitors were selling boots that could withstand 14,000 volts of electricity. Give us *something* to sell against that to the utilities, the sales staff urged Caparrelli. Sure, he said, but why would a customer switch to ours? Again, *how can we differentiate ourselves?* His solution: a boot that withstands 20,000 volts. Since 1983, sales have climbed steadily to about 10,000 pairs a year. "It's a nice margin of protection and a great selling point," says David Forsthoffer, president of Shoes & Gloves Inc., a safety-equipment distributor.

Servus added a few extra touches, as well. Based on an idea that Caparrelli got from a customer in the utility industry, Servus added a two-and-a-half-inch heel to the boots, enabling workers to climb poles more easily. The dielectric boot was in another market where quality was more important than price, and Servus could reach it through direct mail.

In some markets, Servus created a flagship boot through sheer positioning, rather than technological innovation. The three-eyelet Northerner boot, for instance, hasn't changed much in the thirty years Servus has been selling it to farmers. But the label looked slapped on, and the box featured a drawing that looked too much like pigs frolicking. Farmers are not only a price-sensitive market, but expensive to reach — and they don't like their pigs made fun of. So Caparrelli upgraded the packaging, drawing attention to the boot's benefits, and added color to a new package illustration, which now looks like a polar bear. He used point-of- purchase hangtags, with instructions for care and a two-year warranty. Inside each boot, he added an inspection tag. "It creates an image that 'these guys are really proud of this boot,' " says Cappy. "You behave like it is a superior product."

Making a superior product has its rewards. A year after Cappy took over, Servus cleared about $150,000 after having lost more than $1 million the year before. Sales reached nearly $20 million in 1986, with "substantial pretax earnings," according to the company. Employment has swelled from 350 to 500 since 1982.

How easy it is to drift back into bad habits. Servus had learned a lesson from its pursuit of the Koreans and had also rediscovered its own strengths — or *had* it?

The innovation that got the company moving again has slowed. "We're somewhat frustrated with Servus's lack of ability to develop new products," Cappy admits. Some attempts seem halfhearted. Last year, Jalayer wanted to extend the Northerner brand name into cover-alls. Cappy says he agreed because Jalayer "got all hot and bothered about it." Servus sold only about 7,000 pairs in 1986, and Jalayer predicts it will sell 10,000 this year. He even talks about acquiring a coverall maker. Cappy has other ideas. "We ought to be out of that business," he snaps. "It's not even a business. It's a distraction."

Worst of all, Servus tested the low end of the market once again. In 1985, Jalayer noticed that Servus's sales of Tomahawk, an overshoe for farmers and construction workers, were only a fraction of what they had been six years before. The Korean boot makers, who were selling similar overshoes at around half the price, offered to become Servus's suppliers.

But after visiting Korea, Jalayer strolled into Caparrelli's once and announced his intention to revive Tomahawk. *Revive Tomahawk?* Don't be silly, replied Caparrelli. We can't compete on price. But maybe we could import the boots from the Koreans and market them here. No, that would damage the integrity of our own lines, countered Jalayer. What are you going to say to the union workers who don't get a change to beat the Koreans? Then Jalayer presented his own plan. Drop the price by about 20 percent, he said, and make up the margin in volume by offering it only to customers who buy at least 150 pairs. And use incremental price increases after that. Well, they finally agreed, it *would* be a great way to absorb overhead and use excess capacity.

Jalayer returned to Rock Island and plastered stickers of angry bald eagles all over the factory.

"We are fighting back," they said, referring to the Korean footwear. The market responded to the drastic price cuts, and sales shot up 500 percent between 1985 and 1986. Suddenly, the Tomahawk line was becoming the company's most visible product. The local newspapers were even writing about it.

Tomahawk developed into a marketing blunder, though. The "fighting back" theme was in danger of becoming Servus's image in the marketplace. It wasn't at all consistent with the slogan "Servus Sets the Standard." "The last thing I want to tell our customers is that we're fighting back," says Cappy. "Implicit in it is an admission that we got our asses kicked." Cappy was also concerned that the low-margin items of the Tomahawk line might eclipse the company's more profitable lines of boots.

If that happened, Servus could find itself back where it started. "You can be a genius in turn-arounds, but if you don't follow up, it will return to worse than it was before," says Jalayer. That would be more bad news for Rock Island, where mothballed plants have become too common a sight. Since Cappy took over Servus, about 20,000 workers in the metropolitan area have lost their jobs at other companies.

All because of foreign competition, or so they think. Maybe they ought to look at Servus and think again.

47

Corpus Christi
Federal Credit Union

In June of 1989, the National Credit Union Administration (NCUA), the credit union industry's regulatory agency, declared Corpus Christi Parish Credit Union insolvent and took control of the credit union and its day-to-day operations. The major cause of the insolvency was the need to write down or write off a large number of real estate loans made by the credit union. A review of the credit union's loan portfolio revealed that the credit union had over 60 percent of its loan portfolio in real estate, far exceeding the maximum allowed by NCUA. It was also discovered that much of the collateral securing real estate loans was overvalued and that many of the loans were uncollectible. NCUA moved in because failure of Corpus Christi Parish Credit Union, with $26 million in assets, would pose a significant financial threat to the National Credit Union Share Insurance Fund.[1]

When NCUA took control of the credit union, they planned to re-evaluate Corpus Christi's loan portfolio, put new controls in place, correct existing operational problems, train a new Board of Directors (whom they would oversee for two

years), and eventually return control to the credit union's members. Instead, in September of 1992, Corpus Christi Federal Credit Union became a full-service branch of the Liberty Bank in New Orleans.

Brief History of Corpus Christi Federal Credit Union

The Corpus Christi Federal Credit Union was, until 1990, the Corpus Christi Parish Credit Union. The idea for a credit union was that of a priest of the Corpus Christi Church—a Josephite Catholic Church Parish established in 1918 to serve the African American community of the 7th ward in New Orleans. He felt that a credit union was needed to meet the financial needs of the African-American community of the church parish, many of whose needs were overlooked by the larger and more traditional financial establishments. Corpus Christi Parish Credit Union first opened its doors on July 11, 1946 in the

---

[1] The National Credit Union Share Insurance Fund insures credit union deposits up to $100,000. It is comparable to the Federal Deposit Insurance Corporation in the banking industry.

[2] The credit union's name was changed to Corpus Christi Federal Credit Union in September 1990.

Prepared by Karen White, MBA Student and V. Jean Ramsey, Professor of Management, Texas Southern University; Jesse H. Jones, School of Business. Used with permission.

basement of the church rectory. By the time NCUA took over, Corpus Christi had become the one of the largest credit unions in the state of Louisiana and the largest African-American-owned credit union in the nation.

The Credit Union Industry

The philosophy which governs credit unions originated in Europe, and was imported to North America in 1900. Unlike other financial institutions, credit unions are cooperative associations organized to serve members with common bonds of employment, association, or residence. The characteristic that most distinguishes credit unions from other financial institutions is that they operate solely to meet the needs of their members, rather than to make profits. The founders of the movement believed that the organization and operation of credit unions should be accomplished primarily through the use of volunteers.

By definition, credit unions are member-owned. Instead of striving to boost shareholder earnings, earnings are returned to members in the form of higher interest rates on saving accounts, lower interest rates on loans, and increased member services. It has been estimated that by 1993, credit unions nation-wide had over 65 million members and $280 billion in assets.

All credit unions protected by the National Credit Union Share Insurance Fund are governed by the National Credit Union Administration. NCUA operates under the authority of the Federal Credit Union Act which regulates the organization and operation of federal credit unions. NCUA conducts on-site examinations to determine that credit unions are financially sound and being operated in compliance with federal regulations, as well as to assist credit union officials and employees in carrying out their duties and responsibilities. NCUA's objectives are to insure that its regulations do not impose excessive burdens on credit unions, their members, or the public, that they are appropriate for the size of the institution, and are clear and understandable.

The structures of credit unions are prescribed by the Federal Credit Union Act and bylaws, and based on member ownership. Anyone within the domain of the membership—whether it be based on communities, organizations, school districts, hospitals, or church parishes—can become a "shareholder" by having her or his eligibility for membership verified and opening an account.

Credit union members exercise democratic control by attending and participating in regular and special membership meetings. No matter how many shares are owned, each member has one vote. The Board of Directors, elected by the membership, has responsibility to provide general direction for the credit union, establish operating policies and procedures, appoint the Credit Committee (sometimes bylaws provide for direct election of this committee), appoint the Supervisory Committee, and hire the CEO.

The Credit Committee is responsible for establishing lending and collection policies and procedures, appointing loan officers, and acting on any loan applications outside the scope of the loan officer's authority. The Supervisory Committee is the internal audit arm of the credit union and is responsible for verifying member accounts; suspending directors, officers, or Credit Committee members for cause; and ensuring the financial stability of the credit union (see Exhibit 47-1).

Corpus Christi Federal Credit Union—1946-1988

Corpus Christi Credit Union was chartered by the State of Louisiana in July of 1946 as Corpus Christi Parish Credit Union to provide the members of Corpus Christi Church with a place to save and a source of loans at reasonable rates.

Structure

Becoming a member of the Corpus Christi Parish Credit Union entitled individuals to apply for credit, purchase IRAs and money markets, and receive other services provided by the credit

EXHIBIT 47-1 The Responsibilities of Key Elements of the Credit Union

---

Members

Responsibilities:
1. Elect board of directors and credit committee.
2. Participate in membership meetings.
3. Promote participation in and use of credit union services.
4. Repay loans as agreed.
5. Remove any official for cause.
6. Expel members for cause.

Credit Committee

Responsibilities:
1. Meet at least monthly and maintain minutes.
2. Appoint loan officer(s) as needed and delegate authority.
3. Counsel members in wise use of credit.
4. Maintain confidential relations with members.
5. Act on applications for loans and lines of credit.
6. Act on requests for release of collateral.
7. Act on requests for extensions and refinancing of loans.
8. Act on requests denied by loan officer(s).
9. Make annual report to members.

Supervisory Committee

Responsibilities:
1. Make or cause to be made audits at least annually.
2. Submit audit reports to the board of directors and summaries to members at annual meetings.
3. Verify with members their account balances at least once every 2 years.
4. Maintain confidential relations with members.
5. Suspend directors, officers, or credit committee members for cause.
6. Call special membership meetings for cause.
7. Maintain committee's records.
8. Request board approval for compensation of clerical and auditing assistance.

Board of Directors

Responsibilities:
1. Maintain general direction and control.
2. Meet at least monthly and maintain minutes.
3. Establish operating policies and procedures.
4. Elect board officers and fix compensation of specified officer.
5. If bylaws provide, appoint credit committee or loan officer(s).
6. Appoint supervisory committee.
7. Appoint membership officer, executive and other committees.
8. Hire, fix duties and compensation of employees and set personnel policies.
9. Maintain confidential relations with members.
10. Act on membership applications.
11. Determine classes of accounts and fix maximum individual share limit, when appropriate.
12. Fix loan policies regarding loan maximums, interest rate, maturity, and security.
13. Establish collection policies and procedures and fix late charges.
14. Designate depository for funds.
15. Authorize investments and borrowing.
16. Declare dividends and interest refunds.
17. Determine surety bond needs at least annually.
18. Authorize necessary insurance.
19. Provide necessary service facilities.
20. Act on loans to directors, credit and supervisory committee members in excess of $10,000.
21. Appoint a security officer and supervise security program.
22. Establish a records preservation program.
23. Request approval of charter and nonstandard bylaw amendments.
24. Plan and hold annual meeting, report to members, and maintain minutes.

EXHIBIT 47-2 Organizational Chart of Corpus Christi Federal Credit Union

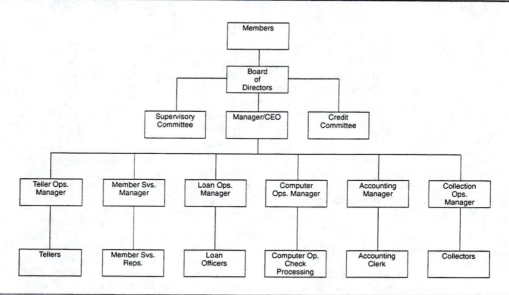

union. The unique structure of one share/one vote allowed members to participate in the election of the Board of Directors and to have a strong active voice in guiding the direction of "their" financial institution. Elected by the membership, the Board of Directors reported to the membership. The Credit Committee and Supervisory Committee reported to the Board of Directors. A manager/CEO was responsible for the day-to-day operations and implementation of policies and procedures set forth by the Board of Directors. The work of the credit union was divided into teller operations, member services, loans, computer operations, accounting, and collection (see Exhibit 47-2).

Culture

Members of the Board of Directors and the Credit and Supervisory Committees of the Corpus Christi Parish Credit Union were unpaid, volunteer members of the credit union. The CEO/Manager and staff were paid employees. Many of the employees, however, were relatives or very close friends of members of the credit union. Many of the children who had attended Corpus Christi Parish School and/or Church re-

turned as proud employees of the credit union. Generations had grown up as members of the credit union, and in some way, each parishioner's life was affected by the presence of the credit union.

One member, Mr. Smith, widowed for a few years, spent at least a portion of his day, every day, at the credit union. He made sure he knew all the employees and that all the employees knew him. He would bring the employees little gifts and always had a special blessing and/or prayer for his favorites. He was thrilled when a loan officer was able to add an extra $100 or $200 to his existing loan to help him pay his electric bill or to meet some other emergency without fussing over his credit report. As one member put it, "I've made so many loans in the past twelve years. I've sent my children to school, I've borrowed $2500 for home improvements, I needed to pay bills...I guess I could be called an apostle for the credit union."

The closeness and concern for the members' well-being and financial success, as well as the actual blood relationships that existed, made Corpus Christi a "family" credit union that everyone loved and respected.

Growth

Beginning with its move from the church basement to its new home in a 10,500 square feet building in 1970, the closely knit community credit union began to emerge from a "vanilla credit union" offering only small consumer loans and regular (passbook) savings to a full-service financial institution. By 1970, share life insurance, a non-fee-based service, was increased to $20,000; in 1971, semi-annual dividends, student loans, auto and homeowner's insurance were instituted; in 1974, share life insurance was increased to $40,000; in 1975, the credit union automated its operations and initiated quarterly dividends; by 1978, the credit union was offering share certificates of deposit and variable dividend rates on share deposits; in 1979, additional services of direct deposits, money market savings, thirty-month certificates of deposit, and interest-bearing share draft accounts (checking accounts) were added; by 1980, a newsletter named "The Informer" was begun; and in 1981, the credit union upgraded its computer system.

Unprecedented growth spawned by good service, excellent financial products, and responsiveness and closeness to members led to tremendous success. By 1982, Corpus Christi boasted assets of more than $25 million, served more than 10,000 members, and employed over twenty full-time employees.[3]

During the period in which the credit union experienced significant growth and increased demand for new and more sophisticated services, a major turning point was 1979, when the Board decided to begin offering mortgage loans to the community. Mortgage loans would allow members who often experienced loan bias and discrimination to purchase a home. The mortgage loan program would also generate a new source of income for the credit union, thereby

significantly increasing its asset base.

With such a move came a new challenge and need for expertise in mortgage lending on the part of the volunteers who made up the Board of Directors, as well as the CEO and staff. This move also brought Corpus Christi under increased scrutiny by the State of Louisiana's Office of Financial Institutions—responsible for regulating the operations of state-chartered credit unions—and the National Credit Union Administration—responsible for regulating federally-chartered credit unions and those protected by NCUA's share insurance fund.

NCUA requires a reasonable balance between long- and short-term lending and restricts credit unions from having too much of their portfolio tied up in real estate loans. In addition, real-estate loans may be granted for residential purposes only: owner-occupied one-to-four family dwellings. NCUA also required that the credit union be listed as the first lien holder and that qualified appraisals be obtained for all real estate loans.

1989-1992: Enter NCUA

In 1989, after reviewing Corpus Christi's financial statements, NCUA became very concerned that the credit union's real estate loans had exceeded 60 percent of their total assets. This prompted a more in-depth, on-site visit by NCUA examiners. During the on-site visit, the examiners found that some loans had been made for purposes other than those specified by NCUA—for example, real estate loans had been made for rental property and other investment purposes. In addition, loan documentation did not consistently meet regulatory requirements: documentation was often either incomplete or nonexistent; appraisals were not available for many of the properties; many of the appraisals that were available were inflated; and in some instances, the credit union was not listed as the first lien holder.

After further review, NCUA determined that certain real estate loans would have to be "written down," i.e., recognize in the financial state-

---

[3] In 1993, the average credit union in the U.S. had a membership of 4,775 and assets under $20 million. Approximately 78 percent of credit unions are occupational, including government, education and manufacturing; 14 percent are associations; and 6 percent are residential. The largest credit unions tend to be those organized by employees.

EXHIBIT 47-3 Organizational Chart After NCUA Takeover

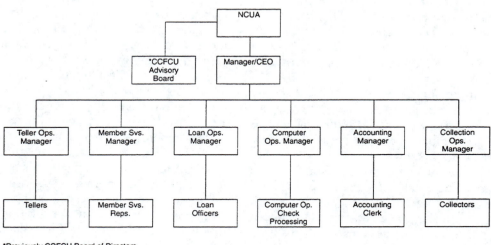

*Previously CCFCU Board of Directors

ments that the full amount of the loan would never be recovered. The result was a reduction of the credit union's loan balance and an increase in expenses (since the difference between what was on the books and what was written off had to be charged against the credit union's net worth). Many of the real estate loan balances had to be totally written off and the credit union had to absorb the loan balance—once again reducing the credit union's net worth and increasing expenses.

Because of the magnitude of the losses resulting from the write-downs and write-offs, the credit union found itself insolvent. The potential failure of the Corpus Christi Parish Credit Union, with $26 million in assets and ranked 17th of the top 50 credit unions in the State of Louisiana, became a significant threat to the National Credit Union Share Insurance Fund. Given this, NCUA, under the authority of the Federal Credit Union Act, was required to take control of the credit union's operations.

The democratic structure was gone. The members of the largest African-American credit union in the country had to relinquish control of their credit union to a federal regulatory agency. The leadership role of the Board of Directors, who had been elected by the membership, was usurped by NCUA examiners. The current CEO/Manager was relieved of his duties; the Board of Directors was demoted to an advisory board; and the assistant manager, now given the title CEO, reported directly to NCUA representatives rather than to the Board of Directors (see Exhibit 47-3).

NCUA's first order of business was to stop the "bleeding." The collection department was beefed up to begin recouping funds lost because of inadequate documentation, improper lending procedures, or noncollection of delinquent accounts. A collection manager, hired from outside the credit union, was brought in; new written policies and procedures were developed and implemented; accounts were reassigned based on the collector's expertise and experience (consumer collections or mortgage collections) and their relationships with the members; new controls were put in place—daily telephone logs were kept and reviewed, daily recording of calls and responses from members was made, weekly reviews of payment plans were conducted and weekly departmental meetings were held. The survival of the credit union, at this point, depended on the efforts of the collection department. The lost funds from delinquent mortgage loans, as well as delinquent consumer loans, had to be collected in order to get the credit union moving toward recovery.

As the reality of NCUA's presence began to set in, conflict and frustration began to rise: employees resented the agency's presence, the department managers and collectors felt the collection manager should have been promoted from within the organization instead of being brought in from the outside, and all employees were frustrated when their benefits were reduced on top of having had no salary increase for over two years. Members also resented the intrusion of NCUA, especially the demotion of the Board of Directors, and became increasingly upset when fees were increased and services decreased.

As 1989 came to an end, some progress was being made, delinquency was decreasing, controls and procedures were being implemented in the loan department, and income was beginning to creep up, but acceptance of the transition of authority from the Board of Directors to NCUA officials was very, very slow. Although the actions of NCUA were taken in an effort to rebuild the credit union, to increase income, to reduce expenses, and return the control of the credit union to the membership, the membership and the staff found it difficult to accept the presence of NCUA, or their actions. Both the staff and membership wanted to maintain the previous organizational arrangements, and they continued to act as if the policies and procedures set forth by the previous management were still in place. In order to speed up the transition, NCUA decided it was necessary to "clean house" completely.

As word got around that NCUA had decided to disband the Board of Directors completely and fire the current manager/CEO, members became very upset. Individuals who had played leadership roles in the credit union for many years, who had come to be respected and trusted by the membership, would no longer be there. In spite of numerous phone calls and letters from members supporting the current CEO and Advisory Board, and personal meetings with NCUA representatives, all were dismissed. Leadership

by peers was about to be replaced completely with leadership by outsiders.

In August of 1990, NCUA hired Ms. Andrea Lucas, an African-American CPA practicing in the State of Louisiana, to direct and control the credit union's daily operations. At the time, all of the managers and 95 percent of the staff were also African-American females. With the exception of a few skeptics, they were looking forward to working with "one of their own." All the employees, including the skeptics and the small number of male employees, offered her a warm welcome and made many offers to assist her in any way, at any time.

During her first week, the department managers spent a great deal of time in meetings with Ms. Lucas discussing their roles as managers; the progress their departments were making in meeting the goals set by NCUA and where they were falling short; information regarding their staffs; their future plans for their departments, as discussed and agreed upon with NCUA; and background information on the credit union industry generally and Corpus Christi Parish Credit Union particularly.

By the end of the second week, Ms. Lucas restructured the entire operations of the credit union. Managers were transferred to other departments, halting work on a number of major projects. The collection manager had been in a year-long process of foreclosing on three major real-estate loans, the lending department manager had been in the process of drafting new policies and procedures, and the computer operations manager had been developing and redesigning system reports to meet requirements set forth by NCUA. There was no preparation for the personnel changes and no transition period. The newly-transferred staff members were unable to bring closure to their old duties and had little understanding of their new duties. This led to a great deal of frustration and stress.

Entire departments were left in disarray. For example, the collection manager was made the manager of the lending department, one collector was transferred to Computer Operations, two additional collectors resigned, leaving just one experienced and one inexperienced collector to maintain what had previously been a five-member department. By the end of the third week, all controls were gone and members, once again, had slowed down repayment of their loans; delinquency increased dramatically and income took a nose dive.

Member services began to erode rapidly. In an effort to reduce expenses, the credit union no longer provided share life insurance free of charge to the members; if members wanted to provide life insurance benefits for beneficiaries upon their deaths, they would now have to purchase the insurance. The minimum deposit to purchase a certificate of deposit increased from $1000 to $5000, share draft accounts (checking accounts) were no longer interest-bearing, and service fees were increased, in some instances from no fees or very minimal fees to significant ones. For example, the fee to pull a credit report for loan review went from no fee to $5. Members were given no forewarning of these changes.

After her initial meetings with department managers, Ms. Lucas communicated with the staff through written directives and memos; very seldom did she address any concerns with employees face-to-face. She also refused to meet with members to discuss their misgivings about such things as fee increases, the safety of their deposits, the financial soundness of the credit union, or collection issues. In contrast to the previous open door policy for both members and staff, Ms. Lucas's policy was "closed door." Every issue, every problem, every comment, had to be screened by her administrative assistant. She was often heard to state, "I don't have time to deal with those people."

Conflict and tension replaced care and concern. Ms. Lucas was determined to run a "tight ship," while the staff and membership were fighting to maintain the "family" credit union they had grown to love. Members became increasingly frustrated. In the past, they could wander into the CEO's office and chat about their everyday concerns. Now they had no one to whom they could express their concerns about the reduction in services or their fears about the credit union being liquidated. Familiar faces—staff and board members—

were disappearing, and loans were more difficult to obtain than before. Loyalty began to wane; many members began to close their accounts and suggest to family members and friends that they do the same. In addition, six of the department managers, with two- to twenty-plus years of experience, resigned their positions.

By 1991, NCUA realized that the credit union's situation was getting worse, and in August, fired Ms. Lucas. At this point, NCUA decided to hire a management team instead of a CEO. In theory at least, the day-to-day operations of the credit union were to be overseen by a three-person management team, each member of which brought different expertise to bear (see Exhibit 47-4). Two of these individuals were hired from outside the credit union. Mr. Martin, whose specialty was preparing credit unions for liquidation and who had worked for NCUA on a contract basis for the past 6 years, was to have major responsibility for the collections and loan operations. Ms. Height, with 20 years experience in large banks and credit unions, was to have major responsibility for accounting and computer operations. Ms. Klein, who had six years' experience in the credit union industry and had served as both Collections Department Manager and Loan Department Manager for Corpus Christi, was to have major responsibility for member services and teller operations. The team reported directly to the acting CEO, an NCUA representative, who reported to NCUA's Project Case Officer, who in turn reported to the Regional Director of NCUA. The chain of command was increased from four levels to six, further distancing the NCUA officials who made decisions about the credit union from the staff who actually ran the credit union and the membership.

The team concept failed. The Acting CEO from NCUA was assigned responsibility for an additional credit union and was unable to devote all of his energies to Corpus Christi. Mr. Martin began to function as the acting CEO, having Ms. Height report to him, and Ms. Klein report to Ms. Height. The African-American females, who made up 90 percent of the staff at this time, resented this new chain of command. The female employees and managers

EXHIBIT 47-4 Background Information on Management Team Members

Jules Martin: *NCUA Resource Specialist*

1. White male in his late 40s to early 50s
2. High school education and some additional junior college courses
3. Contract worker with NCUA for six years with experience in preparing credit unions for liquidation
4. Initial responsibilities:
   a. redesigning system reports
   b. drafting new policies and procedures: employee handbook, lending and collection procedures, procedures governing check cashing and deposit
   c. overseeing daily operations

Valerie Height: *Operations Manager*

1. White female in her early 40s
2. Bachelor's degree in accounting
3. Twenty years experience in financial institutions (large banks and credit unions
4. Initial responsibilities:
   a. overseeing computer operations
   b. managing all accounting functions
   c. providing accurate financial statements

Nancy Klein: *Assistant Operations Manager*

1. African-American female in her early 30s
2. Bachelor's degree in education; pursing a Master's degree in Business Administration
3. Six years management experience in the credit union industry (two years management experience at Corpus Christi, including Manager of Collections and Loan Departments)
4. Responsibilities:
   a. resolving member problems
   b. marketing and promoting credit union products
   c. training and development of the tellers
   d. other duties as assigned by the Operations Manager

had developed relationships based on trust and understanding. They had become used to having their complaints and suggestions about the new policies and procedures and job duties considered in the decision-making process, and their personal concerns, such as children's doctors' appointments heard. They felt Mr. Martin would not be as understanding or as concerned about their well-being as Ms. Height and Ms. Klein had been.

And they were right. Mr. Martin would make comments such as, "Your job should be your first priority"; "I am the only one in this credit union that works from 7:00 a.m. to 7:00 p.m. every day." He would get upset if an employee had to leave suddenly to take care of a family emergency or would take sick leave to care for an ill child. His most common saying was, "The suc-

cessful people are those who do the things unsuccessful people will not do," often made when employees had to leave early to take care of a sick child, or even left to go home at 4:30 p.m. (the credit union's closing time).

Ms. Height and Ms. Klein could do nothing without consulting Mr. Martin. Any decision to be implemented, any meeting to be held with an employee to discuss credit union operations, any termination of an employee had to first be discussed with Mr. Martin. He had been empowered by the Problem Case Officer of NCUA to approve or disapprove any decision made by Ms. Height or Ms. Martin.

At this point, the staff was frustrated. It was increasingly difficult to get decisions made, since they had to be approved by at least two additional levels of management. As Ms. Height and Ms. Klein became increasingly powerless, employees who had previously reported to them became unsure about who they were to report to, or who they could depend on to look after their interests.

The credit union was on a collision course. Service deteriorated, operations continued to take a nose dive, and members no longer trusted management. Fees were charged without prior warning, holds were placed on checks, additional identification was required to cash checks. Meanwhile, NCUA representatives refused to meet with members as a group to discuss the future of their credit union. Employee morale also plummeted; they were discouraged in their efforts to save the credit union. The closely-knit family credit union had evolved into a sea of darkness.

Since NCUA had taken over the credit union, it showed no signs of improvement; in fact, the situation was getting worse. Despite the increase in fees, income continued to fall; losses from real estate loans continued to surface; the deposit base was shrinking quickly; it was becoming more and more difficult to foreclose on defaulted real estate loans and to sell the properties that had previously been foreclosed. NCUA's efforts to save the credit union had failed; the decision now was to liquidate or merge the credit union with another financial institution. On September 28, 1992, Corpus Christi Federal Credit Union became a full-service branch of Liberty Bank in New Orleans, the oldest and largest African-American-owned commercial bank in Louisiana.

48
Montgomery Hospital

Montgomery Hospital, a non-profit, tertiary care facility, was established in 1903. The hospital has 488 beds and does not come under any governmental jurisdiction. The Chief Executive Officer (CEO) of the hospital in 1987 was Ed Thompson. He received a graduate degree in hospital administration in 1952 from Northwestern University. Straight out of that program, Thompson was named head administrator for a 58-bed hospital in Columbus, Ohio. Three years later, he accepted a position as the head administrator for a 150-bed community hospital in Burlington, Indiana, and remained for 15 years to see the hospital grow to 175 beds. He was at Montgomery for 17 years (1971-1987), its CEO for 16 of those years.

During his time at Montgomery, Thompson described the hospital as "a quality institution that provides excellent basic health care through a fairly stable set of services but refers out cases that are esoteric, highly complex, or require sophisticated medical machinery." In 1987, the hospital employed roughly 1800 people and had an operating budget of over $73 million. Up until 1985, the hospital had seen moderate profits (and still retains a moderate amount of cash reserves). However, from 1985 to 1987 occu-

pancy and market share had fallen and Montgomery had come under increasing financial pressure.

The Environment

Montgomery Hospital is located on the east bank of a river on a bluff overlooking a medium-sized midwestern city. This town of approximately 200,000 is divided both physically and socially by the river that meanders from the north to the south. Since 1903, Montgomery has been the primary medical facility for the eastshore residents along with Loganton Memorial Hospital (established in the early 1900s). Smaller community hospitals, including Paxton Hospital and St. Mary's Hospital, are the major care providers on the less-densely populated and more affluent westshore.

A study published in 1985 revealed that nearly 10% of the local population was ineligible for health insurance coverage or government-funded health cost assistance. The study also suggested that HMO and PPO market penetration would increase steadily through 1990. These alternative delivery systems, the report

Written By James B. Thomas, Penn State University and David J. Ketchen, Jr., Louisiana State University. Used with Permission of the authors.

EXHIBIT 48-1 Organization by Function

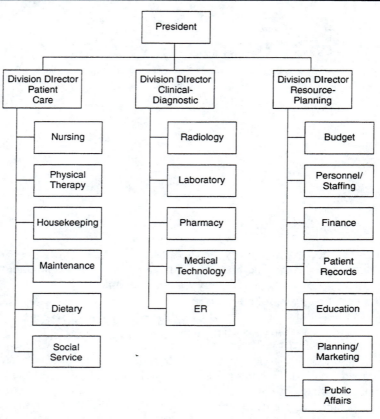

went on to say, would likely be used by 30-35% of the area employees and their dependents by 1990 and could go to 50% by 1995.

A local marketing firm was hired in 1987, at the urging of the Montgomery board of directors, to report consumer trends in the area. Their report to Thompson indicated that the population on both the east and west shores would be increasing through the year 2000. The report further stated that 75% of the population was under 44 years old. It was expected that this percentage would remain constant during the growth period.

The Hospital

The organizational structure at Montgomery un-

der Thompson had a functional focus. That is, units vere organized around three divisions: patient care, clinical diagnosis, and administrative support (as shown in Exhibit 48-1). The top management team at Montgomery consisted of the three division directors and Thompson. Thompson considered this type of structure a "corporate" structure that stressed managerial efficiency and control. Though Thompson referred to himself as a "benevolent dictator," most major organizational decisions were arrived at through consultation with the top management team. Medical staff leaders were frequent participants in the strategic decision process. Further, Thompson recognized the need to bond physicians more closely to the hospital. As a result, he established a number of physician services, including data processing support, purchasing assistance, and practice-management support.

From 1977-1987, the stability of the hospital's goals, structure, and performance was quite striking to the outside observer. There had been a relative lack of growth in either the number of beds or the scope of medical services offered. Any changes in services that were made reflected consolidation and retrenchment rather than diversification or growth.

Montgomery's Controller in 1987 described the hospital as a "lean and hungry" organization. Wages below the division director level were lower than at other hospitals and the ratio of employees to patients was also low. The principle that "everybody here does some bench work" applied to all supervisory and administrative personnel. No administrator had an assistant or private secretary. The low turnover of administrative personnel and infrequent changes in hospital policy allowed departments to operate within largely autonomous spheres of activity. Any changes that were made involved "fine-tuning" for increased efficiency. Consequently, inter-divisional communication and coordination were informal and relatively infrequent.

For many years, Thompson felt that Montgomery's policy of responding to external change should be to "wait until the dust clears. We don't want to be first — it's a waste of time and money in many cases. We want to be able to respond as needed." He estimated that 75% of his time and energy was devoted to the hospital's internal operation and about 25% to monitoring events and solving problems related to the external environment.

The physical location of Montgomery had been an issue for a number of years. The hospital juts out on a small bluff overlooking the river. This prevented any expansion on three sides of the campus. A dense residential area borders the hospital on the fourth side. Though expansion in some service areas seemed warranted, it was, for the most part, physically impossible. Ambulatory services was one such area that was considered for expansion. Nearly 47% of the surgery being done at Montgomery in 1987 was out-patient surgery. However, this surgery was being performed in a facility that was designed to take in 5% ambulatory patients. Additionally, 59% of the radiology patients were outpatient; and the outpatient physical therapy center, located in the basement of the hospital, could not comply with many of the usage requests and referred the overload to the Valley Recovery and Rehabilitation Center. A critical issue facing Montgomery in 1987 was its inability to expand existing facilities to meet the need in ambulatory services.

The Competition

While located approximately 50 miles away, University Medical Center has the best image for quality health care in the region. In 1986, the center announced a $60 million, multi-phased construction project and considered the development of satellite centers throughout the region, including the Montgomery area. They have a medical education affiliation agreement with Logan Memorial Hospital, a local competitor, and plan to house a major nursing education program in 1990.

Loganton Memorial Hospital, along with Montgomery, is located on the eastshore. This 155-bed medical facility was also engaged in a construction prospect in 1987 that would cost over $25 million and would significantly improve the operating rooms and obstetric facilities of the hospital. From 1982 to 1986, Loganton entered into affiliation agreements with five family medicine centers on both the east and west shores. It continues to be known for its quality medical staff, many of whom also have privileges at Montgomery. In 1987, Loganton announced the anticipated 1989 opening of the Mill Hollow Health Center—an outpatient treatment and rehabilitation facility. While considered a quality institution, Loganton was in 1987, and continues to be today, debt rich and cash poor.

On the westshore within sight of Montgomery, the 112-bed St. Mary's Hospital is an affiliate of the Sisters of Mercy Hospital System headquartered in St. Louis. Since 1986, the hospital has engaged in a marketing program that focuses on opthamology, podiatry, and obstetrics programs. Its opthamology program has always contained the best, state-of-the-art equipment available and is considered to be one of the best programs in the state. By 1987, the podiatry program had captured 60% of the market and the obstetrics program was promoting a "Birth Place Privacy Program." It still has the only drug and alcohol treatment program in the region.

Paxton Hospital is a 45-bed institution with strong ties to the westshore community dating back nearly 100 years. Since 1986, they have had a medical staff of approximately 60 active members and 50 consulting members. While its strength continues to be in its skilled nursing wing, the Paxton board has always insisted that the hospital continue as a full-service facility despite the approximate $500,000 loss in 1986 that was repeated in 1987. Since 1986 Paxton has operated a series of ambulatory medical centers in the outlying areas of the county. The chairman of the board for Paxton, who refers to the three centers as "docs in a box," has actively lobbied the board to discontinue the centers.

An Information Processing View

Ed Davis, the manager of data processing, has worked at Montgomery since 1977. Born in the area, Davis graduated from State University with an undergraduate degree in computer science in 1974. After three years of working for a major vendor, he was hired away by Thompson in 1977 to oversee Montgomery's implementation of a patient accounting system, a system that Davis helped design. The initial success in implementing that system paved the way for the rapid promotion of Davis to manager of data processing. Davis has a staff of 20 programmers, systems analysts, and operators. In 1987, he reported directly to the division director of resource and planning.

Up until 1987, Montgomery's information technology environment was primarily built around an IBM System 38. In addition to the 10-year-old patient accounting system, the environment also supported a general ledger and payroll system. A large percent of the development effort was centered around maintaining these relatively old and complex systems and trying to keep up with a constant stream of demands by regulatory agencies for increased reporting. Users' request for customized reports required months of lead time, or could not be filled at all. While there were pockets of personal computer usage, primarily in accounting and finance, centralized managerial control was felt by most to be the key to effective data processing.

In 1987, Davis was focused on a project to attempt to update the hospital's aging patient accounting system. As Davis observed, "Our old system was designed around the concept that the patient came to Montgomery, received all of their care here, and then they were released. Today, whole surgical disciplines have begun to disappear from in-patient care facilities at the hospital. It's quite common now for a particular patient episode to involve diagnosis in one place, surgery in another, and rehab/follow-up in a third." Davis went on to explain that, "What we need is something that allows us to link our case mix and patient flow to our cost accounting system. For example, right now I can't tell top management which DRG's (or even which physicians) make or lose money for us. Ed Thompson has approved development money for such a system but I don't know when it will be on-line."

"I might also mention," explained Davis, "that I think we'll see a 20% reduction in head count in our accounting department as a direct consequence of this improved system. With the new system, each of our division directors should be able to get the information they need to help meet our cost-cutting and productivity objectives."

Transition

In early 1988, Thompson was appointed as the President of the Board of Directors at Montgomery. Upon assuming his new duties, he stated that top management had become "too provincial and too narrow for these turbulent times. We are going to have to come to grips with the change in this area if we hope to prosper." Thompson initiated a search for a new CEO who "has the ability to identify business opportunities, analyze them, and decide whether we want to pursue them."

James Gainer

In June, 1988, with the unanimous approval and support of Thompson and the Montgomery board, James Gainer became the new CEO. Gainer had been with the hospital since 1984, most recently as the division director of resource and planning. Before joining Montgomery, Gainer had worked for a national consulting firm specializing in strategic healthcare issues.

Managing interpersonal relationships with present and potential stakeholders would make up, in Gainer's opinion, 60% of his new job. Participation and interaction served as the foundation for his managerial philosophy. He believed that teamwork, mutual respect, and a concern for fairness and equity coupled with a results-orientation based on accountability could make the hospital successful. Gainer set out, through both formal and informal ways, to spread that message.

The New Face of Montgomery

Gainer describes Montgomery as, "promoting the health and well-being of the people of the area by providing community-oriented primary medicine, either directly or by 'acting as a catalyst for the development of affiliate-based health services." Gainer goes on to explain that, "in 1987 we faced the question of whether Montgomery should continue to define its mission in its own terms or in terms of the community's needs. We could have maintained our traditional operations, avoided risk, ridden out the bad times, and perhaps eventually seen a reasonable return on our investment. Alternatively, we could redefine the hospital's mission in community terms (both east and west shores) as an organization that would extend itself beyond familiar bounds and ally itself with other organizations capable of answering requests and demands from people, whether or not they were among our current group of patients. The board of directors at this hospital chose the latter."

This latter direction required that Gainer act to meet the health needs of the entire area. He felt that it called for a flexible and expandable organization that had Montgomery at its core but was fully supported by decentralized family care centers in different communities and by other organizations that could impact every phase of the hospital's care delivery from diagnosis to rehabilitation. Of critical importance, was the hospital's ability to monitor a wide range of environmental trends, conditions, and events since Gainer saw that achieving the hospital's growth objectives rested primarily with the location of new markets and the development of new services/products. To that end, he felt that Montgomery would need to push to develop and refine its links to vendors and outside agencies, and increase the involvement of physicians in the strategic decision process.

Gainer is currently able to devote about 70% of his time to managing the hospital's expanding arena of external relationships because virtually all responsibilities for day-to-day operations have been delegated to the division and even program levels. The top management team now consists of four vice- presidents and Gainer (see Exhibit 48-2). The Vice-President for Programs is now charged with directing 4 program units: (1) Cardiology, (2) Perinatal, (3) Neurology, and (4) Orthopedics. These programs were identified by Gainer as those services that could create a competitive advantage for Montgomery if managed well. Each program area is responsible for all patient-care functions related to that area. The Vice-President for Medical Services is charged with providing capital-intensive ancillary services to all of the medical-diagnostic units as well as therapy, housekeeping, and

EXHIBIT 48-2 Organization by Product & Function

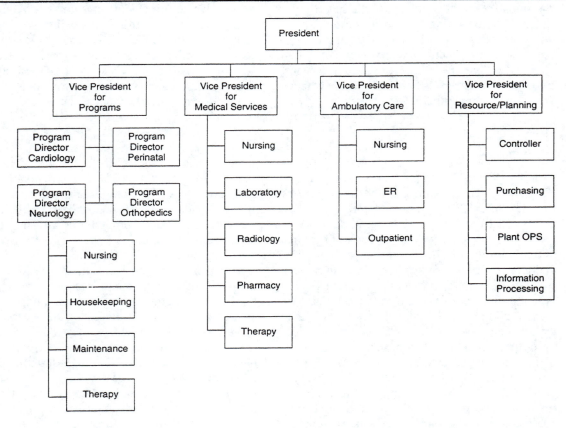

maintenance services to the Ambulatory Care Division in the hospital. All resource/planning support services are grouped under one vice president.

Strategic Direction

At his first meeting with hospital managers, Thompson described what he felt had to be done to implement Montgomery's strategic goals. "I see four key areas that we need to concentrate on. First, we need to think how we can build alliances with physicians, other health care institutions, and appropriate institutions outside of health care to strengthen our strategic position in the region. With frozen Medicare payments, massive losses for insurers, and the renewed growth of managed-care plans, we must seek collaboration so that we can control how resources are going to be used to treat patients. Second, we have to have meaningful cost and usage information across functions within the hospital and across alliance members. Our goal here should not be to worry about the efficient transmittal of information, but how information can help us meet the community's needs. Third, we need to stake out positions in ambulatory surgery and home care for the chronically ill — two big health care growth markets. Finally, we need to think about accurate measures of quality so we can develop clinical protocols to manage a patient's illness according to its seriousness and eliminate wasteful clinical practices."

Against the backdrop of these four critical success factors, Gainer went on to explain how he

EXHIBIT 48-3

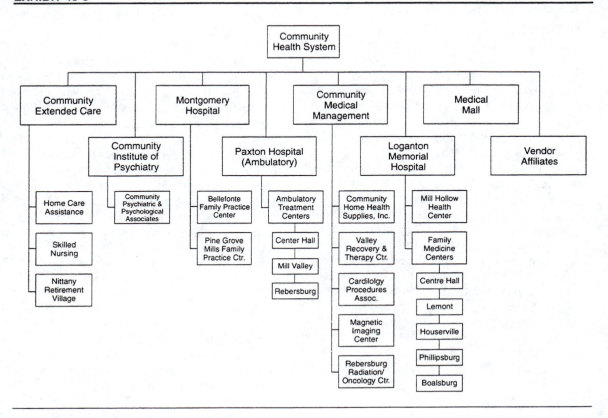

felt the strategic vision of the hospital could be realized:

"I have initiated a series of informal conversations with the chief executives of Paxton and Loganton Hospitals about the possibility of building a multi-institutional alliance. This alliance would create a highly integrated health care delivery system encompassing the east and west shores of the river. I see us allying with not only other healthcare organizations (for example, a joint venture with physician groups, rehab facilities, ambulatory care providers to construct a one-stop "medical mall") but any organization that will help us replace or strengthen weak aspects of our service delivery such as vendors and reporting agencies. All of this adds up to new and creative ways of supporting and delivering healthcare. The handout that's being distributed (see Exhibit 48-3) gives you some idea of what such a system of alliances might look like."

Many of the participants expressed interest in Gainer's discussion of new ways of thinking about inter-organizational relationships. However, questions concerning coordination, ownership, and even anti-trust were posed and discussed. Indeed, under the surface, the alliance concept was both misunderstood and threatening to not only some potential external participants, but also to internal management. As one manager voiced later, "I think one of the things that bothers many of us about the whole thing is that this hospital is moving very quickly from a having a care-taker role to a risk-taker. This may require a very different type of manager set. And suppose this whole thing doesn't work right away? Do we shed our skin again in another two years?"

Medical Information Integration

In early 1989, Gainer called together his top management team and other key personnel at Montgomery, including Ed Davis. "To make this hospital's strategic goals a reality, it's clear to me that we need to think through the capabilities of our current information processing system. How well we can mesh the information across functions and institutions seems to be absolutely critical. I'm not sure that our present system can do that irrespective of how many changes we make in it. I'm also aware that designing a new system will not take us into the 21st century because we'll be there before the new system is completed. Therefore, I'm forming a committee to explore the different technology and financing options available to us. The major criteria for selection of any system that is reviewed by the committee is that it provide for a completely integrated data base and can be on-line within the next two years."

The Future

At present, Montgomery and other area institutions not only lack information for a marketing program to reach into the community, they're not even sure what information they need. Specific information such as patient satisfaction and needs, and the identification of possible new clients is either not available or there is a lack of understanding concerning how the information can be used. These shortcomings have led to the inefficient use of marketing dollars, poorly thought-through programs for the attraction and retention of patients, and information-poor marketing tactics.

Gainer envisioned the focus of the marketing function in the alliance environment to be on harnessing and using information gathered from all of the alliance members to actively promote the products and services of all the alliance members individually and collectively. Information would be captured on service usage, satisfaction, and demographics to be used to (1) identify needs of patients in the community, (2) identify those patients with the highest affinity for making future purchases of services offered by the alliance members, and (3) provide physician, service and medical information referrals. This information would automatically be supplied to an external marketing firm for use in a comprehensive marketing program to include mass mailing and "power dialing" efforts.

As Gainer explained to his top management team, "Each 'node in the system' will need to serve an information gathering function to be used for the construction of comprehensive data bases for use by our marketing people and by the outside marketing firm we use. Further, I don't see why this idea of, what I call, 'elimination of organizational boundaries' can't be applied to other functions such as supply and banking. Perhaps managed health care is another area that presents an opportunity to ally ourselves with outside firms and reshape how we deliver health care. Let's call these opportunities Creative Alliances and get to work on what other functions might benefit from direct, mutual ties with outside folk. However, I'm concerned as to whether we have, or have thought to obtain, the information technology necessary to drive such alliances."

49
Palace Products Company

You are J. C. Kramer, executive vice-president of Palace Products Company. John Maguire, president of Palace Products, hired you from another company and you began work only one week ago. You were to train under Walter Hopkins, who was executive vice-president for one year until his retirement. You have twenty-two years of experience working in manufacturing companies, with ten years at middle and upper management levels. You have a bachelor of science degree in engineering.

Walter Hopkins is critically ill and will not be returning to work. You have not been with the company long enough to learn very much about the management system. You have just had time to learn the names of other managers. John Maguire wants you to assume full responsibility as executive vice-president because you are an experienced manufacturing executive. He told you that you are in complete control of internal operations. He does not want to interfere in your decisions because his role is to work with people in the environment and with International Controls Company, the company that purchased Palace Products two years ago.

History

Palace Products was started in 1948 by John Maguire and two other World War II veterans. They invented a flow control device and pooled their resources to develop and manufacture it. Palace Products grew rapidly and now produces control valves to regulate almost anything that flows through pipe. Palace originally established a niche as an innovative new product leader in the field of control valves and flow control instruments. Over the last ten years, however, innovation has been less frequent. The products are rather standard. Other companies are gaining a new-product edge, and Palace has gradually experienced a decreasing market share. Palace Products was taken over two years ago by International Controls Co. in a friendly merger. To date, Palace has kept substantial autonomy from International.

Prepared by Richard L. Daft. This case is adapted from several sources, including James B. Lau, "Crofts Products Company," *Behavior in Organization: An Experiential Approach* (Homewood, IL: Richard D. Irwin, 1975), 269-277; Harry R. Knudson, Robert T. Woodworth, and Cecil H. Bell, "Electronics, Incorporated," *Management: An Experiential Approach* (New York: McGraw-Hill, 1979), 128-138; E. Paul Smith, "You Are Bob Waters, Assistant Administrator at Unity Hospital," distributed by the Intercollegiate Case Clearing House, Soldiers Field, Boston, MA 02163; and the author's own management experiences.

The Situation

Palace Products is located in central Ohio. It has a capital investment in excess of $30 million, and produces seven major products for civilian (82 percent) and government markets (18 percent). Four products represent distinct types of control valves, and three products are instruments for flow control regulation. A control valve and instrument are typically combined to fit a specific flow control application. Palace also produces many valves on a custom order basis to meet unusual applications. A fifth major product, called the 830 Butterfly Valve, is under development.

Flow control products have a variety of applications in refineries, pipelines, and utilities. Industrial applications represent 70 percent of Palace's business. Small control valves are used in virtually every home and building, and account for about 30 percent of total sales.

Palace's employees now include sixty-four engineers and thirty-eight technicians. There are approximately twelve hundred production employees who work two shifts. The manager in charge of production is Keith Malone. He has been in his current job for less than a year, but has been with the company about twenty-one years. His previous job included manager of quality control and manager of the machine shop. The marketing manager is Ray Thomas, who has been in his job four years. He was promoted from field sales manager into his present position. He is now responsible for the field sales manager (Mike McKay) and for the advertising and research manager (Bruce Parker). Marketing functions include promotion, merchandising, market research, market development, and direct sales to customers. Sixty-five employees work in the marketing department.

Pete Tucker is the manager in charge of research and development. Tucker has a Masters Degree in Electrical Engineering. Prior to his promotion thirty months ago, he was the manager in charge of electrical engineering. The Research and Development Department includes nineteen engineers and several technicians. Pete Tucker refuses to appoint anyone to supervisor roles because he believes his people should work as a team. Because of John Maguire's strong interest in research and development, nearly 8 percent of Palace's profits are allocated to this function.

The Engineering Department is managed by Bill Urban. Engineering typically implements the products created in Research and Development. Several engineering specialties are represented within the department, including electrical, mechanical, product, and systems engineering. The contracting specialist handles technical details involved in contracts with clients.

Al Wagner is in charge of employment and administrative services. His responsibility also includes community relations. This department has a staff of nineteen people. Wagner transferred from the corporate personnel department over eighteen months ago.

The finance manager is Ed Brock. He has been in his job about two years. Brock has an M.B.A. and is a specialist in management information systems. He is responsible for general and cost accounting, payroll, the computer unit, and accounts receivable and payable. Finance has a staff of about twenty people. (see Exhibit 49-1 for Palace's current organizational chart.)

The demand for control valves has traditionally fluctuated with general business activity, especially construction. When construction and business activity is high, the control valve business booms. For the last two years, industry output has been stable, and the number of units shipped by Palace has declined slightly. Palace is not yet in financial trouble, but money is tight. High interest rates on short-term loans are drawing off cash.

Control valve innovation follows developments in electronics, metallurgy, and flow control theory. Developments in these fields are used by manufacturers to increase the sensitivity and efficiency of valves and instruments. Recent developments in electronics have led to new control valve applications based upon miniaturization and automatic controls. Palace has been working for three years on a new control valve design called the Butterfly. This design has the potential to regulate the flow of liquids at 75 percent of the cost of traditional designs.

Palace has a reputation for product quality and reliability. Engineering, research, and production have traditionally been important departments in the company.

In the single conversation you had with Walter Hopkins before he became ill, he confided to you that Palace should retrench for the next two years or so until economic conditions improved. He insisted that Palace's reputation for product quality would hold the customer base if the marketing department concentrated on servicing established customers rather than on finding new customers. Hopkins said that Maguire always wanted more money budgeted to R & D for new developments, but he disagreed. New products have been an enormous hassle, and Hopkins could not see their contribution to profit. He believed new products were more trouble than they were worth. Hopkins planned to concentrate on improving internal effciencies. "Cutbacks now will leave us lean and strong for the economic upturn ahead." He also said, "One dollar saved in production is worth three dollars in sales."

Hopkins also confided to you that a staff member from International Controls Company headquarters suggested to President Maguire that a project or matrix form of structure be adopted at Palace. Maguire isn't sure whether that is a good idea, but most managers, including Hopkins, don't see any need to change organization structure. They are more concerned with human resources — finding and keeping good people.

Saturday, March 7

You were appointed executive vice-president on Thursday, March 5. On Friday morning you got word to all those reporting to you (see Exhibit 49-1) asking them to write you a memorandum if they had any issues to be discussed with you. By Friday night, your in-basket contained the memoranda below. You take these memoranda home for evaluation so you can plan your next week's activities.

Your Assignment

Study the memoranda and answer the following questions.

1. What are the four most important problems facing you? Specify and rank the problems in priority order of importance. What are the two least important problems facing you?
2. What techniques will you use to work on the problems during the coming week? Be specific. State exactly how you plan to approach and solve the problems listed in response to question 1.
3. What overall strategy should Palace Products adopt? Should the company cut back, retrench, and stress efficiency? Should it invest heavily in research and development in order to be innovative and reestablish itself as a product leader?
4. Based upon the information available to you, is a change in organization structure warranted? What would you recommend to Maguire?

EXHIBIT 49-1 Organization Chart for Palace Products Co.

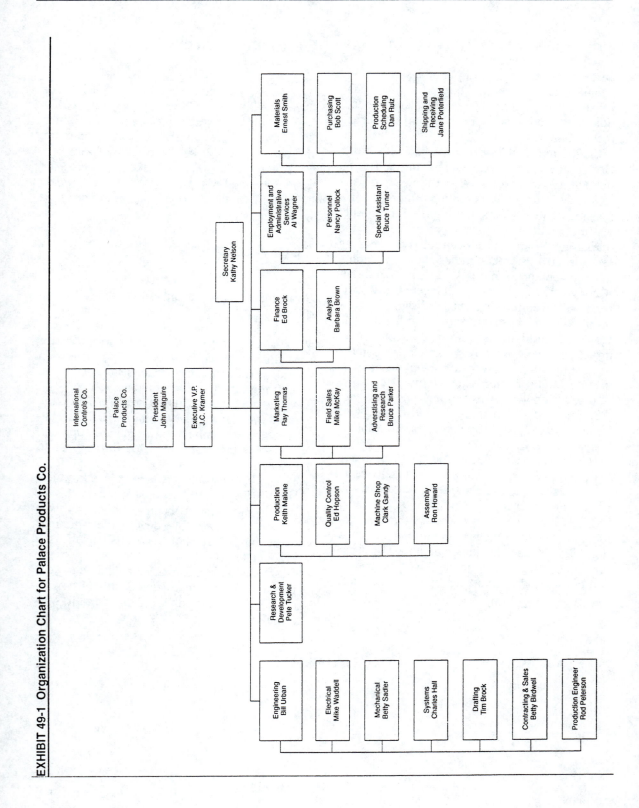

PALACE PRODUCTS COMPANY

OFFICE MEMORANDUM   DATE: March 6, 1983

TO: J. C. Kramer
FROM: Kathy
SUBJECT: Your Meetings and Correspondence

Here are the memos that came in today. Mr. Maguire's memo is on top. Your luncheon appointments for the week are as follows:

Tuesday, March 10	11:30 A.M. 1:30 P.M.	Award lunch
Wednesday, March 11	12:00 A.M. 1:30 P.M.	Peter O'Reilly of O'Reilly Construction Co.
Thursday, March 12	10:00 A.M. 1:00 P.M.	Corporation meeting
Friday, March 13	12:30 P.M. 2:00 P.M.	Mrs. Rogers of the United Way

The following meetings were already scheduled by Mr. Hopkins.

| Tuesday, March 10 | 8:00 A.M. 9:00 A.M. | Weekly staff meeting. This will include a discussion of new policies and procedures by Al Wagner and expanding opportunities for women by Nancy Pollock. A program for using less energy will be proposed by Bruce Turner. |
| Wednesday, March 11 | 9:00 A.M. 10:00 A.M. | Meet Chamber of Commerce representative. |

See you on Monday.

PALACE PRODUCTS COMPANY

OFFICE MEMORANDUM   DATE: March 6, 1983

TO: J. C. Kramer
FROM: John Maguire, President
SUBJECT: New Products and Corporate Meetings

J. C., let me welcome you aboard once again. I'm looking forward to working with you. I will be out of town for the next two weeks but will get together with you immediately upon my return.

I am quite concerned that Palace continues developing new control valve products and adding to our line. New developments have not been progressing very well, and decisions will have to be made in the near future for allocating funds and people to this endeavor. Could you get together right away with Pete Tucker and find out what new developments they would like to work on? We need to have these ideas consolidated and to select promising projects in the near future.

By the way, would you also check into the progress of our new model 830 butterfly valve? I've heard grumblings from two customers, but told them I didn't believe there was any problem. Where is the monthly report? It should have been on my desk by March 1. Would you please have that completed and bring it to my office?

One other thing. I'm scheduled to attend the international Controls Company meeting on Thursday at 10:00 A.M. Since I will be out of town, could you attend for me? We do not have to make a presentation, and the corporation will send me a copy of the minutes. The executives from the other companies within International Controls will be there, and you can meet them.

I look forward to seeing you when I return.

PALACE PRODUCTS COMPANY

OFFICE MEMORANDUM   DATE: March 6, 1983

TO: J. C. Kramer, Executive Vice-President
FROM: Ray Thomas, Marketing Department
SUBJECT: Model 830 Butterfly Valve

I understand that the new model 830 butterfly valve will not begin production for another two months. We have had repeated delays introducing this new system. It was originally scheduled to begin production last August, then January 1 of this year. Now the earliest date appears to be May 1. This is creating a serious problem for us, because we've been telling our customers about it and they want to have an opportunity to experiment with it. I anticipate a thirty- to sixty-day lag from the beginning of production before we will have products ready for delivery to customers. One of the salesmen heard from a customer that a small control valve company in Texas was about to introduce a new butterfly valve.

Another urgent matter is the model 820 retrofit. This should go on the market immediately. It also needs to be priced low or it could affect sales. Our retrofit is a small item, but it is badly needed because it will provide the precision control our competitior's products already have. Mr. Hopkins agreed with me that every effort should be made to have this product in the field immediately. We have promised our customers that the retrofit would be ready for delivery on April 1.

The sales forecasts for this year were based on the expectation that new products would go into production and sales as planned. Further delays in the introduction of the model 820 retrofit and the model 830 butterfly valve could seriously reduce sales forecasts for the year.

PALACE PRODUCTS COMPANY

OFFICE MEMORANDUMDATE: March 6, 1983

TO: J. C. Kramer, Executive V.-P.
FROM: Ernest Smith, Materials Manager
SUBJECT: Material Costs and Inventory Needs

I have been concerned for a long time about our steadily increasing materials costs. Due to the nature of our business almost 30 percent of our direct costs are materials related. Walter Hopkins agreed with me that we should do everything possible to increase efficiency at Palace Products. Reducing materials costs was a top priority for him. My people work hard to reduce costs and establish decent manufacturing schedules, but we can't do it alone. We always have to revise production schedules because of manufacturing problems, especially with the new models. My purchasing people don't get word on what to buy until the last minute, and then their materials need to be rush ordered and expedited. This increases costs at least 10 percent. By the time we get the materials, another design change may be underway, so the parts we rush-ordered may not be appropriate. Because of the way Engineering, Research, and Production work, our material costs are almost out of control.

Another important matter is the inventory problem. During the spring and summer we receive many small orders for one or two items. Setting up and manufacturing a special order is expensive. Sometimes after we complete the order, the customer will decide they want one or two more of the same item. This means two setups for the same product and customer. For approximately $275,000, we could keep these small orders in inventory and fill orders much more efficiently. Ed Brock in Finance tells me he doesn't have $275,000 for inventory. Walter Hopkins agreed with me that this was another priority in our efforts to increase efficiency. An investment in inventory would be the best thing for this company right now.

The final problem is the designs for the model 830 butterfly valve. We need to get these designs finalized so we can establish decent manufacturing and purchasing schedules. The model 830 is supposed to go into manufacturing shortly, but as yet we have not been able to get a parts list that we can rely on. How can we go into production without acquiring parts? I wish the people in Engineering and Research would be more cooperative on this.

PALACE PRODUCTS COMPANY

OFFICE MEMORANDUM   DATE: March 6, 1983

TO: J. C. Kramer
FROM: Barbara Brown
SUBJECT: Request for Appointment

Since you have an open door policy, I must see you. I am about to resign from the company and want to discuss it with you before I make the final decision. I have been here for six months. The assignments I am receiving from Mr. Brock simply are not challenging. I am not having any impact upon Palace Products Company. The projects I have been assigned are small and do not utilize the theoretical and analytical abilities I acquired during my M.B.A. training.

My mid-year progress report was excellent, which frustrates me even more. I would rather be rewarded for making a major contribution to this company than for doing small projects. I have tried to explain the problem to Mr. Brock, but he hardly has time to discuss it. He says he understands, but still hasn't assigned me to do anything really important. It is becoming clear to me that the Finance Department does not control anything here at Palace Products Company.

PALACE PRODUCTS COMPANY

OFFICE MEMORANDUM   DATE: March 6, 1983

TO: J. C. Kramer, Executive Vice-President
FROM: Al Wagner, E. & A. S.
SUBJECT: Employment of the Disadvantaged

I received important information at a personnel meeting last night. The word is out that federal equal opportunity agencies will be looking at industrial plants in this area during the next six months. Currently, we have a very low ratio of disadvantaged employees. We may be in serious trouble.

I believe we should begin a crash program to employ fifty non-whites in all areas of the company. In order to save time, we should not use our normal testing procedures for these employees. Besides, our regular aptitude and intelligence tests may open us to charges of discrimination. Of course we can continue to use these tests for our normal employment of whites.

A crash program may involve some increased training and labor costs. Increased costs are better than losing government contracts. Besides, employing the disadvantaged is the right thing for Palace Products to do.

PALACE PRODUCTS COMPANY

OFFICE MEMORANDUM   DATE: March 6, 1983

TO: J. C. Kramer, Executive V.-P.
FROM: Bill Urban, Manager, Engineering
SUBJECT: Engineering Activities

There is really not too much to report from here. Things are in good shape. I would like to give you a complete briefing on our activities and plans whenever your schedule will allow it. For now, I would like to call four things to your attention.

1. I heard a rumor that International Controls was planning to centralize many of the contracting and engineering activities to the corporate level. This would mean a transfer of people to corporate headquarters, and many of our activities would be done away from this plant. I think this is a terrible idea because centralized engineers wouldn't know the details of what we're doing here. The International people seem to think it would save money by consolidating engineers into a central facility and allow them to use up-to-date equipment. That would be a poor tradeoff, in my opinion.

2. We continue to be short-handed by two engineers. Betty Sadler and Charles Hall both told me that some of their people have job offers from other companies. We may have to make counteroffers in the next few weeks.

3. A related item is the need to send five people to the American Engineering Society meeting in Las Vegas. Some of the engineering and research people want to report in a scientific paper some of the theoretical work behind the 830 butterfly valve. They will conduct a full-day session. This would be a great reward for them, but it will cost $7,500. We will need your approval because this will be well in excess of the travel budget.

4. The model 820 and model 830 developments seem to be coming along quite well. There is no urgency, but we do not have the most recent data and the final report from R & D. R & 0 claims we already have the data, but I think they are too busy to write the final report. We can't make the final decisions about production designs until we know the exact figures. I discussed this with Walter Hopkins last week, and he was going to see Pete Tucker about it.

PALACE PRODUCTS COMPANY

OFFICE MEMORANDUM   DATE: March 6, 1983

TO: J. C. Kramer, Executive Vice-President
FROM: Nancy Pollock, Personnel
SUBJECT: Award Lunch

Don Jameson, a machinist, has been with the company thirty-five years and is being given an award as the most senior employee. He has been with the company since its founding, and a luncheon has been scheduled for him on Tuesday, March 10, from 11:30 to 1:30. It will be held in the luncheon room at the Townshire Hotel.

Walter Hopkins was going to present a company pin and give a brief talk. He always believed it was good human relations to emphasize the company's interest in those working here. Several of the senior production employees will attend the luncheon. Keith Malone agreed to substitute for Walter, but I'm sure you will also want to attend Don's luncheon.

PALACE PRODUCTS COMPANY

OFFICE MEMORANDUM   DATE: March 6, 1983

TO: J. C. Kramer, Executive V.-P.
FROM: Al Wagner, E. & A. S.
SUBJECT: Reporting on the Model 820 and
             Model 830

I have attached a note from Bruce Turner, a bright young employee with the company. It reflects the problems he is having, and I have not been able to do much about it. The memo illustrates the lack of cooperation when we try to coordinate new product developments.

Dear Mr. Wagner:

One of my most important jobs is coordinating the monthly report for the Model 830 butterfly valve. In the initial meeting with you and Ed Brock from Finance, we worked out a monthly reporting plan for the 830 project. The plan was designed to record budget expenditures, and to keep upper management informed on the progress of each aspect of the development. We have tried to use a similar procedure for the Model 820 retrofit.

I'm getting no cooperation whatsoever. As it turns out, I am nothing but a pencil-pusher. I am having no influence at all on running and coordinating the 830 program. The departments are not taking this project seriously, no matter how many memos I write. R & D wants to do its own thing. Pete Tucker tells me that I give too much emphasis to reporting procedures and that I can expect the final report in a month or so. He says he is busy with important new developments, and the 830 is now old stuff. Keith Malone in Production says that they are having problems, and have not yet started production, but I don't know why. Marketing is pressing me to get the report moving, but they don't provide any useful information either. None of the departments bothers to meet my deadline for a monthly report. As an administrative coordinator, I can't enforce compliance. What should I do?

Bruce Turner

PALACE PRODUCTS COMPANY

OFFICE MEMORANDUM   DATE: March 6, 1983

TO: J. C. Kramer, Executive Vice-President
FROM: Edward Brock, Finance
SUBJECT: Integrated Management Information
             System

After a long struggle, we finally completed our computer-based integrated management information system last month. It cost $110,000, but will be well worth it. The new system will provide daily, weekly, or monthly information about sales, production scheduling, the status of customer orders, vendor deliveries, and the like. The system will also provide me with more detailed cost accounting data.

Unfortunately, although we debugged the computer software, the system is not working very well. One problem is that the managers are not providing the correct information and they are not using it. They are maintaining their own reports. They don't seem to want me to have the detailed figures I need for the cost-accounting reports. This system is important to the efficient operation of this company. Another problem is that we aren't using the most recent technical developments for data processing. I've set aside $60,000 for acquiring updated equipment. We will have the best MIS in the industry.

Walter Hopkins gave me his full backing to install the MIS. Would you talk to the other managers about adhering to the rules and procedures necessary to make the system work? Any assistance you can give me will be greatly appreciated. My staff and I have spent almost full time on this project for several weeks.

PALACE PRODUCTS COMPANY

OFFICE MEMORANDUM   DATE: March 6, 1983

TO: J. C. Kramer, Executive V.-P.
FROM: Pete Tucker, Manager, Research and
             Development
SUBJECT: New Products

Our most pressing need is to get budgets approved for new developments. John Maguire has always supported new-product development in this company. Our people in R&D have a number of original ideas, and they are ready to start working on them. We will need a budget allocation of about $325,000 beginning April 1. We will have the people to allocate full time to the projects then. Would you contact Ed Brock about assigning the needed budget to us? He hasn't even responded to my memos. And please don't ask for a lot of formal plans and approvals. My people are very creative, which is their strength, and paperwork inhibits them. Palace Products has been a success because of new-product developments, and we need to maintain our momentum.

I also want to call your attention to problems in Production and in Engineering. The Model 820 retrofit has turned into a joke. We gave those people a perfect retrofit design, and somehow things have been screwed up so that it is not yet in production. It may be the people in production engineering or a lack of cooperation in the machine shop. Somebody was not able to follow through on an excellent design.

I have also heard that Engineering and Production are having problems with the new Model 830 butterfly valve. I want to assure you that everything is under control. We have completed the design work and the final report will be written as soon as we have some free time. Engineering has all the figures they need. I admit there were some slippages in the development of the 830. One hangup was due to the failure of the system to pass the high pressure flow control tests, but we anticipate no further difficulty. I don't see any reason why Engineering and Production should not be able to meet their schedules. By far the most important thing for us is to get the $325,000 so we can commit ourselves full time to new developments.

PALACE PRODUCTS COMPANY

OFFICE MEMORANDUM   DATE: March 6, 1983

TO: J. C. Kramer
FROM: Keith Malone
SUBJECT: Model 820 Retrofit

I can't possibly make the production schedule for the Model 820 retrofit if I also have to be concerned about beginning production of the new Model 830 butterfly valve. The research, engineering, and marketing people are driving us crazy. Engineering keeps making design changes, and marketing people keep coming out to the shop to see when they can get their hands on the finished products. My people are working overtime to make production changes to meet design changes so the 820 won't be delayed any further. I strongly recommend that we stop all production activities on both the 820 and the 830 until all design issues are resolved once and for all.

I see that I made a mistake in accepting the 820 for production. The engineering people convinced me that there would be no more changes, but they did not have the final figures ready for me. It turns out they weren't clear about the final design. I won't make that mistake again.

By the way, can you get the Finance people off my back? They have installed a computer system and want to have us run everything into that computer. It creates a lot of extra work for us at a time when we don't need extra work. The computer has not been debugged, so my people still have to keep their own reports.

50
Panalba

The purpose of this exercise is to analyze the decision-making actions of an organization faced with conflicting responsibilities to its constituents and to society. This exercise may be conducted as a role-play, with members representing various constituents, or as an "unaffiliated" group decision process.

Strategic actions/planning in an organization may take into consideration constituents internal and external to its operations. Stockholders, employees, the board of directors, competitors, and government are a few of those to be considered. In the following exercise you will be challenged to determine the course of action to be taken by a major pharmaceutical manufacturer in the face of various demands.

Step I. Group Assignment (5 min.)
The class will be divided into groups of seven people. Each group will read the problem description below; the instructor will assign either the "Financial Accounting" or the "Social or Interest Group Accounting" to each group.

Step II. Group Decision (20 min.)
After reading the problem description each group will discuss and propose a course of action

to be followed for the U.S. market. Select from the possible solutions A, B, C, D, and E.

Step III. Group Decision (5-10 min.)
Repeat step 2 for the foreign markets, again selecting from solutions A, B, C, D, and E.

Step IV. Class Discussion (20 min.)
Each group will briefly present its proposal and justification. The class will then discuss the relevant issues in relation to the theories and models that may have been presented earlier in classroom lectures and discussions. The following questions are provided to stimulate the discussion.

Discussion Questions

1. Which constituents and environmental factors must the company consider? Which are most important?
2. What role should the constituents play in the decision-making process? Should the company involve each in making a decision?
3. How would you describe the strategy of the Upjohn Corporation before the Panalba inci-

Abstracted from "Social Irresponsibility in Management," J. Scott Armstrong, *Journal of Business Research*, 5 (Sept. 1977), 185-213. Prepared by Dick Daft.

dent? What strategic shift, if any, would your course of action require?

4. What do you think are the internal cultural values of the Upjohn Corporation? How would these support the strategic goals of the company?

5. Can you cite other instances when an organization's cultural values conflicted with society's? How was this resolved?

6. Can organization theory teach managers to act ethically?

Background Information for Panalba

Assume that it is August 1989 and that Upjohn Corporation has called a Special Board Meeting to discuss what should be done with the product known as "Panalba."

Panalba is a fixed-ratio antibiotic sold by prescription, that is, it contains a combination of drugs. It has been on the market for over thirteen years and has been highly successful. It now accounts for about $18 million per year, which is 12 percent of Upjohn Company's gross income in the United States (and a greater percentage of net profits). Profits from foreign markets, where Panalba is marketed under a different name, are roughly comparable to those in the United States.

Over the past twenty years, there have been numerous medical scientists (e.g., the AMA's Council on Drugs) objecting to the sale of most fixed-ratio drugs. The argument has been that (1) there is no evidence that these fixed-ratio drugs have improved benefits over single drugs, and (2) the possibility of detrimental side effects, including death, is at least doubled. For example, these scientists have estimated that Panalba is causing about fourteen to twenty-two unnecessary deaths per year, i.e., deaths that could be prevented if the patients had used a substitute made by a competitor of Upjohn. Despite these recommendations to remove fixed-ratio drugs from the market, doctors have continued to use them. They offer a shotgun approach for the doctor who is unsure of his diagnosis.

Recently, a National Academy of Science National Research Council panel, a group of impartial scientists, carried out extensive research studies and recommended unanimously that the Food and Drug Administration (FDA) ban the sale of Panalba. One of the members of the panel, Dr. Eichewald of the University of Texas, was quoted by the press as saying, "There are few instances in medicine when so many experts have agreed unanimously and without reservation" (about banning Panalba). This view was typical of comments made by other members of the panel. In fact, it was typical of comments that had been made about fixed-ratio drugs over the past twenty years. These impartial experts believed that while all drugs have some possibility of side effects, the costs associated with Panalba far exceed the possible benefits.

The Special Board Meeting has arisen out of an emergency situation. The FDA has told Upjohn that it plans to ban Panalba in the United States and wants to give Upjohn time for a final appeal to them. Should the ban become effective, Upjohn would have to stop all sales of Panalba and attempt to remove inventories from the market. Upjohn has no close substitute for Panalba, so consumers will be switched to close substitutes that are easily available from other firms. Some of these substitutes offer benefits that are equivalent to those from Panalba, yet they have no serious side effects.

The selling price of the substitutes is approximately the same as the price for Panalba. It is extremely unlikely that bad publicity from this case would have any significant effect upon the long-term profits of other products made by Upjohn.

The following possible solutions were considered by the Board:

A. Recall Panalba immediately and destroy.

B. Stop production of Panalba immediately, but allow what's been made to be sold.

C. Stop all advertising and promotion of Panalba, but provide it for those doctors who request it.

D. Continue efforts to most effectively market

Panalba until sale is actually banned.

E. Continue efforts to most effectively market Panalba and take legal, political, and other necessary actions to prevent the authorities from banning Panalba.

You, as a member of the board, must help reach a decision at today's meeting. The chairman of the board, Ed Upjohn, has provided this background information to each of the board members. He is especially concerned about selecting the most appropriate alternative for the U.S. market. (You must decide which of the possible alternatives is *closest* to your preferred solution.)

A similar decision must also be made for the foreign market *under the assumption that the sale of Panalba was banned in the United States.* This decision will be used as a contingency plan.

Financial Accounting

To assist with this decision, the chairman had asked the Controller's Office to make some quick estimates of what would happen as a result of each course of action. These estimates are summarized in the memo from the controller.

MEMO: To E. G. Upjohn, Chairman of the Board
FROM: Samuel Hardy, Controller (copies to Board of Directors)

The following estimates were prepared on very short notice by the Controller at Upjohn. As a result, these figures should be regarded as crude estimates as to what will happen. After-tax profits at Upjohn prior to this crisis have been predicted to be $39 million for 1989. The figures below are estimated losses from this prediction under each alternative. The figures represent only the financial losses to Upjohn stockholders.

Alternative	Estimated Losses* (In millions of dollars)
A. "Recall Immediately"	20.0
B. "Stop Production"	13.0
C. "Stop Promotion"	12.0
D. "Continue until Banned"	11.0
E. "Take Actions to Prevent Ban"	4.0

* This estimate represents present-value loss to Upjohn and covers all items (e.g., lawsuits, legal fees, expenses involved with recall). The losses would be spread out over a number of years.

Social or Interest Group Accounting

To assist with this decision, the chairman had asked the Controller's office to make some quick estimates of what would happen as a result of each course of action. These estimates are summarized in the memo from the controller.

MEMO: To E. G. Upjohn, Chairman of the Board
FROM: Samuel Hardy, Controller (copies to Board of Directors)

The following estimates [see page 373] were prepared on short notice by the Controller of Upjohn. As a result, these figures should be regarded as crude estimates as to what will happen. After-tax profit at Upjohn prior to this crisis had been predicted to be $39 million for 1989. The figures below are estimated losses from this prediction under each alternative for each group. All other important effects from this decision have also been estimated.

Alternative	Estimated Losses* (in millions of dollars)			
	(1) Stock-holders	(2) Customers	(3) Employees	(1)+ (2) +(3) Total Losses
A. "Recall Immediately"	20.0	0.0	2.0	22.0
B. "Stop Production"	13.0	13.6	1.8	28.4
C. "Stop Promotion"	12.0	16.8	1.2	30.0
D. "Continue until Banned"	11.0	19.6	1.0	31.6
E. "Take Actions to Prevent Ban"	4.0	33.8	0.2	38.0

*These estimates represent present-value losses to each group that is affected by this decision. The losses to customers represent deaths and illnesses caused by Panalba for which no compensation is received; losses to employees represent lost wages and moving expenses beyond those covered by severance pay and unemployment benefits.